# THE RIGHT TO DO WRONG

# THE RIGHT TO DO WRONG

## MORALITY AND THE LIMITS OF LAW

MARK OSIEL

Harvard University Press
Cambridge, Massachusetts
London, England
2019

Printed in the United States of America

First printing

*Library of Congress Cataloging-in-Publication Data*
Names: Osiel, Mark, author.
Title: The right to do wrong : morality and the limits of law / Mark Osiel.
Description: Cambridge, Massachusetts : Harvard University Press, 2019. |
Includes bibliographical references and index.
Identifiers: LCCN 2018025427 | ISBN 9780674368255 (hardcover : alk. paper)
Subjects: LCSH: Law and ethics.
Classification: LCC K247.6 .O85 2019 | DDC 340/.112—dc23 LC record available at
https://lccn.loc.gov/2018025427

*To Joëlle*

# CONTENTS

Should there happen to be a country whose inhabitants were of a social temper, open-hearted, cheerful, endowed with . . . a facility in communicating their thoughts; who were sprightly and agreeable . . . and beside had courage, generosity, frankness and a certain notion of honor, no one ought endeavor to restrain their manners by laws, unless he would lay a constraint on their virtues.

—Baron de Montesquieu, *The Spirit of the Laws,* 1748

It is the manners and spirit of a people which preserve a republic in vigor. A degeneracy in these is a canker which soon eats to the heart of its laws.

—Thomas Jefferson, *Notes on the State of Virginia,* 1782

Standing within the law, we are always in danger of allowing law to fill our entire vision . . . Not to see the end of social order as the rule of law strikes us as unnatural—the equivalent of imagining a world without gravity.

—Paul Kahn, *The Cultural Study of Law,* 1999

# Introduction

## Defining the Puzzle

The websites of all the largest internet companies now expressly commit themselves to honoring "community standards" in public discourse.[1] These standards, as the companies articulate and interpret them, well exceed the demands of law, they acknowledge. Their websites exhort those posting there to respect prevailing norms of basic civility, snappily illustrated at times, and to report their violation to web administrators. This commitment to policing community standards prompts these businesses to regularly remove postings deemed to breach social mores against hate speech, graphic violence, advocacy of terrorism, and even demeaning and aggressive expletives.

In appreciation of this commitment, the Home Affairs Committee of the UK House of Commons in April 2017 formally declared, "We welcome the fact that YouTube, Facebook, and Twitter all have clear community standards that go beyond the requirements of the law."[2] With these words, the lawmakers of a leading Western democracy openly acknowledge their considerable dependence, for the effective governance of the peoples they represent, on nonstate entities for this role in sustaining and refining social mores deemed essential to an acceptable public order. In fact, the legislators express their gratitude.

Yet what do we really mean when speaking of a community's moral standards, beyond those enshrined in its laws? And what confidence can we have in those—not only internet companies, by any means—to whom, through no formal legal delegation, we thus entrust the definition and enforcement of these apparently indispensable standards?

The relationship between law and common mores raises vital questions for both social understanding and policymaking, questions systematically examined by no field of study.[3] From disparate sources, in this book I take stock of what we may glean of that relationship, identifying fruitful directions for its further investigation.

Since the Second World War, Anglo-American philosophers have had much to say about the relationship between law and "morality," by which they generally mean moral truth, rightly understood. In more recent years economists have shown sharp interest in the relation between law and "social norms," including standards of conduct and appraisal embodying notions of right and wrong.

Yet it is sociology that offers the most perspicacious guidance in making sense of the interaction between a legal system and what most people governed by it consider just and unjust. Common morality is found in the ways people employ and rely upon these notions within a given milieu, in their daily language and observable behavior. In speaking of sociology, I refer specifically to the writings of Montesquieu—which is to say, sociology in its most theoretically far-reaching and currently unfashionable register.[4] To Montesquieu's capacious concerns we must today add careful, ground-level inquiry into how ordinary people respond to lawful activities they deem reprehensible. By comparing and contrasting these activities and responses, we can identify empirical patterns enabling us to generalize, still more broadly, about the relationship between "law and society,"[5] and that at times can even guide our lawmaking efforts on this basis.

The interaction between common morality and the law has been of occasional curiosity to legal theory generally, but it is no longer of serious interest to legal sociology, a discipline whose aspirations have narrowed greatly since the work of its famous founders. What chiefly defines the broader enterprise of legal theory, as widely understood, is its commitment to posing the most comprehensive questions about law's intersections with life's myriad nonlegal dimensions. To this end, legal theory today draws on diverse currents of thought—notably philosophy and economics, but also psychology, anthropology, and other fields. A sustained effort to uncover and account for law's intersections with commonsense morality should therefore naturally elicit interest among those in many corners of this spacious endeavor, whatever their formal niche within the division of academic labor.

Though these intersections have many aspects (several here assayed), one of these demands special attention—perhaps urgently so, some insist. It may at first seem ingenuous to observe this, but a major reason the law permits considerable moral wrongdoing—much of it petty, some profound—is that lawmakers often assume that people will exercise their rights "responsibly,"[6] with some measure of concern for others' welfare, beyond the law's demands. This simple, little-noted fact, I shall show, turns out to explain crucial features of the gap between law and everyday morals. This fact also often accounts for why law's apparent moral failings do not inexorably conduce to societal breakdown. Common morality provides what political theorists call an "enabling constraint."

Only because common morality decisively limits the way we actually use our rights[7]—including those we most cherish and celebrate—do we possess many of these entitlements at all. This includes the rights on which we construct some of our most fundamental political and economic institutions. It follows that if we could no longer trust to common morality in performing this task, we would need to rethink major portions of our legal system. We would need to redesign it upon assumptions less innocent, less hopeful about the capacity of individuals and institutions for self-restraint in the exercise of their entitlements. That would entail a step both daunting and momentous.

To begin with a humble example of what is at stake, consider the law of personal bankruptcy. Though it entitles us to absolve our debts, both lawmakers and the general public remain ambivalent over whether people should feel entirely comfortable in taking this path. We thus grant a right whose exercise, we know, carries a certain aura of stigma. We do not like to admit to stigmatizing others. Yet most of us do not wish to entirely dispel such stigma *here*. In fact, not a few may secretly welcome the feelings of shame induced in some such people, even at this already-stressful moment in their lives. For many suspect that these moral sentiments will discourage the right's "abuse." We sincerely believe that people should have the option to go bankrupt—when they really need it. But we don't want them to believe *too readily* that they need it. And we know we cannot draft the law so perfectly as to prevent that danger from materializing, more than occasionally, perhaps especially among well-lawyered high-flyers.

At such points within our legal systems, a curious interplay develops between a lenient law and a more censorious morality that we depend on to dampen the law's use. Lawmakers often have that dampening at least vaguely in mind even as they devise the law's very terms.[8] This general configuration—ample rights, joined to stigmatizing restraints on their use—recurs in patterned ways at various points across the legal landscape. We nonetheless remain sheepish about admitting and defending our practices here. The result is that stigma, as a mechanism[9] of rights-restraint, is wrongly stigmatized, and shaming becomes too often shameful.

But why do we do things this way? Why do we knowingly establish entitlements considerably broader than the conduct we're truly prepared to countenance?[10] Once we recognize the law's deep debt to stigma, we must ask how far the implications of this recognition run. Might it mean that even those rights we regard as most central to our democratic way of life—to engage in offensive political speech, for instance—turn out to depend for their very existence on our expectation that few will ever invoke them? If that is so, does this make us hypocrites? If we dismiss these questions, we succumb to mystification in defending treasured rights entirely in terms of the high moral principles they enshrine.[11] For these rights rest at least equally on our tacit sociological assumptions about who will exercise them, under what circumstances, and how frequently. It is not only explanatory questions that are here at stake, but normative matters too, because we cannot fully assess the defensibility of a given legal right until we discover how it does or doesn't influence actual activity.

Our expectations about its likely real-life effect often rest on little evidence, however, and so regularly prove unfounded. Though accurate predictions are sometimes easy enough, at times it's a shot in the dark. A serious challenge for the lawmaker is that more people may show up at the door to claim the rights she blithely created but secretly hoped few would employ. Informal constraints against what she considers the "abuse" of rights may prove weaker than anticipated. The converse is always possible as well; under-claiming can prove as troublesome as over-claiming.

These considerations prompt us to wonder: Why does resistance to the exercise of rights arise acutely at certain points within a legal system and not at others? And how does the contemplation of this resistance come to shape the law itself? Specifically, how does such anticipation influence the drawing of lines between what the law will and will not allow, encourage or discourage? For social and legal theory, these questions are unfamiliar.

We may delude ourselves, in ideologically problematic ways,[12] whenever legal rights allegedly central to our system of government and the legitimacy of our social order exist only insofar as they are almost never put to use. Yet many situations exist, I'll show, where there is good reason to create—even commend ourselves for championing—de jure entitlements unlikely to be invoked. These rights are sometimes central to what we (most of us) wish to be as a people. Yet they are ultimately agreeable to us only insofar as we successfully stanch their de facto usage in nearly all situations where they formally apply. To grasp this paradox and its implications—the goal of this book—is to appreciate the workings of our legal system in a distinctive and perhaps unsettling light.

If we should be concerned about mystification in how we understand our legal rights, it is especially in places where we mistakenly imagine that these informal counterweights to abusive rights-claiming are safely in place. We should also be wary of places where such weights grow too heavy, imperiling the vitality of rights whose active, real-life exercise we deem essential to a decent society. Conservatives tend to worry about the first of these dangers; liberals, about the second. It is helpful to put polemics momentarily aside, however, and investigate these twin dangers as opposite sides of a single coin, complementary aspects of the same sociological question. This is the question of how to design our rights for situations when we realize that the conduct they authorize will nonetheless invite wide reproach.

The legal system is only one part of a larger normative order and often stands in tension with other parts, requiring us to consider their respective workings and their interactions with law itself. How this mixing of legal and extralegal elements occurs, and with what ramifications, is my central question. One aspect of the problem is that we regularly acknowledge moral duties to refrain from, and to discourage in others, activities the law expressly allows, just as we sometimes feel duties to encourage lawful activities that, we fear, suffer undue impediments. In either case, the law provides inadequate guidance to what we believe that we and others ought to do. Yet it is a common pathology—observed since Tocqueville,[13] of Americans especially—to think that law offers sufficient basis for action and its evaluation.

Thus, when a person is accused of murder, journalists and others consider themselves publicly obliged to uphold the law's standard of proof—"beyond a reasonable doubt"—in assessing the likelihood of his guilt. Yet there is little reason we should adhere to so high an evidentiary burden outside the courtroom,[14] where the stakes and objectives are quite different from those within. As neighbors and citizens, our concerns and legitimate curiosities are by no means identical to those of jurors. Still, as one legal scholar observes, "When law and morality are so much conflated in popular (and even sometimes professional) thought, it is hardly surprising that people should want to place the same limit on morality's ambit as on the law's."[15]

When nonlegal restraints greatly influence how we exercise our rights, the result is that we obey unwritten rules far more demanding than any we would wish the law to impose, even as it quietly depends upon their efficacy. We preoccupy ourselves with the dramatic moments when these informal impediments break down, as when neo-Nazis march through Jewish neighborhoods. More sociologically significant, if less conspicuous, is how frequently such inhibitions succeed, sometimes to excess. Without them, our law would necessarily look very different, as in other lands, with sharper curbs on even our most fundamental liberties. When this foundation of extralegal inhibition seems to shake, the edifice of rights and institutions dependent on it threatens to totter. Whether this scenario fairly describes our recent history—if not across the board, then in crucial corners of this country—has been a central, if implicit, question within much public discussion of its recent direction. This formulation of our seeming predicament can help us better understand and grapple with current challenges.

We live in a time of intense political polarization, institutional dysfunction, societal fragmentation, disorienting change.[16] Almost inevitably, we Americans turn quickly, instinctively, almost inevitably, to our legal system for some semblance of normative order. We sometimes do so without appreciating that there are distinct limits, at times readily discernible, to what the law can offer. At such points we must find other, further ways to address our dissatisfactions and our distempers with one another. In so doing, we begin to learn what it is about law that requires it to seek regular supplement from other regulatory mechanisms, in patterned ways, at predictable places.

In fact, thoughtful lawmakers regularly formulate our rights in full awareness that we may "misuse" and employ them in an undesired fashion widely deemed reprehensible. When creating our entitlements, legislators and judges thereby gauge—at least implicitly, sometimes quite openly—the counterbalances that are likely to obstruct the unwelcome exercise of these very authorizations. (This is the "ideal-type"[17] of a right to do wrong, as I will use the term.) What exactly are lawmakers thinking at such times?

And how accurate are their assumptions, during these key moments, about the world's true workings?

These questions lead us to ask whether social changes of recent years make it no longer credible to rely upon this tacit tempering of rights-assertion. If so, then the tasks of lawmaking and legal interpretation themselves become very different from what they have been in the past. It would seem that the law must then penetrate ever farther into areas of our lives, such as parenting practices,[18] once governed almost exclusively by subtler promptings, through social pressures and processes more informal. What would law's permeation into these further crevices entail for the preservation of personal and public liberty, for the proper relation between state and society?[19]

Many people find themselves vexed by how the quality of collective life suffers when people cannot trust one another to resolve their differences independently of the legal system, through more casual, everyday practices and the shared ethical understandings these embody. Such concerns today pervade the work of several leading political thinkers and social scientists of diverse theoretical orientations.[20] These same worries intermittently suffuse the thoughts of many citizens as well. A recent Gallup poll thus finds that 72 percent of Americans themselves believe the morals of the country are in significant decline.[21]

A frequent recent criticism of the United States—from across the ideological spectrum, by both Americans and foreign observers—has been that conventional notions of moral duty no longer seem to effectively push back against rights-based ways of speaking and acting in relation to others. Influential work in social science attributes Americans' increasing reliance on law in recent decades to a decline in social trust and the "social capital" permitting such trust.[22] Putnam thus contends that "we are forced to rely increasingly on formal institutions, and above all on the law, to accomplish what we used to accomplish through informal networks reinforced by generalized reciprocity."[23]

The social capital Putnam has in mind moderates not only the invocation of legal rights but also the uncivil behavior that common morality and the social practices embodying it once seemed effortlessly to suppress. It is precisely this uncivil behavior that now increasingly inspires us to invoke such rights. An apparent weakening of inhibitions on rights-talk calls into question the continued vitality of common morality and the hesitations it imposes on such language use, even as this morality has itself come to indulge a greater measure of this talk.[24] It is credible—from evidence not merely anecdotal and memoiristic, but archival and ethnographic as well[25]—that in many corners of America prevailing mores and the social capital on which they depended did indeed hold such inclinations in substantial check, as professed "communitarians" stressed not long ago,[26] and as others of diverse theoretical leanings today continue to claim.[27] And yet, as this book shows, there are many places within American society where social mores remain quite effective in restraining the abusive exercise of legal rights, in ways that the law itself heavily (if tacitly) relies upon.[28]

Eyebrows often ascend with suspicion in progressive circles when anyone suggests that others should exercise their rights responsibly. Distrust wells up at the very moment words like "duty" or "responsibility" pass one's lips. In deference to these sensitivities, Samuel Moyn begins his defense of duties, written for ideological compatriots on the Left, by observing "the anxious sense that to legitimate talk of duty is to flirt with disaster—that, all things considered, it is best to stick exclusively to the vindication of hard-won rights."[29]

This distrust of duty may be initially surprising. Public talk of responsibility should resonate with certain feminists, at least. Gilligan showed empirically that women find its language more congenial than that of rights.[30] Yet there is much fear that talk of responsibility, invoked in connection with another's rights, aims to discourage their exercise entirely. And legal rights *exist* to be exercised, many assume. One moral theorist thus insists, "When people refuse to press their rights, there are usually others who profit"—unjustly so.[31] Concerns of this sort lurked not far beneath the many excited liberal rejoinders[32] to communitarian critiques of "rights-talk." In that spirit, several Oxford dons vigorously urge, with respect to human rights especially, that "citizens should not be required to justify their exercise of these,"[33] as by defending their motives for such use. These academicians exhort that "a duty to respect the rights of others is to be preferred to a duty to 'exercise rights responsibly,' which confuses the moral appeal of living a responsible life with the existence of a legally enforceable duty."[34]

This stance fails to recognize that much of what people reasonably expect of one another in acceptable conduct—fulfilling routine promises, for instance, and exhibiting elemental civility—does not find its way fully into the law, for the several reasons (often wholly defensible) here examined in Chapter 6. Even so, many instinctively associate all talk of extralegal responsibility with the indefensible suppression of lawful entitlements. And this instinctive mental reflex renders "responsibility talk" problematic for anyone much imbued with rights consciousness, as are many Americans[35] (and increasingly others too,[36] even the Chinese[37]), and certainly all Western law professors.

Though this book chiefly concerns the relation between law and morality, the problem at issue arises within morality itself, even before we begin to consider its relevance to the law. Thus, when moral theory sets out, as it often has in recent decades, by first asking what moral rights we have, it naturally proceeds to ask who holds the corresponding duties, for these are designed to ensure that those rights are satisfactorily respected. We therefore naturally come to think of our duties in relation to others' rights, to which these duties "correspond" or "correlate," as both ordinary parlance and familiar legal theory has it. Duties thus enter our frame of contemplation at this second stage in the analysis.[38] The possibility that we may have genuine duties independent of others' rights-claims upon us is rejected as illiberal,[39] and then recedes from routine consideration—perhaps beyond our imagination, some maintain.[40] Many of these "obligations without rights," as O'Neill calls them,[41] arise from particular social roles, which vary acutely by place or period and hence derive from no general theory.

When rights are said to precede responsibilities, and when responsibilities attach only to those with "corresponding" rights, it becomes difficult to get a conceptual handle on certain kinds of responsibility—that of men in preventing unwanted pregnancies, for instance. Because women alone possess the right to abort, the conduct putting them in a position to exercise this right—often a failure to employ contraception—seems naturally to become her responsibility alone. This suggests a deep deficiency, not only in how we think about responsibility, but perhaps even in how we think about rights themselves.

Within liberal moral theory, the prevalent view is that any moral commitments we may have to other individuals, beyond our generic duty to honor their universal moral rights, are discretionary and supererogatory. Yet for much of history, even within the modern West,[42] this way of thinking about morality's claims upon us, and about our responsibilities to others in particular, has not been widely embraced. It has in fact rarely been much accepted, as best one can discern, beneath the academic ether, and in most of the world it remains peculiar even today. This is especially evident from recent work in the promising new field of "moral anthropology"[43] (discussed in Chapter 9), which employs ethnographic methods to discover how ordinary people throughout the world manage the ethical issues encountered in their daily lives.

The aversion to talk of extralegal duty becomes especially acute in progressive responses to those urging that the poor, in exercising their rights of public provision, take greater personal responsibility for how they conduct their lives, and for how they fare in the world.[44] The apprehension here is that calls for greater responsibility are intended not merely as a supplement to public assistance, but as a substitute for it. In this "personal responsibility crusade,"[45] as one prominent scholar derisively calls it, we uncover yet another insidious tactic of "neoliberalism,"[46] it is said. Be that as it may, these suspicions are unconvincing when extended across the board, to contexts where the normative stakes and valences are quite different, where such scholar-critics would be the first to call for the greater recognition of nonlegal duty.

Within Western scholarship, the question of law's relation to morality is today almost exclusively the concern of analytic philosophy. Philosophers generally understand the query in *conceptual* terms: Does law logically entail some form of morality? And can positive law be truly binding if it is inconsistent with claims of morality, properly understood?

In contemporary moral philosophy, "the right to do wrong" refers to something entirely different from present concerns. The philosophical discussion poses the question of whether it is coherent to speak in such terms at all—a question of logical possibility.[47] As I here define the notion, there can be no doubt that such rights exist, that we are not chasing a dybbuk. To speak of a legal right to engage in moral wrong is avowedly to make "a mid-sentence shift in domains of reasons,"[48] but without confusing the two enterprises. My concern is with how this type of legal right presents itself in our lives, how we create and cope with its myriad manifestations. In short, the relation between law and morality has sociological dimensions no less than philosophical ones, prompting the question: When and why do law and morals overlap, or part company? In other words, when do societies incorporate their common morality into their laws? Why do they often fail to do so, even where its claims are clear and forceful? And how do people then manage the resulting gap between these 'warring' normative orders? Once we settle on a few basic definitions, these become empirical questions, their answers inviting causal explanation, implicating theories and methods chiefly within the social sciences.

If the key questions here are then not conceptual in character, neither are they *normative* and prescriptive. I do not ask whether it is *desirable* to incorporate a given moral principle into the rules governing a particular activity. Normative matters will interest us here only insofar as people choose to act on their understandings of what morality demands. The two points at which they most prominently do so are when collectively deciding what laws to create and when determining where and how to bring this shared morality to bear upon their daily life as individuals.

Every legal system defines itself largely in terms of how it answers the question of where prevailing views of morality, insofar as these exist, will receive juridical recognition, and where they will not. Without implicitly resolving this matter, one cannot construct a legal system at all. There seems no more suitable academic pigeonhole for this question than the field of sociology. For my overriding concerns originate in key texts of Montesquieu, on the relation of law and "mores" in differing political regimes.[49] Also pertinent are Émile Durkheim's observations on how the law often embodies and reinforces a "collective conscience," manifested in our "collective representations." These become increasingly individualistic in character, he believed, in response to profound changes in the West's economic and social structure. Yet neither Durkheim nor the contemporary sociology of law (or the still-broader field of socio-legal studies) has conceived the relevant questions to be those just raised, nor have these questions been examined in relation to a wide range of pertinent empirical materials.

We law professors most often pursue a third type of investigation, which we describe as *doctrinal*. We analyze the intricate intersections and assess the implications of particular statutes, constitutions, and judicial opinions, in light of their express terms and underlying purposes. We view our professional task as integrating specific texts within a larger fabric or ecology of surrounding legal rights, duties, and official processes. The present study does not fall into this category any more than within the preceding two, those of normative and conceptual inquiry. Still, it will sometimes be necessary to scrutinize with some care the content of particular legal rules—for instance, those on "abuse of rights," insurance contracts, and offensive speech under the First Amendment—a task that legal sociology undertakes only infrequently. Without determining the content of legal rules, it is impossible to assess how much they comport with prevailing moral sensibilities and the social practices embodying these.

This study is conceived as an elementary introduction from an advanced standpoint—or perhaps better, an advanced introduction to some elemental questions. It is intended for university students, undergraduate and graduate, and for scholars beyond legal academia with a curiosity about relations between law and society. I suspect my fellow legal scholars will find much to argue with here as well, especially those with some wonder about legal theory, broadly understood. The book provides an empirical look into the ways that widely shared normative commitments find expression in mores restraining the exercise of legal rights, with the result that individuals and institutions behave more attentively to common morality than the law requires. To assess these issues is to inquire into when and why these moral ideals at times find their way into our law, but sometimes instead only into the social practices moderating its use. My purpose is to crisply formulate the concept of a right to do wrong, identify some of its sources and empirical expressions (with no pretense to exhaustiveness), suggest its significance within our legal order, and prompt its further study.

My primary concern is with rights to do *serious* wrong. But I will often refer more broadly to wrong *tout court,* speaking simply of "rights to do wrong." This is because the gravity of the wrongdoing at issue in a particular situation itself regularly proves a subject of contention among those concerned—and therefore, for sociological purposes, cannot simply be stipulated. Matters that some people will deem merely etiquette and arbitrary convention will by others be considered more fundamental, as raising profound issues of justice or of a person's character. Differences of opinion over the perceived gravity of a given wrong often influence the law's measure of response, or nonresponse.

Even where there exists some consensus on perceptions of gravity, these may exercise greater or lesser weight in shaping the response—social and legal—to the particular type of wrong. Some of these responses, though widely deemed draconian (or too indulgent), will endure unperturbed for long periods, locked in by inertial forces. We must examine multiple cases of perceived wrongdoing lying at various points along this spectrum. Only in this way can we discover how differences in gravity influence the range of responses, legal and otherwise, to moral wrong. It is important as well to investigate the reasons different groups of people mark out gradations of moral gravity as they do. Also significant and revealing are how these markings alter over time, whether in response to legal change or, more often, for other reasons entirely. The ensuing analysis will therefore necessarily shift in focus, as context requires, between the larger genus (all wrongs) and the specific species (grave ones) of chief interest.

In employing the term "rights to do wrong," I mean to include both the type of rights intentionally created by lawmakers when they seek affirmatively to protect a specific form of disfavored conduct, and the type of rights arising only from the absence of a prohibition, where legislators deliberately decline to intercede against what they acknowledge to involve misbehavior. My usage in this respect is consistent with ordinary language—with how most people within the Anglo-American world standardly employ the term "legal right." Rights of the first set present the greater puzzle, and most of my examples therefore draw from it. The rationale for including the second type of right to do wrong is that it is often said, with only slight exaggeration, that Western liberalism, in its classical philosophic understanding, holds that everything not expressly prohibited by the law is permitted, and that authoritarianism insists on exactly the contrary.

Without explicit proscription of a given activity, countries whose law adheres to liberal principles presume a "right" to engage in it, and I shall use the word accordingly. It is entirely possible that rights to do serious wrong may therefore come into being not only through a lawmaker's deliberate acts but because common morality no longer looks so leniently upon forms of lawful conduct once widely regarded as acceptable. At that point, a disparity arises between an indulgent legality and a common morality newly less forgiving. This disparity will often present serious challenges for both lawmakers and ordinary citizens—challenges little different, at their core, than in the first situation. Whether the disparity comes into being deliberately or spontaneously, through legal changes "from above" or a transformation in common morality "from below," the essential questions will be how to understand and manage its implications.

Consider now several brief cases of real-life situations where the law is considerably more charitable than common morality, often in the expectation that potential problems thereby generated will resolve themselves extralegally:

1. Under the label "collateral damage," thousands of innocent civilians may be lawfully killed in combat, provided that those

responsible do not intend this result and anticipate that battlefield gains will outweigh such carnage.

2. American law allows us to completely disinherit our children, including young minors, even if they have done nothing to deserve this fate.
3. We may construct buildings on our property that are profoundly offensive to our neighbors. In some countries, including the United States, we may even do such things *in order to* offend our neighbors.
4. International law allows Western museums to retain masterworks looted long ago from their rightful owners.
5. When we purchase insurance to protect our property, we are usually free to behave with considerable indifference in safeguarding it from destruction.
6. We may lawfully engage in highly offensive speech, such as (in one Supreme Court case) denouncing—even at the funerals of fallen soldiers—the military's acceptance of homosexuality among the ranks.
7. We may decline medical attention even when our physicians correctly tell us that we will otherwise promptly die. Any perceived moral obligations that we may owe—to our children, other financial dependents, or to ourselves—receive no legal recognition.[50]
8. In most societies, it is legally permissible to terminate a pregnancy on the grounds that the child would be a girl.[51] This is true even in some Western countries with substantial immigration from parts of the world where sex-selective abortion is common.[52] There is ample basis to suspect the practice continues in recipient countries.[53]
9. An adult woman in the United States may employ abortion[54] as a means of birth control, for no other reason than that she and her sexual partner find contraception unpleasant or burdensome.[55]

These illustrations have something crucial in common: the law permits what ordinary morality—widely shared notions of right and wrong—reproaches, sometimes severely.[56] These common features reveal a great deal, not only about the social context within which the law operates in a given situation, but about law itself, its nature as an instrument of human governance. It is helpful to think of these situations as involving rights to do wrong or, more simply (if less evocatively), lawful wrongdoing. The reader, now familiar with the general idea, will easily call to mind similar situations. Though these will likely vary somewhat with one's political proclivities, there will nonetheless exist much agreement on many cases. What do we learn from their empirical incidence, and from its explanation; what do we come to understand, in particular, about the character of law, as one regulatory modality among others, fully intelligible only in working relation to alternative forms of normative ordering, with which it is often complementary, though sometimes in conflict?

The illustrations just mentioned differ greatly in several respects, of course. The conduct involved in each is objectionable to different people in distinct ways. The mix of reasons why the law permits each such form of disfavored conduct is distinctive as well. In seeking to constrain such behavior, we succeed to varying degrees—in some cases almost entirely, in others scarcely at all. From each situation to the next, people also employ very different methods—some coercive, others more consensual—in restraining the conduct deemed objectionable. In some cases the preferred means to this end are readily apparent to any observer; in others they are known only to institutional insiders, invisible to the uninitiated.

There exists an entire class of such entitlements. These are rights we at once deeply enshrine within our law yet actively, even aggressively at times, discourage one another from exercising. We are often sincere and justified in regarding them as important to protect, through legal rules sometimes grounded in high constitutional or humanitarian principles. We nonetheless treat such rights as advisable to frustrate at nearly every turn. We recoil especially at the possibility of facilitating their wide usage, beyond a very restricted set of circumstances, which the law cannot adequately define and delimit. Many feel ambivalent, even deeply troubled, in recognizing these rights at all. It is therefore unsurprising that though they may endure for long periods, these entitlements occasionally face strong challenge and regularly dissolve. The only thing about such rights that endures is the *category* of such rights itself—its social dynamics and suppositions regarding the strength of informal pushback—not its particular content at a given time.

Despite our persistent doubts about such rights, we very often act in good conscience and on defensible grounds in establishing them. For we have some reason to believe that various mechanisms will press upon people and institutions to exercise these rights "responsibly," attending to moral considerations that the law itself cannot fully entertain and absorb.[57] We may regret that it proves impossible to devise a legal rule that clearly distinguishes prohibited from permitted conduct, which would enable the law to more perfectly track the terms of common morality. For practical purposes this slippage becomes immaterial, however, because we are confident that social forces will close the gap.

This socio-legal configuration, as we might call it, arises with some regularity. Its distinct mix of features may be neither immediately recognizable nor readily intelligible. It presents a recurring puzzle that, at some level, everyone has at least casually considered. It arises not only in weighty matters of national and global concern, but in ordinary lives. We often encounter it when wondering why our legal system allows conduct by others, individuals or institutions, that elicits within us strong indignation at perceived injustice,[58] whether the justice we seek is corrective, retributive, or distributive.

It bears emphasis here that unlike mere personal resentment (in most forms), indignation regularly has salutary consequences for social change, though it is an often poor guide to immediate individual action and lawmaking. "The feelings of moral indignation with which human beings react to insult and disrespect contain the potential for an idealizing anticipation of successful, undistorted recognition,"[59] observes Honneth, in an Hegelian idiom. At the moments and places within social life where these feelings receive no legal recognition, we occupy the realm of rights to do wrong.

## Elements of the Argument

Chapter 1 defines what I mean by common morality, and why the very notion—though controversial for some—harbors much of interest and unexamined import. Chapter 2 sketches many salient examples of rights to do wrong, observing similarities and differences among them. These examples provide a basis for the analytical comparisons to follow. Chapter 3 explores three such rights in greater detail. Chapter 4 examines the notion of "abusing" a legal right. Chapter 5 discusses the place of rights to do wrong within our ordinary language and assesses the two leading explanations for why the law converges with or diverges from common morals. Chapter 6 looks deeper into the sources and sites of the divergences, in particular, beyond those recognized by these two broad theories. Chapter 7 does the same for sites and sources of congruity between law and morals.

Chapter 8 critically assesses the view, widely shared among legal scholars, that there is no reason to be much troubled by even the most glaring gaps between common morality and the law. On this account, the legal system must follow a path entirely independent of common morality, to facilitate its frequent intercession against prevailing moralities and, in particular, the objectionable prejudices they authorize. This chapter also defends the need for a specifically sociological perspective on the relation between law and morality, though this is not the species of sociology today undertaken in academic departments of that name. In further support of this approach, Chapter 9 indicates the serious limitations of other scholarly disciplines in confronting the present questions.

Chapter 10 assesses the shifting stance of American lawyers toward common morality, while Chapter 11 undertakes a similar appraisal for financial professionals. In Chapter 12, I inquire into the reasons particular responsibilities attach themselves to particular rights, contrasting the present, sociological approach to this question with philosophical and economic alternatives. Chapter 13 describes how law's relationship with common morality has changed over time, with the advent of liberal modernity, in particular. The Conclusion draws these several strands of analysis into a single argument concerning the meaning and significance of rights to do wrong. I show how an adequate understanding of the law itself, in the most general terms, depends upon proper understanding of this crucial category of rights in particular.

## The Cautionary Tale of the "Ground Zero Mosque"

The question of when and by what means it is acceptable to discourage others from exercising their legal rights in ways we deem wrongful is of practical importance on virtually a daily basis, despite the limits of our ability to discuss and answer it, even to satisfactorily formulate it. These limits are vividly revealed, to pick an illustration from the headlines, in the 2010 controversy over an initiative to construct a Muslim cultural center, with a prayer center, near the site of the former World Trade Center.[60] The public debate elicited, on both sides, several ill-considered intercessions from some of the most refined voices in national life.

*New Republic* editor-in-chief Peter Beinart curiously proclaimed, for instance, "If you say that people have the right [to build the cultural center], but they shouldn't take advantage of that right, in fact, it seems to me you're denying them that right."[61] This implies it is never permissible to question any exercise of legal right on grounds of prudence, social sensitivity, wisdom, or moral defensibility, a position Beinart obviously does not actually hold. He undoubtedly believes, for instance, that we should all refrain from public speech fairly described as anti-Semitic or white-supremacist; and he surely supported those many "moderate" Muslims who argued, following the Danish cartoon controversy, that "while free speech has its place, the sensitivities of the Muslim community should be respected," as Bret Stephens explained their views. To which Stephens then added: "But tolerance isn't a one-way street, and sensitivity is not the preserve of Muslims alone. So what do they make of the sensitivities of 9/11 families in the face of their mega-mosque?"[62]

Opponents of the center's construction offered little better than Beinart. While acknowledging their legal right to build, Charles Krauthammer—whose weekly *Washington Post* columns betrayed nary the slightest theological inspiration—urged the developers to manifest greater "respect for the sacred," suggesting their intentions would amount to "sacrilege."[63] This is odd wording for someone well-steeped in the liberal political theory[64] averse to such invocations of religious language in public discourse. Krauthammer might have sought to proffer a liberal theory of geographical space ritually resonant with special or ultimate value, sacred in this specific sense. That would have allowed a more secular argument for limiting the morally acceptable uses of such symbolically charged terrain, if one may loosely so characterize the site. This could have presented Krauthammer a difficult but worthy philosophical challenge. He did not attempt it—though some have, in other contexts.[65] In light of his standard mode of argument—militantly tough-minded, profanely unsentimental—his vaguely pious offering here was entirely out of character and, it would therefore seem, disingenuous.

Among opponents of the cultural center, still more overheated was the intervention of *New Republic* erstwhile owner Martin Peretz, once an influential intellectual voice within the Democratic Party: "I wonder whether I need honor these people and pretend they are worthy of the privileges of the First Amendment, which I have in my gut the sense that they will abuse."[66] Peretz's comments sparked a firestorm of criticism, alleging racism and Islamophobia. As a rare defender observed, however, "the promiscuity with which proponents of the mosque project . . . tried to make a constitutional issue out of what is really a debate about propriety . . . validates Peretz's concern about First Amendment abuse."[67] It is unlikely, however, that this was the particular species of rights abuse Peretz had in mind, given that he had not criticized Muslim leaders for slighting concerns of propriety; he had criticized them for failing to speak out more fulsomely in criticism of jihadist terror attacks on civilian populations, of which the World Trade Center attack was only one notable instance.

It is tempting to dismiss all three authors' unpersuasive, even histrionic, remarks with the charitable concession that for none of them was this his finest moment. Their shared failure nonetheless suggests that the problem resides in limitations of our available ways of thinking or speaking—and hence grappling adequately with—the very notion of a right to do serious wrong.[68] The failure here therefore runs deeper than any momentary lapses in reasoning by prominent public thinkers.

Wherever one may come out on that particular, passing controversy, we should be able to discuss significant moral questions—those the law undoubtedly touches but leaves largely unresolved—without resorting to such debased forms of argument. There should be no need to call in divine thunderbolts against our opponents (Krauthammer), to abuse the sometimes-valuable notion of an "abuse of rights" (Peretz), or summarily dismiss others' arguments as pure bigotry (Beinart), as if appeals to graciousness or solicitude for others' grief could in principle have no place in public conversation.[69] Accusations of bigotry were indeed common from those defending religious liberties of the Center's imam and developer.[70] Yet if bigotry were the only source of possible doubts about the wisdom of the selected site, then the considerable majority of polled Americans who opposed the location[71] would have to be condemned in just those terms. Almost certainly, most people simply thought it defensible to wish that nearby property owners might respect the emotional sensitivities of 9/11 families.

Even a supremely eloquent president found himself struggling to articulate anything more coherent than unequivocally celebrating the religious freedom of the center's sponsors on one day, while embarrassedly insisting the very next on the qualification that he "was not commenting . . . on the wisdom of the decision."[72] The wisdom of the decision was, however, the only matter ever in contention.[73] Few Americans denied the legal right to build a house of worship on the site.[74] The president's second interjection therefore failed to join issue with anyone's actual concerns (about wisdom), just as his first (about law)—however principled and passionate—was both obvious to all and entirely off-point. His undoubted intellectual powers (and those of his agile speechwriters) came up dismayingly short in helping us bridge the discursive chasm between his disjointed intercessions, between the law and common morality.

Among the dozens of interventions on the subject by prominent political and journalistic figures, perhaps the most appealing was that of New York City Mayor Michael Bloomberg. He not merely defended, but *advocated,* construction of the cultural center with a prayer area. He did so, not on the anodyne grounds that the site's owners had a legal right to do so, but because building such a center, *especially* on that hallowed site, would powerfully send "a great message . . . of tolerance and openness [to] the world."[75] By "the world," he notably meant not only those Muslim lands where the state routinely persecutes its ethno-religious minorities, but also certain *Western* countries, where the burqa and minarets were then being outlawed, and where discrimination against Muslims was apparently increasing in other ways as well.[76]

To Bloomberg's good fortune, a decision to defend the center did not require him to survey the hypothetical terrain on which it might be wrong to exercise legal rights to use one's real property for religious purposes (or any other). Bloomberg's stance thus put him on the side with the better arguments, perhaps, but also the easier, the most familiar ones, most readily couched within our standard normative idiom. If "abusing" one's rights to religious expression were theoretically conceivable to him, his remarks gave no such indication. Still less did they convey any sense of when those rare circumstances might arise, even for purposes of distinguishing such a hypothetical state of affairs from the facts before him.

The disappointing episode of the Islamic cultural center at Ground Zero painfully reveals the absence of even a preliminary vocabulary for acknowledging something like "legal rights being invoked for unacceptable purposes, the wrongfulness of which law fails to see." It behooves us to find a language by which to more fruitfully entertain that possibility. This book is a modest invitation to that end. I propose that we begin modestly, by introducing the concept of a right to do wrong into our ordinary speech—an idiom of lawful wrongdoing.

All my chief illustrations of such entitlements display this same perplexing property: they arise in situations that for many people elicit strong intimations of an accompanying duty, unacknowledged by law, often for admittedly good reason. These situations reveal as well the absence of any widely acceptable terms for the public articulation of that moral duty.

Though ordinary language often offers a useful window into common morality, everyday speech here generally fails us. It fails us not only as a guide to individual action, public policy, and legislative initiative, but also as a source of raw material for reflection on our daily sentiments and practices. We here resemble those unfortunate primates who, while lacking "speech" (as we humans understand it), clearly wish to express to us their intense indignation at perceived injustice in how we treat them, as when—with no apparent reason—experimenters offer better food to one than to another in the next cage.[77] A better lexicon, or simply greater confidence in deploying some existing one, would help us discern when we should hesitate in fully exercising our rights. Chapter 1 begins this task by further elaborating the idea of common morality employed throughout the book.

# 1

# Common Morality, Social Mores, and the Law

We must have some level of comfort with the notion of common morality, in its own right, before we can begin to examine its relation to the law. And if common morality, like the law, contributes to elementary social coordination—as to more ambitious forms of solidarity—how might it do so, exactly?

Certain observers militantly affirm that a shared sense of moral fundamentals is necessary in enabling people to cooperate with and rely upon one another in basic ways—necessary even to say that a society exists at all. This common morality is essential, they believe, to any social order in which one would wish to live, at least. For social order of this baseline sort is a threshold condition for thereafter attaining loftier ideals of justice, freedom, and human flourishing. Many also see common morality as essential to uniting a society against its enemies, present or anticipated, distant or residing just next door.

Others passionately deny not only the existence of a common morality (in any nontrivial sense) but its very possibility—indeed, its conceptual intelligibility. On both sides of this sometimes-heated dispute, large numbers apparently believe that acknowledging or repudiating the sheer fact that moral standards are shared within a given national territory has clear and decisive implications for its governance, though these are rarely articulated or explained with any care. Those implications they find either simpático or profoundly unpalatable. To offer a few concrete illustrations: Some people today consider it appalling that persons of modest wealth perceive injustice in a new tax upon the rich that is adverse to those (like

Mark Zuckerberg) who earned their billions through technological innovations that much enhance the well-being of most people in the world. Other people, generally of opposing ideological inclinations, find it equally outrageous that so many African Americans do not share the view that, apart from a few "bad apples," most police officers adhere to acceptable ethical standards, treating criminal suspects with sufficient respect, refraining from excessive force.[1]

It is by no means obvious what truly follows from according or rejecting a prominent place to common morality in our understanding of national societies and their workings. The question nevertheless appears politically momentous, and there is no doubt that it is ominously large. We might best work up to it gradually, indirectly, by first inquiring what evidence there is for the existence of a common morality, treating this simply as an empirical puzzle. Here is a question that might be resolved on a factual basis, one might hope, even if the answer is unlikely to be a simple yes or no. Before we could examine the issue in such terms, though, we would need to resolve a few thorny conceptual issues, some of which this chapter assays. I therefore sidle up to the bigger questions only somewhat laterally, rather than seeking directly to resolve them. Still, it is possible to begin by naively asking of the available data: How strongly does a national population hold common views of right and wrong? How broadly do members share sentiments on questions of justice, whether in general terms or in reference to more specific issues (conceived in this fashion)?

We would have to adopt a pluralistic stance on pertinent methods for approaching these questions, seeking answers not only in expressions of opinion to survey researchers and in experimental philosophy, but also in many other places, including the everyday mores of various milieus, as ethnographers describe these. Where differences among people initially seem more evident, we would need to consider the possibility that principled commitments, though fundamentally shared, may assume distinct forms in specific subcommunities. The virtue of "personal respectability," in particular, appears no less weighty in the minds of many who find themselves trapped in poor ethnic enclaves, according to several urban ethnographers,[2] as those living in Park Avenue penthouses. Conversely, acceptable mores that initially seem quite similar in different places might in fact signify deeper value commitments wholly at odds.

Though the two greatly overlap, we should not entirely equate the *concept* of common morality, as here employed, with the *verbal expression* "common morality," its use within ordinary language. Philosophers of language are correct to insist on some separation between the social realities with which we are consistently concerned—and which scholars may help us conceptualize—and the particular patterns of wording we routinely employ, at a given place or period, to navigate within these realities. It is nonetheless of some interest that an Ngram Viewer search finds that, since 1800, the term "common morality" has alternately waxed and waned, today enjoying a frequency of usage attained only twice before, in 1811 and 1883.[3] We cannot, however, assume that the term retained the same meaning throughout this long period. We can be more confident in interpreting sharp changes over short periods. So it warrants mention that the largest upsurge in American usage of the term for over a century occurred during the 1980s and 1990s, which saw the advent of America's "culture wars." Usage of the expression has not much declined since then.

Common morality is an elusive notion, both conceptually and empirically. "We live during a time when the very concept of a single unifying moral order is hard to fathom,"[4] write two leading scholars—in evident exasperation. The idea of common morality has long been quite "thin," in Bernard Williams's sense.[5] Such thin concepts as good, fair, ought, permissible, blameworthy, and praiseworthy are strewn across the language of public discussion in modern liberal societies. These words are rather amorphous, however, too remote from any recognizable social context or moral content—hence, too abstract—to assist much in practical tasks of understanding and evaluation.

We can distinguish these terms, readily and intuitively, from equally positive expressions like honest, rude, brave, heroic, courageous, generous, and wise, and from words with negative valence like cruel, boorish, selfish, barbaric, obscene, and gaudy. These concepts are thick, in that they effectively merge descriptions of fact with judgments of value. They are thick also in the sense that, to use them properly, one must know a great deal about the specific contours and commitments of one's society, and often about someone's place within it.

Thick concepts are essentially absent from liberal moral and political philosophy, as they are from the elite political discourse of the societies that spawned it. Yet they still suffuse the language of evaluation in nonelite political discussion and in the private life of nearly everyone within these same countries, if perhaps less so than in the distant past. In certain parts of the world that are more culturally homogeneous than the contemporary West, areas lacking the experience of mass immigration, people continue to employ thick concepts even in their public discourse, it would seem.[6] This is because the stronger commitments we make when employing thick concepts often stem from the contemporary expression of a long-standing culture or civilization. Despite continuing differences over the proper interpretation of its legacy, this common heritage can instill some confidence among interlocutors that even their sharper judgments, positive and negative, will be shared—or at least not dismissed as incomprehensible, incoherent, wholly barbaric. By contrast, prevailing understandings of liberal modernity demand that, when engaged in public justification of our political views, we seek to extricate ourselves from precisely such culture-specific commitments. Admittedly, this proves not merely difficult in practice, in the heat of the moment, but impossible fully to imagine, when of cooler head, even in theoretical terms, some insist.

For common morality to become a thick concept, its idea of "wrong" would have to take on much richer coloration, denoting "wrong in this particular way, for these reasons, in those circumstances, when dealing with that kind of person, given an appreciative understanding of our group's shared criteria of judgment." Today, within modern liberal societies, the freestanding notion of wrongdoing tells us almost nothing, and so in these respects common morality seems to ascend or, as it were, recede into thin air. Even so, within a given country or professional community, concepts once quite thin can thicken over time. Within the law over recent decades, this is clearly the case with "due process" in U.S. constitutional law and "good faith" within the contract law (and attendant commercial mores) of Western Europe.[7] Thick concepts sometimes have to begin their legal life rather ethereally. And concepts once densely specific in reference, evaluative and descriptive, can conversely wizen over time. This is as true within professional communities—of lawyers, physicians, and military officers—as it is of entire national societies. A certain measure of thinning is nearly certain to occur, in fact, whenever any such social entity becomes more internally variegated *and* seeks to accommodate, rather than suppress, this increasing ideational differentiation, whatever its sources.

This is one way of fairly characterizing the fate of common morality, as personally experienced and articulated among North Americans and Western Europeans in recent years. It should be clear that this way of characterizing our moral history is evaluatively neutral—necessarily so, because, thick ones are by nature no more ethically defensible than thin, not from an avowedly universalistic or cosmopolitan standpoint, at least. Nor are thick, normative concepts particularly helpful in avoiding tension within conversation, for thinner ones enable an adroit speaker to remain somewhat vague, where greater clarity about what she truly thinks could readily invite conflict. The word "inappropriate" is even thinner than "wrong," still less committed to anything much in particular. This is one major reason the former has so substantially displaced the latter, certainly in interpersonal communication among non-intimates.

The term "common morality," slippery enough at the conceptual level, turns still more vexing when we confront the political ramifications of its real-life usage. For many people, the very term—along with "moral order"—has become quite controversial, carrying a distinct whiff of Victorian stodginess. An inevitable objection to my purposes, in fact, is that in a given time and place there may exist virtually no common morality at all, in any coherent, robust, or otherwise acceptable sense of the term. After all, subgroups of a national society often feel keen indignation toward very different practices, institutions, and people. Even where moral judgments are widely shared, there is certainly no reason to assume they are defensible.

Yet the questions implicated by the term "common morality" are by no means antiquarian. It is these questions, more than any possible (and certainly contentious) answer to them, that are the focus of this chapter. Their incendiary character should be clear from the observable fact that, when they are not simply deemed too sensitive to broach openly, ensuing disagreements threaten to set us nearly at fisticuffs, even in scholarly settings.[8] This is true not only of empirical questions about whether any common morality truly exists and, if so, what its 'contents' or implications might be in the here and now. It is true even of the meta-questions, concerned with the vagaries of what precisely it might even *mean to speak* of a common morality.

Though we today find it hard to believe, in late-nineteenth-century America opposition to the sale and consumption of alcohol was for many people no less intense than indignation against human slavery a generation earlier.[9] It is especially difficult to determine the empirical contours and even the existence of common morality when ethical sensibilities and opinions are clearly in flux.[10] At such times, new understandings of moral acceptability coexist with those much older, whose adherents vigorously defend these in face of vociferous challenge.[11] Where there exists no genuine agreement on what morality demands—beneath the level of ponderous platitude, perhaps—one cannot intelligibly compare these demands with the law's. (The reverse is also true: when there exists no settled or clearly emergent law on a given question, we cannot intelligibly compare law's demands on us to those of prevailing morals.)

An essential question here concerns the empirical scope of common morality within a given social order. The methodological obstacles to answering that query are daunting. We can confront them only by employing the widest variety of available instruments, taking up each wherever it best suits the immediate circumstance, from survey research and archival inquiry to participant observation and interviews with insider informants. Even their combination will sometimes leave us well short of the confidence to which we aspire. Yet if the substantive questions impelling such an inquiry are clearly important, we cannot simply discard them upon acknowledging the limitations of our present methodological tools. We must do the best we can with what we have. In the social sciences, there often seems to exist an inverse correlation, alas, between the measure of confidence we can have in our answers and the relative importance of the questions to which they respond.

Let us start with the most ambitious arguments for moral commonality. It may be possible, some plausibly contend, to identify a meaningful form of morality shared universally, everywhere on earth, if we confine its content to a few basic, broad beliefs: do not kill persons; do not cause pain; keep your promises.[12] These commitments rest on no particular philosophical "foundations": they are "primitive, pre-theoretical."[13] They "make no appeal to pure reason, rationality, natural law, a special moral sense, or the like,"[14] write two proponents. Following from such commitments are certain "ordinary virtues," Michael Ignatieff recently writes, "unreflexive and unthinking." These virtues amount to "a life skill, a practice acquired through experience, rather than an exercise of moral judgment or an act of deliberate thought."[15] They provide "the necessities of living together"[16] in any form whatever, Heinich observes, and are therefore "the very foundation of sociology."

Heinich's observation will seem innocuous to those untutored in contemporary social thought. Yet she then draws out from these seeming platitudes a number of implications decidedly more challenging, bracing, and politically pointed. With the intellectual climate of contemporary France chiefly in mind, Heinich thus adds that to deny the indispensability and reality of shared moral values is to succumb to the "psychologically infantilizing and politically dangerous delusions" of "an individualistic Left, systematically anti-state and anti-institutional," whose adherents "consider it normal to give free rein to fantasies of omnipotence," believing that "the law is simply a tool of domination to discredit legitimate human desire."[17] Heinich here refers to the strong and continuing influence of Pierre Bourdieu and the early Foucault on French thinking today about morality, of any sort, an influence she only slightly exaggerates.[18]

In its universality, the panhuman consensus identified by philosophers of common morality resembles the logical structure of grammar apparently underlying all natural languages,[19] though this may offer only a helpful metaphor, not a more literal claim. And like a universal grammar, this consensus apparently originates in the early history of our species. "To facilitate living together in groups," Lindsay argues, "certain patterns of cooperative behavior" came into being, "and at some point in human evolution norms fostering this behavior began to be deliberately inculcated in each succeeding generation."[20] These shared norms must be formulated in very general terms, to be sure. That fact does not mean that they are necessarily vacuous, that they offer no serious guidance in conducting one's life or in drafting further rules, more detailed than these, for regulating society as a whole. In fact, these fundamental moral beliefs are the most significant of all. For as H. L. A. Hart observed, "If conformity with these most elementary rules were not thought a matter of course among any group of individuals, living in close proximity to each other, we should be doubtful of the description of the group as a society, and certain it could not endure for long."[21]

Because these rules are scarcely ever questioned, they have little immediate salience in our minds, though we depend and draw upon them daily. Both private conversation and the mass media inevitably focus instead on issues more controversial. "There is far more moral agreement than there is moral disagreement," one scholar in this camp contends, "but the areas of moral disagreement are much more interesting to discuss and so are discussed far more often . . . The fact that legitimate moral disagreement on some issues is compatible with complete agreement on many other issues seems to be almost universally overlooked."[22]

It is nonetheless also true that the abstractness of these fundamental commitments requires a spelling out of specifics before they can closely guide our actions and acquire much practical significance. The substance of these specifics varies greatly by place and period. This is especially glaring in regard to the 'detail' of who shall and shall not, within the morality of a given society, enjoy protection from lethal harm by others. Throughout history, members of *other* societies have often been accorded only very limited such protection. And as Lindsay concedes, though "all cultures have applied certain core norms within the boundaries of the moral community, the common morality cannot determine where those boundaries lie."[23]

Like the blanket rule "Thou shall not kill other persons," the proposition that one "should not lie" is immediately subject to several qualifications, distinct from one society to another. When we add up these exceptions and observe their considerable scope, we inevitably begin to wonder whether they do not entirely swallow the putative rule, or at least render it only loosely presumptive.[24] To each of the purported "moral universals" we must then extend this line of inquiry into the qualifications restricting its true field of operation. The cumulative effect is to call seriously into doubt the entire notion that there exist any nontrivial moral principles shared by humankind in all its extravagant heterogeneity, throughout its convulsive history. What remains of common morality emerges as not merely gossamer in its thinness, but nearly vaporous. Or so one might fairly conclude.

Until we turn our attention to the matter of punishment, at least. Cross-cultural studies reveal extraordinary congruence in intuitions on criminal justice among respondents of diverse nationalities and demographics.[25] The commitment to punish perpetrators of major wrongs (and not merely to compensate victims) is essentially ubiquitous, as is the societal effort to distinguish states of intentionality, degrees of personal culpability, and actions under one's control from actions beyond one's control.[26] Species-wide concurrence is also evident on a remarkable number of criminal legal rules still more precise. These concern such diverse matters as the relative seriousness of particular offenses and the recognition of various exculpatory principles, even the seemingly rarefied difference between excuse and justification.[27] In fact, people throughout the world agree not merely when voicing highly abstract principles, those that skeptics of moral universalism dismiss as glittering generalities. Worldwide, people concur as well in their moral responses to many detailed factual scenarios.[28]

It was these extensive commonalities of moral sentiment that made it relatively easy for global negotiators to reach agreement on the Rome Statute of the International Criminal Court, on so many of its first principles and their juridical formulation. Rules of criminal law and their violation simply touch people more profoundly than other legal rules. "In a world of secular diversity," writes Garland, "punishment continues to protect a sphere of sacred values, and draws its force and significance from this fact."[29] This is not to deny that there is greater variety between societies in the details of these rules than in those universal commitments essential to society as such, in any form whatever.

Turning to questions less abstract and more controversial, we must ask: What sort of moral order, what agreement on normative fundamentals (if any), is essential to *social* order, to the continued existence of a national society over time, one in which most people could comfortably imagine living? And how much of this moral order must find expression within its law? To many readers, these questions will be the weightiest, whereas others may dismiss them as antiquated Westphalian prejudice. The skeptics plausibly wonder: Why should we *care* about an apparent debilitation of the shared moralities that once sustained the nation-state? These were very often deeply nationalist, in that moral duties were owed only to fellow citizens, and often endorsed massive bloodshed against others. On this view, the distinctive form of political entity responsible for these peculiar moralities is also historically anomalous and increasingly superannuated by more progressive entities and identities, transnational and subnational. Even at the height of its political power and psychological salience in its citizens' minds, the sovereign state may have rarely been the predominant source of shared moral sensibility among a national population, whatever the wishful thinking of its leaders. Often just as influential were other wellsprings of common morality—a religious faith, most notably, but also subnational regional identities or the culture of one's caste. Even today these competing sources of individual self-understanding and social mores remain more powerful in many parts of Asia and Africa, as they did in much of Europe until the late nineteenth century.

Then there are those of sensibilities more truly anarchistic, who find the very idea of *order*, moral *or* social—and certainly the two combined—insufferably constraining, inherently oppressive. Often inspired by poststructuralist theory, they too imagine themselves untroubled at prospects of the disorder that would ensue from a decline of the national identities and institutions through which social morality was long ostensibly transmitted. Central to this agenda is an avowed deconstruction, at once polemical and scholarly,[30] of the collective carriers of these particularistic and "intellectually discredited" ideas: the historic nations of Europe. Many thoughtful young people especially find it curious, indeed bizarre, that anyone should ever have thought it natural or desirable that the task of sustaining widely shared morals should lie at the door of nation-states, through their transmission of distinctive political moralities (and other elusive properties allegedly unique to their national "cultures").

There have occasionally existed non-invidious forms of nationalism—liberal or civic in spirit and self-understanding,[31] based on general normative commitments claimed as irreducible to the culture and historical experience of a given people. The founders of many modern nation-states have in fact often proclaimed their commitment to liberal values,[32] including that of equal respect for the rights of other peoples to national self-determination. And public schooling in Western countries has frequently sought to actively propagate such civic virtues as commitment to democratic governance, political tolerance, respectful treatment of opponents, and freedom of speech.[33]

Still, throughout modern history the actual forms of common morality championed by nation-states—and especially by nationalist social movements—have not proven nearly so agreeable. With scarcely a handful of exceptions, commendable but short-lived, liberal or civic nationalism seems to have existed chiefly in occasional political rhetoric. This has sometimes been soaringly eloquent, yet of limited mass resonance. One finds it chiefly in the laudatory treatises of a few Jewish political thinkers; for as a small people, diasporic throughout most of our history, Jews have been understandably quick to recognize the appeal of national identities founded on broader bases than the culturally particularistic and allegedly primordial, still less the genetic. Some will say that the much longer legacy of illiberal national identity, in Europe and beyond, accounts for today's deep doubts over whether prevalent forms of national polity can be much entrusted to cultivate within their citizens any felicitous forms of shared morality, political or otherwise.[34] It is by no means clear, though, that such distrust as now exists toward nation-states is chiefly attributable to the illiberalism of the moralities they long imparted. For recent data suggest that many people throughout the democratic West—the young particularly—are decreasingly committed[35] to key principles of liberal philosophy, notably including tolerance for views they strongly oppose. Against such opponents, in fact, violence is sometimes warranted and well-deserved: so say nearly a fifth of American university students.[36]

This chapter can do no more than briefly entertain the possibility that common morality in some form, to some extent, may be indispensable to the forms of social solidarity that have historically sustained the modern state.[37] This includes the solidarity long integral to its provision of material support to those unable economically to sustain themselves.[38] This book does not straightforwardly offer any answer to that capacious query, but—for those few who may continue seriously to care—seeks only to suggest how present findings bear indirectly upon it. It is helpful to start with a brief history of how we have discussed these matters.

Beginning with Talcott Parsons's early work of the 1950s,[39] sociological theory for nearly a generation ascribed great significance to the role of shared moral values in holding societies together, in solving "the Hobbesian problem of order,"[40] as it was often called. This empirical claim was at once highly ambitious and poorly substantiated. It was soon deemed ideologically suspect as well, politically unacceptable to the ensuing generation of sociologists, spawned by student rebellions of the 1960s. The disciplinary pendulum swung toward an opposite excess: Western society lacked any significant moral consensus whatever, sociologists now claimed to discover. "Once upon a time, sociologists believed that people were motivated by the values they learned from society."[41] So reports a distinguished member of their tribe. Today, however, even to speak of common morality or common culture is unacceptably to "brush aside all questions of diversity, oppression, contestation, resistance, uncertainty, and change."[42] Modern capitalism was rife with seething, subterranean conflict, if not ripe for revolution.[43]

The proper question, therefore, surely could not be how much of common morality should or would find its way into the law? The only serious question was that of *whose* morality—and whose material interests thereby rationalized—will win legal recognition, and whose morality the law will spurn.[44] Virtually barred from consideration was the possibility that there might exist any meaningfully shared moral values binding all members of a capitalist society. As Trotsky put it, there are only "Their Morals and Ours,"[45] the two inevitably at war, until we crush them, or they us.

Empirical evidence of values that were accepted generally—embraced by even "the working class"—could not at times be entirely denied,[46] however. This acceptance was then ascribed to "bourgeois hegemony."[47] The worldview of the dominant class within capitalist society deeply permeates every aspect of our mental lives, it was widely argued. This influence extends to the moral sensibilities informing our daily deference to authorities, such as workplace superiors, and to our decisions concerning what, as capitalist consumers, it is acceptable to purchase from whom. To deny the reality of any truly common morality and at once ascribe its (grudgingly acknowledged) existence to class domination allowed a substantial portion of the academic Left to have it both ways: if we must admit to any ethical sensibilities shared across class lines, these simply cannot reflect any genuine form of consent. Shared moral sentiments could arise only from manipulation and imposition by the powerful. Millions of people, it seems, enthusiastically embraced this theory.[48] It was neither conceptualized with analytic precision however, nor anywhere treated impartially as susceptible to serious possibility of genuine empirical disconfirmation.

It is scarcely a controversial proposition that the dissemination and adoption of ideas throughout a national society are influenced in some measure by the distribution of resources within it, though systematic studies of this influence are very few.[49] To warrant such lavish scholarly attention and allegiance, it should have been necessary—but for winds of intellectual fad and fashion—for the theory of bourgeois hegemony to offer something rather more perspicacious, precise, or counterintuitive than so mundane a truism.[50] The political submission of people poor and powerless to their socioeconomic superiors does not, in fact, present so deeply vexing an explanatory challenge. Elster's answer, willfully humdrum, is terse but trenchant—and still the best we have: "The inability to conceive of anything beyond local alternatives reduces the range of what is perceived as possible, while . . . the pursuit of consonance [that is, overcoming cognitive dissonance, between what is and what ought to be] reduces the range of what is desirable."[51] Shared moral sentiments play little role in this; yet neither does clever brainwashing, much less brutish coercion.

Still, few would deny that in contemporary Western societies the experience of conflict over the requirements of justice has often been no less pervasive and fundamental than has a cohesion grounded in moral consensus. In fact, recent scholarship suggests[52] that *most* known societies combine, if in quite different proportion, three very different "modules" of morality: preventing harm, respecting authority, and avoiding impurity. These find their respective foundations in prevailing ideas about human nature, cultural tradition, and religious sanctity. Inevitably, elements within each of these modules, as they bear on a given issue, periodically run afoul of the other two, generating moral discord.

Common morality—though it does exist, on this account—simply displays an internal complexity and multiplicity militating against any easy societal convergence on many matters of ethical significance, major or minor. To hope so much from such morality in seamless, day-to-day agreement among those who work or live together in acute scarcity or other challenging circumstances is to hope for too much. On the other hand, we should also be careful not to define common morality in such robust and demanding terms that it could never possibly exist in the world, as our species has ever known it. That move would render the concept entirely unworkable for purposes of social science, which does not much concern itself with worlds wholly hypothetical. In fact, to construe common morality so that the very idea becomes self-evidently preposterous or simply unintelligible appears to be precisely the tacit agenda of those most fearful of what might be learned by rendering it amenable to disinterested empirical inquiry. To them, the very idea apparently seems too dangerous to accord it even the modest but respectable status of a testable scientific hypothesis.

We might say of common morality, as we encounter it in day-to-day experience, what Clifford Geertz once said of "common wisdom": that it is "shamelessly and unapologetically *ad hoc,*" reaching us chiefly "in epigrams, proverbs, *obiter dicta,* jokes, anecdotes, *contes morals*—a clatter of gnomic utterances—not in formal doctrines, axiomized theories, or architectonic dogmas."[53] Common wisdom, so understood, would seem to encompass common morality. In any event, common morality is equally disorderly, certainly from the standpoint of modern moral philosophy, which has generally sought much greater coherence to our ethical life.

Even within a particular profession that holds its members to shared standards, "practitioners live with a fragmented moral consciousness," observes a seasoned teacher of professional ethics at Harvard's Kennedy School of Government. Practitioners in all professions inhabit "a world of multiple sources of obligation, for which no general formula is at hand for granting priority automatically to one consideration over another."[54] The common morality of professional communities often consists less in our answers than in agreement on the proper questions, in how they should be framed, in why certain ones are now most vital, others no longer so. Scrupulous professionals may meaningfully concur only over the range of considerations they deem relevant in discussing such matters, allowing that among colleagues there will exist reasonable differences of opinion in assigning proper weights.

In real life, people often also agree on how to handle a particular moral challenge at a given moment, though they differ over which principles—"consequentialist" versus "deontological,"[55] most often—to invoke in arriving at shared results. And where they agree on the abstract moral principles to guide their deliberations, they nonetheless regularly disagree about how to apply them, with what results. (Thus, we agree that killing other humans is presumptively wrong, but differ in concrete cases on whether some essential factual predicate is present, as over whether the concept of human being extends to the human fetus.) Morality may be "common" at either level or at both, but not necessarily at both simultaneously.

The earthiest modes of moral expression, to which Geertz pungently refers, appear especially prominent among non-elites, for whom morality is entirely a matter of "practical engagements," some anthropologists report.[56] In their moral reasoning, those of higher socioeconomic status are apparently more comfortable with appeals to general principle, and hence to thin concepts no less than thick.[57] This hypothesis has not been systematically tested, but recent laboratory experiments suggest its eminent plausibility.[58] Moral discourse among elites is not entirely indifferent, though, to pithy specificity. Above the rank of "peasants," Geertz continues, ethical expression may take the somewhat different form of "polished witticisms à la Wilde, didactic verses à la Pope, or animal fables à la La Fontaine; [and] among the classical Chinese . . . embalmed quotations."[59] To say nothing of elegant Persian *ta'arof*.[60]

In certain premodern societies, in fact, the line between how people of high and low stature conceived or spoke of morality seems to have been almost undetectable. One historian of premodern "popular morality" thus writes, "In the classical world, as Erasmus said, popular sayings were valued . . . collected by the greatest philosophers, cited by the best authors, quoted by the most distinguished jurists, inscribed on temple doors as worthy of the gods and carved on columns and marble tablets as worthy of being eternally remembered."[61] A contrast to present practices is inevitable: "Nowadays, proverbs and their close kin *gnomai*, fables, and exemplary stories do not receive the same attention from high culture as they did until relatively recently,"[62] in broad historical terms.

It is striking that nearly all known societies, even those experiencing deep instability, remain quite effective for long periods in fastening their members' capacity for moral censure upon certain objects while diverting it from others, often without heavy reliance upon the law. Still, even within the most entrenched forms of social order, people cannot and do not act bovinely on unreflective habit. They interpret their long-standing mores with a view to meeting new challenges, resolving questions to which these normative standards, however rich and resilient, do not supply an unequivocal answer, or an answer still wholly satisfactory. It is such reflection that gives a "living tradition," as it is tellingly called, such adaptability as it may possess. This capacity for adaptation proves essential to bracing an increasingly unstable environment. Such instability virtually defines the contemporary world as most of us know it, and threatens in particular the survival of many non-Western communities, small and vulnerable, from the upper Himalayas to the lower Orinoco.

As best we can tell from myriad sources, social scientific and otherwise, shared ethical sensibilities and the mores embodying them undergo revision largely through the ongoing stream of interaction whereby people informally propose 'amendments' to the ongoing terms of a life together; these terms identify the forms of conduct that warrant censure and approval. Others assess such casual 'proposals' in light of second-order standards, widely shared, for appraising a proffered revision. These encompass such criteria as prevailing notions of what counts as logical coherence and as acceptable evidence, both of which are widely variable by time and place. There will exist some agreement over which lines of justification—personal intuition, divine revelation, appeals to human nature, the laws of history—offer acceptable argumentative moves and which lie beyond serious consideration. In such ways, along these several paths of persuasion, people induce one another to newly accept and celebrate gay rights, for instance, or to denigrate Mormons, stigmatize the obese, disdain those who read *Breitbart.* (Contrary to a prevalent view among scholars, feelings of disgust toward others and the practice of stigmatizing them are not the monopoly of any particular ideological orientation, nor is there clear evidence that any such orientation proves especially prone to it.)

Changes in social mores governing reactions to perceived injustice have multiple sources, subtly interacting. Over time, broad cultural and intellectual currents work to shift the line between what conduct most people will regard as acceptable or objectionable. For these shifts to alter actual behavior, though, people must decide to shame those who violate new norms and refrain from shaming those engaged in conduct deemed newly tolerable. Novel abstract ideas must, in other words, find concrete footing in altered mores, including those of praise and reproach. Large notions about justice must touch down on myriad micro-interactions between individuals, usually by first influencing "opinion leaders" at key nodes in social networks, local and global. The efforts of such people, coordinated and scattershot, may then accumulate into larger patterns.[63]

To take only one likely example: throughout nearly all of Western civilization, the rape of women by men was a familiar feature of relations between the sexes. This is graphically evident in the many painted portrayals of the classical narrative called *The Rape of the Sabines,* some of which clearly depict the women as taking lascivious frolic in it all.[64] Seizing the women of other social groups, to ensure the reproduction of one's own (and so its survival), has been standard practice, in fact, throughout many parts of the world. Only very late into the twentieth century did such depictions of mass sexual violence become widely repudiated as intolerably indifferent to the indignities and suffering there represented, arousing ire among certain vocal visitors and leading several museums to remove such works from their walls. The law's mandates play no role in this.

No one ever knows or controls exactly when diffuse ethical criticism of this sort will prompt shifts in social mores. We know only, from a long history of our professional efforts, that the place law occupies in this is usually quite slim, until very late in the game, finally bestowing official imprimatur upon social changes already established or well under way. The law offers a modest tributary, cascading into a river composed of many currents, some of these rather stronger than it. In the case of marital rape, in particular, these currents notably included the activism of feminist movements.[65] Yet feminists won their legal victories on this issue only a full century and a half after first insistently raising it.[66]

In allowing for its own revision (in the ways above suggested), common morality incorporates important elements of *critical* morality, though more so in certain societies than in others. Integral to the mores of liberal society alone is a principled willingness to tolerate criticism of even its most fundamental institutions, including those (such as freedom of speech) grounded in tolerance itself. Waldron thus writes, "For whatever our modern mores are, they are anything but unsophisticated . . . there is a lot of self-consciousness about all this . . . [with the result of] *making critical morality a community norm* . . . So one does not have to embark on an allegedly liberal repudiation of our traditions and take off into abstraction in order to raise questions about whether this or that local standard should be enforced. It is part of our particular heritage to address moral questions in this reflective mode."[67]

Even so, the social mores of liberal tolerance cannot be limitlessly indulgent. "Only a thoroughly demoralized community can tolerate everything," Robert Post rightly counsels; and as Daniel Bell long ago observed,[68] philosophic liberals profoundly disagree among themselves on the acceptable limits to permissible behavior. "If pursued with single-minded determination, tolerance is incompatible with the very possibility of community," Post continues. "If community life is to survive, on either the local or national level, tolerance must at some point or another come to an end."[69] Post wrote here specifically in support of prohibitions on defamatory speech, enacted to ensure respect for individual reputation—by then hardly a matter of great controversy in the West.

Yet Post further intimates that community members may share still other moral commitments, so integral to their collective identity that major breaches should enjoy neither legal authorization nor immunity from stigma. Through both their law and mores, liberal societies may defensibly suppress cultural practices seriously inconsistent with their central ethical commitments,[70] and deny admission or citizenship to those refusing to genuinely accept these.[71] More generally, it is axiomatic that—for better or worse—a civilization that fails to defend its most fundamental and constitutive values is lost, though the question of what those values truly are and require in a given circumstance is often subject to legitimate contest. The converse danger—"equating difference with disorder,"[72] with inevitable anomie and imminent chaos—has historically been still greater, in any event, a more frequent actual failing.

The root problem here is that neither Post nor anyone else has offered a remotely satisfactory account of the relation between moral order and social order, especially for the unit of the sovereign state. That account must be convincing in its causal claims about what truly connects the two species of order—about the respects in which either of these truly and significantly depends for its existence upon the other.[73] An acceptable account must also be nontautological. It turns tautological when social order is defined so as to implicitly incorporate (some nontrivial form of) moral order, shared standards of right and wrong. This entails a difficult conceptual challenge: "Not just any busload or haphazard crowd of people deserves the name of society," keenly observes anthropologist Mary Douglas; "there has to be some thinking and feeling alike among members."[74] Yet this shared thinking and feeling almost immediately begins to identify the proper sites for shared sentiments of indignation at injustice, a key element of common morality.

There is a problem of tautology as well in accounts implying that a particular society no longer recognizably exists once many of its members surrender some practice or commitment that a given critic happens to deem ineliminably sacred. For religious conservatives such as Lord Devlin,[75] these constitutive commitments fall heavily within the realm of traditional sexual mores. Even the partial abandonment of these commitments by those around them leaves these people sincerely feeling like aliens in their native land. Those particular legal controversies have now largely been put to rest in many Western postindustrial societies, though public sentiment still lags well behind, to judge from polling data.[76] The scope of heated moral conflict today, in any event, is considerably wider.

The chief challenge for a national society in this connection is to distinguish between those moral commitments it may legitimately regard as nonnegotiable—which its law or mores will therefore expect all to honor—and those amenable to revision, reinterpretation, perhaps even discarding, in recognition of moral heterogeneity. Some will consider this form of diversity desirable, while others simply acknowledge its inevitability. More than a few will seek to reduce it, by means lawful or otherwise.

The tension Post identifies between liberalism and the preservation of cultures was a prominent theme in contemporaneous writing by other notable theorists.[77] The central question was: in light of the human right to preserve one's culture,[78] must the liberal state tolerate all practices fairly attributable to the culture of any social group among its citizens? Or must a liberal state tolerate only those cultural practices consistent with ensuring equal respect and autonomy for all individuals,[79] in their treatment not only by the state but by private parties as well? If the latter, then liberalism is clearly compatible with, and may even require, a great deal of cultural suppression, often of non-Western immigrant groups who regularly seek to deny their members (especially though not only their women) the essential freedoms now enshrined in international human rights law.

Within a given country, differences between subcultural groups have often also been a significant source of differences in moral perspective. Yet in all those prior discussions among political theorists of various stripes, the question of whether any shared sense of morality is necessary to an adequate measure of social solidarity and public order floated only very obscurely in the background, never rising to an articulated source of anxiety. Cohesion was simply not their concern. Despite some variation among these (largely liberal) theorists of multiculturalism, all seemed generally to assume—without offering any supporting evidence—that a sufficient basis for social coordination exists in our shared acknowledgment that others possess the legal rights they do, that this offers a foundation adequate to whatever form of solidarity is necessary to staunch the conflicts leading to societal dissolution.[80] By implication, no self-inhibition in the *exercise* of these rights would be necessary.

In response to conservative laments over declining morals, H. L. A. Hart wondered in 1967, "What are the criteria in a complex society for determining the existence of a single recognized morality or its central core?" Only some compelling answer to that question could identify which departures from this core might credibly count as evidence of "disintegration," as signs of "drifting apart," in Devlin's ominous words.[81] To be more specific, let us suppose that we were indeed reaching a point where mutual intolerance and (in Hart's words) where "quarrels over the differences generated by divergent moralities must eventually destroy the minimal forms of restraints necessary for social cohesion."[82] How would we know that this fate was imminently upon us, that we truly heard the whisperings of Cassandra and not merely delirious ravings of minor prophets? To this question, conservatives of Hart's day ventured no serious response, by which I mean a sociological response, empirically and theoretically informed, more careful than Devlin in its use of key terms. Today's prophets of doom offer little better, though they may prove correct in their forebodings nevertheless.

What Post had to say of the need for "shared culture" must be said as well of shared morality (which he had no less in mind), if only because the two much overlap: "At some point . . . cultural disagreements become so intense that they lose their intramural character. They cease to occur between those who imagine themselves as struggling to define the destiny of a shared culture."[83] The factions, each encased within its cocoon of thought and feeling, occupy parallel universes, moral and ontological. They must ultimately go their separate ways, peacefully if possible, otherwise if necessary. Post is thus driven to conclude (though he offers no historical examples) that at these extremities of moral discord, societies simply meet their end.

Even when the key question receives a clear and forceful formulation, as this chapter seeks to provide, it continues to elude a compelling answer. What kind of moral consensus is both necessary and possible in a country very large and culturally diverse? How much agreement is it reasonable to expect and enforce, through law and mores, on ethical fundamentals fairly understood? How much of such agreement now actually exists? We may linger pensively over these questions and their perplexities. As we do, the empirical evidence continues to mount that deep dissensus, reflected in sharp judgment of others and their worldviews, can be greatly destabilizing to a polity, especially to its least stable members, already prone to violence. This presents a predicament and a policy choice irresoluble by comforting talk of pluralism.

Plurality can take very different forms—sociological, political, and moral (among others)—and the relations between these can be intricate, in ways alternately vexing and reassuring. Sociological plurality is officially welcomed, though there is now substantial data indicating that religious, ethnic, and racial differences much weaken social trust and civic engagement.[84] Plurality in politics presumptively carries a positive valence as well, for robust electoral competition, sparking vigorous debate, ensures that a variety of reasonable views will find a public hearing. Beyond a certain point, however, political plurality becomes "polarization," and the evaluative valence turns negative.[85] In extremis, political polarity eases into ontological: this is what Mark Zuckerberg had in mind when lamenting the "fragmentation in our sense of shared reality . . . our loss of common understanding."[86]

A further type of plurality—sometimes empirically correlated with the political, yet analytically distinct—concerns differing sentiments about justice and injustice. What sorts of activities trigger strong feelings of indignation and attendant practices of reproach (public or private), among distinct elements of a national population? It is likely that what we really valorize in this moral plurality is not the diversity itself, but only its tolerance, for which we pride ourselves. This tolerance is apparent mostly within liberal polities alone, for that matter, and in practice only to a modest, uncertain extent.

Tolerance of social mores embodying greatly different conceptions of right and wrong is genuinely valued only insofar as actual differences do not challenge anyone's core commitments. For some people, such commitments extend well beyond those few, universal principles with which this chapter began, to matters much more detailed and culturally specific.

Even seemingly minor differences in mores—in others' "scandalous" beachwear, for instance, or in the "strange smells" (evoking disgust)[87] their cooking emits—are in practice regularly tolerated less on grounds of high liberal principle than in grudging resignation to brute requirements of a modus vivendi tenuously won, where greater agreement, despite occasional efforts to foster it, has proven simply impossible.

It was Montesquieu's *Persian Letters* that first alerted modern Europeans to the fact that acute moral alterity can be acutely disconcerting. In that epistolary novel, this meant the consternation—sympathetically portrayed—of Persian elites at the liberal West's tolerant and gaily sociable ways,[88] especially among its women. Now as then, for large numbers of people throughout the world, those who do not pride themselves on their cosmopolitanism,[89] ethical alterity and the cultural differences engendering it (of which Post speaks apprehensively) often prove not merely disorienting on first encounter, but persistently rankling, setting the temperature of intergroup relations at just short of a low simmer.[90] Sociologists have found that physical proximity to groups with differing morals can enhance the perception of this threat.[91]

What are the long-term repercussions of living under conditions of acute moral plurality—the consequences for individuals, national societies, and democratic polities? This question has not received serious social scientific attention, nothing remotely comparable to the attention accorded to plurality of the sociological or politically partisan sort. Moral plurality is conceptually identical to neither. There have regularly existed major differences in moral sensibilities among those of common social background and party affiliation, as where political parties successfully strive to offer a "big tent."

Yet recent social science suggests a growing division of Americans into insular and homogeneous enclaves.[92] "Cross-cutting cleavages" once leavened political conflict with the mutual respect and civility more readily displayed toward those with whom we share some salient affiliation (as neighbors, workmates, fellow Elks members) beyond the realm of electoral politics. This unfortunate development helps explain the increasingly hard edge to discussion of many policy issues over which most people, even those politically engaged, were once prepared to allow that "reasonable people will differ."[93] For the reasons that Post identifies in speaking of cultural plurality, we should doubt the desirability of sharp moral plurality, certainly in the civic realm and probably well beyond. We should appraise it not as we officially judge the sociological variety—with presumptive sympathy. We should view it as we do extreme political plurality, intense ideological polarization. As a society fractures along any number of possible lines, common morality becomes at once more important for securing public order (in defensible form) and much more difficult to attain.

This book ventures no further reflection on these momentous matters, for my focus is on the workings of common morality at levels of life both smaller and larger than the national society. It is as members of governmental entities that our mores as citizens—our felt sense of civic duties and civic virtues—come clearly into play. Yet it is at other tiers of social organization, and in the interactions these afford, that common morality is today often more vibrant and consequential, more significant to social change no less than to social order, in ways that Chapters 2 and 3 suggest. And yet, if democratic states require any robustness of shared political morality among their citizens, it would be naive to hope that we might substantially overcome its grave weakening by way of rights-restraining mores salubriously at work above and beneath the sovereign state.

The notion of common morality, sketched in the Introduction and central to my ensuing analysis, is integral to the concept of a right to do wrong. Rights of this type consist precisely in their inconsistency, each in its way, with distinct elements of the moral commitments shared within a given social space, large or small. Let us therefore next consider several brief illustrations of rights to do wrong, and the societal efforts to hinder their abusive exercise. This provides a rich trove of empirical material from which the later analysis will draw in identifying and explaining the locus and significance of such rights.

# 2

# A Sampling of Rights to Do Wrong

This chapter summarily introduces a number of rights to do wrong and the considerable attempts to restrain their disfavored exercise. These pages thus offer a solid factual basis on which ensuing inquiry will rely in seeking to discern the place and meaning of such rights within our socio-legal order.

## Offensive Speech

In the United States, the Constitution allows people to engage in highly offensive speech. They may express their hate of minority groups, for example, as long as this does not constitute "fighting words"[1] and poses no clear, immediate danger of violence.[2] Data suggest that only a very small number of people have actually employed such speech,[3] however. And they have generally been met with widespread recrimination. When incidents of hateful speech become widely known, public protest is a regular response in the United States and many other parts of the Western world.[4] At such times, two legal scholars note, "citizens often perceive a gap between having a right and doing the right thing, and raise their voices to close the gap."[5]

Violent "hate crimes" often elicit still stronger protests, such as those after German "skinheads" burned down buildings housing Turkish immigrants some years ago.[6] By historical and comparative standards, today such violence is very infrequent, certainly in the United States.[7] A few insensitive remarks by a handful of young students in a small Iowa community[8] now merits sustained attention from the *New York Times,*[9] whose coverage then draws worldwide effusions of sympathy and moral support for the two students thus targeted. Violence conducted *by* members of the same minority groups today frequently elicits responses indistinguishable from reactions to violence *against* such groups. Thus, as Sohrab Ahmari writes of recent American events, "When a jihadist would go boom somewhere, pre-emptive hashtags expressing solidarity with threatened Muslims are never far behind."[10]

Mass protests against "hate speech" effectively rejuvenate what Durkheim called the "collective conscience" of liberal societies—our commitment to mutual respect and tolerance for members different from ourselves. A more modest view might simply observe that public protest creates such conscience where prior evidence of its vitality may have been spotty. Public protest also affirms the legal rights of victim groups whose members have been mistreated and stigmatizes offensive speakers, who often retreat from public view, curtailing overt efforts to enlist adherents.

We lawyers usually assume it is chiefly the First Amendment that restrains the law's regulatory hand in these matters. Yet other, subtler mechanisms are also powerfully at work. In the back of our minds, Americans realize that few will exercise this particular right. We at least dimly sense that if many more were to do so, we would almost certainly have to reassess its acceptability and constrict its scope. To be more specific, the political import of organizing a Nazi political party, exercising one's right of speech and association in this manner, is very different in a country that has experienced right-wing authoritarian rule in recent history than where constitutional democracy has had a long and stable history.[11] The rules defining the scope of these entitlements are therefore generally very different within these two sorts of society.[12] German constitutional law, in particular, includes several provisions specifically designed to ensure that no one may again employ liberal freedoms as vehicles to destroy the democratic process.[13] Legal restrictions on hate speech often also prominently appear in societies just emerging from civil war among tribal and ethno-religious subgroups.

Americans have been able to take it comfortably for granted that extralegal impediments are in place on violent ideological extremists and those they might otherwise recruit.[14] For this reason alone we have been able to accord them such indulgent legal treatment.[15] A revolutionary leader of Left or Right might plausibly complain that our law compels him to endure a form of "repressive tolerance," along much the same lines

Herbert Marcuse had in mind.[16] America's willingness to indulge highly offensive speech thus depends on a great deal more than our constitutional law. Such law itself rests upon certain key sociological assumptions, indispensable yet rarely articulated or acknowledged. A European observer might well dismiss our much-vaunted First Amendment and the shelves of adulatory scholarship it long inspired as mere liberal philosophical froth atop a deeper conservative sea of common morality and the informal devices by which we police it.

The most telling current evidence for this conclusion may lie in recent federal prosecutions of Islamist radicals accused of providing "material support for" or "solicitation" of "terrorist acts."[17] Justice Department officials find it increasingly necessary, with the guarded approval of federal courts, to interpret these criminal offenses so that they now encompass what some would still regard as constitutionally protected speech.[18] The government's fear has been that such utterances—artfully couched to fall just short of "incitement to violence"—will, as in Western Europe,[19] successfully spread radical Islamist ideas and spur the violence these sometimes inspire. Conferences of pro-Palestinian activists in the United States today openly invite attendees to "come navigate the fine line between legal activism and material support for terrorism."[20] This species of activism employs speech and related rights of association as its chief weapons. As Islamist attacks increase throughout much of the world,[21] political pressures build within the United States for further prosecutions,[22] seeking to move the evolving jurisprudence still further down the path of criminalizing speech. And as the American public perceives ever graver security threats, it will almost inevitably consent or acquiesce more readily to greater legal restrictions on forms of speech deeply at odds with common morality and the informal practices embodying it.[23]

The contingent quality of our American commitment to free speech reveals itself still more starkly, perhaps, in President Barack Obama's 2011 decision to assassinate Anwar al-Awlaki,[24] the American imam whose recorded sermons preached violent jihad against the West.[25] The United States alleged that al-Awlaki held operational responsibilities within Al Qaeda and had planned particular attacks,[26] but evidence for that claim was not strong.[27] Much more compelling was the view that his spectacular oratorical gifts had attracted many millions of sympathetic online viewers to the jihadist cause. A number of individual attackers throughout the world had, in fact, specifically credited him as a major influence on their thinking and activity.[28] There existed only a tenuous legal basis for his assassination,[29] but that question was never mooted before the court, which declined to address the merits of his father's early legal objections. These were dismissed on procedural grounds (lack of standing) and the separation of powers.[30] Though a U.S. citizen, engaged in expressing his political opinions, Al-Awlaki was—with only the wispiest of legal process—unceremoniously murdered: his speech was deemed too great a threat to national security, to public order.[31]

It is true that highly inflammatory and offensive rhetoric constitutes only a small fraction of all political speech. Offensive artwork, however, has been a significant portion of the most "sophisticated," commercially prized, and culturally influential of twentieth-century art. Creators of entire aesthetic genres—from surrealism and situationism to performance art—self-consciously understood themselves, on several accounts,[32] as engaged in challenging dominant moral sensibilities, in opposition to which they often found their very raison d'être. *Épater la bourgeoisie* became the proud banner for generations of the cultural avant-garde, with each new wave laboring to "transgress" whatever diminishing residue of truly conservative morality had somehow escaped adequate attention of the preceding.[33]

This specifically aesthetic critique of capitalism has always differed from the moral critique.[34] It directs its indignation not at alleged injustices but at philistine vulgarity. It condemns the plodding indifference that capitalism's stolid denizens allegedly display toward true beauty and the emotional intensity of "limit experience," probing the uncertain line between pleasure and pain. Straying far from common parlance here, American constitutional law conceives of the arts as involving "speech," and as a form of speech expressing "opinion" rather than asserting "facts." The result is to insulate artists from state censorship and other governmental policy animated by the impulse to "protect public morals" from the provocations of willfully subversive aesthetes.

Here we must pose a question that is necessarily counterfactual:[35] In what direction would our law likely move if Americans came to believe that intentionally inflammatory artwork was apparently succeeding in its attacks on common morality? It is inconceivable that its indulgence would long endure, little more so than if a fascist or communist political movement were to gain a significant following on our shores. It is a seriously mooted question throughout much of the world, especially in Muslim lands, whether Western-inspired mass culture,[36] demonstrably influenced by the modernist arts, presents a genuine threat to "sound morals," as state authorities and large publics understand the notion. Concerns with that possibility are no longer only the quirky hobbyhorse of a few crotchety culture critics. It is true that actual demand for truly transgressive artwork of the avant-garde has never been large. And when public curiosity strays beyond bohemian enclaves, those claiming to speak for common morality frequently take up the challenge, opposing its public funding and display.[37]

As with hate crimes and hate speech, the official endorsement of offensive artwork regularly has effects quite paradoxical, reawakening public antipathy toward what many continue to regard as "obscene" and therefore wrongful. The open depiction of certain sexual acts, even where this can no longer be lawfully prohibited, still often entails a significant breach of shared moral sensibilities. The very process of indignant public reaction to their profanation, whether lawfully or otherwise (as by child pornography[38]), serves above all to invigorate these moral sentiments. It adds only a telling condescension to dismiss those engaged in this moral rejuvenation as mindless slaves of "moral panic."[39] Of authors employing this term, "it is always possible to suppose," Garland gingerly allows, that they "are simply refusing to take seriously the moral viewpoint of those who are alarmed."[40]

In summary, Americans indulge their more 'eccentric' exercises of First Amendment freedoms precisely because—and only when we're quite certain that—those engaged in these pose no serious threat to the survival of these freedoms, and of liberal society itself. We trust to the efficacy of common morality to satisfactorily restrain the practice, and limit the wide impact, of any expression, political or aesthetic, broadly deemed as deeply disruptive.

The United States remains unique in the measure of legal freedom it grants to morally offensive speech and association. Yet the essential issues are by no means confined to that country. A scholar of Islamic law writes to similar effect that "the constitutions of many Muslim countries would seem formally to allow critical inquiry into Islamic scriptures, the open practice of non-Muslim religions, and apostasy from Islam. It seems generally to have been assumed that these would not happen very often—and that when they did, they could be dealt with, if necessary, via laws permitting the suppression of . . . activities likely to cause unrest."[41] This much is little different from practices in the United States. The courts of Muslim-majority states often characterize such speech and activities, in legal terms, as "contrary to public order and morals,"[42] here invoking statutory provisions earlier imposed, ironically, by Western former colonizers, and now sometimes interpreted through the analogous *Sharia* concept of *hisba*.[43] This scholar continues,

> As both the human rights movement and Islamic revival have simultaneously spread, we find that this solution works less well. Indeed, countries and courts are finding it very hard to continue the practice of formally allowing behavior on the assumption that social pressures will keep it from happening. For one, encouraged by global human rights movements and local NGOs, members of dissenting Muslim groups and/or religious minorities are increasingly defying social pressures and are demanding the right to speak and act in accordance with beliefs that are deeply unpopular.[44] At the same time, most countries have also seen factions [voicing revivalist versions of Islam] arise that believe it is important symbolically to outlaw these types of practices—rather than simply let social pressures work on them or suppress them on "secular" grounds.[45]

## Bankruptcy

To declare personal bankruptcy would often be materially advantageous to thousands of working Americans who are experiencing severe financial difficulty.[46] Many such people also believe, however, that it is wrong to dodge one's financial obligations when one's plight owes to one's own imprudence rather than to sudden medical expenses. Such individuals therefore delay for long periods before acknowledging the inevitable.[47] These feelings of personal obligation toward those who placed trust in one's financial probity combine with the considerable stigma (as some data suggest)[48] still associated with going bankrupt to deter significant numbers from exercising rights to so discharge their debts.[49] Their self-understanding as "morally responsible" persons also leads many to defer that step, even when virtually inescapable, to their considerable detriment.

Yet if stigma were to decline greatly, as some scholars believe is occurring,[50] and everyone for whom bankruptcy was advantageous then declared it, current law could quickly become unsustainable, economically and politically. The increasing numbers of bankruptcy petitioners repeatedly (in 1976, 1990, 1998, and 2005)[51] led federal legislators—expressly invoking "weakened stigma"—to tighten requirements,[52] at the urging of consumer credit companies.[53] Until well into the twentieth century, at least, Christian ministers effectively imparted "the presumption that some moral failing lay behind each and every business failure,"[54] writes one historical sociologist. Bankrupts were often shunned by fellow believers.[55] And though large parts of American society have secularized in many ways, these long-standing views continue to exert nontrivial influence, especially on those of lower socioeconomic status, whose appreciation of economic forces is often unsophisticated. This ingenuousness may exercise some salutary influence, ironically: there is a positive correlation, even today, between favorable credit scores and self-identification as "religious."[56] The bankruptcy proceeding is itself richly steeped in moral symbolism and continues to display, with its unmistakable tone of anticipated penance, the hallmarks of what sociologists call a "successful degradation ceremony."[57]

We might claim to wish that people of modest means, facing severe financial distress, better understood the extent to which factors beyond their control often prejudice their economic plight. And yet, as a polity and society we implicitly bet upon the continuing efficacy of more 'innocent' views (which enjoy some empirical support).[58] We depend upon the self-restraints these subtly impose when we draft the law of bankruptcy eligibility as generously as we sometimes have. We let people weigh the costs and benefits of declaring bankruptcy, assuming that pecuniary calculations will be foremost in their minds. Yet we also quietly hope and expect that, among the relevant costs of doing so, the possibility of suffering social stigma will be duly counted in the balance. If we could no longer trust to stigma's quiet, sub-rosa workings, we would almost certainly have to tighten our law of bankruptcy to a degree many would regard as unpalatably draconian.

Other countries appear to rely on stigma less than does the United States. But their law invites courts to take a finer-grained look at how the debtor arrived at his present predicament, at how maturely he has been addressing it, and on these bases to distinguish forgivable from inexpungible arrears.[59] In other words, courts more closely scrutinize the moral defensibility of a debtor's purchasing behavior, in light of his income, savings, familial duties, and age (which bears on the level of ethical maturity reasonable to expect of him). Most Americans would presumably reject such intimate and extensive governmental inquiries as unduly paternalistic encroachments on their private lives and liberties.

Stigma provides a serviceable alternative. In the United States stigma attaches not only on account of the presumed financial imprudence of those declaring bankruptcy; it arises as well from fears that sophisticated debtors exploit the bankruptcy process itself, shrewdly shifting assets offshore or to states with generous "exemptions," a practice not uncommon among wealthy Americans.[60] Common morality revolts at these opportunistic stratagems and at a system acquiescing in them. Where requirements for bankruptcy are drafted more stringently and hence fit more closely with common morality (as in certain Scandinavian societies), stigma does not so heavily attach to the people who resolve their financial problems under the relevant regulatory architecture. For fellow citizens can be confident few will gain relief from the natural and foreseeable consequences of economic extravagance, at least, and certainly not by "gaming the system." As a result, there is also less need for stigma, for its extralegal pressures to fill a considerable gap between law and prevailing morals by deterring recourse to rules that many perceive as unduly generous.

## "Welfare" Entitlements

Several federal programs for social provision to poor people create economic entitlements that frequently go unclaimed by many of those eligible and in apparent need.[61] The intended beneficiaries are sometimes simply unaware of their eligibility or are disinclined to complete the necessary paperwork,[62] in exchange for benefits they regard as paltry.[63] Until the late 1960s, at least, only some 40 percent of Americans eligible for Aid to Families with Dependent Children (traditional "welfare," in common parlance) exercised their right to it.[64]

Recent studies suggest that disinclination to do so is often due partly to the cognitive and psychological repercussions of material deprivation itself.[65] Such people are demoralized, in a word, though some policy analysts believe that simpler paperwork might induce greater rights-claiming. For Medicaid, those who qualify yet decline to register—estimated as some six million people in 2016[66]—sometimes blithely assume that they are simply too young and healthy to require its services, and that they will easily cover minor medical expenses out of pocket.[67]

There is no direct evidence to suggest that those who decline to exercise their right to these federal entitlements feel any specifically moral duty to refrain from doing so. There is substantial indication, though, that many potential beneficiaries fear the stigma of negative moral judgment from others, directed against all who seek such assistance. Some scholars contend that this has been a significant obstacle to benefits-claiming in several Western countries,[68] notably including the United States.[69] Other researchers demonstrate simply that welfare recipients feel that they are stigmatized for seeking a "public handout."[70] It requires no great leap beyond these surveys to surmise that the negative self-characterizations they have uncovered lead recipients and eligible nonrecipients—persons deliberately declining to assert this right—to pejorative self-appraisal. If this is so, they feel badly about themselves not in some generic way but in what should be described as a distinctly moral sense. From available evidence, it is impossible to determine whether these feelings are ones of guilt or of shame.[71]

The stigma attached to seeking this form of public assistance originates almost certainly in the view prevalent within common morality that able-bodied adults should somehow find a way to financially support themselves.[72] At very least, one should turn for help to family members before resorting to governmental support. Scholars nonetheless believe that stigma in this regard has waxed and waned over the years, for a variety of reasons, including the relative activity of "welfare rights" movements encouraging greater rights-claiming.[73]

## Disability Benefits

Over only the last generation, the novel diagnostic category of "disability"[74] has become the rationale and foundation for major institutions that today effectively encourage people to understand themselves in this fashion, classify themselves under this conceptual category, and claim legal entitlements on its basis. This development is now evident not only in wealthy Western welfare states but throughout much of the world.[75]

"As many as one in four students at some elite U.S. colleges," reports the *Wall Street Journal*,[76] "are now classified as disabled, largely because of mental-health issues," notably anxiety and depression. This "entitles them to a widening array of special accommodations like longer time to take exams." The profusion of claimants has reached a point where some professional observers have begun to question the value of the SAT and ACT tests in comparing applicants for college admission. School psychologists ascribe the exploding numbers "to less stigma around mental illness,"[77] among other hypotheses.

In the United States, submitted claims for federal disability benefits have risen greatly in recent years.[78] Policy analysts and administrators within the U.S. Social Security Administration today strongly suspect that the social stigma historically associated with admitting to a disability and being publicly labeled in such terms has significantly declined.[79] The prospect of stigma, they reasonably infer, no longer so seriously deters many claims for benefits.

This may be generally for the best. It is nonetheless also apparently true, as some data suggest, that the diminished risk of shame encourages a higher ratio of "false positives." These are disability claims—successful or otherwise—by those who could in fact find some form of gainful employment if they were prepared to seek and accept it. The recent explosion in certain forms of benefits-claiming reveals how extensively these governmental programs have always implicitly relied upon such stigma as their unacknowledged precondition, their unstated sociological underpinning.

The bipartisan Social Security Advisory Board has urged reforms[80] to a program whose burgeoning annual costs in 2016 exceeded $150 billion.[81] The percentage of Americans receiving such benefits has more than doubled since the mid-1980s, though workplace injuries fell during these same years and self-reported measures of overall health improved.[82] Some portion of this increase in rights-claiming may owe to slightly relaxed eligibility requirements, introduced in 1984.[83] But the rise in "take-up" rates has continued long thereafter, especially in recent years.[84] Nearly one-third of those on federal disability benefits became eligible on the basis of mental disorders,[85] notably depression.

It is also telling in this regard that nearly half of rejected disability applicants ages 33 to 44 manage to return to work despite having formally represented themselves as unable to do so.[86] Equally suggestive is that, irrespective of health status, those who did not complete high school apply for disability benefits twice as often as college graduates.[87] This indicates that diverging prospects in respective labor markets among those with and without college degrees, rather than seriousness of impairment, explain a great deal of this variance in the entitlement claiming. Take-up rates also increase during economic recessions,[88] though there is no reason to believe that disabilities occur more often during these periods than in times of greater prosperity. Several Western European countries, with still more extensive benefits for the disabled, manage to limit the portion of their labor-age population receiving these benefits to much lower levels than in the United States.[89]

There is also informed speculation that "men today may feel less pressure to find jobs because they are less likely than previous generations to be providing for others."[90] Some scholars ascribe this to the well-established retreat from the institution of marriage by males of lower socioeconomic status.[91] Men who do not live with their young children—an increasing percentage[92]—are less likely to voluntarily assume the financial responsibilities of fatherhood.[93] It is scarcely surprising that those with little compunction about shirking such fundamental duties would find little objectionable in seeking disability benefits whenever they believe themselves so entitled, whether or not they could find some form of work, perhaps unappealing to them.

There is even some credible evidence that many of the unemployed seek federal benefits, including those for the disabled, because they are unwilling to accept the type of jobs available.[94] These claimants view such positions—jobs with low wages, strenuous tasks, and longer commutes—as affording conditions of life little better than public provision; or simply as beneath their dignity.[95] The felt sense of moral responsibility, whether to family dependents or fellow taxpayers, to accept whatever work may be available appears no longer so strong as it once was, according to some respected analysts. More venturous speculation advances the possibility that the internet's advent has increased disability take-up rates simply by reducing the boredom and isolation of unemployment, of being stuck at home.[96]

### The Right to Die

A legally competent patient with a sudden, life-threatening ailment has an unqualified right to decline medical treatment essential to his survival.[97] Even so, physicians, other medical personnel, and family members generally do everything within their powers—legal and beyond—to effectively prevent such a patient from exercising this right. They intercede because they think it wrong to allow anyone to die in this way, without what they consider an ethically acceptable reason. There is considerable evidence that their conduct—generally successful to this effect—is fully consistent with prevailing moral sensibilities. Chapter 3 discusses this in some detail.

### Rights in the Workplace

In certain types of workplaces—and not only on the industrial assembly line—formal rules are often much more stringent "on the books" than shop-floor supervisors would nearly ever enforce.[98] If supervisors did so on a regular, nonemergency basis, workers would regard this as unfair.[99]

Through its negotiations over collective bargaining agreements, the company may win formal entitlement to rules draconian on their face. Yet it does so because company representatives and union leaders both understand that such rules will remain largely on the shelf. In other words, the company's legal rights become possible exactly because of anticipated restraint in their exercise.

The second and more important reason union negotiators agree to demanding, pro-management rules is that this facilitates resistance to managerial authority by "working to rule."[100] This form of labor militancy, which some claim to be increasingly salient in recent decades,[101] enables workers to shut down an entire plant, airport, or highway tolling system without violating a single legal duty,[102] indeed by honoring—to the letter—the terms of their formal contractual duties. Workers need only "refuse to cut the corners necessary for things to function smoothly,"[103] as observes one law professor.

## Collateral Damage in War

International law permits militaries in armed conflicts to kill civilians—knowingly, if unintentionally—where such "incidental" harm is not "clearly excessive"[104] in relation to "the military advantage anticipated" from a given use of force. Even so, through more stringent "rules of engagement" and procurement policies for nonlethal weapons, the U.S. military, like that of other Western powers, displays considerably greater restraint in the use of force; it also redresses more of war's harmful consequences, via compensation and condolence payments to victims, than international law requires. As Chapter 3 elaborates, reputational concerns among America's leaders, attentive to global opinion, prompt this rights-restraint. These concerns influence in turn the professional calculations of combat officers. Military elites have become fearful about career-ending accusations of authorizing or failing to prosecute instances of arguably excessive force.

## Whistle-Blowing

To encourage public disclosure of corporate fraud, several federal statutes grant whistle-blowers a sizable share—regularly in the multimillion-dollar range—of sums that the government recovers from criminal defendants.[105] These incentives, though seemingly strong,[106] have not prompted significant numbers of "false positives."[107] Nor have they led to such frequent disclosure of misconduct as to disrupt vital government programs and the industries supplying them with goods and services. Both consequences would have to count as harmful, and undesired by legislative drafters. Their possibility has been a continuing concern to several U.S. presidents.[108]

Despite the law's formal bar against employer retaliation, the right to blow the whistle finds itself much constrained, in practice, by the knowledge that doing so will destroy one's valued relations with co-workers and one's prospects in pertinent labor markets.[109] Joined to this source of hesitation is the counsel of family and friends,[110] discouraging the employee with knowledge of corporate fraud from exercising rights to profit from disclosing it.[111] On one hand, these countervailing pressures ensure that no one undertakes such reporting too lightly, and this reduces inaccurate allegations. On the other hand, the result is that whistle-blowing is almost certainly 'underproduced,' given the demonstrated extent of corporate misconduct uncovered in other ways.[112] An implicit aim of all whistle-blower statutes is to overcome the undercurrent within common morality that leads many to disparage a "disgruntled" fellow employee as a "snitch," "disloyal," a "tattletale," if she discloses organizational misconduct. Here, the prospect of stigma is all too effective a rights-restraint, overriding the forces of material self-interest.

## Family Inheritance

Testamentary law in the United States, unlike in Europe or Latin America,[113] allows parents to entirely disinherit their children,[114] even minors, a right now endowed with Constitutional status.[115] Surveys indicate that most Americans have regarded such conduct as wrongful[116] and, as best one can tell, very few have exercised this right. That was the case, at least, until increasing rates of divorce and remarriage began to weaken the emotional attachment of many biological parents toward children they scarcely know.[117] It is therefore children and stepchildren, not spouses or former spouses, who today most often challenge the terms of decedents' wills and estates.[118] The belief that a parent's financial duties toward his children extends beyond their age of maturity—indeed, beyond the parent's own death—is apparently widespread.

When someone disinherits his progeny, this is often because an adult child has done something considered so awful to the parent as to render the decision, as disinterested observers might assess it, defensible in the circumstances. Many people would nonetheless remain skeptical about whether such extenuating circumstances truly pertained. And for the testator to escape stigma for his act of disinheritance, he would presumably have to publicly disclose his progeny's despicable conduct, which would in turn reflect poorly on him as a parent, inviting his stigmatization in any event. Many people seem to care nontrivially about their posthumous reputation, and not only in non-Western societies that formally practice "ancestor worship." These reputational concerns may have some influence upon their testamentary behavior.[119]

Neither American nor European law seeks to codify the exceptional circumstances that morally warrant disinheritance, to build them into enforceable rules. Europeans, and especially the French, content themselves with an overbroad prohibition, precluding—by means of a statutory "forced share"[120]—complete disinheritance in any circumstances. The United States resigns itself with an overbroad authorization to do whatever one likes with one's legacy, however unjust this may appear to others. We trust to ordinary morality, operative through private conscience and public stigma, to ensure that "unjustified" disinheritance does not frequently occur. Regulating in this manner, we have it both ways: We formally uphold our largely libertarian philosophy of private property, as freely disposable for any purpose its owner may wish. Yet we informally preserve our more traditional and decidedly *non*libertarian views on intrafamilial obligation, the moral duty of parents to provide for their children even, to some extent, from beyond the grave.

European lawmakers were not indifferent to the appeal of liberal individualism, but did not infer that this necessarily mandated a regime of total testamentary freedom. Some were in fact concerned that depriving children of mandatory shares would endow fathers with despotic power by enabling them to threaten their 'errant' offspring with long-term penury.[121] What better means for stifling a child's individuality, legislators feared, even into his adulthood. In France, Revolutionary ideas of individual equality offered the rationale for forced shares; in Germany similar legal rules found their inspiration in more collectivist notions of preserving extended families over time.[122] Shortly before the First World War, Max Weber argued that modernity itself, with its inexorably individualizing animus, would eventually lead European law to abandon the institution of forced shares.[123]

Weber proved mistaken.

## Microfinance

In many poor countries, the conventional sources of finance necessary to start or sustain a small business are unavailable to low-income people.[124] This is due in part to the high fixed costs of processing a loan, relative to its modest size. It is costly to authenticate the applicant's ownership of meaningful collateral, for securing the debt. Community members may universally *regard* the prospective borrower as the owner of a small parcel of land, for instance. She will often be unable to provide evidence of formal title, however, sufficient to satisfy a commercial lender.[125] The borrower's contractual duty to repay her debt is effectively unenforceable in many poor countries, due to long judicial delays. Lenders know this. The result is that only high-interest "loan sharks," as we would call them in rich countries, offer small-business loans. In many places, these lenders fraudulently represent their true rates of interest and employ highly coercive collection methods.

In recent years, though, organizations for small-scale credit have arisen, first in Bangladesh, later elsewhere throughout the Global South. These rely heavily on informal pressures to induce debtors to repay their loans. This local pressure arises because neighbors borrow from and deposit into these same financial institutions. Neighbors therefore share in the costs of each other's defaults. The strength of social ties and the reputational loss from disappointing others with whom one regularly interacts ensures contractual compliance where formal legal duties, on their own, would not.[126]

The courts play a correspondingly minor role within this sociological architecture, relative to communal mores and the stigma attendant upon their violation. The loan contract itself is therefore less stringent in its formal terms than the borrower's material circumstances otherwise warrant. In this way, the transaction proceeds despite her lack of "credit-worthiness," as conventional bankers understand the term. Though microfinance is no panacea for world poverty, few deny that it has improved the material condition and human "capabilities" of many of the world's most disadvantaged,[127] particularly women. In certain rural communities throughout the world, common morality now effectively closes the gap between what the law would normally require by way of secured collateral and what trustworthy borrowers can materially pledge.

## The Right of the Mentally Disabled to Bear and Raise Children

In the United States, even persons with severe mental disability (once called "retarded") have a legal right to create and rear children,[128] subject to very limited exceptions. The U.S. Supreme Court has consistently concluded that the right to procreate is among the most "fundamental."[129] American courts nonetheless long held that compulsory sterilization passed the test of "strict scrutiny" to which legislative limits on the right to "equal protection" are subject. Many states required the procedure, in fact, and thousands of people were involuntarily "neutered," as late as the 1970s.[130] That practice continues on a large scale in other countries, chiefly non-Western, notably China.

Stated in general terms, the rationale was always sensible enough on its face. Parents legally owe their children nurturance and protection. It would be wrong to risk the neglect or unwitting abuse of a child by parents who lack the mental capacity to attend even to their own basic needs, much less those of someone still more vulnerable. The likelihood that children, conceived of such parents, would also be disabled heightens these concerns. After all, *any* parent faces challenges especially difficult in raising a mentally disabled child.

Today our law "on the books" handles these matters very differently. The Rome Statute for the International Criminal Court classifies the practice of mandatory sterilization, when widespread or systematic, as a crime against humanity.[131] No U.S. state today requires sterilization of even the most severely disabled. In certain states, such as California and Colorado, legislatures have entirely banned sterilization of incompetent persons, even when they or their guardians seek it.

Other states allow the procedure only when the mentally disabled person voluntarily petitions for it, with quite high legal hurdles for establishing true "voluntariness."[132] Both neuroscience and the clinical judgment of social workers in the field today suggest that persons of somewhat diminished mental faculties may be competent to make certain reproductive decisions, even if they cannot manage such responsibilities as bank accounts and pension plans.[133] The law continues to require their guardianship by others, but only for the limited purposes to which their particular cognitive limitations directly pertain. Thus, what was once a question of "either/or"—"retarded" or not—is increasingly instead a matter of "more or less," of "yes for this purpose, no for that."

Current law in many American states requires courts to make this species of nuanced judgment when deliberating over whether to authorize voluntary sterilization. Yet judges readily admit to lacking the scientific sophistication to make these determinations with confidence. One aspect of the decision concerns the question of whether the petitioning person fully understands the nature of the procedure to which he is consenting, and that in so doing he is permanently waiving a fundamental constitutional right.[134]

In short, the older and simpler view—that only the legally competent may procreate—has come to seem too rough a cut at justice. Not only do many among the mentally *competent* prove highly unfit as parents, as any viewer of "reality TV" will ruefully attest.[135] But also, some portion of the incompetent (those with only "mild" intellectual disabilities),[136] would also very probably, with periodic home visitation by social workers, prove to be adequate parents,[137] whose love for their offspring could scarcely be doubted. It turns out, moreover, that—when they themselves were finally, actually, *asked*—the mildly disabled often express a strong wish to raise families. In woefully belated recognition of this fact, most states now legally "presume" that such people will be interested in having children, unless there is clear evidence to the contrary.[138] On its face, at least, this legal development is greatly heartening, poignantly so.

The law's new sophistication notwithstanding, there remains great resistance among parents of the disabled—those with perhaps the greatest immediate stake in the matter—to the notion that the mentally disabled should *exercise* their child-rearing rights, now formally acknowledged. By large numbers, both parents and professional caregivers of the disabled disapprove, and strongly "encourage" their charges to undergo sterilization.[139] The percentage of mentally disabled people who successfully persist in having children therefore remains vanishingly small.[140]

That is partly because many of the most severely disabled reside within "total institutions" that separate patients by sex, with the aim—not formally acknowledged—of preventing their procreation.[141] When a mentally disabled girl or woman does give birth, the infant is frequently put up for immediate adoption or, after a time (as evidence of neglect accumulates), removed from parental custody and placed in foster care.[142] This occurs no less often, it appears, where public services are available to help cognitively disabled parents learn the responsibilities of child-rearing. For even then, the problem remains that their cognitive deficiencies frequently render seriously disabled persons, despite their best intentions, unable to make effective use of the instruction they receive.[143]

From this recent experience, it is now dispiritingly clear that our well-intentioned progress toward a more enlightened law of childbearing for the cognitively disabled turns out to be largely a mirage. For our undoubted progress at the level of legal doctrine tacitly rests on quiet methods of rights-discouragement scarcely less effective—if less transparently coercive—than in the "bad old days" of mandatory sterilization. To insist that this right be exercised "responsibly"—as professional caregivers vigorously urge and sincerely believe—is to ensure that it scarcely be exercised at all.

Our law here exalts an enlarging sphere of personal autonomy, inspired by deontological notions of human dignity, for this long-stigmatized segment of the population. After the celebrations on courthouse steps, though, our sub-rosa practices continue to reflect a more skeptical, unsentimental consequentialism, in the belief that everyone is ultimately better off with the status quo ante, in all but a very few circumstances. No less than others, the disabled person herself surely does not wish to become responsible, and feel remorse, for harming her child. In theory, a full-time guardian could be appointed to meticulously monitor each such parent, interceding at every indication of possible danger.[144] And perhaps justice—on some capacious account—so requires.[145] The voting populations of even the wealthiest welfare states are simply not prepared, however, to assume that expense.[146] For many people, the stigma already attached to these fellow members of our species does not diminish, but instead grows still greater as the legal system compels us to confront the prospect of their routinely exercising this fundamental human right.[147] Whether the right itself could then long persist is highly open to serious question.

## Consumer Boycotts, Supply Chains, and Corporate Social Responsibility

International law restricting manufacturing and extractive activities by multinational corporations in poor countries is almost nonexistent, and domestic regulation in these places often goes unenforced.[148] The practices of these companies have nonetheless come under increasing global scrutiny in recent years, often in the aftermath of horrific workplace and environmental disasters. Criticism also concentrates on companies that must act in tandem with national governments that fail to respect their citizens' fundamental human rights—notably including the right to petition the state for change in public policy, and the right to protest publicly when change does not ensue.

Under the banner of "corporate social responsibility," nongovernmental organizations have become increasingly effective in mobilizing global opinion; they often do so through public shaming campaigns and threat of consumer boycott,[149] in opposition to ethically questionable practices. Depending on one's point of view, the increasingly stringent expectations may demand too little or too much. These new expectations find reflection, for instance, in the UN's Global Compact initiative, which seeks to constrain corporate conduct considerably more than does international law. In particular, these guidelines anticipate that by establishing "grievance mechanisms" for public input,[150] a foreign parent company will closely monitor not only its local subsidiary but also a vast number of downstream subcontractors and sub-subcontractors, supplying its subsidiary with production inputs.[151]

It is not merely impracticable to extend international law so far down the commodity chain. Many experts in international trade and economic development believe that it may be undesirable as well, unduly restricting the range of alternative growth policies that poor countries may legitimately choose, capitalizing upon their "comparative advantage" in global markets.[152] If foreign companies should be subject to greater constraints on their operations in such places, this should occur extralegally, many contend, and from the demand side of the trade equation, not the side of supply. It should come about, in other words, through consumers' decisions on whether to purchase a particular product.

The public boycott, in particular, has come into increasing prominence over recent decades as a method for hindering the lawful but ethically objectionable sale of some consumer goods. The perceived wrongfulness of certain sales may stem from the identity of the seller (for instance, South Africa under apartheid), the nature of the product (artificial milk, often dangerous for poor infants), or the process by which it was produced (such as fruit harvested by laborers denied the right to unionize). "Moral entrepreneurs" have repeatedly inspired far-reaching mobilization through informal networks of like-minded consumers, increasingly via social media.[153]

The frequency and periodic efficacy of such campaigns suggests the incipient stirrings of a common morality on the global scale, and its potential as a social force within the world economy.[154] In that economy, however, international law, embodied chiefly in rules of the World Trade Organization, increasingly embodies the policy of unrestricted trade, subject to very limited exceptions, as the preferred method for enhancing global wealth and welfare. That policy gives pride of place to the morality of utilitarianism. This sits quite uneasily with alternative normative considerations—national solidarity among them—that are equally pertinent, many believe, in evaluating today's globalized economic structures and activity.

The periodic success of these moralizing mobilizations is particularly striking in view of the notable failure of most attempts to enact and implement formal trade sanctions[155] that would induce "rogue" states and their leaders to comply with the international law of human rights and of armed conflict. The consumer boycott is now a familiar method of restraint on the legal right to buy and sell. This is especially so in the kinds of markets where activists can readily moralize the issues and make savvy use of vivid visualizations, and where certain companies, among potential targets, are known to be more "shamable" than others.[156] Thus far, though, these efforts have remained ad hoc, independently organized for each such market, by different people, employing distinct organizational vehicles, enjoying the no centralized institutional home. Several such boycotts have failed,[157] often for reasons having no clear correlation to their merits, insofar as these may be impartially determined.

In short, there have not arisen any new, well-settled mores, generally applicable and consistently policed across a wide range of business practices in multiple industries. The UN's Global Compact offers the first approximation to what such a nonjuridical system of constraint might someday resemble.[158] Although more than 12,000 companies have signed up, however, its exhortations are couched at a very high level of generality and are as yet unaccompanied by serious mechanisms of enforcement.[159]

It is notable that corporate participation in the UN's business responsibility initiatives does not arise from any serious threat of new justiciable *legal* rules. There is none on the perceptible horizon, the ambitions of ardent activists notwithstanding. Corporate leaders do not generally choose to incur palpable short-term costs to ward off improbable long-term perils. The normative forces here in play operate instead by way of the market mechanisms just described, over which neither current nor prospective international law casts a strong shadow; and no social science seriously purports to tell us when self-regulatory initiatives within an industry work to stave off more stringent legal scrutiny and when such efforts unintentionally invite it.[160] In 2014, French legislators in the European Parliament introduced a bill that would have made European-based companies "jointly and severally" liable for violations of labor and environmental law by subcontractors of their "controlled" subsidiaries throughout the world. No European company could effectively secure full compliance with local law, however, still less with demanding First World standards, short of sending its monitors into thousands of workplaces, interjecting themselves into fine-grained decision-making on the shop floor. That would also prove a costly obligation to honor, with evident implications for the pricing of goods currently within ready reach of most.

Host countries would also have to contractually agree to routine scrutiny of factory premises as a condition for receiving the foreign direct investment. As a practical matter, it is unlikely that many states, jealous of their national sovereignty, would consent to such extensive foreign "intrusions" into matters of domestic legal enforcement. National leaders would widely regard these as an unacceptable violation—paternalistic and neocolonial to the core—of their country's international right to enact and implement its own law.

To the extent that it were nonetheless realistically possible to enforce, such an enactment could very well induce a significant decrease in investment by multinational enterprises in manufacturing and extractive industries across much of the Global South. Despite the worthy intentions of Western critics—to improve public welfare in those societies—this divestment would seriously prejudice the well-being of hundreds of millions employed in or otherwise dependent upon these economic sectors. There have thus been weighty reasons for continuing to rely in these matters chiefly on "moral suasion" by consumer and human rights organizations (as well as foreign states). It has appeared too perilous to juridically acknowledge the view that foreign enterprises should make greater efforts to encourage legal compliance far down the supply chain, presumably into even the most 'remote' of Bangladeshi villages. For the present, then, and for better or worse, the legal right to "wrongfully" desist from more forceful encouragement to this effect will endure. In sum, the foreseeable future of rights-restraint here lies less in international law than in the deepening of corporate mores, in this particular manifestation of common morality, now gone global.

## Looted Artwork

Throughout the world, many people are greatly troubled by how Western museums obtained much of their collections and by the long-standing reluctance of these institutions to acknowledge and redress the wrongs entailed in such acquisitions.[161] Large portions of these collections were pillaged from their owners, at a time when few Westerners considered that practice morally problematic. During wars, in particular, Western militaries considered the enemy's artwork, like its women, as simply spoils of imperial conquest.

In 1970, however, an international treaty entered into force prohibiting museums from acquiring further "stolen" or "illegally exported" artwork and other cultural property.[162] Museums have no legal duty, however, to return or share in the display of works obtained before that date.[163] The treaty is limited even in its prospective expectations.[164] And many states do not consider it "self-executing," precluding domestic legal claims on its basis without further, accompanying legislation. Savvy lobbying by art museums and other influential collectors ensured that the United States, in particular, did not incorporate the treaty's more demanding provisions into national law.[165]

The result has been to legally permit the continued import of cultural property almost certainly acquired through violation of national law in "source" countries. The failure of Western museums to return or at least share, through lending agreements, artworks questionably acquired today inspires heated criticism from many quarters.[166] The criticism extends to retention of works acquired in ways lawful at the time, in both the source country and the importing state, but at odds with current moral sensibilities. We have grown suspicious, for instance, about lawful "gifts" of invaluable national patrimony by despotic rulers to colonial or erstwhile colonial masters, often in exchange for personal favors from the metropole. This major shift in world opinion has made it increasingly impossible for Western museums to disregard burgeoning demands for repatriation and long-term loans to source countries.[167] These demands regularly issue from politically stable, relatively democratic societies where the artworks originated; many of these countries were imperial outposts of the home countries of these museums. The source countries have strong moral claims, many believe, to at least some portion of what was taken from them.

When drafters formulated the 1970 treaty, Third World nationalism was reaching its high-water mark, and that worldview finds ample reflection within the document. In most respects this ideology greatly waned thereafter. Yet curiously, its insistence on preserving and recovering national patrimony continued to win ever greater sympathy among Western cultural elites. A new generation of curators—first in anthropological museums, then in the non-Western arts—came to endorse several novel, private arrangements for accommodating many of these source-country claims.[168]

To prevent the import of stolen work, the United States has also entered into "memoranda of understanding" with more than twenty source countries, most of them within the developing world. These nonbinding agreements commit the United States to help enforce their "national patrimony" laws, barring the export of designated forms of cultural property. The memoranda now offer source countries still greater protection than the legislation itself.[169] This too suggests the weight of world opinion, even as its full prescriptive influence finds only limited legal expression.[170]

It may be too soon to speak with confidence of any new, stringent consensus here on the future terms of global trade in markets for cultural artifacts. Though expectations are greatly raised, these show no sign of crystallizing into new rules of customary international law. The prospect of further, more demanding multilateral treaties is equally remote. Western states and their museums make it clear that—despite their increasing sensitivity to source-country sensibilities—they do not consider themselves, in selectively sharing and occasionally repatriating, to be acting under any legal duty.[171] Even as operative standards become more demanding, then, they are formulated and enforced chiefly through mechanisms beyond the foreseeable reach of international law. Most leaders of source countries, in voicing their desiderata, are not self-consciously striving to create new global mores, still less to establish any binding international law applicable to all. Rather, they understand themselves as making discrete claims to specific artifacts in the possession of particular institutions, some public, others private. Because such national leadership asserts no international legal basis for its demands, these do not advance any new customary international law.[172]

The recent experience of contemporary Western museums, in short, closely approximates the ideal-type of rights to do serious wrong that meet with significant extralegal impediments to their exercise, grounded in more exigent notions of justice than the law itself enshrines. The progress we here witness may, in fact, render greater legal codification unnecessary as a practical political matter, whether or not such international legal reform might someday prove more readily attainable than today.

## Insurance

What economists call "moral hazard" presents a recurrent and continuingly vexing problem in the design and administration of most insurance. This curious term of art refers to the probability that we will more frequently indulge in harmful conduct if we know that we will not bear all of its consequences.[173] We will cause greater harm—to ourselves, and especially to others—than if we were not insulated from the full repercussions of our indifference.[174] Thus, if our home is well insured against risk of fire, for instance, we will likely be less careful about annually replacing the batteries in its smoke detectors. There is a moral hazard that a financial institution will lend money to borrowers who are not creditworthy, securitize the loans, and pass off the risk of nonpayment to buyers of the securities. And if the state provides very generously for the retired, then their adult children may become less inclined to devote as many resources, including their leisure time, to caring for aged parents; early skeptics of the welfare state raised this concern with some adamancy.[175] The standard economic view is that "*all* of moral hazard represents a welfare loss to society because its costs exceed its value."[176] From a utilitarian standpoint, it is also therefore morally indefensible.[177]

One might suppose that economists would then set out to test this hypothesis, perfectly plausible on its face, against empirical evidence of how often, and in what measure, people succumb to these temptations, from one context to the next. Yet no one has discovered a satisfactory method for doing so.[178] With the single exception of the well-studied health care industry,[179] economists instead generally defend their hypothesis simply by way of axiomatic assertion that, as rational actors, we are naturally driven to exploit every available opportunity to "free ride" on others' contributions to any scheme of social cooperation—in this case, that of insurance. We will "defect," in the game-theoretic idiom, whenever we are able to induce such people and institutions to subsidize our disregard for their interests and their beliefs about what we owe to them. According to this more ambitious claim, our very rationality logically compels what is condemned by aspects of common morality.[180] Economic theory thus suggests an ineradicable conflict between the interests of insurer and insured.

Standing alone, however, this analysis leaves out a crucial consideration: the insured party often considers herself subject to others' expectations, often rooted in common morality; these create acknowledged duties that work to dissuade her from maximally exploiting moral hazard. She owes these duties to those likely to bear some brunt of any harm she may cause if she is morally indifferent to their fate. The insurance will generally protect only her, not them, and never entirely.

Today people must purchase insurance as a precondition of many important life activities, such as acquiring a home mortgage or becoming vocationally bonded. If and when insurance reduces their attentiveness to risk, they are more likely to impose negative externalities on those around them, those expecting more from them than the insurance itself can possibly provide. These parties include both those near and dear, friends and family, as well as peers within a professional firm and insurance companies themselves. Knowing that we are likely to be insured, they have enhanced incentives to scrutinize our conduct more closely for its attentiveness to their interests. This is apparent in how insurance companies monitor the risk-prevention policies of their customers, notably law firms and medical clinics.

The significance of moral hazard, the extent to which it actually increases our "appetite for risk," varies with contextual contingencies. The problem is clearly more serious in connection with certain types of insurance than with others; it is less acute with automobile accident coverage, for instance, than with the coverage of employers for unlawful workplace discrimination.[181] Insurers thus regard moral hazard as a greater obstacle to profitably protecting against some kinds of risk than others, and to protecting *certain* people and institutions against any particular category of risk. What economic theory tends to take as a constant, rooted in an invariant fact about human psychology, must therefore also be understood as a variable—sometimes *highly* variable.[182] Our nature as rational beings, such as it may be, is immutably fixed; logically, it cannot speak to such situational vicissitudes. Yet these become vitally important in real life as we gauge the relative riskiness to us of those on whom our well-being depends.

Today, it is not only those immediately affected by our possible indifference to their interests who monitor us for evidence of susceptibility to moral hazard. The public at large is increasingly sensitive to the reality and extent of insurance fraud,[183] in particular, which is sometimes considered a form of such hazard. In fact, the public now plays a significant role in reporting this species of fraud, on both public and private providers.[184] People with even the most elementary financial awareness understand that the rest of us foot the bill when someone cheats on a cooperative scheme to which we too are parties. Many consider it immoral to free ride upon any such collaborative arrangement, regardless of how much or little such wrongdoing, in a given instance, may affect their premiums.[185] In fact, through their advertising campaigns, insurers' trade associations now actively encourage this sort of reporting, apparently to some effect.[186]

These social constraints on "irresponsible" risk-taking are somewhat inchoate. They often find no consistent institutional expression to which one may confidently point. In this, they much resemble moral hazard itself. To gain any understanding of how such constraints work, we must ask: Where, exactly, are they most and least effective? With considerable promise, sociologists have just begun to look. Insurers themselves will eagerly await the answer, for they appreciate how such checks on vulnerability to moral hazard contribute to the economic viability of their product, by reducing the price they must charge for it.

A single example must suffice here.[187] Officers and directors of large public companies often enjoy generous insurance packages, paid by their employer, protecting them from personal liability for any civil fraud they might commit in the course of their work. This insulation from liability would, on its face, seem likely to create considerable danger of indifference on their part to important professional obligations. However, the problem is greatly attenuated, almost entirely resolved, by the fact that the same set of facts demonstrating an executive's civil liability will usually also establish his criminal liability, against which his insurance does not protect him.

Criminal indictment would immediately, entirely, destroy his professional reputation and career prospects. And that prospect alone serves quite effectively to hold such danger in check. Aware of this fact, insurers pare their product's price in light of these restraints—exogenous to the contract itself, or to background law—on the risk that the insured individual will behave indifferently to his duties. An economist might wish to say here that it is only the executive's material self-interest, not his commitment to common morality, that explains his professional punctiliousness. However, it is in his interest to conduct himself in this more demanding way only because he realizes how others will judge him, judgments made precisely on the basis of prevailing moral sensibilities.

Recent social science suggests, moreover, that insurance companies increasingly draft their contracts in ways designed to encourage self-sufficiency in planning one's life course. In a variety of ways, both direct and circuitous, these contracts seek to discourage reliance on social risk-spreading as the primary means to stave off life's unpleasant surprises.[188] This trend reflects broader currents in public policy that aim to enhance our appreciation of personal responsibility for one's own fate.[189] Some observers describe this trend in terms of "neoliberalism," though other conceptualizations—less ideologically freighted—may be equally defensible for social scientific purposes. Insofar as this trend gains force, insurance companies would no longer need to worry much about moral hazard, at least not so much as they've done historically. As people become more spontaneously accountable for themselves and to those around them, their susceptibility to its siren song would presumably diminish.[190] The temptation to engage in this species of lawful wrongdoing would be further inhibited.

In sum, were it not for the moral restraints informally imposed on us by self and society, through private conscience and public stigma, the institution of insurance would look quite different than it does today, in both legal form and economic substance. In light of our extraordinary dependence on this singular invention, so would the modern world at large.[191]

## Abortion

Until a human fetus attains viability, U.S. constitutional law allows women to receive an abortion for any reason whatever. This is not because most people think all reasons for seeking an abortion are equally acceptable. Terminating a pregnancy after sonography or amniocentesis discovers it to be a girl is almost universally rebuked in Western societies, and illegal in a few countries, though this practice is now common in much of Asia.[192] Rationales for opposing certain abortions vary greatly. The leading liberal thinker Ronald Dworkin argued that "in many circumstances abortion is indeed an act of self-contempt. A woman betrays her own dignity when she aborts for frivolous reasons,"[193] such as her reluctance to cancel a scheduled vacation.

The practical problem, however, is that courts and legislators have found it essentially impossible to draft an enforceable set of rules distinguishing between what people consider morally acceptable and unacceptable reasons to terminate a pregnancy. Several states tried to do that before the Supreme Court's ruling in *Roe v. Wade*.[194] A few other Western countries continue the attempt, no longer criminalizing the practice but authorizing it only "for good cause."[195] They require a woman to demonstrate that her health would be "gravely impaired" if she were denied the procedure. Someone who openly declared that she simply did not wish to have a child would fail that legal test.

In the American experience, however, pregnant women needed only to find a physician sympathetic to abortion rights in order to obtain the required letter indicating a threat to health. This effectively blocked the legislative effort to ascertain a woman's true reasons and to allow the procedure only when endorsed by what were, at the time, conventional morals. The upshot is that in the United States there exists since *Roe* a federal right—subject only to limited procedural restrictions through state law—to employ pre-viability abortion, rather than contraception, as a form of birth control, whether one forms this intention *ex post* (postconception) or *ex ante*.

A full decade after *Roe,* opinion surveys consistently showed that at least 70 percent of Americans believed abortion, under virtually any circumstances, to be morally wrong.[196] Even today, roughly half the U.S. population thinks abortion should be prohibited in all or most situations.[197] There thus exists a substantial chasm between what law permits and how half the country understands morality's requirements. In fact, statistics suggest that abortions are frequently sought by women who, despite having had previous abortions, confess to researchers that they did not practice contraception during the month in which they conceived. Most Americans would very likely consider it immoral for someone—male or female—with at least minimal education, not seeking to procreate, to fail repeatedly in taking reasonable precautions against conception of an undesired fetus.

Even thirty years after *Roe,* a considerable measure of stigma remains associated with the procedure, albeit no longer greatly among the social circles from which this book will draw its readers. Certain scholars believe that, due to the proliferation and easy availability (to most) of contraceptive methods in recent decades, stigma has even increased. Most women who seek abortion report that they would feel stigmatized if others learned of their decision.[198] And physicians still often calculate "that offering the procedure is not worth the stigma of being branded a baby killer."[199]

For these reasons, when *Roe* was decided in 1973, many assumed that continuing societal stigma—as well as private conscience and informal familial dissuasion—would make it possible to authorize the procedure without prompting an exponential increase in abortions. This confidence in the continuing efficacy of extralegal impediments also shaped the method by which the United States established the right to terminate a pregnancy. American law, unlike that in most of Western Europe and virtually everywhere else, chose to ground this right in fundamental constitutional principles. This served to entrench it much more solidly than through mere statute or common law. The American approach rendered the right all but immune from policy reassessment in light of later data concerning the procedure's statistical incidence, including data regarding the circumstances in which the right was regularly exercised.

Belying assumptions of the early seventies, the frequency of abortion among women in the United States rose dramatically in the years following *Roe,* according to epidemiologists associated with a leading abortion-rights advocacy group.[200] In retrospect, it seems that legalizing abortion, combined with a cultural climate of sexual liberation, undermined the stigma that once had significantly restrained recourse to the procedure. Advocates of legalization had overestimated the extent of stigma's continuing influence upon behavior. It is fair to infer that this source of rights-restraint did not close the gap between what federal law permits and what common morality continues to reproach. Though abortions have decreased somewhat in recent years, a significant gap remains.

### Slavery

Let us finally consider how closely the U.S. experience with slavery approximates a right to do wrong that long endures because it meets effective resistance to its most objectionable exercise. Historians report that, among Southern whites, even most who did not own slaves regarded the institution as morally defensible. The question of how poorly slaves could defensibly be treated was another matter; and it eventually became a moderately serious concern even among plantation owners, notably so in the generation preceding the Civil War.[201]

During that period, Southern political leaders sought to "reform"[202] and moderate the system's rigors, not only via the law[203] but also, and at least equally, through efforts at moral suasion.[204] Nowhere did courts or legislators ever put in question the slaveholder's right to employ force whenever "necessary" to preserve order and discipline. Still, lawmakers did move to create doctrinal bases for holding masters and slave "hirers" liable, under criminal and especially tort law,[205] for "neglect," "cruelty" and "inhumanity,"[206] inspired by "anger" or "passion."[207] It became illegal in several states for slave owners to sell mothers separately from their young children, in particular, and to beat slaves with more than one hundred lashes.[208] The rape or murder of a slave became a felony.[209]

Yet slave owners were seldom convicted of crime and were virtually never punished with severity.[210] Whatever measure of serious restraint slave masters displayed in the exercise of their expansive rights therefore inevitably emerged from promptings of common morality, the prevailing ethical sensibilities of place and period. The most ruthless slaveholders thus sometimes found themselves accused by their very peers of abusing—not violating—their rights. These reproachful sentiments found guarded linguistic expression in collegial warnings against "excesses"[211] and even "mistreatment," terms studiously avoiding any direct legal ramification.

Certain slaveholder practices nearly ensured a master's vulnerability to communal criticism of this sort. "Selling slaves apart from their immediate families incurred a social stigma," writes one historian, "and masters when they did this had to find a reasonable excuse for doing so, if they meant to save face."[212] In refusing to punish all but the most extreme cruelty, one historian reports, judges believed or simply assumed that "physical abuse of slaves was dishonorable behavior that would be condemned by the community,"[213] a form of reproach most masters apparently would not risk. Another scholar adds that, in the judgment of slaveholders and political elites, "social sanctions were preferable to legal ones."[214]

The public rationales for both the legal and the extralegal restraints appealed partly to the slaveholder's self-interest by (1) eliciting greater and more willing obedience; (2) increasing rates of human reproduction, as new supplies of slave imports were cut off by the prohibition of global trade;[215] and (3) defending the entire system against challenge from abolitionists,[216] who were then beginning to win a sympathetic hearing among Northern publics.

Yet no less important, several historians have argued, was the self-image of plantation elites. Most wished to view themselves—however inaccurately[217]—as "benevolent,"[218] "considerate,"[219] "forbearing," manifesting "noblesse oblige,"[220] committed to "cushioning"[221] the inevitable burdens of back-breaking manual toil. It was important to their self-understanding and self-regard that plantation owners should be seen to conduct themselves in accordance with "responsibilities"[222] they willingly acknowledged. Distinguished historians have sometimes characterized this normative system, the common morality of the day, in terms of "paternalism."[223] They claim that there developed on this basis—however counterintuitive, even preposterous, it today seems—bonds of genuine "tenderness and affection,"[224] if chiefly with those laboring in "the big house." Each side to the relationship depended crucially upon the other,[225] if admittedly in very different ways. The slaves, as "permanent children,"[226] required "constant protection,"[227] for their subsistence, for insulation from the competitive rigors of a free labor market beyond plantation gates. Masters later also provided the Christian religious instruction that would, they believed, enable slaves to save their souls.[228]

Central to this moral system was the notion that masters and their bondsmen owed duties to one another, duties of a sort resistant to full legal codification. The South's distinctive social structure and elite habitus were in this respect quasi-feudal, resembling the age of serfdom, or at least pre-bourgeois, on one well-known view.[229] Because human relations were chiefly regulated by notions of gentlemanly honor and a species of "mutual love,"[230] many believed that the law could defensibly stand aside, to great degree. The liberal legal niceties that Northerners fetishized—even as they coldly exploited their wretched industrial proletariat[231]—became unnecessary, undesirable, because simply incongruous.[232]

This worldview, elaborately refined by Southern intellectuals of the period, was rooted partly in traditional honorific ideals of the "Southern gentleman."[233] It drew still greater inspiration over time from the evangelical Christianity then spreading among the planter class,[234] as throughout the South more generally.[235] In the United States, slave revolts were relatively few.[236] Planters' fear of such upheavals, which were more common elsewhere in the Americas,[237] hence played little role in recurrent appeals for "moderation," "prudence," "domestication,"[238] and "amelioration"[239] in slave treatment; nor did they figure in periodic calls for the "accommodation" of slaves' reasonable expectations. These expectations were sometimes even loosely described in terms of "customary rights,"[240] though few people took the expression in any strictly legal sense that would encompass judicial enforceability.

If slaves themselves played any role at all in inducing restraint among their masters, it was largely through occasional practices of truculent malingering in response to perceived abuse.[241] These were both spontaneous and partly planned, individualistic and communal. Through such "weapons of the weak,"[242] familiar among subaltern populations across the world, slaves "forced masters to live up more regularly to prevailing standards,"[243] more regularly at least than the most errant, mean-spirited taskmasters desired. To this end, the "slave community"[244] profited from and drew upon the forgiving latitude afforded it by paternalistic theory and practice.[245] For the plantation owner, the result was that arguments for honoring the moral responsibilities of one's class and faith acquired some importance in discouraging practices considered abusive, though their lawfulness remained largely unchallenged, whether "on the books" or "in action."

We should therefore understand certain aspects of slave law, in the broad discretion it granted masters concerning treatment of their human property, as entailing a right to do wrong—wrong, that is, even by moral standards of the day. It was nevertheless a right nontrivially constrained in its abusive exercise, some credibly contend, by extralegal pressures partly aimed at preserving rights deemed still more fundamental, those establishing the institution of slavery itself.

Even so, by the mid-nineteenth century, if not some years before, no equilibrium was possible between the antithetical legal options of human bondage, minimally restricted, and its complete abolition. Nor could opinion leaders on both sides of the Mason-Dixon Line settle upon any mutually acceptable measure or methods of rights-restraint, formal or informal. Even the more "moderate" abolitionists, who were prepared to offer financial compensation to slaveholders in exchange for abandoning their "peculiar institution," recoiled at the possibility of further legitimating it through progressive 'humanization.' The compromises between North and South that had sustained the Union for nearly three-quarters of a century, by which the North acquiesced in slavery's continuation wherever it was already entrenched, could last no longer. Those compromises had never rested, in any event, on any agreement by slaveholders to moderate their exercise of rights by maintaining a minimally acceptable standard of care toward their chattel. And by the 1850s, at least, informal ties among political elites in free versus slave states were too tenuous to allow any effective role for discreet moral suasion across emerging battle lines to yield significant effects.[246]

## Comparing the Illustrations

The preceding situations all involve variations on the theme of rights to do wrong, constrained in their exercise by environing societal pressures. These wide-ranging illustrations display one uniformity: Party A's rights are significantly curbed in practice by informal urgings from party B (or several Bs); party B makes it clear that he regards their unqualified exercise as wrongful. Party A is not in a position to disregard B's views, even where unpersuaded of their merits, because A fears the social stigma and ensuing costs he would suffer if he ignored B's concerns. A and B then often reach an accommodation—tacit or explicit—on terms more demanding of A than the law requires, if less demanding than B desires.

The compromise between them may then at times take a quasi-legal form, as in military rules of engagement or long-term sharing agreements between Western museums and source countries. Still, the legal system itself, strictly speaking, remains at some distance from the main action in all these situations. An equilibrium of sorts, tolerable to pertinent parties for considerable periods, thereby establishes and sustains itself, though not without occasional challenge and attendant instability. To varying degrees, this could be said of nearly all the above illustrations, from military commanders to medical patients, museum curators, whistle-blowers, offensive speakers, corporate social responsibility, and those procuring insurance or making testamentary bequests.

To be sure, the balance just delineated regularly fails, sometimes after many years of success. Thesis and antithesis do not naturally meld into some neat, happy, and long-enduring synthesis. When stigmatized by others for what they consider his wrongful conduct, the right-holder may simply cling unrepentantly to his entitlement.[247] This is the stance that curators of Western art museums, for instance, chose to adopt until quite recently, in face of the world's critical crescendo.

Conversely, the social restraints on a given right may threaten to overpower it, diminishing its exercise to levels suboptimal from a normative standpoint. This may be the case with declarations of personal bankruptcy in the United States and, some contend, with lawsuits alleging employment discrimination. These constraints are sometimes bolstered by those of private conscience, a factor evident to differing degree in the cases described. Like the external constraints, such internal promptings too—through embracing common morality as very much one's own—may be too weak or strong in relation to lawmakers' goals in establishing the relevant right. When we define the law's scope—extending here, curtailing there—we implicitly trust to both of these other, extralegal influences upon us, private and public, in hopes they will (alone or in conjunction) fill the breach between law and morals.

Economists insist at this point that expectations of acceptable behavior influence our conduct even if we do not deeply internalize them—that is, even though we fail to conscientiously embrace them on their moral merits. Most people simply crave the esteem of others, who reward conformity to dominant norms. Social expectations thereby induce conformity regardless of whether we truly share the moral standards and principles from which they derive. We feel no compunction about ignoring such expectations wherever possible.[248] We do so whenever it is not too costly to alter our conduct from one situation to the next in light of whether we suspect others will observe and condemn us. There is no need for any truly internalized morality, then, to ensure social coordination and to maintain society in equilibrium. All that is required is some arbitrary, behavioral "focal point" around which all rational actors will naturally, spontaneously converge.

Some will respond that this hypothesis embraces assumptions about human nature that are cynically simplistic and reductionist. The still greater problem is that the data allegedly supporting it are equally consistent with an alternative hypothesis: that compliance with social norms or mores frequently springs from sincere commitment to the moral principles they embody, whether or not people are able to precisely articulate their content. This second hypothesis also accounts for some pertinent data that the economistic, "rational actor" thesis cannot. Psychological experiments reveal, for instance, that people will voluntarily incur some personal cost in order to vindicate a moral norm where they do not stand to gain anything by so doing because others cannot observe or reward their behavior.[249] Beyond the laboratory, the question thus becomes: To what extent, under what circumstances, may the law reasonably *rely upon* such intrinsic commitments?

It would be foolishly incautious to rely entirely upon this internal sense of moral responsibility where the disfavored conduct is at once very important to the right-holder and unobservable by those who would stigmatize him. The illustrative cases greatly vary in this respect. With early-term abortion, for instance, there is an informational asymmetry between right-bearer and others, undermining any effort to stigmatize. The right to cause civilian deaths in combat is different in this respect, because the misconduct can no longer easily avoid detection and ethical scrutiny by others.[250] In the middle of this continuum lie the rights to declare personal bankruptcy and to decline life-sustaining medical treatment.[251]

Rights to do wrong also differ among themselves in how easily we can persuade one another to accept them; this generally turns on whether they comport with other legal rights already acknowledged, and so with the underlying moralities there incorporated. Thus, for instance, though many people consider suicide to be morally wrong, it did not prove tremendously difficult for lawmakers to link the novel idea of a "right to die"—first, in cases of a terminal, near-death patient, enduring insufferable pain[252]—to long-standing notions of individual dignity and autonomy.

Other rights to do wrong—when we are first introduced to them—strike nearly everyone as counterintuitive at best, perhaps wholly indefensible, even obscene. This is probably the case, for example, with the right of sovereign states and their soldiers to kill innocent civilians in war. That legal right (a "privilege," in Hohfeld's typology[253]) seems incompatible with our deepest moral and legal commitments—indeed, with the central purpose of international humanitarian law—to limit innocent suffering on the battlefield. This is the case, at least, until we recognize, from any fair examination of the history of armed conflict, that unintended civilian harm is to some degree inevitable in war, whether the war's ends be just or otherwise.

Here, the reason our preexisting commitments do not "reflectively equilibrate" at all well with the vexing challenges routinely confronted by military decision-makers is simply that so few of us (readers of this book) have had any immediate experience of armed conflict. Still, even those who created this right—many of whom had considerable such experience—apparently did so only with evident trepidation. Treaty drafters intended this right (to inflict "collateral damage," as it's colloquially called) only as a sober concession to unpleasant necessity, a reluctant qualification to the more essential duty *not* to target civilians intentionally. That is how we continue to think of this right today.

This is why—even with such convincing justifications for its existence—the right does not exercise by any means the same measure of moral appeal as does the right, for instance, to decline medical treatment essential to the dying patient's survival. The justification of this second right does not depend on cordoning it off from all directions by legal responsibilities deemed far weightier. Still, both of these two rights must count as rights to do wrong, in its present meaning. For in neither case are most people content to see the right exercised in many of the circumstances to which its authorizations undeniably extend—that is, to see it employed without due sensitivity to moral considerations that, most admit, the law cannot and should not try to encompass. It is therefore equally important to investigate, as Chapter 3 will do, the ways in which both of these rights, and many others like them in this respect, find their real-life field of operation, for better or worse, much compromised by resistance from a variety of societal sources.

The several rights-cum-restraints enumerated above differ in a number of other ways as well, some of which will be discussed later. Most pertinently, they can differ:

1. In the extent to which the law itself fully incorporates all restraints—those deemed necessary by common morality—upon a given right
2. In the degree to which the restraint of rights is intentional or unwitting—and if intentional, in whether it is overt or concealed
3. In the reasons the law permits so much more than common morality allows
4. In whether the restraint of rights is integral to an established social practice—arising from its essential purpose, rather than imposed upon it externally by others, applying normative standards of more general relevance
5. In the reasons and measure in which the right is susceptible to perceived abuse
6. In the principal motives for resisting disfavored invocations of the right, in light of how its particular exercise contravenes common morality
7. In the methods of resistance to disfavored invocations of the right—such as subtle or blunt, pacific or nearly violent
8. In the relative efficacy of such morality-based resistance in impeding the right's more extensive exercise
9. In the reasons for such variations in relative efficacy
10. In whether the resistance to exercise of the right much affects ensuing changes to its scope, increasing or decreasing the likelihood of greater formal regulation
11. In whether there exists a taboo against admitting that we do not wish to see a given right widely practiced, in whether we are disingenuous in championing its expansive exercise
12. In whether the disparity between law and common morality emerged because law became more lenient, or instead because common morality became more stringent

These variables become pertinent to ensuing analysis of the place and significance of such rights within our socio-legal order. If the present study were to prompt a "research program," we might begin by teasing out and comparing the empirical evidence, drawn from a number of real-life cases, for each of these several sources of variation in the relation between law and common morality. I shall not venture much down that path, but for the moment I shall simply offer a few cursory observations suggesting how intricate (and potentially intriguing) the relations between some of these variables can prove to be.

Thus, for instance, there is no necessary correlation between the efficacy of a given restraint on rights-exercise and its measure of incorporation within the law. Impediments to a disfavored activity may be formally codified into law yet remain relatively lenient (or unenforced) and therefore effectively discourage little "misconduct." Conversely, informal exhortation and the threat of social stigma, though extralegal in form, often prove quite potent in deterring rights-claiming. It is therefore misguided to focus chiefly on the sheer quantity of law in a given area (as does some influential work in legal sociology),[254] or even on how much of common morality it nominally incorporates, when assessing law's significance. It warrants mention here as well that powerful pressures against the exercise of certain rights often receive no legal recognition at all. Or, more precisely, the law formally acknowledges these pressures only in the course of committing itself to their eradication—as with many forms of discrimination, those the law deems unacceptable.

Similarly, the variables of legality and intentionality interact in ways often sociologically revealing. When party B acts to restrain the rights-exercise of party A, his conduct to this effect may be either intentional or unknowing. Start with an illustration of intentional rights-restraint. A Mississippi state trooper blocks the schoolhouse door against entry by African-American students. His intention to obstruct the exercise of their rights could not be clearer. When those intentions inspire corresponding action, the result is illegally prohibited. When it is illegal to restrain another's rights, the party engaged in the restraining is likely, however, to conceal his intention. For instance, for many years, and even today in certain areas, U.S. real estate brokers steered minority home buyers away from white neighborhoods without acknowledging this unlawful practice,[255] which was still a regular practice in certain areas.[256]

The intention to restrain another's exercise of rights is obvious, of course, if the right-holder actively asserts his entitlement and immediately encounters overt resistance from others openly opposing him. When the rights-resistance is perfectly lawful, though, those engaged in it may make no effort to disguise either what they are doing or why they are doing it.[257] In many situations of interest here, however, the desire to dampen others' rights-claiming does not advertise itself transparently, even when the resistance to it is entirely lawful in intent and method.

Sociologists of law would be quick to insist that people may effectively impede others' legal rights without much conscious intention, without fully apprehending what they are really doing in this respect. Our efforts to smother others' rights-exercise may sometimes constitute part of what Searle has called "the background."[258] This is a set of "presuppositions, stances, tendencies, capacities, and dispositions" that we all possess but that are not intentional states, even if they're sometimes called consciously to mind when circumstances require.[259] If that formulation sounds a tad mysterious, consider Wittgenstein's plainer verbiage: quite often "the aspects of things that are most important to us are hidden from us because of their simplicity and familiarity. (One is unable to notice something because it is always before one's eyes)."[260]

There may in fact exist many social practices and institutional mechanisms, imperceptible to current scientific methods, that ensure the right-bearer confronts circumstances quite unreceptive to her exercise of rights. These forces may operate in subtle ways, well short of overt hostility, and therefore can remain elusive to satisfactory demonstration. Where this is so, intentionality and efficacy may even radically diverge: the very absence of self-conscious effort to impede the exercise of others' rights makes their suppression that much more effective. There can then be no unequivocal evidence to which courts might turn in establishing that unlawful conduct occurred. In the absence of such intent, in fact, it did not.

The hypothesis that such subterranean social forces, understood without reference to agents' proffered reasons or conscious intentions, are afoot in the field of labor relations may sound plausible enough when stated generally. It becomes quite controversial, though, when damage judgments in the mega-millions suddenly turn on its scientific validity and demonstrable application to a real-life dispute. Such was the case not long ago in *Walmart Stores, Inc. v. Dukes*.[261] In that litigation, a bare majority of the U.S. Supreme Court rejected this type of analysis, offered by plaintiff and a joint amicus curiae brief from the Law and Society Association and the American Sociological Association.

These organizations argued that courts should infer company-wide sex discrimination from aggregate data disclosing gender disparities in promotion to management positions. Plaintiffs therefore need not offer direct evidence of discriminatory practices themselves—of observable managerial conduct in furtherance of discriminatory ends. Still less must plaintiffs show any official company policy to that effect. The patriarchal habitus works in more surreptitious and insidious ways, these sociologists suggest. Alas, no one has devised an entirely convincing method for operationalizing and measuring these phenomena, which are conceptually undeveloped and empirically intricate. In fairness, the Court here displayed considerable sophistication in its understanding of the difficult statistical and other methodological issues. In the end, it could find no reason to jettison, in the given dispute before it, the law's long-standing evidentiary burdens and presumptions.

In describing my illustrations, it has been necessary to go into some detail, to give more empirical flesh to the bone than analytic philosophers are wont to do in their customary use of "examples," like the familiar "trolley problem." This is also to say more detail than we law professors offer in our condensed classroom "hypotheticals." Such lawyers and philosophers view themselves as extracting from life's vast complexity only those few features necessary to sharpen our intuitions on issues of the very most general sort—about the nature of justice, for instance. That is not my purpose, and so my use of illustrations has required greater richness of particulars, though still well short of true ethnography or historiography.[262]

The reader may find some of my examples inapt, believing that there exists great dispute over the wrongfulness of the given conduct, or simply that few people could consider it seriously objectionable. Some will observe this, for instance, of my example of "collateral damage" in war, which many hold to be often clearly justified, as when a major terrorist leader is targeted in an attack killing a dozen extended family members as well. From a differing standpoint, perhaps, others will say that, among their personal friends and acquaintances, scarcely anyone considers it at all wrongful to indulge the "moral hazard" intrinsic to insurance on our home or health.

There is no need for every reader to accept each of my illustrations as equally convincing. Different illustrations will prove less or more persuasive to different people, depending on their empirical assessment of whether and in what respects a common morality truly exists concerning it. A wide range of alternative illustrations is therefore helpful in developing the general argument: that such a category of rights-cum-restraints exists, sharply displays distinctive features, and presents itself in the most diverse of places, raising a recurring set of questions for social understanding and public policy.

Some will further object that many of my examples do not genuinely involve any wrongdoing at all, or that they do so only until one inquires further into the apparent wrongdoer's specific circumstances, including his state of mind. Thicker description is required to make any confident ethical appraisal. Thus, for instance, it may at first seem wrongful for a parent to disinherit his adult children, but only because we are inclined to assume that the children have not treated their parent so abominably as to warrant this measure of disregard for their welfare. A more complete factual rendering of the parent's situation could cause us to revise or abandon our preliminary conclusion that he acted wrongly in bequeathing his entire legacy to others, or to his goldfish.

Many people may initially think it shameful for anyone to declare personal bankruptcy. However, this may be only because they assume that his debts were undertaken imprudently, that he had clearly been living beyond his means, as by spending lavishly on luxury goods. Most people will alter their assessment of his behavior on learning that he incurred his high debts in order to pay his wife's essential medical services, which were not covered by health insurance. Equally, one may be shocked and appalled at first to learn that a given military operation resulted in the foreseeable deaths of innocent civilians. One may, however, wish to revise this judgment upon discovering that the operation sought to target and successfully killed several ISIS or Al Qaeda leaders, and that military personnel employed due care to avoid unnecessary harm. One presumably amends one's view, initially deontological, that it is always wrong to knowingly kill a human being, as one comes to learn the more specific result of this course of action in the facts at hand. At which point intuitions that are more consequentialist gain salience among one's moral sentiments.

There are two credible responses to this concern about how I have identified rights to do wrong. The first is that it's often very difficult to know whether another's circumstances are more extenuating than first appears. Lacking any knowledge of that relevant backdrop, observers may frequently assume the worst, where prior life experience suggests grounds for suspicion. The result is that conduct not genuinely wrongful by their own lights nonetheless appears as such. Inevitably, it is on the basis of external appearances that they must decide how to react to those whose apparent misconduct requires response. To understand this response, those deeper inaccessible truths—whether exculpatory or still more *in*culpatory—are therefore less sociologically significant than the inferences people will plausibly draw from life's external surfaces, which is usually all that is available to them.

The second response is that the situations described above, in which a further elaboration of specifics proves strongly mitigating, simply do not fall within the scope of present concerns. The situations of interest are precisely those in which nothing much exculpatory emerges from deepening their details. An initial characterization of the relevant conduct as "wrongful" thus withstands a thicker description of particulars. It is almost impossible to imagine circumstances, for instance, in which most people would not consider certain highly offensive speech, targeting vulnerable groups, to be wrongfully abusive. And few would deny that same categorization to the conduct of someone who builds a pork production facility on his property chiefly in order to insult his Muslim neighbors next door. In the modern West, moreover, scarcely any native-born citizen would doubt the wrongfulness of aborting a fetus on grounds that the child would be a girl. Yet in the United States there is a legal right to do all these things.

It will be apparent that I have not cherry-picked my illustrations to accentuate certain aspects of lawful wrongdoing, to vindicate some preconceived hypothesis about its nature or significance.[263] For I begin with no grand theory, and hence harbor no secret desire to bury all data inconveniently in its path. The present work may venture a touch of "the grand style" in sociological theory, assaying the implications of its argument across broad terrain. I have begun however by teasing out the concrete similarities and differences among empirical cases, with the hope of drawing up the bigger questions, inch-by-inch as it were, through modest inductive efforts at comparing and contrasting.

# 3

# Three Rights to Do Wrong

This chapter explores three extended illustrations of how rights to do wrong come into being and how we employ nonlegal means to hold their irresponsible exercise at bay. In these cases, the effect is to establish an equilibrium of sorts—intentional or fortuitous, stable or insecure—between legal right and extralegal responsibility. The right's acceptance by society comes to depend on the attentiveness of its bearers to these extralegal duties, which others understand as being no less obligatory despite "merely moral."

This dynamic is apparent, for instance, in recent patterns of marital dissolution.

## The Unrestricted Right to Divorce

When its law becomes more tolerant of conduct still widely considered reprehensible, a society comes to depend ever more on its informal practices to limit what most consider the abusive exercise of legal rights. The case of parents who choose to divorce while raising young children—an increasing portion of all U.S. divorces[1]—presents these issues with what, for many readers, will be a special poignancy.

For a long time Western law both allowed divorce and actively discouraged it. The impulse to dissuade stemmed from wide belief—common to most religious faiths—that divorce is wrong, except in the most exceptional circumstances. The law therefore imposed impediments, such as long periods of mandatory delay, of the sort still deployed far-afield against other discouraged rights, like the purchase of firearms. These statutory obstacles satisfy scarcely anyone, however. They cause mere inconvenience and annoyance to any persistent right-claimant, without much reducing demand for the regulated behavior in question. At the same time, those who altogether oppose the given practice find such "trivial," de minimis hurdles unresponsive to their deeper concerns. Thus, neither group is satisfied. But more important for present purposes than either the defensibility or efficacy of such mandatory delays is how they are to operate: by creating a space for social mores to do their desired work.

For centuries the most onerous obstacle to a divorce decree was the limitation on acceptable reasons for seeking it. Legal rules required that the marital partner seeking the divorce demonstrate that his or her spouse was at "fault" for the relationship's breakdown. In the law's eyes, it was not enough that one marital partner simply no longer loved the other. The law here sought to closely track traditional moral understandings, still prevalent within the United States until midcentury. In short, the law successfully restricted divorce to circumstances in which common morality then authorized it.

Starting in the 1950s, public views began to endorse greater liberty in many matters deemed private or personal—changes that culminated in the "sexual revolution" of the late 1960s and the 1970s. These shifts in prevailing moral sensibilities led many to the conclusion that divorce should be available whenever "irreconcilable differences" had arisen between partners, in the opinion of either. Divorce began to shed nearly all stigma, all implication of wrongdoing, much as happened for gambling and alcohol consumption. Legal reform quickly ensued, a process lasting scarcely a generation. To many people, "no-fault" divorce appealed on grounds of abstract moral principle: respect for autonomy of the individual in private, romantic matters. The decision to banish moral appraisal from the law of divorce seemed, at first, unequivocally salutary.

As the reality of no-fault reform began to take sociological shape over time, however, the new rules soon began to elicit a quiet current of ambivalence.[2] These reservations are today apparent even among feminists, who had been the first and most vigorous champions of no-fault. As one such scholar writes, the law of no-fault runs powerfully at odds with a fundamental empirical fact of moral psychology:

> The underlying problem with both fault and non-fault regimes is that judging human behavior in intimate relations . . . sometimes

> seems morally necessary. Fault regimes tend to blame some parties for things that society no longer finds reprehensible and to create new, blameworthy practices in which litigants can take advantage of the system. No-fault regimes, on the other hand, exclude even the most awful behavior from consideration, so that physical abuse—even attempted murder—does not affect property division upon divorce, a conclusion that seems perverse. People have a persistent need to make fault judgments.[3]

The decision to eliminate moral fault as a legal precondition for divorce has been only one source of the growing public doubts inspiring recent legislative proposals for revisions. These initiatives have sought, as yet without great success, to curtail the conditions under which one may obtain divorce. Some of these efforts went so far as to seek restoration of the fault requirement—against all odds.

Many people clearly think, with some empirical support,[4] that marital dissolution often has harmful psychological consequences for young children. And they believe this is not entirely attributable to its economic effects on the remaining custodial parent. Law's liberalizers had failed to seriously apply their minds to the possibility of such effects, thereby creating a species of right to do wrong, as many now see the matter. There is no doubt today that children of single-parent families suffer a variety of serious pathologies with much greater frequency and severity than other children.[5] In particular, boys raised in fatherless homes later fare far worse in the labor market than those reared in two-parent households.[6] Statistical evidence to this effect began to emerge only a generation after divorce reform. Legal reformers thus could not easily have contemplated the full empirical repercussions of their efforts. When later reconsidering what they had wrought, legislators could find no practicable, acceptable way to limit the availability of divorce to circumstances that would be unlikely to prejudice the developmental needs of young children. The only measure some states now venture is to require a longer waiting period for a final decree,[7] equally applicable to all seeking divorce. The "best interests of the child" remains legally irrelevant to obtaining a divorce itself, even as that verbal standard became central to the question of which spouse would obtain custody.

There exist no reliable data enabling a judge to determine whether the divorce sought in a given case would harm or help the child. For there is no compelling evidence that children are worse off when raised by a single parent than by two parents whose relationship has broken down, and who fight constantly.[8] It is impossible to gather reliable evidence bearing on this question, due partly to the difficult methodological issues. There is the further obstacle that such a study would require extraordinary official intrusion into what the law regards as a constitutionally protected domain of privacy within the nuclear family.

The single-parenting of children has sources other than divorce, of course; many children—45 percent in the United States,[9] still higher elsewhere—are born out of wedlock. Yet divorce is nevertheless very often a proximate cause of single-parenting.[10] Many clearly believe that divorce is a significant cause of single-parenting. They also believe that such parenting often has harmful effects on young children, and that the process of divorce itself is often highly disruptive to such children, emotionally and psychologically.

An avowed aim of no-fault laws was to eliminate the stigma traditionally associated with the decision to divorce, reducing its costs to personal reputation. The stigma attached to divorce had been vastly overinclusive, for it penalized many who had good reason—notably, abusive treatment—for leaving their spouse. Even so, the prospect of suffering stigma had certainly induced greater hesitation, at least, among others also contemplating marital dissolution, including the parents of young children. According to opinion surveys—a fair indicator of common morality here[11]—Americans believe that parents should make all reasonable efforts to preserve a marriage whose dissolution could imperil the well-being of youngsters.[12] To this end, many people consider therapeutic counseling as desirable. Yet no credible social science, scholars acknowledge,[13] purports to tell us when such counseling succeeds and fails in restoring a "satisfactory" marital relationship; indeed, that very concept is highly freighted, acutely contested, and hence nearly impossible to convincingly define except within the broadest outlines. Without such necessary evidence, it is impossible to construct a workable legal test for evaluating the sufficiency of parental efforts to save a faltering marriage.

Still, many Americans clearly harbor a fear that the law, in authorizing divorce so unconditionally, has taken leave of common morality. Though it once fully enshrined more traditional moral views, the law now displays a seeming indifference to enduring ethical considerations over child welfare that many continue to view as rightly within its concern.[14] These public concerns are manifest in the recent movement for "covenant marriage."[15]

By contract, couples entering into wedlock agree to limit the conditions—to adultery and domestic violence—under which they may later obtain divorce. Several states authorize this marital option, but only a small percentage of wedding couples adopt it. If there is any social pressure to marry in this fashion, it presumably arises from the religious community to which a particular couple belongs. The law of covenant marriage seeks to accommodate this gentle form of communal influence over individual choice. We may describe this influence as an expression of the morality common to a distinct, self-selecting subcommunity. Advocates of covenant marriage believe that it is possible to induce greater "responsibility" in the exercise of the right, now otherwise unrestricted, to divorce one's spouse.

Yet divorce rates today are higher among Christian evangelical couples than among more secular Americans.[16] This largely reflects the fact that divorce rates are now also much higher among those of lower socioeconomic status than in the upper middle class.[17] It is hence safe to infer that covenant marriage has had a minimal effect on divorce rates even within the subcommunities now regularly employing it. For similar reasons, there is little basis to believe that any new forms of societal impediment to divorce could much persuade those seriously contemplating that step to acknowledge and act upon traditional notions of personal responsibility. A number of social changes ensure that these notions—though still widely salient among a large public—now lie beyond law's effective reach.

And yet clearly no polity and its society can remain indifferent to the measure of parental attention with which its next generation will be raised. Germany's Basic Law provides that the "care and upbringing of children are the natural right of the parents and a duty primarily incumbent upon them."[18] Jeremy Waldron, a leading legal theorist, lauds this close linkage in the statutory language, the way it acknowledges that the right itself "is kind of synonymous with a responsibility."[19] He continues:

> We may even say that the right is something which a person, if she is a parent, has a duty to exercise. It's her job, it is something incumbent on her; but it's *still* a RIGHT that she has; it's something which (in the normal case) she holds against others. And the duty aspect of the right is not just a matter of submitting to a set of rules. Often what is involved is continual and active exercise of intelligence and choice; these are her choices to make; her intelligence to exercise. She is privileged in this regard.[20]

The German Basic Law establishes an exception, of course, if the mother exposes her children to "serious neglect." This wording contemplates misconduct far worse than the sort here at issue. Still, most Americans believe that the responsibilities of a divorcing parent include some concern with how the anticipated breakup may affect young offspring.[21] Failure to honor such a responsibility is by no means so deplorable as to warrant such intrusive forms of official intercession as triggered by graver forms of parental misbehavior.

If the misconduct here were more severe, as with genuine child abuse or actionable neglect, it would not then occupy the regulatory void in which neither law nor mores effectively governs. In those other, more dire circumstances, the law directly resolves the problem through a child's removal from the parental home and placement in foster care. Where the law withdraws its regulatory reach, however, as it has concerning the availability of divorce, we inevitably gauge the strength of extralegal restraints on conduct that is still widely questioned by many, who continue to regard it (in certain circumstances) as irresponsible. We then discover that these residual restraints appear weaker than we had imagined, insofar as we ever seriously considered the question at all.

To summarize, the experience of divorce reform in the United States over the last half-century reveals that public expectations of divorcing parents, grounded in common morality, continue to demand more of parents than the law can realistically require or than informal pressures any longer induce. We endure the diminished restraints with some equanimity here, at least for the present. This is presumably because we do not perceive the wrongs in question, though by no means trivial, as truly severe, at least not when compared with others here examined, such as civilian deaths in war.

The next two illustrative explorations are more encouraging, or at least less dispiriting. This is so despite enduring doubts about whether common morality is suitable or sufficient to the task in either case. In both situations to which I now turn, the stakes are still higher, for the loss of human life on a significant scale is immediately in issue. Still, as we will see, the acute moral gravity of these wrongs provides no guarantee that the law will address them comprehensively. In fact, it regularly proves unnecessary or undesirable, as these cases will suggest, for the law to ambitiously "occupy the field" of normative ordering.

## The Right to Decline Medical Treatment

American law, under the Constitution's Fourteenth Amendment, affords a right to decline medical treatment even where one's very survival depends on receiving it.[22] When the patient is terminally ill, unlikely to live much longer, and in severe, irremediable pain, the exercise of this right is no longer widely controversial, except among the traditionally religious.[23] The legal right to decline lifesaving treatment is much broader, however. It extends to all competent adults under any circumstances whatever, irrespective of whether they suffer these supremely grave conditions.[24]

Among those therefore entitled to spurn essential treatment is the surviving victim of a catastrophic accident who cannot bring herself to accept the inevitability of life with a permanent, profound disablement. Such a person may suffer acute emotional trauma, in the moment, yet remain legally "competent" to decide her medical fate. She may be extremely pessimistic about ever again enjoying life in any way; she may therefore experience intense thoughts of suicide, which only her bedridden hospitalization prevents her from enacting.

Yet if her physicians can successfully prevail upon her to promptly accept highly invasive treatment—though it entails painful recovery and lengthy rehabilitative training—she will frequently make the mental adjustment, empirical studies suggest, to living thereafter with even the most profound of disabilities.[25] Through this felicific recalibration, most such patients find a way to devise for themselves a new "utility function" whereby they discover traces of the sublime in what, for the rest of us, would seem the very smallest and most inconsequential of pleasures. This scholarly finding naturally emboldens medical staff, on its basis in deliberation with reluctant patients, to plead energetically that they accept radical surgical procedures, sometimes entailing immediate, emergency-room "heroics."

Situations such as this present the staff of any major modern hospital with a challenging professional predicament. Thus, in one reported case, a 21-year-old college student, delivered by a friend to the hospital emergency room, is legally entitled to decline the penicillin that would—because he suffers advanced pneumonia—save him from near-imminent death; immediate medical intervention will grant him several healthy decades. The patient offered no reason for his decision and displayed no evidence of mental disability apart from the decision itself, which the law does not classify as such. Situations of this general sort arise with a regularity initially surprising to those outside the health care professions.

Most physicians consider it morally unacceptable to withhold treatment in this circumstance, as in the preceding one. Common morality would seem to endorse their reluctance to respect patients' assertion of legal right at such times.[26] In both cases just described, the patient's decision amounts to suicide. Some 80 percent of Americans regard suicide (except in final stages of terminal illness) as not merely irrational, but wrong.[27] The most plausible rationale for such views is the prevalent belief that people have moral duties to dependents and to themselves, duties that are violated in taking one's life. These moral sentiments, originating in the theologies of nearly all world religions, are especially strong when a young person threatens to take her life in a passing moment of self-destructive fury or existential doubt.

Reliable reports suggest that, at such times, medical professionals routinely seek to circumvent the patient's expressed desire to exercise his right to decline treatment.[28] Seldom do physicians effect this result through juridical means, however, winning a court's order requiring the patient to submit, for example, to a blood transfusion or cesarean-section delivery declined on religious grounds.[29] More often, extralegal urgings are brought to bear upon the patient, via family and friends—those best situated to exercise "moral suasion," as ordinary language sometimes captures the notion. Persuasive efforts will be respectful at first, but if these subtle approaches fail, a shift quickly occurs from reasoned argument, based on scientific facts about recovery prospects, to increasingly manipulative forms of emotional arm-twisting.[30] These must, of course, stop short of overt physical coercion, such as obstructing the patient's departure from the hospital. Scholars of medical ethics in real-life settings report that these diffuse forms of "irregular" pressure are pervasive—and rarely ineffective. They must remain surreptitious wherever they directly involve a medical professional. For past a certain point, such measures entail an outright refusal to honor the clear intentions of a legally competent adult who is insisting upon her unequivocal rights.

For medical professionals there is some nontrivial risk of liability, personal and organizational,[31] when they participate in such efforts. Admittedly, the person whose life is saved through a nonconsensual medical intercession is, as a practical matter, unlikely to pursue legal action against her caregivers. Her legal claim would also be so jarring to common morality that she would find little sympathy from a jury, in most cases. The law's effective influence on human conduct is doubly weak here: both in deterring medical professionals[32] and family members from violating the patient's right to decline treatment, and in empowering her to sue them successfully thereafter.

The claims of law and common morality stand much at odds here. It is hence only through informal practices—the social mores of hospital and clinic—that we succeed, as a society, in dissipating the potential for frequent and severe clashes. We live comfortably with a legal rule authorizing the patient to abrogate common morality, because we anticipate that she will face intense remonstrance, where 'necessary,' to forswear her right. As the gap between common morality and the law began to widen with each new extension of patients' rights, the felt necessity for stern exhortation against their "irresponsible" exercise grew ever stronger.

Beyond this point in our analysis, we must indulge a modicum of informed speculation. The American public is apparently comfortable with allowing physicians to resist a patient's early insistence on declining lifesaving treatment, to the point in extremis of altogether ignoring her most heated and strenuous protestations. We indulge as well the dissimulation involved in describing, on the patient's bedside chart, her vigorous objections to recommended treatment in terms of "provisional reservations" or "preliminary doubts." We resign ourselves to the fact that our moral views in these matters will not find full reflection within our legal rules. We tacitly trust to a jury's likely nullification of the law for ensuring that medical professionals and hospital organizations have little reason to fear liability. This is a process blithely indifferent, however, to the "rule of law," itself a moral ideal to which we profess abiding commitment.

As we observe the real life of "law in action," recounted only through whispering in hospital corridors and clinic stairwells, we find an impenetrable thicket of subtle obstacles. These are virtually invisible to outsiders, obstructing the effective discipline of those who furtively employ illegal means to prevent a patient from "abusing" her right to end her life. We may wish to think of such practices as continuous with the efforts—entirely lawful—of physicians and family members to dissuade patients, through reasoned argument or emotional appeal, from the self-destructive path initially chosen. That is decidedly *not,* however, the standpoint of our positive law, "on the books."

One might say, in Weberian idiom, that we secretly hope the physician's personalistic, charismatic authority before a mesmerized jury—recounting her valiant efforts to save an uncooperative patient who was teetering on the brink of death—will somehow miraculously mediate between the inconsistent claims of our moral judgment and our law. I refer not only to the specific law of "informed consent," here clearly breached, but to the larger, legal-rational authority, which in Weber's view provides the very legitimacy of a modern state and its health care institutions. Clearly there are many ways in which this bizarre arrangement could easily go terribly awry. Still, it has rested in relative equilibrium for many years, insiders report, with quiet, private resolution of the rare, incident-specific challenge. We may thus fairly describe this set of nonlegal restrictions on patients and their most fateful of life decisions as something of a settled social practice. Initially it seems remarkable that today a profession that is accustomed to multimillion-dollar judgments against its members and faces declining public trust[33] remains content to venture upon this perilous legal terrain.

A breathtaking measure of trust lies in that calculation of juries' probable behavior, the gamble that the depth of their commitment to common morality will overpower the law, even as the judge instructs them to punctiliously obey it. As the general counsel to any hospital will soberly intone, the prohibited conduct here is astonishingly risky from a legal perspective. From a moral viewpoint, though, most jurors would find it disarming—winningly, radiantly so, in its nobility of spirit (to risk a hackneyed phrase). From a socio-legal standpoint, the magic of such luminous moments lies in their seeming transcendence of self-regarding caution, in their impulsive humanitarian indifference to mere positive legality.

A more innocent age, untutored in our sophisticated embarrassment at the notion, would have felt little hesitation in defending this indifference in terms of "the natural law." Even today, some may suspect that it is only within the terms of that antique doctrine that quaint notions of duties to oneself[34] (not to end one's life), and of others' responsibilities to guide us in fulfilling such duty, could possibly make any sense at all. It may indeed be on some such basis, and its sociological foothold in common morality, that we can maintain this curious accommodation between the de jure rights of patients and the de facto responsibilities of medical professionals, both of which nearly everyone acknowledges.

If we harbor doubts about these odd arrangements for bridging this particular gap, it is chiefly because we remain uncomfortable about their nontransparency, with how they occlude so much of our quotidian practice on matters of such profound ethical import. What is crucial for immediate purposes, though, is simply that such countervailing pressures (lawful and otherwise) brought upon truculent patients combine to make it possible for the law of informed consent to uphold a more pristine "Kantian" ideal of individual autonomy than we are ultimately prepared to deliver. But for our unspoken anticipation of medical intervention in support of common morality, we would surely not continue so unequivocally to endorse broad readings of patient entitlement. Even once enshrined into law, that noble philosophical ideal, this finest intellectual flower of "critical" morality, simply promises greatly more than common morality, and the social practices by which we instantiate it, will abide.

What, then, can explain why most people are seemingly untroubled by the recurrent practice of medical professionals in surreptitiously subverting patients' rights? After all, these are rights whose creation, by elected legislators as well as judges, has been much-celebrated for two generations in public discourse no less than in judicial rulings and philosophy journals. Why can't (or shouldn't) we write the law to track common morality more closely in these matters?

To answer that question, some brief history is necessary. Beginning in the mid-1970s, state courts began to realize and conclude that it is possible for people to become so ill that further treatment imposes on them greater burdens than benefits. Their right to refuse treatment received ever wider recognition; and the perceived "state interest" in preserving their life diminished, as prognoses dimmed and treatment became more burdensome.[35]

This proved a legally unstable equilibrium, however. It required the state, through its courts, to determine when someone had lost enough "meaningful experience of life" that he should be permitted to choose death. That initial approach proved unacceptable because few were truly prepared to trust the state with this power to "play God."[36] In the balance of competing constitutional concerns, it was far more important to ensure that the state did not violate fundamental duties to its citizens than that an individual honor whatever moral duties he might arguably have to his dependents and himself.[37] And it proved impossible to draft a satisfactory rule preventing judges from imposing their own, necessarily arbitrary notions of when human life ceased to be worth living.[38] A jurisprudential consensus began to emerge that this is a decision, which, in a liberal society, one can only make for oneself, and that the law had best extricate itself as much as possible from the process of reaching it.

Our rules thus evolved toward the stance that all competent individuals enjoy an absolute right to refuse treatment. Two factors combined to yield this "categorical" approach, as Orentlicher calls it: first, the "infeasibility of case-by-case determinations"—that is, the difficulty of "trying to decide whether the decision to die is morally justified in a given case"; and second, the fact that "treatment withdrawals *typically* involve morally justified deaths," in that the vast majority of patients requesting such withdrawal are clearly at death's door from a long-standing and deteriorating terminal condition.[39] Combining these two considerations, the danger of legally imposing medical care where its repudiation is morally acceptable is therefore far greater than the danger of legally permitting such rejection when morality (common or critical) would clearly require it.

And yet, by all indications, common morality continues to endorse the long-standing view that a patient's prognosis for recovery is highly relevant to whether he may defensibly refuse medical care. By implication, his prognosis is also relevant to how far others may legitimately go in discouraging him from exercising his right—that is, beyond the point where the figurative arm-twisting turns at once more literal and clandestine. This feature of common morality—the relevance of prognosis for recovery—does not operate only sub-rosa. It finds its way back into law's implementation where the patient becomes no longer competent (as when unconscious), so that treatment decisions are made by surrogates.[40]

The law clearly provides that an incompetent patient (though acting through her surrogate) has just as much right as the legally competent to refuse treatment or to have it withdrawn. Yet in practice, courts employ a sliding scale, demanding much clearer evidence of an incompetent patient's wishes to that effect where she is neither terminally ill nor likely to be permanently unconscious. By this route, patients with grimmer prognoses *do* turn out to enjoy better de facto prospects to decline treatment.[41] Common morality here infuses the law's implementation, further dampening the exercise of this right. Though these situations arise periodically, one need not exaggerate their incidence to establish their considerable sociological significance. When lifesaving treatment is likely to be very painful and highly risky, patients often express strong disinclination, then find themselves subject to overwhelming pressure against acting upon it. There is stunningly little acknowledgment of all this, much less sustained discussion, within the vast scholarly and professional literature on medical ethics.

What one does find is confirmation that "advance care directives," though now signed by a large share of all in-patients, often fail of their purpose because physicians simply decline to honor their express terms.[42]

These documents are often admittedly somewhat vague—perhaps not entirely by chance—too imprecisely worded to provide clear guidance in distinguishing between acceptable and unacceptable means of artificial resuscitation, for instance. Even so, there is evidence to suggest that physicians, like clever lawyers, strive to unearth any such ambiguities in order to read the document as inconsistent with a wish to die.[43] And from influential scholarship in cognitive psychology, there is reason to suspect that, in presenting alternative treatment possibilities, physicians may regularly engage in "overestimating some risks and underestimating others, as well as allowing . . . choices to be manipulated by subtle and apparently irrelevant aspects of how options are presented."[44] So speculate two leading scholars, at least, one on a major medical school faculty. The result is that physicians may end up circumventing a patient's preference to exercise her right to decline medical care, including treatment essential to her survival.[45]

Our acquiescence in this peculiar configuration of practices owes little, if anything, to an uncritical deference toward medical authority. Few people any longer supinely endorse the surgeon's peculiar "virtue ethics"[46]—his tunnel-vision commitment to "saving life," irrespective of its quality—conceived of as his vocation's intrinsic telos. That singular self-understanding induces him, we now widely believe, to overvalue his technical skills, proudly putting them on maximal, self-aggrandizing display, thereby imperiling other, more important values.

The better explanation of our settled mores is instead that common morality holds that an individual owes some measure of duty to herself, to "respect [her] objective and inalienable human dignity,"[47] Waldron writes, and hence not to "throw her life away," as ordinary language registers this intuition. An individual owes a moral duty as well, most believe, to those who care deeply about her, because her life is profoundly enmeshed with their own. These are people whose well-being depends in no small part on her continued vitality, though she owes them no legal duty in that regard.

In sum, when medical professionals intercede against the will of self-destructive patients, saving their lives during the ephemeral crises here observed, they act in the knowledge that common morality stands firmly in their support; for most of us are here prepared to turn a blind eye even to certain outright violations of law. Though it may be tempting at first to dismiss this fact as a quirky anomaly of no general significance, it has become an integral feature of our modern medical system, and therefore too of the society it serves.

## The Right to Kill Civilians in War

International humanitarian law offers another fruitful example of a right to do perceived wrong that is informally constrained in ways that render it widely acceptable and politically sustainable. It is impossible to understand the law's true significance here without due attention to why and in what respects the dispensations it affords combatants are held in reserve, increasingly so, at least by the armed forces of the developed world.

This body of law seeks to limit the extent to which belligerents may cause unintended harm to civilian persons and property, and thereby establishes the acceptable means and methods of armed conflict. When at war, states may not target civilian interests intentionally, but may inflict "incidental" damage to them if it is not "clearly excessive" in relation to the "concrete and direct military advantage anticipated" from a given use of force.[48] The law here authorizes (and at once restricts) such harmful conduct because it is generally impossible to make war in any other way; and from the perspective of common morality, some wars—of self-defense and humanitarian intervention—are just.

All agree that, in seeking to restrict the scope of permissible civilian harm, international law here engages a laudable objective. Once war has begun—however wrongfully, aggressively—it is better to limit its destructiveness than to let it follow a course entirely indifferent to humane values. Yet though it has long been part of customary international law, and more recently embodied in multiple treaties,[49] the proportionality rule—as it is colloquially called—has never been well defined. It has attained no greater precision in recent years, despite the proliferation of international criminal tribunals and considerable scholarly attention to the matter.[50] Commentators who agree on little else here concur. Soldiers themselves have little idea what the rule really requires of them, except in the most obvious circumstances where the ethically proper course of action can be readily ascertained without it.[51] Military prudence alone—under the "economy of force" doctrine—often dictates the same measure of restraint, without need for recourse to law's guidance. The rule itself therefore has little real-life influence on combat conduct, officers readily acknowledge. Prosecutions for disproportionate force have been nearly nonexistent, in no small part because the legal test is so lenient, encouraging judicial deference to the military commander's situational judgment.

There are good reasons for such deference. Where they provide the basis for criminal liability, legal rules must display a measure of generality and specificity inconsistent with the extent to which proportionality determinations in war involve fine-grained assessment of unique factual particulars.[52] And no one really has any well-developed idea about how to conduct the required balancing between civilian lives and military gains—that is, about how the relative weights are to be attached.

The stress of combat and its disorienting "fog of war" also set powerful limits on what can be known *ex ante* about the precise measure of force, and of attendant civilian harm, necessary to achieve a given battlefield goal.[53] This uncertainty often originates in the elusiveness and inscrutability of enemy "morale." Further distortion in judgment is introduced through the mental processes recently explored by cognitive psychologists, even as armed forces today strive to redesign training programs and decision procedures with a view to overcoming these same biases. The efforts display only modest prospects of success.[54] Epistemic limits and decisional uncertainties are still greater regarding broader operational and strategic aims.

Experts cannot agree on whether the civilian harm relevant to proportionality assessment should be only short-term or also longer-term, though much depends on which position the law adopts on this question.[55] All these problems arise even before one reaches more familiar concerns about practical obstacles to attaining jurisdiction or custody over ostensible violators. These obstacles are rooted in the de facto power of states, especially major military powers, to thumb their nose at international law.

Many people throughout the world are greatly dissatisfied with this state of affairs, however.[56] Civilian deaths in war today are closely scrutinized by human rights NGOs and academicians, employing accepted epidemiological methods.[57] These deaths evoke wide international uproar,[58] especially when caused by modern militaries considered capable of greater restraint and "discrimination."[59] States are now widely expected to formally apologize for military errors that cause significant unintended casualties.[60] Critics of today's military practices concerning collateral damage are not deterred by the leniency of long-standing legal "technicalities," as they would call them. These critics demand greater moral accountability than the law requires.

"People should not be allowed," Waldron writes, "to think that they are insulated from moral criticism of their irresponsibility simply because they are exercising a legal right that is not subject to any legal limitation."[61] A recent international illustration of this comes vividly to mind. A UN commission ultimately cleared the State of Israel of widespread accusations that it had violated international law in forcefully stopping a flotilla of Turkish protestors on the high seas.[62] The ships had been seeking to break Israel's blockade on the Gaza strip, a blockade which the commission held to be lawful as well. A commission thereafter appointed by the Israeli government itself found, however, that in these events the country's prime minister had been gravely at fault in violating the state's settled procedures for national security decision-making.[63] The commission found that his failure to consult sufficiently with military leaders had led the country's troops to be inadequately prepared for the type of resistance they were likely to encounter; and these inadequacies were partly responsible for the extent of the ensuing bloodshed. In this case, as is quite common, international law proved more lenient than widely accepted standards of moral assessment, domestic no less than global.

A distinguished Israeli expert in humanitarian law can still today affirm that collateral damage often "emanates from human error or mechanical malfunction, and when that occurs there is no stigma."[64] Yet younger scholars now respond that "human error is sometimes (although not always) caused by putting people in situations where such errors are more likely."[65] This suggests that it would then be entirely appropriate to stigmatize those doing the "putting." In fact, the view is now widespread that the international law of "distinction" and "proportionality"—designed to accommodate, even facilitate, the lawful progress of war-making—accords insufficient weight to the lives of innocent civilians who are likely to be caught in harm's way. Many today believe, in other words, that such law creates a right to do serious wrong.[66] This remains true even if we acknowledge that, due to the intractable impediments just described, there can be little realistic expectation that international law will, in these matters, become significantly more stringent.[67] These concerns do not concentrate simply on the inadequate state of legal doctrine, in the abstract. There is also a broadly shared perception that these legal limitations are being frequently exploited in practice, that such rights are "abused" on actual battlefields.[68]

Despite the wide berth international law allows them, U.S. leaders have come to believe that they cannot afford to remain indifferent to international criticism if the country is to have any hope of sustaining its stature as benign world leader.[69] Every reported incident in which civilians are killed in a drone strike on terrorist leaders elicits a public explanation of the target's strategic importance.[70] Official U.S. government studies express concern that public anger over civilian casualties appears to have contributed to the growth of insurgencies, both Sunni and Shiite, opposing American military presence in Iraq.[71] Thus, when President Barack Obama eventually agreed in August 2014 to let U.S. bombers target ISIS positions in Syria and Iraq, he imposed such restrictive rules of engagement that nearly three-fourths of all aircraft, according to Central Command, returned to base without dropping their ordnance.[72] Concerning ground operations, the considerable resources today devoted to refining counterinsurgency doctrine,[73] with its emphasis on "winning hearts and minds" through a more discerning use of force, offers further evidence of such concern over the moral assessments by ordinary Iraqis and Afghans, in particular.

All of this suggests that concerns over reputation for ethical attentiveness now exert a nontrivial influence on American commanders, inducing them to display greater attention to saving the innocent civilian from war's horrors than international law requires of them. Military deference to such "ideal" considerations arrives quite circuitously, and by a decidedly "material" route. The moral sentiments first manifest themselves in world opinion, which then registers in the geostrategic calculations of a superpower that cannot afford to ignore others' views on matters of such acute global concern.[74] By this route, a tough, "realist" concern with preserving power results in increased sensitivity to the more idealistic considerations of common morality. This sensitivity finds reflection in the regulatory restraints the superpower at war chooses to impose upon itself. Given its doctrinal laxity and weak enforcement, international law will long remain less significant a protection against needless civilian harm than the enigmatic workings of something so seemingly ethereal as humanitarian sensibility—which is to say, common morality, now embryonically at work on the global level.

Military officers themselves, at all levels, regularly report serious concern that their career prospects will be compromised—destroyed in a heartbeat, in fact—if they so much as initially appear to cause unnecessary loss of civilian life.[75] To speak of career incentives is not to minimize the abiding influence of nonselfish motivations, based in martial virtue,[76] as an additional fetter on excessive force. In fact, even in Western countries widely considered the most "pacifist," the study of martial virtue is "currently the most popular underpinning for ethics education in the military."[77] However, such virtue is a species of what philosophers call "role morality"—distinct from the truly common morality stressed thus far in identifying social encumbrances on how people exercise their rights. The global movement to limit acceptable levels of civilian harm asserts a moral cosmopolitanism strongly distrustful of any such military virtue.[78] This distrust of virtue ethics is clear in the obvious fact that, for instance, no one expects the civilian beneficiary of this professional probity, across the battle lines, to feel or express any gratitude toward his benefactors for graciously sparing him the violent death they were lawfully entitled to inflict.

We doubt the capacity of this soldierly self-understanding to satisfactorily address the moral crisis of collateral damage, or even to conceptually register its normative magnitude. Common morality, one could therefore credibly say, today insists on a more stringent standard than does either international law or military ethics. We may strongly suspect, for that matter, that the traditional preoccupation of the professional soldier with upholding martial honor—that of his country no less than his own—has throughout history encouraged too ready a recourse to force.[79] This is militarism, in its most dangerous form. We Americans, in particular, will be inclined to think immediately of our country's South, where the defense of honor was long associated with guns and other violence, much as in Germany it was long identified with the duel.

Still, anyone who listened regularly to Western officers discussing their recent battlefield experiences in Iraq and Afghanistan will attest to the obvious sincerity of their belief that this "internal morality" of professional soldiering fetters their use of force in ways far more demanding than the law.[80] Many officers accept, often even embrace, current public demands for greater moral scrupulousness,[81] but view these as inalterably "beyond the call" of legal duty. One almost suspects here that they insist on a right to do great wrong precisely in order to receive extra kudos for graciously declining to exercise it. There could be some truth to that, as a matter of human psychology. It would have to count as a corruption of virtue, on most accounts, not its genuine expression. For it is in the nature of a virtue, classically understood, to desire nothing from its beneficiaries in return.

Yet clearly so pristinely purist an account of virtue, unsullied by any yearning for others' recognition, cannot much guide us in deciding how far international law may trust to mores in restraining civilian carnage.

There is necessarily an element of willful individuality in honor, martial or otherwise, which led Montesquieu to deny it the status of virtue at all. Krause thus observes of honor generally:

> It can, as Montesquieu said, inspire the finest actions, risky undertakings that yield great public benefits. Yet honor achieves the effects of virtue without oppressing the particular passions or individual ambition. Indeed, much of the power of honor lies in the fact that it is a mixed motive. As a duty to oneself, it builds on the particular attachments and private desires that make us who we are and move us to act. It channels and directs personal ambitions rather than suppressing them in the name of a comprehensive common good or a universal standpoint. It does not require the state to cultivate character or submerge diverse identities into a homogeneous collective one. And . . . honor reminds us of the aristocratic capacities in ourselves that have survived the rise of modern man and of liberal democracy's need for them.[82]

To rest any serious measure of hope for minimizing war's horrors on such "irreducibly aristocratic"[83] foundations is at once deeply disconcerting to egalitarian sensibilities and utterly inescapable in the face of law's persistent, transparent failings. Not only is martial honor premodern in origin, and often in tension with "rule of law" commitments; there is also good reason to question its real-life efficacy in restraining the exercise of humanitarian law rights. One searches the record in vain for substantial indications that aspirations for honor had actually inhibited significant numbers of soldiers from inflicting excessive harm, though this evidence may simply exceed the reach of our methodological tools (so much the worse for them, perhaps). As one might expect, such evidence is sparse and anecdotal, even in the more insightful meditations on the military calling by its most distinguished practitioners.[84] Admittedly, this extralegal restraint in preventing incidental civilian losses is precisely the avowed aim of certain novel forms of professional recognition. In the U.S. Air Force, for instance, awards once given only for lethal bravery in battle are today sometimes granted to pilots who *declined* to use lethal force in circumstances where it would have been lawful but where their decision to wait saved civilian lives.[85] This reflects a larger Pentagon policy discourse of "winning through courageous restraint."[86]

We might characterize the self-understanding that Western officers today evince as conjoining rights and responsibilities in ways that lend a distinctive dignity to their calling and social role[87]—distinguishing it, at least, from murder, in this case. Here, unlike in most of my other illustrations, there exists a long-standing vocabulary for formulating and expressing such deep intimations of duty. It is a vocabulary of "my station and its duties," however, and strikes most outsiders as redolent of mothballs, faintly Victorian, anachronistic, intolerably elitist.

In fact, it almost seems as if the special dignity of the officer's social role, insofar as such dignity today endures, does not derive primarily from its core activities—violent and sanguinary, after all. This dignity derives more decisively from the very fact that his weighty responsibilities do not and cannot find full reflection, complete specification, within the law governing him.[88] That he is formally authorized to operate in this grey zone becomes central to the elusive charismatic nimbus (today well-routinized) historically surrounding his station. For it is his commitment to martial honor, a species of moral virtue, that warrants us in *expecting* him to act beyond the call of legal duty.

It is this very disparity between legal and moral duty, this failure of law to adequately capture and cognize our ethical expectations, that grants him the broad authority over grave matters with which we endow such positions of special dignity. The esteem accorded the military officer (such as it is, in modern societies)[89] therefore arises not merely from the intrinsic importance of his chief societal function—national self-defense. It springs as well from our reluctant acknowledgment that we simply cannot entirely subject him, as thoroughly as we do most others, to the rule of law.

We are obliged, willy-nilly, to place enormous trust in someone who, we concede, must operate to great extent in a domain of literal lawlessness. This is true not only of war, though it is most conspicuous there. It is also the case wherever we expect people—as professionals, parents, or medical patients—to behave in morally demanding ways that we cannot quite pull under law's umbrella, cannot bring the legal system to precisely require of them. "Discretion" is the prosaic, flatfooted term we lawyers employ to describe the net result. Yet the artful alchemy by which professional groups win and sustain public legitimacy for their considerable autonomy from greater legal scrutiny can be nothing short of theatrical; this is a conjuring game of self-enlargement, by which the merely human quickly becomes superhuman, grandiosely so. It would be inaccurate to say, without clearer law on the meaning of military proportionality, that there exists an internationally accepted common morality filling the regulatory shortfall. For there is no more agreement on the term's meaning in the wider political discourse than in the juridical.[90]

Without any clear agreement on these matters, however, what does step into the breach, within certain contemporary armed forces at least, is a norm not of substance but of process. The central idea here is not to directly challenge the legal right of the commander to cause a given measure of civilian harm. The chief idea is to assess whether she has abused that right by failing to take all reasonable steps to limit whatever incidental damage would ensue.[91] If she is then legally disciplined in any way, it is not for having violated the substantive international law of proportionality, as such.

To reduce civilian losses, Western armies today also employ "rules of engagement" (ROE) that impose unprecedented self-restraint on use of force by both ground and aerial services. The restrictive ROE imposed by General Stanley McChrystal on U.S. soldiers in Afghanistan, in particular, received much attention at the time. The increased risks to which these rules exposed U.S. troops understandably led some to chafe at their considerable restraints.[92] Some critics even contended that stringent ROE seriously compromised mission objectives, at times.[93] In both Afghanistan and Iraq, restrictive ROE were adopted in response to exhortation from local leaders, reflecting public opinion in these countries.[94] Eventually, close air support (aerial bombardment) could be called in only when Western troops were in serious danger of being overrun.[95] Data suggest that, as ROE in Afghanistan became more restrictive, civilian deaths declined but deaths of U.S. soldiers increased.[96] Civilian victims of such force also regularly receive compensation from the American military, a practice that international law does not require.[97]

Significant here as well are the new, nonlethal weapons in advanced stages of Pentagon research and development.[98] These promise to disable enemy fighters without killing them, and to reduce attendant harm to enemy civilians and their property. To this effect, such technologies are of a piece with a generation of improvements in precision-guided weapons, employing laser and GPS electronics.[99] These are embodied especially within drone technology, which has come to be the chief tool of U.S. counterterrorism policy in recent years, and has been consistently effective in disrupting the operational capacities of terrorist groups, according to the best recent data.[100] International law does not require states to develop and maintain such weapons. No one would contend that it should, insofar as this would entail allocating increased revenues to weapons acquisition, a commitment of resources that states could otherwise direct to programs for general well-being.

In sum, then, the responsibilities most vigorously urged upon states and their soldiers are today, and must remain, nonjuridical. Even so, in deference to emergent common morality on a global scale, the armed forces of certain Western democracies, at least, have clearly incorporated a measure of legally supererogatory moderation into their formal routines, technologies, and institutional structures. Professional soldiers themselves increasingly view such restraint as being within their core vocational function, and not as an alien, exogenous imposition. The result is that, in authorizing considerable civilian losses, the international law of proportionality legalizes what many throughout the world consider great wrongdoing. World opinion has nonetheless brought considerable extralegal pressure to bear, to some notable effect, in persuading major military powers to exercise such rights responsibly. Through these responsibilities, soldiers subject themselves to greater restrictions on force than the law itself imposes. Because it proves impossible to incorporate all pertinent moral considerations into law, we have knowingly created a right to do severe wrong. Its full exercise is then impeded, however, by responsibility-inducing mechanisms and social mores that operate independently of international law. Anyone defending the leniency of international law here would certainly emphasize that these environing encumbrances on modern military organizations are indispensable to such law's continuing legitimacy and essential to understanding its true workings and significance.

These recent forms and sources of inhibition on the measure of force employed in war have paradoxically become integral to accepting the law of proportionality itself. This is what accounts for the measure of equilibrium that today exists here between a lenient law and a common morality far more exigent. It would probably be too much to claim that the law fails to do more in safeguarding civilians *because* the world is content with what common morality and informal pressures accomplish to that end. Rather, the increasingly stringent mores of recent years simply make the current state of affairs more ethically defensible than one would surmise from simply a reading of applicable law, which is all that some critics of current law deign to do.

To conclude, the right to cause collateral damage in war implicates all three of the weighty concerns mentioned at the outset: (1) The legal right to which responsibilities attach arises from an essential task or position authorizing one to cause grave harm; (2) the scope of the right would hence be very limited, were it not for our confidence in assurances that concomitant moral duties will be honored; and (3) the extralegal supports for fulfilling these duties are uncertain, apparent only via difficult and uncertain empirical inquiry, or simply defy description in a satisfactory modern idiom.

These concerns must give pause over whether we may reliably trust to extralegal practices and pressures to satisfactorily plug all gaps in current law, even as the alternatives remain unclear. Certainly, there is some reason to wonder about the stability of these new expectations, how they will fare over time, whether their efficacy may wax and wane with the measure of a country's concern about others' views. It may therefore be premature to suggest that emergent mores have attained much genuine equilibrium, a measure of solidity enabling them to continue their currently significant influence without greater legal bolstering. It is further noteworthy that the United States, in particular, is always careful never to allow the inference that its present commitments in this regard reflect any acceptance of newly customary international law.

The true challenge to the ostensible new mores would arise when nearly the entire population of country A regarded the entire population of country B as "the enemy." This scenario may be hard to imagine with respect to present public attitudes in developed Western societies, though some data suggest otherwise.[101] It was certainly the case there, however, not long ago, and remains characteristic of most wars of "ethnic cleansing,"[102] which are common in several parts of the world.

Finally, it is likely that the notable shift in prevailing moral expectations on the issue of collateral damage in war, though lacking legal foundations, has been influenced by the growth of international human rights law, even where that law is not strictly applicable. This body of law, like that on crimes against humanity, prohibits state-sponsored atrocities during both war and peace. There is no doubt that the idea of human rights, if not the details of the international law embodying it, has captured the imagination of conscientious people everywhere,[103] informing their moral judgment of belligerent behavior in war. In this respect, it would be wrong to imply that the recent strengthening of extralegal mores against collateral damage is advancing in ways entirely unaffected by legal developments. Still, it may be more the general notion of fundamental human rights, as a moral ideal, that does most of the work here in fostering public concern and creating the impetus for new mores.

International lawyers have long acknowledged, at least in private, that self-restraint has proven and will likely continue to prove no less important than international legality as a source of moderation in war. As early as the early seventeenth century, Hugo Grotius, a founder and early advocate of public international law, adduced some historical evidence to the effect that statesmen—even when entitled to wage just war—generally recognize significant responsibilities beyond those of the law itself. According to these acknowledged duties, "it is an act of greater piety and rectitude to yield a right than to enforce it."[104] For him, this notably included rights to employ lethal force on a massive scale. If we could translate his theological terminology into more acceptably secular idiom, we would surely say the same today, notwithstanding the notable advances and refinements in this legal area since his time. Restraints on the use of force in armed conflicts today depend heavily, perhaps still largely, on the moral rectitude of professional soldiers and the state's civilian leaders in yielding their acknowledged legal rights.

Let us now step back for a moment from the empirical analysis, assayed in these last two chapters, and pose a number of larger questions that these descriptive materials and their sociological analysis immediately invite.

# 4

# How to "Abuse" a Right

It is noteworthy that, with some regularity, we lawyers privately describe certain rights as "disfavored."[1] This casual expression is not a legal term of art, and we use it in a number of distinct but related senses, all pertinent to present concerns.

Throughout much of Continental Europe, many consider it distinctly suspect, if not quite repellant, to publicly report the criminal activity of others, a view quietly shared even by certain authorities themselves. This attitude is counterintuitive to some, and certainly counterproductive to law enforcement, as we law professors sometimes lament.[2] Although this attitude has several sources, it has become especially noteworthy since the Second World War, during which collaborators with Third Reich occupiers employed this particular right for the purpose of incriminating their neighbors, notably those who harbored Jews. Collective memory of that somber experience continues to hang heavily over European perception of the relevant legal prerogative. In fact, the entire history of twentieth-century totalitarianism evokes in many a lingering distaste toward the idea of reporting on others' misconduct. Quick to mind here, in particular, may be the Soviet Union under Stalin, where schoolteachers actively encouraged children to report their parents for errant remarks over the dinner table.[3]

To this day, many decades after all these events, the right to report another's wrongs to the police or other regulatory authorities continues to meet with significant social disfavor.[4] That this right could be so easily employed in these objectionable ways, if only for a few years long ago, seems to have cast enduring doubts not only on those who exercised it in these ways but also upon the right itself. Its societal utility notwithstanding, it is little employed, except in response to the witnessing of ongoing violence against the obviously innocent—if then.

Under liberal democracy, there may be little defensible basis for this continuing aversion, a significant share of which surely arises from factors other than a healthy recollection of how the right was historically abused. The public aversiveness to reporting crime amounts to more than a mild disinclination, for it is a significant social fact. Even those of us beyond Europe's shores, for whom its peculiar history in this department has no personal bearing, sometimes frown on people whose voluntary assistance to law enforcement agencies springs from motives we find unappealing. This is notably so when such informants act in service of political objectives we do not share, or where they (certain whistle-blowers, most notably) seek something of great material value in return for their services, in which case they begin to approximate "officious intermeddlers,"[5] whom law itself discourages.

More often today, though, when we think or speak of a disfavored right, we have in mind that people tend to invoke it mistakenly, because they inaccurately understand its terms and purposes, believing that it extends to their situation when it does not. The right thus often generates an unacceptable number of meritless, even frivolous causes of action, or prompts people to undertake activities that will, to their unpleasant surprise, subject them to liability. Due to the very low success rate for plaintiffs in suits alleging employment discrimination,[6] for instance, many lawyers and judges quietly think of this category of disputes in an unfavorable light, though they remain prepared to neutrally assess the evidence in a given case.

We may be similarly suspicious of a given right when we believe its definition or judicial interpretation misconstrues the problem it professed to address. Legal redress is thus genuinely available to those asserting these rights, so that there is no significant problem of "false positives," in the normal sense. Yet there remains a widespread sentiment about these cases that the particular right is itself inaptly articulated, even misconceived; it is only very imperfectly responsive to the underlying issues that lawmakers hoped to resolve. Though the right-holder acts consistently with the law, fully within his rights, he does so in ways widely considered to be misplaced, even wrongful. Here too we are averse to granting the right-holder what he wishes, though we are obliged reluctantly to acknowledge that his claim satisfies the factual and doctrinal predicates for what he seeks.

Consider a particular context of concern. Legislators in many U.S. states recently came to believe that punitive damages in civil litigation were being awarded too often and in excessive amounts.[7] Lawmakers did not directly challenge the right to collect such damages, nor did they seek to narrow the substantive standard—defendant's "malice"—used to determine their availability. This suggests that the problem was perceived to lie not so much in the law itself, but chiefly in its extravagant misreading by jurors unduly generous to sympathetic plaintiffs. Identifying the problem in this way, legislators intelligibly responded by requiring that plaintiffs meet a higher standard of proof. Anyone claiming punitive damages must now, in some states, establish the defendant's maliciousness not merely by "a preponderance of the evidence" but in a manner "clear and convincing."[8]

All these disfavored rights, as well as those explored in Chapters 2 and 3, differ importantly among themselves. Yet in all of them we find significant numbers of people wishing—with varying candor and intensity—that pressures could lawfully be brought to bear upon the potential claimant to dissuade him from asserting his right. People hope that, like a house guest who has overstayed his welcome, he can be gently induced simply to go away.

Among laymen especially, it is more common to speak of a right's recurrent "abuse" than to describe it as disfavored. Within the common law, however, one succumbs to oxymoron if one speaks of abusing a right. Either you have a right or you don't. And if you do, then you may use it in any way you wish. If another person may lawfully stop you from doing what you desire, it is because your right does not extend as far as you thought. The very expression—an abuse of rights, as a legal term of art—is therefore effectively absent from lawyerly discourse in the English-speaking world.

Yet when we drop our professional guard and garb, we lawyers too sometimes say that a person has abused his rights. This colloquialism registers our recognition of the points at which law permits activities reproached by prevailing morals. Much the same may be said of "loopholes." The two terms warrant ethnographic attention, as they enjoy some linguistic salience in everyday interaction. Readers will easily recall a personal experience or incident eliciting the urge to invoke one of these familiar turns of phrase. We may most often refer to an abuse of rights in connection with highly offensive speech, like that involved in the notorious case of *Snyder v. Phelps*.[9] There, members of a Christian religious congregation whose members oppose homosexuality carried posters reading "Fag troops," "*Semper fi* fags," and "Thank God for Dead Soldiers," at the funerals of U.S. soldiers killed in Iraq and Afghanistan. Such speech is very different from that involved in perjury and libel. To libel another or perjure oneself is to exceed the scope of one's speech rights; such conduct therefore escapes First Amendment protection altogether.[10] One cannot abuse a right one never had.

Only certain rights are susceptible to abuse, or so our linguistic practices suggest, as Fred Schauer observes.[11] Other rights—as to privacy, to marry, to vote—are not. Schauer does not tell us, however, what it is about a certain right that renders it amenable to abuse. We might first suspect that, say, contractual rights would be least susceptible to abuse, because we create them through mutually beneficial exchange without force or fraud. Yet contracts classed "unconscionable" will not be judicially enforced; the legal concept itself is a creation of American lawyers but inspired by ethnographic observation of the Cheyenne[12] and thus modeled on how Native Americans incorporated social mores into legal interpretation. The doctrine came into existence to facilitate law's more ready integration of prevailing moral sensibilities—when these prove much more restrictive of the defendant's conduct than the terms to which parties had agreed.[13]

In these rare and exigent situations, the law of contract extends its protective reach, according supremacy to common morality. That it is indeed *common* morality, rather than some more rarefied notion of "critical" morality that animates this move within legal doctrine is apparent from the relevant judicial opinions, in their failure to specify any particular tradition of moral thought. It is enough that the defendant's conduct "shocks the conscience" of pertinent publics, as a jury will discern it; this is conduct deeply at odds with "the mores and business practices of the time and place," in Corbin's often-cited wording.[14]

Schauer does not tell us what it is that turns *some* forms of offensive speech into the abuse of a right. He allows that much of the distasteful, even repugnant speech that we routinely hear does not fall within that particularly noxious subset. In fact, people sometimes consider it entirely defensible to speak in ways likely to offend another. Not merely does the law then fail to prohibit such speech. People do not even consider it wrongful. There's even a finely honed art to giving clever offense. As Oscar

Wilde famously quipped, a proper Victorian gentleman never says anything likely to offend another—unintentionally.[15] And though the etiquette of inter-state diplomacy is finely drawn and well-known to all insiders,[16] "the calculated breach of diplomatic norms about civility retains a force which can be exploited to make, or score, a point," observes a perceptive scholar of international relations.[17]

We are thus left to wonder what makes certain forms of speech not merely offensive, but "abusively" so.[18] In the common law, neither "offense" nor "abuse" is a freestanding concept, though sometimes both notions—their meaning varying from one context to the next—become incorporated into the definition of particular legal wrongs, as with the rules against "abusive tax shelters."[19] Nor is there much overlap between the notion of offensive speech and that of abusive speech. Just as offensive speech need not "abuse" the right to speak, so too certain rights may be abused in ways that offend no one, if only because no one learns of the misconduct, spoken or otherwise. Offensive speech may be obnoxious in forms the law forbids (defamation and fraudulent misrepresentation) or in ways that elude its prohibitions (constitutionally protected "opinion"). Perceived abusiveness therefore need not—and often does not—entail illegality, even if illegal speech presumably entails some form of abuse.

Let us put such conceptual intricacies aside, however. Ordinary language usage among the English-speaking middle classes, at least, does closely track the points where Schauer invites us to draw more rigorous analytic lines. In real life, people at least occasionally say that someone has abused his right to speak, whereas no one (other than certain Islamic jurisprudents)[20] would assert that someone has abused her right to marry. When disapproving of her choice in spouse, one says instead that she has shown poor judgment, as by allowing her emotions to distort her thinking, override her reasoning. Friends and family would describe her choice as ill-considered, unwise, or unsuitable—all terms that seem to deliberately skirt overt moral judgment.

Though a right may be the sort unsusceptible to abuse, in Schauer's view, it may nonetheless entail a right to do wrong, in my sense. The right need only be defined under-inclusively in relation to common moral expectations of the person holding it. This is not the more familiar species of under-inclusiveness Schauer himself later examines.[21] For there he identifies situations where the wording of a legal prohibition simply falls short of the broader goals legislators sought in drafting it. Facing that challenge, common-law courts sometimes conclude that lawmakers intended to prohibit a wider reach of conduct than they managed explicitly to bar. Judges then interpret the law accordingly, if they can credibly read the legislative history to this effect. Alternatively, a judge may hold that the way a defendant exercised his statutory right is inconsistent with public policy encoded in other areas of law.[22] In either case, the court concludes that the offending party has no right to do what he has done, not that he has abused his right.

In the "civil law" world of Continental Europe and its former colonies,[23] by contrast, the judicial response in such a situation would often be to acknowledge that the challenged party *does* have a right to engage in the objectionable conduct, but then find he has abused that right and may not exercise it in this manner.[24] He abuses his right insofar as his activities—though authorized by a statute's express wording—may be inconsistent with the statute's underlying purposes, which generally are discerned without reference to independent evidence of legislative intent. Alternatively, the court may simply characterize his conduct as "socially reprehensible," at odds with "moral order," "societal conscience," or demands of "social responsibility."[25] These two tacks combine to do much of the same work as those employed by tribunals in the Anglo-American world.[26]

They do so in a very different way, however, with differing implications for the relation between law and common morality. The second of these rationales for disallowing an exercise of acknowledged legal right is pertinent here, for it involves an express overriding of clear positive law on the basis of prevailing moral sentiment. Courts notably do not couch this move in terms untethered from common notions of moral responsibility, in terms of a "critical" morality, as philosophers use that expression. Even so, this judicial step is more controversial, from the standpoint of democratic theory and the rule of law, than common-law approaches to the problem. We in the Anglophone world demand demonstrable evidence from legislative history or facts about policy objectives clearly manifest within closely related bodies of law. We then interpret the relevant statute or precedent in their light, *in pari materia*.

George Fletcher, a leading scholar of comparative law, nonetheless defends the "abuse of right" doctrine on the grounds that its workings are clearer than those of the common law, and clarity is always a virtue in legal analysis. In particular, the doctrine enables both citizens and courts to more easily distinguish between formally enacted law and the "just or sound" law.[27] Courts will generally seek to find and apply the second of these, he contends, even though this means the result will sometimes turn on "extra-statutory considerations."[28] Fletcher draws his examples chiefly from German criminal law. That enterprise heavily incorporates principles of Kantian morality, he contends, principles that we today consider too sternly retributive in many situations. German law classically committed its agents to punishing all serious wrongdoing, irrespective of whether this served any "productive purpose."[29] Such a notion is altogether alien to the professed goals of American criminal law. For the Germans, as in certain other civil-law systems, it is important to acknowledge the "absolute"[30] and "supposedly dispositive," character of Kantian-inspired rights, such as that to defense against violent attack.[31] To preserve such principles from messy compromise, the first stage of any legal analysis will always do exactly that.

Yet if courts were to stop there, Fletcher contends, the result would often fail "criteria of human solidarity"—it would fall short of the law's inherently "humanitarian" aspirations.[32] This second, 'softening' set of moral intuitions finds expression, within many European languages, through an entirely different word for "law" (the single term we English speakers must employ). One of these words always reflects a positivist conception of the enterprise, the other a nonpositivist notion. A legal analysis considered fully satisfactory will always move sequentially from the first to the second, Fletcher argues. At this latter stage, the question arises of whether the pertinent party, in exercising his right to self-defense against armed attack, has abused this right by not treating his attacker with sufficient "compassion."[33] One who employs greater force than necessary to his self-defense would be so characterized.

The common law holds such a person liable, as the Germans do, but does not separate the analysis into two steps. We ask only the single question: Was the person's use of force "reasonable" under the circumstances? One norm alone is at work, not two. This ensures that the single norm—behave reasonably!—is unavoidably "vague,"[34] however, because it must serve as a "placeholder for everything one needs to know to resolve a particular problem."[35] These include norms both legal and moral. Fletcher concedes that the end result in decided cases is exactly the same. He concedes as well that "a sophisticated American lawyer would presumably respond that these ostensible virtues of German law are illusory, and that it is better to work with vague and qualified, but at least non-deceptive, legal norms."[36] It is deceptive to suggest both that a right is absolute and that it is always potentially defeasible by countervailing considerations that no judge could defensibly ignore in the final analysis. It is misleading, in other words, to offer with one hand what the other will immediately snatch away. This is precisely what the "abuse of right" doctrine does.

One finds noteworthy German cases where the doctrine yields an appealing result unavailable to civil lawyers via any other route of reasoning. For instance, toward the end of the Second World War, a German woman was convicted and imprisoned, based on evidence provided by her neighbors, for making "defeatist" statements. There is no doubt that the neighbors had a legal right to report what they had heard her say. But a provision of German law, long antedating the Third Reich, allows one citizen to sue another for acting in ways that, though otherwise lawful, are at odds with "sound morals." The neighbors had abused their right to share with authorities the criminally inculpatory information in their possession. The injured woman could therefore later recover from those who had betrayed her confidences in ways foreseeably resulting in her incarceration.[37] In fact, postwar courts and commentators,[38] coping with the legal aftermath of the Third Reich, found this doctrine invaluable.

In England, the law of rights abuse developed in response to a quite different set of challenges. The law found its small footing at a time, just over a century ago, when private property possessed an aura of sanctity and near-absolute protection it no longer enjoys. In those years, we may "doubt whether without the animus attaching to the notion of 'abuse,'" one scholar speculates, "inroads could have been made on so exceptionally well-established and buttressed a concept."[39] To accuse one's neighbor of abusing his property rights was then presumably more resonant and evocative than merely to allege his malice, though it was precisely his malicious use of property that gave rise to the claim against him. Within the ordinary language of the day, there occurred, in the descent from abuse to malice, "an undoubted sacrifice of emotional content." It may be precisely the word's emotional charge, even today, that quickens the pulse of legal thinkers still skeptical of private power and the property rights on which it rests. The emotional register rises even higher in the current climate, when to speak at all of "abuse" is necessarily to allude, tacitly yet inescapably, to the physical abuse of women and children, sexual or otherwise. For these are the legal contexts in which the word now often finds its most frequent and familiar public expression.

The doctrine of rights abuse is very helpful for coping more generally, beyond such singular circumstances, with situations where rapid changes in prevailing moral sensibility profoundly redefine how people believe certain rights may be acceptably exercised. The European Court of Justice regularly finds that legal rights have been abused,[40] as do the domestic courts of many civil-law countries. The European Court must periodically assess, for instance, whether cross-border investors take unfair advantage of continuing differences between the domestic laws of member states.[41] The judges seek to draw a line—predictable in advance to investors—between acceptable "arbitrage" among countries (over tax law, for instance) and the unacceptable exploitation of such national dissimilarities.[42]

International law at times goes still further than European views on the abuse of rights in authorizing direct recourse to common morality. This recourse appears in two distinct situations, always with a view to narrowing the range of situations dispositively governed by international or foreign law. First, international law has long authorized national judges, in civil litigation, to decline enforcement of foreign judgments deemed *contra bonos mores*—"inconsistent with public order and sound morals"[43] in the country whose courts would do the enforcing.[44] These are situations where, to oversimplify only a bit, common morality in country B, as reflected in its laws, is simply too different from that of country A to expect B's courts to enforce A's law, as determined by A's courts. Yet despite loose talk about public morals, judges in these cases generally cite their domestic law—chapter and verse—seeking to show how radically it differs from that of the foreign jurisdiction whose judgment they must therefore reject.

Second, in recent years disputes have also regularly arisen when a citizen of minority religious faith within a given country invokes an international human right, adopted by her country, to engage in religious practices offensive to national majorities; these practices include wearing her head scarf in school, which is sometimes barred by national law. In these cases, the question before international human rights courts has been whether the objectionable practice is compatible with *bonos mores,*[45] as the country's majority appears to understand these. Essentially an appeal to common morality, that wording—however amorphous and potentially expansive—today provides the formal test under international law for determining the reach of human-rights-based claims to religious freedom. The international court will not treat the nature and content of common morality as an empirical question, requiring direct evidence from national authorities concerning what their publics truly believe.[46] Instead, the legal question concerns only the nature and extent of discretion properly afforded such authorities in the face of worldwide standards, increasingly exigent, to which their state has formally agreed.[47]

Within the common-law world, there existed an early analogue to the civil-law notion of rights abuse, which had been abandoned by the modern era. In the late medieval and early modern English Courts of Chancery, it was perfectly acceptable for litigants to loosely invoke ethical considerations, including "abuse of rights,"[48] whenever settled rules of common law proved uncongenial. Historians report that these invocations remained accepted if periodic practice until the late eighteenth century. Yet even during the centuries of freewheeling "equity" jurisprudence, each courtroom result was (in relevant respects) taken as unique unto itself, without future legal import. This conveniently allowed an idiosyncratic judgment, based on little more than common morality, to set no nettlesome precedent, as it would have done at common law.

In any event, this early equity jurisprudence soon hardened into more formal rules of its own, for these were easier to reconcile with "the rule of law," with accepted notions of due process. Those subject to the law's dictates must not fear, after all, that they will later find themselves judged by a magistrate's singular sense of what common morality requires, plucked from air. It is notable how often, even today, civil-law judges and scholars appeal vaguely to something called "the social order" (and verbal variants thereof) or the "moral order" when condemning what they consider, often without elaboration, an abuse of rights.

Defenses of this practice often succumb to rampant reification, pitting one ethereal phantasm against another. The isolated asocial individual, indifferent to other's interests and suffering, goes into battle against the putative needs of "community cohesion,"[49] of "society's concerns that transcend individual interests."[50] Some defenders claim to discover the deeper source of all difficulties here, the true reason we require such a legal doctrine, in "the philosophy of classical individualistic liberalism," even "the problem of human greed."[51]

When extended beyond instances of outright malice, in fact, the law of rights abuse has almost amounted to "a socialist doctrine," one scholar asserts. For "it implies that a man's right is no longer, as it were, a sphere within which he is sovereign, over which he may dispose according to his own view of his interests and his own ideas of right and wrong."[52] That Soviet law afforded the doctrine wide breadth thus comes as no surprise, though jurists even there expressed concern about its reach.[53] In litigated cases throughout the West, those alleging that another has abused his rights usually turn out to be simply other human individuals, downstream property owners for instance, or neighboring sovereigns.[54]

In loose notions of abuse, it was once possible to seek judicial recourse more casually than today. There have been eras when judges—rather like certain French intellectuals—could effectively anoint themselves the privileged guardians of universal and critical values, of all things noble, in the face of life's pervasive pettiness and inhumanity. Anyone today confidently laying claim from the bench to privileged insight into "the public interest" knows she is nearly certain to meet vigorous rejoinder from others, equally well informed, who reach conclusions diametrically opposed. Even among federal appellate judges, deciding cases where mooted legal questions often betray considerable indeterminacy, scarcely anyone—with the noteworthy exception of Richard Posner[55]—openly confesses to ever having decided cases directly on the basis of what's morally best for society, all things considered, as he or she happens to see it.

In the United States, at least, sundry "realisms"—at both ends of the political spectrum, from law and economics to critical legal studies—have conquered the centrist political terrain once staked out with such wooly nostrums. If they concur in nothing else, adherents of these disparate movements agree on the intellectual bankruptcy—when issued gratuitously from the bench—of such earlier atheoretical language and, we now realize, the professional complacency it entailed. Even within the civil law, some now repudiate the abuse of rights doctrine for inviting and indulging high-handed judicial arbitrariness of a similar sort.[56] They accuse it of offering cover for a court's partisan evaluation of litigants, where the challenged activity—though wholly lawful—is morally controversial in certain precincts.

Some skeptics go so far as to insist that contemporary judicial resort to the doctrine often entails "the abuse of the abuse of rights."[57] These "promiscuous" and "indiscriminate"[58] invocations risk discrediting it altogether. The ease with which the doctrine lends itself to such manipulation warrants its outright repudiation. Such critics—in a spirit akin to the common law—even decry the very idea of abusing one's rights as "self-contradictory."[59] They enlist Roman law's ancient anthem (tripping lightly off the tongue), *neminem laedit qui suo jure utitur:* no one wrongfully harms another when he merely exercises his own rights. Within the common-law world, we simply assume that proposition to be true, without need for its explicit articulation in maxim or doctrine.

Yet a moment's reflection reveals that this 'heroic' stance cannot be quite correct either,[60] any more than dismissing outright the very idea of rights abuse can be. The legal doctrine of rights abuse rests on an irrepressible intuition that chasms between positive law and common morality, as they arise within litigated cases, must somehow be closed. If we cannot bridge the gap through some such formal doctrinal device, we will have to attempt it extralegally—at times a momentous step, posing dangers of its own.

In any event, continental doctrine on abuse of right captures and addresses remarkably little of what I'm here calling rights to do grave wrong. At times the doctrine springs into action when a litigant's motives for invoking his right are malicious. In the situations of interest to this study, however, that is rarely the case. A second situation also triggers the rule: Party A, in order to exercise right X, would effectively prevent party B from exercising right Y. The court must decide which of the two rights, in the given situation, will receive priority, curtailing the other's scope. This is a perennial quandary in all legal systems, arising much further afield than in the special circumstances of immediate concern. The judicial "balancing"—as it's often imprecisely called—of conflicting rights-claims is nonetheless irrelevant here: Party A's right to engage in what others consider serious wrong is not inconsistent with any legal rights of parties B, C, or D. Those people have no basis to complain that A's conduct, however morally objectionable and socially reprehensible, is also illegal.

The third situation in which civil-law courts find an abuse of rights arises where we exercise our entitlements in ways their creators did not contemplate and would not have wished. This consideration does cover many of my illustrations of rights to do wrong, but much else besides. It therefore "proves too much" as an explanation for what specifically concerns us here.

Only in its fourth and final form does the abuse of rights doctrine speak relevantly to the present analysis: judicial invocation of "the public interest," "social responsibility," or "moral order," as the particular judge will understand their requirements. Yet as indicated, this is the most questionable of all its usages. The upshot is that none of its four purposes grapples trenchantly and helpfully with the special problems posed by rights to do serious wrong, as here understood.

A single example must suffice to illustrate the doctrine's limitations in this regard. Waldron recently argues that it was, loosely speaking at least, an abuse of the right to freedom of the press for several European newspapers to have published a cartoon mocking the prophet Mohammed by depicting him as a bomb-throwing terrorist.[61] Waldron does not object to such publication on the grounds that it sparked lethal protests throughout the Muslim world. That would be a consequentialist appeal to prudence, as the reason for restraint. Rather, the essential harm occurred earlier, he contends, in the act of publication itself. That publication evinced profound disrespect, not simply for Islam as such, but for the human dignity of individual Danish Muslims,[62] prominent among its foreseeable readers and presumptive targets. That is reason enough to abjure publication. Here, there is not only a moral duty to refrain from exercising one's legal rights, Waldron adds, but a duty that the law itself should enshrine—and, in Europe, often does.

European rules on "abuse of rights," however, require that complainants show more than this, and therefore do not address Waldron's concerns. The disrespect these publishers displayed arose from their indifference—negligent or reckless—to others' feelings. In civil law that does not rise to actionable abuse, because their motives were not spiteful and malicious. Almost certainly, the publishers did not intend to give offense to Muslims who reject terrorist violence, who view its rhetorical justification in the name of Islam as a perverse distortion of their faith. Publishers may have exercised a right to do wrong, but they did not abuse their rights, within the term's legal meaning.[63] Critics couched their charges of unlawful conduct in terms of hate speech rather than "abuse of rights."[64] Those few who did complain of rights abuse almost certainly understood themselves to be engaging in moral criticism, not legal argument, for which there was no cognizable basis.

The European rule on abuse of rights readily finds a receptive ear, in my experience, among American legal scholars when exposed to the idea. Two Columbia Law School professors thus chime enthusiastically over how the doctrine "offer[s] a more powerful tool" than ordinary equity jurisprudence "for disciplining and deterring . . . [conduct that] comes across as deceptive or self-serving."[65] They immediately see its potential value in such circumstances as our rules on professional ethics, which authorize attorneys to do much apparent mischief in the name of "zealous advocacy," often for large businesses. Though they may be careful not to violate firmly settled rights of others, corporate counsel are abusing their rights (and those of their clients), many believe, when engaging in practices—just this side of illegality—that imperil third parties or macroeconomic stability. Or so some are quick to conclude.

We are slower to recognize the dangers that such a doctrine could pose to rights we wish to see exercised, not with greater moderation, but with enhanced vigor. When they contemplate our most essential human rights, in particular, contemporary "progressives" recoil at the possibility that we might have "human rights to do the right thing"[66]—that we may employ these rights only in ways consistent with what others consider honorable and desirable. We blanch at the thought that, as one European scholar observes, the "failure to exhibit civic virtue in your own motives may result in the loss of the remedy that would normally entail your rights."[67] In other words, if you exercise your human right irresponsibly, the scope of your justiciable redress will be correspondingly curtailed.

And yet, on what grounds could we defensibly deny even the conceptual possibility that a human right might on occasion be abused, while welcoming the possibility of doctrinally treating every other species of right in this fashion, judicially delimiting its exercise on that basis? For that matter, the right to "freedom of expression," though long characterized within the United States in terms of domestic constitutional law, is in most of the world today more often articulated through key documents of international human rights law, beginning with the Universal Declaration.[68] And as Schauer observed, our ordinary language amply reflects our recognition that freedom of speech is a right we very much regard as susceptible to abuse. In light of the breadth with which we often state its purposes, it seems simply a historical oddity that this legal doctrine has thus far been confined to such cubbyholes as the structuring of business transactions for propitious tax treatment and the malicious use of one's real property to offend a neighbor.[69]

The question of whether to recognize and extend the rule's reach may display some urgency if we acknowledge the great expansiveness with which regional human rights courts have sometimes interpreted their charters,[70] eliciting impassioned repudiation by member states,[71] including their democratic publics.[72] Large numbers of people share moral sentiments, polls suggest,[73] that lead them to chafe against key aspects of these legal judgments, which contributed significantly to the populist uprisings of 2016–2018, not only in Poland, Hungary, and the Czech Republic, but also in Britain, France, Italy, and the Netherlands. After all, the more extravagantly one construes a given entitlement, extending its scope well beyond the "plain meaning" of its canonical formulation or its drafters' demonstrable intentions, the more likely it is that situations will arise where some will plausibly conclude that the right at issue has been, if not formally exceeded, then at least abused.

Though the "abuse of rights" doctrine originated in private law (as Europeans still understand that notion), Continental courts there since the mid-twentieth century have amply extended it to public law and constitutional law specifically.[74] If the judicial restraint of rights abuse is now moreover truly "a new general principle of EU law,"[75] as some maintain, then it is difficult to see how so general a principle should not extend to some portion, at least, of the rights called human, as certain leading legal thinkers acknowledge.[76] In fact, the European Convention of Human Rights contains two provisions directed specifically against the abuse of rights, by individuals and nonstate groups (Article 17)[77] and the state itself (Article 18).[78] (The German interwar experience weighed heavily upon the minds of those drafting both Articles.) The European Court of Human Rights has developed significant case law on the crucial question of how democratic states, consistent with their duty "to hold free elections,"[79] may lawfully restrict the political speech and related activities of those who seek—through the electoral process or once in office—to destroy fundamental freedoms that the Convention assures to all citizens.[80]

To recognize that human rights, like other rights, may be unlawfully "abused" is not to deny attendant dangers of starting down this path. These only burgeon as this preeminent category of contemporary entitlement finds ever wider application to ever new "generations" of human rights, as their eager advocates breathlessly describe them. One wonders whether it may be conceivable to abuse, for instance, one's human right against "arbitrary . . . interference with [one's] family."[81] On what other legal grounds might one challenge the claim of a convicted jihadi terrorist who, after serving his sentence in Europe, resists extradition on the grounds that, though his other wives reside in his Muslim homeland, one of them still lives in Europe and his deportation would preclude conjugal relations with her?[82] It is no longer enough to observe that such a result would be inconsistent with what treaty drafters wrote or intended; for the appellate judicial gloss on human rights treaties long ago abandoned any pretense of adherence to interpretive strictures so "antidiluvian."

My immediate point is both practical and theoretical. Acute real-life controversies, otherwise avoidable, are certain to ensue if we take seriously the idea of rights abuse for addressing situations wherever others, we believe, do grave wrong by exercising their rights irresponsibly. And this danger arises chiefly because the expansive theoretical rationales offered in support of this doctrine suggest for it no natural boundaries, permit no evident stopping points.

In sum, even if we Americans were to follow the Continental Europeans, adopt their well-developed law on abuse of rights, it would be to little avail in grappling with the peculiar puzzle of rights to do grave wrong. As shown in the preceding two chapters, major disparities between law and morality arise in situations and from sources generally quite different from those involved in the abuse of rights, as civil lawyers understand the term. That doctrine regularly fails, in any event, to satisfactorily cross the chasm between legality and common morality which Europeans, no less than us common lawyers, regularly encounter. There can thus be no neat doctrinal trick for banishing the predicament of lawful wrongdoing or the daunting, real-life challenges it creates. To meet those challenges, there will be an abiding need for social mores, including those for shaming, even as these mores will sometimes sit uneasily with the law.

No one genuinely denies that certain legal rights are susceptible to abuse, in some meaningful if conceptually elusive sense of the word. A Dutch scholar even insistently proclaims that this doctrine is essential to "keep law and society together, inasmuch as it prevents lawyers from declaring legitimate the exercise of rights where ordinary citizens would see only their abuse."[83] To speak of the need to "keep law and society together" is another way of voicing the view that the exercise of certain legal rights cannot be allowed to stray too far from predominant moral sentiments; it is to insist that—where all other interpretive techniques fail—the law itself, through this particular doctrinal conceit, must retain some last-ditch device for bringing the two back into acceptable equilibrium.

And yet, as many acknowledge,[84] no one has constructed an adequate account of the matter, much less a workable legal answer to the vexing practical questions it presents. Neither of the world's two leading legal traditions has made much progress in resolving them. Exasperating at times, the questions remain—inviting answers from beyond the law.

## When Human Rights Entail Responsibilities

If the law on abuse of rights is ever someday to intelligently address the problem of rights to do grave wrong, it will be chiefly by recourse to recent philosophical thinking concerning the nature and requirements of human dignity. Some prominent legal thinkers today contend that our very status as human beings endows us with an inherent dignity that we violate or dishonor when we engage in forms of conduct entailing profound self-abasement.[85] The dignity reflected in one's personhood gives rise to certain responsibilities of self-respect, which the law should often require of us.[86]

The impermissible forms of self-degradation would include such acts as suicide and "dwarf-tossing."[87] An individual dwarf might believe himself entitled to consent to such treatment (when well-compensated, his safety ensured, in the litigated French case).[88] He nonetheless abuses that right insofar as its exercise, for the rowdy entertainment of drunken revelers, violates his entitlement to protection from "inhuman or degrading treatment."[89] Because this right is intrinsic to his human status, it follows that he may not waive it without violating that status in ways no decent society may choose to allow.

From our understanding of the dignity within us, the dignity intrinsic to our humanity, we frequently deduce and defend our most basic human rights. The legal implications of human dignity here point us, however, in a different and unfamiliar direction, ominously "moralistic and non-emancipatory," Waldron acknowledges.[90] Both he and Dworkin find themselves compelled to admit the possibility that not only dwarf-tossing and suicide, but abortion as well may, on the woman's part, entail so great a contempt of self as to violate her essential dignity.[91] (The status of the fetus per se plays no role in this analysis.)

These "responsibility-characterizations of dignity,"[92] in Waldron's wording, may extend as well, he contends, to certain statuses and social roles occupied not by all of us, in virtue of our sharing a species, but by relatively few. The dignity enjoyed by those occupying these positions arises from the importance and esteem accorded to the social function they serve. For military officers, this entails risking their lives to defend their country from foreign attack. For parents, it means producing the next generation and, in this way, enabling the reproduction of society itself. For both types of role, it is the particular social order, not the human condition as such, which chiefly defines their contours. And the anticipated victim of rights abuse is here no longer the right-holder himself, but others whose welfare is prejudiced by his exercise of legal entitlement.

## Criticizing Others for Abusing Their Rights

There are several distinct ways we deliberately constrain legal rights to ensure they are not exercised in ways widely deemed wrongful. The law incorporates some of these devices within its very terms. Of greater present concern, though, are those the law leaves out yet nonetheless depends upon for its efficacy and satisfactory operation. Central among these are the ways we criticize others for how they exercise their rights. When we criticize an individual or institution on these grounds, we do so in the belief that those rights—and the social roles to which they attach—entail correlative duties not fully reflected within the law.

We sometimes succeed so spectacularly in persuading others to refrain from exercising a given right that it eventually disappears. This is rare. The process nonetheless proves quite revealing about the sociological relation between law and common morality. When moral opinion changes decisively, taking a more negative view of a given activity than does the law, those initially inclined to engage in it confront increasing efforts to dissuade them. These may become so effective, for so long, that the right itself falls into "desuetude"[93] and, on that legal basis, becomes unenforceable. The U.S. Supreme Court explains, in affirming the doctrine of that name, that "deeply embedded ways of carrying out state policy—or not carrying it out—are often tougher and truer law than the dead words of the written text."[94]

A state of desuetude had developed by the 1930s, for instance, with respect to the crime of "adultery" and so-called heartbalm civil actions.[95] These had enabled jilted fiancées to sue for "breach of promise to marry" and spouses for "alienation of affections."[96] By that time, anyone seeking to invoke these rights in litigation risked ridicule and embarrassment.[97] If the lovesick claimant overcame her fear of stigma and litigated nonetheless, she would for some years have won legal vindication, at least. These rights entered into true desuetude only after the prospect of ridicule, contempt, disdain, and stigma had, for several decades, effectively deterred virtually all claimants. (The same had earlier occurred with dueling, which was prohibited in some countries only after its stigmatization had already much diminished its incidence.[98]) Thereafter, even a plaintiff who remained blithely indifferent to public contempt could no longer obtain redress.[99] Humiliation—the prospect or fear of it, more precisely—though wholly inconsistent (many believe) with respecting human dignity, here proved indispensable to advancing modern liberal understandings of the acceptable relation between love, sex, and marriage.

Desuetude can also come about when juries nullify a legal prohibition so consistently that prosecutors no longer wish to waste scarce resources pursuing its violation. Until well into the nineteenth century, for instance, English juries generally refused to convict young, unmarried women for infanticide or abortion.[100] Both practices were then subject to draconian sanction, in evident excess of anything prevailing moral sensibilities endorsed.[101] These criminal prohibitions became effectively unenforceable and shrank nearly to nonexistence for a long time. De facto societal obstruction, expressed in chronic acquittals, all but annulled the state's continuing de jure right to punish them. Prosecutors gave up.

At times the law authorizes a practice most people privately oppose. The practice remains pervasive only because many people do not realize that most others oppose it as well. Those opposing the practice fear they will be stigmatized for not engaging in it or at least not publicly endorsing it. These people harbor what we might call "concealed preferences,"[102] an obverse of the "revealed" ones on which economists near-exclusively dwell. Some social scientists, including female ethnographers who have interviewed African women, believe that we may understand the practice of female genital mutilation in these terms.[103] Confidential opinion surveys of opinion in several African societies, those with highest indices of "human capability," disclose that men too increasingly harbor serious doubts about this procedure,[104] which remains widespread. Desuetude stands at one end of the spectrum by which we may measure the relative efficacy of moral criticism. It is a limiting case, for it marks the point where our criticism of those who insist on exercising a disfavored right becomes so effective that the right not merely falls into decreasing use, but—on that very basis—disappears entirely.

A chorus of concern has arisen in recent years that our collective capacity and individual facility in employing this form of rights-restraint has atrophied in ways that are perilous to our society and its moral order, indeed to the fate of the Republic. The concern is voiced from opposing poles on the political spectrum, if in reference to differing forms of perceived abuse. This shared preoccupation trades in part upon an empirical claim about changes in our prevailing linguistic practices. These are, however, extremely difficult to establish with any precision, employing methods yet available. We must therefore seek evidence, more informally at times, wherever it offers itself. To this end we must closely observe how we speak and write on given issues, for particular audiences, in specific social milieu. If patterns exist, this is how we will find them. I end this chapter with one example.

The evidence sometimes comes at us obliquely, as when by chance we encounter texts from an earlier day that are more candid, more congenial to the notion that it is acceptable to criticize others, on ethical grounds, for how they employ particular rights. Hence this archaeological shard—almost ancient from today's perspective, yet in fact from only 1995—by Harvard law professor Cass Sunstein, who first seeks to position himself as a critic of communitarian attacks on "rights-talk," then allows this concession to those whose views he otherwise claims to reject: "Under the Constitution, women have a right to have abortions. But it is important to insist that this is a right that ought not to be exercised, or to have to be exercised, very often, and that in a society with 1.5 million abortions per year, something is extremely wrong . . . Efforts to discourage pregnancies that will result in abortion, and even to discourage abortion itself through moral suasion, should not, as a general rule, be taken as unfortunate interferences with a 'right.'" Sunstein then adds that "one possible pathology of a culture of rights is that people will think that because they have a right to do X, they cannot be blamed for doing X."[105] To this hypothesis, which Sunstein immediately sets aside, the present study devotes sustained attention by exploring the points at which people in various milieus exhort others to exercise their rights "responsibly," consistently with moral commitments widely shared yet escaping law's grasp.

We can discover how far contemporary "progressives" have traveled since Sunstein's remark above, once entirely anodyne among liberal Democrats, by examining a recent book from Columbia Law School professor Carol Sanger. She specifically argues that we must "destigmatize"[106] abortion by "normalizing"[107] its discussion among women who have undergone the procedure. We should, for instance, encourage online blogs in which women openly discuss their abortions, much like the chat rooms where they discuss "their knitting."[108] "Normalizing abortion talk aligns ordinary discourse with experience,"[109] since abortion is "not rare"[110] and has in fact become a "much-exercised *right.*"[111] Sanger thus suggests that the legality (and frequent practice) of abortion makes it improper and unacceptable to express disapproval of those exercising this right. Still, surely, there are many other rights whose regular exercise, in certain situations, Sanger thinks it entirely appropriate to criticize. So the logic of her argument extends to many situations where she would never actually want to apply it.

It is true, as she observes, that when women are made to feel ashamed and become reluctant to speak openly about their abortion experience, this conveys "that what they are doing," though lawful, "is wrong."[112] Yet as Sanger would certainly also acknowledge, as do all educated people, there are many wrongful activities—some quite seriously so—that remain lawful, often for good reason. The sheer fact that abortion is lawful therefore has no particular implications for—and no significant bearing on—whether it is morally defensible in given circumstances.

Rather than engage the normative issues on their philosophical merits, Sanger simply announces that because "the right to choose abortion is *an absolute good,*"[113] its exercise cannot involve a wrong that needs to be "forgiven."[114] In fact, it is necessary to "Shout Your Abortion . . . for this message is optimistic and confident."[115] Sanger declares with satisfaction that, though President Bill Clinton prudently maintained the compromise position that abortion should be "safe, legal, and rare," his wife Hillary, running for that same office in 2016, tellingly revised the slogan to read that abortion need only be "safe and legal."[116] Sanger then adds, here endorsing the views of sociologist and pro-choice activist Tracy Weitz,[117] that the word "'rare' creates an immediate normative judgment about abortion, suggesting that there is already too much abortion going around; it ought to happen less. This in turn increases the stigma for aborting women generally because maybe theirs isn't one of the good, properly rare abortions . . . 'rare' is a linguistic trick, affirming the right to abortion on one hand while devaluing it as part of women's lives on the other."[118]

In this way, the possibility that there might exist any circumstances in which one might acceptably scrutinize—ethically, and on the basis of reliable data—the reasons some portion of women exercise their right to abort passed almost undetected, within influential quarters, from intellectual innocuousness into ideological heterodoxy, indeed into the world of inexpressible taboo.[119] Both authors are studiously vague over whether they actually believe the right to abortion is one of those (Schauer offered several genuine examples) by nature truly insusceptible to abuse, or whether it is simply inexpedient to publicly acknowledge even the slightest incidence of such abuse, for fear of affording ammunition to political adversaries. If the latter, as one strongly suspects (and as Weitz herself scarcely conceals), then these authors deny "inconvenient facts" with too strong an evidentiary basis to satisfy Max Weber's definition of what it means to undertake "scholarship as a vocation,"[120] by far the most influential and convincing account of that enterprise.

In the United States, at least, opinions on abortion like those of Weitz and Sanger today clearly occupy a cutting edge of feminist thought. Weitz herself holds a prominent position at the Buffett Foundation in policy programming on family planning issues, where she commands a substantial budget, helpful to advancing her views.[121] Be that as it may, Sanger's wording above consistently betrays the now-familiar tissue of confusions about the relations between morality, legality, and society. We have encountered these confusions before,[122] and will here witness them again. In fact, we should come to recognize them as widely at work all around us. They do much damage to our capacity to understand the social world and to act intelligently upon it.

# 5

# Law and Morality in Ordinary Language and Social Science

## How We Speak about Rights to Do Wrong

The very idea of "disfavored" rights seems counterintuitive, at first. In my experience of teaching at several U.S. and foreign law schools, those just entering the legal profession find the notion especially odd, and some consider it perverse, if not oxymoronic. These are eager young people for whom legal rights all but exist to be robustly exercised. That rights-exercise might at times defensibly be met with active discouragement seems inherently questionable, even politically pernicious. Informal discouragement, behind the backs of our legal system, is little better than the official variety. In fact, its lack of transparency to public scrutiny renders extralegal dissuasion especially suspicious.

The arguments of civil libertarians suggest that offensive speech, in particular, does not only deserve our legal protection against efforts at its suppression. Offensive speech and artwork are not a mere "necessary evil" to be regrettably endured. Instead, they are a frail flower that we must scrupulously cultivate and affectionately treasure. We are deficient in our appreciation of our liberties if we do not, as a society, regularly and actively set ourselves to occupy the outer boundaries of the terrain these rights demarcate.[1] According to the American Civil Liberties Union, one skeptic bemoans, "The extreme exercise of a right comes to be the only true exercise because the best test of commitment to a principle is thought to occur at its furthest reach . . . a right is not a right unless it can be . . . used irresponsibly."[2] We mistakenly regard the law like an aerobics workout, such critics claim. As if our Greek forum were the local Equinox fitness club, our rights must be vigorously exercised, preferably three times per week! "Flex Your Rights"[3] is in fact the very name of a civil rights group devoted to improving the "constitutional literary" of Americans regarding the use of force by police.

The ACLU's understanding of free speech, whatever its merits, then becomes an attractive model for thinking about individual rights more generally. There is serious danger here of succumbing to a misplaced "moral heuristic."[4] A principle derived from one area of law becomes a tempting template for thinking about a much larger class of seemingly similar phenomena, without giving sufficient consideration to important contextual differences. Thus, if we believe that the protection of fundamental speech rights will seriously suffer if we do not often aggressively employ them, we may come to think the same about certain other legal rights, if not quite all rights as such. Yet a moment's serious reflection reveals that this heuristic can quickly lead us astray, at times in directions profoundly perverse.

When Americans first contemplate the notion of a right to do wrong—that is, when I first suggest it to them in conversation—what most often comes quickly to mind is the right to express one's political opinions in ways others find offensive. For this entitlement is central to our national political identity, many have observed, far more so than in other liberal democracies. Our sensitivity to the danger that officials will wrongly suppress controversial speech seems to make us acutely sensitive to the danger that they and others will suppress a broader category of constitutional and nonconstitutional rights as well.

Yet the risk of too easily analogizing speech to other rights may not chiefly be that we will interpret all rights too broadly, insist on affording them greater scope than they warrant. The opposite danger is at least equally real. We may cabin the scope of many rights unnecessarily if we fail to appreciate how social processes often work unobtrusively to restrain their abusive deployment. These informal restraints enable the law to authorize a wider range of potentially suspect activity than is ever likely to materialize to significant degree.

The peril here is not merely that we will misunderstand what goes on all around us, how law and society interact. When we underestimate the myriad mechanisms pushing back against the irresponsible exercise of legal rights, we are very likely to overregulate in ways that civil libertarians, among others, have warned against. We will interject the law into corners of social life where it is unnecessary and in fact likely to have unwelcome effects. Scholarship now suggests that this may regularly occur where the type of behavior we most value in others can arise only from public-spirited motivations, which are "crowded out" when such behavior is mandated or materially incentivized.[5] As observes Paul Kahn (a Yale law professor), we need periodically to "remind ourselves not only that people have lives of meaning outside of law's rule, but also that many of our richest and deepest experiences must be protected from the imperialism of law's rule."[6]

The many examples of lawful wrongdoing discussed in Chapters 2 and 3 indicate that our most fundamental constitutional entitlements by no means exhaust the category of rights to do serious wrong, extralegally restrained. This notion of rights-cum-restraint helps us to understand a much wider range of situations and to reflect on how the law should treat them. Once exposed to the general idea of a right to do serious wrong, other situations will likely spring to the reader's mind, similar in relevant respects to those here examined. Here, our ordinary language provides a better guide than legal scholarship. For in everyday speech we readily recognize what legal academicians, with their constitutional preoccupations, generally do not: that some of the most powerful burdens we place on the exercise of our legal rights emanate not from the state but from a variety of specifically social mechanisms—admittedly more difficult to discern, sometimes, or to channel in any determinate direction.

This is sometimes true even with respect to rights against the state itself, rights that such mechanisms discourage us from invoking. The Constitution even precludes the state from prohibiting efforts by third parties to impede the exercise of certain rights. That is the case, for example, when one set of public marchers and demonstrators, supporting a given policy, seeks to protest a simultaneous demonstration by opponents of that policy. Constitutional law allows the state to regulate the use of public space by both groups, to the extent necessary to prevent violence between their members. But the state may not preclude the second group, through its own demonstration, from impeding successful demonstration by the first group, as by seeking to heckle its speakers or drown out their oratory with electronically enhanced harangues of its own. The state's mandatory *in*action, not its action, is what here hampers rights-assertion. This hampering has then found expression not in the law, but through "society," through social mobilization. The contribution of public law is in fact to *protect* that private hampering.

This book therefore accords little attention to First Amendment doctrine—where present issues are already well mooted in any event. It instead brings several other doctrines and social practices, ranging far afield, into a single field of theoretical vision, inviting their reexamination in a novel way. My chief interest lies in why we sometimes neither prohibit nor broadly permit an activity, but combine a formal dispensation to engage in it with its active discouragement, publicly or privately. Of little concern here, then, is the much narrower question of how to determine when such discouragement, officially sponsored, becomes unconstitutional.

First Amendment rights are not the only basis for keeping the state from more onerously burdening morally suspect activities. So too, categorical prohibition is by no means the only (or most prevalent) method for inducing people to abandon them. As a restriction on what the state may do to establish orthodoxy of opinion, the First Amendment has virtually nothing to say about official methods for dissuading adherence to particular viewpoints, or for discouraging participation in a given activity, which do not, through their "chilling effect"[7] at least, amount to state censorship. Acting well within the limits imposed by constitutional law, government officials often employ a variety of indirect stratagems, which we might describe as symbolic or semiotic, aimed at inducing people to think and feel differently about the lawful activity that officials wish to discourage. Modestly effective in this regard, if for only a time,[8] were recent policy efforts to combat self-destructive behavior by young people, by correcting their mistaken impressions of the frequency among their peers of such conduct—binge drinking, smoking, and illicit drug use.[9] Through these few experiments, policymakers have come to believe that the best way to dissuade us from engaging in a disfavored activity is frequently not to ban it, but instead to alter how we perceive it, how we interpret its "social meaning."[10]

This may, ironically, entail a re-moralizing of issues not long ago deliberately *de*-moralized, as when they were "medicalized."[11] Through public-interest advertising, it may require, for instance, the official depiction of tobacco consumption,[12] drug use, excessive drinking, and even obesity (some contend)[13] as not merely unhealthy, but disgusting and reflecting a personal ethical failing. This remains controversial. Such efforts to cast the consumption of certain products in immoral light are also now promptly countered with advertising campaigns, from their manufacturers, evincing clever forms of counter-moralization. Corporate management may issue a barrage of press releases proclaiming its "social responsibility"[14] in urging only the "responsible" consumption of its products, after "informed" decision making by consumers, in light of their personal circumstances and obligations.[15] The moral burden thus subtly shifts from manufacturer to consumer.

Lawmakers sometimes avoid outright prohibition of a product or practice, where constitutionally permissible,[16] because they believe this unnecessary, even counterproductive. For young people especially, the criminalization of a pleasurable activity often lends it a transgressive cachet, turning it into tantalizing "forbidden fruit." The law of discouragement, as it might be called, operates optimally when it works more subtly, almost subliminally, though it remains quite unclear how or when this approach genuinely works for very long.

The law's role in reforming common morality is generally quite limited, however. The rapid acceptance of gay marriage by most Americans[17] represents, by almost any measure, an oceanic transformation in common morality. Yet some data suggest it owes less to the long years of arduous litigation than to certain widely watched television programs and commercially successful movies, depicting gay characters in a favorable light.[18] This is to say that the debt is owed not chiefly to us lawyers,[19] though most of us are happy to take the credit and undoubtedly played some part, but to a few dozen Hollywood producers, directors, and screenwriters. From the start, their results were thoroughly intended, insiders report.

Public backlash against the more brutish legal methods of moral transvaluation has a long history. These can be almost comic in their crudity. In medieval and early modern Europe, for instance, the very effort by Catholic prelates to suppress public drunkenness and sexual infidelity during Carnival lent such simple, 'innocent' indulgence an element of social protest it would never otherwise have acquired—but did thereafter.[20] To similar effect, the frisson of transgression explains the fascination of 1960s-era sociologists with the right to be rude. It also helps account for the long-standing ACLU rhetoric, arising in those same years, celebrating not merely the right to engage in offensive speech but offensive speech itself.[21] Much like a Lenny Bruce shtick or a *Mad* magazine article—all of the era—the lurking subtext in these period discourses was always a thumb in the eye of social complacence in general, and of bourgeois decorum in particular. The stodginess and "phoniness" of common morality was conceived as the problem, liberalizing law as its solution.

In placing the emphasis where I have, my aim is not to diminish the importance of constitutional law. It is rather to suggest that what we already accept as normal within that legal domain actually operates much beyond it. And in these farther places too, we should be no less comfortable about acknowledging and exploiting the relevant forces in play. In other words, we are already familiar in one limited locale with the reality of rights-cum-restraints and, to some degree, with how this kind of sociolegal configuration in fact functions. We should simply recognize and appreciate its powerful, often-agreeable presence in other legal areas as well. In staying our inclination to ban morally objectionable speech and association, the First Amendment reflects a commitment to the principle of antipaternalism. That principle operates much farther afield, where it regularly guides law and policy in areas wholly beyond reach of Constitutional protection.[22] In fact, as shown in Chapter 6, there are several additional reasons we often curb our impulses to employ the law for discouraging others' moral wrongs.

We reach instinctively for the Constitution when someone burns a U.S. flag or assembles fellow neo-Nazis to march through a Jewish neighborhood. Yet there is more at work in limiting our regulatory activities in the areas of offensive speech and association than the First Amendment; so too with the hate speech that frequently accompanies such extremist political activity, the speech by which adherents seek to mobilize the like-minded. It is not ultimately because our Constitution enshrines a right to engage in such speech that we are willing to endure it. The very intensity of this constitutional commitment—however appealing it may be on its own terms—rests on a tacit supposition still more basic and essential.

We know that whenever someone conspicuously exercises this particular right to do wrong, it will frequently elicit broad attention. Others will publicly condemn the offensive speakers, if only by expressing their solidarity through conversation with members of the targeted group, alongside whom they may work or reside as neighbors. Such displays of "moral support," as it is often tellingly called, reinvigorate the liberal conscience, an important slice of common morality within the United States. More precisely, these public expressions of beneficence reflect and reinforce moral sentiments already at least mutely pervasive among fellow citizens, whose "moral emotions" (as psychologists call them) rise up in support of their public reasoning.

There comes into being a "collective intention" or "collective attitude" to this effect, as philosophers of mind today describe this phenomenon,[23] often empirically fleeting. Although very few may directly enter the fray, it is enough that citizen A knows that his neighbor, citizen B, shares A's indignant reaction to the abhorrent speech, and vice versa. This provides the intersubjective basis not only for collective intention, but more importantly for what Durkheim called "mechanical" social solidarity. Though there is a collective character to this process, it is sustained by a certain natural propensity, which psychologists have discovered among people in many cultures. Parsing Thomas Jefferson,[24] Jonathan Haidt describes this in terms of our "emotional responsiveness to moral beauty,"[25] producing in us heightened feelings of "spiritual purity." This at once entails a sense of emotional elation and ethical "elevation," in Haidt's wording.

These sentiments are precisely the antithesis, he believes, of the disgust elicited in us when witnessing or learning of atrocious violence. We observe such moral beauty, most obviously perhaps, when we find ourselves among those engaged in offering charity or expressing gratitude, but also among those protesting severe injustice. Very little is often necessary, by way of initial counter-speech and political activity to set this dynamic in motion. The moral entrepreneurs who organize public protests against hate-mongering will never be very numerous. Yet through well-staged rituals inducing "collective effervescence,"[26] they vitalize many sympathizers, now unified in thought, feeling, and action.[27] This is not entirely what it claims to be: "love conquering hate," as organizers often describe their purpose. Righteous indignation is a form of anger, dictionaries tell us. It finds ample expression in speeches, slogans, and banners designed to passionately arouse and forcefully channel this particular moral sentiment. These efforts and mobilizations restore our confidence not only in our political efficacy as individuals, but in our fellow citizens and in the values we share with them, articulated through both conventional and creative forms of "collective representation." As Hans Joas observes, "outrage remains the most reliable indicator of the violation of key values,"[28] often also their most reliable source of regeneration.

There is no slight irony in how these public gatherings, during which large numbers psychically merge and effectively erase their particularity into a mass, prove so valuable for ritualistically affirming our esteem for the individual, her dignity and autonomy. Still, there can be little doubt that the protesters reactivate sentiments of liberal tolerance by arousing acute antipathy, even disgust at times, toward the intolerant. Such protest also notably exerts extrajuridical pressure against the abusive exercise of this singularly American species of lawful wrongdoing.

Political theorist Andrew March well captures the sentiments of these protestors when he observes that public use of the n-word, in particular, "does more than offend, harm, or intimidate African-Americans. It harms a certain kind of public good that many Americans are striving hard to attain . . . a society where people feel safe, valued, and at home in their social home. There is a way in which all Americans are the victims of such speech; for as a white American I have an interest in an America where my sense of belonging is not achieved at the expense of others."[29]

Notably, this language does not defend resistance to racist speech on the basis of anyone's constitutional rights, or legal rights of any sort. In fact, the immediate targets of vicious speech scarcely figure in March's observations. When such victims invoke their claims, they are disappointed to learn that, in the United States at least, the verbal antagonism directed against them enjoys generous legal protection. Indeed, by its intrusive monitorings and inessential surveillance,[30] the state violates the constitutional right of their hate-mongering ill-wishers to free political "association."

March focuses instead on what he calls a broader "public good," beyond the interests of the particular people immediately attacked. Racist discourse, he observes, equally imperils that larger good, "a society in which people feel safe, valued, and at home." March may here seek to establish, in the lexicon of U.S. constitutional law, a sufficiently "compelling state interest" in restricting such speech, beyond its mere "time, place, and manner."[31] The "public good" he has in mind presupposes shared feelings of "belonging," in his words, of strong emotional connections to others. These are based in the similar sentiments evoked in response to violent or near-violent challenge. A peculiar feature of hate speech, in particular, is that it seeks to break apart this sense of solidarity, to divide a community upon itself, so that its members no longer understand it as constitutively committed to purposes and principles shared by all.

The suggestion that liberal political freedoms are possible in such generous measure only because social pressures weigh heavily upon their effective exercise bears a certain, superficial resemblance to central claims of the early Foucault. Those who find his idiom congenial could in fact observe that the mores by which we restrain the irresponsible exercise of legal rights provide the conditions of possibility for many of these rights themselves. We therefore truly understand the workings and meaning of our rights only when we grasp them in relation to such mores, their shifting contours and vicissitudes, their sources and areas of weakness and resilience.

According to Foucault's early influential stance, extravagantly extended by many others since, virtually everything we do, think, and desire in the modern West is "governed" by the discursive practices of the various vocations determining what will count as normal, and therefore acceptable. These disciplining discourses (of medical clinics, criminology, the military, insurance, the welfare-state and public health bureaucracies, and counterterrorism) render us "docile," so estranged from our own inner yearnings and unruly urges that the state can then afford us the most plentiful of political liberties without risk we will employ these to deeply disruptive ends. It is precisely by granting us such freedoms, and conceiving each of us as unique in his employment of them, that liberal society can more effectively detect and correct our individual deviations from the standards of normality these well-meaning regimes of truth serially propound.

Our self-understanding as political creatures is hence gravely mistaken. We are not in fact democratic citizens of a true republic, free-spirited, sallying into political and legal agora to defend our rights, individual and collective. We are not as we imagine ourselves: ever-questioning and skeptical of authority, continually wary of its susceptibility to corruption and illegitimacy. As under earlier undemocratic polities, we moderns are not genuine republican citizens at all; we remain "subjects," occupying "subject positions" severely limiting our ability to freely think, feel, act, and imagine. We are no longer repressed by law's coercions, to be sure. We are governed instead through our very freedom, including our juridical entitlements, and the deceptive sense of personal autonomy, of self-determination, these inspire in us. From the perspective of those urging radical change, this species of freedom, though hardly "meaningless," subsists against a tacit, enabling background approximating its very opposite. That backdrop, unperceived and taken wholly for granted, quietly quashes much of what within us is willful, quirky, intemperate, refractory, immodest, spontaneous, instinctual, assertive, irreverent, and potentially rebellious or politically subversive—everything *interesting* about us as individuals, precisely insofar as we, each in our own fashion, are *ab*normal.[32]

This book makes claims neither so arresting nor intoxicating. Foucault's rendering of contemporary restraint flamboyantly exaggerates, in any event, the disciplining power of scientific discourse and the professions deploying it, not least because these groups themselves are often hard at work undermining one another's competing claims to authority. Foucault also ignores several potent countervailing pressures where disciplinary power runs up against acute atomistic self-interest, intense in-group affiliation, or simply the aimless anomie ensuing from debilitated social bonds.

Anomie entails the weakness of authoritative norms both within individual selves and across society at large. Social psychologists, employing recent methodological refinements, today compare its empirical distribution across many countries, seeking to explain the sources of its relative incidence, at times considerable.[33] Anomie represents the very antithesis of the suffusing normativity that Foucault discerned nearly everywhere around us, powerfully at work *within* all of us. Any attempt at a fully satisfactory picture of modern society would have to instruct us about the interplay between these several contending forces, rather than fix our attention exclusively on one of them.

It is nonetheless true, as J. S. Mill observed of England a century and a half ago, that the fear of what others will think of us plays a central role in hampering the expression of unorthodox political views, and in constraining the exercise of many further legal rights to self-expression. It's true as well that the "others" in question here are sometimes practitioners of the scientific or helping professions, as in my illustrations of the right to die and the right of mentally incapacitated persons to bear children. Yet more striking in this book's factual illustrations of restraints upon rights to do wrong is how these intercessions remain so often cast—hesitantly, uncomfortably, inarticulately, sotto voce—in the language, not of science, but of morality, of personal responsibility. When we wish to exercise our rights to spurn treatment or others' exhortations, the question that most people, even medical professionals, more often put to us is not so much "Why be abnormal, in light of what we learn from statistical and other modern science?" The more common query, certainly after that initial approach fails to persuade, remains: "Why disregard acknowledged duties to others whom you presumably (or ought to) care about, to say nothing of what you owe yourself?"

## Observing Common Morality through Ordinary Language

The use of language is relevant to the present inquiry in ways apart from the subject of hate speech. Prevailing views of moral acceptability often manifest themselves within common parlance. Daily patterns of speech would therefore offer a credible starting point in identifying the contents of common morality. "Ordinary language analysis"[34] was an early method for studying the workings of morality within society, and is still of some value though no longer much practiced under the name. That field's mid-century practitioners generally limited their search for relevant evidence of everyday linguistic practice, however, to the confines of their immediate social circle—effectively, the Oxford drawing room. There was much over-confident talk about how "we" speak of normative matters, what kinds of things "we" normally say in ethically appraising others' conduct; the composition of this implicit speech-community remained innocently unspecified. It requires no great sociological sophistication to observe that—though they may sometimes employ the same terminology of moral appraisal—members of distinct social strata often lend it quite different connotation, apply it in quite variant ways.

Acts of speech amounting only to mild reproach among one subgroup might well, within another, prove an immediate invitation to altercation, perhaps to lethal violence. That was certainly so in early modern Europe, where a carelessly abrasive remark might require any self-respecting aristocrat to defend his honor—to the death—by duel. In certain hands, ordinary language analysis nonetheless sometimes proved the very opposite of ethnocentric, and was in fact quite relativistic in its view of morality. A given "form of life," including those of tribal Africa, would inevitably turn out, on close inspection, to maintain its own terms of normative appraisal, a hypothesis since then abundantly confirmed.[35]

Where the philosophers of ordinary language clearly fail us, we must today turn to discourse analysis and especially linguistic anthropology, also known as sociolinguistics. Its practitioners lift themselves from the academic armchair to painstakingly examine language use in situ, sometimes in what—for white, middle-class academicians—must seem rather dodgy dens. What they find there, unsurprisingly, is that ordinary language beyond the elite university is rife with moral talk as well,[36] much of it rather more passionate, uninhibited, and certainly no less playfully inventive than at an Oxbridge High Table.[37] Despite the wide linguistic variation they reveal, these ethnographies also disclose that even denizens of crime-plagued urban ghettos regularly appraise the moral acceptability of one another's conduct, often sharply, by way of general categories often approximating those operational within more privileged precincts.[38] These categories centrally include multiple variants on "respectability,"[39] such as maintaining one's self-respect, respecting authority figures (including gang leaders, at times), in-group loyalty, shame at its violation, and taking pride in self-discipline, understood as a personal virtue necessary for sustained achievement in nearly any kind of labor, including organized criminal activity. Whatever the prevailing standards of personal appraisal within a given milieu, they are regularly invoked and appear often quite effective in disciplining disfavored conduct.

A small sampling of linguistic usage among the middle classes of the contemporary United States provides an easy point of embarkation to broader issues. One periodically hears such people describe themselves as feeling "wracked," "troubled," or "vexed" by "pangs" of conscience, as "stricken with" or "consumed by" guilt. They are relieved when they conclude that their "conscience is clear." They suffer "resentment" when others mistreat them and feel "indignation" at the mistreatment of others with whom they "sympathize" or "empathize." They think critically of someone for his "moral indifference" to a certain problem, describing him as "blind" to its ethical implications. They commend others for virtuous conduct and the personal character it reflects:

"He's a generous godparent."
"That was noble of her."
"He is a person of integrity."
"She behaved selflessly."
"He displayed such dignity in adversity."

People express their "moral support" for the victims of major wrongdoing, and "disgust" toward its perpetrators, to whom they may express their "contempt," or over whom they may seek to exercise "moral suasion." They may feel "ashamed" in not having done more, where possible, to prevent a given injustice that passed before their eyes. They suffer "remorse" for their harmful actions and inactions, whether intentional, reckless, or negligent. They may experience "regret" for having caused serious harm, even when they could not reasonably anticipate or prevent it.[40] These are merely several illustrations; the reader could easily add prodigious examples of her own. It bears observation, at least, that this sort of ordinary language rings quite differently in the ear from more abstract talk about "what justice requires"[41] or "what we owe to each other,"[42] the idiom of leading thinking in analytic moral theory.

The philosophical scrutiny of our moral discourse virtually began with "the excuses" we employ to mitigate our blameworthiness when others accuse us of wrongdoing.[43] This scholarly preoccupation may be unsurprising: most of us are reticent about accepting blame, voluble in denying it.[44] The ordinary language of moral condemnation follows a path of its own, distinct from that of exculpation. When moral philosophy began to secularize its mission and vocabulary, it soon ceased speaking of "sin," and has had astonishingly little to say since Victorian days about the vices, even the secular, pre-Christian ones.[45]

And yet, within ordinary language the nontheological lexicon for moral condemnation of perceived misconduct continues to be vast. This is the case despite periodic laments over our alleged failure to deploy it more often against worthy targets. Apart from the religiously devout, it seems that few speak seriously any longer of "evil." It is quite common, though, for people to say that someone has "not acted in good faith" or has "abused his rights" through "lack of consideration" for others' feelings or their legitimate concerns, and thereby behaved "inappropriately," even "wrongly." One regularly hears, in myriad contexts:

"That's unfair!"
"That would be a lie."
"That was awfully sleazy."
"She's so materialistic!"
"He's a chauvinist pig!"
"What a bastard!"

Our morality-talk, the way we articulate our indignation in particular, heads quickly downhill from there, in ways alas unprintable, even today, in a scholarly work. (So I've been instructed.)

In any event, ordinary language offers only an imperfect guide to the place of common morality within social life, for the simple reason that we often do not say what we really think and feel. Within "polite company" we Americans—more than in certain other societies, apparently[46]—regularly avoid use of words clearly indicating moral censure, in particular, for fear of giving offense, being thought "too judgmental,"[47] unduly "moralistic." Moralism describes "a tendency toward overconfidence in one's judgments," an inclination "to present [one's] substantive positions as having a high degree of internal coherence and purity, thus drawing upon the aesthetic and psychological appeal of clarity and simplicity."[48]

Moralism disposes us toward "punitiveness," even "cruelty," on a Nietzschean view.[49] As members of a liberal society, many prefer to justify their conclusions, especially on public issues, in terms acceptable to those of diverse moral and cultural persuasions. This precludes appraisals derived from any controverted conception of the good life.

Those who think and live this way would reject the communitarian complaint that we lack any shared, meaningful moral vocabulary, responding that ours is simply a morality of liberal tolerance, and properly so. It is our commitment to liberal political morality that makes even informal reproach seem so atavistic a means of upholding moral order and renders the vocabulary of its expression often so awkward and uncomfortable. From this perspective, at least, the apparent reduction in social practices of moral reproach—still pervasive in less liberal societies—may appear entirely salutary. The retreat from overtly censorious speech, then, represents not a weakening of common morality but instead simply a modification in its substance, signaling not anomie but maturity, modernity.

We may today prefer to describe an objectionable practice as "inappropriate," though we actually abhor it. This wording suggests that the behavior perhaps arouses in us only "annoyance," "irritation," "frustration," "exasperation," or "perplexity," as we are likely to publicly couch our sentiments. When we employ these weaker words, we may intend to signal that we're prepared to treat the perceived misconduct as a violation merely of etiquette or social convention, rather than of morality, or at least as not a moral wrong of any magnitude. American usage nevertheless lacks consistency here.

In fact, the line between demands of politesse or etiquette and those of morality, more strictly speaking, often proves quite indistinct. It is unclear whether, in real life, most Americans, at least, accord the distinction any practical significance. Scholars find it unable to bear much analytical weight. The scope of what counts as "rudeness"—a frequent converse of politeness—varies cross-culturally as well, profusely so.[50] This in turn raises questions about what kinds of objectionable conduct a given legal system will prohibit, and what kinds its drafters will implicitly trust to more informal, nonlegal mechanisms of discouragement. There is vast variation here: forms of speech and conduct today deemed "merely impolite" not long ago provided solid basis for legal redress.[51]

## Competing Theories of Why the Law Converges with and Diverges from Common Morality

What explains the wandering boundary between law and common morality? How are we to account for the law's occasionally flagrant deviations from prevalent moral views, and when might such deviations make good sense? Do they amount merely to an intriguing paradox, ultimately intelligible from the perspective of some comprehensive theory, explanatory or normative? Or do they show no coherent pattern, so that the relation between law and common morality discloses no more than a shifting patchwork of our periodically warring commitments, stitched crudely together in ways neither explicable nor defensible?

In answer to these questions, two alternative models immediately suggest themselves: the first anticipating nearly complete correspondence between these normative orders, the second virtually none. In speaking of correspondence or convergence, I refer to circumstances where the law adopts and incorporates within its terms the same normative understandings and commitments as those embodied in social mores. Law and mores then require (or prohibit, or permit) the same conduct, on the same basis.

It is true that even when its authors self-consciously seek to codify a widely shared moral intuition, positive law is always more than a straightforward application of moral ideas. It requires some specification for the intuition or principle to assume a form that could possibly work as a legal rule, situated amid other rules, integrated within a complex *corpus juris*, including rules of evidence and procedure. This also "makes it harder," writes Waldron, "for law to function as any sort of great public morality, embodying officially endorsed moral absolutes."[52]

Many scholars long embraced the first of the two models mentioned above. They imagined that, as Roscoe Pound put it, in "all cases of divergence between the standard of the common law and standard of the public, it goes without saying that the latter will prevail in the end."[53] In ways at once natural and spontaneous, law and mores move closely into sync. Through some mysterious osmosis, legality would unproblematically absorb and "reflect" or "mirror" community morals, to employ the naive terminology of some early socio-legal scholarship.[54] Still today, as Tamanaha observes, "So strong is the assumption . . . [that law mirrors socially prevailing morals], that it is routinely asserted by social and legal theorists without supportive evidence, with a sense of the self-evident."[55]

Thus, Greenawalt rhetorically ponders, "Does the law within a society reflect dominant cultural norms? . . . To ask this question is to answer it . . . a society's law will *reflect* its patterns of life and morality."[56] Such views find their most self-confident expression in the serene words of a midcentury law professor and master of University College, Oxford: "Although few people would be prepared to argue that there are no parts of English law today which do not lag behind the generally recognized moral standards of the community, these 'gaps' are comparatively rare and are of minor importance . . . We can truly say that the common law is our common heritage,"[57] that is, our moral heritage.

The essential task of the common-law judge, as articulated by Lon Fuller and epitomized (for many) by Benjamin Cardozo, was "to discern antecedent expectations and entrenched norms of the community," writes one contemporary exponent of this view, "to give these norms official expression, and perhaps refine them or bring them up to date."[58] The judge should thus embrace "the natural flowerings of behavior in its customary forms," because a "respect for extra-legal practices or social mores [lies] at the center of the judicial task." Replacing Cardozo on the U.S. Supreme Court was Oliver W. Holmes Jr., who went so far as to write that "the first requirement of a sound body of law is that it should correspond with the actual feelings and demands of the community, whether right or wrong."[59] A judge may therefore resolve interpretive ambiguity, Holmes inferred, in light of such feelings and demands. These may prove helpful in discovering the correct answer to a given legal question.[60]

Simply ignoring prevailing moral sentiment, on this view, would also likely elicit public backlash, prejudicial to respectful attitudes toward legal institutions at large.[61] Contemporary authors still regularly affirm such views. One thus contends that "written law will have no purchase on a community unless it reflects the practices of that community in some way: even a law that sets out to correct custom will necessarily reflect other aspects of the customary practices of a community, or it will lack purchase."[62] When Pound and the early Holmes spoke of common morality as the basis for our law, they had in mind a national society organized around its members' shared commitment to certain core principles—and to whatever these principles might entail for the law.

This first hypothesis, that common morality naturally and effortlessly finds its way into the law of a democratic society, does not withstand the slightest serious scrutiny, however—not in so simplistic a formulation, at least. First, it failed to specify any exact process or causal steps by which common morality might actually come to penetrate the law, certainly not in any manner susceptible to empirical disconfirmation. The method by which common law judges were to discern community sentiment remained entirely mysterious, though it is scarcely surprising that a theory so describing even their most expansive, assertive law-making activity would find a sympathetic judicial ear. Second, we have learned too much from empirical political science about the complexity of legislative and judicial process to ignore the fact that any influence of common morality would have to be heavily mediated through the dynamics of large institutions, possessing limited resources, controlled by individuals with conflicting interests and priorities. Third, if the law simply absorbed common morality through so casual an affair as the public-spiritedness of good-hearted lawmakers, we would expect to find evidence of such absorption broadly and evenly distributed across the panorama of legal life. We find no such thing.[63] At certain points, common morality clearly encounters significant obstacles to permeating the legal system.

At bottom, the first hypothesis simply trades too heavily on the undoubted fact that all lawmakers are, well, . . . *people, too*. It relied as well on the related and confused notion that because common morality is much like the air we breathe, lawmakers will spontaneously, organically, intuitively breathe it into the law. Our powerful affinity for the mirroring thesis invites comparisons perhaps initially counterintuitive, even subversive. As Tamanaha observes, when we think of the law as a mirror of society, "The implied threat of disorder works on our primal fears to render law in heroic terms, as a savior or protector; the metaphor of the mirror makes it *our* savior, *our* protector, a power to identify with, not fear."[64] The evident analogy to how tribal Africans were thought to employ the "fetish"[65]—to ward off dangers, misunderstood or exaggerated—is inescapable (if a bit uncomfortable: Tamanaha soon became the dean of a distinguished American law school). For it is law's putative power to reflect what is best in us, our deepest ethical commitments, that enables us to project onto it such curative powers as we believe it to possess. To peoples of certain non-Western cultures, often less confident in or hopeful for their legal institutions, this faith in law's extraordinary restorative potency seems nearly indistinguishable from their belief in magic, as they are quick to observe.

The second model of law's relation to common morality adopts an antithetical view. Shared moral commitments, in any nontrivial sense, do not exist across a large society; or when they may occasionally arise, they are too diffuse and disorganized to articulate themselves as a political force. What stands in need of explanation, then, are those few aspects of law that do closely comport with common morality, such as it is. Congruity between the two, not divergence, presents by far the more curious puzzle.

The passage of time alone allows, and often nearly ensures, that the two normative orders will drift apart. A new legal rule frequently endures long after the impetus inspiring its creation. The balance of political forces and moral passions enabling its enactment may have passed from the scene. Yet the current legislative balance prevents its modification.[66] "Assuming some short-term coalition gets the law passed," observes a prominent legal scholar, "such a law can operate very independently of current social mores, depending on voters' or politicians' inattention to the laws, or on some more complex politics underlying the law's persistence."[67] He refers particularly to criminal laws still popular with prosecutors, though now widely deemed "draconian in light of social mores." These notably included prohibitions on the use of marijuana and rules mandating lengthy incarceration for its possession with intent to sell.

The theory of "public choice"[68] predicts that law will overlap with "the public interest" and, by implication, with common morality only where there exists some well-organized group actively dedicated to moving the law in this direction. Its members must concern themselves greatly about the issue, far more than the population at large, most of whom may care little about it. Enthusiasts will lobby energetically for their views, in the face of indifference, inertia, and organizational dispersion among potential opponents. For the enthusiasts to prevail, the particular practice they find objectionable will often already be so widely reproached by the general public that those engaged in it risk severe stigma even in publicly identifying themselves as endorsing its authorization.[69]

Though it does not anticipate a close match-up between common morality and the law, public choice theory is at least consistent with certain observable correspondences between the two.[70] Majority opinion did not endorse the goals of the American Temperance Movement,[71] for instance, and juries regularly nullified ensuing restrictions on the sale of alcohol. Yet the Movement's active promoters successfully advanced their legislative program and kept it in place for thirteen years.[72] Lead organizers sprang chiefly from rural Protestant churches[73] whose members, on one long-influential view,[74] experienced deep status anxiety over perceived threats to the cultural authority of their class. Movement activists saw these threats emanating from the millions of recent immigrants to U.S. shores, and especially from poor Irish and Italian Catholics.[75] Competing "status groups,"[76] old and new, each sought from the state an official imprimatur of respectability for its favored forms of private life. The struggle over Prohibition has long fascinated social scientists because it is unrecognizable, on either side, as a conventional quest for material advantage and its worldly accoutrements.

Public choice would predict certain further areas of convergence and divergence between law and common morality. The conditions under which one may lawfully obtain an abortion are much more restrictive within heavily Catholic societies, notably in Latin America, than in other (non-Muslim) countries.[77] Leaders of the Roman Catholic Church were once unassailable in such places, and often remain quite politically influential. They actively press their views, often through back channels,[78] upon sympathetic legislators, a large share of whom attended Catholic educational institutions in their youth, adolescence, and young adulthood.

Still, in Italy and Portugal, only a minority of the population regularly attends the Catholic mass.[79] As in Latin America,[80] most other citizens consider themselves Catholics, but endorse only mildly or merely acquiesce in the Church's moral teachings. A majority may even favor a legal right to abortion, some polling suggests,[81] and support for gay rights has grown considerably.[82] Throughout Latin America, decreasing percentages identify themselves as Catholics at all. Yet those opposing Church policies are often poorly organized and have lacked strong allies well-positioned to help achieve legal change on favored issues, most of these concerning gender.[83] These general conditions are propitious, as public choice theorists will observe, for considerable overlap between traditional Church doctrine and national abortion law.

The experience of Western Europe has been nearly the reverse, in a sense, though the pattern there as well proves arguably consistent with the expectations of public choice. Political elites support abortion rights much more than the general public they represent and govern. By considerable majorities, Western European respondents have often told survey researchers that they believe abortion to be morally wrong in all but a very limited range of circumstances (rape, incest, serious threat to the mother's life), representing only a very small percentage of abortions. In fact, nearly half the citizenry of Western countries describes the practice as tantamount to "murder."[84] Such data suggest that even in highly secular societies, abortion law has generally been less restrictive of the practice than has prevailing moral sentiment.

This feature of common morality nonetheless remains politically inert. Though churches are politically influential in Eastern Europe, they are weak elsewhere on the Continent, lacking even the pedagogical and diffuse cultural influence enjoyed by Catholic clergy in Latin America. Both there and in Western Europe, common morality on its own—even on so seemingly freighted a question—is simply too desultory to exercise significant causal impact over lawmaking. Successful impact has required the active, enduring intercession of a well-organized Church, even where it is officially 'established.' Prevailing public views on abortion do not strongly predict the measure of that influence, compared to such alternative causal contributions.[85]

Abortion politics within the United States has been much more heated and its partisans on both sides much better organized. An early influential ethnography found that female opponents of abortion rights defend their views with such righteous indignation because they believe that pro-choice advocates implicitly tarnish the societal value of women who choose to become full-time homemakers[86]—women like themselves. These informants observed that it is chiefly upper-middle-class professional women who serve as spokespeople for abortion rights. Thus, contrary to initial appearances, it was not the question of whether the human fetus possesses human status that chiefly establishes the lines between supporters and opponents of abortion rights. Though invariably couched in more elevated idiom, this conflict thus also displays deeply socioeconomic features and fractures, unintelligible when approached entirely in philosophical terms.[87] Luker thus writes:

> The political constituencies—primarily women—have vested social interests in whether the embryo is defined as a baby or as a fetus . . . [T]o attribute personhood to the embryo is to make the social statement that . . . women should subordinate other parts of their lives to that central aspect of their social and biological lives . . . Conversely, if the embryo is held to be a fetus [i.e., to lack personhood], then it becomes socially permissible for women to subordinate their reproductive roles to other roles, particularly in the paid labor force.[88]

These accounts of abortion politics and of Prohibition are compelling in their close attention to the social promptings of moral arguments for legal change (or stasis). Fascinating as well is their richness in recording subtle shadings of emotional register concerning how informants articulate their ethical views. Yet this very richness, essential to the sociology of motivation for political activism, sits uneasily with the elegant simplicity of public choice theory. The theory also inquires chiefly into the nature of backstage legislative maneuverings, not the prior question of what animates people, in the first instance, to thoroughly immerse themselves in such processes at all.

The theory's leading proponents privately concede that "moral reform" movements like those concerning Prohibition and abortion are ultimately quite peculiar in their wellsprings, in ways greatly reducing the theory's ability to explain activists' behavior. These movements implicitly focus on advancing large social visions of the world rather than the immediate material advantage of their adherents. Activists on both sides scoff at the very idea of "splitting the difference" in hopes of reaching legislative compromise, which they view as an intolerable betrayal of fundamental principle. It is hence unsurprising that public choice theory fails to account for the tactics and strategies of moralizing movements nearly as well as for more familiar kinds of electoral alliance.[89] In any event, if the predictions of public choice theory comported more closely with observable empirical patterns across the board, as it claims to do, we would not find nearly so many legal fields and rules (see Chapter 7) where the law tracks common morality quite neatly. From a public choice perspective, these vast swaths of life—where legality mirrors society with surprising ease—are utterly unintelligible.

Partisans of the theory will rejoin that in these areas of legal doctrine, no organized group at least actively *opposed* law's incorporation of prevailing morals. This concedes a great deal, however: that common morality may find ample legal expression *unless* those with strongly held minority views organize effectively to resist that result. By implication, we should anticipate at least a rough correspondence between common morality and the law wherever there exists no aggressive rent-seeking to throw the law off its natural course.[90] To concede this much is to acknowledge backhandedly the explanatory force of our first or "naive" theory, holding that law tends spontaneously to reflect prevailing morals. For the political issues we Westerners generally describe as "moral" in character[91] do tend to stir passions altogether more agitated and different from—less readily subject to compromise than—the material concerns centrally at stake in more conventional political disputes.

The persistent correspondence between common morality and much of our law provides the dull grey background against which moral entrepreneurs, whatever their ideological stripe, must mightily labor. Until recently, activists for rights to gay marriage, in particular, would certainly have concurred. Reformers long confronted prevailing views that effectively blocked their efforts at legal reform through legislation and litigation, whereas their opponents effectively tapped into a common morality still strongly averse to such change.[92] The result was a series of constitutional amendments in many states that defined marriage as the union of man and woman.

Yet even on this issue, as public choice enthusiasts would retort, the widespread moral understandings averse to gay marriage did not seep effortlessly, unobtrusively, into the law. Advocates for allowing homosexuals to marry confronted a phalanx of moral entrepreneurs and nonprofit organizations—better organized, better funded, racially more diverse than their progressive adversaries. Until 2004, at the earliest, broad currents of moral opinion blew powerfully at the back of those opposing gay marriage. During this considerable period of effective resistance to change, there was close alignment between the claims of common morality and those of organized political power. This temporal co-occurrence renders it very difficult to extricate the respective influence of each such causal contribution, and hence to assess the relative explanatory power of public choice.

From these several illustrations, and others to follow, it is clear that each of the two general theories concerning the measure of common morality's influence upon the law can account only for a distinct subset of legal life. We must therefore approach this question from an altogether different angle, more attentive to a wider range of causal influences pushing the law into and out of harmony with common morals. That is the goal of Chapters 6 and 7.

# 6

# Divergences of Law and Morals

## Sites and Sources

Chapter 5 sought to deflate exaggerated claims of the two grand theories purporting to tell us everything we need to know about whether the law and common morality will converge and where such convergence is most likely. The general failure of both theories should prompt us to address these questions at a lower level of abstraction. This demands that we delineate the particular forces prompting convergence and divergence across a wide array of factual circumstances. This chapter seeks to identify the forces within society that tend to drive law and common morality apart. These forces are more numerous and generally more powerful than those, discussed in Chapter 7, drawing the two normative orders into harmony. I will start with the better-known of the centrifugal forces, then discuss the less familiar.

Little will be said about philosophical accounts, drawn from the largest normative theories, of why and when we may properly prohibit certain conduct. For as Leo Katz shows, none of these theories—utilitarianism, for instance, even Mill's harm principle—"really stand in the way of criminalizing what we disapprove of."[1] In any event such ideas, though sometimes present within policy discussion, usually exercise only very limited influence on how a given society resolves which forms of objectionable conduct will and will not face penal or civil sanction.

### Legislative "Capture" by Special Interests

The influence of well-organized "special interests" over the lawmaking and regulatory process will probably be first to the minds of most readers when wondering why law and common morality sometimes go separate ways.[2] Thus, common morality may clearly endorse enactment or repeal of a given rule, but well-entrenched interests wield sufficient political power to block that result.

For instance, Americans across the political spectrum may feel deeply indignant over the federal rescue of major financial institutions during the 2008–2009 financial crisis.[3] Yet financial leaders may effectively discourage the federal government from adopting more aggressive regulatory policies against their industry,[4] in the area of antitrust for instance. Much the same could be said of those few issue-areas where organized labor exerts considerable political influence in ways discordant with views prevalent among the general public. Labor unions of prison guards, for instance, press actively in some states to preserve policies of lengthy incarceration for small-scale drug possession offenses[5] that the public no longer views as morally meriting severe sanction.[6]

Comparing opinion surveys with current law and policy, one prominent political scientist recently writes that "Under most circumstances, the preferences of the vast majority of Americans appear to have essentially no impact on which policies the government does or doesn't adopt."[7] Other scholars reach more measured conclusions, finding that the influence of organized interests on law and policy varies greatly from one issue-area to another.[8] Still others convincingly show how the very concept of industry "capture" is itself problematic and essentially contested, if not simply confused.[9] Still, it would be misguided to minimize the likelihood that interest-group influence at times seriously contributes to cleaving law from common morality, at least in those societies with few legal limits on the role of private money in electoral campaigns.

The strongest correlation between Americans' attitudes and congressional votes is found on issues usually described as "symbolic" and "moral," such as abortion and capital punishment.[10] "Issues" of *any* sort, though, are not central to the electoral choices of most voters, according to recent political science.[11] Data suggest that people generally vote for candidates on the basis of "group identification"[12] rather than the policy substance. This is not to deny that moral considerations sometimes greatly shape voting behavior, for there is more to political morality than intuitions of justice. The emotion of intense disgust that voters may feel for candidates whom they vigorously oppose, for whatever reason, is no less a matter of morality than the belief that their preferred candidate will advance policies they deem morally just.[13] In fact, a wide range of moral emotions—love, for instance—influences electoral choices: parents consistently manage to convey their party loyalties to their adult children.[14] The child's voting behavior presumably here reflects some uncertain, elusive mix of duty and affection.

Political scientists have long noted that the most effective way for organized interests to capture the legislative process is to keep their favored issues off the radar screen entirely, and thus to profit from the public's inattention.[15] An invaluable means to this end is to rhetorically characterize an issue in value-neutral terms, so that sentiments of indignation at injustice become simply inapt, a species of category error, a mark of elementary misunderstanding, of rude unsophistication. As research with focus groups confirms,[16] most citizens will then likely say to themselves, "Let's leave it to the experts" or "It's too complicated for the likes of me." And those professionally engaged in the issue thereby become free to conceptualize and resolve it publicly through idioms entirely technical or scientific. Talk of justice—or revulsion at injustice—has no recognizable place.

Elite insiders sometimes unguardedly confess, and social scientists report, that it is regularly a self-conscious political strategy to induce others to construe a policy issue,[17] potentially controversial, in ways so technically complex and notionally value-neutral as to imply that nothing of any moral import is at stake—nothing authorizing the public's attention, still less its censure.[18] The question of how and why legislative capture occurs thus becomes, in major part, a question about how and why certain issues—by coincidence or contrivance—manage to remain beyond the moral domain. There are nonetheless effective ways to increase the prospects of bringing them within that realm. "Moralization is a psychological state that can be turned off and on like a switch," Stephen Pinker confidently writes, "and when it is on, a distinctive mind-set commandeers our thinking."[19] For present purposes, social scientific in nature, we can say that a moral issue (relevant to the law) is simply one to which sentiments of indignation at perceived injustice have successfully attached.

Particular questions enter and exit this domain by way of stratagems and vicissitudes today the particular concern of "cultural sociologists."[20] This scholarship examines the rhetorical techniques employed by those striving to moralize or de-moralize a given issue, or to turn its existing moral valences in their favor. These techniques serve to press issues and antagonists into antithetical categories—pure versus polluted, sacred versus profane, elevated versus base, truth versus lies, rational versus irrational, well-balanced versus mentally unhinged.[21] These binary oppositions deny relevant complexity by portraying one's adversaries not as merely misguided, in need of greater instruction, but as irredeemably contaminated, tainted by evil, warranting contempt and disgust more than respectful engagement.[22] Transposing a given issue from the technical to the moral domain often entails not merely a depreciation of genuine scientific complexities, but a vast oversimplification of normative ones as well.

## The Limits of Language

Rights to do wrong can arise simply from the limitations of language in fully capturing our objectives for the law.[23] These limits are at times inherent, but also often contingent on the relative foresight and ingenuity of lawmakers. In crafting an enactment's wording, it may prove impossible to perfectly distinguish the morally acceptable from the unacceptable exercises of a given right. The express terms of a statute can thereby turn out to be broader than its drafters' purposes. It thereby authorizes a wider range of conduct than they intended, conduct they and others deem wrongful.

The result is frequently to authorize the objectionable, for fear that a broader prohibition would discourage the unobjectionable. This is a periodic concern, one that skilled legislative drafters routinely confront, and strive valiantly to minimize, but never wholly banish. We have largely learned to live with it. We handle it chiefly after the fact, through methods of interpretation designed to bring law's verbal form into better alignment with its normative content, as best that may be ascertained. Yet we may be unable to determine law's exact content (and scope-conditions)—what it actually authorizes—except through scrutinizing its form, the particular language that drafters employed to articulate their intentions. That language will regularly lend itself to alternative readings, at times equally plausible, so that the true nature or scope of what they have enacted remains inscrutable. Still, even in such difficult cases we have well-settled methods for thinking this problem through, and there are standard grooves into which our arguments and counterarguments will fall. Complete surprises are very rare.

In fact, it is a truism of legal thought that *all* legal rules are under-inclusive or over-inclusive, to some extent, vis-à-vis their intended purposes—and sometimes suffer both defects at once.[24] This means that the rights created by almost any rule could, in some situation, be exercised inconsistently with the aims of those establishing it, who would (with others) find such exercise morally objectionable. It is conceptually possible that literally any legal right could come to be utilized in unanticipated ways, or so greatly in excess of what legislators contemplated, that such "abuse" generates serious concern for policymakers and the general public. Yet it is only the points where this abuse actually transpires, and where lawmakers should fear it may occur, that concern the present inquiry, focused as it is on sociological realities, not speculative possibilities.

Legal philosophers engage the specifically linguistic issues here, and the intrinsic limits of human language as a tool for expressing our complex purposes presents a problem endemic to all lawmaking. This problem arises even where all those involved in the legislative process view the issues in technical terms implicating no moral controversy. When the law employs very unclear language, legislators may appear to be deliberately backing away from more complete regulation in anticipation of stigma against exercising a given right. Alternatively, they may intend their enactment to be comprehensive in scope, to "govern the field." Yet practical constraints—of cost in time, energy, foresight, or the requirements of political compromise—prevent them from agreeing on words any more precise, on language more clearly foreclosing the objectionable conduct to which right-holders will later believe themselves entitled. Greater clarity on the factual predicates for a rule's every application hence proves impossible.

This is again a regular feature of legal life, to which courts respond with standard interpretive devices, normally satisfactory. The result of such legislative "failings" may be effectively to invite extralegal resistance to the exercise of rights so vaguely defined, whose bearers interpret them more capaciously than other people thereby prejudiced. Yet in their resort to loose statutory verbiage, lawmakers need not have contemplated this salutary resistance (though they would be wise to do so); still less will they have anticipated the forms it will take, their particular sociological configuration.

This book's preoccupations do not lie in such linguistic concerns, their undoubted practical import notwithstanding. The major disparities between the law and common morality do not often originate in the very nature of legislative drafting as a lawyerly skill, still less in the nature of language as such. And the disparities that *do* owe to uniquely linguistic issues rarely assume the largest real-life import. Of present interest are precisely those disparities that acquire political and sociological salience. How and why does this come about? It is never the strictly linguistic challenges alone that turn them from semantic brain-teasers—most famously, the meaning of "No Vehicles in the Park"[25]—into raging, real-world controversies over which much blood or money will flow.

## Distrust of Authority

We frequently do not trust public officials with the power necessary to enforce common morality, even on issues where most people concur about what morality requires. Though they are notionally our "agents," and we their "principals," officials may do our bidding only through exacting large unanticipated costs. We suspect they will exceed their lawful authority; or they will act lawfully but in ways we regard abusive nonetheless. We fear that in turning laudable moral principles into legal rules, we will unwittingly invite the state and its agents to violate other principles about which we care equally. Americans in particular, compared to Western Europeans, harbor great doubts about the good faith of those who must at once administer justice upon others and behave justly themselves.[26]

Because this problem will be familiar to many in a domestic legal context, let me illustrate it with an example drawn from international law. Consider the issue of armed "humanitarian intervention" to protect human lives threatened by ongoing mass atrocity. During such events, many throughout the world allow in principle that common morality warrants and perhaps even requires military intervention against the perpetrators. Many equally believe, however, that power-hungry statesmen are likely to exploit such occasions to extend their sphere of influence, turning cosmopolitan sympathies for suffering victims into convenient rationalizations for imperial adventurism. Universalist principle will be insincerely invoked in service of nationalist *machtpolitik*.

There has nonetheless arisen over the last fifteen years a novel moral and political doctrine urging members of the international community to accept a shared "responsibility to protect" regarding all victims of ongoing, large-scale atrocities.[27] International law does not authorize inter-state force, however, except in self-defense or with express approval of the UN Security Council,[28] which has been very rare. The result is a moral duty to protect—widely acknowledged as such in international discourse, including a UN General Assembly Resolution[29] and U.S. presidential proclamation[30]—without any accompanying legal right to honor it. In short, it appears that the world widely acknowledges that common morality sometimes allows, even demands, actions that the law forbids and—most believe—should continue to forbid.

In the domestic context, when the public opposes a stronger state role in barring morally objectionable behavior, the animating concern is usually that officials will illegitimately intrude upon our personal liberty and familial privacy. They will sometimes do this in sincere belief that the public interest so requires, but sometimes also simply for power or profit. In the most pernicious cases, they may abuse their trust by at once employing the prejudicial personal information they acquire about fellow citizens (the FBI under J. Edgar Hoover, for example)[31] as well as their monopoly on legitimate violence (the Los Angeles Police under Chief Daryl Gates, for instance).[32]

The standard academic analysis usually stops here, with vague invocations of our deep distrust of looming Leviathan, an overly powerful state. Yet we nonetheless proceed to make more refined judgments when we decide, as we inevitably must, which features of common morality to enshrine into which legal prohibitions and which government agencies to entrust with their enforcement. Within any society, the measure of citizen trust in certain institutions will be greater than in others. Americans trust the National Park Service and U.S. Postal Service much more than they do the Internal Revenue Service or the Department of Veterans Affairs.[33] The less confidence we have in a given state agency, the more we are inclined to tolerate the morally objectionable behavior otherwise naturally within its jurisdiction to prohibit and police.

One reason certain agencies enjoy lesser public trust than others is that they regulate in issue-areas peculiarly susceptible to abuse. Drug enforcement, in particular, is notoriously prone to corruption. Leaders in countries where the rule of law is not well established therefore often choose to tread gently when criminalizing drugs. Their doubts stem not necessarily from any principled opposition to "legislating private morality," but from recognition that the integrity of law enforcement agencies, including military and police, cannot credibly be assumed. Better-governed societies—with well-compensated public servants, less susceptible to bribery—can afford to take greater risks in this regard. These considerations sometimes powerfully influence how much the law will neatly follow common morality, or instead leave unregulated a great deal of conduct to which large numbers of people morally object.

## Public Ignorance

Most people simply don't know much, if anything, about certain lawful practices, sometimes far-reaching, that they would regard as ethically unacceptable. The obstacle here is not that issues become construed as entirely technical, and hence beyond our ken, but that we are entirely ignorant, or only faintly aware, that the questionable activity even exists, or occurs with some frequency. In such terms we may fairly describe, for example, the legal rules allowing corporate boards of directors to set compensation for the chief executive officers (CEOs) who appoint their members. These rules authorize board members to award very generous remuneration packages to CEOs and to themselves even as the company itself teeters on bankruptcy.[34] Only in the last several years has there arisen any significant public awareness of this practice or the legal rights on which its possibility depends. And only very recently is there much recognition that these rights are not conjoined to any legal duties of a sort that many laypeople would imagine must exist.

In particular, there remains little empirical correlation between how well a company performs economically and the size of its CEO's annual increase in compensation.[35] No law requires that individual salary be limited by measurable institutional achievement. This has been the case for decades. It continues today, notwithstanding the "shareholder value" movement and the leveraged buyouts of underperforming companies it sparked, developments aimed at better aligning incentives between manager-agents and shareholder-principals.[36] The business practices ensuing from the right to set compensation independently of company performance came into being and persist for reasons having nothing to do with legislative anticipation that shareholders would obstruct its abusive exercise. Lawmakers might very well nonetheless have assumed that responsible officers and directors themselves simply wouldn't seriously dream of employing this right with so little self-restraint.

In the years shortly following the 2008 financial crisis and ensuing recession, at least, a certain moral fervor—powerfully evident as late as the 2016 presidential primary campaigns[37]—accompanied the public's growing awareness of such issues. Even so, the political obstacles to drafting legislation designed to satisfactorily address them,[38] notwithstanding the enactment of Dodd-Frank,[39] prevented great progress (most observers concur) in addressing "moral hazard," in closing this particular crevasse between common morality and the law. In fact, the political power of affected elites, where attributable to public ignorance, clearly comes to the fore in several of my illustrations of rights to do wrong. It varies widely in its causal significance, though, in accounting for particular disparities between law and common morality. Nor should one discount the possibility that it is sometimes those most invested in and concerned about a given issue who best understand the true stakes of policy choice concerning it, even the specifically moral stakes.

## Harms of Prohibition

A further factor militating against outlawing conduct at odds with common morality is that it frequently proves preferable to legalize an objectionable activity precisely in order to regulate it. In this fashion its most pernicious manifestations and societal ramifications might be most effectively discouraged. To proscribe it altogether simply drives it "underground." In certain black markets, effective demand is virtually a force of nature and, like water, inexorably finds its own level. This is especially so when many consumers perceive the good as a necessity, for which demand will therefore be relatively inelastic.

Goods and services viewed as luxuries in the mind of a majority, moreover, often become necessities to a minority, sometimes a substantial one. Prohibition de jure then raises prices more than it decreases de facto consumption. Prices ascend on account of the greater risks involved in producing an illegal product. Proscription proves especially misguided where most people find the now-verboten activity too pleasurable to abandon, such as the generous consumption of alcohol. When formally banished, it simply burrows into certain socioeconomic crevices, now governed only by stigma, of which there may be little. The result will often be to cause still greater harm than when it remained in public sight, subject to surveillance,[40] at least.

These are broad generalities, however. Whether proscription in fact causes greater harm once forced into the dark is always an open question at the outset, empirical in nature, often susceptible to answer only through legal experimentation. Stated merely as an abstract proposition, the prospect of such harm is ever-present and hovers vaguely over much of policy discussion. More an adage than an argument, so broad an observation does not tell us where the hypothetical dangers will significantly materialize. We may pride ourselves in our awareness that every policy intervention yields unintended consequences. This world-weary realization cannot, however, much guide the law in any given issue-area. Myriad other considerations, more sociological than strictly economic in nature, invariably intercede, complicating the assessment of alternative policy options.

A few illustrations of the general problem will immediately come to the reader's mind: fatal back-alley abortions that maim or kill women, bathtub gin that blinds its drinkers, unmonitored prostitution that spreads AIDS and venereal disease. Less familiar examples deserve brief mention too. In poor countries with weak legal institutions, the decision to criminalize child labor often simply leads to surreptitious employment in black markets, frequently sex work, rather than in "above-ground" industries, where law-abiding employers treat their young charges better, studies suggest.[41] And if the law were to prohibit credit card companies from charging "usurious" interest rates for those with poor credit histories,[42] the underprivileged would instead inexorably turn to payday lenders, whose rates are far higher and who sometimes employ coercive methods of collection.

Also, for a given object or activity, there often exist both beneficent and reprehensible purposes. Legalization in such circumstances often facilitates effective suppression of wrongful, harmful uses. Thus, the Nuclear Non-Proliferation Treaty permits international transactions in fissionable material because there are some perfectly legitimate uses for it. "Above ground" markets, such as those in certain nuclear energy technologies, also facilitate the task of international officials in identifying unauthorized diversions of regulated materials to wrongful ends.

A closely related variable is the degree to which potential wrongdoers are able to operate under the radar, keeping the most objectionable of their activities invisible to official overseers and other concerned observers. When the law starts to seriously scrutinize a given industry for potentially wrongful activity, these informational asymmetries enable firms to take their wrongful activities underground without great disruption to lawful operations. More generally, the easier it is for reproachable conduct to avoid detection, the less effective its legal prohibition will be, other things equal. Such considerations enable us to anticipate regulatory failure in certain recurrent types of situation. And when we do not expect to succeed, we become concerned that the law—in pursuing a fool's errand—will at once waste its scarce resources and needlessly humiliate itself; it will depreciate the currency of public trust and legitimacy on which its efficacy depends across all other issue-areas. As Aquinas observed long ago, when prohibition proves ineffective, its conspicuous defeat is likely to engender an undercurrent of public disdain for the legal system itself, inciting at least a diffuse inclination to disobey it.[43]

Even those who endorse and obey the prohibition at immediate issue will—once it's widely ignored by others—begin wondering why they themselves should follow *other* such prohibitions, those that *they* oppose, when it becomes possible to evade detection in flouting them. Savvy regulators are not inattentive to this danger, in contemplation of which they sometimes produce a set of legal rules more lenient toward the disfavored activity than indulged by prevailing moral sensibilities, thereby creating a right to do wrong. In addition to prudently regulating the production and use of disfavored products, it will sometimes also make good sense to adopt educational programs and advertising campaigns discouraging demand, rather than turning suppliers into scofflaws.

Black markets are always, to some extent, a "perverse" and predictable effect of any prohibition. They vary greatly in the degree of their perversity, however. We worry less about creating such a market in marijuana or sex work than in fissionable nuclear materials. Where we consider the misconduct entirely unacceptable, we will—in banning it—knowingly embrace the risks of failing at its effective elimination. The international community thus chooses to criminalize the recruitment of child soldiers, for instance. It is nonetheless well understood that, in much of sub-Saharan Africa, most efforts to halt the practice will fail—and that international criminal law itself may suffer some discredit in the failing, whatever points it may arguably earn for trying.

## Ensuring Proper Motives

It is no less important at times that we perform a given act for the right reason than that we perform it at all. And in assessing his conduct, we sometimes care about the virtuousness of the individual actor no less than the consistency of his observable, exterior behavior with general principles of morality. We regularly regard his act as virtuous only when undertaken "as an end in itself," as ordinary language has it, not to further another aim, even that of cultivating a reputation for virtuousness. The law can mandate our outward conformity to the demands of common morality. But for conduct to be truly moral, on some accounts, we must freely choose to do what morality demands of us.[44] In order for our rightful conduct to be freely chosen, we must have the right to choose otherwise; we must therefore sometimes have a right to do wrong. From this viewpoint, the law should not foreclose that possibility if its drafters wish to help citizens become truly moral.

This has always been the rationale invoked by certain Christian (non-Catholic) denominations and sects for refusing to baptize children, authorizing this sacrament instead for adults alone. The enduring Amish practice of *rumspringa,* sometimes explicitly acknowledged in these groups' rules of "*ordnung,*" offers perhaps the most immoderate expression of this stance. Adolescents of age 16, until then rigorously secluded from the outside world, are encouraged to explore and indulge its temptations, which—with wild abandon—they often do. These indulgences usually extend to television and movies, driving automobiles, video games and cell phones, social media, junk food, dancing, smoking, swearing, rock and rap music, and premarital sex.[45] Amish adolescents must then willfully and entirely renounce all these activities if they choose, a year or two thereafter, to rejoin their religious community as full-fledged members, facing excommunication and lifelong ostracism if they later change their minds.

Concerns with ensuring that moral standards are freely chosen, not legally mandated, first arose in connection with the worship of "false gods." This preoccupation might initially seem peculiar to the ancient Greek and non-Western worlds and, since then, to Christian thinkers. One need not look far-afield to find them today at play in entirely secular situations. Thus, there now exist global mores, reasonably well settled, that a sovereign state recently responsible for a mass atrocity, particularly genocide, has a moral duty to apologize for its misconduct.[46] Some have sought to turn these mores into a legal duty. The Inter-American Court of Human Rights, in particular, now regularly orders states that have been found liable for large-scale, violent violations of their citizens' basic human rights to issue formal apologies to the victims and their families.[47]

Others plausibly reply that the very notion of a legally mandated apology is a category mistake. An apology is genuine, only worthy of the name, in fact, if truly voluntary and sincere. It is impossible to convincingly establish either property if the apology is court-ordered. This remains the case even if, in its wording, the apology is forthright, not equivocal or incomplete. International law should therefore preserve the possibility that states, by declining to apologize, may exercise this right to do wrong. A state may most credibly demonstrate its apologetic bona fides if its leaders retain a right *not* to do so. In any event, we should not deprecate the importance of "mere ritual" in public life, including that of public apologies.[48] For rituals steeped in shared symbolism have historically played a significant role in fostering social solidarity around common moral ideals, old or new. In the immediate aftermath of mass atrocity and the severe social conflicts engendering it, such solidarity is widely sought, hard-won, and often precarious.

Advocates of a legal duty to apologize retort that, as applied to nation-states, the key concepts in play here—voluntariness, sincerity, remorse, worthy intention—represent the true category error and are hence irrelevant. To insist upon firm evidence of their presence makes little sense, for they pertain only to natural persons, not to such 'fictional' legal constructions as "the sovereign state." On this view, what matters more than motives and inner repentance for prior wrongs is the message that current leaders now choose to send, through their sober act of atonement, about the state's commitment to a future very different from its past. Still, a signal designed to communicate peaceful intentions evinces greater clarity, less "noise," if leaders have no obligation to issue it.

Of course, this is not exactly what Aquinas had in mind in arguing that positive law should indulge some measure of "depravity" in order to foster reflective choice and authenticity of adherence to "the moral law." Sometimes the best way for the state to mold our souls is to leave us alone to mold them ourselves or, more precisely, to submit consentingly to the more delicate, kinder intercession of those we love, admire, and respect. In any event, contemporary liberal societies, on most accounts, stand opposed in principle to deep "soulcraft" by the state, to the very idea of "making people moral" by manipulating their inner motivations. We are wary of any role for government in character formation, beyond the particular, delimited species of virtue necessary for liberal citizenship,[49] for responsible participation in a democratic polity.

Modern law can therefore derive no moral guidance from historical theories holding that the state's central telos is precisely to cultivate our heartfelt dispositions to live in accordance with natural law. We tell ourselves, at least, that it is enough for people to obey the positive law and thereby honor the shared morality it embodies. This is central to the political philosophy of liberalism (on most accounts), with its emphasis on the personal autonomy and legal rights that enable us to develop and act upon our individual conception of the good.[50] Contemporary liberals regard the rest of personal morality—whatever it may be, however genuine its claims—as no longer within law's proper ambit. The upshot is that, from the standpoint of that larger moral domain, we acquire a considerable range of rights to do wrong, some of these serious indeed.

## Motives Are Inscrutable

In judging others' conduct, our civilization ascribes an importance to "mind reading," to discerning another's precise mental state, a task that is altogether absent among certain non-Western peoples, who deem it immaterial or impossible.[51] Even for us, others' motives differ not only in their moral defensibility, but in the ease with which we are confident that we can discern them. A person's intention to engage in particular conduct is usually easier to establish than the motivations inspiring him to do so. His intention—to hire or fire a given employee, for instance—can often be "read off the face" of his observable conduct.[52] Not so his motives (or purposes, wording that some here prefer) for forming this intention, though these too entail states of consciousness. He may choose not to share with others his motivations—the reasons that recommend his action to him—especially if it is precisely these that render his conduct unlawful or otherwise objectionable.

Consider an example. In filing a legal document with the court, Party A registers his intention to obtain a divorce. His motive for developing this intention, more likely than not, will be that he believes the marital relationship has irremediably broken down, that he and his spouse have developed "irreconcilable differences." Until two generations ago, however, U.S. law did not acknowledge this as an acceptable ground for seeking divorce. It was therefore necessary for him to allege that his spouse had engaged in infidelity or abuse, which placed her legally "at fault" for the marriage's failure. The result was that millions of Americans found it necessary to perjure themselves if they wished to end an unhappy marriage. Their lawyers found themselves lured into suborning these criminal acts, and judges into turning a blind eye. The entire problem arose only because the law saw fit to inquire into the petitioner's motivations. The legal profession came to conclude that this pervasive practice of perjury was doing serious damage to public respect for the law as a whole.[53] It was easy to develop disdain for a system demanding such a dishonest charade from all before it. It was this conclusion, no less than humanitarian sympathies for the parties, that drove legislators to retreat from insisting upon any legal inquiry into motive.

That painful recent episode illustrates a larger class of problems, arising across many areas of law, whenever a defendant's conduct would be morally acceptable if motivated by one reason, yet wrongful if by another. If it was the second, unacceptable rationale prompting his intention to engage in the questionable conduct, he has every incentive to conceal this fact. And on the witness stand in his defense, he may be convincing in doing so. When we cannot ascertain his motive, and when motive is crucial to our appraisal of his observable behavior, the law sometimes demurs, tempers its ambition. The result is effectively to allow certain forms of conduct, universally deemed reprehensible, to remain lawful—again, a right to do wrong.

This paring back of law's ambitions may seem indefensible, and it may well be so in certain circumstances, as when fundamental constitutional principles are at stake.[54] Yet we take this step where the alternative proves no better, perhaps far worse. That alternative is to proceed in the face of these evidentiary obstacles, continuing to outlaw conduct whenever inspired by illicit motive. It then proves nearly impossible, however, to establish the culpable mental state (or, at times, organizational policy) required for liability. The law then risks humiliating not only those before it in a given dispute, but the courts themselves, on whose continued public authority much depends.

The problem becomes still more complex where law must acknowledge that motives may be mixed, and hence prohibits certain conduct only if the objectionable element in a given mix "predominates."[55] It is still more difficult, however, to determine the relative causal weight among mixed motives than to identify, among the facts in evidence, the presence of a prohibited one.

## What Does Common Morality Really Require of Whom?

Legal rules do not track common morality very closely at the many points where it proves impossible to sufficiently specify its requirements, to say exactly what it is that morality demands of anyone in particular, in the relevant circumstances. To count as law at all, on some accounts, and certainly to be consistent with the "*rule* of law," a governmental norm must attain a certain threshold level of clarity.[56] Yet even our deepest moral commitments sometimes do not attain this requisite measure of precision and hence do not well translate from abstract principle into workable rules. The limits of moral theory as a guide to lawmaking are again here evident. Kant famously acknowledged as much in describing the moral rights and duties inhospitable to juridical codification as 'imperfect,' contrasting these with those amenable to embodiment in and realization through positive law.[57]

Consider a contemporary illustration, mentioned before in another context: the international "responsibility to protect" victims of ongoing mass atrocity.[58] It is clear who is to benefit from this moral duty, and in what respect: particular human beings, those currently subject to violent attack, must be saved from genocide, crimes against humanity, and war crimes. Yet it is unclear what this responsibility requires of the rest of us. In seeking to honor our responsibilities at times of such moral moment, who must do what, exactly? A convincing answer is hard to identify. Even insofar as we can state an answer in general terms, it is by no means clear how we might draft the law, with enough precision, to give it adequate expression.

Moral rights and duties can remain imperfect in other ways. It may be clear who possesses a particular moral duty and what it demands of him. Yet it may remain uncertain who, if anyone, has a corresponding right to assert a claim upon him.[59] Consider, in that regard, the question of who should recover the invaluable antiquities now held by Western museums. Many of these were looted from political entities now long extinct, whose once-thriving populations no longer exist or exist only residually in diaspora. It is entirely uncertain who, if anyone, would be morally entitled to claim repatriation of such artifacts—to the extent that *re*patriation (the term invariably employed in these disputes) generally turns out to be a misnomer. In sum, when determining what we should actually do through the law in these situations, nothing follows directly from the conclusion that museums have a moral duty to redress these wrongs. Even as we sincerely acknowledge morality's new claims, in general terms, we find that this offers little guidance in determining what anyone should then actually do or receive from whom. The result is species of right to do wrong.

Kant's distinction between moral rights and duties that are 'perfect' or potentially perfectible and those that must remain imperfect finds helpful application in Amartya Sen's recent efforts to construct a satisfactory philosophical basis for international human rights.[60] Sen is anxious to refute those who believe these rights are not merely vague at the margins but entirely meaningless, due to the profound ambiguities and "essentially contested" character of key terms. In other words, such documents, even where officially binding, do not actually "perfect" into law most of the moral entitlements and obligations we have in mind when we speak confidently in terms of "human rights" and "human rights law." We can often agree that a particular human right exists, Sen insists, and that it imposes certain general responsibilities, without concurring in how we should concretize it into administrable legal rules, applicable at this time and place, enforceable in a particular way. We may acknowledge disagreement on such legal "details," as he puts it, even as we concur on underlying moral essentials, each of us seeking to advance these as best we may, under our differing circumstances.

Sen here invokes Kant's distinction not to deprecate imperfect duties, but precisely to accentuate their importance.[61] They require us to ask what we may realistically do to ensure that others' essential moral rights are not transgressed. We must then proceed with some effort to that end, the details of which the law need not fully address. We may even have a responsibility to organize ourselves to seek the reform of large-scale international institutions so that it becomes possible to perfect a larger subset of our moral rights and claims upon one another. Yet Sen contends that this possibility does not exhaust the meaning, nor define the essential place, of human rights within our lives.

Some have misread Sen to imply that social and economic rights, as opposed to civil and political ones, are those that must remain unperfected.[62] He makes clear, however, that there is no connection—logical or empirical, inherent or contingent—between whether a moral right is legally perfectible and whether we characterize it as civil/political versus social/economic/cultural.[63] Scheppele's misreading, in particular, suggests that Sen believes we should not legally codify human rights that cannot yet be enforced effectively through litigation—that such "aspirational" entitlements are not yet ready to enter law's domain.

This is not Sen's position. He instead believes that the concept of human rights has great value in our public discourse, national and international, entirely *apart from* its further value in providing arguments for particular legal enactments. We should not even regard moral principles, including those today widely described in terms of human rights, as "potential legal rights in waiting," as he puts it. Sen would grant that decisions about whether to seek greater legal perfection of a given moral right or duty present questions not of moral philosophy, but of public policy, political strategy, and legal craftsmanship. He is simply uninterested in the questions, integral to the present inquiry, of when and why moral rights and duties come to be recognized as such or when they should find full expression within legal doctrine. His interest, rather, is precisely in preserving a vital field of operation for their *non*-juridical influence.

In fact, even where some of our human rights seem susceptible to juridical "perfection," they might nonetheless do more good, he implies, if preserved in their status as moral ideals and strengthened in their efficacy as "*social* norms," a term he regularly employs in this connection. We should not await the juridification of fundamental moral rights, in other words, before holding ourselves bound, individually and collectively, to guide our lives in their light.[64] Still, insofar as "imperfection" remains inevitable at given time, on a certain issue, the result will be a breach between common morality and the law.

## A Moral Right to Do Moral Wrong?

Several liberal theorists suggest that people have a *moral* right to engage in forms of immoral conduct.[65] The law should generally acknowledge these moral rights, to protect the choices we make in exercising them, to afford a certain dignity to the very act (in such situations) of choosing.[66] These moral rights are emphatically not confined to a "private" realm of intimate relationships or care of the self. Thus, one of Jeremy Waldron's examples suggests that it is morally wrong to contribute money to the electoral campaign of a racist politician, but that one nonetheless has a moral right to do so, which the law should acknowledge.

This is decidedly not a prudential argument about how it could prove ill-considered or impracticable to draft, enact, and enforce a suitable legal prohibition to this effect. Nor is Waldron offering a causal account of why the law has often seen fit to enshrine such rights to do wrong. One further doubts whether any intention to that effect could possibly much explain why our legal system regularly allows conduct greatly at odds with common morality; for even to speak of a moral right to do moral wrong has a quite odd ring in ordinary language and would strike the layperson as thoroughly counterintuitive. Still less could such an intention explain the law's particular doctrinal contours in this regard. Waldron rightly observes that we nonetheless routinely, if implicitly, rely on the notion of a moral right to do moral wrong when we engage in the common practice of "moral and social criticism of someone for the way they exercise their rights."[67]

## Moral Debauchery as a Political Salve

A final explanation offered for disparities between law and common morality is that the law has sometimes allowed to poor people a range of indulgences that elites, those who devise and enforce such law, regard as immoral. These activities, at times beyond the merely lewd or bawdy,[68] permitted the poor to "let off steam" and thereby served as a "safety-valve," releasing accumulated pressures that could easily assume overtly political form. The most renowned and esteemed exponent of this position was its first: Frederick Douglass, who denounced the slaveholder class for manipulating public holidays, during which alcohol was sometimes lavishly distributed with a view to "keeping down the spirit of insurrection." Otherwise, he insisted, "the rigors of bondage would have become too severe for endurance, and the slave would have been forced to a dangerous desperation"[69]—conducive to open revolt. Throughout history, as in dystopian film and fiction, brief release from normal restrictions on "immoral" conduct has taken other, related forms as well. At such moments, the law itself authorizes release from everyday inhibitions, whether formally or informally, "on the books" or "in action." In the latter case, the police are simply instructed to turn a blind eye to most misdemeanors.

The Carnival of medieval and Renaissance Europe, in particular, gave open expression to the inversion of social hierarchies, with the powerless—their faces prudently masked—symbolically assuming the role of elites.[70] The powerful themselves were in turn depicted in grotesque caricature, engaged in disgraceful acts, making them target to ridicule and disdain, even mock violence. Men dressed as women, women as men. Reversing a meaner reality, wives (albeit in costume) semi-playfully "beat" their husbands, whose identity remained concealed as well. In Carnival's classic incarnation, the ruling class and ruling gender were symbolically defenestrated. All the better, scholars argued, to ease their prompt return to pomp and power on the morning of the very next workday, with the deference of their underlings solidly reinstated.[71]

In the early modern period, minor criminal assaults occurring during traditional English festivals received formal exemption from prosecution.[72] In more recent times, legal authorities have enacted, for these few days per year, explicit exceptions to city ordinances barring public nuisance, loitering, vagabondage, and other petty offenses.[73] The mere casting of plastic "throws" by Mardi Gras crews, for instance, whose members include New Orleans's most prominent personages, would amount to multiple littering infractions, each legally 'aggravated' by the preceding. Levying such sanctions would prove highly embarrassing, of course—hence the need for these statutory exemptions.

A New Orleans ordinance today also rehabilitates the moribund "assumption of risk" doctrine to relieve crew members from tort liability for throwing objects that unwittingly cause bodily harm.[74] The public authorities—there as elsewhere[75]—actively organize and commercially promote these festivities, implicating the state in encouraging widespread breach of social mores. Thus, with the law's wink and nod,[76] even its proactive facilitation, conduct once viewed by Catholic theology as unadulterated vice now officially receives free rein, in that very Catholic city, to romp and frolic.

To what end? The safety-valve hypothesis is tantalizing and certainly appealing to anyone with a taste for conspiracy theories and Marxist variants of functionalist sociology; these are arguments that certain practices and institutions come into being because they function to preserve a repressive social order. The defects of such theories, once immensely popular, are today widely acknowledged. And no one has introduced serious evidence from any place or period—despite the considerable sleuthing of innumerable scholars—that, in authorizing a couple days of drunken debauchery, anyone of political significance ever actually thought in these terms. Still less did such savvy, far-sighted elites go about organizing others of their ilk in devising legal dispensations to that effect. There is also far greater evidence, from many more places and periods, that social elites in highly hierarchical societies have generally preferred the repression of nonelite sensuality to its celebration, fearing that—once loosed—it would indeed issue into genuine political unrest, even revolution. Slave masters of the American South, for instance, clearly felt "the greater lapse in mastery" to lie in excessive "laxity," in allowing "too much freedom"[77] to their human possessions, not in their excessive repression.

This is not to deny the possibility that legally endorsed, ritualistic release from social mores may sometimes help preserve the social order, even if no one has ever adduced any real evidence of this.[78] After all, none among those foppish aristocrats or complacent Church elders, upon entering his parish on Lent, seems to have been caught gloating over having just pulled one over on the unsuspecting plebs.[79] And none of the latter seems to have left a record of suddenly renouncing his *resentiment,* concluding—upon recovering from the decadent indecencies of Fat

Tuesday—that all those nasty, dastardly autocrats really weren't such bad sorts after all.

In any event, other learned academicians retort that, whatever the elites may have wished, the legalization of carnivalesque sensuality was, on closer inspection, not really so politically cathartic after all. It showed no evidence of attenuating serious tensions—if indeed any could be empirically discerned—beneath the tranquil surface of daily, manor-house interactions between residents upstairs and down. This is not to imply that Carnival was all "just innocent fun," of course. For the turbulent passions that Carnival undoubtedly uncorked were not only carnal but *moral* as well—passions for justice. How else to decode those flamboyant rituals of socio-symbolic topsy-turvy, hierarchical higgledy-piggledy? The events ensuing in the later stages of these occasions, moreover, often slipped the bounds of law's brief benevolence, suggesting a more serious challenge to prevailing mores and social structures.[80] Properly understood, the socialist scholars intoned, Carnival—and other such lawfully routinized forms of moral transgression—must be understood as a repressed, subterranean expression of revolutionary yearnings among *les misérables*.

It was never clear from this account, though, why the impulse—perfectly intelligible—to periodically escape life's quotidian constraints, the dreary decorum of our constricting societal roles, should be confined to "the dangerous classes." Why wouldn't the rest of us equally appreciate the annual opportunity for an idyllic respite from tiresome courtesies, sundry social inhibitions, and pedestrian decencies toward those we may disdain? Why should only the proletarian rabble have the right to be so rude, behave so outlandishly, have so much fun? And indeed, it turns out that in many places and periods—at least before the Reformation—all socioeconomic groups *did* routinely partake of Carnival's delights,[81] as today's New Orleans Mardi Gras continues to illustrate.[82] This would also suggest that those rigidly repressed elites, often accused of squelching their own unruly passions no less than those of the masses, weren't really so 'puritanical' after all.

So then, was Carnival—and the law authorizing its pleasurable peccadillos—truly a safety-valve, staving off social rebellion, perhaps even consciously advancing that ideological endgame? Or did it represent only the brief sublimation and veiled expression of an incipient sedition that would ultimately, irrepressibly, take more manifestly political shape? Such were the bizarre terms of serious debate for at least a generation, starting (as one might expect) in the late 1960s.[83] It is hard to know where to begin in untangling the twisted knot of conceptual conflations,[84] empirical evasions, murky methodology, and theoretical sloppiness to which both sides in that now-dated—but alas not defunct—debate sadly succumbed.[85]

Leave that for another day. For present purposes it is enough to observe that many reputable observers in several scholarly disciplines for thirty years found quite credible the suggestion that law sometimes authorizes the breach of social mores with a view to venting our pent-up frustrations with the iniquities, otherwise unbearable, of a miserable lot in life. That notion today still lingers as an intellectual cobweb, at least, in the mustier corners of social thought.[86] At its most plausible, it pertains only to depravities far more modest than the serious wrongs I here chiefly discuss. Yet the very gravity of the perceived wrongdoing I proceed to examine ensures that, were it to go wholly unchecked, it would throw into disarray some central lineaments of moral order; it could thereby overpower common practices of rights-restraint that equilibrate many of today's social conflicts and controversies. And all that without any nefarious, cabalistic machinations from those peering down on us from power's commanding heights.

There is reason to suspect that fear of revolution may have done more to raise moral standards among the elite than to bring about their legal lowering among the downtrodden. One historian observes that, during and shortly following the French Revolution in particular, influential English publicists urged a "conspicuous piety . . . at least the appearance of virtue"[87] among ruling elites. These publicists believed that the upper orders of British society inevitably set the moral tenor for the country at large, offering exemplars "whence the vulgar draw their habits." Satirical broadsides, widely circulated, were then "lifting the lid on the seamy world of upper-class sexual depravity," lampooning flagrant, notorious incidents of adultery, gambling, alcoholism, out of wedlock births, and divorce among the aristocracy. The view was then generally shared among the landed classes that the stability of public order rested upon popular belief in their own ethical integrity, in their evident adherence to moral standards governing matters most people today would view as private. Hence the perceived "urgency of self-reform," as revolutionary fervor convulsed the Continent, as the conduct and moral character of the hereditary rich came under unprecedented public scrutiny. This urgency would soon find legal expression in such proposed legislation as the Adultery Prevention Bill of 1800.[88]

Such are the chief sources and significance of incongruities between the law and common morality, illustrated with some examples of their location across the legal landscape. These sources are far more numerous than those to which we now turn in Chapter 7—those that tend to bring law and morality into accord, though there is here no necessary "strength in numbers." Still, the forces militating in favor of convergence are in many legal areas considerably weaker than those against it. This helps to explain, and to locate within social space, the vast reach of rights to engage in conduct widely regarded as seriously wrongful.

# 7

# Convergences of Law and Morals

## Sites and Sources

Having examined the forces driving law and common morality apart, let us now consider where and why the two sometimes come into greatest harmony.

The incidence of overlap turns out to be less frequent than suggested by the classical sociological view of Durkheim, Pound, Holmes, and early socio-legal scholars, whose theories (rehearsed in Chapter 5) lead us to expect the terrain of these respective normative orders to be virtually coterminous. The overlap is nonetheless much greater than one would expect from a straightforward application of public choice theory—that is, from the most influential 'sophisticated' account of contemporary lawmaking. This theory, we saw, derides as naive the expectation of any such congruence at all, except perhaps where the material interests of well-organized rent-seekers somehow coincidentally match others' moral understandings.

That unabashedly cynical view of law's relation to common morality, however, leaves far too much of legislative life and output unexplained (this chapter will show), indeed utterly mysterious. Any effort to ascribe disparities between the claims of law and common morals to single-minded rent-seeking thus proves overconfident and incomplete, at best. This approach is misguided not least in its indifference to the question of when people consider such disparities intolerable. For these very intolerances regularly turn out to influence how much (and which elements) of common morality the law will later proceed to incorporate and which it will continue to leave aside. It is therefore impossible to disregard, even for strictly explanatory purposes, the reasons people offer one another—within legislatures, en banc judiciaries, over kitchen tables—when voicing dissatisfaction with the law, whether they view it as overly lenient or too stringent. The challenge for socio-legal theory here is therefore to identify the empirical strengths and weaknesses of these contending theories, each wildly overreaching in its claims; and because both approaches so frequently collapse, this task (pursued in this chapter and in Chapter 6) demands that we descend into enough empirical detail to locate the actual situations where, and real reasons why, law and morals move into and out of harmony. This requires a finer-grained analysis, with a greater sensitivity to contextual variation, than either of those dueling grand theories deigns to offer.

## Points of Empirical Convergence

In seeking sites of confluence between law and common morality, a few data-points immediately suggest themselves, within the law of tort, contract, crime, evidence, and intellectual property. The following observations are confessedly sketchy, sometimes quite speculative, and intended chiefly to prompt further reflection and inquiry by others, those specializing in any number of discrete legal fields.

### *Tort Law*

Empirical research in experimental psychology discloses that common morality tracks the law of tort in largely accepting the familiar distinction between corrective justice and distributive justice. Tort law devotes itself to the first of these objectives, and most respondents believe it right to do so.[1]

The law of "negligence," in particular, governs vast areas of our lives and, in doing so, incorporates prevailing notions of morally acceptable or "reasonable" conduct. These establish the "standard of care" governing when we will be civilly liable for harms we unintentionally cause to others. To determine the reasonableness of a given act or practice is chiefly an empirical inquiry, turning heavily upon the contours of common morality, deviating from this touchstone only very rarely.[2] In other words, it is the moral expectations most widespread within society (or some pertinent portion thereof) that determine where the line will lie between reasonable behavior on our part and our imposition of unreasonable risk on those around us. By incorporating a broad and important slice of common morality, the law of negligence thus places great confidence in the vitality and defensibility of prevailing ethical sensibilities. Tellingly, it is usually a jury of laypersons, not the judge, who—as better Geiger counters of prevailing moral sentiment—make these determinations at trial. The question for fact-finders is always: Would a reasonable individual or institution within our society, in the defendant's place, have taken greater care against the risk that here materialized? Would he or it have displayed greater concern for the well-being or dignity of the claimant before this court?

With other tort actions, courts invoke social mores in fleshing out key terms within statutes or judge-made law. These torts are obscenity,[3] defamation, privacy invasion, false arrest, intentional infliction of emotional distress, and offensive battery (without accompanying physical injury). All expressly incorporate community standards of "offensiveness," "outrageousness," or community "expectations," deciding live disputes on this empirically elusive basis. And historically, the law of punitive damages instructed jurors to ask themselves simply whether the defendant's conduct is not merely unlawful, but also "shocks the conscience" of their community.

### *Contract Law*

Within the United States, at least, the law of contract finds its sociological footing within common morality as well, if in a somewhat different way. American law professors report that nearly all of contract law (in contrast to the law of evidence) elicits in their first-semester students an almost immediate, intuitive recognition of its ethical acceptability, even obvious correctness. The right to enter into mutually binding agreements, with only the fewest restrictions (against force and fraud), reflects the wide compass that we Americans, in particular, accord the principle of personal autonomy to choose the terms and conditions of our duties to others. This is the rationale most often proffered for contractual freedom,[4] though "reasonable reliance" on raised expectations provides a further basis, at times, for enforcing a promise or other representation.[5] When a contractual dispute comes before a court, the judge will often formally presume, until shown otherwise, that the autonomy principle has found adequate expression within the agreement.[6] That legal presumption reflects our factual assumption that, when entering a contract, most people are indeed exercising the personal autonomy that our social mores so highly prize.

Enhancing liberty is the aim of even our rules on "mutual mistake"[7] and "impossibility" of performance,[8] exempting counterparties from their formal commitments. For these rules limit the scope of enforceable duties to those that the parties could themselves possibly have accepted. "Default rules"[9] may appear different in this respect, in that they fill gaps in what parties actually agreed to, and hence do not give expression to anyone's genuine acts of choice. Increasing numbers of judges—influenced here by economic analysis—now believe, however, that default rules should impose the terms that parties would themselves have reached had they considered the question, possessed all relevant information, and incurred no transaction costs.[10] This sort of autonomous choice is admittedly "constructive" or "fictional," in the jurisprudential sense. Yet the intended result of this interpretive strategy, like those preceding, is the same as if the voluntary consent were actual.

With a further view to keeping law in sync with common morality, the Uniform Commercial Code encourages courts to resolve contract disputes between businesses on the basis of widely accepted practices and usage of terms within the relevant trade or industrial sector.[11] Drafters even contemplated that juries would be composed entirely of fellow traders and merchants, people intimately familiar with the thick social mores of the pertinent vocational milieu.[12] However, empirical studies of several trade communities suggest that when their intramural disputes reach the courts, judges find it very difficult to incorporate these mores.[13] The evidence necessary to prove their existence, and that the parties in question had them in mind when forming their agreement, is often weak. When reading contracts that are incomplete and gap-ridden, most judges hence prefer a more formalistic approach to interpretation. The "relational" alternative (as it is called), committed to unearthing implicit mores, simply proves beyond their competence, and therefore unworkable.[14] This means that the relevant mores do not in fact so often become infused into the law through judicial decision-making. These particular mores continue to exercise their influence on commercial conduct in ways effectively beyond law's reach, resembling in this respect most others here examined.

International commercial arbitrators periodically invoke a transnational form of customary law—the so-called *lex mercatoria*—allegedly springing from prevailing commercial mores. This body of law was said to encompass the general principle of "good faith."[15] This appeal to good faith offers yet another doctrinal device for incorporating prevailing moral sensibilities into the law. Empirical studies again counsel skepticism, though. Historical evidence indicates that at least medieval and Renaissance merchant courts and arbitrators hardly ever drew upon any recognizable set of commercial mores, certainly none so far-reaching as their trading networks.[16] Merchants themselves considered their mores, such as they were, too unstable and variable between regions to provide a solid, predictable basis for resolving their disputes. This community, covering a vast geography and of great economic significance, was apparently engaged in serious if informal self-regulation. Yet its members consistently declined to seek the legal incorporation of any international mores.

Though many contracts grant one party the unilateral right to decide a given issue, they also explicitly prohibit him from acting unreasonably. Where the contract itself does not expressly so provide, rules of common law may be drawn upon to yield the same result. The effect is to allow multiple angles of entry, in the event of dispute, for common morality into a contract's interpretation.

Psychological experiments suggest that their moral intuitions lead most people to reject the notion of "efficient breach"—that one may violate one's contractual duties as long as one is prepared to pay for harm thereby caused.[17] It is unclear, in any event, whether the law itself truly authorizes such conduct, a question that turns largely on what one means by "truly authorize." If the law does not do so, as most courts would say, then it closely tracks common morality here too. Still, it is fair to observe that contract law affords less significance than does common morality to the defendant's motives for breaching a binding agreement.

"Unconscionability" departs from contract's core principle, in blocking judicial enforcement of certain kinds of voluntary agreements—for instance, freely to sell oneself into slavery. Some judges of liberal political persuasion once experimented, in the late 1960s and early 1970s, with reading this doctrine in ways unprecedentedly broad.[18] Today, though, it is successful at trial only in very narrow circumstances,[19] where contractual terms are so flagrantly oppressive that prevailing public sensibilities would not endorse their enforcement. Through the doctrine of "good faith," however, European law continues to advance where U.S. law generally retreats.[20] In both places, those whose "conscience" must be "shocked" to trigger these doctrines are not judges alone, but the relevant community, as best the judge can determine this. Both doctrines were designed to bring the judicial interpretation of agreements into consonance with common morality where its demands are extremely exigent yet manage to escape law's more specific embodiment. The law of unconscionability tracks prevailing moral sentiments insofar as most people deem certain agreements simply too unfair to justify judicial enforcement, to warrant this questionable use of the state's coercive power.[21]

### *Criminal Law*

Criminal law offers a third legal field whose rules today closely approximate the terms of common morality. A considerable body of careful social science, inviting survey participants to assess detailed factual scenarios of arguable wrongdoing, finds few significant disparities between the two.[22] The notable work of Paul H. Robinson concludes that the U.S. Model Penal Code, in particular, adopts "an unspoken principle of heeding lay intuitions of justice . . . on issues touching essentially all criminal cases."[23] Where respondents disagreed with the Code's approach to a given question, they turned out to prefer earlier, long-standing rules of common law, rather than departing from recognizably legal standards altogether. This was true, for instance, in their greater emphasis on the defendant's completed acts and the harm he actually posed or caused, rather than his mental state (*mens rea*) and the probability of success as he perceived it.[24]

This congruence between law and lay morals is evident not only on matters of broad principle. Robinson and other criminal law empiricists find convergence concerning some very rarefied doctrinal details. These include the details of our rules on fraud,[25] insider trading on corporate information,[26] and the distinctions between different types of robbery.[27] The congruity extends even to such seemingly abstruse questions as what it means to "excuse"[28] a defendant's misconduct. Like their law, most Americans understand this notion to entail a complete defense, to exculpate rather than merely mitigate. And like the law, they understand a legal excuse as vitiating the defendant's blameworthiness while leaving the wrongfulness of his conduct intact—seemingly a fine point indeed.

These studies nonetheless do discover a few discrepancies between law and morals. If asked, the public would, for instance, extend criminal liability to far more instances of "negligent" misconduct than does the law.[29] They would also punish those who fail to act as "good Samaritans," who forego the chance to save another's life when at no risk to their own.[30] Yet though American law declines to criminalize this kind of wrongful omission, much of the globe does so, including most of Continental Europe, at least "on the books." In a small number of other contexts, by contrast, the American respondents view criminal acts somewhat more indulgently than do our legal rules. This is true of "unconsummated attempts," "felony-murder,"[31] and euthanasia.[32] Laypeople were also more forgiving than that law toward those who "stand their ground," employing lethal force where they could instead safely retreat.[33] Elsewhere, as for certain types of perjury and bribery, most people are more demanding of their fellow citizens than is the law.[34]

Available data suggest that prevailing moral opinion is also at odds several sentence-enhancing doctrines, such as "three strikes," mandatory minima, the prosecution of juveniles as adults, strict liability, and the narrowing of the insanity defense.[35] In these instances, common morality is less punitive than a well-settled jurisprudence. Finally, whereas criminal law now consolidates theft offenses under a single category, most people continue to draw distinctions of moral gradation on the prior basis of the type of property involved and the means by which it was wrongfully taken.[36] It is nonetheless fair to describe nearly all these areas of discrepancy between existing rules and prevailing morals as lying rather far from the core activity of criminal law, certainly in comparison to such central matters as the "grading" of offenses and of mental states for their relative wrongfulness.[37] (Alas, no one has yet done, for any other area of law, what Robinson and co-authors, plus Green and Kugler, have done for criminal, which requires us to rely, in further fields, on indicators less methodologically punctilious.)

For centuries Western societies have criminalized essentially all forms of conduct that almost everyone regards as highly wrongful. Only at the margins and interstices of current rules does one observe any serious, present-day efforts to criminalize still further; these efforts entail plugging relatively small gaps,[38] rather than opening whole new vistas for the criminal justice system. Some of these new crimes, such as schoolyard bullying,[39] involve wrongdoing already long subject to civil liability, now simply deemed more serious in moral import than before, deserving of greater sanction. Where Americans today apparently seek more substantial change, it is in the frequency of prosecution and severity of punishment, notably for corporate fraud,[40] rather than within the terms of legal prohibitions themselves.

Congress has also thought it necessary to revise federal criminal law in certain respects to address contemporary terrorism. These recent statutes penalize "material support" for organizations the State Department designates in this fashion,[41] and effectively transform conduct traditionally considered mere "aiding and abetting" into forms of perpetration,[42] facilitating their more severe sanction. This legislation encompasses circumstances where the defendant might not necessarily have known to what end his "support" would ultimately be employed. Given the intense public concern and indignation immediately following the 9/11 attacks, when the relevant statute was first enacted,[43] we may infer that this legislative extension of criminal law was entirely consistent with prevailing moral sentiment of the day, registering itself quite directly upon a bipartisan legislative process.

Virtually no one questions the serious wrongfulness of the conduct prohibited by any of the major offenses at common law: murder, armed robbery, rape, and so forth. It is only a few of the statutory additions to the criminal code, notably drug use and small-scale possession—relatively recent, historically speaking—that give rise to live controversy over continued criminalization. Many people across the American political spectrum, studies suggest,[44] have in recent years come to regard as deeply draconian the official federal guidelines for sentencing certain kinds of drug offenders. Today there also exist serious doubts among the well-informed—those familiar with sentencing metrics in other advanced Western democracies—over the disproportionate severity of our penal sanctions even for crimes much more serious. These reservations are moral in nature, insofar as they find their basis in concerns about injustice to defendants. Still, there is somewhat less indication that these concerns have much reached the mass public, among whom strong retributive winds of "penal populism"[45] still sometimes blow, especially during violent "crime waves," as in the "crack" epidemic of the 1980s and 1990s.

It would nonetheless be a mistake to concentrate on the few, isolated areas of divergence, recent or long-standing, between common morality and criminal law. For present purposes it is more essential to acknowledge and account for the wide swatches of intimate consonance between law and contemporary morals. Yet because criminal law relies so heavily on statutes, it generally employs strategies of moral incorporation very different from those in contract or tort. The interpretive maxim that penal prohibitions must be "strictly construed"—that is, in favor of the defendant when their terms are not abundantly clear—precludes any easy evocation of diffuse community standards as the basis of legal liability. For these standards, when they exist, are often amorphous, certainly at the edges, and evolve over time in ways often elusive to adequate anticipation of how they may be applied to one's actions post facto.

There are discrete pockets of criminal law where the law nevertheless finds it impossible to fully codify its prohibitions entirely in advance of contemplated action. The crime of battery, like the tort bearing the same name, prohibits "offensive" touching, requiring jurors to fill in the content of that term with their best understanding of prevailing mores. The criminal offenses of extortion and blackmail make similar moves. They prohibit the threat to reveal secrets likely to expose a victim to "hatred, contempt, or ridicule."[46] With these three crimes, at least, to grasp the relevant law demands that one plumb the content of current 'extralegal' mores.[47]

It bears emphasis that none of the legal rules expressly incorporating an evolving common morality—in tort, contract, and criminal law—can do so if there in fact exists no such morality to begin with. Here again we find that, in a particularly conspicuous way, the law's effective workings depend on the vigor and vitality of the social mores to which it must defer, yet over which it can rarely exert much influence.

### *Intellectual Property*

In recent years the law of copyright presented a notable contrast to that of contract, negligence, and crime, as just described. The generous protections afforded to holders of copyright fell decidedly out of sync for a number of years with the moral sentiments of large numbers of young people. Hundreds of millions throughout the world felt no compunction about illegally sharing files of their favorite music and movies,[48] inflicting billions in damage on copyright-holders, including struggling musicians. Though no one doubted the illegality of such conduct, few violators apparently found in it anything seriously objectionable, viewing it as "victimless crime," on a par (at worst) with prostitution and marijuana consumption.[49]

Moral censure was in fact reserved instead for the huge corporate entities, such as Sony Inc., when these went so far as to file suit against a small number of individual file-sharers. Over time the problem partly resolved itself, not through changes in either copyright or prevailing moral sentiment, but through new business models enabling consumers to purchase songs and videos online, for streaming or downloading at modest expense.[50] This new model did depend on a species of legal change, but only through the network of contracts entailed in implementing it, not through revision to statute or common law.

### *Judge-Made Law versus Legislation*

From its beginnings in seventeenth-century England, copyright has been more dependent on legislation than has the law of contract, crime, or negligence. The latter three legal fields were almost entirely the creation of common-law judges. This is not to imply that common law and common morality tend strongly to flow in tandem, more than legislation, throughout their history. When we describe the law as "common," we refer simply to the fact that it applied to the entire realm of England, rather than only to certain parts. Historically this law was the creation of the socioeconomic elites who sat upon the bench, in nondemocratic eras much less egalitarian in ethos and social structure than our own. There is no reason to suppose that the moral sensibilities of these legal dignitaries in early modern England bore any close relation on many important issues to those of most other British subjects of the time.

This was especially so with respect to the common law of theft, and almost certainly that of private property generally, since most people possessed very little, certainly nothing of commercial significance.[51] Copyright is itself a form of private property owned almost exclusively, then as now, by the highly educated, at least, and often by those with other, more material forms of capital as well. The creation of elites in a monarchical and aristocratic age,[52] touching upon matters remote from the daily affairs of most subjects, copyright did not speak to the morals of common people, which in turn did not speak to it.

There are good grounds to suspect that elite and non-elite views would have stood leagues apart not only on moral issues concerning early capitalism and the law embodying it. The common law of evidence continues to harbor certain major "testimonial exclusions"—notably the prohibition on hearsay—originating historically in a pervasive judicial doubt about the mental capacities and political trustworthiness of jurors.[53] In bench trials, judges today nonetheless often admit hearsay evidence, granting themselves a de facto exception to its continuing strictures.[54] We must surmise that jurors would do the same if given the chance. It is clear that hearsay—perfectly admissible in most courts throughout the world—is often "probative" and hence legally "relevant" to assessing a case, however little "weight" jurors or judges may conclude it ultimately merits. In sum, there can be little doubt that this age-old evidentiary prohibition—others too, perhaps, such as the priest–penitent privilege—now deviates from prevailing moral sensibilities among lawyers and laypersons alike.

I have said that, in light of the social rank its early authors enjoyed, there would be no reason to anticipate that the common law, including that of evidence and property, would track common morality very closely. And yet, very often it does just that, as indicated in my observations concerning the current law of contract, negligence, and crime, fields created by common-law judges and rendered into statute only much later.[55] This invites the hypothesis, worthy of investigation, that modern courts have glacially revised these three fields over time so as to bring them more closely into harmony with the prevailing public morals of societies whose standards of ethical appraisal in key respects no longer diverge so starkly along socioeconomic lines.

Still, it would be very odd if even contemporary common law were to harmonize with common morality more than the legislation of modern democracies, the law enacted by elected legislators and executives. Legislators are far more vulnerable than judges to displacement through infusions of public sentiment and opinion. Those owing their position to these periodic interjections would therefore seem more likely receptive to promptings of common morality than federal judges at least, those enjoying life tenure[56] and elevated into office through appointment by like-minded political elites. In some parts of the world, the institution of public referendum—more readily than ordinary legislation—allows still greater, direct input of popular sentiment into lawmaking.[57] Yet on issues where organized interest groups "capture" the legislative process,[58] and indeed directly write much legislation,[59] there is no reason to assume that legislators will be any more attentive than judges to even the clearest indicators of profound public indignation at perceived injustice. Alas, we lack satisfactory methods—social scientific, historiographical, legal doctrinal—to convincingly answer the question of whether judge-made law or enacted law is more likely to cleave to common morality.

Some appear confident they know the answer, at least with respect to their particular professional bailiwick. They make this point most often concerning the regulation of particular industries whose legislative influence meets little resistance from an unwitting public. It is true that a federal judge enjoys greater independence from lobbyists than do legislators, but this need not render her more consistently responsive to common morality, even when clear. And state judges who must stand for electoral retention may face incentives little different in this regard from those of legislators, certainly those without "safe seats."

If *any* generalization seems warranted, it is that neither source of law, legislative or judicial, more consistently tracks common morality than the other, across the entire panorama of legal life. The better part of wisdom here—as in other, equally overheated theoretical debates here engaged—is simply, for now, to resist the temptation to overgeneralization.

Let us now observe and examine several reasons for the congruities observed between law and common morality. These reasons assume different import within various legal fields and for particular doctrines within them. Identifying the distinct locations within the law where each reason for confluence becomes most influential offers a fruitful point of entry for fathoming the place of rights to do wrong within our legal and social order. Particular rights and the rules creating or abolishing them assume their shifting shape, define their exact contours, at the intersection of the forces moving law and morality into alignment and forcing them apart.

Legal scholars will rightly say that the law of tort and contract, at least, so closely track common morality because they pervasively employ the doctrines of "reasonableness" and "good faith" (in Europe). Though that observation is correct, it is unresponsive to the question of why certain bodies of law come to employ such mechanisms of continuing moral incorporation at all, so extensively, whereas others do not, or only much less so. In other words, what is it within a given social order, within human experience generally perhaps, that leads particular bundles of legal rules to so thoroughly incorporate the common morality of the people they will govern?

## Sources of Convergence

There are three factors regularly working to bring law and common morality into accord. On their basis it is possible to venture some predictions about where, in what areas of social life, this accordance will likely be greatest, ceteris paribus. There is no need here to take sides over whether these factors mostly operate directly upon lawmakers' reasoning, largely unmediated by complex institutional processes, or instead through more circuitous causal paths, an issue assayed in Chapter 5. That is an empirical question we must independently pose in each case of interest to us.

The law is most likely to incorporate an element of common morality when many people *intensely care* about the issue at hand, to which their concerns attach. This caring has two conceptual elements. First, the issue must acquire mental "salience," in the terminology of cognitive psychology,[60] so that it stands out prominently from competing claims upon our attention. For salience to endure, it must enhance our appreciation of the issue's deep or lasting importance in our lives, which makes us more likely to act upon our understanding of it. Moralizing an issue is one major and frequent way to render it more salient. For once it is construed to fall within "the circumstances of justice,"[61] people are no longer prepared to allocate its competent appraisal entirely to those qualified to employ pertinent scientific standards. We no longer so confidently "leave it to the professionals." Salience in the public mind is neither necessary nor sufficient for legal change, notably so where well-organized rent-seeking and agency capture occurs. Yet salience can and does often make a considerable contribution.

Though moralization increases salience, there are other sources of salience besides moralization. And in any event, we must ask what factors increase the chances that an issue will become moralized. Ordinary language throughout the Western world has been quite consistent in recent decades concerning which issues count as "moral"[62]: those involving marriage, human reproduction, and the end of life (including euthanasia, assisted suicide, and—in the United States—capital punishment). This folk categorization is nonetheless inadequate to social scientific purposes, because (as explained earlier) nearly any issue, in the proper circumstances and the right hands, is capable of arousing indignation at injustice. Even so, though it is conceivable in theory that any matter might be moralized, certain aspects of life appear more readily amenable to this distinctive social classification than do others. Apart from the deliberate moralization campaigns of political activists, by what other routes might certain issues acquire the measure of salience necessary to exert much influence upon the law?

### *How Often Do We Directly Encounter a Legal Rule in Our Daily Lives?*

A first source of salience is the regularity with which most people confront a certain body of legal rules in their ordinary experience. One might hypothesize that the more frequently we personally experience the events triggering a given rule's application, the more salient a place it will occupy within our minds; and the greater the dissatisfaction we will then feel if the rule wanders markedly off the path of common morality. These dissatisfactions would in turn tend, other things equal, to find their way into the lawmaking process, drawing the content of legality into closer correspondence with this morality. Thus, we enter into contracts on almost a daily basis, and contract law—its most essential principles—tracks common morality very closely. And as Luker writes of abortion, "perhaps because pregnancy is such a common experience in all corners of the social world, people have firsthand ideas and feelings about it and are less willing to defer to experts."[63] At the other end of the spectrum we find legal rights and rules that, though of great import to a small number of people, rarely touch the lives of many, certainly not very directly: the ancient "rule against perpetuities"[64] in property law offers a clear instance.

This general hypothesis is certainly plausible, and almost certainly explains some nontrivial portion of the empirical variance. It is nonetheless extremely difficult to test, and—with any precision—impossibly so. A legal rule may enter our awareness in a number of ways, some of these unrelated to the frequency of our immediate encounter with it. A given rule sometimes taps us firmly upon the shoulder as we go about our lives, influencing decisions we must take on a regular basis. Such rules include those governing how physicians may interact acceptably with their patients, and how parents may treat their children. The law of civil negligence governs at least a dozen choices we must make every day of our lives, as when backing our car out of the driveway and onto the street.

Other bodies of legal rules, such as those of antitrust and administrative law, lie quite distant from the ordinary person's routine experience. In the United States, administrative law has profound consequences for the making of public policy. Yet there exists no common morality at all in respect to its details, only as regards "thin" principles of due process applicable there but also in legal places far beyond. Most people are only very dimly aware, if at all, that this important legal field exists. The law of antitrust differs slightly here in that it taps into common morality at least obliquely; educated Americans at least vaguely appreciate the importance of competitive markets to economic efficiency and hence to the general well-being. Examples of legal fields at other points along this spectrum come quickly to mind: few people encounter firsthand the rules that criminalize grand larceny. And hardly any—certainly among the American middle and upper-middle class—will in their lives become victim of a major violent crime.

Yet murder and larceny are staple, even inexhaustible, themes of popular entertainment. This likely owes to the fact that certain forms of wrongdoing trigger questions intrinsically central to the human condition. Such questions thus become more psychologically salient in the mind than one would anticipate from their remoteness to everyday experience. This is one reason the criminal justice system and the legal rules it enforces enter actively and regularly into our consciousness. We are often free to decide—as by choosing what to watch on TV or at the movies, and what kind of fiction to read—just how salient within our mental lives to make a given activity; and hence, too, how salient will be the legal rules shown to govern it. Salience is thus not entirely forced upon us, and need not arise through regular face-to-face encounters.[65]

Even once we admit this qualification, the hypothesis that direct personal experience with an issue renders it psychologically salient, and thereby draws law's attention to it, confronts some glaring counterexamples. The recent experience with rampant violations of music copyright must undermine any simplistic expectation that the relative number of people directly encountering the law's workings within their daily lives would somehow bring about a closer fit between common morality and the law. In that experience, by no means entirely resolved after several years,[66] direct encounters with applicable legal rules not only were frequent but concerned issues highly salient in the minds of millions of music consumers throughout the world. One could easily enumerate other circumstances where conspicuous breaches between law and common morality endured on a given matter for long periods despite its acute salience in many minds. Yet it is also true, in the case of music file-sharing, that the very pressure placed upon the law by common morality and the illegal behavior thereby massively engendered played a great role in prompting the creation, within less than a decade, of a novel contractual armature significantly redressing the conflict.

### *How Greatly Do These Rules Affect Our Collective Life?*

This question suggests a second source of salience, and hence too of convergence between law and common morality. The question arises whether or not we directly encounter the workings of these rules or the activities they regulate in our ordinary life experience. Certain kinds of misconduct, more than others, exercise a significant impact on the public at large, often in ways that cannot easily escape detection. We might hypothesize that those much affected will readily identify, and then call lawmakers' attention to, how current rules grievously depart from prevailing moral standards.

Thus, for example, American law treats corporations—not just their top managers—as possessing moral agency and therefore susceptible to penal sanction. When Americans themselves are asked whether they find this intelligible and defensible, they concur, notwithstanding the inherently abstract and legal-fictional nature of any corporate entity.[67] One likely explanation is that Americans have become increasingly aware in recent decades that large-scale corporate conduct, as in an oil spill or a product fraudulently represented, can greatly affect their own personal well-being.

Though perfectly plausible, this hypothesis, like the preceding, demands qualification. It is true that there are wide-scale forms of perceived misconduct—lawful and otherwise—that easily draw the immediate heed of the many people thus victimized. Yet other forms, equally far-reaching in effect, elude detection for long periods, or never at all become widely known; information asymmetries—between wrongdoers and those they wrong—prove insurmountable. Here we might contrast the perceived misconduct giving rise, respectively, to a large oil spill in a well-traveled sea lane, on the one hand, and the sophisticated design of aggressive tax shelters or the intra-firm "transfer pricing" practices of multinational corporations,[68] on the other.

All three forms of conduct may contravene prevalent moral sensibilities, and all have substantial socioeconomic effect. Yet only the first is legible to the untrained eye; the second and third become conspicuous only very rarely, as when many well-known companies formally relocate offshore to tax haven jurisdictions. Of these three types of perceived misconduct, that involving waterway contamination is much more likely to draw the awareness and stir the passions of citizens, and hence too of democratic lawmakers. Its likely effect upon vast numbers of humans and on nonhuman forms of life is, through mass media coverage, virtually transparent, hence highly salient. In fact, with all these forms of perceived misconduct by large businesses, it is more the degree of information asymmetry than the magnitude of wrongs or harms themselves that explains the measure of common morality's incorporation by the law.

### *How Closely Does a Given Issue Lie to the Very* Core *of Common Morality?*

We might anticipate that the law would tend increasingly to approximate the terms of common morality insofar as a matter subject to potential regulation touches closely upon social mores and principles widely deemed most fundamental, often raising the most vexing and profound questions. Certain bodies of law and particular doctrines within them meet this test more than do others, and hence occupy a greater salience within our minds and hearts. For instance, only very rarely in her life, and often with little impact on others already born, does a Western woman face the question of whether it is morally acceptable to abort a fetus she carries. Yet women regularly report that the moral magnitude and existential stakes of the decision, when in fact personally confronted, can be life-altering, inducing a reversal in their prior views on the normative question, in either direction.

Even when rates of violent crime are low, penal law (both substantive and procedural) registers more prominently than nearly any other legal field within the consciousness of most ordinary Americans, as in many societies. Other, less colorful areas of law we more often palpably encounter in our daily lives, exerting equal or greater impact upon our well-being, individual and collective. Yet certain legal rules touch us where we live, as it were, arouse the most primordial emotions, likely hardwired into our brains through evolution of the species. Violent crime and the law's response to it often evoke the strongest moral sentiments, largely retributive (those of the brain's "System 1,"[69] in the lexicon of contemporary psychology), and raise the deepest existential doubts, for reasons I'll suggest.

Empirical studies in experimental philosophy show clearly that retributive impulses, rationalized deontologically, are far more potent within prevailing attitudes toward crime than are concerns with deterrence and incapacitation.[70] In fact, it is only a slight exaggeration to observe that, with regard to serious criminal wrongs, common morality is nearly indifferent to utilitarian considerations of the general population's well-being. Concerns of that sort seem coldly consequentialist, requiring that we make the considerable mental effort to retrieve the content of our brain's "System 2." Such carefully reasoned deliberations are not what truly drive the periodic popular demands to "get tough on crime." As Judith Shklar observed, "For most people, retributive justice *is* justice."[71] And to do retributive justice, no close expert analysis of aggregate data on punishment's deterrent effects is required—or particularly welcome.

The strong reactions, emotional and existential, aroused by violent crime are presumably a major reason so many people choose to entertain themselves with the salacious YouTube postings, tabloid reporting, television programs, and movies concerning such wrongs. Some forms of illegality, like first-degree murder, grant extravagant rein to these moral sentiments, whereas others—*mala prohibita* rules, in particular—do so scarcely at all; with the latter, we feel indignation only when their violation happens, on particular facts, to endanger lives. When a given practice strongly evokes our retributive sentiments, we are especially unlikely to tolerate its legal regulation in ways wildly at odds with these reactive attitudes.

First-degree murder contravenes our deepest fears and firmly-held convictions concerning the inviolable dignity of human life. Especially when it occurs in some proximity to us, an act of murder also compels a revisiting of everyday assumptions about how much trust we may confidently place in those around us. Murder thus not merely reminds us of the inherent frailty of any individual's life. It also intimates the fragility of "the social contract." These are the most basic arrangements by which we implicitly agree (at a minimum) to forego our violent impulses, in exchange for protection from the state against the violence others would do us. Debates over the precise terms of this contract are less important here than the simple fact that its very contemplation calls prominently to mind, often with some intensity, the most elemental questions and lurking concerns about the fact that we necessarily spend our time on earth among some who wish us ill, at times passionately so.

This also helps explain why so much criminal prohibition of interpersonal violence, in particular, comports very closely with the contours of common morality. For the law of violent crime seeks to redress those forms of misconduct most highly offensive to the moral principles dissuading us from acting upon our very worst impulses, never far from the surface of many lives. These principles centrally define our common morality. This is why it is intelligible—as we vaguely intone in the first ten minutes of every introductory course on criminal law—to speak of the true victim of all criminal activity as "society at large."

The law of civil negligence raises questions about the human condition nearly as fundamental as those in criminal law, if perhaps less transparently so. This area of tort poses a decisive issue about social reciprocity: In any acceptable moral order, how much risk of serious harm is it permissible for us to foist on others, and how much should we ourselves fairly expect to assume in our relations with them? The answers to this question too, like those at the core of criminal law, establish the central terms of shared existence with others and hence speak to the very nature of "the social bond," in a given time and place. Though necessarily abstract, this puzzle bears closely on how we conduct our daily lives, often eliciting an apprehension greater than many others matters the law addresses. It is therefore unsurprising that our law here gravitates into especially intimate congruity with common morality.

This chapter has briefly identified some of the major sites and sources of convergence between common morality and the law. I have sought to pose new questions and gesture at how we might begin to answer them, without urging firm conclusions. With frequent references to relevant illustrations, I have hypothesized that, despite a few necessary qualifications, a given matter or activity will attain psychological salience and become legally cognizable insofar as it increases in three respects. These are (1) how frequently we encounter it within our immediate face-to-face interactions, (2) how greatly and conspicuously it injures large numbers of people, and (3) how profoundly it challenges the most central, core principles of common morality, those raising transcendent questions of timeless concern about the nature and meaning of life with others.

What I have offered here are mere speculations, though informed by relevant evidence, where pertinent and available. They operate at a level of generality rather higher than any of this study's other chapters. Our methodological tools remain too crude to confidently assert that any of the three contributing factors, alone or in conjunction, actually explains very much of the empirical variance in how greatly the law comports with common morality on a given issue, in a particular society. The modest purpose of this chapter has therefore been simply to sketch a few provisional hypotheses and join them to a few concrete examples, in hopes of prompting more sustained inquiry into how they may bear upon many areas of the law, beyond those few here summarily surveyed.

# 8

# Questions of Method and Meaning

## The Law at Odds with Common Morality

The configuration of social forces reflected in rights to do wrong involve the opposite of a more familiar situation: where the law prohibits an activity, perhaps even criminalizes it, yet there is little effort at enforcement. That scenario generally occurs when moral opinion has so shifted that few now regard the activity as wrong, or few at least still find it so objectionable as to warrant public expense in its discouragement.[1] The upshot is a de facto authorization of what remains proscribed de jure. Thus, for instance, in several U.S. states, "blue laws" continue to prohibit businesses from operating on Sundays[2]—laws never enforced. Similarly, and more politically significant, to protect fundamental human rights the world sometimes tacitly acquiesces in (indeed, sometimes privately encourages) violent forms of "humanitarian intervention" unauthorized by the UN Security Council and prohibited by the UN Charter.

No less intriguing, and certainly far less closely examined, is the opposite of such situations, where we permit de jure what we prohibit de facto. One aim of this book is to help us in assessing when and whether we should place our collective trust in such extralegal regulation. The answer depends on two considerations. First, what are the reasons for particular breaches between law and common morality? Which of the several forces driving the two apart, those discussed in Chapter 6, are at work in a given circumstance? Are they influential, inevitable, and defensible in the situation at hand? At times there will be a number of these forces at once potently in play. Second, how strong and salutary are the social mores potentially at work in closing the resulting gap between what law allows and what a shared moral order reproaches? Do these significantly diminish any need for the law's greater intercession, with all the perils that itself can entail, as by crowding out more spontaneous sources of salutary behavior?[3]

This is not to imply that "private ordering" is necessarily or even presumptively superior to public, as both libertarians and religious conservatives often believe.[4] Nor should there be a presumption *against* such ordering, a view common among progressives, who today often deny the very existence of any inherently private realm demanding unqualified legal protection.[5] My point is simply that when creating and interpreting our law, we must become more reflective and self-aware in assessing the strengths and weaknesses of the kinds of nonlegal ordering here examined.

The specific instances of rights to do grave wrong that I've explored, though often important on their own terms, serve only as an empirical point of entrée to these larger issues. Some of these rights first strike many people as surprising, even bizarre. Legal thinkers tend to casually dismiss such public apprehensions as simply ill-informed and certain to dissolve once law's mysterious and circuitous workings are unveiled. This is a mistake. When the legal professoriate turns a back hand to such doubts, we treat law's departures from laypeople's morality as requiring no serious consideration, easily explicable with a handful of nostrums, ready to hand and quick to the tongue.

"Of what relevance to the criminal law are the musings of unsophisticated lay people?" ponders Slobogin.[6] "The community upon which [Robinson and Darley] rely for their input on moral intuitions is generally uninformed," he observes with some empirical basis. "Therefore . . . even knowledge that the community resoundingly disfavors a particular legal formulation should usually be irrelevant [to informed lawmaking]."[7] Lawmakers should not bow, in particular, to the public's strongly retributive sentiments on matters where scholars, judges, and legislators favor other, more "progressive" goals. "So what?"[8] Slobogin wonders of common morality's claims upon the law, a view widely shared among law professors, though rarely expressed so straightforwardly, with such candid disdain.

Yet like the air we breathe and water we drink, law's departures from common morality turn foul at times, requiring urgent reconsideration. They imperil the legal system's very legitimacy among the public, some plausibly claim,[9] though serious evidence for this conclusion is equivocal.[10] When *are* those times, exactly? And how much should we worry about them when they arise? Does anything then need to be done, or are we fated to live with them?

We legal academicians turn a brave face to outsiders here, largely united in our conviction that the reasons for disparities between law and common morality are well established, quickly comprehensible, and readily explicable to anyone willing to hear us out. That agreement is skin-deep, however. It collapses into discord as soon as we're asked *which* such reason is actually at work in explaining *which* legal/moral disparity or empirical distribution of disparities. The question that legal scholars would most likely ask about these disparities, were they widely noticed at all, is straightforwardly normative: When are they justified? We are much less concerned with explaining where they actually come into being, how they rise to social or political significance, and why they meet a hostile or more indulgent response from affected parties and larger publics. Our arguments of principle and policy, like those of the philosophers or economists on whom we here rely, contribute only one set of variables in this larger and more complex causal equation.

A further reason legal scholars ignore these questions is that most of us do not consider them sufficiently "theoretical." We prefer to view our law in terms of the fundamental principles and policies underlying it, which we understand in terms of justice or efficiency. These considerations help us interpret legal sources in their best light, resolving doctrinal ambiguities accordingly. Whether we are deontologists, consequentialists, or something else, we at least agree on that much. There exist many inquiries into how the law departs at various points from what particular theories of justice or efficiency demand. There is little curiosity, though, about how, when, or why our law reflects or rejects the moral views of our fellow citizens.

A third source of incuriosity is the prevailing suspicion that such sociological inquiries—much like the political science on "judicial behavior"[11]—inevitably devalue legal doctrine or the ideals it serves. We regard ourselves as the rightful stewards of both. This fear rests on a misunderstanding. To improve the law, to refocus its efforts more effectively, it is often helpful to understand how it works at ground level, in relation to its societal setting, which creates both constraints and opportunities for realizing its drafters' goals. For these several reasons, it is a mistake to stop with merely observing that incongruities arise between legality and lay morality, and that there are several abstract reasons why this is so.

Once beneath the clouds of such generality, we immediately descend into our comfortable "case by case" analysis of particular facts, within specific legal disputes. At this lower level of abstraction, each empirical situation threatens to become infinitely unique. Regularities between disputed cases interest us intensely, but only insofar as the law itself incorporates these patterns as principled qualifications to rules of more general application. Other forms of regularity lie beyond our professional ken. Trapped within our cabined vocational vision, we miss many important features of the very social landscape we seek to tend and, at times, redesign. Reform-minded academicians would thus do well to more closely monitor the points where social mores successfully resist law's attempt to transform them, and where the legal system is therefore essentially forced to retreat. Some of this recalcitrance will strike us as highly objectionable, other features of it rather less so. And some of this obduracy will also show itself more readily amenable to further challenge, through revised efforts at legal reform.

This picture turns dark, though, where the legal right in question authorizes an indispensable task entitling its bearer to cause grave harm. Examples include parenting, lawyering, and soldiering. If the task were not indispensable and we were not confident that concomitant duties would be honored, the right would not exist, given the serious dangers its abuse presents; or it would be far more narrowly drafted and more strictly construed by courts. We know that this confidence regularly proves unwarranted, just as we recognize that conscience, remonstrance, and incentives *do* often satisfactorily restrain such rights abuse. In deciding how much trust to place in these restraints, our knowledge as lawmakers is frequently quite limited. For these impediments often exercise their undoubted influence in an empirical netherworld, requiring arduous inquiry to uncover its murky operations. We tell ourselves, "Let's hope for the best," even when the evidence counsels greater caution. We must ask, with respect to a given right: Do common morality and the social mores embodying it direct right-holders, when employing their entitlements, in desirable directions, in proper measure? Rarely, if ever, do we pose these questions in any concerted, self-conscious way. Still less often do we seek empirical data responsive to them. Our lawmaking nonetheless inevitably reflects our implicit answers.

Most of this study focuses on situations where the chief concern is that common morality does not constrain the exercise of rights as much as we wish it would. We must attend as well, however, to the situations where these social pressures prove all too effective to that end. We might observe, for instance, that by declaring bankruptcy millions of Americans could be saved from financial ruination. For fear of incurring stigma, many debtors fail to take this step.[12] Some would say that common morality, in generating feelings of shame, has all too powerfully dissuaded them from exercising this legal right.

Others believe, to the contrary, that a certain degree of stigma is essential to the defensible operation of personal bankruptcy law at all. Its workability and continued existence rests upon the sociological speculation by Congress that those entitled to exercise the rights it creates will regularly decline to do so. The question becomes whether we have established the optimal measure of stigma. In public, we invariably describe stigma as reprehensible. To acknowledge its indispensability and seek its rehabilitation runs powerfully against the grain of modern moral sensibility.

Concern over how much the social environment deters the exercise of rights may call to mind a long-standing lament of Marxist thought that capitalist society systematically betrays the promise of freedom held out to us by liberal legality. The present point is quite different. Marx did not condemn, as have later Leftist critics, the failure of capitalist society to deliver on the liberal rights it formally proclaimed. Rather, he rejected the conception of freedom reflected in the very notion of individual rights,[13] however exercised, for encouraging various forms of selfishness.

He criticized the importance that capitalist societies ascribe to individual legal rights as such, not only to those of private property, but also to rights protecting personal autonomy and individual self-expression,[14] which he viewed as modeled on the property right. Such rights, Marx wrote, "are simply the rights of a member of civil society, that is, of egoistic man, of man separated from other men and from the community."[15] Individual rights thus betray us not in failing to make good on their promises, but precisely through their success in doing so. That law is little more than bourgeois ideology is a charge more recently reiterated by certain prominent proponents of "critical legal studies."[16] These doubts about the value of legal rights *per se* do not much bear on the question of how we *employ* our rights—particular rights, in particular circumstances.

Compared to Marx, the doubts of interest to me here do not run nearly so 'deep' (or so Marxists would say). They are nonetheless today greatly troubling to large numbers of people throughout the world, particularly within the United States. Many conscientious citizens are demonstrably dismayed, in ways generally quite distinct from Marx, by the direction their society is taking.[17] Yet common to these varied vexations, for us as for him, lies the problematic character of legal rights within a liberal society, of the relation between de jure entitlements and the de facto social relations that these purport to govern and describe.

One salient aspect of this problem may be strictly semantic. To so observe is not, however, to minimize its significance. It is to underscore a point in the sociology of language, about the sources of inexpressibility, about why certain thoughts and feelings remain consistently, systematically unsaid, whereas others find uninhibited voice. There can be little doubt that—for many people, much of the time—the moral duties they accept as binding upon themselves, beyond those to friends and family or enshrined into law, *do* often dissuade them, in heartfelt and forceful ways, from the potential abuse of legal rights.

Yet these acknowledged responsibilities, often historically originating in theological and "civic republican" ideals, frequently defy description in satisfactory contemporary idiom. So proclaimed one influential qualitative study of thirty-five years ago,[18] at least, a finding confirmed by later sociologists with better data.[19] Even when engaged in acts of obvious altruism, such as anonymous charitable contributions, people explain their conduct chiefly in terms of how it advances their self-fulfillment, avoiding all reference to ethical considerations.[20] Lacking a congenial vocabulary to convey our non-egoistic motivations and defend our actions, these scholars concluded, we often only half acknowledge these moral sentiments, or do so only with evident embarrassment. A keyword search within the *New York Times* recently found that the word "duty" appeared with decreasing frequency over the twentieth century.[21] And an Ngram Viewer search of books in English reveals a great decline in the use of such virtue-related terms as "honesty," "patience," "compassion," and "fortitude," accompanied by a rise in words and phrases associated with the "self" and the "individual."[22]

From very different intellectual and ideological quarters—philosophical and sociological, Right and Left[23]—there has been influential and continuing criticism of our allegedly undue reliance on the language of legal rights in thinking and talking about the legitimate claims of citizens upon one another. Thus, in one trenchant formulation:

> Rights talk . . . leads those who use it to neglect important virtues such as courage and beneficence, which are duties to which no rights correspond . . . [T]he use of rights language encourages people to make impractical demands, since one can assert a right without

> attending to the desirability or even the possibility of burdening others with the corresponding obligations . . . The modern discourse of rights is characteristically deployed by those who see themselves or others as potential recipients, entitled to insist on certain benefits or protections.[24]

To some extent, though, the problem may indeed exist merely at the level of "talk," in our ordinary language. We should not confuse any lack of regularly employed discourse of moral responsibility, evident in my excursus on the "Ground Zero mosque" controversy, with what is surely our deeper concern: whether people actually *conduct* themselves in ways consistent with the extralegal duties we think they possess. Even so, the absence of a comfortable lexicon for discussing such matters makes it more difficult to perceive and describe what may actually exist in the way of such adherence to extralegal duty. The problem might then not be as grave as it seems (to some). A limited, inadequate framework for conceptualizing our condition could simply make it difficult to see what lies before our eyes, discernible upon closer empirical scrutiny.

That our predicament may substantially reside in our linguistic practices does not, however, entirely eliminate its vexations. There is legitimate concern that our relative muteness about extralegal duty,[25] compared at least to the Victorians[26] and many non-Western cultures, may contribute to its debilitation. As historian Thomas Haskell writes:

> If talk of duty is discouraged or even silenced, may not the substance of it atrophy as well? . . . for practices and values that we hesitate to express, much less commend, are unlikely in the long run to retain their grip on us. Rights-talk, with its endless variations on the inherently self-centered and polarizing theme of "Don't tread on me!" leaves much to be desired especially when a culture tries, as ours has, to make it virtually the only acceptable vocabulary for policy-oriented public discourse. Given the rhetorical hegemony of rights-talk in America today, there is much to be said for selectively rehabilitating the language of duty.[27]

The language of moral duty is not entirely alien to our law, however, which has long sought to discourage, while not prohibiting, certain forms of lawful activity in the name of fostering its more "responsible" exercise. This is true to some extent even of international human rights law,[28] often considered one of the chief 'offenders.' Nor is there any inherent contradiction in striving at once to protect certain forms of legal choice and to guide its exercise in such a way. This remains the case even if some such restraining counsel may be disingenuous, as arguably by tobacco companies in encouraging only the "responsible" consumption of their products.[29] The guidance sometimes involves putting our collective thumb on the scale, in strenuously seeking to influence how an individual employs his freedom, without denying his right to thumb his nose at that attempt. Such guidance often takes juridical form.

In this dissuasive mode, the law employs such methods—"choice architecture," as behavioral economists call it—as procedural hurdles, obligatory waiting periods,[30] geographical restrictions,[31] deliberation requirements,[32] default positions ("nudging"),[33] as well as enhanced tax burdens.[34] Another regulatory method sometimes employed is mandatory warnings, appearing within the texts of commercial advertising.[35] The law often adopts a mix of the above. The situations of chief concern here, though, are not amenable to effective regulation through such mild prodding. They stand apart in fateful ways from de minimis, garden-variety wrongdoing (and irrationality) of the sort that law routinely hinders through such modest methods—and thereby often, in practice, blithely indulges.

Our limited and seemingly deficient vocabulary for articulating intimations of moral duty further hinders us from more fully enshrining our subjective experience of common morality into legal rules, where we wish to do so. This is because legal terms and rules often incorporate our everyday ethical lexicon. "Good faith," "reasonable" behavior, diligence that's "due," prudent business "judgment," even the notion of "rights" themselves: these are all moral terms too, not only specifically legal ones. When we are at a loss to articulate our moral experience within our ordinary language, the law itself will therefore sometimes suffer. For many people, the call of common morality may nonetheless still subtly influence their thought and action, inhibit their abusive exercise of right.

Yet when we lack shared terms to describe and defend the process, it almost certainly becomes enfeebled over time. If we so much as speak of these matters today, of the classical virtues in particular, we risk seeming faintly antiquarian, stuffily "Victorian." That fact itself is telling evidence of a certain problem. The reality of rights-cum-restraints, this essential armature to any socio-legal order, remains only half-glimpsed, leaving one to wonder whether its apparent debilitation is genuine or merely linguistic. Very real, however, is the fact that we are stuck with this perplexing class of rights, even as we struggle to decipher its peculiar place and significance within a legal system and social order, from the neighborly to the national and beyond.

Rights to do wrong regularly arise as a particularly acute expression of a familiar legal conundrum: distinguishing between closely related acts—one of these acceptable, the other intolerable. We sometimes respond to this difficulty by criminalizing nonblameworthy acts, relying on prosecutorial discretion and judicial lenience *ex post* to compensate for law's overly inclusive ex ante prohibitions. Scholars devote much attention to this method for bringing the law into sync with morality. I here focus on the opposite situation: where we render the law under-inclusive of our moral concerns (that is, overly broad in what it permits) because we trust[36] that common morality and the stigma attached to its violation will dissuade most people—with the exception of tolerably small numbers—from abusing their more expansive entitlements.

By placing this measure of confidence in something so elusive and ethereal, we are sometimes grievously mistaken. It is therefore necessary periodically to ask: How much stock should modern law continue to place in such morality for preventing the abusive exercise of rights, at just the proper times, in the proper places, to the proper extent, for the proper reasons? To what degree can we tightly tailor law's measurements to match the shifting contours of such moralizing pressures, capitalizing on their strengths, compensating for their frailties? This is to treat morality as a "social fact," in Durkheim's sense,[37] much like birth rates, mortality tables, or the statistical incidence of belief in God.

There is no reason to assume that the gap left by the law's under-inclusiveness of all relevant normativity will be satisfactorily filled in these ways. Social scientists today repudiate the functionalist sociology, which once posited that "society" would inexorably ensure that "its needs," or at least those of its "ruling classes," were somehow met.[38] Many "societal needs"—insofar as the concept is even passably coherent—go unmet entirely. (Here again, the reader may, without difficulty, supply her own preferred examples.) It is difficult to envision—in light of "collective action" problems—how the weakening of anything so often diffuse as common morality, its benefits widely dispersed and little-recognized, could directly inspire organized efforts at its restoration. Occupants of political office, for instance, cannot simply, by force of law or agencies of its enforcement, *command* the reinvigoration of something so apparently elusive to our grasp.[39]

An intriguing feature of rights to do wrong, in ideal-typical form, is that those who create them are often conscious of authorizing conduct they themselves regard as gravely immoral. They do so not merely (or not exclusively) as accommodation to ephemeral exigencies or lack of current political momentum for more restrictive rules. Instead, they fully understand that they authorize wrongdoing, which for the foreseeable future, will be much resistant to further legal tinkering. This intentional authorization of acknowledged wrong is what distinguishes such circumstances from more familiar ones where lawmakers must simply strike a mutually acceptable deal between those preferring more straightforward policies toward the activity or institution in question: outright prohibition or unrestricted authorization. To the extent they approximate the ideal-type, rights to do serious wrong thus do not emerge as a mere patchwork of philosophically irreconcilable commitments produced by brute brokering among warring factions.

These rights all but invite some serious unethical conduct, and therefore portend genuine peril. They nonetheless present a fitting stance and coherent response to a certain regulatory predicament: where legal restrictions suffer irremediable limitations in scope, yet prevailing mores substantially mitigate resultant risks through informal practices effectively limiting the abusive exercise of rights. We must neither exaggerate the incidence of such propitious conjunctures nor deny their existence. We should instead aim to discover their empirical distribution and theoretical significance, the task this book undertakes.

## A Social Scientific Angle on What Seems a Philosophical Problem

In speaking of "morality," I do so throughout this study in a sociological register, intending what legal and moral theorists often call common morality, ordinary morality, conventional morality, folk morality, or commonsense morality. Philosophers generally distinguish this from "critical" morality, or simply morality tout court. Common morality refers to widely shared belief, often largely unspoken[40] yet vividly observable in its behavioral effects, about what is right and wrong, about what justice permits or requires. Critical morality purports to describe the claims of true morality, of morality properly understood, irrespective of prevailing views on a question.

It may be mistaken to draw this distinction very sharply, though. John Rawls constructs his account of justice on the basis of "considered judgments," concerning a variety of concrete topics, judgments he takes to be pervasive in the culture of democratic societies, asking how we may bring these together more coherently.[41] Critical morality thus builds on common morality, which provides the raw material, familiar to most people, for reflection more theoretical in character. "Kant sought to vindicate the deontological moral intuitions of the ordinary German peasantry," writes Leiter, "while Sidgwick found that the 'unconscious' morality of the English 'peasants' was utilitarian."[42] Both viewed themselves as elucidating, elaborating, and extending the moral theory implicit within their society, embodied in its daily practices, already embraced by their contemporaries, humble and haughty.

A certain strand of analytic philosophy has expressly understood its task as seeking chiefly to render our extant ethical intuitions "more systematic." The professed aim is to lend "greater clarity" to moral concepts already widely employed within the everyday vocabulary of thoughts and feelings—not to eagerly override these whenever a more pristine reason and logic so dictate. This view of the philosopher's task does not date from mid-century Oxbridge, in fact, but from its very inception.[43] Still, there is always a revisionary aspect and animus to this method. And the "clearer" understandings of what morality requires very often depart markedly and systematically from those predominant among most citizens, to judge from opinion surveys.

This is conspicuously true concerning a number of specific policy issues, often quite politically salient, such as torture,[44] abortion, the death penalty,[45] euthanasia, gay marriage, immigration, affirmative action,[46] and income inequality.[47] The views of most Americans and Europeans have been considerably right of center compared to those of moral philosophers writing on all these issues. Moral philosophy in the Anglo-American orbit, as Haidt observes,[48] does not deem such 'conservative' values as in-group loyalty, respect for authority, or preserving the purity of the sacred, to occupy the moral domain. If these do not merit analytic attention, it is not simply because they lack serious weight in moral deliberation, but that they do not count as genuinely moral concerns at all.

Haidt's empirical surveys suggest that large numbers in many societies, both within the West and far beyond, think otherwise.[49] One major philosopher confesses her profession's "prejudices" in this regard, its "contempt for commonsense ways of thinking about ethical problems."[50] Empirical studies today helpfully identify the considerable differences in how professional philosophers and ordinary folk—each with its own predispositions—reason about moral issues.[51]

Differences are evident not only in their conclusions, but in the methods by which they reason. For in routine interaction we do not usually ask one another what we would choose "behind a veil of ignorance," in an "ideal speech situation," or even "what we owe each other."[52] In ordinary life, as Bernard Williams writes, "rather than how a universal program is to be applied," we wonder how our own "concretely experienced form of life can be extended."[53] A "form of life" may encode general principles. These prove of practical value to us, however, only when we invoke and employ them, Winston contends, not "in isolation from the background of interconnected norms and institutions and interpersonal relationships that give them concrete meaning."[54] On this account, he adds, learning how to think and live in accordance with a common morality "requires close observation and practice, being initiated into particular ways of feeling and acting and responding, mastering standard techniques, and eventually innovating within acquired understandings."[55] This stance toward morality and its workings has implications for how people transmit and revise its terms over time. There are indications here as well for how one should go about studying morality, where one should look to discover it at work, the places it does and does not take on strong significance within human lives.

The work of Williams, Haidt, and Winston is helpful in suggesting the limits of professional philosophy in its "analytic" mode, as a method for making sense of morals, conceived of as infusing social practices. There sometimes nonetheless occur more abrupt ruptures in belief systems than such authors acknowledge; these are situations where abstract principles and concrete practices cease to be as inextricable as such authors suggest, and are in fact violently sundered. Transformations of this sort affect prevailing views of both collective life and individual conduct. The personal virtues most highly prized within society may then cease to be those of good neighborliness or liberal tolerance, for example. They instead become fervent dedication to "The Revolution" or passionate commitment to "the nation" facing urgent mortal threat. Highly theoretical texts may then inspire radical change in dominant standards of appraisal,[56] of both institutions and individuals.

This "transvaluation of values," as notably occurred with Mao and Hitler, strives at times virtually to reverse the magnetic poles of good and evil, courage and cowardice. To induce uncoerced cooperation in genocide, for instance, the psychological trick has been to convince potential participants that, should they fail to join in the mayhem, their peers will consider them cowards. It then paradoxically requires great courage to go on as before, adhering to humane principles once universally endorsed and wholly conventional. Since the French Revolution at least, the modern age has repeatedly witnessed such transvaluation as the explicit goal of states, social movements, and their leaders. To fathom how common morality changes over time, we must look to such mass campaigns at "moral reeducation," as they are sometimes tellingly called, no less than at the slower shifts in more intimate patterns of interactions that Williams and Winston affectionately delineate.

It is nonetheless true that those 'heroic' historic campaigns do not often effect lasting change in how most people make their moral judgments, in what they regard as the proper objects of indignation and veneration. Common morality, especially when grounded in spiritual practices that are ritualized and routinized, proves remarkably resistant to such efforts, on the whole, regularly bouncing back from long years of official efforts to suppress or transfigure it. In recent decades, the resurgence of Islamic sensibilities in Turkey, of Catholicism in Poland and Lithuania, and of Russian and Serbian Orthodoxy after sixty years of Communism offers only the most familiar examples. Perhaps the most moving and astounding is found in the quiet endurance of indigenous Andean religiosity in the face of Catholicism's four hundred years of assiduous efforts to expunge it, succeeding chiefly in deflecting it into infinitely ingenious forms of syncretism.[57]

It is also true, however, that those ancient, companionable methods of moral reasoning and propagation, as Williams and Winston sympathetically paint these, themselves today prove quite fragile in many places. All manner of mass and social media vigorously disseminate standards of normative appraisal at once more lenient and more demanding, in differing respects, than those known to prior generations, transmitted face-to-face. To judge from some scholarship, these 'charming' practices of slow habituation into ethical wisdom, of gradual intergenerational enlightenment, are today often frail even in parts of the world historically least subject to Western influence. There is thus an unmistakably nostalgic cast to the loving renderings of long-standing moral practices, as Williams and Winston describe these—entrancing as they are even (perhaps especially) to those of us who have never known them.[58]

Some may protest that a social scientific approach to the relation between law and common morality is impossible, because it cannot dodge the question, logically preceding all others, of what defines the realm of morality in the first instance. In other words, which questions are moral questions, and which are not? To what portions of our lives does morality lay claim, whatever its substance, its true terms? Any answer would seem to require an a priori definition of morality, a map of where it begins and ends. For instance, the issue of whether the state should pay for abortion inherently presents a moral question, whereas that of how to repair an automobile engine does not. The present inquiry must therefore delineate and defend some account of the boundary between the moral and nonmoral, as intrinsically distinct dimensions of life. How else can one then proceed to compare and contrast the claims of morality with those of the law?

This way of thinking sails us wholly off course. As should by now be clear, this book's concerns are chiefly empirical and explanatory. They demand only that we identify the range of issues that most people in a given place and period *deem* to be moral ones, which they *consider* to raise questions of right and wrong, in relation to which they subjectively experience sentiments of indignation at perceived injustice as entirely apt.[59] These are matters that, even in modern societies, people regard as transcending issues strictly scientific or technical, governed by such explanatory laws as those of chemistry and physics.

The moral domain often overlaps empirically with the legal realm because lawmakers specifically seek—though none would put it so portentously—to incorporate a great deal of morality into legality. Hence, intentionally killing another human being is illegal precisely because it is considered wrongful. The extent to which legislators perform such incorporations—in what ways, at which times—are empirical questions too, to which the causal theories of social science should help in offering answers. To identify the boundaries of the moral domain in a given locale and point in its history demands close attention to prevailing patterns of language usage (among other indicia), despite the reticence and lexical limitations observed above. It is via language that people routinely reprimand one another for breaches of common morality and stigmatize those who exercise their rights in ways regarded as reprehensible. And it is through these practices of reproach—again, empirically observable, in large part—that we inject our feelings of indignation into the social world.

Indignation at perceived injustice is *the* reactive attitude most acutely and routinely aroused by the law[60]—in litigation, almost invariably so, usually on both sides to the dispute, though not centrally in the legal negotiations entailed in most commercial transactions. Other such attitudes undoubtedly occupy the moral domain as well, of course, including gratitude, kindness, compassion, sympathy, generosity, loyalty, propriety, regret, and remorse. These too regularly inspire the creation of new rights, duties, and dispensations. Feelings of mercy, for instance, often provide the emotional basis for executive acts of clemency and pardon, though these last two juridical measures are unusual in drawing directly on moral sentiments at the very moment of application.[61] Far more often, the moral sentiments spawning legal rules are accorded no official place or recognition at the stage of implementation and enforcement, when the law leaves them behind.[62] By contrast, feelings of indignation—acutely felt and publicly displayed—lie on the very surface of virtually all legal disputes, transparent in the demeanor of accuser and accused.

For present purposes, then, we may demarcate the moral domain—the portion most pertinent to law—as that range of issues and circumstances evoking strong feelings of indignation at perceived injustice among significant numbers of people in a given time and place. In short, the relevant subset of common morality is the reach of our shared indignation, manifested empirically in myriad ways. Because ordinary language is one of these, we learn greatly by attending to the places in social life where we do and do not employ wording in this register. This understanding of morality and its scope-conditions is avowedly sociological and, as such, immediately yields an implication, mentioned earlier in passing, quite counterintuitive to anyone approaching morality from more familiar philosophical standpoints. The implication is that people may conceivably construe literally any question in moralizing terms, any question whatever,[63] just as it is possible in principle to construe anything (far beyond the fine arts) from an aesthetic angle.[64]

To prove the point, we need only identify a few issues, long viewed exclusively in technical or scientific terms, that people now often discuss in a decidedly moral idiom. Most people once regarded the question of where to site a contemplated sewage treatment plant as simply a matter of locating the least expensive, permissibly zoned parcel of land. Today it is for many people a question of "environmental justice."[65] They believe that their commitment to distributive justice, or simply justice *simpliciter,* bears directly upon the question of how to allocate the burdens associated with our collective reliance on certain modern technologies, including those of waste disposal. To similar effect, only fifty years ago few would have identified any specifically moral issue—concerning our duties to other species—at stake in decision-making over how or whether to build a transcontinental gas pipeline.

The empirical examples I employ to help understand the phenomenon of rights to do wrong vary significantly in moral gravity, from the cardinal to the relatively venial, the monumental to the mundane. I am not much concerned, though, with deviations between law and common morality that most would judge trivial in political import. Neither am I especially interested in situations where a gap between the two quickly dissolves, as one of them moves effortlessly into harmony with the other. More intriguing and significant from the perspective of public policy and socio-legal theory are the points at which a tension between them long persists because each is relatively resilient to pressure from the other. A certain equilibrium develops between them, with the frailties of each regulated or redressed by its opposite; in this sense the tension is fruitful, productive. There is much variation between cases in the extent to which anyone actually planned this or foresaw its emergence.

Though my chief concern is with the gravest and most vexing of lawful injustices, similar causal mechanisms prove regularly at work among virtually all such iniquities, great and small. These mechanisms help to create, to manage, and sometimes to close breaches between law and common morality. To gain some understanding of all these processes, Chapters 2 and 3 examined a variety of situations across an expansive legal landscape, differing in several ways—relative moral gravity among them. A phenomenon widespread across many spheres of life, banal in garden-variety circumstances, can become ethically inescapable and politically charged when matters of life and death on a large scale are suddenly at stake. Once the lawful wrongdoing becomes serious or grave (terms here used interchangeably), public policy can hardly remain indifferent. At these times, the rationales we ordinarily find acceptable for discrepancies between law and morality become decidedly less so.

There should be serious concern when we create rights to do serious wrong on the basis of an assumption that the law can make adequate use of extralegal restraints. These are the situations on which this study concentrates: where lawmakers believe, or simply take for granted, that these restraints will reinforce policy objectives that the law itself cannot directly attain. Were it not for their confidence in a certain baseline adherence to common morality—ensured by private conscience, moral suasion, and social stigma—many legislators would likely forge ahead with more stringent rules.[66] That is the case in several of the situations here examined. At these key moments, we may see ourselves placing a prudent measure of trust in our fellow man. Yet often we are making more a leap of faith,[67] a wager we may lose, with heavy costs that we discover only later, when it may be too late to shift course without extraordinary difficulty. When stakes are high, such a path is defensible only after due consideration of its likely ramifications, which it too rarely receives.

We should here distinguish the situations of present interest from those where, for whatever reason, law simply drifts far apart for short periods from common morality, as when the former moves at a temporal pace—or even, more rarely, in a direction—different than the latter. There is no productive equilibrium, even for a short period, between an indulgent right and a more stringent moral norm. Legal history is littered with discontinuities of this sort. It is worth mentioning a couple of them, to show how they differ from situations where rights to do wrong are made possible by the environing social restraints upon their exercise.

Consider, for instance, the prehistory of life insurance. In the United States, early nineteenth-century lawmakers enacted legislation authorizing this ingenious new commercial service. Yet several decades passed before the general public came to consider it morally acceptable.[68] Most people viewed it as sacrilegious to 'gamble' on the death of loved ones. Life insurance finally became commercially viable only when people no longer saw it as ethically objectionable. That transformation occurred when insurance companies found they could successfully market this novel product as an ideal way for a father to demonstrate his moral responsibility to family members by providing for them in the event of his early death. To convincingly dissociate the sale of insurance from "immoral" gaming, Congress enacted legislation requiring that the purchaser possess an "insurable interest"—a direct personal stake—in the continuing well-being of the potential decedent.[69] Influenced by these changes, common morality gradually moved into harmony with the law, making possible the spectacular growth of an industry long shunned by potential consumers. Similar obstacles continue to bedevil the industry in certain non-Western lands, notably China,[70] again for reasons rooted in religious attitudes.

Despite initial revulsion in certain quarters, an American public now comfortable with the moral implications of life insurance had little difficulty accepting the novel recent market in "viatical contracts." These are agreements whereby HIV victims sell the eventual proceeds of their life insurance to complete strangers.[71] Some philosophers and legal theorists still cavil at such "self-commodification." But few people today object to the practice of organ donation; this won early acceptance through the intercession by religious leaders and the creation of secular rituals, rich in gravitas, for securing consent from family members.[72] In these recent American experiences, law and mores moved quickly into harmony, with relative ease.

The early history of personal bankruptcy law presents a converse shift in the relation of law and common morality.[73] Here, morality changed faster than the law, demanding that the latter address a series of novel issues. The incipient capitalism of Renaissance England posed the novel challenge of encouraging productive risk-taking by early entrepreneurs without fostering "immoral" speculation. The common law long preoccupied itself with the risk that people, whether cunning financial schemers or the merely indolent, would unethically exploit the possibility of legal release from their debts. Such people would, in so doing, recklessly imperil not only the solvency of responsible creditors, but their own immortal souls. The law here proved slower to accommodate changes in economic life—later crucial to modern industrial and postindustrial economies—than the evolving mores of the marketplace itself, the commercial culture of its nascent merchant class. Lawmakers' skepticism began to subside only as fears of "moral hazard" diminished. Such trepidation eased with increasing evidence that default rates on commercial lending would be acceptable to lenders, because interest rates on this lending could viably "price" that risk.

To bring law and prevailing social mores into harmony sometimes proves much more difficult than exhibited in these two historical experiences. To prohibit slavery in the United States (though not elsewhere), to draw American law into line with the stiffening moral sentiments of mid-nineteenth-century abolitionism, required a war and the deaths of more than 600,000 people. Harmonization can be anything but harmonious. There have existed other such rights, so antithetical to common morality of the day that their continued existence cannot be secured through any measure of prudent moderation in their exercise. This has been the case for lawful injustices well short of slavery, though the history of human bondage in mid-nineteenth-century America can well serve as the archetype of such equilibratory impossibility.[74]

These historical episodes, and others more prosaic, stand apart from my primary concerns in that they involve determined efforts to increase the measure of overlap between morality and the law, whether through means sudden and violent or gradual and peaceful. In the experiences of greater present interest, we find relative equilibrium between these two countervailing normative forces, and a curious kind of dependence, in particular, of the law upon the restraints of common morals. The disparate claims of law and morality here persist, often for considerable periods, frequently without arousing great objection.

It was Montesquieu who offered the first sustained analysis of the relations between law and "mores," which he took to mean widespread, everyday social practices embodying prevailing moral sensibilities. These relations, on his account, were multiple and intricate, yet lent themselves to a simple three-part typology, a helpful starting point for my own, to follow. Montesquieu's original, eighteenth-century prose style strikes the contemporary reader as cumbersome or ponderous, and the pertinent passages are scattered about his sprawling volume. So let us turn for guidance to an able recent interpreter:[75]

> First, Montesquieu argues that when mores are good, or "pure," as he says, laws are often unnecessary. The early Romans, for instance, had no law against embezzlement.[76] And when embezzlers started to appear on the scene, they offended the mores of the Romans so much that the law's demand merely for the restoration of goods seemed like a great penalty. Thus, as long as corruptions offend mores, then the law need not respond too harshly. Laws are simpler to the extent that mores are purer. As mores become more corrupt, then the law must anticipate more problems.
>
> The Frenchman's next example involves Roman laws regarding guardianship of a ward and inheritance. Early Roman law gave guardianship to the closest relative—the person who most often was entitled to the inheritance. Montesquieu argues that these laws reflected the fact that the Romans had no worry that in such a system the life of the ward "was put in the hands of one to whom the ward's death could be useful."[77] Later Roman legislators were forced to take steps that anticipated plots to kill the ward for his inheritance—"fears and precautions unknown to the first Romans."[78]
>
> In the last example, we learn about Roman law's recognition of legitimate causes of the repudiation of a husband by a wife. Among these was the whipping of a wife by her husband—a chastisement "unworthy of a freeborn person."[79] Montesquieu indicates that later Roman laws did not recognize this as a legitimate cause for

> repudiation. The Romans had exchanged the mores of the East for those of Europe.
>
> Let us look back at these examples—together they provide a sober lesson about the fundamental weakness of law in relation to mores. In the first example, we see that because mores are offended by the crimes of embezzlement, Roman opinion makes a minor penalty seem great . . . Next, when mores become more corrupt, the law must consider things that it never had to before. The law began to punish crimes that mores themselves used to prevent. Finally, mores can become so corrupt that the law simply gives up. The law no longer recognizes corruption as corruption—it tolerates what mores have come to tolerate.

These observations are today considered unscientific and largely ignored by current social science.[80] There is some accuracy in this critique. If it is examined closely, however, the work of today's cultural anthropologists—Montesquieu's closest heirs—generally reveals itself to be scarcely more systematic.

Aspects of Montesquieu's analysis merit rehabilitation if we can reformulate and evaluate them somewhat more rigorously.[81] Though we need not accept his final counsel, of course, we cannot—in light of law's recurrent failures—ignore his case for chastening our modern hopes that law can chart society's direction indifferently to prevailing ethical sensibilities. In none of his three scenarios does the law display any nontrivial power to prevent the long-term degeneration of mores. Rather, it is mores that give the law whatever force it may have,[82] if only for a time, enabling it to fulfill its formal promise.[83]

Legal rules can prohibit and punish perceived violations of social mores, yet cannot staunch these abuses at their source, nor even long hold them at bay, Montesquieu contends. For in the end, the law will necessarily reconcile itself to consistent violations of long-standing mores by no longer regarding them as intolerable, as violations at all, and hence ceasing to combat them. As writes a distinguished commentator, for Montesquieu "each constitution [monarchy, aristocracy, despotism, and republic] is preserved thanks to the *moeurs* which are proper to it [honor, moderation, fear, and civic virtue, respectively], and becomes corrupt when those *moeurs* are no longer adequate."[84] Still, Montesquieu insists that though a wise legislator will not attempt to regulate all activities, she will seek to influence prevailing mores when these are corrupt.[85] He concludes that as long as a potential tyrant does not directly offend our mores, to which we have become ardently attached or complacently accustomed, he may otherwise revamp our laws in ways profoundly inimical to our freedoms and welfare.[86] Most people have greater concern about preserving prevailing mores than with the fate of their laws, certainly those not discernibly affecting their immediate experience.

Let us sketch out a few further analytic possibilities, inspired by Montesquieu's analysis but beyond those he fully contemplated. Thus, consider this two-by-two table, with the two axes identified by the *possibility* and *necessity* of legally codifying a social norm of communal morality.

First quadrant: where it is both possible and necessary for law to step in and supplement weak mores, there is no problem. The law can fill the breach where mores fail to regulate conduct satisfactorily, restating and reaffirming a common morality which may have weakened.[87]

Second quadrant: it is impossible but also unnecessary that law assume an active role in normative ordering, because common morality is at work in successfully moderating the exercise of overbroad rights. The world is, again, all sweetness and light.

There is usually no problem in the fourth quadrant either. Here it is both possible and unnecessary for law to intercede—unnecessary, again, because mores are well entrenched, effectively dampening abusive exercise of a given right. The only complication is that if law *does* nonetheless interpose itself, it might not necessarily reinforce healthy mores but instead "crowd them out." In that case, legal entrenchment of moral duty is possible but undesirable.

The serious problems arise only in the third quadrant, where legal absorption of a social norm is both necessary and impossible. Here, informal processes of equilibration between law and morals simply fail. The law cannot effectively intercede to solve critical regulatory problems. At the same time, extralegal mores prove equally inadequate in addressing them. Dire consequences may loom. It is often difficult to know when we face this predicament, and even harder to address it. Several situations of this sort may spring readily to the reader's mind.

One of these near-insuperable predicaments may exist, for example, in the uncertain efforts of the United Nations to induce greater restraint by multinational corporations operating in poor, politically repressive countries. These are places where national law or its nonenforcement often allows such companies to operate at ethical standards well below those

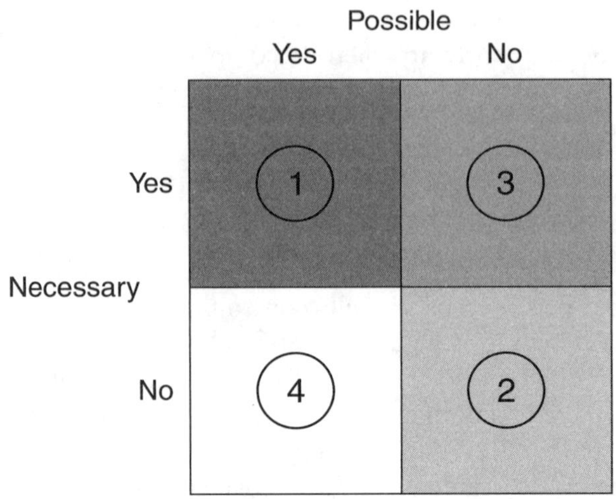


imposed by richer, democratic countries, standards protecting labor, the environment, and rights to political participation. In the judgment of many, though recent progress is notable, neither mores nor law have here proven entirely satisfactory to essential regulatory tasks.

Some of my case-illustrations of rights to do serious wrong discussed in preceding chapters fall felicitously into the boxes where social mores fill the regulatory breach. This is the case, for instance, with the right to inflict civilian harm in war, and the right to decline essential life support. Further legal restriction appears largely unnecessary, undesirable, or impossible. Vigorous normative ordering remains necessary, however. If private ordering proves insufficient at first, moral entrepreneurs will often go to work—as with consumer mobilization against Bangladeshi "sweatshops"—in closing the gap, strengthening dissuasive mores without enlarging law's formal prohibitions.[88]

In how it apprehends and investigates the relationship between law and morals, this book will strike many as quite odd. Its approach differs greatly from how others, across several fields of study, have seen fit to conceive of and examine that relationship. Chapter 9 briefly scrutinizes these alternative lines of analysis. I indicate how—their many merits notwithstanding—they miss key aspects, accessible to understanding through the present approach alone.

# 9

# Why This Book Is Not What You Had in Mind

There are several lively intellectual enterprises that might first seem best-suited to examine the relations between law and morality, and to answer the more particular questions this book poses. To make the case for my preferred approach, it is therefore helpful to show how these fields of study fall short of essential tasks. The fields are philosophy, economics, the sociology of law, and moral anthropology. Because they do not directly join issue with present concerns, as I will demonstrate, they shall not serve as genuine "foils" in the familiar sense. This chapter does not directly refute any of their claims, though in places I will voice relevant reservations. To students and scholars in these several disciplines, my aim is instead to extend an open, friendly hand in pan-disciplinary dialogue on a very general question of perennial curiosity to legal theorists and other thinkers in a number of fields.

I must, however, first address the fellow lawyers among my readers, who may be tempted to confuse my concerns with those of what we call the law of "equity."

## Equity Jurisprudence

This body of law, to which I earlier referred in passing, authorized early English Courts of Chancery to invent novel and sometimes ingenious means for resolving conflicts between what the common law allowed and "public conscience" forbade. A landowner might claim, for instance, that his neighbor utilized a shared waterway in a manner that, though consistent with the common law, breached conventional notions of neighborliness. To decide whether that was so, courts had to take "judicial notice" of moral understandings prevalent within society, at least among its "upright" members.

These concerns of equity jurisprudence, which today find analogous expression within capacious European doctrines of "good faith,"[1] differ crucially from my own. Courts of Equity understood their task as reintegrating the common morality of their day into judicially enforceable rules, when the two had drifted widely apart. At that time, however, there existed no truly democratic institutions through whose legislative institutions the moral sensibilities of the day might find legal register. It was only courts and kings who made the law. Equity courts came into being precisely in order to help close the gap between law and common morality by packing ever more of the latter into the former, in ways that settled precedents of "common law" could not. Chancery judges thus sought to create a body of law more closely approximating prevailing moral sensibilities. The goal always remained: more and better *law*.

My concern is instead in finding ways to live with that gap, and manage it intelligently, because closing it often proves impossible or undesirable. This approach reflects a more modest, realistic assessment of law's claims upon us than "Herculean" theories of the prior generation,[2] which staked out a considerably broader reach for "law's empire"[3] and insisted that the legal system colonize ever wider swaths of life, extending the reach of its underlying principles.

## Philosophy: Rights to Do Wrong as a Conflict of Law and Morality

The "conflict between law and morality" is a timeless theme in modern Western thought and a central concern of this book. Most such conflict, though, involves two situations quite different from those of present concern. These arise where the law either prohibits a given act but morality requires it, or law requires the act but morality forbids it. In both cases, the actor must choose between obeying the law and answering the claims of morality.[4]

This study is concerned, by contrast, with situations where the law authorizes an act that it may also seek to inhibit, and that community morality may further hinder, at times decisively. The right-bearer in my cases does face a choice between what law allows and morality discourages. Yet whether or not to obey the law—with all the gravity of that decision—is simply not at issue, because he violates the law in neither case. The same is true of those who would lawfully attempt to discourage such a person from exercising his legal rights in ways at odds with societal morality. In any event, the predicament that an individual confronts at these moments—whether to exert or forgo her rights—is less significant for social theory than the larger question of what place and purpose this peculiar species of rights occupies within our legal system as a whole.

Some readers will assume that my reflections must necessarily address the perennial puzzle within legal philosophy over the "separation of law and morality."[5] The greatest Anglo-American legal theorists of the last half-century chose to concentrate their considerable intellectual powers on precisely this question. It was long believed that weighty political matters must turn on the answer: notably, whether it is necessary or possible for judges—consistent with their professional duty to uphold the law—to enforce the wicked laws of evil regimes. Yet as the scholarly discussion advanced, it became increasingly clear to all that little of practical import truly turns on that controversy, as its leading participants now generally acknowledge.

Analytic philosophers are fascinated by whether the law is linked to morality at the conceptual level—analytically, logically, or linguistically. This is a question about the very nature of law as such, and sometimes too, by implication, about how we should interpret its authoritative materials. Theorists seek the answers by reflecting on how we lawyers argue among ourselves when applying these materials to the resolution of live disputes (Ronald Dworkin), or by describing how all of those governed by a given legal system and attentive to its demands employ the "concept of law" in their ordinary language and in guiding their lives (H. L. A. Hart).[6]

Philosophers observe that we cannot define the nature of law through empirical inquiry into the normative content of a given legal system—that is, into what its rules happen (as a factual matter) to permit, prohibit, and require. Countries A and B may both have law yet incorporate within their rules very different understandings of morality. Whether the law of a given society *ought* to incorporate these particular understandings rather than others is equally immaterial to the task of answering the question "What is a legal system?" Philosophers correctly observe that the answers to questions about how actual legal systems selectively incorporate elements of common morality are necessarily "contingent," dependent on peculiarities of place and time. Answers of this sort cannot speak to more universal concerns, transcending "empirical ephemera."

My interest in law's relation to morality is very different from that of analytic philosophy. For more intriguing to me—and to most others, I would suppose—is instead the question: How does the law determine which elements of common morality it will take up and which it will leave aside? This presents a tall task, nowhere currently assayed I believe, and my answers are hence necessarily sketchy and provisional, at times conjectural. I wish to suggest a research program, and to initiate it by closely examining several situations that entail a right to do wrong, then compare and contrast these to learn what accounts for their similarities and differences. This is a task for social theory, not analytic philosophy, whose practitioners—as I read them, and when I ask them—expressly disavow it.

There may first appear some tension between my formulation of the relevant, researchable questions and Ronald Dworkin's understanding, in particular, of the relation between law and morality. Dworkin viewed the judicial task centrally to involve unearthing the moral principles already immanent within the law; the judge must then extend these to situations where the positive legal materials, taken merely as expressions of lawmaker's immediate intentions, might seem to require an ethically unsatisfactory result. Applying the law hence always draws upon morality in ways seemingly inconsistent with acknowledging even the possibility of serious tension between the two.

Yet even Dworkin did not go so far as to argue that all of relevant morality, rightly understood, invariably finds adequate embodiment within the legal materials immediately pertinent to resolving a given case. One sometimes had to look quite farther afield, he believed, into entirely different areas of law. Still more important, the morality he had in mind is largely that of the philosophers, bearing no close or necessary relation to what I am calling common morality. Very often, we entirely fail to discern this second form of morality in the pertinent legal materials, however broadly we conceive their legitimate range.

We discover it instead in available indicia of how and when people feel indignation at perceived injustice, when this particular moral sentiment is widely and observably activated. Thus, even if we adopt Dworkin's expansive view of morality's claims upon the law, we are left with the very real possibility that law and common morality will often fail to fall entirely into sync, that they are significantly at odds. To this empirical proposition, Dworkin would have no objection. It would have no interest to him, though, for it lacks implications specifically "jurisprudential," bearing on how we should properly interpret legal texts.

## "Morals Legislation"

There is a second, very different way that modern Western philosophy interests itself in the relation of law to morality. Here the question is no longer conceptual, with whether the very idea of law entails morality (or at least an important subset of its claims). The question now becomes straightforwardly normative: When *should* the law prohibit conduct that—though immoral, in the view of most—appears to harm no one? "Morals legislation" is the familiar term to describe legal restrictions on matters widely deemed "private," a highly contested concept in this context.

In philosophical debate,[7] self-professed liberals generally contend that the law—as when it bars pornography—is *over*-inclusive of common morality, particularly of its illiberal elements. Common morality condemns the given conduct, yet the law should nevertheless allow it, liberals contend, because it harms no one except perhaps arguably the person immediately undertaking it. "That's his choice," we often say. In other words, roughly speaking, liberals criticize an existing law where, in proscribing certain acts, it incorporates elements of common morality inconsistent with J. S. Mill's famous "harm principle."[8]

My concern is instead with situations where the law is *under*-inclusive vis-à-vis common morality, allowing what most people condemn, though they would not necessarily outlaw it. Here, there is no "legislation of private morality," hence no grounds for opposing "state paternalism,"[9] which is always the chief objection invoked against criminalizing "personal vices."[10]

## "Applied Ethics"

The field of applied ethics seeks to bring various moral theories, notably deontology and consequentialism, to bear directly upon practical problems in public policy and daily life.[11] Yet applied ethicists display essentially no interest in the relation between law and common morality. The policies and practices these authors critically appraise—for instance, national restrictions on immigration—often find ample endorsement within both of these normative orders at once. In other words, common morality and the law (both quite restrictive) are nearly in sync. The problem for ethicists lies elsewhere: both common morality and the law are often inconsistent with what they consider "critical" or correct morality. Critical morality disabuses us of our unreflective assumptions and conventional precepts. It is this species of morality that tells us what we really owe to one another, what it is that justice, properly understood, truly requires of us. Wherever possible, both law and common morality must cede to such true morality, these thinkers believe. They generally evince no professional curiosity about the ways in which, or the reasons why, common morality deviates empirically—here, but not there—from either true morality or the law.

Consider, nonetheless, how an applied ethicist might approach my central questions. Suppose that lawmakers draft a particular legal right while under the sway of "rule-consequentialism," the view that overall consequences determine a law's moral acceptability. That right will then sometimes permit conduct a Kantian would consider wrongful, because it violates some aspect of essential human dignity, if only with respect to a small number of persons. She would then discourage the right-holder from exercising his entitlement. One could say that the right-bearer holds a consequentialist-inspired right to do deontological wrong. Conversely, the law may reflect lawmakers' commitment to protect the right-holder's dignity, come what may, irrespective of societal cost. In exercising his entitlement, the right-bearer will then, at times, likely cause some harm to others, who may in turn discourage him from acting upon his legal right in this fashion. One could say that law here establishes a dignity-protective right to cause consequential harm.

This way of thinking does not carry us any further, though, which is to say it does not carry us very far at all. For many philosophers themselves, all this appears an unsystematic temporizing, a muddled and inconsistent hedging, in any event, an incoherent tacking back and forth on matters requiring consistent adherence to first principles. What does philosophy bring to the table in such matters if it cannot help us think more systematically and coherently about them than we already do?

## The Economics of "Law and Social Norms"

Some readers will consider it natural and inevitable to take up the economic analysis of law and social norms, a subject recently treated to considerable scholarly attention.[12] That body of writing, though at times insightful, alas proves largely immaterial to present concerns, for the following reasons.

First, the economic literature shows great interest in how we might employ *good law* to weaken *bad norms,* notably those dissuading us from honoring our legal and moral *duties to others.* Social norms are said to impose, on those violating them, psychological and emotional "costs"[13]—a word employed very expansively, at times to the point of near-meaninglessness. My chief concern is instead to understand how and when *good norms* discourage people from exercising and extending their *own rights* in *bad ways.*

Second, though its central concerns are largely confined to norms of mere coordination, the most ambitious and influential writing in this economic literature fails to disaggregate this very broad notion—norms *simpliciter*—into its vastly different subsets.[14] Distinctions of this sort are admittedly irrelevant where the aim is precisely to locate and account for regularities in all manner of human behavior through a single, simply stated axiom about the corollaries of rational self-interest. As legal economists understand them, norms are important (and interesting) because, and only because, they are what make these behavioral regularities possible, by providing "focal points" for cooperation, thereby enhancing efficiency, overall public well-being. Compared to the law's formalities, norms can often better reduce transaction costs, if only because norms do not require police, courts, prisons, or collection agencies. Yet many would say that such norms are not truly "normative" at all.[15] For they need not directly involve matters of fairness, justice, or virtue. Fairness becomes relevant only in those special circumstances where one gains unfair advantage by violating a coordination norm to which others consistently conform.

This book concerns itself with norms only of the latter sort, which I've called mores, not norms in general. Mores generally involve conduct deemed *mala in se* (inherently wrong), not merely *mala prohibita* (wrong because unlawful).[16] Only *mala in se* norms uniformly generate indignation at perceived injustice. In fact, my interest in *mala in se* mores consists exclusively in how they block the exercise of particular legal rights in particular contexts, where such exercise runs afoul of common morality. By no means does this type of norm necessarily facilitate cooperation, for that matter. In fact it regularly leads its adherents into conflict with those who understand morality's requirements quite differently.

Third, in the interest of conceptual parsimony, the economic analysis of norms generally travels at so high a level of generality as to adequately explain very little of actual life.[17] It is scarcely of great surprise, for instance, to discover (as influential works in this field instruct, often after several pages of refined mathematical modeling) that most people seek "esteem,"[18] or wish to "signal" (i.e., convey) that they are "trustworthy types."[19] Or that they strive to meet the expectations of those around them, whatever these may be.[20] Observations of this sort could offer novel insight only to those apparently operating on the prior belief that all human behavior, when the state does not suppress it, originates in the decisions of discrete individuals bereft of any significant attachment to others, lacking any concern with how others view them.

Fourth, in its more generalizing formulations, the economic analysis of social norms has displayed little predictive power[21] or even clear, compelling policy implications.[22] It chiefly offers "just-so stories" coincidentally matching up an author's favored, a priori theory of human motivation to a smattering of cherry-picked facts, with case-illustrations "selected on the dependent variable," a violation of basic social scientific protocol. Untested in any systematic way, such a theory can do little more than loosely illustrate its authors' metaphysical intuitions. The economists of norms largely content themselves with identifying discrete micromechanisms of self-aggrandizement and self-preservation. These are arguably present, in some measure, essentially anywhere and everywhere. The more significant questions concern differences in degree, from one context to another. Virtually never do economic analyses undertake the more challenging task of assessing a number of alternative hypotheses derived from conflicting theoretical premises. These would necessarily include the possibility of morality's genuine internalization, a scenario rarely foreclosed by available data.

Fifth and finally, though economists admit the periodic superiority of informal norms over law as a regulatory modality, they favor norms because (and where) these yield greater efficiency. Norms are often preferable to law, however, for reasons very different. That is especially so when the norms in play are not utilitarian in inspiration, not focused on overall well-being, however conceived. Social norms sometimes work to foster virtue in individuals and to protect their human dignity. When the law sees fit to rely upon norms, it is often in hopes of attaining these same aspirations. And because such nonutilitarian norms do not always enhance cooperation, they sometimes *reduce* efficiency.

In any event, economic writing on the relation between law and social norms chiefly concerns itself with accounting for when, within a self-enclosed communal enclave, disputants seek redress in legal venues and when via informal mechanisms. These inquiries show little interest in explaining, beyond these tightly circumscribed contexts, the extent of law's formal reach into areas of society already intensely governed by informal norms. Here, a sociologist of law, Eric Feldman, offers greater insight.[23] Though he too studies dispute resolution, he finds that even where informal norms are strong, as among Tokyo's tuna traders, people may still choose to resolve their disagreements through courts, in this case a court administered by members of that particular occupational group. Economists and sociologists largely agree that it is more efficient to resolve disputes informally where there exist strong intragroup bonds establishing shared moral standards. But if so, then the tuna traders, in preferring juridical formalization, appear wildly irrational in not acting upon their clear self-interest. That seems not merely an ungenerous interpretation, but an improbable one, Feldman observes.

Like Feldman—and Montesquieu, in this book's first epigraph, for instance—I too am curious about what happens when law and its institutions permeate a social order already rich in mutual moral expectation, dense in extralegal ordering. At these times, the law may formally authorize morally disfavored conduct, yet not actually embolden and encounter much of it. At least not nearly as much as lenient rules "on the books" would seem to augur. The economic literature provides a variety of micro-inquiries into the inner workings of such insular enclaves as diamond dealers, sumo wrestlers, medieval European and Maghrebi merchants, Chinese cross-border family-business networks, and Shasta California cattle ranchers—to cite the leading case-studies.[24] Unlike these works or Feldman's, I am not chiefly concerned with the norms governing how people choose to resolve legal disputes *after* unlawful conduct has occurred. Though these experiences do fall within my compass, I wish to broaden our attention and train it as well on situations where no legal disagreement exists, nor could arise, because the objectionable conduct at issue is perfectly lawful, and acknowledged as such even by those who find it objectionable.

A further frailty in the economic analysis of social norms lies in how it lavished much attention on the ways we farsighted elites might tinker cleverly with law to alter prevailing moral sentiments toward this or that discreditable practice,[25] such as our disinclination to donate harvestable human organs. In assessing the prospects for success, scholars mostly ranged from guarded optimism to extravagantly wishful thinking. Even the most cautious seemed to intimate that auspicious practical answers lay just ahead: Can we "evaluate different kinds of interventions" with our innumerable tools of law and policy, pondered Eric Posner, "according to the likelihood that they will enhance desirable forms of nonlegal cooperation and subvert undesirable ones?"[26] The long history of public campaigns at moral reform—certainly those on a broad scale, like the American Temperance Movement and China's Cultural Revolution—strongly suggests, however, that social mores follow a more elusive and convoluted course, recalcitrant to most such machinations. And though major changes in mores undoubtedly do occur, these changes have proven largely opaque to genuine scientific explanation. Such explanation seeks to assess alternative hypotheses and disentangle the relative influence of competing causal factors.

Still, it is clear that state power, whether exercised within the law or through its violation, generally proves too crude an instrument for permanently transforming prevailing morals in intended directions, certainly not without undesired consequences, often vast. This is not to deny that governmental repression can effectively drive underground—even thoroughly suppress, for a time—practices officially disfavored yet still cherished by many. These include the sacrificial rituals of banned religious groups, as well as cockfighting, bearbaiting,[27] and dwarf-tossing,[28] or more contemporary indulgences like potato chips, soft drinks, overeating, binge drinking, marijuana, and "problem" gambling.[29]

One encounters no effort within the considerable scholarship on the relation between law and social norms to identify the sources of this consistent failure, nor to uncover reasons for the few, arguable exceptions to the rule. Still less does one find any candid recognition of the extent to which prior attempts to officially denigrate popular practices—deemed immoral by legal elites of the day—resemble more contemporary proposals, even for purposes of distinguishing these seeming precedents from current campaigns. What one instead encounters are continued celebrations of law's transformative powers, exaltations of its ability to conjure new social and cultural realities into being.

Typical is this rousing peroration from Robert Post, later the dean of Yale Law School: "Law can create the preconditions of its own legitimation, because it can establish values that 'seem natural and necessary.' Law is in this sense performative, constituting the very culture in whose service it purports to act."[30] He then adds the proviso, "Of course law may fail in this task of cultural creation, in which case a social crisis may ensue."[31] Post clearly intends this as a reservation to his bold, preceding assertion. Yet his 'qualification' is in fact bolder still. For it suggests that law is the preferred method to "establish values," the primary source of "cultural creation," perhaps the only fully acceptable means, in fact. And therefore "a crisis may ensue" if society had to rely in significant measure for its values and culture on wellsprings not chiefly juridical. This is "legal centralism" with a vengeance, the view that law, and law alone, is what acceptably holds together a modern social order. This stance is wholly hegemonic among American law school faculties. Until not long ago, it has been widely shared in few other places. This fact alone is enough to mark it as exotic, an anthropological curiosity, an anachronistic eccentricity.

We law professors sometimes accede—passingly, grudgingly—to a weak version of law's limitations, of history's cautionary tales.[32] We nonetheless stop well short of acknowledging the true magnitude of the obstacles to our task. This is scarcely surprising: no one enters a professional field with a view to demonstrating its severe limitations in solving the central problems it sets itself. While we bemoan our disappointing track record, those of Foucaultian leanings and vaguely anarchistic impulses, temperamentally averse to all such authoritative efforts at "normalizing," will have every reason to rhapsodize about it. In fact, they should rejoice in the resilient spirit of subaltern resistance to all such ephemeral policy enthusiasms, each deploying its own peculiar "biopolitical technology of governmentality" against so wide an array of pleasurable practices.

## The Sociology of Law and the Frailty of Individual Rights

Scholarship in the sociology of law, on "law and society," would initially seem a natural place to look for sustained engagement with present questions. Yet answers are virtually absent there. What one does find, closely related, is the frequent insinuation—not quite an argument, really—that there is something wanting, almost morally deficient, about asserting one's experience of discrimination (racial, gender, or disability) in the law's individualistic categories; for such victimization actually emerges from larger institutional structures and social practices.[33] It would seem woefully misguided, in short, simply to invoke one's own legal rights when broader change is necessary to secure them, for oneself and others.[34] It is too much to realistically expect that, simply through pressing one's own, isolated legal claim, one might succeed in calling significant public attention to what remains inherently a systemic problem, one that must be attacked root and branch. And it is surely correct, of course, as these scholars urge, that truly large-scale injustices—where discrete wrongs are truly integral to a larger problem—cannot be fully redressed by any single piece of litigation.

The worthy victim of discrimination, these scholars observe, is unlikely to pursue his individual claims unless he understands them as part of an encompassing pattern, which he learns to recognize and resist only with support from "a wide social network"[35] of fellow victims and legal activists, urging him on. Without this awakened sociological awareness, his "rights-consciousness"[36] is simply alienated consciousness, on a Marxian view of the matter. Raising a consciousness of rights is thus a worthy political aim only when this fosters a collective consciousness of shared victimhood; and this is highly unlikely to occur without prompting from an elite vanguard of "cause lawyers."

Somewhat at odds with this view, others within the law-and-society canon do regularly suggest that individuals are too slow to claim their antidiscrimination rights, at least, and that victims confront herculean obstacles to that end.[37] A number of identifiable mechanisms operate, elusively yet potently, to discourage them from taking even the first steps down the long, arduous path to legal vindication. This path requires several independent steps, from recognizing the injury itself to "naming" it as wrongful, then identifying and "blaming" a culpable party, to formal "claiming" against that party.[38] Only then does one confront the challenge of "prevailing" in court.

Yet if there were ever a circumstance when it is fitting and proper for the potentially meritorious claimant to demur from asserting her full battery of legal rights, we never learn about it in this considerable literature. This may admittedly be because the particular rights these studies investigate are ones that, most of us believe, should never be foresworn, their possible violation never endured. We would then require some account, though, of why these certain rights, and not others, fall into this category, an analysis offered nowhere in this body of scholarship.[39] From its standpoint, informal encumbrances on exerting one's rights—of employees against employers, minorities against majority institutions, women against men—are (put bluntly) bad.[40] To invoke one's individual rights is fully commendable, however, only insofar as it reflects and fosters political solidarity with others whom the right-bearer should recognize and embrace as comrades in arms. Whatever social forces may help raise the right-bearer's consciousness in this respect are what truly deserve our praise and support, not the particular claimant and his isolated act of rights-assertion.

This long-standing scholarly tradition does not purport directly to address the question of immediate concern, that of when people consider it wrongful to exercise their rights, and acceptable to dissuade others from doing the same. Still, the canon of law and society does implicitly offer the answer just outlined. This answer relies too heavily on broad-brush categories—of race, gender, class—to serve any present purposes, equally sociological in nature. It accords no place, in particular, to the moral discernment that ordinary people themselves display in distinguishing among the many types of situations in which these questions arise. The questions I pose at this point are entirely empirical and explanatory, not at all normative. They invite no flights of metaphysical fancy, and bear centrally on the relation of law to society, however one wishes to define these terms. It is therefore lamentable that this distinguished intellectual tradition has found virtually nothing to say about them.[41]

## Moral Anthropology

This scholarly field, writes a leading proponent, "explores how societies . . . found their cultural distinction between good and evil, and how social agents concretely work out this separation in their everyday life." Moral anthropology thus "helps understand the evaluative principles and practices operating in the social world, the debates they arouse, the processes through which they become implemented, the justifications that are given to account for discrepancies observed between what should be and what is actually."[42]

Scholarly curiosity of this sort is rather new. For cultural anthropology has long been mired in a "hermeneutics of suspicion"[43] discouraging investigators from treating ordinary moral sensibilities as worthy of close sympathetic attention.[44] The importance of moral sentiments resided chiefly in how they serve as a smokescreen for something else, always more sinister.[45] Anthropologists of Nietzschean persuasion, in particular, have understood nearly the entire enterprise of moral 'discourse' in the West—over which the Christian churches long predominated—as aimed chiefly at suppressing sensual pleasures that many contemporaries deem entirely legitimate. The intellectual architects of such discourse sought to normalize relations of domination, as by preaching the moral duties that wives owe to their husbands.

Talk of morality fared no better among those whose theoretical tastes inclined toward Bourdieu. He conceived of morality as integral to the "habitus" and "cultural capital" by which certain elements of the dominant class improve their standing relative to other such elements, by exchanging their symbolic (including moral) capital for material and political forms.[46] When the individual exercises his capacity for moral judgment of others, this is actually a thinly veiled weapon for "distinguishing" himself from members of social classes that he disdains, for denigrating their moral failings and highlighting his own virtues.[47] From either theoretical perspective, that of Bourdieu or Nietzsche, the resources of moral language as a supple, probing instrument of collective self-assessment and social criticism, regularly employed in fact to justify rebellion, are largely ignored when not simply denied. This failure of appreciation is especially evident concerning the resources of liberal moral theory for the powerful criticism of actual liberal societies. It is scarcely surprising then that, when two leading French scholars argued that most people are sincerely committed to offering moral justification for their actions, and that social integration emerges from the resulting interplay of convictions,[48] many initially greeted these findings as scandalous.

Social scientists of more conventional stripe than Bourdieu or Nietzsche may lack their visceral antiliberalism, yet often succumb to a second pitfall. We often perceive our professional stature intolerably sullied when we allow ourselves to draw up "too closely to the taken-for-granted stuff of everyday life,"[49] writes one of our number. Such homely "stuff" notably includes the moral appraisals that life invites, even requires us to make, on literally a daily basis. It is just such quotidian encounters, however, that arouse our most acute concerns and emotions, suffuse our "life-world."[50] The scholarly result of this inattention is a strange desolation, a dead space of the sociological *un*imagination. To which sociologist Andrew Sayer issues a rare and moving dissent, warranting quotation at length:

> We are ethical beings, not in the sense that we necessarily always behave ethically, but that as we grow up we come to evaluate behaviour according to some ideas of what is good or acceptable. We compare and admire or deplore particular actions, personal traits, social practices and institutions. How people behave and should behave with respect to one another is undeniably important to us, indeed it is hard to imagine anything more important, yet social science tells us little about our sense of what is good or bad in these

> matters and why it is so important to us. Its third-person descriptions typically drain away the normative force of such considerations, making it appear that we are mere pursuers of self-interest, creatures of habit, followers of conventions and norms, or puppets of power. . . .
>
> Given the care and attention that people sometimes give to deciding what to do for the best in their dealings with others, given the subtlety and difficulty of some of the issues that they agonize over in running their lives, and given the power of . . . sentiments such as respect, compassion, gratitude, shame, guilt, pride, hate, disgust and resentment, this bland rendering of the ethical dimension of social life is almost insulting. If we encounter someone who is disrespectful, dishonest, callous or selfish we are likely to react strongly. Even if we wish to be tolerant and nonjudgmental about others' actions, characters and lifestyles, this too is a moral stance. As social beings, we simply cannot live without developing some sense of how actions affect well-being and how we ought to treat one another.[51]

With the historical weight of so much scholarly skepticism against it, it is hardly remarkable that the serious study of how we bring sincerely held moral standards to bear upon the intricacies of our daily lives—deciding how to adhere, when to depart—has been so long in arriving and remains still incipient.[52]

The new field of moral anthropology, heavily inspired by Foucault's later works, offers much promise here. Through ethnographic inquiry, its practitioners seek to gain some methodical purchase on what one scholar calls "lay normativity . . . the first-person evaluative relation to the world."[53] The best of this writing, though theoretically informed, operates quite close to the texture of immediate experience, often one of cruel indifference and terrible anguish,[54] though also, intermittently, of extravagant generosity, of both the spirit and the pocketbook.[55] Texts in this vein can defy all conventional genres of writing, scholarly and literary, scientific and humanistic; they intermix interior monologue with the meticulous description of external surfaces, unobtrusively conveying, for instance, the salty scent of drying tears on a sorrowed face.[56]

In any event, moral anthropologists have only begun to reach some of the pressing questions Sayer intimates. Such an enterprise would examine how people directly experience a range of moral sentiments when confronting quandaries on which they are daily compelled to reflect. These reflections, often wordless, concern what people owe themselves, what is right or wrong, and the relevance of these very categories in interpreting their intimate encounters. How do people make nuanced sense of their choices when they are confident they know what morality requires of them, but must weigh the considerable personal costs of acting upon such knowledge? What goes through our heads and hearts, in other words, when we deliberate—within ourselves and among those we most trust—over how to meet the moral challenges, ordinary and extraordinary, that life throws at us?

These few questions naturally invite several others. What place might the law occupy in these earnest self-reflections, where it clearly authorizes conduct we or others deem unethical? In appraising our conduct, will others—those whose good opinion we value—more heavily weigh the legality of our action over its immorality, or the reverse? How much importance do we accord the fact that others consider our conduct wrongful, though they acknowledge it to be lawful? How much significance do we ourselves accord the apparent wrongfulness of our conduct, even as we correctly reassure ourselves of its legality?

Finally, how do the answers to all these questions vary between cultures whose members may or may not accord the law much inherent authority?[57] How do those answers differ, within a given society, according to variations in social stature among those engaged in these appraisals? And if we exaggerate the inclination to consider such matters at all (even haphazardly), then what might ethnography teach us about the subjective experience of moral indifference, the phenomenology of "simply not giving a damn"?

One hopes that this promising new field of inquiry will soon address such questions, treat them as integral to its promising new research program. It has not yet done so.

# 10

# The Changing Stance of Lawyers toward Common Morality

## Moral *Certainty* as the Basis of Professional Authority: Or, How We Lawyers Once Viewed Our Vocation

Individuals and institutions regularly seek professional counsel in situations where the applicable law clearly authorizes a great deal more than do prevailing mores. The client may therefore lawfully engage in conduct that most people consider reprehensible. As best we can tell from the historical record,[1] American lawyers once felt authorized and impelled at such moments to call a client's attention to extralegal considerations of this sort, as he deliberated over how to act upon his rights. Through these intercessions, attorneys sought delicately to suggest that their clients behave more "responsibly"—as prevailing moral sensibilities understood the term—than the law itself unequivocally required.

The bar's ethics rules have long permitted us to offer such nonlegal counsel.[2] These rules do not require us to do so, however, even where a client's interests could be well served by hearing it. Like the rules to which clients themselves are subject, those of legal ethics leave lawyers free to disregard common morality if they so choose. It is surely fair to surmise that the general public—defensibly or otherwise—wishes us firmly to intercede against prospective client conduct widely deemed highly unethical. In failing to require such intercession, the rules of legal ethics thereby create a species of rights to do wrong, as this book employs the term.

And yet, if this is how most people view such rules today, we should recall that they were first drafted in contemplation of a profession whose members were not so uncomfortable about discouraging clients from "sharp practices" not clearly illegal. "Statesmanlike" appeals to "public morals" were apparently not uncommon, though it would be mistaken to magnify these intermittent rhetorical forays into some long-lost "golden age"[3] of hyper-ethical lawyering. The occasional resort to gentle ethical exhortation may have nonetheless been integral to professional self-understanding, on some accounts,[4] though these longstanding inclinations came under increasing pressure within the new corporate bar at the beginning of the twentieth century. It is no small irony that early American lawyers could speak with such apparent confidence in what common morality required of their commercial clients while adopting a decidedly *un*common stance of "noblesse oblige."[5]

This haughty habitus is all but avowedly aristocratic in character, as many since Tocqueville[6] have observed. The bar's cultural authority[7] over extralegal aspects of client conduct thus rested on its members' confidence in their elevated social stature—and, by implication, on their moral superiority in relation to clients deemed "mere merchants." In hindsight, what is most unfamiliar, counterintuitive, even astonishing in this picture is that the clients, captains of the country's emergent large industry, were apparently willing to accord their attorney, despite his far inferior wealth, some deference of this sort, even to hear him out.

Few Americans now view the legal profession in such terms, of course—as a serious guardian of common morality, valiantly pressing back the tides of unrestrained commercialism, preserving nonmarket values increasingly frail. Opinion surveys consistently suggest, in fact, that we are not held in especially high ethical regard,[8] to put it generously. Most Americans would today surely scoff at the notion that we lawyers exercise any "civilizing influence" on our corporate clients, infusing moral considerations into their decision-making beyond any the law itself unambiguously adopts. Some of us may have won the wealth of aristocrats but have surely lost all trace of leisurely gentility.

Some evidence suggests that, over the last half-century, we American lawyers have retreated from that earlier self-understanding.[9] Like our corporate clients themselves, we increasingly view this willfully aristocratic persona as indefensibly paternalistic, reflecting a certain diffidence, almost indifference, toward the pressing challenges of our business clients. The rationale offered for our current stance is that we live in a morally pluralistic society, whose members subscribe to very different conceptions of the good. Only the legal system can hope to hold together so potentially fissiparous a social order, and we lawyers are essential to that system's operation. We must therefore suspend any moral appraisal of our clients' ends, assisting them by whatever lawful means may advance these lawful objectives.[10] Our rules of professional responsibility hence provide what philosopher Joseph Raz calls "exclusionary reasons"[11]—that is, grounds for excluding any broader normative considerations from our professional purview. Within this field of vision, such common morality as may exist is immaterial to, and indeed likely to be often at odds with, our proper role and duties within such a society.

This view finds abundant colloquial expression in the ordinary language of American lawyers. From his survey of them in the early 1990s, Nelson quotes one as saying: "I personally would have a problem even conveying my own view of the morality of the situation to a client. I think morality is a very slippery concept, primarily in the eye of the beholder."[12] There are several areas of legal practice where attorneys still largely control how a dispute will be handled: criminal defense, personal injury, divorce, and bankruptcy. However, corporate clients today directly determine key details of their representation, especially in litigation, on such matters as witness preparation, discovery,[13] and even spoken objections in court.[14] The litigator's immediate 'client' is generally the company's in-house counsel, who is the "most vocal partisan of the litigator-as-agent model,"[15] according to one empirical study. A prominent historian of the American legal profession thus concludes,

> In recent decades the claims that lawyers are the exemplars and transmitters of public values, guardians of the public purposes of the law and the system of restraints on liberty, and mediators between excesses of democracy and plutocracy, have almost completely disappeared from the rhetoric and self-image of the elite business bar . . . Business lawyers see themselves simply as part of the financial and business service industry, selling complex technical skills to help clients minimize legal costs and manage risks in the global economy.[16]

There is some indication that our present, unsentimental way of thinking about the relation of law and common morality may explain the profession's apparent contribution to the 2008 financial crisis. A leading corporate-law scholar thus finds that in-house counsel for major investment firms, those promoting subprime mortgage securitization in particular, felt themselves trapped in "co-dependency" on reckless clients. These attorneys faced a "Darwinian . . . career tournament" ensuring that they would "predictably frustrate focus [by their clients] on ethics beyond minimal legal compliance."[17] In other areas of practice, too, a perverse symbiosis often develops whereby lawyer and client—viewed through the lens of common morality—bring out the worst in each other. The lawyer tells herself, "I am only acting at the behest of the client. The injustice is his responsibility, not mine." The client rejoins: "I would never have considered doing this, but my lawyer says I should."[18] Each is passing the buck, some will say, yet neither is telling an untruth.

Until recent decades, few would have considered it ironic or paradoxical that corporate legal counsel would "arrogate" to themselves a professional duty to dissuade clients from employing rights in ways at odds with prevailing morals. Lawmaking itself was necessarily a somewhat different endeavor in such conditions. Until the early 1970s, legislators—when deciding the scope of law's authorizations—could assume a legal profession whose members counseled restraint when these authorizations proved unclear. The law of business corporations, in particular, could therefore formally indulge certain sorts of questionable conduct, at the margins; for drafters knew that informal remonstrance would limit exploitation of this slippage between law and morals. Any reputable legal counsel would moderate the ethically uncouth impulses of our nouveau riche clientele, dispelling dangers of rights abuse. More intrusive legal proscriptions would be unnecessary.

As the American practice of law became ever more commercial in focus throughout the twentieth century, the social foundations on which generations of legislators and judges established these rights to do wrong have eroded. This is not to say those foundations have dissolved; nor have the professional sensibilities restraining the objectionable exercise of these entitlements. There remains, moreover, much argument over how fast or extensive these changes have been. Yet in creating early instances of rights to do serious wrong, lawmakers had implicitly assumed the vitality of these restraining sensibilities, whose full significance and precariousness we can only now begin fully to appreciate.

The analysis just offered should call into question the continued defensibility of long-standing rights adopted on the basis of sociological assumptions no longer valid. These rights could include, for instance, those authorizing companies to compensate managers and directors chiefly on the basis of quarterly profits rather than longer-term performance. For generations these rights were uncontroversial, because few imagined that corporate decision-makers might someday exercise them in ways so greatly at odds with shareholder and societal expectations.[19] Economists will predictably reply that such people were simply responding to then-prevailing incentives. Yet the rights creating these incentives were already long available. It must therefore be that shifting moral sensibilities among business and legal elites played a role in attenuating self-restraints, in causing these elite professionals to newly act upon long-present opportunities (in ways that many business leaders in other Western lands find almost obscene).

There is also reason to believe that, though they have lost their prior self-assurance in addressing moral questions their clients faced, lawyers today continue to rest their authority in no small measure on a certain, distinctive relation to common morality and its demands. That is a relationship quite different than in the past. Though our societal influence once required great self-confidence in our own powers of ethical discernment, today our influence rests far more on our skills in eliciting mistrust and suspicion toward the competence and moral integrity of others, in evoking reservations about how much we may rely upon their professed good will toward us. To be sure, it will be initially puzzling why it might come to pass, as the next section contends, that *in*certitude could today become as essential to our professional authority as, in the past, was its very antithesis.

## Moral *Doubt* as the Basis of Professional Authority: Or, How Lawyers Now View Their Jobs

We law professors make a living by helping our students mostly get, not "to yes"—the aim of real-life negotiations—but "to maybe," as we put it.[20] This requires sowing doubt, where most people crave certainty. Few of us view our aim as conclusively resolving disputes, pointing the way toward a single, definitive "right answer." Mostly, we seek to suggest how cases might credibly "go either way," more often than our students would initially suppose, so that results will regularly turn on the relative analytical firepower brought to bear by contending legal counsel and their well-coached witnesses.

To this end, it is often helpful heuristically to pay closer attention to the places where law departs from common morality than where it conforms. Thus, common morality may suggest one result, the law another. Such situations invite counsel with the weaker legal argument to find clever ways to appeal to common morality, where it can be found, especially in disputes likely to go before a jury. In settlement negotiations, "getting to maybe" sometimes involves planting the possibility that the jury may choose to rely more on prevalent moral sentiments than on the law, even where the applicable law does not explicitly authorize such reliance (as it rarely does).

Many of us law professors take a certain sober satisfaction, even an inside-dopester glee at times, in drawing back the curtains and disclosing to our students the myriad ways that law regularly departs in key respects from what the dewy-eyed novitiate, in thrall to her simplistic lay sense of what morality requires, innocently supposes it must be. We discreetly distance ourselves from what Felix Cohen, an influential "legal realist," belittled as "the spontaneous outpourings of a sensitive conscience unfamiliar with the social context."[21] The dialectician in us may even revel in showing how the law must tack in one direction so that it can then move in the opposite, ending often somewhere in between. We sometimes relish in showing why law indulges seeming immorality—through a circuitous cunning, mysterious to outsiders—in order to advance the good. We, the worldly-wise, take guilty pleasure in revealing the counterintuitive to the uninitiated.

Thus, for instance, many of us love to shock the conscience of our entering students—with stunning effortlessness, in their first semester—by showing how top Ford Motors executives decided to put the Pinto on the market despite knowing full well that hundreds of lives could be saved by inexpensively fixing a small design defect.[22] We then show how Ford executives ran the numbers to their cost–benefit analysis, thereby "attaching a dollar value to human life," stunningly so, when declining to make this essential, lifesaving modification. We next disclose how those numbers, examined unsentimentally, establish the greater societal efficiency of paying out *ex post* compensation to victims of foreseeable accidents than solving the design problem *ex ante,* preventing many fatal injuries. This means that, far from warranting the $125 million dollars in punitive damages that an outraged jury awarded,[23] Ford executives did exactly the sort of calculations we very much *want* corporate decision-makers to undertake (provided they get the numbers right, a very different question). Within a mere twenty minutes, the moral sentiments of our students often shift from utter abhorrence to plaintive appreciation, at least, of the problem's normative complexity. Students exit the classroom much less confident in their ethical bearings than when they entered.[24]

We might describe this recognition, without exaggeration, as something of an ethical epiphany—though of a decidedly unwelcome variety. The initial response of our students, when first learning of Ford's conduct, had been impulsively Kantian, to the effect that human beings must never be treated in ways so disrespectful of their inherent, essential dignity, as mere means to others' material ends, including those of society at large. It is simply wrong for the law to so regard and handle them, in other words, even if the aggregate result will be to deprive many thousands of the only kind of car they could afford, consigning them to long hours on the bus.

When we suspect that our students' moral sentiments now tilt toward consequentialism (of roughly utilitarian sort[25]) we will tack back in the opposite direction. We show them how the law now instead adopts a stance more deeply protective of personal dignity and individual autonomy, regardless of society-wide repercussions. The law does so, for instance, through the unqualified right to decline essential life-support, even when a patient facing an ephemeral medical crisis (but otherwise with no terminal condition) will certainly die, and where she and others—notably young dependents or aging parents reliant upon her—would clearly be better off if she remained among the living.

Whether we move in one direction or the other, consequentialist or deontological (or to virtue ethics, when sentencing criminal convicts), our pedagogical purpose is the same, and well served: to show how law's seemingly arcane mysteries are ultimately intelligible, and that its superficial absurdities often disclose—beneath their surface—moral judgments entirely defensible, all things considered. For these are matters of great normative complexity, implicating all leading theories, disclosing the limits of each, its failure to capture central aspects of a factual configuration, aspects undeniably relevant. As real-life counselors, our task is not that of engineers (social or otherwise), to cut a wide swath through the Everglades, so that big ships might pass; it is instead to run a thin thread through a pathless jungle, so that a given client might find her individual way to safety from pursuing beasts.

When our aim is merely to disconcert, to undermine our students' frequent overconfidence in their moral discernment, we introduce disturbing distortions of our own. We depart from any honest effort to make sense of when and why disparities between law and common morality arise and, no less importantly, when they do not. We may pride ourselves on appreciating the many subtle reasons (see Chapter 6) why our legal rules depart from such morality—often in service of a more "critical" moral thinking, or simply because we base legal rules on better factual information than most laymen possess.

We should acknowledge, though, that many of those recalcitrant commoners—even after hearing out our refined rationales or rationalizations—will remain skeptical, if not thoroughly unconvinced. We spokesmen of the law may be perfectly prepared, in our intellectual sophistication, to accept its frequent indifference to common morality.[26] Yet most bearers and vocal representatives of this parallel normative universe will continue to insist upon law's acute attentiveness, even subordination, to it and to them. This disagreement plays out not in the classroom or the pages of a learned treatise, but in the political arena, where they, not we, are much more likely to prevail. Oliver Wendell Holmes Jr. cheerfully championed this result, even when thoroughly convinced that the law's path would thereby lead directly "to hell."[27]

There is some similarity here in how we law professors and lawyers establish our authority over others, students or clients, and how the more modern, scientific professions do so. We all emphasize the complexity of what we know and do, and by implication its remoteness from common knowledge or popular intuition. Those in professions whose authority rests upon the achievements of modern science, though, make much bolder assertions about what their practitioners can know, with confidence and precision, through their unique and specialized learning.

The type of complexity we lawyers routinely manage so dexterously for our clients, by contrast, leaves much of importance unsettled, even at the end of the analysis, where uncertainties will remain. In fact, our own assertions of professional authority often rest precisely on our disconcerting facility in displacing what seemed so certain—just a moment ago—with unanticipated doubt, notably in cross-examining opposing witnesses.[28] We do not so much "seek the truth" per se as we probe persistently for evidence that others, through their incompetence or moral failings, have distorted or even suppressed the truth.[29] We thereby appeal to our listener's recognition of life's unpleasant underside, because this move so often makes for a more credible account of contemporary society than narratives more rousingly upbeat.

Nonlawyers may here fairly ask of us: But what sort of authority and expertise is *that?* We live in a global society, after all, in which the most successful practitioners of science and technology, from Nobel Prize physicists to Steve Jobs and Bill Gates, enjoy supreme stature. Little of such cultural authority is left, one might first suppose, for those who can only quibble at the margins of the modern world, for us whose vocational self-understanding entails a certain agnosticism toward all confident claims, cognitive or normative.[30]

And yet, on further reflection, the contemporary world displays another key feature rendering the lofty status and accompanying wealth of us lawyers entirely intelligible. For we occupy an era, we're often told, pervaded by acute skepticism toward all "master narratives" of universal human progress, all ambitiously comprehensive worldviews, scientific or political. The law stands apart from all this in making *no* such confidently progressive claims. This is apparent above all in its "moral pluralism,"[31] in how it shifts kaleidoscopically among differing and seemingly inconsistent normative perspectives and commitments. Each may be incompatible with the rest, according to its more academic exponents, certainly when formulated at the highest levels of abstraction. In confronting the unavoidable messiness of real life, the law intermittently adopts this moral theory or that, from one moment to the next. As advocates, we draw upon these alternative theories to elicit differing moral sentiments,[32] those most congenial in the instant to our cause or client. For the career of the contemporary American lawyer, a belief in moral pluralism (as philosophers employ the term) is quite simply—irrespective of its strictly philosophic merits—extremely convenient.

These dueling theories must of course find some textual footing within applicable authorities whose strictures we must honor. Still, our social authority trades heavily on a deftness at invoking, as suits the occasion, the shared moral sentiments of others, often nonlawyers. Any accomplished advocate (well short of the most silver-tongued) is able to interpret the law and fashion the facts in a given dispute so as to evoke this or that broadly shared moral sentiment—deontological, consequentialist, or virtue-based—as behooves her client's immediate interests or ideals. We generate even a certain, curious kind of 'trust,' precisely through our acuity in inspiring distrust toward others. In complex commercial and financial transactions, for instance, we celebrate our savvy at finding myriad ways to protect our clients against the devious designs by which their counterparty might later exploit their vulnerabilities, designs which may exist only in our own ingeniously florid imaginings.

Our pinpoint skills at unmasking others' seeming arrogance, at puncturing their hot air balloons, accounts for a second, telling feature of the classroom encounter just described. Our students may depart the place convulsed in moral doubt. Yet we ourselves, their teachers, exit in quiet confidence that we have demonstrated the unmistakable value of our wares. We admit that these remain embarrassingly premodern, largely inherited from the Sophists and other ancient rhetoricians. Even so, these skills enable us, and those to whom we lend our services, to survive what some call "the postmodern condition," to emerge still standing, more or less unfazed, in the ruins of others' exaggerated pretensions to resolve life's mysteries scientifically, quantitatively, definitively, incorruptibly. We ourselves, whatever our undoubted failings, at least chain our star to no such misplaced certainties.

The danger here is that we may thereby acquire more than simply a sophisticated appreciation of normative complexity, a virtue by nearly any standard. We further succumb, writes a prominent law professor, to "an occupational hazard in becoming morally weightless, detached, never committed to any person or cause, never responsible for any consequence."[33] To this peculiar fate, more precisely, many of us do not so much succumb, in fact, as actively aspire.

It is also true that still more of our number, much like our students here, feel a painful personal loss in abandoning our early certainties on many an issue, even as we still silently wish we might someday recover them. As a faculty colleague writes (in response to this chapter), "The same questioning voice that I've always deployed in the classroom now lives firmly in my own head and speaks just as vigorously against me when I wish to take a strong position on an issue [like abortion, he adds] about which I was once much more certain I knew the moral truth." In other words, this "same questioning voice" opposes him just as energetically as when he challenges the moral overconfidence he sees so clearly in his students. This loss of the self-confidence essential to any committed activism, he ruefully admits, is greatly dismaying. "You cannot raise the standard against oppression, or lead into the breach to relieve injustice," wrote Judge Learned Hand, "and still keep an open mind to every disconcerting fact or an open ear to the cold voice of doubt."[34]

Who really desires the kind of worldly wisdom my colleague here finds within himself, so inward-looking and politically quietistic? As we pose this question to ourselves, we find that we cannot, in the final analysis, draw great satisfaction from instilling such enervating doubt even *in others,* whose headstrong, cocksure convictions we ourselves, to our own ambivalent regret, can no longer quite bring ourselves to share. Still, we ultimately recognize that it is this search for doubt, not for truth, that defines our true stock and trade, that earns our bread and butter.

Beyond the courtroom and its grueling cross-examinations, the story is similar. A growing portion of our work consists of "legal auditing," chiefly on behalf of large organizations. This often involves helping reorganize their internal life and external relations with a view to reducing prospects of legal dispute. Stirring trouble is no one's immediate aim here—just the contrary. Still, it is the present possibility of conflict, perceived as credibly on the horizon, which generates the demand for this increasing share of legal services. When we seek to supply it, we could scarcely be condemned for sowing conflict, it might seem.

Laypeople themselves, after all, routinely counsel one another to "get it in writing," to ensure that others' avowals can later be enforced.[35] Students at major business schools are today taught that "law remains the last great untapped source of competitive advantage."[36] They are assigned books by prominent law professors with titles like *Proactive Law for Managers: A Hidden Source of Competitive Advantage.*[37] Europeans are advancing similar ideas and pedagogies.[38] We lawyers do no more than respond sympathetically to others' self-defined need, on this view. We behave "like the supplier of artificial hormones that supplement the diminished supply coursing through the body," writes Galanter. "The lawyer contrives enforceability to supplement the failing supply of reciprocity, moral obligation, and fellow-feeling [within the society she serves]." We devise and market forms of "artificial trust." We are simply "the beneficiaries of the decline in its low-cost rival,"[39]—the real McCoy, we admit. If more informal practices of conciliation have atrophied—those long endorsed by common morality, embodied in prevailing mores—this then has nothing to do with the law's allegedly invasive tendencies. This position amounts to claiming that the new, burgeoning business of recent decades has fallen effortlessly into our laps, owing to a process of moral decomposition within society at large, in which we ourselves play no active part.

That view is incomplete, at best, and disingenuous at very least. It observes only one-half of the cycle, of a deepening spiral. If social distrust has significantly increased, as considerable social science suggests, our efforts to market ourselves, to generate new business on its basis, has nonetheless contributed to this result in no small part. These marketing efforts are recently much enhanced: large U.S. law firms spend considerable sums on promotional workshops and seminars touting our services to fearful managers in the private, public, and nonprofit sectors,[40] highlighting that we no longer limit our professional activities to dispute resolution, transactional structuring, or political lobbying.

The successes of preventive medicine provide the ostensible inspiration for what is now sometimes called "preventive law."[41] We understand this in terms of our enhanced "proactivity" and our "growing focus on risk management," write Richard and Daniel Susskind (in an influential work).[42] This is in keeping, we may tell ourselves, with larger macro-sociological trends marking the rise of "risk society"[43]: a new type of social order in which altogether eliminating catastrophic risk—from chemical spills and technological system failures to "natural" disasters and epidemics from new diseases—is deemed impossible. In a risk society, we instead acknowledge the near inevitability of periodic catastrophe and seek only to structure our activities intelligently around it, to minimize its harmful consequences. We believe that with great risks often comes the chance for great rewards, societal no less than individual. In this spirit, we seek to develop sophisticated methods of legal "risk analysis," loosely analogous to those in fields more quantitative and respectable by modern epistemological standards. We orient our legal practices toward offering comprehensive packages of "risk protection," touching on all aspect of our clients' present and prospective activities.[44]

In these expansionary ventures, we necessarily sell ourselves through inducing some doubt in others' trustworthiness. We subtly propagate our distinctive worldview—once peculiar, no longer so—in which the human universe assumes a visage full of imminent peril at nearly every turn. But it is impossible to inculcate this idea—that we should become warier of others' designs upon us—without insinuating that they too will in turn be growing increasingly wary of us. There arises a version of "the security dilemma,"[45] familiar from international relations: no one really needs certain weapons until one's potential rivals begin acquiring them, at which point they may become truly essential.

Advocates of preventive legal auditing highlight "strategic advantage" as among its central objectives.[46] A recent empirical study even finds that large companies whose CEOs are trained attorneys stave off litigation more effectively than those managed by people holding only MBAs. Reducing disputes serves to maintain shareholder value by diminishing both litigation costs and liabilities (civil and criminal) to unhappy customers, competitors, or the state.[47] The authors plausibly infer that our professional training and prior legal practice enable us to entertain genuine doubt, more easily than can most nonlawyers, not only regarding others' competence and integrity, but about the strength of our own legal position in areas of potential dispute.

Having shown how this book's animating questions bear on the practice of law, and on corporate law especially, let us now see, in Chapter 11, how these questions bear upon the conduct of corporate business activity itself.

# 11

# Commercial Morality, Bourgeois Virtue, and the Law

The questions this study addresses arise as well with respect to commercial activity, no less than in other areas of life, but here inevitably take on a distinctive configuration. We must thus ask: Does the law of business regulation capture all the major moral concerns raised by business activity, and by high-level financial activity in particular? Does this body of legal rules, in other words, incorporate the whole of relevant morality, leaving no remainder, no need for further and more informal modes of governance?

It is striking that scarcely anyone who has seriously entertained these questions answers them in the affirmative,[1] even the most uncompromising defenders of contemporary American capitalism. The "responsibility of the corporate executive," writes Milton Friedman, "is to make as much money as possible [for the company] while conforming to the basic rules of the society, both those embodied in law *and those embodied in ethical custom.*"[2] In light of the vast disagreement over how to regulate commercial activities, this measure of implicit agreement is notable, even remarkable. There is broad concurrence, in other words, that the law cannot possibly encompass all that society ethically expects of businesspeople, cannot force them to internalize all significant externalities, in particular, ensuing from their activities. It cannot perfectly align incentives between principals, agents, and affected third parties. Extralegal mechanisms of some sort are necessary, at times, to hold business entities and those who manage them to a different and presumably "higher" standard. Given the law's limitations (contingent or inherent), that standard demands something more than law-abidingness. Judge Richard Posner thus readily enumerates a number of profitable business practices, entirely lawful yet widely regarded as unethical[3]—regarded as such by many businesspeople themselves (though far fewer would likely favor their legal prohibition).

What, then, *are* the extralegal restraints, precisely, within the world of business, on conduct seriously at odds with common morality? How do these restraints operate and sustain themselves over time? Have they become debilitated, and if so, at what points precisely, for what reasons? How might we strengthen these informal mechanisms, if that indeed be necessary? And at what points must we give up on extralegal constraints and instead formally interpose additional law? I shall venture a few brief observations regarding the first three of these questions. Attempts to answer them fall into two camps. Let us call these the internalist and externalist perspectives. Each standpoint has very different implications for the law. If the chief moral restraints on commercial activity issue from within, from the self-interested calculations of individual businesspeople, then the law needs to adopt a different approach to their regulation than if the more important and effective moral restraints must issue from without.

On the first, internalist view, lawmaking should address its attention above all to those points within the economy, national and international, where mutual trust among market participants is weakest. These are generally the locations where network ties among them are only intermittent and limited in scope or depth.[4] Here, "the shadow of the future" offers poor protection, through the likelihood of retaliatory tit-for-tat, against predacious conduct. With this in mind, post-crisis financial regulators evinced great concern for inter-firm "connectedness."[5] Yet they focused chiefly on the sheer size of each such institution,[6] examined individually, in isolation from the particular ecology of organizations with which it transacts, from its nodal centrality within such a network. Still broader forms and sources of "contagion" were left unaddressed.[7]

On the second view, legal regulation ought to focus on issue-areas where common morality within society at large, rather than only among immediately pertinent enterprises, is most tenuous and can therefore exert little pressure on those within the business community. Most clearly, these would be the points where there exists no common morality at all, or only in very "thin" form.[8] Such is the case when the matters at issue seem too complex for ready lay comprehension, or because the public remains ignorant of the relevant activity, of its relative incidence and impact on the well-being of large numbers. There is little likelihood in such circumstances that businesspeople will defer to expectations of common morality in resolving difficult questions about how to act where the law authorizes conduct arousing ethical doubts. In identifying where social mores will likely fail to induce restraint, we must again locate the relevant information asymmetries between pertinent parties and the power imbalances thus engendered. In this case, however, the relevant asymmetries are no longer chiefly those among immediate market participants, but now also between such participants and larger publics. In deciding where and in what ways to concentrate law's efforts, we must ask where it is that social mores succeed in exercising most influence, in dampening the abusive exercise of rights. This is true both of existing rights and of those whose creation we may contemplate.

In light of these general considerations, let us now consider in more depth the two opposing answers to the question of how moral pressures on business activity may become effective. What I have described as the internalist stance holds that needed restraints on the exercise of rights emerge naturally from within the very practice of business. More precisely, these inhibitions spring spontaneously from a farsighted concern with preserving a positive reputation, among customers, suppliers, and professional peers, for law-abidance and ethical integrity—because such a reputation is essential for long-term success, of both entire enterprises and individual businesspeople. This would mean, for instance, that the law of securities fraud exists to catch only those few irrational outliers who cannot see where their own self-interest ultimately lies. Economists view this simply in terms of how we all respond to material incentives.

These incentives would never come into being, however, but for the workings of common morality and the fear of stigma through which it exercises social influence. This is a process more deeply assayed by other social sciences. Shared moral understandings are what generate the negative reactions to perceived misconduct that render it costly for individual actors, attaching to it a certain personal price in relevant labor markets. It is therefore impossible to speak intelligibly here of micro-incentives without implicitly invoking the effects of moral ideals operating macrosociologically. The bluster of economists notwithstanding, all such hard talk about individual incentives 'free rides' on soft talk about shared values, about common morality.

Many would nevertheless seriously question whether business activity requires or entails any particular moral "virtue." None of the virtues identified by premodern Western thought, classical or Christian, directly endorse commercial activity of any sort. Many of them in fact sit very uneasily with the personal traits widely deemed essential to economic success. If it is nonetheless meaningful to speak of "virtue" in this connection, it is likely to be virtue distinctive to modern capitalism and therefore still relatively novel in historical terms.

According to the first view, "bourgeois virtue," as it is sometimes expressly (if ironically)[9] described, thus emerges organically from capitalism's very nature, its constitutive internal workings. Lawmakers should therefore largely allow competitive markets to operate freely from fetters extraneous to their nature. This view finds prominent early defense in the writings of Adam Smith[10] and Benjamin Franklin,[11] later in Max Weber to some extent,[12] as well as in such contemporary thinkers as Michael Novak, George Gilder, and Deirdre McCloskey.[13] Novak, a leading Catholic commentator, thus writes, "The ethic of commerce furnishes a school of virtues," which "enhances the cooperative spirit, since economic tasks cannot be accomplished on one's own . . . [Capitalism also] singles out the self-determination of the individual as the main source of social energy . . . inciting imagination and industry."[14] Philosopher Robert Solomon defends similar conclusions with slightly greater guardedness, in texts adopted by U.S. business schools.[15]

Trustworthiness, in particular, is intrinsic to the operation of capitalism and an aspect of bourgeois virtue, on this view. Like prudence, this concept has a long history in moral thought, but has been reshaped to fit the contours of market society. It had to "embourgeoisify" itself, as McCloskey puts it.[16] To succeed in any modern business enterprise, the argument goes, one must win and retain the trust of suppliers, employees, lending institutions, and clientele. Before the advent of credit-rating agencies, which rely on more impersonal sources of data, this required that one cultivate a personal reputation among immediate acquaintances for honesty and "good will."[17]

A circular relationship thus arose, writes a historian of debtor–creditor interactions in the late nineteenth and early twentieth centuries, whereby "character functioned . . . at once as the basis upon which lenders extended credit to borrowers and consumers, and as a broader social and cultural measure of personal worth. Perceptions of personal worth, in turn, registered in the successful use of goods and services obtained on credit to construct creditworthy characters. Credit thus reflected character, but also constituted it."[18]

A further virtue endogenous to capitalism, some have thought, is "sobriety" or seriousness of manner, a credible demeanor of self-control and respectability. What might strike us today as "mere appearances," others long thought to disclose matters of much genuine substance.[19] Sobriety, creditworthiness, and commercial achievement were widely understood as mutually reinforcing, the lines between them rather indistinct, in fact. Of the Victorian age, as Barrington Moore observes, "Just as success in business was taken to be a good indication of moral probity," in private life no less than public, "so was failure in business treated as an immoral act requiring religious censure."[20]

Assessing the sobriety of a potential counterparty required considerable fine-grained "local knowledge," elusive and often uncertain, about the personal life of the particular individual, whether borrower or banker. "A creditworthy man," writes a historian of nineteenth-century England, therefore "outwardly gave no sign of emotionally or financially distracting ties and expenses. His house, furniture, horse, and carriage should be of good quality, indicating solid financial resources, but definitely not showy. Above all, there should be no signs of a taste for champagne and sexual variety."[21] To disclose one's character to strangers, one must also literally carry oneself in a certain manner. For moral rectitude would undoubtedly find reflection in bodily rectitude,[22] a view still common in certain investment banks, no less than within the armed forces. Physical stature would naturally 'embody' social stature, an equation virtually continuous throughout Western history.[23] Under the influence of early Methodism, Moore adds, ideals of "respectability conquered a goodly segment of the urban workers as well as a large sector of the gentry and aristocracy."[24]

Trustworthiness and sobriety rely upon a curious species of empathy, however counterintuitive this may initially sound. To some, this feature of bourgeois virtue evinces no small moral appeal in its own right. The more competitive a given market, the more that sellers within it must attune themselves to the concerns of potential customers, not merely serving current desires but anticipating future ones. In this way, competition between competing enterprises—though a form of social conflict—exercises "an immense sociating effect," Georg Simmel observed.[25] For such competition creates "a web of a thousand sociological threads . . . of conscious concentration on the will and feeling of fellowmen," one's potential customers. He adds (in seriousness) that business competition can "achieve what usually only love can do: the divination of the innermost wishes of the other," through a kind of "clairvoyance."[26]

In sum, those who champion the morality of capitalism insist that—in valorizing trust, sobriety, empathy, and steady self-application to one's work—this economic system does not celebrate greed, nor abandon "the virtues" as such. It reformulates some to suit its nature, discarding those actively hostile to itself or simply inessential, irrelevant to *any* form of modernity, capitalist or otherwise. These include the bravery of the Spartan warrior, the asceticism of the Carthusian monk, and the chastity of the Renaissance courtly maiden. Theorists of bourgeois virtue further maintain that the appealing traits fostered by commercial activity in the individuals so engaged lend attractiveness to the larger economic system authorizing and engendering it.[27] Moral acceptability travels both directions at once, from micro to macro and back again, with each iteration of the cycle reinforcing the previous, in a virtuous circle.

American lawmakers displayed great confidence in the theory of bourgeois virtue—though they would not have couched it that way—when deregulating financial markets in the 1980s and 1990s. Legislators drew guidance from economists who, in thrall to the efficient-market hypothesis, anticipated that prudential considerations alone would adequately discourage reckless risk-taking. This was because such conduct is seen, not as immoral, but instead as simply inconsistent with the enlightened self-interest of these institutions themselves. Their managers were certainly intelligent enough to adopt a sufficiently long-term "view," in their idiom, of where those interests lay. No deeper sources of private scruple or public stigma were necessary to discourage wrongfully reckless behavior. These forces are not only inherently elusive to the law. They are unamenable to the statistical modeling so integral to contemporary finance, and hence lie beyond the conceptual repertoire of contemporary economics, beyond the mental universe to which it can lend intellectual expression.

More careful assessments today suggest, however, that though we professionals often sell ourselves precisely as "reputational gatekeepers,"[28] vouching for the integrity of those we represent, concerns for high moral regard proved largely ineffective in chastening voracious "appetites for risk" among key market makers in the decade preceding 2008.[29] "Reputational capital" among peers came to stand exclusively for one's renown in winning the highest short-term performance,[30] rather than garnering more consistent returns over a longer period.[31] Most financiers may have remained acutely sensitive to their private portfolio and career prospects. But any such attentiveness to impending dangers did not extend to certain forms of what we now call "systemic risk"[32]—that is, to the massive perils that one's conduct, when joined to that of others similarly engaged, might pose to the financial and economic system at large.

Some might contend that because bourgeois virtue proves so clearly inadequate to the task, common morality ought to exercise some influence here, help fill the breach, impart a broader acknowledgment of responsibility than the law itself could require or permit. Few seriously argue, however, that specifically legal liabilities of such breadth should attach to these roles, that is, to financiers engaged in creating or advising clients regarding the purchase of system-risking securities.[33] Faced with the prospect of such expansive civil liability, no rational manager or director would accept the job, some observe. The prevailing view hence remains that responsibility for system-wide externalities resides with government, however severe its recurrent failures to that end.[34]

This chapter began by nevertheless observing the broad consensus that law cannot do everything necessary to ensure the ethically satisfactory conduct of business. It may also be true, as perceptive observers suggest, that common morality—shared by publics and business professionals alike—once induced greater self-restraint, rendering closer official scrutiny superfluous. How was it possible, we now ask, that (as in other capitalist countries) nonlegal inhibitions proved more effective here in the past than in recent U.S. history?

There is informed speculation, at least, that one cause of our recent economic crises has been that the U.S. financial elite is no longer nepotistically self-perpetuating. When it was clubbier and preppier, its members allegedly felt bound by unwritten norms of gentlemanly restraint, their horizons elongated by hopes of passing their business on to progeny. These restraints have broken down with the rise of labor markets now more competitive and meritocratic.[35] This is much the same story—the discrediting of noblesse oblige as mere aristocratic presumption—told in Chapter 10 concerning successive generations of legal counsel to large U.S. corporations. Thus, writes Brooks,

> If you went to Groton a century ago, you . . . were taught how morally precarious privilege was and how much responsibility it entailed . . . The best of the WASP elites had a stewardship mentality, that they were temporary caretakers of institutions that would span generations. They cruelly ostracized people who did not live up to their codes of gentlemanly conduct and scrupulosity . . . [people

> who lacked] restraint, reticence and service . . . Wall Street firms . . . now hire on the basis of youth and brains, not experience and character. Most of their problems can be traced to this. If you read the e-mails from the Libor scandal you get the . . . sensation: these people are brats; they have no sense that they are guardians for an institution the world depends on; they have no consciousness of their larger social role.[36]

Even from the few richly textured historical accounts,[37] however, it is impossible to discover whether such ruminations are more than fanciful nostalgia. Some historical evidence does suggest that "the narrative of the gentleman" was once centrally important to the self-understanding of London's financial elites,[38] at least, but self-understanding is often self-deceptive. Following 2008, in any event, respected observers nonetheless became convinced that older generations of financiers, more than the current crop, inhabited a life-world of social "embeddedness,"[39] in the terminology of economic sociology. Transactions that bankers today conceive of as strictly economic were traditionally enmeshed in a web of tacit expectations and human relationships understood, as Brooks suggests, to encompass generations past, present, and future.

It may seem a matter of only theoretical interest whether the moral codes thereby entrenched and policed were in fact ever deeply internalized, or were enforced merely through self-interest in cultivating reputational capital. Not so, it seems. As Durkheim observed[40] (and as others have since), the species of trust and loyalty engendered by competitive markets is more limited, shallower and less extensive in scope, than that arising within certain other social spheres, notably the kinship group or religious community. Commercial forms of these virtues ("brand loyalty," "customer trust") do not form or transform one's moral character—the human soul, if one prefers a theological idiom. The defining principle of the economic sphere, on the utilitarian account at least, is simply the mutual enhancement of well-being through self-interested transactions. When trust and loyalty are reconfigured for such a context, they provide little stable basis for sustained reliance on even the most consistent of counterparties, when their interests diverge significantly and sustainedly from one's own.

The self-restraints to which Brooks fondly alludes rested on deeper, nonmarket ties of kinship ("generations," "stewardship") and social class ("privilege," "Groton"). This was a class still self-confident in its singular sense of morality, more aristocratic ("gentlemanly conduct") than bourgeois. Its normative habitus and nonmarket ties are today not only much weakened in strictly sociological terms, those that Brooks delineates. They are no longer considered even morally defensible. Such a personal identity—if it remains nontrivially intact at all—thus cannot provide a widely acceptable basis of public behavior, certainly not within the professional milieu of modern financial markets.

An altogether different form of professional identity now arises from one's immersion in the labor markets where investment bankers sell their services. Because personnel move so quickly between firms, it would be irrational to identify very closely with the long-term interests of one's immediate employer.[41] Both employers and employees view themselves as operating, moreover, under conditions of near-permanent emergency. Scholars report that urgent "course corrections," major and minor, are anticipated and routine.[42] These notably include changes in currently needed expertise and experience, hence in the composition of workforce teams, temporary by clear intention. Between employer and employee, there runs little loyalty in either direction. Still broader loyalties—certainly any to so nebulous a conceit as "society at large" or "the world economy"—are literally unimaginable. The perceived scope of personal duty becomes more constricted than in the past, confined strictly to the law, and indeed only when the law's constraints are absolutely clear (as often they are not).

Firms and bankers defend the fickle, fleeting quality of their attachments as directly and necessarily reflecting objective "market conditions." These forces have undoubtedly accelerated. Yet when glimpsed from a longer horizon, the perpetual state of unrest they create is little more than the familiar workings of an energetic capitalism, immersed in the perennial turmoil of "creative destruction."[43] On this account, economic theories of financial behavior, by firms and their employees, simply mirror the palpable empirical realities, merely lend them clearer conceptual expression, in no way altering their course.

Cultural anthropologists plausibly reject these "materialist" accounts as reductionist and hence insufficient at best. The few, careful ethnographic inquiries into Wall Street workplaces find that the abstract "models," held out as merely descriptive and explanatory, in fact subtly inform concrete, real-life decision-making.[44] "Financial theories get *performed* . . . they play a constitutive role in actively shaping market practices."[45] Through their everyday performances, investment bankers ensure that such theories "become incorporated into the very infrastructure of market action,"[46] subtly metamorphizing from scientific hypothesis to self-fulfilling prophecy. The result is that "investment bankers can 'act like the market' that they espouse and impose on others."[47]

The economic theories at first appear to preclude normative commitment of any sort by those whose behavior they purportedly explain. These economists equally disavow any implications for how the rest of us should evaluate such business behavior. Questions about how the law should attend to these evaluations therefore simply cannot arise. Yet on closer examination this literature implicitly endorses the expectation that all will obey the stern, implacable promptings of "market forces," without compromise or hesitation, on pain of irrelevance (i.e., unemployment). Still, it would be mistaken to classify such views within the camp of those defending the market's "internal morality" as sufficient for filling law's gaps. This latter stance is at least self-conscious about offering an argument in capitalism's defense. It thus displays a measure of candor absent from those claiming to practice a purely "positive" economic theory while tacitly interjecting their normative views.

In markets less volatile or competitive than high finance, social embeddedness and the nonlegal pressures it creates may elicit a greater measure of moralizing restraint. "Repeat players" are often highly interdependent, their fate rising and falling in tandem. Their differences are complementary, creating the type of solidarity Durkheim described as "organic." Nearly all players recognize that, in pursuing self-interest, they must find ways to trust one another in honoring certain duties beyond those fully and readily amenable to contractual or regulatory codification. They have learned, as writes philosopher Elizabeth Anderson, that "once people extend self-interested reasoning to consider whether they should lie, cheat, and steal, market transactions become very costly or break down."[48] In fact, where organic solidarity and its corresponding morality develops among market participants, it becomes unnecessary and inefficient for them to secure full protection of their interests within the law, whether through contractual negotiation or legislation.

There have been a few serious empirical inquiries into how such embeddedness arises and may restrain conduct widely deemed ethically objectionable. Yet we lack much evidence or insight into larger patterns, revealing when and why the network-embeddedness of businesses and their managers successfully inhibits their exercise of rights to inflict great risk on others. In fact, we have not yet greatly advanced beyond

Max Weber's discerning observations a century ago on how the American businessman ostentatiously attends his local Christian congregation so that he may signal to his neighbors—before the age of federal deposit insurance—his dread of damnation for misconduct with their savings.[49] More than a century earlier, Adam Smith offered a similar explanation for why certain Protestant sects, by evidencing their members' good morals, flourish in the anonymity of cities, where other, earlier indicia of upstanding character were newly elusive.[50]

As recently as the mid-twentieth century, it was still possible for a distinguished Oxford University law professor to write, "Commercial law and moral law are closely related, because commerce and industry depend on good faith. It is difficult to envisage an economic system which does not assume as a basic premise that men can rely on each other's promises. These promises may be given the additional force of law, but even in the absence of law they must be recognized as obligatory by the commercial community if it is to exist at all."[51] Some still hold such views today, but can do so no longer as self-evident truths; no one could write or utter these words with such perfect equanimity and unequivocal self-assurance, that is, without immediately adding significant qualifications.

The second stance on business ethics, of much longer historical pedigree, is more pessimistic than the first—the theory of bourgeois virtue—regarding capitalism's inherent capacity to generate a satisfactory morality of its own, on its own. A defensible capitalism relies indispensably, according to this alternative view, on continuing assistance from a common morality sustained by forces exogenous to capitalism, forces that capitalism (or perhaps liberal modernity more generally) tends powerfully to deplete.[52]

This position begins with a critique of capitalism inspired by moral traditions extrinsic, even foreign to it, by claims that capitalism fosters the vice of avarice. Avarice is then not a mere, unfortunate by-product of this economic system, carried to unnecessary extremes, an exaggeration or distortion of its otherwise salutary tendencies. Rather, avarice is a condition of capitalism's success, and the success of individuals living and working under its institutional aegis. Anyone possessing this disposition in insufficient measure will ultimately be lost—surpassed, if not quickly crushed, by others around him. Some infer that, left to its own devices, the capitalist system cannot internally generate the normative materials necessary for its satisfactory governance. That task requires the external correction of common morality, operating partly through its reflection within the law, but at key points through social mores as well.

This intellectual tradition reaches back to the origins of Christianity, indeed to certain thinkers of the ancient world. It reaches a crescendo perhaps in the anguish of Calvinist theologians over the material abundance generated by seventeenth-century Dutch capitalism, concerns then well described in terms of an "embarrassment of riches."[53] Even today, similar preoccupations find vigorous expression among certain prominent thinkers maintaining that capitalism's continued vitality depends on traits of character increasingly debilitated by its very success. Only common morality, not business activity itself, can imbue these traits. Historically, this morality found its grounding in religious ideas, and was conveyed with pride, as a cherished patrimony, from one generation to the next through churches, families, and stable communities, whose members were few, interacted regularly, and were therefore tightly bound.

The capacity for sustained self-denial and resilience in the face of apparent defeat—what psychologists today call "grit"—is essential to consistent achievement in any demanding "calling," they observe. The very notion of a calling rests on theological convictions seriously shaken, however, through more than a century of secularizing critique. A long history of sober Calvinist toil in God's service has brought us a world of economic institutions continuing to yield up a vast cornucopia. This is seemingly unending, despite intermittent crises, even as much of the population shifts from industrial employment to work in human services, notably information and culture-production. Ever since those Dutch theologians, at least, there have been acute concerns that spectacular wealth and the leisurely opportunities it affords begin to enervate sterner habits of yore. Only long thereafter would thinkers of a more secular cast further add that, in undermining the precapitalist virtues on which its own institutions still rely, capitalism sows the seeds of its destruction, in ways Marx did not at all foresee.

Contemporary critics of this ilk hoped that the same habits of moderation and self-restraint impelling reinvestment of hard-earned profits into one's business and professional endeavors would also inhibit impulses to engage in business conduct that, though lawful, stood greatly at odds with common morality. Noted professors of "business ethics" sometimes still adopt this reassuringly high-minded stance, writing in tones that sometimes teeter into treacle.[54] Yet skeptics rejoin that the freewheeling culture of contemporary capitalism confines the scope of perceived moral duty to those near and dear; even immediate clients are sometimes left in the cold, to say nothing of society at large. This diminished sense of moral duty fosters reckless attitudes not so much in private behavior, as conservative culture-critics once feared, but more importantly toward financial activity on which the economic security of entire populations relies. Here the apprehension has been that contemporary capitalism foreshortens the horizon of human concern so that it no longer extends to situations where our lawyers tell us that particular conduct—profitable in the present, but systemically risky and likely reprehensible to many—is not clearly prohibited. In the United States, this was a central theme during the populist electoral uprisings of 2016, vigorously voiced by Elizabeth Warren, Bernie Sanders, and Stephen Bannon,[55] who was raised in the Left-leaning tradition of "Social Catholicism."

When the customary bearers of commercial virtue apparently succumb to old-fashioned avarice, premodern greed, many will naturally demand greater legal regulation, however difficult in practice to formulate, enact, and enforce.[56] The "internal morality" of business itself will not suffice, nor will the broader forces of common morality, originating in and transmitted by institutions no longer salient in the lives of financial elites. Thus, neither of the regulatory approaches sketched at the outset, alone or in conjunction, is today sufficient. Yale political theorist Steven B. Smith recently asked: "How did the idea of the bourgeois, once considered virtually synonymous with the free and responsible individual, become associated with a kind of low-minded materialism, moral cowardice, and philistinism?"[57] The preceding analysis offers an answer.

In summary, social theorists differ greatly over the form of morality that capitalism requires: Is it mere bourgeois virtue (prudence, trustworthiness, and sobriety), triggered by reputational concerns? Or does it involve the sincere internalization of more diffuse cultural inhibitions, religious at their roots and difficult, if not impossible, to reestablish on more secular foundations? Theorists therefore differ too over whether the necessary species of virtue springs from commercial activity itself or requires the external influence of a common morality evidently precapitalist in origin and propagated by cultural forces in increasing tension with the nature of marketplace 'relationships.'

We should acknowledge, as their ardent advocates scarcely do, that these two "opposing" views are not logically incompatible: the forces at work in depleting capitalism's moral foundations may well coexist and contend with those operating to replenish them.[58] Whether one or the other becomes more powerful, in differing circumstances, is an empirical question still largely unexplored, despite Hirschman's call to do so.[59] Admittedly, it has proven virtually impossible to measure either set of competing forces, and hence empirical support is not especially compelling for either of these grand theories.[60] That fact does not render the questions they raise any less vital in grappling with the relation between law and common morality in contemporary business. And despite their differences, these opposing accounts concur that—because the law cannot fully incorporate all of morality's pertinent domain—the normative commitments of individual human beings remain indispensable to the satisfactory operation of markets. This leaves us, alas, not far from where we began, with the question: To what extent may legislators and judges, in crafting the law of business regulation, rely upon the continuing efficacy of moral pressures—whether capitalist or precapitalist—to restrain the objectionable exercise of market rights, particularly by those administering large financial institutions?

Very little, it would appear. For in the years preceding 2008, at least, it seemed entirely rational, with even a long horizon on self-interest, for the most reputable financial institutions and those managing them to maximize present returns in the expectation that eminently predictable risks of disastrous later costs could be shifted to others,[61] a prospect they expressly anticipated.[62]

In fact it may no longer be entirely true that "scarcely anyone" (as I initially remarked) seriously believes that the law, on its own, can restrain unacceptable business practices to an acceptable degree. In leading American graduate schools of business, at least, long-standing theories of "business professionalism" and "managed capitalism," whose human representatives evinced a chummy esprit de corps and ritually professed their civic or social responsibility, have recently given way to a worldview quite different and historically novel. This is a "renegade capitalism" in which, it is said[63] that those who once serenely applied a settled "administrative science" must now cast aside such "technocratic," "bureaucratic," and "sclerotic" thoughtways to embrace instead an "essentially subversive attitude . . . entirely rebellious and loyal to nothing other than their own sense of possibility." This new species of men and women is composed of "true entrepreneurs, inspired individuals . . . cocksure and refractory . . . aggressive, anti-social, edgy." Fierce market pressures compel them to defy prevailing norms with a view to effecting efficient forms of "creative destruction." In order "to propel economic innovation," they must act with utter "indifference to custom." This is less the hidden curriculum, the unspoken subtext of B-school doctrine than its explicit agenda, the militant manifesto of its leading theorists, Rollert contends.

A deep skepticism toward a common morality within and beyond the stolid "business community" lies at the heart of this altered understanding of the ideal enterprise and those who should govern it. Among corporate leaders influenced by these views, there comes to prevail a "contempt for convention," especially for practices prevalent among risk-averse companies whose complacent managers "simply imitate"[64] their competitors. These changes in prevalent self-understanding provide a "warrant for recklessness," of just the sort amply evident in the ill-informed use of certain financial practices preceding the 2008 crisis. Because the law enshrines so much of social convention, the question at this point may no longer be that of what place common morality must have in the extralegal regulation of business. From the perspective of contemporary financial theory, the question instead becomes whether there is much proper place—except as servile handmaiden, facilitating any and all commercial activity—for law itself.

# 12

# How We Attach Responsibilities to Rights

In the modern West we routinely employ both law and mores to link particular rights with particular responsibilities, affixing both to the same person or institution, in combinations that, we hope, will prove sensible, compatible, and effective for our purposes. We do this in several ways, on several grounds.[1] This chapter offers real-life examples of each, highlighting limitations in prevailing accounts of how these linkages should and do come about.

I propose a distinctively sociological alternative, covering much of the pertinent empirical territory. On this account, such linkages result not chiefly from 'high' considerations of logical entailment or the disinterested search for economic efficiency, on one hand, nor from 'low,' self-interested rent-seeking through raw power politics, on the other. They result instead from discussions among members of a given vocational or other social group concerning good-faith differences of opinion over the proper meaning of normative commitments sincerely shared.

Summarily stated, the several methods of linkage involve (1) "responsibility-rights," a philosophical notion (described below) proposed by Jeremy Waldron; (2) "least cost avoider/provider" theory in economics; (3) virtue ethics, sociologically construed; (4) doctrinal revisions to the law, so that it incorporates changes in common morality; and, often after all of these fail, (5) informally enforcing social mores against those deemed to exercise their rights "irresponsibly," a practice often best examined ethnographically. Thus, at once several disciplines—philosophy, economics, sociology, law, and anthropology—seek respectively to address the question in issue. It is helpful to bring them into conversation, so that they genuinely join issue on the question, as their respective advocates and practitioners fail to do. We might then ask such novel questions as: If there are empirical patterns here, what explains them? Why do we employ one or another of these methods of right-responsibility attachment at different times? And what are the strengths and weaknesses of each such method in certain circumstances?[2]

The immediate focus will be on Waldron's theory, its singular insights and explanatory possibilities, as well as its evident frailties, its ultimate inability to make adequate sense of even the few concrete illustrations he offers. These weaknesses become clearest when we compare his perspective to a sociology of virtue ethics, the sort here offered as a superior alternative in most situations.

## "Responsibility-Rights"

A striking and intriguing feature of many of the gravest and most vexing rights to do wrong is that they often arise from well-established social roles to which correlative responsibilities attach in ways elusive to the law, irremediably beyond its reach, intrinsically or contingently, for the foreseeable future. A right to do wrong thus emerges willy-nilly when law adequately captures the rights defining a particular role, but not all of the responsibilities that prevailing mores attach to it. In other words, both right and responsibility emerge from a single, critical task that a given society considers indispensable. In implicit exchange for honoring the accompanying moral duties, there is bestowed a broad range of rights to cause serious harm, at times. Because both the rights and responsibilities spring from activities deemed societally essential, it is impossible simply to dispense with (or massively curtail) the rights, upon discovering that attendant duties have been consistently breached—the rights thereby "abused," as we are wont to say.

One potentially fruitful way to think about all this is through the notion of "responsibility-rights."[3] To Jeremy Waldron—perhaps the leading living legal theorist today—what is distinctive about this category of entitlements is that "the importation of the element of compulsion" through an associated set of responsibilities "is not necessarily to be conceived as something . . . brought in from the outside to limit the right but as part and parcel of the right." Four features coalesce to link rights with responsibilities in this singular fashion: (1) the delineation of a task especially important for society; (2) privileging someone as uniquely situated to perform it; (3) in view of the singular concern and stake that someone has in the matter; and (4) on which grounds we grant legal protection against interference by others, including the state (except in extreme cases), to the sphere of decision-making deemed necessary for one to satisfactorily honor this responsibility. On a strong view,[4] these rights do not merely cry out for responsible behavior in their exercise. They in fact arise and take shape precisely in order to enable the fulfilling of functions which a given society deems indispensable, so that individuals charged with these can meet their obligations.[5]

Because the package of rights and duties implicates public concerns of great moral moment, a measure of social "dignity" attaches to exercising such a right, especially as one demonstrates maturity in honoring attendant duties. The considerable wealth or power that may accompany those tasked with responsibility-rights, such as physicians and military officers, is inessential and even extraneous here, it would seem. For this is a peculiar species of "social dignity" (Waldron's wording), unfamiliar to the contemporary mind and ear, meaningfully distinct from what sociologists standardly have in mind by "social status."[6] Thus, in one of Waldron's central examples, the parents of young children enjoy this special dignity as well, regardless of socioeconomic or political position, due largely to their responsibilities for inculcating basic moral standards, from very young age, into a new generation.

Some of the social roles to which Waldron refers are freely chosen; others are imposed by fiat, as with public service on juries and in early modern militias. Even when law mandates the particular status, the right-holder derives its characteristic dignity, Waldron suggests, from the fact that "the element of compulsion" is conjoined to "a clear sense of empowerment and choice." The law seeks to embody a widespread expectation that anyone occupying such a status will apply her mind with special conscientiousness in determining how best to exercise its particular amalgam of rights and responsibilities in any real-life situation she may confront. Because the law fails to incorporate all relevant duties, it accords those occupying these roles a measure of discretion, frequently considerable, in employing the rights bestowed. This ample discretion over matters of such moral gravity adds still further to the enhanced respectability that society ascribes to these positions. That esteem does not derive, then, simply from the intrinsic importance of these roles in serving essential public functions. If functional importance alone were here at stake, the same could be said of plumbers.

The notion of a responsibility-right may offer a nutshell way to formulate what we sometimes have in mind when we speak colloquially of certain rights and responsibilities as "inextricably intertwined." Though hackneyed, that phrasing is very much a part of how ordinary language captures this peculiar normative configuration. What we mean by this admittedly loose locution is that we view the paired elements, these particular conjunctions of normativity, as naturally congruent, inherently interdependent, mutually reinforcing, salubriously symbiotic. It is further telling that such formulations are somewhat metaphoric—inevitably so, it seems. A couple of quick illustrations of responsibility-rights: When serving as jurors, Americans have both rights to decide the legal fate of a defendant and weighty duties, to that end, governing their deliberations and decision making. And historically, the constitutional right to bear arms was paired (on some historical accounts) with a duty of service in a local militia with civic responsibilities to defend the republic.[7]

But what is it, exactly, that holds the elements of a responsibility-right together? Here, Waldron draws upon the ancient Roman notion of *dignitas* to distinguish his preferred concept of merit-worthy status from more modern notions.[8] The latter includes that of John Austin, in which a particular status—of the priest or aristocrat, for instance—is merely "an abbreviation for the list of rights, powers, etc. that a person in one of these situations has."[9] Rather, Waldron continues, "we may say that dignity is a status that *comprises* a given set of rights," and hence "the list is not arbitrary; it . . . *makes sense* relative to some underlying idea that informs the status in question." Thus, the particular rights and responsibilities "make sense *together,* as a package, in response to that idea." This idea displays "an underlying coherence . . . and unifies them."

This suggestion is tantalizing, if studiously vague, and Waldron's attempt to clarify it through very brief illustrations remains undeveloped. Any attempt to remedy this, however, brings quickly to the fore a second query: To what extent can the concept of responsibility-right accommodate the fact that the particular configuration of rights and responsibilities associated with any given social role varies by time and place? Not much, it would seem. And this greatly undermines the concept's value (unless further elaborated), despite its seeming affinity with present purposes, for a sociology of law's relation to common morality.

We recognize immediately that most rights don't fit Waldron's theory of a responsibility-right, which he couches tentatively as a provisional foray and work in progress. Any relation that most legal rights bear to their holder's associated duties is contingent, adventitious. This is most transparent perhaps in the lobbying efforts of professional associations to expand their members' rights and to limit their obligations and liabilities to others.[10] It might first seem that such elegant philosophical notions as Waldron's offer no insight into what we observe at such times. Yet when a professional group increases its cultural and social authority, the range of issues over which it legitimately speaks,[11] the scope of both its rights *and its duties* generally expand. The arguments its leaders make in favor of enlarging its jurisdiction then at times take a form resembling Waldron's account: we must now be authorized to do *this,* because the law imposes a duty on us to do *that,* and the two are inseparable. In this fashion, even the most ambitiously self-aggrandizing efforts by occupational groups at collective empire-building are in most cases publicly defended with straight-faced arguments of policy and principle, accompanied by at least a patina of empirical evidence.[12]

Waldron himself does not claim that responsibility-rights occupy a very large portion of legal life, and expressly invites others to explore the notion's scope conditions. So let us consider a number of alternative ways by which certain rights and responsibilities become entangled and jointly associated with a given social status.

## The Economic Theory of "Least-Cost Provider"

A particular connection between right and responsibility may often reflect simply a legislative or judicial calculation that public policy is well served by assigning obligations in this fashion. The rights might have been established long before the duties to which they are later attached; or vice versa. As economists observe, we sometimes ascribe legal duties simply because the party chosen to bear them offers the "least-cost provider" of a socially desired good.[13] Thus, chemical manufacturers are more knowledgeable about and hence better positioned to purchase insurance against the far-reaching consequences of a large chemical spill they might cause than are the thousands of small businesses likely to be thereby harmed.[14] And the contractual party who is most fully informed about the distinctive harms likely to ensue from his counterparty's possible breach is ideally situated to protect himself against them, by negotiating for that protection within the agreement itself; so that if he fails to do this, he alone should shoulder the losses.[15]

More suitably than Waldron's theory, the notion of least-cost provision explains many additional admixtures of duty and dispensation, visible across the legal landscape. Thus, nearly no one would say that a legal right protecting corporate employees from retaliation by employers on whose fraud they "blow the whistle" is hardwired, in the very nature of such employment, to a duty to protect the company's shareholders or general public by disclosing its wrongful practices.[16] Rather, it is simply that company insiders are better positioned than others to learn of information relevant to public policy and more vulnerable to retaliation for publicizing it. The law should therefore seek to limit the cost to them of providing information highly valuable to society at large. No one has yet systematically sought, however, to pose the large empirical question of where and why the theory of least-cost provision does and does not account for the actual linkages of rights and duties that we find arrayed across our (or any other) legal system. The theory tends to be invoked more often in a normative than an explanatory key,[17] with a view to proposing particular such allocations, as yet untried, or defending existing ones.

The resulting configurations of normativity come into being with a view to general public welfare, though there may be little self-conscious planning actually involved. Though small in scale when glimpsed in isolation, these little arrangements provide essential building blocks from which a larger social order arises. We thus employ the law to assemble workable packages of rights and duties into roles and institutions with distinct locations in a division of labor, including a division of duties specifically moral in character, eliciting clear indignation if violated. When engaged in such institutional design, modest or more ambitious, we seek to combine these discrete socio-legal blocks into larger organizational entities. We try to arrange the respective individual roles—those of physician, nurse, and medical patient, for instance—so that those occupying them will interact in compatible and reciprocally supportive ways.

This is why prominent scholars, inspired by theories of "fields" and networks,[18] today speak of a "'sociology of expertise" rather than of experts or professions, conceived of as individual practitioners or distinct vocational groups.[19] On this recent view, we cannot satisfactorily understand the social significance of any given profession's activities until we closely examine its network of patterned interactions with members of other such groupings. Like everyone else, lawmakers experiment with available tools for combining, in ways both practicable and ethically acceptable, rights and responsibilities —within a school, for instance, those of children, teachers, school administrators, parents, and policemen. There is often an appealing air to this experimentalism, as a regulatory architecture shifts gradually over time in light of its perceived failures and our creative, collaborative responses to them.

This experimentalism is absent from Waldron's more strictly philosophical account of how particular responsibilities come to attach themselves to given rights and to the people holding them. Still, least-cost-provider theory excludes from consideration the real-life power disparities among pertinent parties, and hence exaggerates the measure of impartial rationality involved in the actual decisions really linking rights to responsibilities. The division of labor we observe before us in a modern economy often, in fact, comports more greatly with such inefficient political distortions than with this highly idealized "scientific" account of how such questions should be answered.

We should distinguish Waldron's contention that there exists a conceptually distinct category of responsibility-rights from the platitude that every occupational role entails certain responsibilities. All employees and independent contractors have obligations to perform workplace tasks designed to serve the organizations engaging them. An employer grants her employees the right to perform these tasks on condition of their accepting those responsibilities. As Bernard Williams observed, "there is no notion of a 'bank teller' which does not involve a reference to responsibilities, and the term refers to a role which can only be explained in relation to social institutions which give someone with that role certain functions and duties."[20]

The job of bank teller is also clearly crucial to the workings of certain financial institutions, themselves essential to a market society. Yet this form of employment does not involve responsibility-rights, on Waldron's understanding. The teller does not, in his wording, acquire his work-related rights in light of his "particular interest in the matter" of personal banking. The stake of even a bank manager in the responsible operation of a given financial institution differs categorically from the stake of a mother or father in the matter of raising their child or of a professional soldier in defending her country. That is why the law of bank management does not seek to protect any essential, bank-specific "sphere of autonomous decision-making from the interference of others," or by the state. None exists.

Certain roles that Waldron has in mind fall readily into the familiar legal category of fiduciary, with loyalties often diffuse, codified only to limited degree. A trustee, for example, holds rights of administration naturally paired with her duty to manage trust assets in a responsible fashion, consistent with the terms of the trust instrument, in the interests of a designated beneficiary.[21] In fact, there is an element of "constructive trusteeship" in virtually all of Waldron's examples.

It is significant, though, that the *law* of constructive trusteeship does not extend nearly so far and fails to encompass this larger realm of perceived obligation. The law imposes a constructive trust whenever there has been some form of "unjust enrichment" because the constructive trustee has acquired property in an "unconscionable manner."[22] This broad wording at first gave "fear that it would be difficult to contain [the doctrine] within manageable bounds,"[23] that it might turn a notion so thoroughly contested as "injustice" into a freestanding basis of civil liability. Taken to that extreme, the law of constructive trusteeship would threaten to swallow up, incorporate by reference, essentially all of morality, as the particular judge happened to construe it. In practice, courts soon narrowed the reach of this equitable doctrine, initially amorphous, to a few well-delineated situations, readily foreseeable to most of those likely to find themselves there. These include, for instance, the mistaken bestowal of goods upon someone who did not order them. Courts thereby channeled the expansive but elusive claims of justice and unjust enrichment into a small number of rules,[24] several of them quite "bright-line."

The puzzle of present interest for both public policy and social-theoretical understanding is that we see fit to place such profound trust in those charged with these dignifying duties, despite the law's refusal to specify very much of what they entail. We may fruitfully so understand the main rights examined in this study. Thus, for instance:

1. The right of a state and its soldiers to knowingly kill enemy civilians, as an unintentional consequence of war, is acceptable only because we view that right as bound up with a responsibility (imperfectly codified) to take great precaution to limit this form of harm.

2. The right of a hospital patient to decline medical treatment, though his life depends on it, is tolerable in practice only because the autonomy this right protects is qualified by a nonlegal responsibility, informally enforced, of care for oneself, to treat and treasure one's body as the inalienable repository of an inherent human dignity.[25]
3. A woman's right over her reproductive capacities is associated, many believe, with an uncodified responsibility to take reasonable precautions against conception of an undesired fetus.[26]
4. We generally conceive of the citizen's right to vote as indissolubly connected to a civic responsibility to do so, though this responsibility lacks any legal basis in the United States. Nearly 90 percent of Americans express the view that all eligible citizens have an obligation to vote.[27] Before mass urbanization in the late nineteenth century, Americans experienced significant communal pressure to turn out at the polls, according to some accounts.[28] Even today, policy experiments in shaming individual citizens to vote, by informing them that electoral records reveal they have previously failed to do so, have been relatively successful.[29] Many other countries do join the right to vote with a legal duty to exercise that right.[30] There is little indication, though, that those who feel obligated to vote feel themselves subject to any further duty of attending closely to the policy positions and moral character of candidates for public office. Still, scarcely anyone would seriously contend that, should you fail to honor this possible further duty, you should lose your right to vote. Such a duty would be effectively unenforceable, in any event.

In justifying the discretion that law accords to them in their work, physicians, military officers, and lawyers all invoke certain notions of "professionalism." The concept acquires sociological import precisely for how it signals one's acceptance of certain duties beyond those fully justiciable. Still, we the public are presumably ambivalent about law's failure to codify these more completely, and more reluctant to trust to informal constraints as a sufficient check on the corresponding rights where the duties at issue bear powerfully on matters of life and death. Our inevitable reliance on the wise intercession of pertinent professionals, especially those in scientific fields, to resolve innumerable personal and societal problems manageable in no other way, enhances the concerns arising where the overbroad rights are those of professionals themselves. This is the case, for instance, with the right of military commanders to inflict "proportional" damage on civilian property and persons, discussed in Chapter 3.

The several case illustrations I invoke throughout this study vary greatly in the degree to which people with special nonlegal responsibilities are self-conscious about occupying any recognizable role or distinctive status. Those suffering a short illness rarely think of themselves in such terms. Yet as Talcott Parsons observed,[31] a society defines sickness in relation to its prevailing understanding of health, and imposes upon those it deems healthy certain expectations from which it exempts those it labels "sick." Once we acknowledge that someone is ill, she immediately acquires new rights and responsibilities, some of these juridical in nature, others not so. She is entitled, in particular, to relief from many of her normal responsibilities at work and home.

In implicit exchange for these moral and legal rights, she assumes a corresponding moral duty, widely accepted, to defer to medical counsel, with a view to restoring her well-being and resuming those obligations as soon as realistically possible.[32] If she is perceived as "malingering," unduly extending and exploiting this ephemeral status, others begin to retract the scope of these normative dispensations. Anyone who appears to be shirking her acknowledged obligations enters this normative grey zone and will soon likely find herself gently reminded, with increasing firmness, that pressing duties of ordinary life await her attention. Others will eventually begin to withdraw the accompanying legal entitlements as well, retightening—as she begins to recover—the tort "standard of care" she is deemed to owe her legal dependents, for instance.

Unlike those afflicted by illness, licensed professionals understand themselves to occupy a specialized role by which society, largely through its law, assigns them a particular bundle of expectations and authorizations. These people lie at the opposite end of that continuum in how much those subject to a particular conjunction of rights and responsibilities are self-conscious about inhabiting a distinctive social status. Whether biological or adoptive, parents of young children occupy a middle point. When they neglect or abuse their offspring, the state firmly reminds them—if their kinship networks, neighbors, or co-workers have not already done so—that they are not entirely free to define the responsibilities of childrearing as they see fit. In creating a family, new parents constructively consent to occupy a role defined, both legally and nonlegally, by a shifting set of entitlements and encumbrances; neither of these is entirely chosen. Only a subset of each is open to voluntary redefinition by the people immediately concerned.

Oddly, though the concept is sociological to the core, Waldron's notion of a "social role"—central to his notion of a responsibility-right—is almost *anti*sociological in spirit. Scholars in sociology today do not think of a role so much as a discrete packet of rights and duties inhering in any single person; when they consider roles at all,[33] they do so more in terms of the occupant's position within a complex relational grid,[34] potentially far-reaching, and an organizational structure, often expansive. Roles are defined in relation to one another, with their respective jurisdictional boundaries often the object of ongoing contention.[35] It is possible that each of the social roles to which Waldron alludes harbors a certain essence, transhistorical and pan-cultural, as he apparently believes. If so, that essence must be stated so abstractly—"the collective defense," for military officers, for example—as to tell us little of substance or genuine interest about what the occupants of that role actually do, how they are organized, or how others understand and interact with them. In these matters, the sociological variables become more essential than the philosophical constants.

At times the responsibilities associated with a given role find nearly full expression within the law. Yet even there, the role itself—as its occupants experience and practice it—will often evolve autonomously from the legal system. It does so through shifts in mores among members of a given profession, for instance, often affected by their interactions with the people they serve. These extralegal changes in role-requirements—in what medical patients reasonably expect of their caregivers, for instance—regularly assist in revising the legal rules themselves, those governing the given profession. Such accretions of responsibility, both within and beyond the law, can come to feel, for all affected, no less real or integral to a given role than those Waldron contemplates, which he infers from rights essential to its practice, anywhere and everywhere.

Thus, in the United States today, the legal "standard of care" that parents must meet in ensuring their children's safety is coming under some modest pressure, "in the age of the helicopter parent,"[36] as one scholar writes. American parents in 2011 spent over four hours more per week on child care than in 1965.[37] Moreover, after a few widely publicized kidnappings beginning in 1979,[38] parents came to perceive that particular risk as greater than they had imagined.[39] The result has arguably been to lower the threshold of parental inattention amounting to actionable tort and triggering still more intrusive official intercession.[40] In this way, informal societal mores defining the meaning of "responsible parenting" begin to place increasing pressure on existing law,[41] which has to date remained remarkably indulgent of parental neglect, even when such misconduct results in a child's death.[42]

The law sometimes intercedes still more directly to enhance the measure of responsibility expected of parents, and thereby reconfigures their rights as well. Medical professionals in neonatal intensive care units must sometimes struggle to instill a keener sense of responsibility in parents whose infants are born very prematurely. These parents—distressed by their child's great physical and mental disabilities—may initially prefer to leave the infant in hands of the state, or simply allow it to die.[43] Yet if either the parents or professionals participate in causing such a death, they face severe liability under recent federal legislation designed to protect gravely handicapped infants.[44] Until that enactment, it was not uncommon to withdraw care from such an infant, without great compunction.[45] In responses to changes in common morality and the associated urgings of certain religious denominations, the responsibilities of parenting such a child, and of professionally assisting parents in honoring those obligations, have greatly enlarged.

Consider now a still starker example of threatened increase in the scope of responsibilities, with far-reaching repercussions for attendant rights. In this case, the desired changes in professional responsibility augured poorly for constitutional rights integral to the American republic. It would be hard to argue that the social role of news reporter harbors any invariant function, apart from the highly indefinite task of providing the public with "relevant information." The news media's accepted purpose in a liberal democracy is so fundamentally distinct from in a Communist or Fascist regime that the kind of information deemed publicly pertinent becomes hugely different,[46] if not quite wholly at odds.

Yet it is also true that, even within a single society, prevailing interpretations of informational needs may undergo periodic change in the face of sustained challenge. In the early 1940s, for example, there arose considerable skepticism among certain American elites and segments of the public toward the emergent mass media, notably large news outlets whose reporting had militantly opposed key features of Franklin Roosevelt's New Deal.[47] This skepticism much inspired the "Commission on Freedom of the Press,"[48] chaired by University of Chicago president

Robert Hutchins and peopled by celebrated dignitaries in public and university life.[49] Their report fiercely proclaimed the "social responsibility of the press" to serve the "needs of society" and "the public interest," leaving both concepts scarcely defined.[50] The authors argued that, due to its increasing concentration of ownership, the press—though privately owned—had implicitly acquired the status of "trustee" or "common carrier," with duties to provide "public access" for a wider range of views; it must assume an "educational" mission, and resist the temptations of "sensationalist" scandal-mongering.[51]

The commissioners earnestly urged that the news media have weighty obligations not fully reflected within the law, nor fulfilled in practice. These had become intrinsic to the practice of journalism, properly understood, even if journalism itself did not yet acknowledge them or recognize their full importance. The Commission's dignitaries warned, even threatened, that continued "abuse"[52] of the media's First Amendment rights, its failures of "self-regulation,"[53] could and perhaps should lead to greater governmental regulation, even "amendment" of the U.S. Constitution.[54] Owners of major media outlets volubly repudiated these criticisms,[55] and nothing came of the Commission's energetic exhortations.

Such conflictual episodes disclose the precariously constructed character of social roles, the possibility of reconfiguring their terms and conditions in light of changing times. The current assignment to a given social status of particular rights and duties becomes recognizably open to contest. Particular responsibilities cannot then simply be logically deduced from some eternal property of the rights inherent to news reporting, parenting, doctoring, soldiering, and so forth.

The several case illustrations here examined vary in other respects than those yet mentioned. They differ in how far other parties, those counseling restraint upon the right-bearer, see themselves as enforcing norms peculiar to that person's special role and status, or simply urging him to do what a more society-wide moral standard requires of us all. Sometimes, as in the case of American litigators, a profession's formal code of ethics seeks to establish a "role-morality"[56] very different from, even much at odds with, normative expectations operative within society at large. Litigators often view themselves as not merely entitled, but professionally bound in the name of "zealous advocacy," to flout such general social strictures as "fair play" and respect for others' human dignity. Any pressures that may fall upon them to do otherwise, to exercise their professional dispensations more consistently with common morality, are tremulously weak.

There are still other sources of intriguing variation in how, from one situation to another, people tend to understand the relations between rights and responsibilities. When we informally enforce norms of common morality, in reproaching others for how they exercise their rights, we sometimes believe only that we have a right to do so. In that case, the impulse to exercise this right must come from elsewhere. In other circumstances, we feel as if we are under a moral duty to this effect, leaving us little choice in the matter. The distinction has some practical import. Enforcement can be costly to one who assumes the burden of enforcing common morality. One who intervenes to stop a barroom fistfight, enforcing social mores of nonviolence, may find himself beaten up by one or both belligerents, suddenly united in opposition to his impudent intercession. Empirical evidence suggests that many people will nonetheless at times accept certain costs to themselves in privately sanctioning moral and legal infractions, though they stand nothing to gain from their commendable conduct.[57] Still, the psychological cost one incurs may depend in part on whether one perceives oneself to act under a right or, instead, a duty. Opposing hypotheses, equally plausible, here suggest themselves.[58]

## Responsibility-Rights for Sovereign States?

It may be that not only human beings, but institutions too, can be said to hold responsibility-rights. This possibility becomes easier to entertain if we do not cleave too closely to the particulars of Waldron's account, allowing greater scope for culture and history. (The ensuing section on virtue ethics takes this tack still further.) Consider, for instance, a recent revision in thinking about the place that state sovereignty occupies within public international law. Until scarcely a half-century ago, international law regarded states as largely subject to only such legal duties as they themselves embraced[59] through affirmative acts of treaty ratification or consent to emerging norms of customary international law. Yet though statehood as such imposed few, if any, inherent duties, this legal status conferred many entitlements. A state's rights within the international community derived from the very fact of its legal personhood, whereas its duties derived almost entirely from its own choices.

Then as now, states remain generally quite discriminating in which such duties they choose to embrace, whenever there is reason to anticipate nontrivial consequences for breaching them. This is the chief reason today's most successful, concerted attempts to alter normative ordering at the international level—to introduce new global mores—involve, not treaties, but instead more informal agreements, expressly nonjuridical. To achieve their goals, these efforts must sometimes involve both states and nonstate organizations (notably multinational corporations) lacking legal capacity to enter into treaties at all.

The foremost historical right of any sovereign state, codified in UN Charter Article 2(4), protects the state from "the threat or use of force" against its "territorial integrity."[60] Today, however, most people throughout the world consider it an abuse of rights, an irresponsible exercise of this entitlement, for a state and its leaders to thereby shield themselves from global objections when turning the sword on innocent citizens. Mass atrocity itself violates innumerable agreements within international criminal and humanitarian law. The right to do wrong lies not in any formal authorizing of such acts, but at one step removed. It arises from the failure of international law in practice to allow,[61] still less to require, that other states intervene militarily against those engaged in these grievously illegal actions.

There has emerged in recent years, however, a very different understanding of the relation between the rights and responsibilities of states. On this view the sovereign state no longer enjoys any inherent dignity attaching to it automatically, a view once elaborately theorized by Hegel[62] and still widely shared among elite civil servants, including leading judges,[63] across Western Europe.[64] The dignity of the state now derives instead from the polity's effective commitment to honoring its citizens' most fundamental human rights. A state may exercise exclusive authority over its territory only insofar as it respects these rights. Every state has the "responsibility to protect" all persons within its territory from mass atrocity, in particular.[65] The state owes this duty not only to those who dwell within it, but to international society at large, whose members therefore acquire a legitimate stake in the matter. If a state fails to honor this duty, it forfeits the right of territorial exclusivity, to the extent necessary to halt continuing wrongs, to put a stop to its abusive behavior. The responsibilities of statehood are thus no longer contingent on their self-imposition. Rather, they derive from an altered understanding of the nature of statehood, now conceived as a species of responsibility-right.

To date, however, it is only the political theory of sovereignty that has undergone this recasting. International law itself has not adopted it, and is unlikely to do so. To clarify what such a responsibility would require of whom remains too difficult.[66] Even if one could do so, states and their leaders would never consent to subject themselves to a legal obligation putting them at risk of liability to victims of genocide a world away,[67] over whose fate they may have little control. These considerations aggravate each other: the more thoroughly we "perfect" this putative responsibility, concretize it into precise legal form, the greater the obstacles in persuading states to ratify it. The UN General Assembly in 2005 unanimously "resolved" to embrace this new norm, amorphously formulated, and the Obama administration expressly invoked it when intervening militarily in Libya. Far more would be necessary, though, if the doctrine were to enter into customary international law and acquire real-world efficacy in this way. Most states, and certainly "leading" ones, would (through their *opinio juris*) have to describe the doctrine as legally binding upon them, and act accordingly—as "state practice" does not currently reflect—in the many situations throughout the world to which its mandates pertain.

In sum, if the "responsibility to protect" ever comes to exercise any nontrivial influence over the martial response of other states to mass atrocity, it will be through mechanisms other than those the law itself provides. It will be through the mores of public leaders and citizens throughout the world. To describe this new norm as "soft law"[68] is, from one well-established standpoint, vainly to finesse the fact that, insofar as there exists a settled "rule of recognition" or "rule of change" within public international law, such norms fail to satisfy it. To acknowledge this is not to deny their possible efficacy, at times, in restraining abusive exercise of the right to territorial integrity.

In fact, over the last generation the most promising developments in global governance have taken precisely this form. Because international law inevitably remains quite sketchy in key areas, nonlegal forms of normative ordering necessarily assume a greater place than in most domestic contexts. In the now-familiar manner of "democratic experimentalism,"[69] so-called soft law offers a method for states to quickly establish and test out new, potentially promising modes of interaction among themselves and others without requiring formal legal commitments of a sort (like multilateral treaties) that would later, if they prove unfruitful, be hard to reverse or significantly revise.

A responsibility to protect may one day gain real-life influence through nonlegal mechanisms encompassing both traditional diplomacy and "bottom-up" campaigns to shame national leaders for failing to act decisively against states that violate their citizens' rights to physical integrity.[70] Here too, we find extralegal stratagems regularly impinging on how rightholders exercise their entitlements. The world's failure to legally codify and judicially enforce the responsibility to protect need not fatally diminish its practical import. It has been no small achievement to alter so decisively the basic terms of diplomatic discourse and public conversation throughout the world, on matters of such normative import. To revolutionize the ordinary language of international affairs has itself long been an integral aim of much human rights advocacy. Several major moral thinkers, notably Amartya Sen, contend it should so remain, irrespective of whether our new, broadly shared moral commitments ever find their way fully into the law.[71]

It requires no vaulting prophetic vision to anticipate that if sovereign states survive in recognizable form a century from now, this will be in no small part because their leaders will have come to embrace (or at least acquiesce in) a robust understanding of their responsibility to protect their citizens from mass atrocity. There is no minor irony here in the fact that the enduring strength of sovereignty itself, as a *legal* norm, will come to turn so heavily on a successful strengthening of the "responsibility to protect" as a *non*legal one; the new extralegal duties will have circuitously restored the legitimacy of a legal right both very old and, in an increasingly common view, morally scandalous. This is but one example of how a strengthening in mores can render acceptable a legal regime otherwise deemed intolerably weak.

## Back to Ground Zero

Recall here my early discussion of the proposed Islamic Cultural Center near the site of the former World Trade Center. In medieval England, ownership of property in land, associated with the name of a given family and kept intact through mandatory primogeniture, was a right associated with a distinctive role and stature in the social order. That is obviously not the case in contemporary America or other Western societies. This historical contrast again illustrates the contingency, in so many circumstances, with which particular rights and responsibilities come to be linked. In few if any circumstances can one accurately say that a given right is logically "inextricable" from a corresponding responsibility, irrespective of time and place. This is true even for professions whose essential purpose—human healing, for instance, in the case of physicians—

seems invariant, if only when characterized in terms so vaporously vague.

Today, compared to other forms of wealth, land does not accord its owner any unique dignity. The essence of all property is simply the owner's right to exclude others.[72] In parts of Western Europe at least, the law's more prominent concern is, in fact, not with preserving the dignity of a property owner but with whether he employs his land in ways sufficiently respectful of *others'* human dignity.[73] Most modern accounts of the nature of property, shaped by "legal realist" thinking of the early twentieth century, conceptualize it in ways that suggest no essence at all.[74] We do better to understand property as a shifting "bundle of sticks"[75]—a metaphor useful in indicating how its elements are susceptible to periodic addition, subtraction, and rearrangement, with a view to enhancing its just and efficient use. The precise contours of rights in property are always in flux, subject to change in the law of, for instance, zoning, housing codes, rent control, public nuisance, environmental protection, air rights, "wastage," and inheritance, among others.

Private property is obviously central to market society. Still, nothing in today's common parlance would suggest that one's right in a particular piece of land bestows upon its holder an inherent dignity of the sort evident in any of Waldron's responsibility-rights. Its owner may lawfully put his land to disparate uses, after all, none of these more essential or archetypal than the rest, none logically or conceptually derived from its very nature. Rights in land thus do not designate for its owner any single, unique societal function. Other claimants, holding future or partial interests, often have a stake as well, to the extent that, some argue, it is not exclusive possession at all, but indeed mandatory forms of sharing—through a complex web of rights and duties—that becomes real property's essential and defining feature.[76]

This means that whatever dignity was once associated with real property ownership would today have to be subdivided, and potentially sliced quite thin. Land is today also readily alienable from one person to another in exchange for money. Through "eminent domain," the state may "take" it at any point, in exchange for due compensation, to achieve any number of "public purposes,"[77] broadly understood. We may all accept that *personal* property (one's toothbrush, for instance) belongs entirely and unequivocally to its owner. Yet some noteworthy thinkers have also long believed that large tracts of *real* property, bestowing great wealth and influence, are necessarily held in an implicit 'trust' for society at large, on the condition that they be put to uses enhancing the general well-being.[78] All this further negates the possibility that land, through some feature intrinsic to it, accords its present owner some elevated social stature, and still less any special moral worth.

Real property owned in common with others does often attach informal responsibilities to rights of use, effectively enforced in extralegal ways. Economists traditionally viewed private property as the optimal solution to overuse of a "commons."[79] Empirical studies now suggest, though, that no such "tragedy" need ensue if social mores firmly regulate its usage. Such mores sustain the peer-to-peer trust that effectively discourages abusive exercise of rights to its exploitation,[80] establishing a stable equilibrium among competing claims on a collective bounty.[81] There would appear to be no special social dignity, moreover, in the exercise of rights to share in a commons, because these rights extend to so many people, often to all those resident in a particular locale.

Waldron's general point about the dignity and inherent duties associated with exercising certain rights nonetheless likely influenced the public dialogue over possible use of the Ground Zero locale for an Islamic cultural center. The duties associated with real property rights have a fluid, inconstant character that may have led many Americans to assume we could readily impose further obligations—based in no more than a widely shared, intensely felt sense of moral appropriateness—on the owners of this piece of land. The technical legal vocabulary of "bundles" finds no place within ordinary parlance. Yet many people apparently viewed the right to build an Islamic center in that particular location as merely a particular "stick" easily plucked from such a shifting sheaf.

Still, it is a right that we must formally pluck *by law,* not through the rough justice of extralegal intimidation, notably the veiled threat of arson.[82] Since the right to own land—unlike parenting or soldiering—subjects no one to any intrinsic, inalterable responsibilities, its owners acquired no elevated stature in possessing the land; and they therefore did not subject themselves to any duties correspondingly enhanced. This intuition likely informed the views of those many other Americans who found the center's location unobjectionable. For the intuition suggests that the owners had no particular responsibility to use their property in any way other than they might lawfully desire.

On the other hand, it is true that the more familiar, layperson's view of property trades on an essentialist notion of land—in particular, as a single indivisible thing, resistant to decomposition into constituent conceptual elements. "So simple was the belief that personhood and ownership stood and fell together that Americans hardly knew they believed it, save when it was challenged," writes Alan Ryan.[83] This simpler understanding of property, as attached to a given person, finds early theoretical grounding in Locke[84] and still enjoys many defenders. Entirely consistent with this view is the notion that a piece of property might become deeply imbued with a certain public purpose, precluding its use for entirely private ends. The state might then formally "take" this piece of turf, duly compensating its owner.

No one argued, however, that the federal government or the City of New York should go so far, acquire the property outright. And yet most people clearly wished to see its use restricted in ways that, they acknowledged, our law could not otherwise constitutionally effect. It was therefore difficult to conceptualize, within any of the legal terms readily at hand, the widespread public apprehensions over the site's prospective use as an Islamic cultural center, the diffuse sense that this would constitute an abuse of rights. Neither did ordinary language, as I earlier observed, offer any other satisfactory terms with which to speak of the moral issues and extralegal responsibilities that many felt to be powerfully at stake.

The entire debate over constructing an Islamic cultural center near Ground Zero might have been more fruitfully conducted in terms of some notion of responsibility-right. This approach offers no unequivocal answers, of course, yet draws us closer, at least, to posing the right questions.

## Virtue Ethics, Sociologically Conceived

A further variation among my empirical cases lies in the source of constraints on rights-exercise. In what way does a constraint on a given right originate? Does it emerge from within the very social practice in which rights-holders are engaged? Or do others impose it from the outside? In other words, are these "impediments" partially "constitutive of the practice"[85]—of doctoring, lawyering, parenting—and hence not truly impediments to it at all, properly speaking? Or are they instead overlaid upon it by those not directly involved, on the basis of ideals extrinsic to its own criteria of excellence?

Virtue ethics (as mentioned before) regards a person's moral character as the key element in understanding and appraising her actions. Virtue consists in her settled disposition to display such habits or traits as benevolence, prudence, judgment, fortitude, charity, and forgiveness. Though some such virtues pertain to all walks of life, they often do so in greatly different measure and take on distinctive meaning within particular vocations and in different historical eras. To engage in serious reflection on the ethics of virtue, at this level of specificity, is always at least to make certain sociological assumptions, perhaps even to engage in sociology itself, as Alasdaire MacIntyre famously argued.[86]

The military officer offers the most ancient archetype of virtue ethics, so conceived, for he occupied an esteemed social role with moral responsibilities understood as integral to its competent practice. Within Europe, professional soldiering entailed obligations of chivalry once owed chiefly to opposing belligerents—fellow members of a pan-European, aristocratic knightly class.[87] These duties were later extended to noncombatants as well. Until the late nineteenth century, however, such responsibilities found only the most limited expression in anything one could truly call positive international law. Respecting these obligations was nonetheless very much part of what it meant to be a good soldier, as officers themselves widely understood their vocation, to judge from their writings.[88]

These seemingly antiquarian notions turned out to play no small role, centuries later, in prompting U.S. Judge Advocate Generals to oppose certain now-infamous methods for "enhanced interrogation" of terrorist suspects during the presidential administration of George W. Bush.[89] This resistance entailed express objection to interpretations offered by the Justice Department's Office of Legal Counsel of federal law ratifying the Convention against Torture. The JAGs' arguments were legal in nature, but the animus behind them was extralegal, to significant degree. Many critics of martial honor, since Thomas Hobbes at least, see it as fostering needless violence and deserving no place in modern societies. Yet in that significant recent experience, honor instead worked to *civilize* it. This memorable episode also strikingly illustrates and confirms Montesquieu's argument about how the martial honor of an aristocratic elite can sometimes put an effective brake on tyrannical temptation.

Like professional soldiering, other social practices frequently combine behavioral norms (often clear) and methods for their enforcement (sometimes strict) with ample opportunity for competitive positioning (frequently fierce). The rivalry generally operates within certain self-imposed constraints, within "rules of the game" defining the nature of the given practice. These constraints can be quite effective, though the law is conspicuous chiefly in its absence.

Even an ethical expectation broadly accepted as internal to their practice may, among its members, become subject to acute disagreement over its proper meaning. Within the American legal profession, for example, there has been some dispute over whether the attorney's acknowledged role and duties as "officer of the court"—a concept long solidly established within our codes of ethics[90]—entail the obligation to report a client's past or prospective illegal activity. Tellingly, those arguing for such an obligation do not often invoke general theories of justice, nor theories of responsibility bearing on "the professions" at large.[91] Robert W. Gordon, for instance, invokes traditions of collective self-understanding intrinsic and specific to the practice of law. Though these traditions originated long ago, many current practitioners, outside the largest cities at least,[92] report considering their standards still authoritative.

It is their critics who seek to tar these legal ethicists—though ensconced within the profession's most distinguished academies—with the brush of pushing ethics *simpliciter* and hence being, in a certain sense, 'unprofessional.' These critics contend that general lay notions or philosophical theories of ethics brought in by others are necessarily alien to the nature of good lawyering; for its standards of virtue, sufficient to its tasks, have emerged historically from within, in the course of sustained efforts by many people over many years to solve recurrent practical problems, specific to this vocational endeavor.[93]

Like other professional activities, the practice of law accords participants an authoritative status and the effective power, if they abuse their rights, to do grievous wrong. The rights in question are tied so closely in common understanding to responsibilities that it is again fair to speak of "responsibility-rights"—though not in Waldron's way, with its essentialist cast[94]—for the terms of this normative conjunction are here always open to dispute and possible revision.

Shifts in the perceived duties and dispensations associated with particular vocational roles initially arise not only from in-house express disagreements among current members, or between members and dissatisfied nonmembers. New mores spring also from the subjective experience of intense personal turmoil within individual members. Goffman writes of the evident self-distancing in which professionals of various sorts regularly engage, through myriad subtle cues and clues, so as to signal their discomfort with what their well-settled role demands of them in a given circumstance, even as they largely honor its requirements.[95]

Insofar as these discomforts stem from concerns fairly characterized as ethical in nature, there is no anomie in this self-distancing, only alienation. These individuals are simply identifying themselves with certain normative understandings somewhat at odds with those currently regnant within their field or discipline. Their inchoate understandings implicitly gesture at the possibility of revision in the mores of their job. The human self evinces great multiplicity,[96] and macro-social change occasionally begins in such humble, micro-level dissatisfactions, first evinced through a momentary grimace, welcomed with an appreciative passing glance.

In many contexts beyond the licensed professions, there is no discernible social practice by whose internal standards one may appraise the conduct at issue as reprehensible or commendable. When people hesitate to declare bankruptcy or terminate a pregnancy, for instance, they often fear stigma and anticipate feelings of shame or qualms of conscience. Though these moral sentiments undoubtedly influence conduct, one could not point in these cases to any established practices or specific institutional settings within which they arise. The rights themselves—to abort, to declare bankruptcy—are not part and parcel of any determinate social role or distinguished status, the predicate for a responsibility-right. The responsibilities associated with these less elevated rights find inspiration in the shared moral sensibilities of society at large—broad portions of it, at least—not those peculiar to any single professional milieu, for instance. The causal processes at work, though often potent, are also diffuse, organizationally inchoate, and elusive to convincing scientific inquiry. Still, we know they exist, because they allow us to accurately anticipate how most others will judge us for engaging in such conduct, should they learn of it.

We may observe much the same concerning the occasions when family members intercede to prevent a medical patient from exercising her right to die, especially where she suffers no enduring terminal condition. The demands of common morality here at work again far exceed the law's. These are moral duties of care both to youthful dependents, if any exist, and to herself. Family members appeal to these duties in dissuading the patient from forgoing treatment. If these people consider *themselves* under any moral obligation to dissuade her, it is to assist her in honoring her own.[97]

When a *physician* intercedes at such moments, though, we more readily, convincingly describe her conduct as grounded in institutional practices. She conforms to the long-standing virtue ethics of an entire profession that continues to prize patient survival above all else, though contemporary law no longer embraces that goal unequivocally. The modern hospital regularly, if surreptitiously, acquiesces in "heroic" efforts to suppress patient resistance to essential, life-sustaining care. It is therefore accurate to describe this tacit administrative accommodation as a settled practice within American society.

This chapter has identified five ways that, through both law and mores—alone or in combination—responsibilities become attached to legal rights. To summarize: First, policymakers and legislators may conclude that a given type of right-bearer simply offers the least-cost provider of a certain societal good. He happens to be better situated, for the moment, to perform certain important tasks more easily or effectively than anyone else. The responsibilities thereby affixed often ensue from some informal variety of cost-benefit analysis. Lawmakers will readily reallocate these responsibilities if and when altered circumstances so indicate. The moral reasoning involved in these calculations is consequentialist, of roughly utilitarian variety. It is that allocating these legal responsibilities—in this particular way, in this type of circumstance—is most propitious for advancing overall public well-being.

Second, there are responsibility-rights, on Waldron's understanding of the notion. The duties attendant on a given societal role, from parenting to soldiering, here follow naturally and inexorably from its very nature, understood in ways largely irrespective of historical and societal context. The core rights and responsibilities concomitant to a given role virtually entail each other. At this level of abstraction, however, there is little from which a sociology of rights to do wrong may profit. As a philosopher, Waldron's professed aims are understandably different, but his formulations veer unmistakably into territory that sociologists, with some reason, customarily consider their own.

His theory is of some help in conceptualizing the most stable, enduring conjunctions of right and responsibility, at least those whose mode of admixture is relatively "hardwired" into a given role's inner essence and therefore changes little with time and place. This is a small subset, however, of all vocational roles and status positions within society. And as with the idealized economic theory of least-cost provision, here too there is no conceptual space for periodic dispute—still less ongoing political struggle—over who, on account of holding certain rights, should also bear certain duties. More precisely, with the philosophic and economic approaches to distributing rights and duties, such disputes as may arise can concern only whether we have properly understood the essential nature of a given role or have correctly tallied up, from the standpoint of some impartial master planner, the aggregate costs or benefits of any given such allocation. If we wish to delineate and explain any actual lay of relevant empirical land, neither theory carries us very far.

Third, and far more promising, there are rights and responsibilities intrinsic to an evolving social practice, whose conception of virtue changes importantly over time in light of collegial in-house conversation. One might argue that these situations, too, represent a form of responsibility-right. For there is again, if only for a time, a certain natural intimacy to the connection between the normative ingredients thus paired, each with unmistakable affinity for the other. Yet this is not a matter of logical entailment (the second view, above) any more than a result of institutional design with a view to cost-efficient provision (the first view). And there is much cross-cultural variation in relevant respects. Thus, though both "healers" are committed to their patients' well-being (and enjoy elevated societal stature), a London heart surgeon and an Andean shaman[98] inhabit occupational roles in which rights and duties are defined and distributed very differently, if perhaps with an equal sense of perceived congruity between the corresponding elements.

Because these social roles and statuses lack any inalterable essence, practitioners regularly revise them experimentally, through trial and error, in light of acknowledged failures and opportunities newly apprehended. And it is practitioners themselves, on this view, who must settle upon a unified understanding of their duties to their clients and to society at large. This intramural deliberation takes the distinctive philosophical form of virtue ethics. The central question is therefore always: What does it mean, precisely, to be truly accomplished in our unique vocational endeavor, meeting the very highest standards of excellence we collectively set for one another? Inevitably here, the line between virtue and virtuosity then becomes willfully vague.

The deepest debates within all professions nonetheless ultimately move on to the question of whether the standards that practitioners generate internally are fully adequate, in all cases, to normative challenges their members confront, challenges increasingly raised not only from within their ranks but from beyond.[99] There thus appears a fourth method of linking rights to responsibilities. Those beyond a vocation's ranks may conclude that its practitioners are not to be entirely trusted in answering all central questions on their own. Society at large and its elected representatives make a necessary and legitimate contribution as well. The ensuing public discussion of potential legal changes inevitably involves not only reasoned argument, but the expression of righteous indignation over perceived abuses of existing rights. This effusion of moral sentiment—often revulsion at current practices, approximating disgust at times—ensures a more freewheeling, open-ended conversation, among a much larger number of people. Debate no longer focuses on the quantitative intricacies of least-cost provision or the seeming solipsisms of virtue ethics, now seen as unduly insular. By means both juridical and otherwise, existing roles are redefined, with the objective of assigning new legal responsibilities to those (soldiers, physicians, journalists) perceived to be abusing their rights.

Fifth and finally, where many people remain dissatisfied with lawmakers' response to their concerns, they regularly proceed, through myriad means this book examines, to exert more informal pressure on right-holders, so that the latter may honor responsibilities that law declines to incorporate. Social mores, revised or reinvigorated, here become more important than the law, independently chastening right-holders' behavior. Within public discourse, the central concern becomes: How might we, the interested public, induce the profession to better respect the human dignity of its clients while enhancing their well-being, along with that of affected third parties?

As the public's role becomes more prominent, common morality finds its voice and asserts its influence upon the law as well as on human behavior more directly. Deontological intuitions acquire especial influence here, because these are more readily accessible to most minds—even those well-schooled—than a cooler, consequentialist/utilitarian calculus. Most of us are content to follow our initial visceral emotional reactions, and psychologically averse to the lengthier deliberations necessary to assess complex second-order ramifications.[100] Easy intuitions of "just deserts," especially of retribution for grievous wrong, become most prominent in our thoughts and in relevant policy discussions. Criminal law and its sanctions then inevitably assume greater salience within the repertoire of available responses to major departures from common morality, however much "the experts" counsel differently.

This book's chief interest lies in the final method of attaching nonlegal responsibilities to legal rights, whereby concerned parties push back against the perceived abuse of rights, without any immediate effect upon the law, often without any clear intent to alter it. This chapter has offered only a nutshell conceptual typology, necessarily static, illustrated with a few examples; in real life, many of its constituent types are in simultaneous operation. A typology can tell us nothing, moreover, about historical changes, those tending to increase or decrease the incidence of a given method, relative to others, for tying duties to dispensations. And I have not yet asked whether rights to do wrong, and the relation they establish between law and common morality, assume distinct form in various historical epochs, in contemporary Western society as contrasted with earlier or non-Western social orders. Let us now turn to these large questions, fateful and inescapable.

# 13

# Common Morality Confronts Modernity

## The Law's Ascendance in the Modern West, and the Decline of Common Morality—or Any Need for It?

There has been much skepticism over whether, in the contemporary West, maintaining an acceptable social order requires any nontrivial sense of shared morality at all. At least since Bentham, a widely held view has been that it does not. This has in fact been a leitmotif across several competing schools of modern legal and political thought. Liberal theory in particular—while directing a steady stream of criticism at *particular* laws—has virtually never challenged the supposition that the law in general remains our last best hope of constructing a decent society, whose members are well treated and passably content. Even libertarian forms of liberalism, ever fearful of the state's encroachment beyond its due domain, consistently stress the importance of official protection for "the private realm," secured through *the law* of contract, of property, and of the family.

The view that law's potential contribution to social amelioration is inherently limited arises largely from those (loosely) to liberalism's Left and Right. It has come from Marxists, denouncing the fraud of "bourgeois liberal legality," and from "historicist" strands of conservatism—from Burke and Savigny[1] through Oakeshott—avowedly antimodern in spirit. This latter strain of thinking consistently celebrates "the social organism," its spontaneously regenerative capacity for preserving and gradually improving its health, along with that of its members. Such traditionalist diagnoses maintain that this process, operating independently of the state, is generally superior to the law in attaining a morally satisfactory polity and society.[2] When it seeks to alter mores, the law tends to do more harm than good—*much* more, at times.

A view often heard today is that, whether its aim be stability or change, positive law should essentially supplant society's reliance on common morality. As the basis of normative ordering, common morality and the social practices embodying it are too frail or corrupt. It follows that there is little reason to be much concerned with identifying the points of strength and weakness in their sociological supports. Because the very idea of common morality is something of a quaint Victorian cobweb, on this view,[3] its importance should and will decline as societies discover that they must rely ever more upon their legal system, and specifically (one hopes) on "the rule of law."

In a formulation not untypical, Jürgen Habermas thus strongly affirms, "Today legal norms are what is left from a crumbled cement of society; if all other mechanisms of social integration are exhausted, law yet provides some means for keeping together complex and centrifugal societies that otherwise would fall into pieces."[4] He regards this trajectory as virtually inevitable and destined to continue, but does not celebrate it (as do many others) without ambivalence; he openly acknowledges that an unfortunate consequence of our increasing reliance on positive law as the near-exclusive source of normative order is to "*relieve* the judging and acting person of the considerable cognitive, motivational, . . . and organizational demands of a morality centered on the individual's conscience."[5] Others further infer that the displacement of individual conscience by law in assessing our actions not only allows but encourages—subtly yet powerfully—the irresponsible exercise of legal rights.[6]

"Legal centralism" is the prevailing term for these developments, seen in a positive light. It was also prevalent in the time of Montesquieu,[7] who argued strongly against its versions of the day. Montesquieu sought to show how allowing some measure of social regulation through mores does not lead to chaos, and that admitting their inevitable role is entirely consistent with a prominent place for individual freedom and human agency. To this moment, some of his scholarly critics still deny this claim,[8] seeing no way to reconcile his political liberalism, which they share, with his sociology, which they feel therefore compelled to reject.

Habermas states the centralist case with especial militancy. It remains widely held among legal thinkers, both in the United States and in other lands. Centralists believe that the extralegal norms by which we appraise and guide others' conduct usually display, in the words of J. L. Austin (an early, influential legal positivist), "uncertainty, scantiness, and imperfection."[9] These properties render common morality unworthy of law's solicitude. It is important to record in passing, at least, that this view, its pervasive current influence notwithstanding, would appear wildly eccentric to most people in most cultures and world civilizations throughout human history. For millennia, billions of Confucians, for instance, have firmly regarded the law as necessarily a very imperfect mechanism for establishing and enforcing morality, which they understand as better transmitted and refined in other ways.[10]

Insistent codifiers like Bentham wished to make every possible human action the subject of law's scrutiny. He believed, in fact, that he himself had written a legal code in which "there is no *terra incognita,* no blank spaces; nothing is . . . omitted, nothing unprovided for."[11] In a similar spirit, a recent author contends that "the more coherent and consistent a legal system, the less the need for . . . customary rules and practices." The law's deference to customary morals is inherently suspect because "the relevant customs prove to be those of an influential group of insiders."[12] The law expressly incorporates these mores when, for instance, courts interpret disputed terms within a contract in light of "trade usage,"[13] and defer to "standards of care" (in negligence litigation), including those specific to established industries whose oligopolistic elites exercise undue influence in establishing prevailing mores.

The law relies on common moralities even when it does not expressly "incorporate by reference" a moral terminology—such as "moral turpitude"[14]—already prevalent in society, Doubts about law's deference to conventional ethical sensibilities will be still greater here. For the judiciary is not authorized in these circumstances to monitor social mores and so to ensure their objective "reasonableness" and ethical acceptability. When tort and contract law defer to current social practices and the prevailing moralities these embody, the courts remain at least nominally sovereign, insisting in the final analysis upon their own criteria for determining whether the law should admit any such prevailing practice into its domain.[15]

In the situations of present interest, by contrast, the law imposes no such formal limit on prevailing moralities and in fact rides largely upon their back, unsure of where, in what direction, they may travel. In this respect, the socio-legal configuration on which this book focuses differs from what we observe in tort or contract, and its defense will be more controversial on that account. To allow that extralegal mores will significantly limit the exercise of our rights is anathema in the view of most modern legal theorists who have seriously considered the matter, with the singular exception of Lon Fuller.[16] And when the social practices by which we enforce common morality all but prevent someone from exercising her rights, these apprehensions are often well warranted. Exceptions may arise where we regard the rights themselves as morally indefensible. Yet most believe that, even so, we should then change the law rather than allow its express promises to be denied in practice. Such change is not always quick or easy, however, and often proves impossible (for reasons discussed in Chapter 6).

## Shame and the Law

The most effective way to ensure general adherence to social mores not legally enshrined is through the public discrediting of those violating them. Scholars in the humanities delineate the shifting borders and areas of historical overlap between such words as "reproach," "disrepute," "disesteem," "dishonor," "shame," "disgrace," "ignominy," "infamy," "obloquy," "opprobrium," "stigma," and "humiliation."[17] And for certain purposes it is indeed important to maintain the subtle distinctions among them, however elusive at times. More significant to this book's aims, however, is the shared capacity of all such discrediting to restrain the abusive exercise of legal rights. "Lumping" these several notions is therefore preferable here to "splitting" them, registering and cataloguing every nuanced shading of denotation and connotation. The public discrediting of others is morally defensible in certain situations and not in others, all would presumably agree. The proper way to distinguish the two is by way of straightforward moral argument, however, not by observing differences in changing historical uses of these several terms.

Skepticism toward alternatives to legal sanctions against disfavored conduct has focused in recent years on the dangers of "shaming sanctions." These are analogous to scarlet letters, the punishment pillories of Renaissance Europe, and the ducking stools of colonial America. Historically such sanctions were formally imposed by law. They were nonetheless intended to invite more spontaneous popular expressions of indignation toward their human targets—in full public view, unlike when one is punished through fines or incarceration. Today, shaming sanctions include mandatory bumper stickers on automobiles of those previously stripped of their license, for driving while intoxicated.[18] This has been notably successful, on some accounts,[19] in decreasing accidents resulting from inebriation.

Though the law here continues to employ its formal procedures in imposing such sanctions, there is serious concern that these violate the wrongdoer's essential human dignity. Yet the same can be said, often in much greater measure, of the wrongdoing eliciting these sanctions, and deterred by them; and there is much to be said for expecting people, in the interests of overall social well-being, to be thicker-skinned in these matters. Most Americans agree: when asked in surveys to consider the effect of modest shaming sanctions on human dignity—without even being invited to weigh these drawbacks against positive effects in diminished wrongdoing—a large majority report that they find such measures "very acceptable" or "fairly acceptable."[20] We are not so different here from contemporary East Asians, who (researchers report) "expect that people should be able to handle shame,"[21] provided that opportunities are quickly afforded for ready reintegration.

Still, when we rely upon public shaming and informal social stigma *without* any official guidelines and protections, the dangers grow. It is precisely these nonlegal sanctions—their nature, significance, and effects, for good and ill—that this book strives to better understand and, with due qualifications, to defend. Some insist that shame and stigma are the stuff of archaic social orders, not the legitimate tools of liberal justice. This finds some modest reflection in the fact that, according to an Ngram Viewer search on the word, references to "shame" declined in use from 1800 through 1980, though it has risen steadily and significantly since that latter year.[22]

It has been a celebrated hallmark of the modern West to have eliminated—in the name of greater "humanity"—the public use of shaming for state-imposed punishment, as Foucault famously observed.[23] Sanctions of this sort "typically involve a type of mob justice and are problematic for that reason alone," writes Nussbaum.[24] Yale legal historian James Whitman adopts a similarly stringent stance: "Justice by the mob is not the impartial, deliberative, neutral justice that a liberal-democratic society typically prizes."[25] From this standpoint, law alone is the reliable source of public order, the only truly legitimate basis of our obligation to others.

The law's use for shaming is still more reprehensible, Nussbaum contends, than the less disciplined forms employed by private citizens, precisely because law puts the state's official imprimatur on the humiliation.[26]

And the criteria by which we appraise the law's defensibility in a given circumstance must remain independent of prevailing "prejudice," of the shifting empirical contours of popular indignation. These societal influences are always potentially and perilously at odds with our commitment to "critical" morality and to "rule of law values," these authors contend.

To be sure, whenever the law sees fit to grant wide berth to rights-restraining mores, its drafters and interpreters need to carefully assess how much trust to place in processes largely beyond their control, about which they should therefore learn as much as possible. No one should deny that there are times when the law rightly overrides prevailing moral sensibilities within a given community, where these threaten vital human interests. The unacceptable standards may simply be those of an insular subcommunity, deviant in this respect from standards within the wider society, embodied in its law.

That is the case, for instance, with members of the Jehovah's Witnesses, a religious group whose adult members regularly refuse to let their children receive blood transfusions essential to survival. These are situations where the law clearly cannot depend upon fellow members of the relevant subcommunity to wisely and effectively resist the exercise of legal rights by one of their number—here, the parent of a legal minor. The law strongly presumes that a child's parental guardians will act responsibly when exercising the well-accepted right to accept or reject medical treatment.

The legal system nonetheless intercedes when there is a compelling basis to rebut that presumption. Here, subcommunal sentiment is just as misguided as legal centralists and positivists like Austin assume. In seeking an effective regulatory stance, the law cannot rely on these sentiments and mores to ensure satisfactory parental behavior. From this perspective, the question becomes: When, if ever, is it defensible and desirable for the law to place so much reliance on something as questionable as extralegal morality, over which it retains so little control? The concern may be at least equally acute if this is the morality of an entire national society, no less than of some parochial subsection.

Whether it is defensible to employ shame in eliciting conformity with social mores, existing or emergent, depends on the ends sought and particular means employed. It is necessary to provide some method, as did colonial Americans themselves,[27] by which wrongdoers subject to this species of recrimination may thereafter redeem and reintegrate themselves.[28] Shaming of this variety requires, on all accounts, that criticism be conveyed respectfully—however firm the reproach[29]—and directed against particular misconduct, not at the entire person.

These strictures need not extend to criticism of organizations, certainly so in cases of extreme misconduct.[30] Corporations have a reputation to protect, to be sure, but no intrinsic human dignity to besmirch. Perhaps the objective of reform will be to induce a large multinational enterprise into greater compliance with UN Global Compact norms; and the means to that end will entail public shaming of the company through advertising campaigns directed at prospective purchasers of its products. These campaigns routinely deploy not only reasoned argument, in dry and lengthy position papers. They rely as well on deliberate efforts to evoke feelings of intense antipathy, even disgust, toward the company, its practices, and behavior of top managers.[31] This strategy has periodically proven effective in influencing consumer conduct.[32]

Some will wonder why it is insufficient to speak simply of directing our measured disapproval at others' misconduct, dispassionately arousing their guilt over failures to meet their responsibilities. Why is it not enough to soberly persuade them of their duty to compensate and seek forgiveness from those they have wronged? From this Kantian standpoint, it is important that we each individually engage in an autonomous exercise of reason in adopting the principles that are to guide our lives.

Yet even by our own lights, our reason regularly fails us, and even when it accurately instructs us, our will may prove weak. Many of us thus do not pass this high test, as we readily admit. Our failure greatly limits the efficacy of guilt as a real-life force, in reforming political and social life especially. As Jacquet observes, with only modest hyperbole, "In cultures that champion the individual, guilt is advertised as the cornerstone of conscience. But while guilt holds individuals to personal standards, it is powerless in the face of corrupt institutions. In recent years, we as consumers have sought to assuage our guilt about flawed social and environmental practices and policies by, for example, buying organic foods or fair-trade products. Unless nearly everyone participates, however, the impact of individual consumer consciousness is ineffective."[33]

She proceeds to argue that, in correcting abuses by large companies and sovereign states, "the solution to the limitations of guilt can be found in shame, retrofitted for the age of democracy and social media . . . [S]haming can function as a nonviolent form of resistance that . . . [is both effective and morally defensible] when applied . . . sparingly and pointedly . . . in the right way, the right quantity, and at the right time." These are important qualifications, of course, requiring close attention not only to situational specifics, but also to developing general standards enabling us to distinguish, across a broad canvas, acceptable uses of shame from indefensible ones.[34]

From a Kantian standpoint, however, emotions are generally a distraction from the tasks of reason.[35] Feelings of shame—perhaps the most thoroughly social of the moral sentiments[36]—are particularly misguided. On most accounts, shame chiefly appeals less to our freely undertaken judgments about ourselves than to the judgment that others visit upon us, if only in our imaginations.[37] The discomfort we feel when others seek to shame us reveals that we have come to rely on *their* standards of appraisal when we should be independently formulating and enacting our own. This stern stance regards our emotions as forces inherently irrational, as dark creatures of blind impulse. "The passions" are volatile, ever-threatening to effective social coordination, and always in danger of prompting us to impetuous outburst when we cannot entirely suppress them. This stark choice between repression and tumultuous eruption leaves little space for the reflective alternation between evanescent instants of thought and feeling through which we often strive to sensibly channel our emotions, refocus their direction, recalibrate their intensity, downward or up.

The Kantian view further forecloses the older, Aristotelian and Stoic insight that our most important sentiments—of grief, or love, for instance—are based on beliefs, observations, and judgments about our surroundings, beliefs that we periodically subject to reasoned reassessment. Our moral sentiments also enable us to perceive wrongdoing—cruelty especially, perhaps—when our capacities for reasoning, on their own, may desert us.[38] The moral sentiments of pity, gratitude, and indignation—to take three obvious illustrations—are notable in how they manage to conjoin, from one moment to the next, our capacities for deliberation and spontaneity. We should view shame from this same standpoint. For as a moral sentiment, like the others just mentioned, it is susceptible to intelligent direction, with a view to enhancing our awareness of injustice, in others and in ourselves, and our willingness to act upon that awareness. To *feel* oneself in the presence of profound injustice is often a necessary predicate to openly objecting and interceding against those responsible for it.

To begin with a definition, shame consists in the "shared revulsion at actions and individuals," writes Deigh, "who betray the beliefs, norms, and ideals of a group to which they belong and with which they strongly identify . . . The shame they then experience . . . entails a painful recognition of . . . having acted beneath themselves, of their having betrayed an identity that is a source of their sense of worth."[39] In this much, at least, there is little to argue against. In fact, Arneson adds, "it is *good* to be disposed to be ashamed by perceiving in oneself traits that are genuinely shameful."[40] And "by bringing it about that members of society are fearful of being shamed . . . and by attaching these sentiments to appropriate social standards, the society produces just consequences to a greater extent than would otherwise be possible."[41] Of such standards, Kahan adds, "the question is never whether a society should organize itself around emphatic ideas of high and low, worthy and worthless, but only what the content of those animating hierarchies will be"[42] and what will count as acceptable methods for establishing or securing them. These methods and standards must of course be ones "that orient a person toward promotion of the common good in his community and toward regard for other human beings as his equals."[43] The challenge is to shrewdly harness this "shared revulsion" in service of such laudable and "constructive"[44] aims, without unnecessarily humiliating its targets.

There is no reason to assume that "the ideals of the group" at issue will warrant any such deference, of course, and often they won't. In his defense of shame, Bernard Williams was therefore careful to restrict its legitimate compass to circumstances where the individual has independent reasons to respect the moral judgment of others.[45] For we may then defensibly entrust to them a certain degree of authority in appraising our behavior, measuring its consistency with moral standards we freely share or could readily have come to adopt on our own.

The conclusion thus emerges that a liberal and "decent society trains its members," as Arneson affirms, "to be disposed to feel deeply ashamed at violating the rights of others."[46] It also trains us to respectfully communicate our aversion and revulsion to others engaged in such violation, so that we might evoke their sense of guilt or shame, inducing them by either route to alter their conduct. A decent society should further provide us with a rich and nuanced vocabulary—ample and conceptually discriminating—to accomplish this task. We then employ that language comfortably, in the knowledge that others will find it resonant and share the subtle range of moral sentiments it enables us to formulate and convey.

That is not a society we inhabit, however.

The considerable efforts of these several authors to rehabilitate the sense of shame,[47] to ensure for it a fair hearing among modern liberals, have undoubted appeal, within real life still more than in philosophical reflection. It carries us only so far, though, for it amounts to conceiving of shame as a species of surrogate guilt, something delegated—if only partially and contingently—to others whom we have good reason to rely on in such matters. We should repose such trust when we have some basis to distrust our own judgment, as where we should realize that our self-interest and propensity for self-deception threaten to cloud the understanding of what justice requires of us, or tamp down our inclinations to act upon such understanding.

Even as one endorses these scholarly 'celebrants' of shame, one nonetheless emerges with a lingering, indelible sense that the additional element that shame might add to a fully satisfactory analysis of moral practice, which guilt alone cannot provide, is something in which moral philosophy has had only tangential interest and hence cannot ultimately much help us comprehend. This additional element is the psychology of motivation. It might first seem that guilt would be stronger than shame in actively inspiring measures of reparation. It is the furies of indignation, resentment, and anger that elicit feelings of guilt, whereas shame emerges in reaction to the lesser forces of contempt, derision, and avoidance.[48] These would seem more likely to prompt social withdrawal than energetic intercession directed at moral repair. Shame need not even arise from failures specifically moral in nature, but can stem also from failings in prowess or cunning.[49]

Yet the emotional intensity that shame, even its mere anticipation,[50] can engender in us ensures that its motivational power is often greater than that of guilt.[51] Laboratory psychologists have devised ingenious methods—introducing or withdrawing a third-party observer[52]—to isolate the effects of each from the other. In these experiments, shame consistently emerges the more powerful prompt to public-spiritedness and other conscientious conduct. Real-life policy experiments, beyond the university laboratory and online survey, reach similar conclusions, as when American states seek openly to shame delinquent taxpayers (those owing over $250,000, in California); this policy has much increased overall public compliance with tax law.[53]

Relative to guilt, shame can also be especially powerful in establishing *new* norms, not merely in winning compliance to existing ones. This is because "even when there is no hope of changing the transgressor's behavior," shaming his misconduct "lets others know that such behavior will [henceforth] be punished." This is important, writes Jacquet, "especially in the absence of formal sanctions, or . . . before formal rules are instituted."[54] She goes so far as to contend that "shame resides deeper in human nature,"[55] though here she strays beyond her evidence. The internet greatly enlarges the audience for shaming, of course, in the measure of some three billion people. "Unlike the gossip of the past, which was spoken or printed," Jacquet observes, "Internet gossip is fast, far-reaching, set in digital stone, and often searchable."[56]

Through the power of internalized guilt alone, indifferent to the opinion of others or their reaction to our behavior, it is often difficult to make ourselves fully aware of how we have wronged another and the nature of our responsibilities to make amends. On the Kantian account, we must undertake this challenge largely unassisted, moreover. Only in recent years, Haidt observes, has the question of what motivates us to moral action become of central concern even to the empirical, psychological study of morality. Better than through philosophy alone, we can grasp shame's true significance and ground-level workings through the social sciences, including not only psychology but also sociology and moral anthropology.

With respect to apparent corporate misconduct, casting public shame upon large companies regularly proves more effective than efforts to induce feelings of guilt in consumers of their products. Corporate transgressors of law and mores often respond to consumer guilt chiefly by creating new, up-scale products, like "dolphin-free" tuna, offered at higher prices. Too few consumers are sufficiently wracked by guilt, in any event, for such approaches to produce profound change in many industries.[57]

There are a number of large policy issues—from overfishing and deforestation to the enslavement of child soldiers—that present major collective-action problems to their satisfactory solution. These cannot be seriously addressed by wholly individualizing our understanding of those responsible, then appealing to their capacity for remorse. Thus today, the environmental NGO Greenpeace strives to shame the largest retailers of Chilean sea bass, rather than seeking to instill guilt in the individual people who consume it. When the producers themselves cannot be shamed into altering their practices, Greenpeace then turns to those who finance them. Both producers and financiers are induced to consider the consequences of their activity, not for the fish themselves, but for the firm's societal reputation and market vulnerability.

From accumulating experience of this sort, it is now relatively clear that "small changes by big groups can make a big difference,"[58] as reports a scholar of corporate shaming campaigns. In their efforts to alter the conduct of sovereign states and large companies, NGOs like Human Rights Watch have developed sophisticated "shaming methodologies,"[59] calculated for maximum efficacy on the basis of what has worked and failed in prior campaigns. Before launching any such effort, these activists systematically assess the relevance and weight of each among a long list of relevant variables.

It seems safe to say that, to ensure the persistence of any society over time, some mixture of shame and guilt is necessary in eliciting adherence to its most basic principles,[60] for the simple reason that these principles can never receive full embodiment within its law. The more modern and liberal the society, the more this is the case, we will now see. These claims are not axiomatic propositions, but thoroughly empirical, and generously supported by evidence from a wide sweep of legal life. Our central concern should not be, as Nussbaum contends, that the shaming of others leads with near inexorability to their indefensible humiliation.[61] The greater problem is that liberal law's limitations ensure that it cannot (for the reasons offered in Chapter 6) do *enough* of the kind of shaming a modern liberal society requires. This is partly because it must be liberal, and partly because it must be law.

## The Sociology of Stigma

Like shame, with which its definition considerably overlaps, stigma too regularly makes a salutary contribution in restraining the exercise of legal rights, limiting their widely perceived abuse. To some, this claim will be still more counterintuitive, preposterously so. Among sociologists, who purport to lend the term a scientific status, prevailing understandings concede nothing to the possibility that stigma could ever be anything but wholly reprehensible. Thus, the most influential recent work on the subject defines it in terms of the conjunction of several elements, each more contemptible than the preceding: "In the first component, people distinguish and label human differences. In the second, dominant cultural beliefs link labeled persons to undesirable characteristics—to negative stereotypes. In the third, labeled persons are placed in distinct categories so as to accomplish some degree of separation of "us" from "them." In the fourth, labeled persons experience status loss and discrimination that lead to unequal outcomes. Finally, stigmatization is entirely contingent on access to . . . power that allows [all of the preceding]."[62]

There is no doubt that, so conceived, stigma does terrible damage, causes extraordinary suffering, in circumstances too numerous to list, well described in a half-century of commendable studies.[63] It represents a massive advance for humane values when those suffering severe physical disability throughout the world come to describe themselves as feeling "stigmatized," rather than—as they long had said—"ashamed" of their condition, and hence reluctant even to venture out in public. For this linguistic revision entirely reverses the poles of opprobrium, its target now the discreditors, no longer those once discredited.

Still, the quoted definition of stigma is very much a sociological term of art. It bears almost no relation to any of the several definitions appearing in the *Oxford English Dictionary*[64] and only very limited consistency with those in published guides to more contemporary usage.[65] *Merriam-Webster,* for example, defines stigma—the only type pertinent here, among its several other meanings—as simply "a mark of shame or discredit." I here employ the term in this expansive sense, more familiar to most readers than the sociologists' more technical understanding. For present purposes, then, it is proper to regard stigma as an acute form of shaming.

There are several differences between the sociological definition of stigma and that of ordinary language. First, the academic understanding entails the targeting of entire groups as such, frequently on grounds having nothing to do with any misbehavior by its members. Second, as the sociologists conceive of it, stigma is not a plight from which the individual member of a targeted group can escape by altering her conduct, bringing it into line with prevailing mores. The "discredit" of interest to the sociologists targets the entire person, not some discrete aspect of her behavior. The conduct at issue in the present study—the behavior that others seek to alter through its "shame or discredit"—is of a very specific sort, moreover: the exercise of particular rights, in particular ways, those which many deem offensive.

Any form of stigma or shaming necessarily entails the "lowering," as Kahan puts it, of some in relation to others, within a particular normative hierarchy, on whose basis the individual acquires greater or lesser status. The species of stigma this book examines and defends does not, however, involve its targets' dehumanization. Thus, to take a few of my illustrations, those who receive disability or welfare benefits may be diminished in the eyes of some of their fellow citizens but are not ostracized. Those who declare personal bankruptcy do not suffer "social death."[66] The treatment of someone as truly "less than human"—Goffman's early definition[67]—is a further aspect of how sociologists understand stigma. There can be no doubt that stigma in extremis does indeed dehumanize, as is evident in how most people treat those who suffer leprosy, for instance. Stigma of this magnitude is notably absent from my illustrations of resistance to the abusive exercise of rights.

Finally, the sociologists are clearly committed to preserving the word "stigma" as a designation for groups having no political power. Ordinary language, reflected in standard dictionary definitions, nevertheless registers the term's usage quite farther afield. Writing for like-minded peers, the sociologists confess that "if we only used the cognitive components of labeling and stereotyping to define stigma, groups like lawyers, politicians, and white people would have to be considered stigmatized groups."[68] Upon reading that sentence, one would expect it to be immediately followed by some intelligible argument for why negative "stereotyping" and pejorative "labeling," alone or in combination, do not suffice for the concept's acceptable application. By this I mean some rationale independent of the fact that a more inclusive definition might suggest its relevance to the disparaging treatment of those from whom sociologists wish to deny the status of victim, a status today supremely elevated within American culture. Instead, to bar the unappealing possibility of their inclusion, an act of definitional legerdemain forcefully intercedes. For these authors and their putative science, stigma thus becomes a perverse species of prize, a reverse badge of honor. It is reserved for those who elicit their ideological sympathies, denied to those who don't—by a form of linguistic gerrymandering more often associated with us lawyers, at our worst.

Several circumstances here discussed, such as the shaming of corporations,[69] nonetheless clearly illustrate that concerted efforts to "shame or discredit" others, individuals and institutions, today routinely find the powerful centrally in their sights.[70] These efforts regularly succeed in effecting some measure of genuine "status loss," costly to companies and their managers. This is often accomplished, we have seen, by recasting issues previously understood as technical and value-neutral as matters to which specifically moral concerns properly attach. Through the very process of successfully stigmatizing their opponents, moral entrepreneurs can themselves acquire no small measure of "power" over the public perception of policy issues. The author of a recent book on the shaming of large companies for alleged environmental abuse thus concludes that, unlike efforts to instill individualized guilt, shame can "be used by the weak against the strong."[71] Yet in the sociological account above—simplistic in this respect as well—the power to stigmatize is a possession necessarily anterior to its use in stigmatization.

The sociologists are, in short, unwilling to acknowledge the bearing of their own definition—these two key elements, labeling and stereotyping—on certain forms of stigma undoubtedly prominent within contemporary Western societies. These forms involve its self-conscious and strategic deployment, with some considerable skill and savvy, in service of avowedly "progressive" ends. This sophistication is evident, for example, in the calculations by which activists decide to target particular multinational companies for shaming. These advocacy campaigns hone in precisely on those enterprises recognized, after careful study, as especially susceptible to such efforts, and susceptible for reasons often unrelated the magnitude of alleged wrongs.[72] That this involves the use of stigma should be readily recognizable, to anyone not blinded by ideological militance.

The consistent question throughout in this inquiry has been: On account of law's limitations, what place must it concede to stigma, what role in ensuring that legal rights are not abused, not exercised irresponsibly? This question should immediately invite objections, however, and it is a formulation that anyone but a law professor would regard as megalomania on our part. From any other perspective, the very opposite question would surely be more compelling: What portion of the larger normative order and its enforcement ought we to entrust to the legal system and those claiming professional authority to administer it?

Our lawyerly hubris here finds expression as well in the flurry of prominent legal theorizing on the subject of "law and social norms," discussed before. This work displayed much greater interest in how law might reconfigure common morality than in how such morality regularly renders law—and hence those practicing or professing it—less important than we would like to suppose. Even those rare authors somewhat curious about how mores felicitously inhibit rights abuse consistently emphasized the efficiency advantages of such extralegal restraints.[73] Yet as indicated, there is far more at stake here than efficiency alone.

## Shame, Social Mores, and Modernity

At this point, skeptics of the law's reliance on common morality will inevitably insist on summoning the familiar story about how contemporary Western society has fatally eroded the foundations for any meaningful measure of social mores. These critics will claim there is no reason to believe that the little insular, thriving coteries examined in those discrete micro-ethnographies[74] represent something broader than themselves, offer any larger lessons for the workings of national societies at large. If the efficacy of modern law really rests on any robust sense of widely shared morals, they observe, we are surely doomed.

The aspect of modernity deemed responsible for this plight will span far afield, according to one's predilections in social theory. It ranges from secularization[75] and spiritual "disenchantment" (so say theologians and conservative culture critics) to alienation by the capitalist cash nexus (Marx), to anomie and atomization (Durkheim), bureaucratic rationalization (Weber), instrumental reason (Horkheimer and Adorno), panoptic surveillance and disciplining discourses (Foucault). Their differences notwithstanding, all these accounts of humanity's fate under modernity make it difficult, if not impossible, to maintain that any genuine form of broadly shared morality, freely adopted, could significantly guide the ways we act in exercising our legal rights. The echoes of such shared morality, if it ever truly existed, have grown too faint, the mechanisms by which it might regulate us too feeble.

Yet modern history strongly suggests that to preserve an essential measure of solidarity among its members, a national society need not require a single, coherent common morality of the comprehensive kind Montesquieu or Durkheim had in mind. That would entail a society, on their accounts, whose mores are equally shared by all and reflect a distinctive national temperament or "spirit." In this view, each people or nation has one such spirit, and only one, shared with no other. This suggestion is of course wholly unsustainable in today's globalized world. It was fantastical even when first proposed. For that was a time when most nation-states—France itself, in Montesquieu's time—were still somewhat inchoate, institutionally incipient, just coming fully into existence, into self-recognition.[76]

Still, the considerable evidence here assembled suggests that particular congeries of mores regularly operate across wide spatial expanses, crossing diverse demographics, influencing the way rights are exercised. In fact, many of my case illustrations indicate the continuing vitality of macro-social morals, beyond the confines of discrete milieus, on rights-exercise in areas quite far afield. These examples include, to name a few, offensive speech, abortion, personal bankruptcy, welfare and disability benefits, the repatriation practices of art museums, state apologies for mass atrocity and the international "responsibility to protect" its victims, as well as the episode of the Islamic cultural center at Ground Zero. The social mores in question at these times appear national—if not broader—in scope. Or perhaps they come readily into view at that level of operation simply because the rights whose exercise they restrain are themselves often creatures of national law. It is international law, however, that establishes the rights of sovereign states, and so it is scarcely surprising that moralizing pressures to resist certain exercises of such rights, or to enforce "soft law" norms against rogue states, are supranational as well.

Mores and informal practices for their enforcement also arise on the subnational plane, often with powerful repercussions for human welfare far beyond. These mores find their home among those occupying particular locations within the division of labor, members of distinct vocational groups, like lawyers, physicians, and military officers (the chief illustrations here examined). Sometimes the source and scope of shared mores and common standards of propriety are not derived from intraprofessional interactions but instead simply from geographical proximity and the interdependencies it can create, such as those between Shasta County herders and cattle farmers.[77]

Mores can be sociologically ambient; they and the ethical ideas they instantiate operate at more than one level at once: micro, meso, and macro. They may migrate fluidly between these levels, in ways that social science yet finds difficult to conceptualize or measure. At all these levels—subnational, national, and transnational—the key question for both policy and sociological understanding is whether perceptions of injustice might be shared with sufficient breadth and intensity that the law can work in significant reliance on them. These congenial forms of conjunction would include, for instance, an English judge's decision to reduce a defendant's normal sentence for "cruelty to animals" in light of the distress inflicted upon him through media and internet publicity.[78] The still broader question (beyond this book's compass) is whether a 'thickening' of stigma at the supranational and subnational levels, in ways my case illustrations reflect, can fill in at least some of the gaps left by an evident thinning out of common morality at the national. Or does a minimally acceptable measure of cohesion, of social order within the modern state, depend upon that entity's continued primacy among the several alternative identities and instruments of interaction today available to its citizens?

To acknowledge that such a thinning has indeed occurred in contemporary America, an assertion I shall not here seek to substantiate, is of course not to embrace sweeping theories of creeping anomie or ineluctable ethical decline, an irreversible saga of world-historical woe, of steep descent from gemeinschaft to gesellschaft.[79] It is instead to urge a focus upon empirical tendencies and potential solutions—employing novel and rejuvenated forms of shame or stigma—available at levels of human association different from those where major problems arise. These levels of moral regeneration would most often be found both above and below that of the sovereign state.

Several of the forces driving law and morality apart (described in Chapter 6) are no stronger, on a consistent basis, in more "traditional" societies than in our own. The inherent limits of language are no more acute, for instance, nor are human motives any less inscrutable at times; neither are the risks of unintended harms from legal prohibition necessarily any greater. It is not the differences between modernity and tradition, then, but rather other considerations that chiefly account for the considerable empirical variation observed in the incidence and magnitude of these centrifugal forces.

Even so, modernity and the quality of ethical experience it affords remain relevant to understanding the relation between common morality and the law. Pertinent here is the question of whether it is always optimal for us to know about our legal entitlements and, if not, which of these may be wholly or partly concealed from our awareness. The legal systems of contemporary Western societies rely considerably more on separation between "conduct rules" and "decision rules" than do many earlier socio-legal orders. Yet in important respects, today's developed societies also find such separation more difficult to defend in legal theory and to maintain in practice, in real life.

The separation sits embarrassingly at odds with the principle, inherent to the "rule of law," that all legal rules must make themselves known to those they govern. Any departure from that principle carries the whiff of "secret laws," a trademark of many dictatorships.[80] It is also more difficult in practice to keep citizens ignorant of the rules by which their disputes will be decided. This is partly due to their higher educational levels and their ownership of advanced communications devices, enabling easy access to vast information, but also to more structural features of modern society as such. The gaps between rules for conduct and rules of dispute resolution present less serious problems, it appears, in many legal systems of preindustrial and non-Western social orders.

Traditional Jewish law, for example, prohibited a significant number of wrongful acts, considered quite serious, which it nonetheless declined to punish.[81] People were aware that they did not risk judicial sanction for committing such misconduct. Consider the situation, for instance, where the husband of a young, Orthodox Jewish woman inexplicably disappears. To lawfully remarry, she must present the court with evidence of his death, evidence of a sort essentially impossible to obtain; otherwise, she must wait many years. She remarries nonetheless.

The conduct rule prohibiting her remarriage would seem to require that when the fact of her second nuptial comes to a court's attention, the judge must invalidate it. Yet though the law clearly prohibited her misconduct *ex ante,* courts did not impose this remedy *ex post,* though it might seem to follow logically, inexorably.[82] The decision rule was more lenient, in other words, than the conduct rule, which remained unmodified. Women apparently faced the predicament with some regularity. And it was well known that the temptations to illegality it aroused were looked upon by courts with a sympathetic eye. Judges nonetheless did not fear that their lenity toward the unlawful behavior would lead to its increased incidence. The explanation reveals a good deal about the relation between law and common morality, not only within such "traditional" societies (as they once were called) but, by implication, within industrial and postindustrial ones as well. Rabbinical law was less concerned—as contemporary law cannot afford to be—that people would exploit their knowledge of the slippage between the two kinds of legal rules, or more generally, between common morality and the law. This confidence arose from the dual nature of this Jewish law. It was at once an officially enforceable rulebook and also a more diffuse corpus of religiously inspired moral teachings, backed by pervasive communal authority; these teachings included the duty "to reprove your neighbor, or you will incur guilt yourself."[83] Courts could assume that most people would not take advantage of the discrepancy between conduct rules and decision rules, or of ambiguities at the margins of conduct rules themselves, at points where common morality continued staunchly to condemn what the law perhaps arguably allowed.

Devout Jews would not casually dishonor social strictures they acknowledged as morally binding. Adherence to these remained essential to any measure of social esteem, even continued membership, in a religious community and nation internally understood as "the indispensable foundation of all life."[84] This allowed the law to become more merciful at the moment of enforcement than on its face, in application than on the books. There was a single, simple reason, legally unspoken yet widely appreciated, why decisional rules could afford to forgive so much more than still-stringent conduct rules: there existed a wide range of stigmatizing practices, effective in restraining all manner of wrongs. These practices embodied a comprehensive system of behavior grounded in a religious doctrine publicly endorsed by nearly all. In other words, the law occupied only one corner of a larger normative space, across which many people were prepared to serve as their "brother's keeper."

The same could be observed of many other ancient, medieval, and non-Western societies. From the Muslim world, for example, one historian brings together a number of Koranic sources for "the duty of one Muslim to intervene when another is acting wrongly."[85] There too, theological sources define both the legally enforceable standards for individual behavior and the shared practices of an entire community. This type of sociological armature allows the law to indulge disfavored practices more generously than does common morality, at times generously indeed. Law can do so in recognition that common morality will, through less formal methods, pick up the slack. We moderns, and we modern lawyers especially, are often puzzled to learn that such extralegal standards of behavior, congruent with the law but still more demanding, possess effective enforcement powers of their own. These run the continuum from backroom rumor and schoolyard scuttlebutt to small-group ostracism and national exile, from polite exhortation to "social death." In many places, some of these sanctions are in fact more potent than any at law, though exile itself—as in ancient Greece—often entailed precise legal procedures.[86]

To accept the preceding analysis is to see why we must qualify the widespread view that religiously inspired legal systems aim to "occupy the field" of normative ordering. They purportedly do this by rejecting any demarcation of legal duty from wider obligations—religious, moral, civic. The experience of Hebrew law, from ancient Israel through Eastern

Europe of the early 1940s, shows how and why this claim is imprecise, to the point of error. What the conventional wisdom fails to recognize is that precisely because religious doctrine permeates literally everything and because virtually everyone embraces it, those who regularly speak up in its support will include not only professional judges, but many ordinary members of society. The reproach of objectionable conduct in others—today a practice we modern liberals regard with much greater apprehension—is a social and civic duty. This grants courts a certain space for lenity in deciding disputes, though legal rules may be facially more comprehensive and draconian. And where judges have some lawmaking authority, they can inject the lessons gleaned from their forbearance back into the legal rules themselves. For their experiments in clemency enable them periodically to gauge the strength or weakness of the social mores restraining rights "in action," and to fine-tune their jurisprudence accordingly.

## Conduct Rules, Decision Rules, and the Modern Division of Labor

Contemporary Western society presents a special challenge for the law's relation to common morality. This is because acoustically separating decision rules from conduct rules becomes at once more important and more difficult, with the result that law begins to 'corrupt' common morals. Even as legal regulation grows increasingly complex in many areas, those subject to it often find it easier to anticipate how the law is likely to address a dispute in which they may someday be embroiled. Participants in a given sphere of regulated activity—oceanic cargo-container shipping, for instance—will be repeat players; they have a strong interest in following every revision to rules affecting their relations with consumers, competitors, international organizations, and a variety of sovereign states.[87] This makes it nearly impossible for courts "in action" to employ rules of decision any more indulgent of misbehavior than conduct rules "on the books" without fear of affecting the underlying, regulated behavior. Nearly overnight, decision rules inexorably *become* conduct rules, because knowledge of changes in all pertinent rules, decisional and behavioral alike, spreads almost instantly within these sophisticated professional and elite milieu.

Thus, for instance, any major IRS regulatory ruling will be quickly incorporated into the standard operating procedure of tax departments at every Fortune 500 company. If the ruling suggests that the Service will now adopt a lighter touch to enforcement on a given issue than the corresponding rule had seemed to mandate, a company's behavior will within a week have altered accordingly. It is the professional duty of every corporate counsel to apprise her client of exactly such legal shifts, often subtle yet potentially of great commercial consequence. It is no coincidence that highly dynamic sectors of modern Western economies and societies, certainly those attracting considerable investment, tend to be those most highly lawyered. The result is that acoustic separation between decisional and conduct rules is particularly difficult to maintain concerning modernity's most characteristic activities. All this issues from an ever-advancing division of labor, which scholars once ascribed to a broader, society-wide process of "structural differentiation."[88] (Critics rightly responded that this capacious notion lends an indefensible air of inevitability and evolutionary progress to it all, and fails to identify any micro-foundations in real-life decision making for its sweepingly macro-sociological assertions.)

Yet just as these features of modernity make it ever more difficult to effectively insulate human conduct from lenient decision rules, this separation becomes in certain respects more important to law's efficacy. It is now more dangerous for a society that its economic elites, especially, so well understand the particular sites where law demands less of them than prevailing moral sentiment may allow, or than law itself would likely permit if the activities were better known. This intimate familiarity with the cracks between law and common morality grows more perilous if common morality itself, beyond the relevant professional milieu, becomes debilitated. Frequent interaction occurs among those within highly specialized fields. These fields may nevertheless be too large and internally competitive to generate the kind of shared moral sensibilities, intensely held and well-enforced informally, evident in the few existing micro-ethnographies (of diamond and tuna merchants, neighboring farmers and ranchers), or in some of my present illustrations (hospital staff, for instance).

Acoustic separation had been hard enough to maintain in many premodern circumstances, with regard to issues in the ordinary life of everyone: birth, death, and marriage. In ancient Israel, one could scarcely get through these basic, inescapable aspects of life without knowing the law's essentials, imparted from sources easily available. In more modern societies, acoustic separation proves difficult to sustain as well, but for quite a different reason. Such separation is absent from legal rules of exactly the opposite variety, those governing discrete, highly differentiated spheres of activity, often carrying profound repercussions.

We modern Westerners too, like others elsewhere and before us, nonetheless still regularly seek, where possible, to deploy shame and stigma to restrain the exercise of disfavored legal rights. These long-standing features of nonlegal regulation within premodern society importantly persist, frequently in propitious ways, within the contemporary West. The pressure of social mores against the exercise of disfavored rights regularly arises from ideals quite novel, in historical terms, inspired by principles of international human rights, for instance. Contemporary methods of push-back, through moralizing an issue, are no more conservative than the aims of such efforts. Their agents regularly find ways, through the latest in "new media" technologies, to veritably shout from the digital rooftops, at times to great effect.

When legislators and judges in contemporary societies liberalize the law (in the philosophical sense), they deflate its aspirations to govern areas of conduct which they decide to consider "purely personal," if still wrongful in the judgment of very many. The progressive retraction of law's reach, by designating ever broader swaths of social life exclusively a "private matter," is a defining feature of liberal modernity. Yet as the law follows this trajectory ever further, those so governed find themselves compelled, paradoxically, to pay ever-closer attention to how dependent both the public and private public realm become for their satisfactory functioning on the extralegal practices by which common morality increasingly sustains itself. In this sense, common morality—within groupings small and large—becomes ever more important over time in governing how we moderns exercise our legal rights, in ways affecting interests and ideals still very much of keen public concern.

To instill among all citizens a strong sense of personal ethics and civic virtue, American and European lawmakers until the recent past evinced abiding confidence in formal instruction on "moral education" (as it was unapologetically called) within the public schools.[89] Republican political institutions could only survive, leaders thought, by cultivating in citizens the patriotic sentiments that would prompt them to defend the country and its laws, a view drawn from both ancient and modern theorists of civic virtue, from Cicero through Machiavelli and Montesquieu.[90]

Today, sophisticated policymakers, with a nod to dominant thoughtways of social science,[91] place their confidence instead largely in a calculative tit-for-tat. This is the natural inclination, grounded in the evolution of our species,[92] to reward others' positive behavior in kind, in anticipation that they will reciprocate one's 'disinterested' gestures of goodwill. Those designing law and policy here draw upon a science—evolutionary[93] and economic—that finds in such "reciprocal altruism" a sufficient basis for interpersonal cooperation at the micro-level, and for social coordination at the macro. Scholars now study these dynamics in application to law-related behavior no less than other sorts.[94] Trust in reciprocity of this variety understands morally acceptable behavior—indeed, society itself—as merely an "emergent property" from individual acts prompted chiefly by calibrations of self-interest, both short-term and somewhat longer. "Norms," including those some naively continue to describe as "moral," are in fact avowedly no more than "equilibria in games of strategy . . . supported by a cluster of self-fulfilling expectations."[95]

The puzzle very much remains, though, of how much a minimally acceptable social order still relies, in ways social scientific thinking apparently can no longer adequately cognize, on deeper forms of common morality—whether society-wide or of more limited scope; I here refer to common moralities more demanding of us than tit-for-tat,[96] where cooperation may be abandoned at early sign of another's "defection." The nuclear family long offered the social setting within which such demanding forms of moral obligation were most conspicuously in evidence. For as one economist writes—straining to apply her profession's unsentimental idiom to this intimate milieu—"unconditional love becomes rational only when relationships lose their exchange quality."[97] Yet many have thought that other spheres of society too require, for their minimally satisfactory operation, some willingness to forego private self-interest, even the most "enlightened" and long-term.

This general view occupies a noteworthy place in all three leading Western theories of morality: those of Kant, Bentham, and Aristotle. Could it really be that a society morally acceptable to us today is possible without some influence on human conduct from any of these long-standing intellectual legacies? Their many differences notwithstanding, all these theories—Kant's and Bentham's uniquely associated with modernity—aim to broaden and enliven our sense of responsibility to others at moments when we must decide how to exercise our rights, in ways likely to arouse others' indignation.

Take utilitarianism, for instance. Leading sociologists carelessly confuse this standpoint with selfishness.[98] Due precisely to its individualism, however, this moral theory requires an almost superhuman self*less*ness.[99] For it asks us to weigh the consequences of our every action as individuals for the welfare of all others.[100] To this end, it does not merely seek, as some suppose, to "align incentives," appealing to our self-interest in a reputation for ethical integrity.

One need scarcely look very far afield to identify sites of moral desolation within contemporary Western societies, in places high and low, where people confront bleak prisoners' dilemmas far more often than cooperative stag hunts.[101] These are precisely the places where we are most often tempted, as others will view it, to abuse our rights, and to become victims of others' such abuse. These are therefore also the places—readers may differ over where they lie—at which social mores remain most indispensable, demanding more from us than farsighted prudence, however elegant the mathematical models rendering that virtue's supposed workings.

Liberal modernity does not entail law's linear retreat from the incorporation and enforcement of morality, common or critical, as we are sometimes told. Rather, there are conflicting pressures and movements at once in both directions. At times what the law once treated as a matter of public concern, governed by law, is now left to unofficial mechanisms of moral ordering. Conversely, prevailing moral sensibilities at times shift in ways prompting law's bold advances into issue-areas hitherto left to the workings of precisely these informal forces. Lawmakers have by then come to believe that private ordering restrains the exercise of legal rights insufficiently, or in morally unacceptable ways.

This second type of change, to offer a concrete example, is apparent in how American law, like that of most Western societies, now limits the scope of medical "paternalism." In its stronger forms, medical paternalism entailed a normative stance authorizing the physician to act on a patient's "best interests," as the physician understood them, with limited regard to what the patient herself desired.[102] Since the Hippocratic Oath, on some accounts, and certainly since Christianity's ascendance,[103] Western physicians have valorized the patient's physical survival above all else,[104] in the face even of imminent death or permanent, unendurable pain. This stance left medical personnel with little opportunity or authorization to acknowledge a patient's moral claims to self-determination, to enact her own conception of the good life, increasingly understood to include a right to end it. Lawmakers stood largely aside, in deference to claims of scientific authority, then considered unassailable.[105] Starting only in the 1970s did courts and legislators start seriously to reassess this position. Invoking the public's evolving moral sensibilities in their defense, lawmakers began to interject the law into the domain of physician–patient relations, once considered an essentially private affair, despite the state's ever-increasing role in financing the health care system.

Along similar lines we may describe the changing relationship, throughout the world, between professional soldiers and their fellow citizens. For centuries the normative ordering of relations between officers and civilians in war remained effectively charged to the profession of arms. Inter-state treaties governing the conduct of armed conflict did not exist until the late nineteenth century.[106] And customary law was only somewhat more developed,[107] with very limited purchase upon wartime military practice, in any event, as best we can tell. Soldiers and statesmen did not regard the common moral understandings of civilians, on either side of the battle lines, as remotely relevant to the regulation of armed conflict.[108] Such ordering remained entirely an in-house affair among military elites, sustained by a distinctive set of mores, to which civilian leaders graciously deferred.[109]

It is hardly surprising that landed aristocrats—who ruled polities that still lacked full adulthood franchise—displayed only the most minimal and "chivalric" of moral sensitivities toward the fate of those suffering war's horrors at their hands. Even the first Hague and Geneva Conventions bore the heavy stamp of self-interested influence by a pan-European officer corps.[110] It required the unprecedented catastrophe of the Great War to dislodge the accepted view that honor—and martial honor in particular—could offer a proper motive in political life. It took the intercession of concerned civilians, beginning only in the 1860s, to press the law gradually toward some faint acknowledgement of the legitimate place of laypeople's moral sensibilities within the international governance of war, beyond the constricted concerns of a hereditary martial caste.

## The Pre-Liberal Inheritance: Virtue among Physicians and Professional Soldiers

In sum, the medical and military professions both traditionally laid broad claims to social authority and self-governance on the basis of practices of moral ordering owing little to any formal intercession by the law. Nor did prevailing moral sentiments among broader publics yet exercise great influence over how these professionals understood themselves or went about their work. Only much later, at the initiative of skeptical outsiders, would a wider form of common morality, enshrined in reformed legal rules, come increasingly to infuse their activities. In both cases, traditional practices of moral ordering embodied views today deemed illiberal and antiegalitarian,[111] premodern or antimodern. And in both cases those practices originated in the particularistic norms of men occupying high social stature afforded by membership within an elite profession of ancient pedigree.

Today many would forgive the unpalatable historical origins of these practices of private ordering if they still seemed, at least, to deliver on their promises in ways liberal legality could not. We might be prepared to live with their embarrassing illiberality, in other words, if they showed themselves effective in inducing physicians and professional soldiers to exercise their rights responsibly, as we would now understand and apply that notion to them. There is otherwise no reason for the law to continue affording members of these vocations any rights to cause serious harm, in ways that so many consider wrongful.

These rights prominently include those authorizing soldiers to "incidentally" kill civilians in war, and permitting physicians, for much of Western history, to override the wish of a dying patient to end an unbearable existence. At present, more problematic than the illiberalism such practices manifest may be simply their debility, their declining capacity to restrain disfavored rights to the extent they once seemingly did.[112] In short, modern society now turns at certain key points to formalities of the law, both national and international, for its chief methods of normative ordering where we no longer trust to the mores of such professional groups and other insular subcommunities to regulate their members in ways sufficiently attentive to common morals. This is a core feature of the historical story that legal centralists seek to tell, from Bentham through Habermas, and the trajectory they seek to advance.

Yet more telling for present purposes is that—despite this increased legal scrutiny of such professions—contemporary Western society continues equally to depend at key points on historic, "anachronistic" forms of extralegal ordering that their members still employ. Though recent changes in the law governing each profession draw the greater attention, more revealing and decisive in sociological terms is what remains almost untouched. Thus, precisely as we enhance the rights of medical patients vis-à-vis those who treat them, we at times increasingly depend on such caregivers to actively restrain—indeed, essentially prevent—these very patients from exercising their new legal right to die. We pride ourselves on creating this modern right, publicly trumpeting it as a triumph of philosophic liberalism, even as we routinely violate it in service of older ethical understandings still prevalent both society-wide and among medical professionals themselves. The same could be said of the right of mentally disabled persons to bear children.

Ideas drawn from modern liberalism now permeate the intellectual ambience and enjoy some footing within common morality, within the West and beyond, in ways inspiring such legal developments as the requirement of "informed consent" to medical treatment and virtually the entire field of international criminal law. These bodies of rules represent an attack on the traditional prerogatives of elite professions, not so much on their social stature per se as specifically on their practices of normative ordering. Those practices have long been and substantially remain antiliberal, with broad implications for all affected, which is to say billions of people worldwide.

Liberal philosophy must not be equated with modernity, or with the necessary future of modern societies, as was once widely, mistakenly done. That philosophy has nevertheless undoubtedly won enormous ground, often through Western influence, colonial and otherwise, in legal systems throughout much of the world. Liberalism has been historically unconcerned with how social mores influence and are influenced by the way people actually use their legal rights. On point of principle, in fact, liberalism (as theorists generally elaborate it) takes no notice of such matters. Alan Ryan thus observes that "liberalism is essentially a political doctrine," in fact "austerely" so, which makes it "none of the political theorist's business what individuals do with their liberty," because her "business is to give a coherent and cogent account of legitimate state action."[113] That, and no more.

Yet the way people exercise their rights necessarily has repercussions for the nature of social order. Philosophic liberals—no less than others—dare not ignore these. The pressing and perplexing question thus becomes that of "how [to] imagine people living within the liberal social world,"[114] as one recent political theorist contends. That inquiry concerns the possibly debilitating effects of liberal political and economic institutions—of "rights consciousness" in particular—on those aspects of shared morals dampening the abusive exercise of rights. These institutions and the ideals they embody have created a world—the liberal *society* we today largely inhabit—by no means "coextensive with the domain of the political."[115] In other words, a liberal polity and its law have spawned a liberal society, which in turn generates unforeseen difficulties that the polity, through its law, must now increasingly confront.

Like many others, the theorist just quoted is vexed by how and why modern liberal legality offers us so little guidance in answering such inescapable questions as: "What do my rights mean to me?,"[116] and "How should I properly put them to use?" A liberal society needs, he argues, to render its citizens "skillful in the art of exercising their rights." It should better enable them to resolve for themselves some of the classical questions of how one ought to live, notably including that of what duties one owes toward others, beyond those imposed by any positive law. In these respects, his gentle provocation to political theory resembles mine to legal thought. For both fields remain virtually obsessed with the question of what rights we should possess, at the neglect of questions about how we ought to exercise, and do in fact exercise, the liberal rights we currently have, in light of a proper regard for those around us, near and far. These concerns of contemporary liberal theory are avowedly more evaluative and programmatic than my own. Their undoubted relation to mine nonetheless lends significance and perhaps some urgency to the task of advancing our sociological understanding of rights to do wrong. For as citizens and lawmakers, our views of what we may reasonably expect of others in the exercise of their rights necessarily inform both our personal conduct and our public policies.

Some will rejoin that contemporary Western legal systems—unlike those insular premodern Jewish communities, for instance—are simply not much concerned with instructing us in what we must do with our lives, about life's purpose and meaning. The law of a liberal society seeks only to establish background "rules of the game," the minimum conditions of mutual coordination we must satisfy in pursuing our own freely chosen life-projects.[117] Liberal democracies and competitive markets exist not to advance any particular, contestable theory of "the human good," other than to assist individuals in advancing their own sundry purposes, often antithetical from one person to the next. The notion of personal autonomy implicit in this picture, however, is *itself* a substantive moral ideal, many observe, and widely endorsed as such within this country and the Western world at large, even well beyond. It is an ideal that our law largely enshrines, increasingly so. It does so most notably in rules protecting contractual freedom, private property, personal privacy (including sexual orientation), as well as rights to speech and association. This *now is* our common morality to a great extent, at least an integral part of it. As some of these examples suggest, moreover, fields of "private" law can embody common morality no less than "public" law.

Still, it is true that much of law in the contemporary West has gradually retreated to the task of protecting a sphere for individual conduct, rather than enforcing an avowedly comprehensive public doctrine of moral or religious truth. Recurrent concerns nonetheless arise among both ordinary citizens and major thinkers within very different intellectual traditions[118] over whether modern legality can succeed in upholding a social order—even one whose terms of cooperation remain ever open to revision—only insofar as key elements of a more full-bodied morality persist, now in more informal, secular, and inarticulate shape than in the past.

These elements could presumably find their sociological footing only in some form of common morality more robust than tit-for-tat,[119] in the personal virtues and social mores embodying it, and in the day-to-day methods we employ for stigmatizing its violation. These are essential where neither the law nor a calculating reciprocity prove sufficient, as many today suspect they don't, in sustaining a tolerable measure of mutual concern, cooperation, and solidarity within modern liberal society. Informal restraints of this sort on rights to do wrong thus become important in a new way as modern legality ceases to lend coercive backing to a panorama of moral responsibilities these extralegal restraints now, for the first time, *alone* underwrite. Yet as this chapter has indicated, philosophical defenders of modernity and of liberal legality remain, on the whole, curiously indifferent to—even actively suspicious of—these restraining mechanisms and of the conditions for their effective operation. This line of thinking doubts not only their desirability, but even—under conditions of modernity—their continued possibility.

Thomas Scanlon offers a rare and revealing exception, in an uncharacteristic moment, while discussing "tolerance."[120] He concedes, "We all have a profound interest in how prevailing customs and practices evolve." Therefore "the liberal response" to conservative calls for the "legal enforcement of morality" is wrong "to deny the legitimacy of any interest in 'protecting society' from certain forms of change." Scanlon even admits to sharing "the concerns" of conservatives over "the evolution of mores," offering a few choice, specific concerns of his own in this regard, amounting to his update of Cicero's *cri de coeur,* "*o tempora, o mores.*"

He then rehearses the familiar, liberal-philosophic opposition to employing criminal prohibitions to this end. He suggests no alternatives, however, no thoughts on "how this informal politics might be regulated," referring to the nonlegal means by which we might hope to influence social mores, alter their direction of movement. Scanlon then confesses that he lacks even any firm idea of "what I mean by informal politics." This confessed and startling inarticulateness, from one of liberalism's most distinguished and able philosophic defenders, could scarcely be more glaring and unsatisfying.

Liberal theorists strongly tend to assume, insofar as the question seriously enters their thoughts, that we may take for granted the continued efficacy of those informal political or social forces and the guardrails they establish on the abusive exercise of rights. These thinkers perceive no need even to carefully identify such forces—their nature, casual mechanisms, or changing factual contours. We may leave all that to the sociologists, they might plausibly respond—at least, if current-day sociologists gave these matters half a glance. Many citizens would, however, infer that our recent experience with several of the legal rights here examined amply indicates that—within certain pockets of modern society, in patterned and predictable ways—we cannot in fact take such efficacy on faith, not at all. To admit this much, moreover, we certainly need not and must not endorse any linear narrative of implacable despair (nor of radiant hope), the sorts extravagantly announced for the last two centuries by so many "master theorists" of modern society, with their totalizing philosophies of history.

# Conclusion

Many of us are keen to enlist the law against perceived defects in common morality wherever we discern them. We are largely deaf, however, to how this morality and the social practices embodying it are indispensable to the workings of law itself, compensating at key points for its inevitable indulgence of widely objectionable conduct. This book revives a certain dormant understanding of sociology, in the tradition of Montesquieu, to right this imbalance and the resulting distortion to our understanding of how law and morality interact. That the law cannot undertake everything necessary to moral ordering in modern society, that it requires informal supplement at so many points, finds vivid evidence in the copious catalogue of factual situations here examined. These begin, in this book's opening paragraphs, with that candid expression of gratitude by British lawmakers to the world's largest internet companies for enforcing "community standards" well exceeding the law's.

Though there are several good reasons, here rehearsed, why law does not perfectly track common morality, one among these is especially important yet least appreciated: that social mores—informal practices embodying prevailing ethical sensibilities—are often assumed to prevent the abuse of rights. When the law relies on these informal restraints and thus 'retracts' its reach, the upshot is often to knowingly authorize activities broadly deemed contemptible. The resulting tension between what law allows and common morality condemns prompts many to employ myriad extralegal devices, subtle and blunt, to ensure that people exercise their rights "responsibly," as is often said. These stratagems range from discreet cues, polite persuasion, and impassioned emotional appeals, to the open expression of disgust, aimed at eliciting feelings of shame. It proves helpful to think of these, though quite diverse in multiple ways, as all of a piece, for all are calculated to bring law and morals into closer harmony.

To speak nonchalantly of restraining others' rights through such legally unorthodox means is jarring to the contemporary Western ear. It is especially disconcerting to those schooled in liberal theory—moral, political, or legal. It is to invite accusations of insensitivity to human dignity, at the very least, indeed of Victorian moralism and reactionary traditionalism. These rebukes are misplaced. There exists no other way to address the genuine regulatory problems created by conduct legally untouchable yet defensibly repudiated by common morals.

Some of these stigmatizing measures are more acceptable than others, of course, but *that* is always the proper normative question to be asking, because as such, the deliberate evocation of shame is not inconsistent with a desirable society and legal order. The acceptability of our censorious practices depends entirely on the particular means we utilize and the ends these practices serve, questions almost nowhere seriously addressed. This study therefore examines many situations where shaming, in forms both old and new, performs essential tasks of normative ordering that law alone should not attempt and, without injurious side-effects, cannot possibly achieve.

Prominent "progressive" voices within legal thought and political discourse object that it is unhelpful to speak in terms of a duty to exercise one's rights "responsibly." The exhortation to do so, we are told, actually requires no more than respecting the legal rights of others,[1] a formulation more congenial to the liberal philosophy underlying most of our law. This objection fails to appreciate that much of what people reasonably expect of one another lacks juridical recognition, for all the reasons—often very good ones—elaborated in Chapter 6. The present study thus focuses precisely on the practices of shaming involved in enforcing these nonlegal responsibilities. Though widely recognized as genuine and authoritative, the duties in question frequently fail to directly correspond to or neatly match up with anyone's rights, whose violation might be called to a court's attention.

Formulating the issues in this way is unfamiliar and perhaps counterintuitive. In fact it is initially uncongenial, certainly among the legally trained. It nevertheless sheds considerable light on the ways we daily encounter the relation between law and morality in ordinary life, beyond the pages of philosophy texts, judicial opinions, or religious sermons. Morality in this register consists of what people within a given milieu consider right and wrong, as these ideas find behavioral expression, verbal and otherwise.

The pertinent questions thus become: What forms of conduct evoke their indignation at perceived injustice, and how do these sentiments find palpable expression beyond the law? To examine the relationship between law and morality in this sociological manner requires close attention to the specific practices deployed in particular contexts when confronting those who seek to exercise their rights in ways widely considered abusive, indefensible. Lawmaking too can sometimes profit from greater consideration, in ways here suggested, to these informal hindrances on rights-exercise, to their relative efficacy and their empirical distribution across the panorama of contemporary life.

Shared understandings of right and wrong inevitably fail to find their way fully into law, but nonetheless assert themselves—at observable points, in recognizable ways—when we seek to put our entitlements to use and encounter others who believe we act improperly. Ethical considerations barred from entering law's front door thus frequently sneak in through the back, influencing our conduct no less for the seeming circuity. Rarely, in fact, will common morality be wholly denied. Legal rights to do serious wrong, and the routine resistance against their abusive exercise, occupy the decisive points where these forces meet, contend, and are compelled to mutually accommodate.

By this route of inquiry we can make some sense—without hope of opening all doors—of a number of law's seeming absurdities. We gain not only in improved understanding of how the world works, and of the law's place within our lives, but also a better appreciation of what is truly at stake in the strictly normative issues themselves. For whether we regard a particular legal right as defensible often ultimately depends on the accuracy of our assumptions about who will exercise it, in what degree, at which times, to what ends, in the face of what impediments imposed by others.

An absolute right to free speech or to form a new political party, for instance, becomes unattractive and indefensible, most believe, where extremist movements seem likely to use it successfully in spreading opinions and activities antithetical to liberal democracy. The empirical record of legal history copiously confirms this hypothesis. Conversely, there are other rights that many people wish to see exercised more extensively. The shortfall in their "take-up"—as with Medicaid benefits, among the very poor—may prompt us to expand such rights or to simplify the procedures for claiming them, facilitating their more robust use.

There have thus far been scarcely any systematic in situ studies of rights to do wrong and the societal restraints upon their objectionable exercise. None of the scholarly sources I draw upon were conceived with the intention of speaking specifically to this study's distinct concerns. Still less has there been any sweeping overview of what existing real-life evidence—we possess a great deal, it turns out—may collectively represent, any general survey or bird's-eye assessment of its ultimate significance. To this end, this study makes a first attempt.[2] It can do so at this early stage, though, only by turning on the lights and partially furnishing the ground floor of an otherwise empty house. The book is thus chiefly a spur of encouragement for others to wrestle with its questions where these arise across many areas of life and law, wherever the right to do serious wrong will now, with this book's prompting, come more clearly into view.[3]

The "relationship between law and society"—so abstractly stated—is a tired topic, about which little of originality has been said for a century.[4] Its study is confined to an academic cubbyhole, drawing little sustained interest today from law students, leading legal scholars, or intellectually serious attorneys. The relation of law to morality, by contrast, raises questions perennially perplexing, eternally fresh, drawing trenchant and original reflection from each new generation. A fruitful way to revive the study of "law and society" is to entertain a sociological standpoint toward the interaction of law and morality.

For every legal system necessarily confronts the challenge of how to define its relation to background moral norms: when to incorporate them, when to resist them, when to let them operate unimpeded and construct itself around them, capitalizing on the restraints they impose upon certain behavior, including that of rights-claiming itself. No legal system can escape these quandaries, and every such system defines itself, to great degree, precisely in terms of how it answers them. Since answering them is something every legal system must do, it is fair to say that—through their ubiquity and inevitability—they disclose not only contingent aspects of the law, but some of its most essential and inherent features. In this respect the present book contributes not only to legal theory, broadly speaking, but also to legal philosophy, more narrowly understood (in the

Anglo-American analytic tradition) as concerned with law's intrinsic features, present in all legal systems recognizable as such.[5]

Common morality, where it exists, and the mechanisms through which it finds expression, where it does, teach us what sorts of behavior are deemed acceptable and desirable. Within a given social order, we identify "the moral domain" by observing the forms of conduct eliciting such "reactive attitudes" as gratitude, admiration, remorse, regret, and certain forms of disgust. The reactive attitude most pertinent to the law is indignation at perceived injustice. This is what we subjectively experience, the sentiment elicited within us, whenever we conclude that an individual or organization engages in serious wrongdoing.

Evidence of indignation's empirical incidence and societal significance emerges from the work of scholars employing diverse methods, laboring in multiple fields. These include experimental philosophy, sociolinguistics, opinion surveys, moral anthropology, ordinary language analysis, ethnographies of rights-consciousness, studies of mass-protest behavior, and archival historiography. Though each has limitations, their respective strengths enable us to capture distinct aspects and expressions of common morality,[6] in diverse social locations. This study draws upon all these approaches in identifying empirical regularities in where and why the law and common morality tend to flow in tandem or to part ways, and how the partings are handled by those who must live with them, day-to-day.

In establishing rights to do serious wrong, a society runs the risk that we will take up this invitation, in more than trivial measure, a risk that sometimes materializes, occasionally to grievous effect. The empirical illustrations I examine disclose no self-regulating "social system" omnisciently at work, no flawless mechanism of self-correction or invisible hand spontaneously setting things aright whenever law and morality grow disastrously apart, unsustainably at odds. Still, the illustrations do disclose the existence and effective workings of crucial impediments to the perceived abuse of particular rights, though the process remains often elusive to scientific method, even to accurate description in an idiom that modern liberals today comfortably employ.

My central contention is that rights to do grave wrong exist, arise with some frequency, and often persist for considerable periods, because (among other reasons) we assume they will be constrained by extralegal methods assuring that right-holders honor corresponding moral duties. These situations elude standard academic cubbyholes. We tend to acknowledge them only in passing, as isolated instances, occasional curiosities. Their larger jurisprudential implications are neglected. We would more fruitfully understand them as forming a distinct category of noteworthy import for both policy and theory. Such rights are neither a daily commonplace nor so rare to warrant dismissal as an intellectual curio, a conversational tchotchke on the jurisprudential shelf. They display the kind of semi-opaqueness of matters that often "go without saying" and "hide in plain sight." In striving to make sense of them, the objective is therefore "not to reveal what is hidden, but to fathom what is seen,"[7] as Foucault writes in another context. Though this category of rights escapes our attention, that is not generally for the insidious reasons regularly ascribed when speaking of social phenomena eluding ready recognition.[8] Their opaqueness does not necessarily or generally serve to conceal oppression.

The proposition that law cannot perfectly track morality—when stated so baldly—borders on the banal. The line between platitude and profundity, between the reactions "ho hum" and "ah ha!," can admittedly prove indistinct. One often-valuable task of theory in any field is to grant us greater awareness of what we already intuitively appreciate "at some level," to articulate more precisely what we may have long vaguely known. At which point our response may inevitably be a yawning "yeah, yeah." Precisely insofar as I've been convincing here, my task thus invites the charge of truism and cliché.

From that fate I have sought to rescue the observation that law and mores at once overlap and diverge, operate both in tandem and at odds, in ways at times felicitous, occasionally disastrous. Loosely inspired by *The Spirit of the Laws,* which introduced these insights to Western thought, I have disinterred and reformulated that observation in terms somewhat crisper and more illuminating, I hope, identifying and explaining, comparing and contrasting, the types of situation where these twin normative orders today move into or out of harmony, where the tensions between them are productive and where destructive.[9] The central questions this book poses are therefore at once quite old—those of classical European social thought—yet fresh of formulation, I trust, answered in novel ways, in light of the many changes, in both social structure and scientific methods, since Montesquieu's day.[10] To these ends, I enlist much recent evidence from across a wide swath of legal life, contemporary and historical, domestic and international.

The gaps between legality and morality may widen, we have seen, to the point where anguished misgivings emerge and assume overtly political shape, ensuring that rights to do serious wrong are seldom laid fully to rest. Because they experience continuous critique and periodic reassessment, the equilibria they may enjoy for long periods can prove fragile. This is especially so when the exercise of a particular right, as to terminate a pregnancy for any reason, is not as strongly mitigated in real life by the countervailing mores its creators anticipated. Effective restraints of this sort are more evident in several of my other illustrations. It may be no accident that they lie farther from the battlefront of any culture war and therefore face less rigorous scrutiny into whether informal promptings of personal or institutional responsibility effectively inhibit their perceived abuse.

Yet even these less agitated situations sometimes flare into heated controversy when it comes to public attention that the law excludes from its ambit moral duties widely considered intrinsic to rights it *has* enshrined, duties "scandalously" neglected in practice. These rights continue to pose nontrivial risks of grave wrongdoing—of conduct widely considered as such—if not fettered in some other fashion. When bankruptcy filings rapidly increase (as they intermittently have), for instance, legislators, economists, and pundits begin puzzling expressly over whether the stigma associated with going broke has weakened, inducing legislative reassessment of the sociological assumptions underlying an existing regulatory architecture.

Helpful here, to some extent, is Waldron's concept of a "responsibility-right," which several of my case illustrations approximate. These are rights associated with a particular occupational role or essential status within society, from which attendant duties emerge organically, yet in ways uncongenial to full codification. By its nature, a given role (say, that of a military officer) may so tightly conjoin these rights to certain responsibilities (to minimize civilian harm) that failure to enshrine the responsibilities fully into law inevitably begins to call the defensibility of the rights themselves (to kill civilians, unintentionally) into question. As long as we cannot dispense altogether with the valued task and those performing it, we must make some extralegal provision for satisfying its attendant duties.

Most roles and statuses (parenting, for example) exist in a continuous state of reconsideration, with their terms and conditions subject to ongoing contention. The nonlegal responsibilities concomitant to a given role and the rights of those occupying it are not therefore chiefly a matter of logical entailments, a domain of philosophic reason. We require an approach more attentive to the shifting societal pressures for behavioral change arising both among those producing a certain public good and those dependent upon its effective provision.

The challenge of optimally conjoining the legal rights and extralegal duties of a crucial role or status is often especially daunting, lending poignancy to many of our cases, distinguishing them from garden-variety rights to do wrongful things. The failure to juridify responsibilities proves especially problematic in three situations: where (1) the right to which the responsibilities attach stems from an essential task or position entitling one to cause grave injury, (2) the scope of the right would therefore be highly restricted but for assurances that concomitant moral obligations will be respected, and (3) the extralegal underpinnings of their fulfillment are uncertain, resist acceptable verbal characterization, or are apparent only through difficult factual investigation. The case of incidental civilian damage in war powerfully implicates all three concerns.

My central conclusions disclose no ideological valence, harbor no partisan agenda. Sometimes the legal right under examination is recent and aims to "liberalize" extant practices, as with reforms in the law of divorce and of abortion. Informal constraints upon its effective exercise spring from enduring attitudes and long-standing practices fairly characterized as "conservative." At other times, as with the right of armies to kill civilians or that of museums to retain stolen artifacts, the entitlement is long-standing, and its exercise only newly disfavored. The people most reluctant to see it altered and curtailed—the right-holders themselves—are confessedly conservative in these respects. When they exercise their rights, they nonetheless today find themselves informally hampered by the mobilization of moral sentiments endorsed primarily by self-described "progressives." Thus, whatever the political orientation inspiring the right's creation or animating resistance to its exercise, the essential process of scholarly interest here, its socio-legal dynamic, is the same.

The law's diffuse but pervasive trust in common morality usually remains implicit. We render it open to view chiefly when opponents of a legal right challenge it as unduly sweeping, posing genuine dangers of serious wrongdoing. Such challenge and response are most conspicuous and energetic, among my chief cases, in connection with incidental civilian harm from war. By contrast, overt challenge to our informal practice is nearly absent concerning the right to decline lifesaving medical care, for there the hindrances we stealthily impose are not merely extralegal but simply, at times, unlawful.

We should understand law's calculated retreat in the face of salutary social mores as a method of institutional design, occasionally fruitful, on which we considerably rely, notwithstanding our frequent lack of deliberation in arriving at it. One may quibble over whether to describe law's deep debt to mores as a "strategy" when, however manifest our deep dependence on it, legislators and judges only infrequently deliberate or defend their decisions in these terms. It remains helpful for us nonetheless—as citizens, lawmakers, and their scholarly kibitzers—to *think of* law's deference to common morality as if it were a strategy, an element in institutional design, and to *make it* so. It is fruitful to thus conceive of our reliance on rights-restraining mores not only in making sense of our own and others' behavior, but also in guiding it. By rendering us more self-aware, fully cognizant of relevant implications, we can better discover the conditions under which this regulatory approach is optimal, or at least defensible, and when it is wholly misconceived. "It is hard to be thoughtful about a practice if you are uncomfortable admitting that you engage in it at all,"[11] as one legal scholar observes. And here, we are not yet comfortable at all.

Contrary to the views of many legal theorists, there is nothing inherently pathological in law's periodic willingness to fall back upon nonlaw in bridling wrongful conduct. The 'failures' of lawmaking here witnessed are untroubling where there is reason for confidence in such extralegal mechanisms to dissuade right-bearers from invoking their entitlements in morally unacceptable ways. The legislative faith in informal rights-restraint arises from this largely unspoken deference toward practices of professional ethics, moral exhortation, and social stigmatization assumed to be operative in particular contexts of anticipated rights-exercise.

A positivist legal centralism is correct to remind us that these implicit encumbrances on rights-exercise may sometimes impede our freedom either too little or too much—though the same can equally be said of law. This inconstancy and imprecision is especially unnerving when human life is at stake, in large numbers at times, even if we are prepared to indulge such uncertainties in matters of lesser moral magnitude. It is this ethical enormity which makes the efficacy and propriety of extralegal counterbalance so important—and at times so affecting—in several of the present cases. This is what sets them apart from the wider legal environment where, in less anguished circumstances, similar counterweights often operate unobtrusively against wrongs less severe. In the gravest matters, it could be disastrous to assume that the level of resistance to the rights in question will prove sufficient.

This must be the response to those, from Edmund Burke through Richard Epstein,[12] who—ever distrustful of the reformist state—urge instead the merits of private ordering through social norms or mores, viewing these as the chief and optimal mechanism for ensuring ethically acceptable behavior.[13] Even when the resistance against disfavored rights is exactly as we wish, this could be mere happenstance. The informal equilibrium between rights and responsibilities encountered in several of my cases may prove less stable over time than what positive law—properly drafted and competently enforced—could secure. One might therefore plausibly insist that we are generally better advised to rely upon the law than something as seemingly nebulous and fickle as common morality. Yet such counsel, offered at so high a level of generality, unconcerned with facts about an immediate issue-area, neither offers much practical guidance nor sheds serious theoretical light.

The legislative and judicial trust we implicitly place in common morality is unwarranted where the countervailing pressures it exerts against the irresponsible exercise of rights prove inadequate to the task, sometimes flagrantly so. Such pressure may weaken over time, for instance with social and economic change, as suggested in the history of American legal ethics over the last half-century. The countervalence may remain undiminished, yet fall behind heightened public expectations of the right-bearer, as with inhibitions on civilian harm in war and attitudes toward museums holding pilfered artwork. The pressure may simply prove weaker than initially anticipated, as with the risks of financial innovation, or with the large percentage of abortions confessedly prompted by failure to use contraception; perhaps also with our qualms about exploiting moral hazard in insurance schemes. As with whistleblower statutes and personal bankruptcy, the corrective counterpoise to the abuse of certain rights, while wholesome and welcome up to a point, may prove too strong and thus overdeter conduct that the law seeks to more broadly encourage.

The relation between law and common morality displays noteworthy differences in societies approximating liberal "modern" and "traditional," though these are not the differences contemplated by classical social theorists of law. The law of highly traditional societies is often surprisingly indulgent of conduct deemed morally objectionable, for lawmakers there can safely assume that more informal pressures are securely in place dissuading the exercise of many such entitlements. Under more modern conditions, the restraining influence of social mores on the exercise of rights becomes not less important, but still more so. This is due partly to the increasing differentiation of economic activity, to the way this expedites the transmission of complex information within a given industry or societal sphere. Extralegal duties and social mores in which they find reflection also grow increasingly essential with the enhanced influence of philosophic liberalism upon the law, in extending the reach of our individual rights and withdrawing many traditional legal duties.[14]

The significance of these rights-restraining mores has been evident, for instance, in the informal impediments surreptitiously placed on the right to die and on the right of mentally disabled persons to bear children. Still, many of the mores here shown to moderate the exercise of disfavored rights are powerfully at work in sites quite diverse—historically, culturally, and geographically—as apparent from the range of my empirical illustrations. We have hence seen significant similarities in the relation of law and common morality across social orders otherwise quite various. The inductive methods here employed draw upon relevant data wherever available, some quite systematic, some less so. This inquiry has often involved little more than sniffing about and sussing out the alternative scenarios, their empirical variations and conceptual contours, to identify and better understand their conditions of possibility and emergence. This sort of patient probing has allowed us to anatomize the dynamics of rights to do wrong, to identify their place within law and society, with a view to determining when it is fitting for the legal system to deploy this perplexing, unnerving, yet utterly inescapable category of rights.

The modesty here is not simply methodological, but theoretical as well. I have chiefly sought to tame the extravagant claims of both those who ingenuously see the law as naturally, straightforwardly "reflecting" or "mirroring" common morality and those who cynically view these twin normative orders as traveling in altogether different orbits, as if lawmakers could afford to remain wholly unconcerned with what elicits keen indignation among ordinary people. I have proposed a number of more fine-grained explanations, specific to delimited areas of law and social life, for why law and common morals at times converge, yet often go their separate ways.

Those seeking a rousing jeremiad or soaring prophecy in these pages will be disappointed. No visionary reimagining of political possibility, the sort for which many today understandably yearn,[15] is here on offer. The "good news," however, is that modern liberal society discloses—here and there, in places both frequent and decisive—a demonstrable capacity for moral regeneration that remains little noticed. We do not depend entirely on the law and on an ever-dissolving inheritance of pre-liberal mores—the perennial fear of conservative culture critics.

There is also reason for skepticism at weepy lamentations, periodically proclaimed from across the ideological spectrum, that we have lost a language of sharp moral appraisal and a readiness to use it in acknowledging or imputing extralegal duty. It is preferable to sidle up gradually to such huge questions. I have done so by way of smaller ones concerning observable patterns of shared indignation within particular milieu and the efficacy of such indignation in restraining disfavored rights. We have seen that this indignation regularly manifests itself quite far afield, intensely at times, in domains from intimate to international, from the face-to-face encounter to the corporate shaming campaigns of global activists. People differ passionately, of course, over how to articulate their indignation and against whom to level it. Yet if we look carefully around us, we find many efforts, often effective, to employ this language in limiting the ways we exercise our legal rights.

Notes

References

Acknowledgments

Index

# NOTES

## Introduction

1. See, e.g., Google User Content and Conduct Policy, https://www.google.com/+/policy/content.html; Facebook Community Standards, https://www.facebook.com/communitystandards; Twitter Rules and Policies, https://help.twitter.com/en/rules-and-policies/twitter-rules.

2. House of Commons 2017.

3. The new field of experimental philosophy, and the work of Paul H. Robinson in particular, has begun to address certain aspects of this large tableau. From data gathered in laboratory settings and online opinion surveys, this research probes the intuitions of ordinary people concerning traditional philosophical questions, such as the grounds for ascribing moral responsibility (see, generally, Knobe and Nichols 2008).

4. Like Montesquieu and Durkheim, the present study conceives of morality as a feature of society, best investigated not through conceptual analysis but instead by empirical inquiry into prevailing *moeurs* or "mores," the everyday social practices that lend concrete expression to people's prevalent moral views. The central source of inspiration is book 19 of Montesquieu's *The Spirit of the Laws* (1949 [1748], 292–315). In this book I differ from Durkheim and Montesquieu in that I do not suppose that there exists substantial uniformity of moral sentiment or collective representations on matters of detail across all members of a national society. Whether such consensus exists—over what issues, in what respects, for what length of time—can be only a scientific hypothesis, potentially testable from one place and period to another.

5. By "law" I shall mean the positive law of the state "on the books," as enacted by legislatures and interpreted by judges. This follows ordinary usage of the word, and I will depart from it, with more technical idiom, only when this is absolutely

unavoidable. By "society" or "social order," I refer to life's social dimension, by which I especially have in mind roles, organizations, and shared worldviews. These all involve a heavy measure of intersubjectivity, arising wherever party A significantly orients itself in relation to party B's thought and conduct (Weber 1978 [1922], 4).

6. Consistent with one major usage recorded in the *Oxford English Dictionary* (*OED*), I employ "responsibility" to mean "a moral obligation to behave correctly toward or in respect of a person or thing." I will sometimes refer also to legal responsibilities, and will specify when doing so. The word has two further senses, not pertinent here. The first involves statements of causal attribution: Party A "is responsible" for bringing about condition X. The second entails impositions of accountability after the fact, as in "holding someone responsible" for his prior conduct through punishment.

7. In deference to readers who are unfamiliar with analytic legal philosophy, I shall employ the words "rights" and "duties" in a conventional way, as embodied in ordinary language. This is more expansive than their use within Hohfeld's influential typology (1923), which introduces several subcategories that are immaterial to present purposes.

8. To examine law's relation to its social context (in the way here endeavored), one need not take sides between positivists and nonpositivists over conflicting definitions of "law." The reader's preferred approach to legal sources and interpretive methods will influence, to be sure, how broadly she understands the boundaries of a legal system. And this will in turn affect how broadly she identifies what lies beyond it, including nonlegal sources of normative ordering. Yet according to nearly *any* current concept of law, the morals or mores here treated as "nonlegal" would be so considered, because these are nowhere defined or enforced by the state, and official law is the only sort with which this book is concerned. In the interests of clarity, "legal pluralists"—who include nonstate sources of regulation within their definition of law—should simply insert the word "state" before every use of "law" in these pages.

9. As contemporary social science often employs the term, "mechanisms" consist of "frequently occurring and easily recognizable causal patterns . . . triggered under generally unknown conditions or with indeterminate consequences" (Elster 1999, 45).

10. This raises a perennial methodological challenge, to which I can reply only cursorily. It is enough for present purposes to suggest that most lawmakers are generally aware that legal rules often depend upon a general conformity by most people, most of the time, to a background of basic social mores. To this extent, at least, we can be reasonably confident we know what is going on within the minds of individual lawmakers. Still, we need not adopt a methodological individualism so extreme as to confine all acceptable explanation of social and legal life to the conscious beliefs and intentions of natural persons, even when their states of mind can be credibly confirmed. There is little doubt that many of the rights-restraints here explored, and certainly the social mechanisms that underlie their workings, frequently escape the lawmaker's explicit consideration. They ordinarily operate in a twilight semiconsciousness.

11. By "mystification," I refer to the obscuring of law's true workings so that they appear more defensible than they truly are. This definition encompasses the specifically Marxist sense of the term, but much else besides.

12. By "ideology," I refer to ideas that systematically obfuscate the nature of social order, generally by making its inequalities appear just, natural, or inevitable, but in other ways as well.

13. Tocqueville 1969 [1840], 237–241.

14. Schauer and Zeckhauser 1996, 31.

15. Schneider 1994, 575.

16. Recent diagnoses of American society to this effect include Deneen 2018, Levin 2016, and Putnam 2015.

17. An ideal-type (Weber 1949, 90) is useful for identifying revealing similarities among a wide variety of situations not previously thought to fall under any common category. Such a conceptual construction loses its informative value once significant differences among its apparent empirical instances exceed the resemblances it once seemed to disclose.

18. Brinig (2010, 133–139), a leading scholar of family law, describes the many ways that American law increasingly governs intimate relations among family members and limits the rights of parents, in particular vis-à-vis children and former partners.

19. Though this book cannot directly address the very largest of these questions, its more limited inquiries will help in advancing their discussion and understanding.

20. See, e.g., Putnam 2015, 218–221; Honneth 2013, 67.

21. McCarthy 2016a.

22. Putnam (2000, 19–22) defines "social capital" as "features of social organizations, such as trust, norms, and networks, that can improve the efficiency of society by facilitating coordinated actions."

23. Ibid., 147.

24. Still, if a weakening of informal restraints on rights-talk has indeed occurred, as Putnam, Honneth, and others contend, this is not uniformly the case across the entire socioeconomic landscape. Ethnographic reports (e.g., Gilliom 2001, 83–85) indicate only limited increase in rights-consciousness among the poor in America. And Ally (2009, 9) finds that such consciousness among domestic servants in South Africa has risen only slightly, despite the many postapartheid enactments designed to improve their work conditions.

25. See, e.g., Ehrenhalt 1995, 35–39, 81, 132–134, 214–216, 230–232.

26. Communitarians among sociologists (notably Bellah et al. 1985; Etzioni 2000) held that American society no longer much displays the shared moral frameworks necessary to sustain social order or personal fulfillment, still less to prompt desirable social change.

27. See notably Honneth 2013, 73, 87–97.

28. Especially in Chapters 2 and 3, the present study offers abundant evidence in support of this claim.

29. Moyn (2016) regards this distaste for all talk of duty as intelligible but unwarranted, because he believes that rich countries owe far greater duties to poor

countries. Be that as it may, he correctly observes—writing here more as intellectual historian than as militant—that "our age of rights, lacking a public language of duties, is a historical outlier . . . Human rights wither without a language of duties."

30. Gilligan 1982, 19.

31. Hill 1991, 7.

32. See, e.g., Eleftheriadis 2009; Lazarus et al. 2009. These authors are correct to observe that such prominent "communitarian" theorists as Etzioni, Glendon, and Bellah, unlike many policymakers later claiming inspiration from them, argued not for change to legal rules but instead for a reinvigoration of social mores.

33. Lazarus et al. 2009, ii.

34. Ibid., iii. Accompanying such talk of social responsibility or civic duty, they warn, "is always the possibility that a court or public body may mistake the statement of a duty as a call for it to be made a precondition for the exercise of a right" (ibid., 31).

35. Even those thoroughly conscious of their rights, however, generally fail to sue. For present-day America in this regard, see Felstiner, Abel, and Sarat 1980; Engel 1984, 20–36. It bears emphasis that rights consciousness is by no means a monopoly of the contemporary world: even in pre-Revolutionary France, a keen awareness of their rights, both legal and "natural," was pervasive among apprentices in certain trades, humble shoemakers for instance (Sonenscher, 1989, 71–75).

36. But see Engel and Engel (2010, 2, 15), who conclude from interviews in urban Thailand that accident victims continue to apprehend their injury and suffering chiefly through non-Western religious lenses, rather than juridical modes of self-understanding. This aversion to "rights talk" stems chiefly from culture, not from low socioeconomic status, functional illiteracy, or roadblocks within the legal system itself.

37. Li 2010, 47–48.

38. Typical of this view is Lazarus et al. (2009, 26–27), who write, "Duties exist, in other words, because rights create the moral and political grounds for their existence. According to this view, once human rights are incorporated into law, the logical priority of rights over duties is accepted."

39. Ibid.

40. Ibid., 27; O'Neill 1996, 127–129, 143–146.

41. O'Neill 1996, 137–139.

42. I shall refer to "the West" or "Western" in a conventional and generally uncontroversial way. I have in mind simply the countries of Europe and North America, along with their political, intellectual, and cultural legacies, leaving open to argument what such legacies may actually encompass. Europe's former colonies are part of the West, in this sense, insofar as they have absorbed these legacies. Even authors wishing to banish the concept entirely acknowledge its frequent invocation and hence its reality as a prominent feature of cultural and political life.

43. See, e.g., Das 2007; Keane 2016; Lambek 2015; Laidlaw 2014; Zigon 2011.

44. Schmidtz and Goodin (1998) offer a helpful introduction to these issues, fair to both sides of the debate.

45. Hacker (2006, 9, 52, 57, 58, 133) here alludes disparagingly to the "Personal Responsibility and Work Opportunity Reconciliation Act of 1996," Pub. Law 104-193 (1996), the "welfare reform" legislation enacted under President Bill Clinton. A common view among those opposing such reforms has been that there exists a moral "right to work," and a corresponding moral duty of states to provide employment to all who seek it, but that right-holders themselves have no moral duty to exercise this entitlement (by accepting jobs they deem unpleasant). The rationale for this singular conjunction of rights, responsibilities, and nonresponsibilities remains unclear, requiring a more careful defense than anyone has offered. Though "progressive" theorists and welfare activists widely hold this amalgam of views, it is far less frequent among Western citizens, most of whom endorse work obligations as a condition of eligibility for key forms of public provision (see, e.g., Doar, Bowman, and O'Neil 2016).

46. "Neoliberalism" is a pejorative term for contemporary reworkings of nineteenth-century laissez-faire economic philosophy favoring such public policies as fiscal austerity, free trade between countries, privatization, and deregulation of the private sector.

47. The contemporary discussion begins with Waldron 1981.

48. Wenar 2015.

49. Montesquieu's word is *moeurs,* which poses notorious difficulties of translation. This French term straddles a line that the English language seeks to mark out somewhat more clearly between "mores," "manners," and "morals." Throughout this study, I generally employ the word "mores," which I understand (consistently with the *OED*) to entail "the shared habits, manners, and customs of a community or social group; the normative conventions and attitudes embodying the fundamental moral values of a particular society, the contravention of which is likely to be perceived as a threat to stability." Unlike Montesquieu or Tocqueville, however, this study presupposes that mores may exist within social groupings both smaller and larger than the nation, and present concerns do not encompass questions concerning "national character."

Scholars have long differed over how to characterize the extralegal mechanisms of interest here, whether to describe these as "social practices," "conventions," "norms," "customs," "mores," or "folkways," to mention only the most popular candidates. Whatever their arguable differences, any such mechanism is equally of interest here insofar as it operates to inhibit lawful wrongdoing and thereby to diminish or refocus the need for law. I prefer "mores" to the alternatives because this seems to comport most closely with lay usage in both English and (especially) the romance languages. Still more importantly, this term registers etymologically that the beliefs and behavior at issue harbor a specifically moral dimension, in that serious departures from others' expectations at these points elicit indignation at perceived wrongdoing.

50. Some will say that such conduct is not immoral, but simply irrational. Yet opinion surveys indicate that 80 percent of Americans regard suicide, except under very limited circumstances, as "wrong" (Saad 2001). Their views here owe heavily to the fact that Christianity, in most of its forms, has long regarded suicide as a

mortal sin. When those of more secular orientation are pressed to explain why they believe suicide to be wrongful, they frequently report that the act of willful self-destruction violates moral duties to dependents or to oneself.

51. A recent study finds that only four countries prohibit sex-selective abortion (Citro et al. 2014, 10).

52. Ebenstein (2007, 3) draws this inference from the skewed sex ratio in several such countries; see also Miller 2001, 1083. One study (Bongaarts 2013, 193) even finds that sex-selective abortion accounts for one-third of all pregnancy terminations worldwide.

53. Egan et al. 2011, 560.

54. Many readers will take offense at the inclusion in this list of the right to abortion, perhaps especially to its mention in the same breath with war's civilian carnage. I am not here concerned, however, with the moral merits of any such entitlements, only with the question of how they can continue to exist, and what purposes they sometimes serve, despite greatly deviating from moral sentiments widely held within democracies. Opinion polls have regularly disclosed that equal numbers of Americans believe abortion should be illegal (either all or most of the time) as think that it should be legal. See, e.g., Rasmussen 2012. Long after *Roe v. Wade,* some 25 percent of respondents have consistently opposed the practice in literally "all" circumstances. More than half the U.S. population consistently expresses the view that abortion is tantamount to "murder" (American Enterprise Institute 2012, at 3, summarizing several surveys over many years).

55. There is reason to believe that abortions originating in this way are numerous. According to a leading and reputable pro-choice organization, half of American women who seek an abortion had already undergone a prior one (Guttmacher 2011, 2016). Further data, from the same organization and other researchers, also consistently indicate that 46 percent of abortions are performed on women who acknowledge that they did not use contraception in the month during which they conceived (Guttmacher 2011, 2016; Jones, Darroch, and Henshaw 2002, 294, 297); compare Brunner-Huber and Toth (2007, 1309). For similar percentages from other countries, see Rasch, Wielandt, and Knudsen 2002, 296, table 2; Schünmann and Glasier 2006; Bajos et al. 2006, 2862. Among U.S. women seeking emergency contraception (i.e., the "morning after" pill), some 40 percent acknowledge that they regularly fail to employ more standard means of contraception (Raine et al. 2005, 60). Due to wide disapproval of recourse to abortion (in lieu of contraception) for birth control, it is likely that such percentages underreport the true incidence of the procedure employed in these circumstances.

Let us now apply those percentages to further data. Approximately one-third of American women will likely have an abortion at some point in their lives, according to the same pro-choice organization and other demographers (Guttmacher 2006; Jones, Darroch, and Henshaw 2006; Henshaw 1998). Women constitute at least half of the U.S. population, which would mean that the present female population numbers some 160,000 million. If one-third of these women receive an abortion at some point in their lives, this would entail some 53 million abortions. The same family-planning organization reports that in recent years approximately 1.2

million abortions have been performed on American women per year (Guttmacher 2016). We may infer from the preceding data that 46 percent of these abortions will be sought by women who admit that they did not employ contraception at the relevant time. It follows that, among the currently living U.S. female population, some 24 million abortions will be sought by women who did not employ contraception, and that some 550,000 abortions of this variety are sought every year.

56. In the interests of conceptual clarity, I do not here employ as examples of "rights to do wrong" any situations where it may be readily possible to reinterpret current positive law to bring it into line with the state of common morality. When the law is unclear, it is impossible to compare it to prevailing morals, just as it is impossible to conduct such a comparison when common morality is itself nonexistent or empirically indeterminable. Both situations are legion, but not the focus of this study.

57. What renders such considerations "moral" in nature raises a more difficult question than many nonphilosophers will suppose. Many legal scholars appear content to use the word as merely a residual category for considerations of a nonjuridical nature. Yet much disagreement exists among philosophers over how to define the nature of moral judgments, and how to distinguish them from other kinds of judgments, such as those of prudence, social convention, manners, or taste.

Recent anthropological inquiry (e.g., Keane 2016, 4, 21) seeks to avoid the question entirely by taking the moral domain to consist simply in whatever people consider their ultimate ends, the objectives of superordinate value in their lives. In any event, the present inquiry requires no commitment to any particular meta-ethics, for it focuses on indignation at perceived injustice, a sentiment falling unequivocally within any remotely plausible understanding of the moral domain. Consistently with ordinary language, as reflected in many dictionaries, I employ the terms "moral" and "ethical" interchangeably. Philosophers and moral anthropologists often distinguish the two, but not in any consistent manner.

58. I use the term "indignation" as defined by the *OED:* "anger at what is regarded as unworthy or wrongful; wrath excited by a sense of wrong to oneself or, especially, to others, or by meanness, injustice, wickedness, or misconduct; righteous or dignified anger."

59. Honneth 1992, 199.

60. The project first carried the name of Cordoba House. Its plans underwent substantial revision since then, including a change of name to Park51. Current plans call for a forty-three-story building of luxury condominiums, to include an "Islamic cultural museum" (Weiss 2016).

61. Citizens against Pro-Obama Media Bias 2010. Here Beinart's understanding of what it means to have a legal right comports with at least one version of "legal realism." Max Weber (1978 [1922], 666–667), for instance, understood the law itself in terms of coercive commands backed by an official staff assigned to enforce them, and defined a "[legal] right as being no more than an increase in the probability that a certain expectation of the one to whom the law grants the right will not be disappointed." Promoters of the Islamic cultural center were undoubtedly

quite disappointed to encounter severe impediments to the exercise of what they considered their rights of religious association and to the use of their property.

62. Stephens 2010. On many American university campuses, those of Beinart's political orientation often further seek—with surpassing efficacy, in many places—to discourage the exercise of constitutional speech rights on the subject of affirmative action by those who privately oppose most aspects of these programs. Defenders of this policy, in discouraging such speech, expressly refer to the alleged need for emotional sensitivity toward local beneficiaries of that policy.

63. Krauthammer 2010. Former New York City mayor Rudolph Giuliani evoked a similarly religious idiom, suggesting that the proposed building would constitute a "desecration."

64. Krauthammer read political theory at Oxford's Balliol College, writing his master's thesis on John Stuart Mill.

65. Chidester and Linenthal 1995, 1–42. As Hassner (2009, 3–4, 11–13, 19–67) observes, we learn that a property dispute engages sacred commitments, on one or both sides, if it proves impossible to resolve through partition or sharing. The antagonists regard such a site as offering privileged access to the divine. Sharing it with rivals is unacceptable because this entails relinquishing control, if only for a short time, in ways that authorize its use for purposes alien and profane, guaranteeing its "desecration." Even sites that seem secular on first appearance may enable people to partake—through the sense of awe their visitation inspires—in analogous forms of ultimate meaning. With Ground Zero, this has meant an opportunity to celebrate one's personal and religious freedom, which many Americans conceive as integral to a national identity consciously shared with millions of fellow citizens.

66. Peretz (2010), who later apologized for the statement. To similar effect, when a derogatory video depiction of the prophet Mohammed sparked lethal riots in several Muslim-majority countries, a professor of religious studies at the University of Pennsylvania wrote in *USA Today* that the film's creators should be arrested for "abusing" their First Amendment rights.

67. Laksin 2010.

68. I do not seek to solve this large problem—only to identify it, delineate its contours, and observe some of its implications for the law.

69. Howard Dean, former Vermont governor and former Democratic National Committee chairman, took an intriguingly idiosyncratic position on this, according dispositive weight to victims' grief, but seeing no need to appraise its reasonableness as a basis for opposing the building's construction. "The builders have to be able to go beyond what is their right, and be willing to talk about feelings, whether the feelings are justified or not" (Montopoli 2010).

70. See, e.g., Kristof 2010; Zakaria 2010.

71. CNN Politics 2010.

72. Stolberg 2010 (quoting President Obama). There was of course no logical inconsistency between the president's two statements. Many people nonetheless interpreted the second as a "baffling retraction" (Nussbaum 2012, 214). It was, however, altogether *non*baffling if seen as the strategic recalculation of a public official

seeking reelection and dismayed by the public's negative reaction to his prior statement.

73. It is pertinent here that promoters of the cultural center showed poor judgment, as all acknowledged, in welcoming financial contributions from Wahhabist states, such as Saudi Arabia, in declining to dissociate themselves unequivocally from all terror attacks on civilians, in refusing to submit to public interviews, and in failing to consult informally with local community leaders before disclosing their construction plans (Nussbaum 2012, 217–220).

74. Mosque-Building and Its Discontents 2010 (reporting opinion survey data).

75. Dean 2010 (quoting mayor Bloomberg).

76. Ibid., 4–5, 44–48, 111, 137 (summarizing considerable evidence to this effect). See also Cumming-Bruce and Erlanger 2009.

77. Van Wolkenten, Brosnan, and de Waal 2007, 18857.

## 1. Common Morality, Social Mores, and the Law

1. In the United States, whites and blacks differ greatly over whether police in their communities are "good or excellent" in using appropriate force on criminal suspects and in treating all suspects equally, regardless of race (Morin and Stepler 2016).

2. I discuss these works briefly in Chapter 5.

3. Ngram Viewer is an online search engine that charts frequencies of any set of keywords found in sources printed between 1500 and 2018 in Google's text corpora, which includes nearly everything published in the English language.

4. Yates and Hunter 2011, 26.

5. Williams 1985, 85–90, 141, 155; Kirchin (2013) offers several trenchant current assessments of this influential idea.

6. Williams 2005, 48–50.

7. Hesselink 2011.

8. That has been my personal experience, at least, in publicly presenting my thinking here—by no means willfully provocative—in several Western countries.

9. On the acute moral and emotional intensity of such opposition, see Hamm 1995, 26–27; Behr 2011, 23–33.

10. Thus, at several points in these pages, regarding questions for which there is only limited evidence, I am compelled to engage in informed speculation about what might or might not be the case, and about the likely future direction of change, social and legal, in light of current tendencies and trajectories. I explicitly identify these uncertainties in just such terms, acknowledging—as scholarly ethics requires—the places where existing knowledge is too limited to allow claims any stronger.

11. On these matters, Garland (1990, 51–54) offers insightful analysis, cast as a critique of Durkheim's concept of collective conscience, understood to apply chiefly at the national level.

12. Gert 2004, 8–10, 20–53. Other such beliefs are said to include: do not deprive of freedom; do not deceive; do not cheat; obey the law; and do your duty (understood chiefly in terms of the requirements of particular social roles). H. L. A. Hart (2012 [1961], 167–176) earlier offered a similar, if shorter, list of rules he deemed "essential to the survival of any society" (167). "The social morality of societies," he argued, "includes certain obligations . . . forbidding, or at least restricting, the free use of violence, rules requiring certain forms of honesty and truthfulness in dealings with others, and rules forbidding the destruction of tangible things or their seizure from others" (167).

From informant surveys, Robinson (2009, 33) finds cross-national and pan-demographic consensus on the necessity of punishing what he calls the "core" wrongs of "physical aggression, taking property, and deception in exchanges." Robinson's most consistent empirical finding across many studies, in the United States and elsewhere, is that there exist certain "core intuitions" generating consensus on basic moral principles, and the strongest of these are retributive (e.g., 34). He concludes that "our existing intuitions" on the moral questions implicated in criminal law are simply "the reality of what it means to be human, and effective social engineers must deal with the world as it exists" (34).

13. Veatch 2003, 191.

14. Beauchamp and Childress 2001, 403.

15. Ignatieff 2017, 27.

16. Bastié 2017 (interview with Nathalie Heinich, concerning her 2017 book, *Des Valeurs: Une Approche Sociologique*. Paris: Gallimard).

17. Ibid.

18. Boltanksi and Thévenot (2006) offer a noteworthy exception.

19. Gert, Culver, and Clouser 1997, 46–47.

20. Lindsay 2009, 32.

21. H. L.A. Hart 2012 [1961], 167.

22. Gert 1999, 58.

23. Lindsay 2005, 340.

24. A further objection has been that even where moral principles are broadly shared within a given group, any two of these principles will sometimes counsel conflicting courses of action, suggesting that common morality does not form a coherent system. And if it doesn't, then it cannot be expected to generate much social stability, which many view as the central purpose of any common morality. Its defenders nonetheless insist that the theory of a universal common morality describes "a single, unified moral system which provides a framework for dealing with all moral problems" (Gert, Culver, and Clouser 1997, 20).

25. Robinson and Kurzban (2007, 1829, 1852–1853, 1862–1866) report results of laboratory experiments in several countries, including India and China. Roberts and Stalans (1998, 42–43) reach similar conclusions from opinion surveys in Canada, Denmark, Finland, Great Britain, the Netherlands, Kuwait, Norway, Puerto Rico, and the continental United States.

26. Robinson and Darley 2007, 8–11; Robinson and Kurzban 2007, 135–139, 1832–1880.

27. Robinson and Kurzban 2007, 1864–1865.

28. Bibas 2012, 120.

29. Garland (1990, 57) here sympathetically parses Durkheim.

30. See, e.g., Bhabha 1990.

31. For theoretical defenses of this possibility, see Tamir 1993, 83–87, 140–145, 158–161. Kohn (1944) offered an influential early account.

32. Armitage (2007) shows the considerable influence of the U.S. Declaration of Independence and elements of its philosophic liberalism on the independence declarations of many other countries.

33. See, e.g., Smith 1997, 216–220, 277–278, 320–324, 392–402, 463–469.

34. Within liberal thought, the term "political morality" generally refers to moral principles, concerning justice particularly, that define the proper limits of state coercion. I here extend the idea in a more sociological direction, to include the sentiments of right and wrong that influence our thought and conduct as individual citizens of a polity.

35. Foa and Mounk 2017. Villasenor (2017) finds that 51 percent of U.S. university students consider it acceptable for a student group to shout down a speaker with whom they disagree, and that 20 percent find it unobjectionable to employ violence to prevent a speaker from publicly expressing her views.

36. Villasenor 2017.

37. These forms of morality are more demanding than readily attainable through extended tit-for-tat, which still rests entirely upon the reciprocal accommodation of self-interest.

38. Data reveal that, both between countries and among U.S. states, "relatively homogeneous areas tend to have more income redistribution and other forms of public spending" than do areas more demographically heterogeneous (Luttmer 2001, 25; see also Alesina and Glaeser 2004, 136–150). Sentiments of mutual obligation apparently provide the intervening causal variable between demography and generosity.

39. Parsons (1951, 41) thus wrote: "The sharing of such common value patterns . . . creates a solidarity among those mutually oriented to the common values . . . Without attachment to the constitutive common values, the collectivity tends to dissolve."

40. Parsons 1951, xvvii–xvviii; Wrong 1994, 1–36.

41. Vaisey 2009, 1676.

42. Reddy 1997, 1.

43. Mann 1973, 45–54.

44. See, e.g., Roberts 2004, 3.

45. Trotsky 1942.

46. See, e.g., Abercrombie, Hill, and Turner 1980, 128–155; Mann 1973, 39–44.

47. Gramsci's prison writings (1992, 141–157) were highly influential here.

48. Anderson (2017, 1) asserts that, "if academic citations and internet references are any guide, [Gramsci] is more influential than Machiavelli. The bibliography of articles and books about him now runs to some 20,000 items." Anderson does not report his search procedure.

49. Martin (2002) offers one exemplary such study, and surveys the best of earlier efforts.

50. Perry Anderson, a prominent Marxist theorist himself, observes that Gramsci, in his analysis of bourgeois hegemony, displayed significant "ambiguities in his use of the term . . ." and "never succeeded in locating definitely or precisely either the position or the interconnection of repression and ideology within the power structure of advanced capitalism" (2017, 94–95). In other words, Gramsci insisted that class domination relies not only on coercion but also on popular consent to bourgeois values, including moral values. Yet he failed to delineate their respective contributions, their relative significance, or the nature of their interaction, the importance of which he conclusorily asserted.

51. Elster 1993, 66.

52. Haidt 2006.

53. Geertz 1975, 23.

54. Winston 2015, 56.

55. I employ such terms as "deontological," "utilitarian," "Kantian," "consequentialist," and "communitarian" as they are standardly employed in contemporary legal scholarship, in full awareness that philosophers argue over the meaning of all these terms, often splitting each into subcategories. Consequentialism is a family of moral theories holding that it is the consequences of an act or rule, not its purposes, that determine its normative acceptability. Deontological ethics maintain that certain acts and policies are morally indefensible regardless of how desirable their consequences might be.

56. Kleinman 1998, 360–363.

57. Ibid., 361.

58. Côté, Piff, and Willer (2012, 490) find significant correlation between higher socioeconomic status and affinity for utilitarian moral views against more empathetic intuitions.

59. Geertz 1975, 23.

60. Beeman 1986, 50–63. *Ta'arof* is a style of personal interaction involving elaborately ritualized displays of respect and humility through which Iranians negotiate matters ranging from taxi fares and dinner invitations to business contracts. In conversation with another, one may seek to establish one's superiority by extravagantly debasing oneself, proclaiming one's demerits, moral and otherwise, in relation to a conversational partner.

61. Morgan 2007, 325.

62. Ibid.

63. Sawyer (2005, 63–99) offers a rare, incisive effort to theorize this elusive process.

64. See, e.g., Charles Christian Nahl, *The Rape of the Sabines: The Invasion,* 1871, Crocker Art Museum, Sacramento, CA.

65. Hasday 2000, 1412, 1425.

66. Anderson 2003, 1480–1485.

67. Waldron 1989, 586–587 (emphasis added).

68. Bell 1996 [1976], 306.

69. Post 1986, 736.

70. We here find the future dean of Yale Law School openly endorsing—under cover of a "communitarianism" then sympathetically entertained among the soft Left—this avowed rehabilitation of Lord Devlin's expressly conservative views (Devlin 1959) regarding the proper relation between law and common morality. Devlin had formulated this theoretical stance in connection with a political intervention defending Britain's antisodomy laws.

71. Liav Orgad (2016, 226–236) and David Miller (2016, 89–92, 102–108, 153–157) argue compellingly to this effect. More pertinent for present purposes, Miller observes that, simply as a observable sociological fact, "people want to feel that they are in control of the future shape of their society," and that "they have an interest in political self-determination, which includes being able to decide how many immigrants should be allowed to enter, who should be selected if more than this number apply, and what can reasonably be expected of those who are allowed in" (13).

72. Sarat 2004, 412.

73. Devlin argued that to ensure a society's very survival, it is necessary for criminal law to incorporate the moral views its citizens share, at least all such views of greatest importance to them. H. L. A. Hart (1967) incisively criticized Devlin's view of the purported causal relation between shared values and social order, showing how Devlin's assumptions in this regard remained largely unarticulated and undefended. Hart extended this same critique to Durkheim and Parsons (ibid., 6–10), observing how these social theorists, although far more sophisticated and intellectually influential, were vulnerable to very similar objections.

74. Douglas 1986, 9.

75. Devlin 1959, esp. 129–133.

76. Hook (2017) shows that declared Republicans, unlike most Democrats, continue firmly to believe that the institution of marriage should be reserved for "a man and a woman."

77. These included Charles Taylor, Amy Gutmann, Seyla Benhabib, Anthony Appiah, and Chandran Kukathas.

78. Int'l Covenant on Economic, Social, and Cultural Rights, Art. 1(1); Art. 15 (1)(a).

79. This is the view of Kukathas (1998, 686–687), for instance.

80. Theorists in the individualist tradition of political thought have usually conceived of such conflict in the form of strife between particular persons rather than between social or cultural groups. In *Leviathan,* Hobbes thus famously described this in terms of a "war of every man against every man" and "a perpetuall warre of every man against his neighbor."

81. Hart (1967, 11) rightly finds this language opaque and dangerously imprecise.

82. Ibid., 13. Hart elsewhere (2012 [1961], 167–176) defines these restraints, necessary for an acceptable measure of social cohesion, in ways quite undemanding.

83. Post 1986, 493.

84. Putnam 2007; Costa and Kahn 2003; Alesina and Glaeser 2004, 136–150; Lewicka 2011, 210; Hopkins 2010, 41; Stolle, Soroka, and Johnston 2008, 71; Habyarimana et al. 2009, 3–5; Wikström et al. 2012, 181–182. Such reputable evidence as exists of positive effects comes chiefly from studies of decision making by teams whose members, though from different countries or ethnic groups, share similar educations, professional experience, socioeconomic status, and elite cultural habitus (McKinsey & Co. 2017; Page 2007, 357). Even here, regarding work teams, the cumulative quantitative evidence that diversity improves performance is highly equivocal, at best (Stahl et al. 2010).

85. There is now general agreement that political polarization in the United States has greatly increased since the late 1970s (see, e.g., Hook 2017, reporting recent polling results), though a few (Fiorina 2017) continue to question how deeply this extends beyond the country's elites. For recent scholarly discussion of the implications, see Hopkins and Sides (2015), whose participants concur in seeing nothing positive to come from such a trend.

86. Zuckerberg 2017.

87. Others' cuisine can easily evoke disgust, and feelings of disgust are regularly accompanied by sharp moral judgments. Yet the disgust some feel toward certain foods is not often specifically moral in character, still less a judgment on others' culture. And yet undoubtedly, at times it is precisely that.

88. Montesquieu 2008 [1721], esp. letters 24, 26, 34, 38, 48, 55, 60, 63, 87, 99, 108, 141.

89. Philosophers generally understand cosmopolitanism as the idea that all people are, and should understand themselves as, members of a single human community (Kleingeld and Brown 2013). This can mean many things, often inconsistent, to be sure. Cosmopolitanism sometimes refers more particularly to a tolerance and even sympathetic curiosity toward differences between cultural groups, in their forms of life, including (up to some point) their differing views of moral acceptability. That is the sense—somewhat idiosyncratic—in which I here use the term.

90. Within Europe today, these concerns focus, of course, on the challenge of integrating more than three million recent immigrants, 80 percent of whom come from Muslim lands (Eurostat 2017). This influx follows several decades of substantial Muslim immigration, many of whose beneficiaries have declined to embrace liberal principles concerning gay rights, women's equality, sexual freedom generally, and freedom of thought or speech, especially when satirizing Islam (Nowrasteh 2016, summarizing Pew and Gallup data). One-third of French Muslims tell pollsters that their religion and *Sharia* law are more important to them than the law of the French Republic (Institute Montaigne 2016). Across Western Europe, some Muslim intellectuals (e.g., Modood and Kastoryano 2006, 172–176) report that they do not share certain liberal values, and if this sharing is what "assimilation" requires, they want no part of it. Instead, they expressly demand sympathetic "recognition" of their cultural differences, in these and other respects.

91. For example, within the United States during the period 1890–1919, geographical proximity to immigrant Catholic groups closely correlated with the par-

ticular counties, composed mostly of small towns and rural areas, that banned the sale and consumption of alcohol (Andrews and Seguin 2015, 475).

92. See, e.g., Putnam and Campbell 2010, 3–7, 34–36, 105–106, 567–580. Thus, for instance, the mainstream Christian denominations with which most Americans of all demographics once identified were politically centrist but have greatly declined in number of adherents. Over the same period, the portions of the population that are evangelical (who mostly vote Republican) or avowedly secular (voting mostly Democratic) have much expanded.

93. See Mutz 2006, 15, 36, 38, 133, 138, 149; Hetherington and Rudolph 2015, 16–33, 72–95; Mason 2015, 56.

## 2. A Sampling of Rights to Do Wrong

1. *Chaplinsky v. New Hampshire,* 315 U.S. 568 (1942).

2. *R.A.V. v. City of St. Paul, Minn.,* 505 U.S. 377, 377 (1992); *Brandenburg v. Ohio,* 395 U.S. 444, 447 (1969) (holding that the First Amendment protects advocacy even of unlawful action so long as it is not "directed to inciting or producing imminent lawless action and . . . likely to incite or produce such action").

3. Southern Poverty Law Center (2017a, 2017b).

4. Several incidents of popular reaction against hate speech and hate crime are reported in Eckert (2012), Eligon and Yaccino (2012), Vitchers (2014), and many others.

5. Fleming and McClain 2013, 43. They add, "There is considerable evidence available in contemporary society that people recognize the distinction between rights and rightness and engage in the sort of moral suasion that communitarians urge" (ibid., 43). They adduce little such evidence, however.

6. For studies of antiracist movements throughout contemporary Europe, see Fella and Ruzza (2013).

7. The Southern Poverty Law Center (2017a), which tracks the activity of nationalist and white hate groups, finds no secular trend in either the number of such groups or the frequency of their gatherings. Both have recently become more conspicuous, though this may be deceptive and attributable to shifting reportorial preoccupations. Though online activity has undoubtedly increased with internet growth, there have in fact been significant declines in the number of active Ku Klux Klan chapters (Southern Poverty Law Center 2017b).

8. Hunter 2016.

9. Bosman 2016.

10. Ahmari 2017.

11. Others (e.g., Holmes 2012, 345–347) have made similar observations.

12. In a comparative study of several Western democracies, Capoccia (2013, 207–226) shows that differences in national history continue to influence "the use of legal restrictions to curb extremist actors." See also de Morree 2016.

13. Grundgesetz Der Bundersrepublik Deutschland [Constitution], May 23, 1949, Articles 9, 18, 20, 21, 33. See also Strafgesetzbuch (Penal Code), §§84–86,

130, 185. De Morree (2016, 185–223) offers recent interpretation of the postwar German experience.

14. One frequent, noteworthy effect of these efforts is to drive such hate speech underground. As Waldron observes, "we want to convey the sense that the bigots are isolated, embittered individuals" (Waldron 2012, 95). We want to thereby shame them into silence.

15. It is true, of course, that the First Amendment protects offensive speech of a sort unrelated to antidemocratic mass movements. My point here is simply that considerable evidence from several countries (see also Garry 1993, 13–14, 18–20) suggests that the scope of this protection would undoubtedly suffer serious legal curtailment if such a movement had ever assumed serious political significance. Also pertinent here is that, during both World Wars, American authorities closed or greatly restricted the operation of pro-German and pro-Japanese publications (Sweeney 2010, 17–18, 119–120), which were perceived as threats to social consensus over war aims. During the first of these conflicts, federal authorities shuttered antiwar publications as well (Garry 1993, 20; Hull 1999, 3; Sweeney 2010, 48–51).

16. Marcuse 1965, 81–123.

17. *U.S. v. Rahman,* 189 F.3d 88, 117 (2d Cir. 1999); *U.S. v. Mostafa Kamel Mostafa,* 16 F. Supp. 3d 236, 249–250 (S.D.N.Y. 2014).

18. *U.S. v. Mehanna,* 735 F.3d 32, 49 (1st Cir. 2013) upholds jury instructions permitting conviction for "material support for terrorism" against someone who translates and disseminates ISIS materials; see also *United States v. Al Bahlul,* 820 F. Supp. 2d 1141, 1202 (CMCR 2011).

19. Tibi 2014, 9–36; Nesser 2011, 178–180.

20. See the online advertisement for American Muslims for Palestine, "Seventh Annual Conference for Palestine in the U.S.: Gaza Teaches Life," Nov. 27–29, 2014, Chicago.

21. Callimachi 2015.

22. An Associated Press/NORC (2015) opinion survey found that 54 percent of Americans said it may be necessary for the government to sacrifice freedoms to fight terrorism; 45 percent disagreed. About half of Americans thought it acceptable to allow warrantless government analysis of internet activities and communications—even of American citizens—in order to discover suspicious activity. Only 30 percent opposed.

23. A number of opinion surveys and other credible indicators so suggest. See, e.g., Associated Press/NORC 2015; Poe 2015.

24. Mazzetti et al. 2011.

25. Shane and Mekhennet (2010) quote al-Awlaki: "I eventually came to the conclusion that jihad against America is binding upon myself, just as it is binding on every other able Muslim."

26. Ross and Ferran (2011) quote President Obama's description of al-Awlaki as "the man who took the lead in planning and directing efforts to murder innocent Americans."

27. The reporters write, "While al-Awlaki was not the trigger-man in any of the 19 terror operations to which he is linked, U.S. officials and terror experts said that his hand was visible in all of them" (Ross and Ferran 2011).

28. Neumeister 2016.

29. Chesney 2011, 3–60.

30. More precisely, al-Awlaki's father lacked "standing," in light of the "political question" doctrine, which allocates policymaking on national security chiefly to the "political branches," especially the executive. *Al-Aulaqi v. Obama,* 727 F. Supp. 2d 1, 44–52 (D.D.C. 2010).

31. I pass no judgment here on the normative defensibility of that presidential action, a question that is immaterial to sociological purposes.

32. Bell 1996 [1976], 53–54. Sowell (2011, 45) observes that "the clear intent of this 'art' is in fact to insult the values and beliefs of the public."

33. Compare Bourdieu 1984, 25, 40, 47. Maggie Nelson (2011) offers a trenchant history of self-conscious assault by Western aesthetic elites on what they have viewed as common (or sometimes "petit bourgeois") morality. Lewis (2015) further shows how American artwork of the last half-century has been "flagrantly, deliberately transgressive" of prevailing moral sensibilities. Still, the deliberate intention to shock or give offense might often simply be one among a shifting set of several motives, jostling about in a sea of semiconsciousness.

34. Boltanski and Chiapello (2005, 37–38) observe the differences between these two types of anticapitalist indignation.

35. As Tetlock and Belkin (1996, 3) observe, "We can avoid counterfactuals only if we eschew all causal inference and limit ourselves to strictly noncausal narratives of what actually happened."

36. Bayles 1994, 47, 388; Pease 2000, 165; Schleifer 2011, 9, 32; Crow 1998, 11, 28–29.

37. This conservative reaction—from groups at times avowedly proclaiming themselves "the Moral Majority"—found conspicuous expression, for instance, in the 1989 public uproar and congressional response surrounding the federal funding of Robert Mapplethorpe's homoerotic photography (Gamarekian 1989). The Moral Majority, founded in 1979 by Baptist minister Jerry Falwell, was a prominent American organization that reflected the views of many conservative Christians. It played a major role in mobilizing these people as a political force in Republican electoral victories of the 1980s.

38. U.S. federal law prohibits child pornography through the Protect Act of 2003, Pub. Law 108-21, 117 Stat. 650, S. 151, enacted April 30.

39. The term refers to "an episode or . . . group of persons [who] become defined as a threat to societal values and interests" (Cohen 2011 [1972], 1; see also Garland 2008). It is better to conceive of these curious contretemps in less polemical terms, as episodes of what Durkheim called "passionate outrage," involving simply an intensification of conflictive worldviews, leading at times to a reinvigoration of the collective conscience, a strengthening of widely shared morality. Those who prefer to speak in terms of panic—a wording more tendentious, suggesting wild-eyed hysteria—consistently fail to offer any determinate standards by which to distinguish a reasonable from an unreasonable response to those challenging majority mores. That task is indeed impossible for most such critics, who insist that our every interpretation of man-made reality, including our perception of risks to social order, is thoroughly a cultural invention, and hence ultimately a matter of predominant opinion.

40. Garland 2008, 22.

41. Clark Lombardi, Professor of Law, University of Washington, personal correspondence, Sept. 2013.

42. Agrama 2010, 507–510; Bowen 2001.

43. See, generally, Agrama 2010, 496.

44. Lombardi here refers specifically to a notable 1996 case in which the Egyptian High Court held Cairo University professor Nasir Hamid Abu Zayd liable, on the basis of his scholarly writings, for "apostasy," a major violation of *Sharia.*

45. Lombardi, personal correspondence, Sept. 2013, adds a second revealing example: *Sharia* does not criminalize relationships of friendship between unmarried men and unmarried women. This is not because such interactions are deemed morally respectable. "Rather, it is because people expect that families who care simply will not permit . . . such relationships."

46. See, generally, Fay, Hurst, and White 2002, 716; Bernard 2011.

47. Lawless et al. (2008, 381) found that over 40 percent of those declaring bankruptcy report that they had struggled seriously with debt for more than two years before filing.

48. Mewse, Lea, and Wrapson 2010. Cohen-Cole and Duygan-Bump (2008) find, from a large data sample of credit bureaus, that stigma from bankruptcy has declined primarily among the wealthy and well-educated, and that the notable increase in bankruptcy filings by other groups since the late 1960s has sources entirely different. Sullivan, Warren, and Westbrook (1989) similarly suggest that their "data show that in this decade, stigma seems to be holding its own as a gatekeeper for bankruptcy, as the great majority of people in bankruptcy are truly desperate." Attorneys who practice personal bankruptcy law (e.g., Las Vegas Bankruptcy Blog 2012) report that feelings of stigma often lead their clients to hesitate and defer filing for protection.

49. See, generally, Sousa 2014. There is considerable evidence (Shah, Mullainathan, and Shafir 2012, 682, 685) that financial decision-making among the poor is often highly subrational, by any standard.

50. Zywicki 2005, 1073; Efrat 2006, 488–517.

51. Livshits, MacGee, and Tertilt 2010. The rate of personal bankruptcy has notably declined since the year of this publication.

52. Bankruptcy Abuse and Consumer Protection Act of 2005, Pub. Law 109-8, 119 Stat. 23, 2005.

53. Liddell, Liddell, and Highfield 2011, 132–133. Among scholars, there is agreement that personal bankruptcy filings had increased, and that the stigma associated with declaring bankruptcy has declined. There is little agreement, though, over whether a strong causal relationship exists between these two developments. Sullivan, Warren, and Westbrook (2006, 253–254) reject that hypothesis.

54. Moore 1998, 26.

55. Ibid., 27.

56. Hess 2012, 11.

57. Garfinkel 1956. The U.S. Bankruptcy Code §343 continues to require the debtor to personally attend a meeting with his creditors, at which the bankruptcy

trustee poses questions to the debtor and creditors may ask further questions regarding the debtor's financial affairs.

58. Zhu (2011) offers support for the view that in the United States, personal bankruptcy often results not from medical emergency or macroeconomic downturns but instead from expenditures—clearly imprudent, in retrospect—on such personal property as houses and automobiles.

59. Graver (1997, 166–172, 175) describes how courts interpret the legal rules on consumer bankruptcy in Norway, Denmark, and Sweden. He observes that Norwegian courts regularly "refuse to give the debtor a discharge of debts, if such a solution would be morally offensive" (ibid., 166). This situation often arises where they deem a petitioner's income simply "too high" or find that he is "unemployed voluntarily" (ibid., 167). This detailed scrutiny is greater than in the U.S. law on "clawbacks" of the insolvent person's recent expenditures and asset transfers.

60. Ahern 2005, 588, 616.

61. Mullainathan, Shafir, and Bertrand 2006. Robert Moffitt, the Krieger Eisenhour Professor of Economics at Johns Hopkins University, writes in personal correspondence (April 20, 2015) that the "take-up" rate for Supplemental Nutritional Assistance Program (Food Stamps) is probably at 60 to 70 percent of those eligible, and at less than 50 percent for the Temporary Assistance for Needy Families. As the term suggests, a "take-up rate" is the percentage of eligible parties actually claiming the benefits to which they are entitled.

62. Irving 2011, 3–4.

63. Moffitt 1981, 753–754.

64. Turner 2004, 277. This program was replaced in 1996 by the Temporary Assistance for Needy Families program, whose eligibility requirements are stricter.

65. Mullainathan, Shafir, and Bertrand 2006, 20–23.

66. Radnofsky 2016.

67. Ibid.

68. See, e.g., Colton 1997, 82, 92.

69. According to Hernanz, Malherbert, and Pellizzari (2004, 21), "the U.S. Food Stamp Program has often been perceived as being particularly subject to such effects, simply because recipients may feel stigmatized every time they go to a shop and use the stamps . . . Despite its vague definition, stigma . . . is considered as one of the main determinants of the observed low levels of take-up for most welfare benefits."

70. Moffitt (1983, 1023) observes, "The stigma has been amply documented in the sociological literature where interviews of recipients have often uncovered feelings of lack of self-respect and negative self-characterizations from participation in welfare."

71. In the conventional understanding, the term "shame" refers to the emotion experienced in recognizing that others judge one poorly, as having violated common moral standards. In feeling guilty, one instead judges oneself harshly by one's own lights, regardless of how forgiving or unforgiving others may be. This distinction has historically been of greater interest to philosophers and psychologists than to

sociologists. This is unfortunate because, as we'll later see, there is good reason to suspect that shame is a more potent potential stimulant to socially desirable behavior than is guilt, and hence more effective in hampering abusive rights-claiming.

72. Gilens (1999, 5) reports opinion surveys finding that most Americans want the state to assist those who are genuinely "trying to make it on their own," not those who take "advantage of the system." People who do not strive "to make it on their own" (ibid., 8) are disdained for free riding on the labors of others.

73. Moffitt (personal correspondence, April 20, 2015) remarks: "There is much speculation that prior to 1996, participation in AFDC was widely accepted and this kept the caseload high. But [thereafter] . . . the caseload dropped because low-income families felt it more stigmatizing." Take-up rates may be affected as well by variations in the activity of "welfare rights" movements that are expressly committed to "overcoming stigma" (ibid.). Thus, "in the 1960s, the National Welfare Rights Organization campaigned in low-income communities for families to apply for welfare, telling them it was their right" (ibid.). See generally Moffitt (1981, 1983).

74. The term "disability" refers, in the relevant U.S. legislation (42 U.S.C. §12101), to "a physical or mental impairment that substantially limits one or more major life activities." Courts have found that the "impairment" need be neither severe nor permanent.

75. This worldwide trend notably extends even to the People's Republic of China (Kohrman 2005).

76. Belkin (2018). The incidence of diagnosed disability at other colleges and universities is now frequently above ten percent, Belkin reports. "Wealthier students are more likely to receive accommodation than poor students," reports a leading lawyer in the field.

77. Ibid.

78. Biggs (2015a, 2915b).

79. Social Security Advisory Board 2006. Erving Goffman's groundbreaking treatment (1963, 12, 52, 117, 146) listed, in passing, physical disabilities as among the possible bases of social stigma, quoting poignantly from those suffering this form of stigma.

80. Social Security Advisory Board 2006.

81. Biggs (2015a, 2015b).

82. Ibid.

83. Ibid.

84. Autor 2011; Merline 2012.

85. Krueger 2017.

86. Von Wachter, Song, and Manchester 2011.

87. Collie et al. 2015, 18–19.

88. Chokshi (2014), referencing Bound, Lindner, and Waidmann (2014), notes that "as coal prices plummeted in the 1980s and threw the industry into a long-lasting crisis, disability insurance beneficiary rates in these regions skyrocketed."

89. Biggs 2015b.

90. Appelbaum (2014) reports, "Only 28 percent of men without jobs—compared to 58 percent of women—said a child under 18 lived with them." See also Kaiser Family Foundation/New York Times/CBS News 2014, 11.

91. Lerman and Wilcox 2014, 3.

92. Kaiser Family Foundation/New York Times/CBS News 2014, 29. American Community Survey Reports (2011, 9) concludes: "For those divorced in the past 12 months [of 2009], 18 percent of men were living with their own children, while 44 percent of such women were living with their own children."

93. Putnam 2015, 69.

94. Appelbaum (2014) reports that "44% of men in the survey said there were jobs in their area they could get but were not willing to take." The Kaiser Family Foundation/New York Times/CBS News poll (2014, 24–25, 28) to which this *New York Times* article refers further finds that 50 percent would not accept a job paying 25 percent less than the last job; 48 percent would not move to a different city; 57 percent are unwilling to commute more than an hour to a job.

95. Kaiser/New York Times/CBS News 2014, 20.

96. Appelbaum 2014; Kaiser/New York Times/CBS News poll 2014. Edward Lazear (2017), former chairmen of the President's Council of Economic Advisers, recently wrote, "Among young men, whose employment is low by historical standards, disability is not a major factor . . . [these] men are opting to spend their time at home in leisure activities, perhaps because their job opportunities are poor." Still, those who, during prime working years, "downshift" from conventional labor markets (middle-to-high-end) to enact an avowed "antiwork philosophy" tell ethnographers that they frequently feel ashamed of themselves, on account of moral expectations and pejorative judgments from family and friends (Frayne 2015, 10, 191–196, 202–206). In other words, though they experience it less powerfully, they too feel the force of social mores sustaining "the work ethic" in the rest of us.

97. This is what Hohfeld (1923) calls a "privilege," since others have "no right" (a term of art) to act in ways that would legally terminate his entitlement, though they may effectively block its effective exercise using rights of their own.

98. Zoghbi-Manrique-de-Lara 2010, 413.

99. Thus, for instance, in one recent incident Chinese industrial workers rebelled when management began newly enforcing strict rules on time limits governing bathroom visits (Associated Press 2013). The managers, held hostage by the workers, "were later freed when police intervened and when managers agreed to reconsider the rules."

100. Bolt and Houba 2002, 206. Shotwell (2012, 58–60, 74, 87–88, 124–127) offers the perspective of a shop floor worker and union activist. *Korea Times* 2016 describes a relevant recent incident.

101. Bloch and Moorman 1993, 170–174.

102. "Working to rule" does not violate U.S. labor law. However, section 7 of the National Labor Relations Act does not protect those participating from employer discipline, including discharge (*Lenox Educ. Assoc. vs. Labor Relations Commission,* 471 N.E.2d 81, 82–83; Jenero and Spognardi 1996, 130–132).

103. Simon 1996, 233.

104. Rome Statute of the International Criminal Court, Art. 8(2)(b)(iv).

105. For two recent examples under the federal False Claims Act (31 U.S.C., §3729), see, e.g., Dale 2011 and Kennerly 2009; under the 2010 Dodd-Frank law, see Engstrom 2017.

106. On the strength of the financial incentives created by *qui tam* statutes, see Vaughn 2013, 125–142.

107. Lipman 2012, 98.

108. Both Presidents George W. Bush and Barack Obama, in official "signing statements," expressed concerns that new legislative protections for whistle-blowers threatened to compromise protected governmental information (Obama 2009) and even, at times, to prejudice national security interests (Sandler 2007).

109. Lipman (2012, 57) quotes SEC general counsel David Becker to this effect. Anyone contemplating such revelation would be deeply sobered and likely deterred by learning that most whistle-blowers, even when vindicated by the proven accuracy of their accusations, "are in some way broken, unable to assimilate the experience . . . to come to terms with what they have learned about the world. Almost all say they wouldn't do it again" (Alford 2001, 1, reporting results of interviews).

110. Engel (2016, 175) summarizes his interview data to this effect.

111. Alford (2001, 1, 10, 19, 49, 118–119) describes how family members often oppose the decision to report, and sometimes entirely cease contact thereafter with the whistle-blower (Miceli and Near 1991, 63). This is a recurrent theme in the autobiographical reflections of whistle-blowers (see, e.g., Rost 2006, 1–3); compare Oppenheimer 2012 (quoting one whistle-blower as saying that even his own mother "was a little embarrassed by him"). To similar effect, Jackall (1988, 146) concludes from research interviews that "professionals who in some way blow the whistle on their colleagues . . . are particularly distrusted and feared."

112. It nonetheless remains impossible to determine, even to estimate confidently, the statistical incidence of corporate and governmental fraud.

113. Martindale-Hubbell Law Digests 2006a; Brashier 1996, 1 (citing statutes to this effect from many countries in both world regions).

114. Martindale-Hubbell Law Digests 2006b.

115. *Hodel v. Irving*, 481 U.S. 704, 718 (1987).

116. Brashier 1996, 11–12. Chester (1998, 5–6) cites opinion surveys from the late 1950s finding that "93% of respondents felt that a parent with no surviving spouse should not be able to disinherit children under twenty-one, and 63.4% believed such a parent should not be allowed to disinherit children twenty-one or older."

117. American Community Survey Reports 2011.

118. Rosenfeld 1998, 186.

119. The perceived wrongfulness of disinheriting a child, even a minor, does not reach the level of gravity involved in certain other cases here discussed, readers will observe. To recall, I have deliberately selected my illustrations of rights to do wrong with a view to introducing some "variance" on this factor.

120. Anderson and Arroyo i Amayuelas 2011, 12. On these issues, Beckert 2008 offers a helpful comparative history of European developments.

121. Beckert 2008, 31.

122. Ibid., 81.

123. Weber 1978 [1922], 370.

124. The discussion in this section draws heavily from Rajan and Zingales 2003, 4–5, 28–33.

125. De Soto 1989, 162.

126. Sengupta and Aubuchon 2008, 9, 12–13, 16–17.

127. Helms 2006, 97; see, generally, Goldberg 2005.

128. Several state supreme courts have reached this conclusion, on the basis of privacy rights to reproductive freedom. See, e.g., *Matter of Grady,* 426 A.2d 467, 472 (N.J. 1981); *Matter of Guardianship of Hayes,* 608 P. 2d 635, 640 (Wash. 1980); *Matter of A.W.,* 637 P. 2d 366, 368–369 (Colo. 1981).

129. *Skinner v. State of Okl. ex rel. Williamson,* 316 U.S. 535, 541 (1942).

130. Gordon 2003, 345. Even such states as Canada and Sweden continued the practice through the 1970s. During the twentieth century some 63,000 Americans were sterilized pursuant to such laws (Robitscher 1973, 1).

131. Rome Statute for the International Criminal Court, Art. 7(1)(g).

132. See, e.g., *In Re Guardianship of Hayes,* 93 Wash. 2d 228, 608 P2d 635 (1980).

133. AHC Media 2003.

134. When evidence is equivocal that informed consent has been truly given, courts generally reject the petition. When it is only the guardian petitioning for sterilization, rather than the parents as well, courts also regularly appoint a second guardian *ad litem,* so that the mentally disabled person may challenge the petition, notionally sought on his or her behalf. In several states, the law even presumes a conflict of interest between the mentally disabled person and her regular guardian (usually her biological parents) and treats the proceeding as "semi-adversarial" (see, e.g., *In re Grady,* 85 N.J. 235, 252, 1981). The party seeking the procedure must establish, often with evidence "clear and convincing," that it is genuinely "necessary," on the grounds that less invasive forms of contraception have been tried and found impracticable (see, e.g., *In re C.D.M.,* 627 P. 2d 607, 613, Alaska 1981).

135. On the advent and sociological implications of "reality TV," see Lorenzo-Dus and Garces-Conejos Blitvich 2013.

136. Until 1992 the American Association on Mental Retardation employed a classification system based on IQ score, designating degrees of "retardation" as mild, moderate, severe, or profound. The organization soon thereafter changed its name to the American Association on Intellectual Disability and Developmental Disabilities. It now categorizes degrees of intellectual disability on the basis of how much assistance an individual requires from others: intermittent, limited, extensive, or pervasive, in the current terminology.

137. There is increasing recognition that the concept of mental disability may therefore require some disaggregation. An individual may lack many mental capacities yet retain those most essential to parenting, notably the capacity for love. On the history of shifting terminological labels for those thus infirm, see Carlson 2005, 133–152.

138. Scott 1986, 816.

139. Human Rights Watch 2011; Kamenev 2013; Sowa 2015, 59–63; Taggart and Cousins 2014, 109; Barton-Hanson 2015, 57.

140. Taggart and Cousins 2014, 111–112; Barton-Hanson 2015, 58.

141. Owen and Griffiths 2009, 192–195; Llewellyn et al. 2010, xiii, 109.

142. Gould and Dodd 2014, 2. Past practices, as reported by Seagull and Scheurer (1986, 493), were little different.

143. There exists a spectrum of parental capabilities relevant to child-rearing, to be sure, and the many nuances involved in distinguishing pertinent breakpoints along this spectrum counsel strongly against simple generalization here.

144. But see Gundersen, Young, and Pettersen 2012, 282, describing the serious challenges faced by experienced social workers in seeking to teach child-rearing skills to parents with intellectual disabilities.

145. Nussbaum (2010, 75–95) argues for extensive use of court-appointed guardians in assisting mentally disabled persons to exercise possible rights to vote and sit on juries.

146. Tymchuk 2009, 59.

147. One might respond that their mental disabilities will often limit their recognition that they are being targeted by stigma. We may still be troubled at the increasing reliance of public policy on deliberate efforts to stigmatize disfavored behavior (efforts urged in, for instance, Bayer 2008 and Callahan 2013), on grounds independent of stigma's full conscious appreciation by immediate victims.

148. Kolben (2011) indicates the limitations of legal regulation at both the international and national levels (in many countries) for protecting workers, those integrated through subcontracting into global supply chains.

149. See, generally, Klein, Smith, and John 2004.

150. See the Report of the Special Representative of the UN Secretary-General for Business and Human Rights, A/HRC/17/31/Add.1, at paras. 29–30.

151. U.N. Global Compact, §II.11.

152. Maitland 1997.

153. On the use of social media in political mobilization, see Fung and Shkabatur 2015, 155–177.

154. See, generally, Glickman 2009, 1–27; Van der Made and Heijnan 2009.

155. On "moralization" as a social scientific concept, amenable to empirical investigation, see Rozin, Markwith, and Stoess 1997, 67 (defining moralization as "a process . . . in which objects and activities that were previously morally neutral acquire a moral component . . . converting preferences into values").

156. Bartley and Child 2014, 669, 673. In the apparel and footwear sectors, at least, large companies that have actively sought and achieved public reputations for "corporate social responsibility" are, ironically, those most likely to draw the attention of labor activists seeking to shame industry management into improving treatment of workers far down the commodity chain.

157. Delacote 2006.

158. See, generally, Ruggie 2007.

159. Advocates for "corporate social responsibility" extol the commercial advantage gained through improved reputation among consumers. The empirical evidence in support of this "business case for virtue" is not strong (Vogel 2006, 54–55; Barnett and Solomon 2012), however, as corporate leaders must recognize. Market incentives to raise ethical standards much above the legally mandatory may therefore remain weak.

160. It would not be difficult to construct a formal model for these alternative scenarios, but such a theoretical construct would tell us little about how or when the circumstances to which they pertain actually arise. Other methods are preferable here. In one careful ethnography, for instance, Rees (1994) concludes that nuclear power within the United States is today an industry in which, in the lingering ethical shadow of the Three Mile Island crisis, self-regulation works quite well. He finds "a well-defined industrial morality that is backed by enough communal pressure to institutionalize responsibility among its members" (67).

161. Throughout this section I rely heavily on conversations with Willard L. Boyd, who served for many years as president of Chicago's Field Museum, which faced several calls for repatriation.

162. Convention on the Means of Prohibiting and Preventing the Illicit Import, Export and Transfer of Ownership of Cultural Property, Nov. 14, 1970, 832 U.N.T.S. 231, Art. 7 (a) and (b)(i).

163. The effect was to "grandfather" works acquired before that date. It is frequently impossible, in any event, to prove that a given work once belonged to a presumptive, long-departed owner. Even if that were possible, there would nonetheless often exist at least one bona fide purchaser in the ensuing chain of possession. Customary international law establishes that the validity of a property transfer is governed by the laws of the sovereign state where the artifact is located at time of transfer. And the national laws of most countries exempt purchasers of stolen art, unaware of its unlawful provenance, from liability for its return (Goldberg 2006, 1039–1053; Montagu 1993, 79–81). There are still further obstacles to legal claims for repatriation, ensuring that any normative basis for such claims must lie beyond the law (see, generally, Merryman 2006).

164. Greenfield 1995, 259–261.

165. The Convention on Cultural Property Implementation Act, 19 U.S.C. §§2601–2613.

166. See, e.g., Democracy Now 2012.

167. Carvajal (2013) and Flessas (2013) describe several repatriation programs of recent years.

168. This has not always been easy. The directors and trustees of American museums generally owe fiduciary duties to citizens of the state of incorporation, precluding any wholesale repatriation of works lawfully within its collection.

169. The memoranda of understanding frequently impose country-specific import restrictions, a step not required by either the UNESCO Convention or the 1983 statute codifying it into U.S. law (Jowers 2003, 153).

170. In recent years American museums and those of other Western countries have repatriated a great deal of stolen art, worth hundreds of millions U.S. dollars

(Donadio 2014); Sgueglia (2011) reports that "since 2007, the U.S. customs agency has repatriated more than 2,500 items to more than 22 countries."

171. The only applicable legal duties of repatriation are those promulgated by the 1983 legislation, which governs only works acquired after that date.

172. When voicing their indignation, these leaders are nonetheless fully aware of similar claims by other source countries and the concessions granted to those states.

173. Hale (2009, 1, 20) may be correct in questioning the common assumption that there is something inherently or nontrivially immoral in exploiting the opportunities afforded by a cooperative scheme (subject to moral hazard). He observes that the dubious behavior at issue does not involve lying, cheating, or stealing. These do not, though, exhaust the realm of conduct generally considered wrongful. And because this is a work of sociology rather than philosophy, what concerns us here is what people widely deem immoral, not what morality—properly understood—may genuinely require.

174. Abraham 1986, 15–16, 35–36; Heimer 1985, 28–48.

175. Lenoir 2003, 382–390, 403–411.

176. In these terms Nyman (2007, 759) characterizes the prevailing view among economists (emphasis in original).

177. From this theoretical standpoint, it is possible to conclude that "in the moral hazard model, insurance makes the individual engage in immoral behavior" (Stone 1999–2000, 46).

178. The very few studies claiming to discover welfare losses from moral hazard, notably the RAND Health Insurance Experiment, are subject to serious methodological criticism (see, e.g., Nyman 2007, 760–762).

179. Farnsworth (2006, 253–259) summarizes empirical studies finding that as health insurance "deductibles" increase in amount, patients reduce reliance on their insurance, yet without significant decline in quantifiable measures of their health.

180. Or at least traditionally condemned, until economic theory began to "educate" the general public, perhaps.

181. Gabel, Mansfield, and Jones 2006, 654.

182. See especially Ericson and Doyle 2004, 322; Ericson, Doyle, and Barry 2003, 71–82, 106–114, 236–271.

183. Tennyson 2008, 1198. There is no legal right to engage in this type of wrongdoing, however, which means it does not entail a right to do wrong, as I employ the term.

184. Ericson, Doyle, and Barry 2003, 540–542.

185. Similar attitudes are evident in how U.S. citizens view tax evasion. Opinion surveys suggest that Americans regard this offense as the breach of a significant civic obligation. The federal government and many U.S. states thus regularly apply the criminal law. By contrast, several southern European states treat this form of wrongdoing as a mere regulatory offense, akin to most types of traffic violation, usually warranting only modest civil liability (Bogart 2011, 118–119).

186. Ericson and Doyle 2004, 150–152.

187. I owe this example to Tom Baker, a scholar of insurance law. Personal communication, Aug. 2012. See also Baker 2008.

188. Baker and Simon 2002, 273–281, 291–294.

189. Hacker and O'Leary 2012, viii, 4.

190. It is unclear, however, whether modestly curtailing the scope of insurance coverage genuinely induces many people to revise their self-understandings in responsibility-enhancing ways. Insurance companies remain greatly exercised over the inducements to moral hazard that are unavoidably latent within their products. This suggests that insurance has not yet transformed our intimate self-assessments in ways Foucaultians like Simon, Baker, Ericson, and Doyle maintain, to varying degrees. Unless insurance companies are greatly mistaken, efforts to harness their products to the task of constituting a "self-policing neoliberal subject" have not been especially effective in overcoming temptations to moral hazard.

191. Consistent with common social scientific usage, I employ the term "modernity" as an ideal-type for societies that display high levels of literacy, per capita GDP, urbanization, scientific activity, secularity, advanced industry, and mobility (social and geographical).

192. Yi et al. 1993; Xue 2010.

193. Dworkin 2011, 376–378. He does not conclude that the law must enforce such an ethical duty.

194. 410 U.S. 113 (1973).

195. Glendon (1987, 145–150) identifies several countries in Western Europe where abortion was then available only "for good cause," with these "causes" specified by statute.

196. KRC/Boston Globe Poll 1987, 7; Granberg and Granberg 1980, 252. The distribution of this belief no doubt varies by social milieu. These particular surveys are also dated, moreover, but more recent ones on the particular question do not exist.

197. Pew Research Center 2012a, 2012b; Rasmussen Reports 2012; Gallup Polling 2012.

198. Shellenberg (2010, 138–149) finds that 67 percent of abortion patients report that they would feel stigma if others learned of their decision. Fifty-eight percent of women reported that they sought to keep their abortion a secret from friends and family.

199. Nieves 2005.

200. The incidence of abortion peaked in the 1980s and has declined since 1990. For relevant data and its explanation, see Guttmacher 2011.

201. There was almost no such concern during the colonial era, when treatment was correspondingly much harsher (Gallay 1987, 370).

202. Patterson (1982, 73).

203. The extent to which legal reforms significantly moderated slaveholder behavior is subject to some dispute among historians. For this debate, see Morris 1996, 182–183; Fede 1985, 93, 101, 132; Rose 1982, 23, 30–31.

204. Gallay 1987, 392. It is of some interest that, in ancient Greece, Plato engaged in a similar moral suasion, counseling "masters" that they "should be especially

careful to do justice to their slaves, because they are persons toward which it is easy to be unjust" (Morrow 1939, 42, characterizing Plato's views). Plato nonetheless concluded that these "are obligations of conscience, not legal obligations which he can be compelled to perform in the city's courts" (ibid.).

205. Gross (2000, 112) observes the greater ease in securing findings of civil than criminal liability.

206. Ibid., 98; see also Morris 1996, 182–83.

207. Gross 2000, 98, 109; see also Morris 1996, 182–183.

208. Gross 2000, 117.

209. Influential reformers on these and related issues included John Belton O'Neall of South Carolina and Thomas R. Cobb of Georgia. Rose (1982, 23–24) describes several other legal restrictions that were increasingly imposed on the permissible treatment of slaves.

210. Gross 2000, 110.

211. Cottrol 1987, 367.

212. Rose 1982, 27.

213. Fisher 1993, 1077.

214. Gross 2000, 112.

215. Davis 2006, 224; Genovese 1974, 5.

216. Personal correspondence with Ariela Gross, professor of law, University of Southern California, a historian of U.S. slave law, June 2013. In answer to abolitionists, Southern newspaper editors also proudly invoked "freedom suits" as evidence that slavery was coming under the governance of a true "rule of law." While radical abolitionists saw no possibility of compromise with the institution, "for a time the more moderate abolitionists," writes David Brion Davis (2006, 224), "searched for a means to ameliorate this conflict" of interest between slave and master.

217. Cottrol (1987, 366) writes that "the paternalistic ideal" was "honored in both breach and observance . . . If the paternalistic ideal did not totally govern the behavior of slave owners, it nonetheless set norms that influenced that behavior." In fact, disinterested Northern visitors confirmed slaveholders' self-assessment in this regard, as have certain recent historians (Genovese and Genovese 2011, 61–62).

218. Genovese 1974, 97–112; Davis 2006, 223.

219. Genovese and Genovese 2011, 61.

220. Ibid., 66.

221. Davis 2006, 262.

222. Genovese 1974, 5; Genovese and Genovese 2011, 66; Cottrol 1987, 367.

223. Genovese 1974, 3–7, 89–91, 133–147. The paternalistic ideal sometimes found its way into legal arguments before Southern courts on behalf of slaves who had been mistreated by their masters (Gross 2000, 102; Cottrol 1987, 366–368). Prosecutors and plaintiffs' counsel would contend that the slaveholder had violated customary duties to protect slaves from their own "helpless infantilism," which rendered them dependent on his superior strength and intelligence, traits bestowing a "custodial responsibility" analogous to that of a legal "guardian" (de Lombard 2002, 94–96). In this way, their legal arguments sought to incorporate

obligations established by norms of common morality. But see Oakes (1982, 8), who contends that masters owning few slaves, i.e., slave owners who were not members of the plantation gentry, often rejected the paternalistic notion of "mutual obligations."

224. Genovese and Genovese 2011, 70.

225. Ibid., 31.

226. Kolchin 1983, 586.

227. Ibid., 587.

228. Genovese and Genovese 2011, 31; Patterson 1982, 73.

229. See generally Genovese 1965, 306–324.

230. Genovese and Genovese 2011, 68.

231. In other words, plantation owners sought in paternalist ideology a basis for morally distinguishing their treatment of slaves from that, allegedly far worse, accorded to industrial workers by Northern and English factory owners.

232. This was a central theme in the proslavery apologetics of Henry Hughes and George Fitzhugh, in particular.

233. Gross 2000, 120, 121.

234. Gallay 1987, 392–393; Genovese and Genovese 2011, 30.

235. Rose 1982, 27. Throughout the pre-independence period in Spanish America, too, the law permitted slaves, when alleging cruelty, to appeal for mercy to the King or his representative, allowing in principle some amelioration of servitude's harshness. The Catholic Church sometimes pressed for moderation as well (Genovese 1974, 178). These efforts offer "an example of trying to attenuate the injustices associated with slavery in order to maintain or enhance its legitimacy," writes Zephyr Frank, professor of history, Stanford University, a scholar of Latin American slavery. Personal correspondence, July 2013. Yet in practice, neither the Church nor Royal authority apparently offered slaves in Latin America effective protection against cruel masters (Mintz 2011, 1).

236. Rose 1982, 30.

237. Ibid., 31; Kolchin 1983, 601.

238. Rose 1982, 27, and, generally, 22–27; Gallay 1987, 370.

239. Morris 1996, 182; Patterson 1967, 77.

240. Genovese (1974, 5, 28–31, 91, 135, 147–148, 569, 575, 584) regularly employs this term. Gross (2000, 110–111) describes "the freedoms slaves had carved out for themselves: cultivating a garden patch, trading in an underground economy, drinking liquor, owning dogs or guns"; see also Gallay 1987, 394. Patterson (1967, 77, 278) explains how, in Jamaica from 1780 through 1817, "the slave had managed to extract certain customary rights which were more often than not respected by his masters . . . the laws of this period became largely a codification of what was already prevalent in custom" (77).

241. Rose 1982, 31.

242. Scott 1985, 29–36, 281–289.

243. Rose 1982, 32.

244. Blassingame 1979. Kolchin (1983, 581) contends, "If once historians lamented the psychological damage wrought upon the victims of bondage, now they

often praise black cultural institutions—religion, family, community, quarters—for protecting blacks from the worst rigors of slavery and for enabling them to lead fulfilling lives."

245. Genovese 1974, 91–93, 133–147; Sinha 2004, 5 (analyzing Genovese's views).

246. Starting in the 1830s, Southern pro-slavery views apparently hardened, as leaders increasingly invoked the Bible, explicitly defending the institution as divinely sanctioned (Davis 2006, 186–192).

247. On the psychological process involved here, illustrated through notorious historical cases, see Scheff and Retzinger 2001, x, xiii, 147–163, 172.

248. McAdams 1997, 376–381.

249. Knoch et al. 2009. Sheffrin (2013, 38–43) summarizes recent experimental research in which participants engage in "ultimatum" and "dictator" games. See also Feng, Krueger, and Luo 2015, 592, 596–599. Bruno Frey and Ernst Fehr offered the key early studies.

250. See, e.g., Khan and Gopal 2017.

251. I refer here to situations where the medical patient has not been hospitalized and therefore enjoys greater effective freedom of movement than when subject to continuous professional surveillance.

252. Opinion surveys vary somewhat in how much support they find among Americans for a patient's right to die. A Pew poll (Pew Research Center 2013c) found 66 percent in support, while a Rasmussen poll (Rasmussen Reports 2015) discovered only 52 percent. A recent Gallup survey (Swift 2016) discloses that 69 percent are willing to let physicians assist certain patients, with advanced terminal conditions, in ending their lives. Heavily responsible for this considerable variation is the fact that respondents' answers vary in their statistical distribution in light of how the question is formulated. In this, there is little consistency across these several surveys.

253. A "privilege" entitles its holder to inflict an injury that is either not legally cognizable or is otherwise lacking in legal remedy.

254. Black 1976, 3–6, 12, 17, 19, 20–21.

255. See 42 U.S.C.A. §3604(d) (2006).

256. A New York Times Board Editorial (2015) describes recent studies concluding that real estate agents continue to steer African-American couples away from majority white neighborhoods.

257. Often these opponents actually claim that the person whose activities they resist does not truly hold the right he thinks he does, in which case there exists simply a difference of opinion over the scope of the relevant right.

258. Several distinguished thinkers offer alternative accounts of how this kind of opaqueness is possible, and differ too over what it tends to conceal from consciousness. In this light, one may appreciate key notions in the thought of Michael Polanyi ("tacit knowledge"), Pierre Bourdieu ("habitus"), and Charles Taylor ("social practices"), as well as John Searle ("the background"). Where these diverse thinkers part company from one another is much less important for present purposes than where they agree. Most owe a good deal to Wittgenstein's analysis of

"the ordinary," and all are concerned, in Searle's (1983) piquant formulation, with "the precondition of intentionality . . . invisible to intentionality as the eye which sees is invisible to itself" (157).

259. Ibid., 154.

260. Wittgenstein 1953, 50, §129.

261. *Walmart Stores, Inc. v. Dukes,* 131 S. Ct. 2541, 2553–2554 (2011) (Ginsberg, J., dissenting).

262. The greater sin here lies in too little detail than in too much. Still, it is easy to quibble that I've not offered enough factual specificity to fully fathom any given illustration. The underlying problem is that we lack a general account of the measure of description necessary and sufficient to such an undertaking. My decisions on where to start and when to stop are hence somewhat ad hoc.

263. Any method for selecting illustrations, informed by any theoretical stance on what is most at issue, would be subject to methodological objections of one sort or another. The empirical examples this book employs are chosen on no particular basis whatever, apart from a desire to demonstrate the breadth of legal fields in which present issues arise. It would have been easy to select an entirely different set of case examples, equally illustrative of my contentions.

## 3. Three Rights to Do Wrong

1. Gleick (1996, 84) reports data indicating that "two-thirds of all divorces involve minor children."

2. I do not refer here to the views of religious conservatives, who had already long been militantly opposed.

3. Tushnet 1998, 2617.

4. Considerable scholarship finds that when parents divorce, their children—particularly young children—"typically experience family breakdown and the consequent disruption to their everyday lives as a form of crisis" (Butler 2003, 33). Compared with those raised in continuously two-parent families, these children more often experience "behavioral, emotional, health, and academic problems" (Clarke and Alison-Brentano 2006, 107). D'Onofrio (2011, 1) summarizes studies concluding that "parental separation/divorce is associated with academic difficulties, including lower grades and prematurely dropping out of school, and greater disruptive behaviors, such as being oppositional with authority figures, getting into fights, stealing, and using and abusing alcohol and illegal drugs." Biblarz and Raftery (1999, 357) find that divorce reduces the probability that children of middle- and upper-middle-class parents will achieve socioeconomic status equivalent to or higher than their parents. Young children of divorcing parents are less physically healthy, struggle to adjust socially, and experience "more subtle" emotional costs, such as pervasive anxiety (Clarke and Alison-Brentano 2006, 107–108). Though the correlations here are strong, it is ultimately difficult, as in many such studies, to infer an equally strong causal relationship, given that the harms children suffer at these times also correlate with dysfunctional family dynamics

and socioeconomic deprivation (Jeynes 2008, 107–130), which offer alternative explanatory hypotheses.

5. U.S. Census Bureau 2011, table 1335.

6. Autor and Wasserman 2013, 37–38.

7. See, among others, La. Rev. Stat. Ann. §9:307(A)(6) (2008) (increasing the waiting period for divorce from six months to eighteen months if the parents have a minor child and were wedded via "covenant marriage," a novel legal institution described herein).

8. Parke (2003, 7) thus concludes that "marriage may or may not make children better off, depending on whether the marriage is 'healthy' and 'stable.'"

9. Curtin et al. 2014.

10. There are, of course, several other causes as well, unimportant for present purposes.

11. One should here add the qualification that, even on issues conventionally labeled "moral" in character, it is mistaken to assume that public attitudes, expressed in response to opinion researchers, invariably correspond to feelings of indignation, as opposed to simple dislike, irritation, annoyance, or alienation. Additional methods are necessary to tap such nuances in emotional register.

12. Kim (1997, 48) reports that 61 percent of Americans "thought divorce should be harder for couples with young children." The Democratic Party policy thinker and political theorist William Galston has urged, to similar effect, "that we could reconsider the availability of no-fault divorce in cases involving young children" (Galston 1988, 153). He proposed a mandatory waiting period of eighteen months for parents who are responsible for young children. Parents would also be legally "obliged to seek counseling and to reach a binding agreement that truly safeguards their children's future" (Galston 1991, 85–86).

13. Orten and Wilson 1982, 408.

14. Scott 2001, 114–115; Cahn 1997, 242; Regan 2001, 119–120.

15. Stewart 1999, 522, 529, 535.

16. Putnam 2015, 75–76; Baylor University 2014.

17. Pew Research Center 2010a; Bramlett and Mosher 2002, 30–31. In the United States the median income of Christian evangelicals is significantly lower than that of the upper-middle class (Sullivan 2010; Pyle 2006).

18. Grundgesetz für die Bundesrepublik Deutschland [German Basic Law], Art. 6.

19. Waldron's looseness of formulation here—candidly self-acknowledged—itself reveals our current difficulty in precisely delineating the nature of this connection.

20. Waldron 2011, 8.

21. That would be especially so if the child was already manifesting strong indications of emotional disequilibrium.

22. *Cruzan v. Director, Missouri Dept. of Health,* 497 U.S. 261 (1990). Among U.S. states, the law varies somewhat regarding the evidentiary standard for establishing a patient's intention to this effect.

23. See, e.g., *In re Quinlan,* 355 A.2d 647, 664 (N.J. 1976). The Pew Research Center (2006) found that over 80 percent of Americans support the legal right to

decline medical treatment, but only 46 percent approve of physician-assisted suicide. Consistent with this pattern of views, American law has approached the possibility of assisted suicide with much greater caution than the right to treatment withdrawal. The U.S. Supreme Court, overruling two federal Circuit Courts, held that there exists no constitutional right to assistance in committing suicide, and only two states have authorized the practice by statute.

For physicians to assist in suicide would require them to make very difficult, case-specific judgments that the suicide-seeker is in fact acting autonomously, not impulsively or in an ephemeral state of despair, nor in a state of clinical depression, and not subjected to undue influence by family members. The medical profession is understandably very wary of allowing its members to become embroiled in such determinations. Any later legal challenge to a physician's decision in a given case would also entail great governmental intrusion into the privacy of the doctor–patient relationship. The result is that nearly half the U.S. public finds morally acceptable a practice that the law continues to proscribe.

24. Orentlicher 2001, 67. See, e.g., *In re Conroy,* 468 A.2d 1209, 1225–1226 (N.J. 1985). The practices of other countries vary significantly here, with only Canada and the UK fully adopting the current U.S. approach (Sprung and Eidelman 1996).

25. Bronsteen, Buccafusco, and Masur 2008, 1526.

26. The official position of the Catholic Church has been that suicide is a mortal sin, and the public stance of most Protestant denominations is similar. This posture and its secular residues within lay opinion ensure that a certain stigma continues to attach to suicide attempts, even if the successful suicide victim frequently elicits pity as well. The possibility of enduring this stigma may weigh seriously into the decision to attempt suicide, since a high proportion of such attempts fail, leaving one to face the moralizing music. According to Richard Posner (2012), when a physician assists in the suicide, this is not the case. The reputational "costs of suicide . . . all disappear if a physician is the agent of death . . . validating its propriety." Sympathetic observers are then free to characterize the death "as lawful medical 'treatment.'"

27. Saad 2001.

28. Orentlicher (2001) reports, "I have heard many doctors describe cases in which they have imposed unwanted life-sustaining treatment on relatively healthy patients. In such cases the physicians indicated their belief that patients should not be able to decline care that would give them the opportunity for many years of healthy life" (69). Orentlicher is a physician, law professor, and consultant to hospitals, who long served as director of the Division of Medical Ethics for the American Medical Association.

29. See, e.g., *Stamford Hospital v. Vega,* 674 A.2d 821, 826 (Conn. 1996); *Fosmire v. Nicoleau,* 551 N.E.2d 77, 79 (N.Y. 1990); *In re Estate of Dorone,* 534 A.2d 452, 455 (Pa. 1987).

30. Miller (1981, 22) describes incidents of "manipulation and undue influence" by physicians and family members as the "less forceful, but more pervasive cousins . . . of coercion." Through ethnographic immersion in several hospital

settings, Zussman (1992, 88) shows how the wishes of family members become increasingly influential on physician conduct as the condition of an intensive-care patient deteriorates and she becomes progressively unable to assert her wishes.

31. Trials courts have occasionally ordered not only young children but also adult parents of young children to undergo lifesaving medical treatment, usually blood transfusions for Jehovah's Witnesses. There is little legal basis for such judicial orders, however, as Orentlicher (2001, 69) observes, and therefore plaintiffs (prospective recipients) sometimes prevail. Measuring their damages presents difficulties, however, because this requires attaching a dollar value to their right to choose death over continued life—a perplexing and unresolved legal puzzle.

32. Many clinicians consider themselves under no legal duty to respect the expressed desire of a nonterminal patient (often one suffering only an ephemeral crisis) to decline essential life-sustaining treatment (Solomon et al. 1992, 14, 20). This has long been the case. Ethnographers who examine end-of-life decision-making reach sobering conclusions about law's efficacy in protecting patients' rights. Zussman (1992, 220) thus writes, "Although physicians often complain about the law [of informed consent], they know little of its details and often ignore its mandates . . . [E]ven in the occasional instances in which patients do withhold consent from procedures physicians wish to initiate, physicians often proceed on their own inclinations." To similar effect, Anspach (1993) observes, "The decision-making process was organized to limit the options available to parents [concerning withdrawal vs. maintenance of life-sustenance for neonates] and to eliminate parents from some decisions altogether . . . staff usually do not employ an informed consent model but rather use practices designed to elicit parents' assent to decisions professionals have already made" (96, 124). A third ethnography (Seymour 2001, 84) describes one hospital's "general strategy of eliciting agreement to decisions that have already been made" as a means to "diffuse responsibility for death by drawing . . . patients' families into the decision-making process." In an older study, Millman (1976) describes hospital practices by which medical personnel routinely deprecated patients' apprehensions about risky surgery, practices through which "the patient loses whatever small amount of autonomy he held" (198).

33. Smith 2012, 187.

34. This is no longer a very familiar idiom, to be sure. Within everyday patois, Americans do sometimes exhort, "You owe it to yourself" to do this or that. Yet if ordinary language retains these moth-eaten nostrums, it does so well to the rear of its closet.

35. *In re Quinlan,* 355 A.2d 647, 664 (N.J. 1976).

36. Orentlicher 2001, 67.

37. Whether we genuinely have duties to ourselves is a notion much contested within moral philosophy. Kant (2001 [1797], 122128) influentially defends the idea, but skeptics have been and remain legion.

38. Orentlicher 2001, 16. There was particular concern that such judicial determinations would come to rely implicitly on utilitarian assessments of the patient's

societal value, rather than on deontological notions of her inherent worth and dignity as a human being (ibid., 71).

39. Ibid., 21.

40. Empirical studies raise serious questions over how well those serving as legal proxies adequately understand and act upon their fiduciary duty to honor the patient's wishes regarding nontreatment (Emanuel and Emanuel 1992, 2068–2069).

41. Further complicating many situations is a lack of clarity over what is going through the minds of family members and medical caregivers. In rejecting the patient's wish to decline treatment, are they negating her decision to invoke that right (at times by treating evidence of such intention as "ambiguous")? Or are they instead effectively refusing to recognize that right at all, denying that it exists? In either case, there is no legal basis for overriding her choice and imposing their own. A patient's oral expressions of intention regarding emergency resuscitation, in particular, are often genuinely ambiguous, to be sure, in that they may shift from one day to the next (Kaufman 2005, 259–266, 272), in relation to his or her level of suffering.

42. See, e.g., Hardin and Yusufaly 2004, 1531; Collins, Parks, and Winter 2006, 379; Burkle et al. 2012; Beach and Morrison 2002, 2060; Geppert 2010, 4; Shapiro 2015, 524; Lynch, Mathes, and Sawicki 2008, 177 (discussing the consistent failure of many physicians to honor the terms of advance directives calling for withdrawal of life support, concluding that "the current legal structure has proven impotent to resolve this problem"). Physicians' resistance to advance directives has been still greater in certain other Western countries (such as France), where doctors take pride in "focusing not only on patient wishes but also on physicians' responsibilities to . . . vulnerable patients" (Horn 2014, 427).

43. Emanuel 1993, 9, 13.

44. Merz and Fischhoff 1990, 323–333.

45. This occurs both where common morality endorses such professional intercession, because the patient's ailment is readily treatable, and where it does not, because she is clearly, inexorably near to death. Data suggest (Pew Research Center 2013c; Swift 2016) that most Americans believe that medical caregivers should honor the wishes of these latter patients.

46. "Virtue ethics" regards a person's moral character as the key element in understanding and appraising her actions. Other ethical theories are not insensitive to virtue. Yet as Hursthouse and Pettigrove (2016) observe, "Whereas consequentialists will define virtues as traits that yield good consequences and deontologists will define them as traits possessed by those who reliably fulfill their duties, virtue ethicists will resist the attempt to define virtues in terms of some other concept that is taken to be more fundamental."

47. Waldron (2011, 22, 26) locates this view within a long history of Christian and early modern thought denying that we possess "a pure right of willful choice" regarding how we treat our body. Instead, "every human being is treated as a repository (but not a proprietor) of a parcel of human dignity, in the name of which that person may be subjected to a number of obligations that have to do with this

parcel's preservation" (ibid., 22). This language has an odd ring to the modern ear. A more contemporary mode of speech would surely be preferable, to give adequate and more felicitous expression to the abiding impulse most people clearly feel to dissuade certain patients (those facing only ephemeral crises) from exercising their legal right to die. Waldron writes that he is unsure about how to classify "the right to refuse life-saving treatment in all circumstances" within a satisfactory understanding of moral rights. He nonetheless suggests that this right may fit aptly within his concept of "responsibility-rights," those to which certain responsibilities attach naturally and inextricably (see Chapter 12).

48. People often colloquially describe this as "proportionality" in "collateral damage," though strictly speaking these are not the applicable legal terms.

49. I.C.R.C. (2010), Protocol Additional to the Geneva Conventions of 12 August 1949, and Relating to the Protection of Victims of International Armed Conflicts (Protocol I) art. 51(5)(b), Jun. 8, 1977, 1125 U.N.T.S. I-17512; Rome Statute for the International Criminal Court, Art. 8(2)(b)(iv), July 17, 1998, 2187 U.N.T.S. 90.

50. Dunoff, Ratner, and Wippman 2010, 851 ("Proportionality in self-defense is an ill-defined concept"); Henckaerts 2009, 470 ("The main problem with the principle of proportionality is not whether it exists, but what it means").

51. Hence the express decision of the ICTY prosecutor (UN International Criminal Tribunal 2000), when investigating the 1999 NATO bombing of Kosovo and Belgrade, to pursue only situations of alleged violations "where the excessiveness of the incidental damage was obvious."

52. Osiel 1999, 246.

53. Lieberman et al. 2005.

54. Janser 2007, 10, 13–14.

55. Commentators are also unsure whether the requirements of proportionality may be satisfactorily distinguished, in application, from those of "military necessity" and "feasible precautions" in protecting civilian interests, doctrines with which they appear to overlap. Nor is there much agreement on whether the mental state required for personal liability is subjective or objective.

56. Ronen (2009, 186) argues that current international law on the subject is "morally unsatisfactory" and endorses strict liability of states for battlefield harm to civilians. These concerns are not widely shared by the U.S. public, however. Tirman (2011, 12, 255) reports, from survey data and other credible evidence, "the public's blasé attitude toward non-American casualties."

57. Tirman (2011) correctly observes that "during the 1990s a sizable philosophical and activist complex had grown that specifically sought to report civilian tolls and assess culpability . . . Global civil society was taking up this challenge" (323). See also Tapp et al. 2008.

58. Pew Research Center 2012c.

59. This has been notably true of casualties resulting from U.S. drone attacks on terrorist leaders in Pakistan and Afghanistan, and of Israel's 2009 Operation Cast Lead in Gaza. For the 2003–2011 war in Iraq, civilian deaths as a proportion of all war-related deaths were credibly estimated at 75 to 90 percent (O'Hanlon and

Campbell 2007, 8, 13–14). On the many obstacles to accuracy in counting civilian casualties, see Seybolt, Aronson, and Fischhoff 2013. There is some reason to suspect that the United States seriously underreports the extent of civilian casualties in Afghanistan and Iraq (Khan and Gopal 2017).

60. Masood and Walsh (2012) describe the "diplomatic deadlock . . . over Pakistani demands for an unconditional apology from the Obama administration for an airstrike" that killed twenty-four Pakistani troops.

61. Waldron (2011, 1114). He here echoes J. S. Mill, who writes in *On Liberty* (Mill 1989 [1851], 140) that, in ethical matters, "we owe to each other help to distinguish the better from the worse, and encouragement to choose the former and avoid the latter."

62. MacFarquhar and Bronner 2011.

63. Druckman 2012.

64. Dinstein 2010, 125.

65. Crawford 2013, 20, 56–57, 77, 94, 157.

66. Not all agree, of course. Some question whether incidental harm is wrongful, insofar as it is unintentional. International law itself adopts this stance, embracing Aquinas's doctrine of "double effect," which holds that when one's intentions are morally acceptable, it is not wrongful to cause harm as an undesired side-effect. Within philosophy, though, many find the theory of double effect unconvincing. Consequentialists stress that the harm produced is identical regardless of whether it is desired or merely anticipated. On different grounds, nonconsequentialists are often equally unpersuaded (see, e.g., Scanlon 2008, 8–36). Soldiers themselves often feel regret or remorse over causing collateral damage, suggesting that they believe they have done wrong in some genuine, if ill-defined, sense (Sherman 2010, 107–110). These sentiments are consistent with having a legal "excuse" and with rightly regarding oneself as morally blameless.

Recent work in experimental philosophy (Mueller, Solan, and Darley 2012) finds that most people regard the harm ensuing from a knowing infliction of risk as "intentional." If we therefore interpret "intention" to encompass much of the conduct here at issue, then the doctrine of "double effect" does not pertain and would not "excuse" it. Laboratory experiments (Robinson and Darley 1995, 124) further indicate that most people believe the criminal law should not treat knowing wrongdoers with much greater lenience than intentional wrongdoers. Thus, there is a greater lay willingness to punish recklessness and even simple negligence through criminal law than authorized in the United States or other common-law countries.

Even where common morality affords some recognition to double effect, the scope of this acceptance appears narrower than in the law. As its critics lament, international law does not uniformly require belligerents to *minimize* civilian harm, nor to accept whatever measure of risk proves necessary to that end (but see Art. 57 (2)(a)(ii), Protocol Additional (1) to the 1949 Geneva Conventions). The law instead generally demands that states and soldiers not specifically intend to harm civilians, nor to cause harm disproportionate to military gains. By all appearances, prevailing moral sensibilities throughout much of the world increasingly demand more than this, especially from wealthy democracies whose soldiers receive significant training in humanitarian norms.

In sum, many today regard the measure of collateral damage that is permissible under international law as not merely unfortunate or tragic, but wrongful. This would be true, as just indicated, regardless of whether one adopts the perspectives of moral theory, soldierly experience, or common morality.

67. Challenges to the legality of drone strikes are frequent but long focused largely on issues—such as violations of "territorial integrity"—unrelated to "proportionality," because attacks on terrorist leaders kill far fewer than does targeting large numbers of low-echelon fighters in training camps.

68. Tirman (2011, 310, 314–315) quotes several U.S. soldiers, some in testimony before Congress, asserting that their superiors authorized lethal force quite promiscuously, e.g., whenever soldiers believed themselves to face any nontrivial measure of danger. To similar effect, see Glantz and Swofford (2008, 17–19), quoting from testimony of Sergeant Jason Lemieux.

69. Schmitt (2015) writes: "American officials say they are not striking significant—and obvious—Islamic State targets out of fear that the attacks will accidentally kill civilians. Killing such innocents could . . . alienate both the local Sunni tribesmen, whose support is critical to ousting the militants, and Sunni Arab countries that are part of the American-led coalition."

70. Tirman 2011, 8.

71. Office of the Director of National Intelligence 2006.

72. Schmitt 2015.

73. U.S. Army and Marine Corps 2007, xxv ("An operation that kills five insurgents is counterproductive if collateral damage leads to the recruitment of fifty more insurgents."); see, generally, Ricks 2009, 24–31.

74. Tirman (2011, 8) rightly notes that "U.S. policy makers and other elites have often demonstrated sensitivity to the potential for a negative public reaction if the U.S. appears to be too unsympathetic to civilian suffering."

75. This is a recurrent theme throughout Sassaman (2008, 9). Colonel Sassaman received an official reprimand for failing to report abusive conduct by his troops; he then elected to accept early retirement. Many officers (and other soldiers) express fears of meeting such a fate. See, e.g., Mullaney 2009, 237–241, 279–292, 313–322; Antenori and Halberstadt 2006, 36–41, 137–194; Buzzell 2005, 6–63, 98–101, 130–139, 248–261; Campbell 2009, 128–130, 144–152, 166–179, 182–185, 198, 211–217; Fick 2005, 22, 182, 210, 237–243; Smithson 2009, 75–77, 102–107.

76. Many today are inclined to dismiss this notion as reflecting merely the self-promotional, self-interested inclinations of an established professional caste. Yet there is little doubt that for much of Western history, this virtue occupied a prominent place in the self-consciousness of many officers. Still, its demands initially focused more on preparing oneself to withstand great pain and personal suffering than on moderating their infliction on others (see, generally, Osiel 1999, 14–41), where its impact on self-understanding may be rather self-deceptive.

77. See Olsthoorn 2017, 78); Olsthoorn teaches military ethics at the Netherlands Defense Academy.

78. But see Osiel (2009, 329–350, 198), on how a version of this virtue inspired opposition by certain U.S. officers to prisoner abuse in Iraq and elsewhere.

79. See, generally, Pinker (2011, 1–30), for a recent statement of this view.

80. Author's interviews, Maxwell Air Force Base (November 2002).

81. Chivers (2012) quotes Navy F/A-18 pilot Layne McDowell, comparing current to earlier, more "robust" rules of engagement: "It's a different mission. It calls for a different mentality." But see Sassaman (2008): "My philosophy—and I think it's still sound—was to crush the ant with a sledgehammer (79) . . . Our primary purpose is to destroy the enemy with overwhelming force at every opportunity" (89). This older self-understanding, however, is no longer well-regarded, or at least publicly acknowledged as such, among upper reaches of the U.S. officer corps.

82. Krause 2002, 189. To make effective use of honor, in ways compatible with their defining principles, liberal societies must therefore find ways to ensure that "honor is less a function of artificially imposed social roles and status and more fully a function of individual action and character" (ibid., 181).

83. Ibid., 181. Unlike basic human dignity (or self-esteem and self-respect), honor is inevitably aristocratic in a sense, Krause believes. For "it requires a measure of courage and ambition that not all of us can or do muster" (ibid.; see also Spector 2009, 68–69).

84. See, e.g., Fisher 2012, 108–133; Stockdale 1995.

85. Author's interviews, Maxwell Air Force Base (2002). For his role in resisting the My Lai massacre, ex-warrant officer Hugh Thompson, for instance, was awarded the Soldier's Medal, the Army's highest commendation for bravery that does not involve direct contact with an enemy.

86. Felter and Shapiro 2017.

87. This is what Waldron contemplates in referring to a "responsibility-right," discussed in Chapter 12.

88. This is a property of all elite professions, certainly of lawyers (Osiel 1990, 2054–2064).

89. Eliot Cohen (1985, 208) correctly observes that in contemporary Western Europe especially, the military is "neglected—if not, indeed, despised—by the bulk of the population," and that therefore "armies fail to attract the best men."

90. To judge from op-eds in major world newspapers, notably in response to Israel's 2009 and 2014 Gaza operations, many nonlawyers appear to misunderstand proportionality as requiring that belligerent 1 bring about no more civilian losses to belligerent 2 than 1 has itself yet endured. Yet if proportionality were so understood, it would be impossible, as one scholar notes, "to explain most accepted exercises of self-defense, including Allied conduct in World War II. Most wars lead to more deaths than their triggering events" (Waters 2013, 221).

91. This duty is not yet well established either in common morality or prevailing understandings of martial honor. In such countries as Israel, however, regulations require any officer contemplating use of lethal force in the vicinity of civilians to carefully follow several determinate steps. She must obtain as much

pertinent information as reasonably possible. And if an operation proves prejudicial to civilian interests, the officer must be prepared to defend her decision by showing that all realistic alternatives were duly considered.

92. Chivers 2010; Sassaman 2008, 303, 141–143, 146, 259.

93. Bowman and Montagne 2009; French 2015; Wong 2015.

94. Kahl (2007, 36) observes that "compliance has improved over time as the military has adjusted its behavior in response to real and perceived violations of the norm."

95. Dadkhah 2010, 3.

96. Crawford 2013, 84–88, 110.

97. If the harm occurs on a battlefield, such victims have no right to recover damages under the Foreign Claims Act, due to its "combat exception." 10 U.S.C. §2736(a)(1) (2006). The U.S. military nonetheless often issues "condolence" payments (§2734), prompted by the considerations here described. Witt (2008, 1456) observes that "American-style damage payments are fast becoming one of the ways the twentieth-first-century U.S. military attempts to win the hearts and minds of civilians in war zones."

98. These include "directed energy systems" (i.e., heat rays), sticky foam, laser guns, and slippery gel (Koplow 2010, 161–178, 192, 194–198, 200, 204, 208, 242).

99. Wrage 2003, 85.

100. Mir and Moore 2018.

101. Sagan and Valentino (2016, 77) gathered experimental data on American attitudes toward alternative military strategies for destroying Iran's nuclear capabilities. They conclude that "the public's support for the principle of noncombatant immunity is shallow and easily overcome in war . . . the prospect of killing more noncombatants appeared to trigger beliefs in retribution and complicity" (1)—i.e., complicity by Iranian civilians in state policy.

102. This expression, which is not a legal term, refers to organized efforts by dominant groups in a population to eliminate a specific ethnic group from its territory.

103. Moyn 2010, 1.

104. Grotius 2001 [1625], bk. 2, chap. 24, 239 (urging moderation by military leaders in war).

## 4. How to "Abuse" a Right

1. Only rarely is this expression used publicly, and even then only to repudiate the very notion (see, e.g., Tribe 1981,144, 145, 146).

2. Robinson and Robinson 2018, 15.

3. Thurston 1991, 562.

4. I owe this observation to Hervé Arsenio, professor of public law, University of Paris, Panthéon Sorbonne, January 2018.

5. *Black's Law Dictionary* defines an officious intermeddler as "a person under no obligation to confer a benefit or privilege to another individual, but

who does so unilaterally. This person cannot expect anything in return for the performance."

6. Plaintiffs in antidiscrimination litigation prevail much less often than those in other civil lawsuits (Clermont and Schwab 2009, 128–129, reporting that 51 percent prevail in other such litigation but only 15 percent in suits alleging discrimination). And the percentage of antidiscrimination plaintiffs winning monetary awards has declined, as has the median amount of such awards (Nelson and Nielsen 2005, 38).

7. Galanter 1998a, 3–11.

8. See, e.g., Iowa Civil Jury Instructions (2004), Iowa Code §668A.1.

9. *Snyder v. Phelps*, 562 U.S. 443 (2011).

10. Schauer 1981, 227.

11. Schauer (1981, 225–235) conceives of an abuse of legal rights from the perspective of ordinary language in the English-speaking world, and hence examines how we use this colloquial expression in everyday speech.

12. Rosen 2006, 30 (discussing Karl Llewellyn's collaborative inquiries with anthropologist E. Adamson Hoebel).

13. Uniform Commercial Code, §2-302 (1952); Williston and Lord 2010, §18:7, 48.

14. Judge Skelly Wright quotes this wording, from William Corbin (*Contracts*, vol. 1, §128, 1963), in the leading case of *Williams v. Walke-Thomas Furniture Co.*, 350 F2d 445, 450 (D.C. Cir. 1965).

15. Berberich 2007, 7. Though the observation is widely attributed to Wilde, it does not appear in his published writings. On the etiquette governing such "instrumental rudeness," see, generally, Beebe 1995.

16. Satow 2009.

17. Sharp 2009, 206.

18. Within the United States, most state constitutions purport to require that one exercise one's speech rights "responsibly." New York's constitution, for instance, provides: "Every citizen may speak freely . . . on all subjects, being responsible for the abuse of such rights" (Friesen 2006, chap. 5, 109). That final clause is judicially unenforceable, however, if taken to encompass anything beyond the law itself, i.e., beyond existing prohibitions on defamation, incitement to violence, fraudulent misrepresentation, and obscenity.

19. See U.S. Internal Revenue Service 2017; Bankman 2004, 925.

20. Dawwas 1993, 3–4.

21. Schauer 1991, 31–34, 47–52.

22. See, generally, Laycock 2010, 122–124.

23. I refer here only to the legal rules now prevalent in these places, because the law of Continental Europe has varied greatly over its long history in accepting or rejecting, narrowing or enlarging, the "abuse of rights" doctrine (Lawson, 1950, 16–19).

24. The issue would arise either *ex ante*, in a petition to enjoin the defendant from exercising his right abusively, or *ex post*, in a cause of action for damages resulting from the alleged abuse.

25. For authoritative legal sources thus employing these expressions, see Byers 2002, 393, 396, 405, 406, 412, 428; Bolgár 1975. In a studiously opaque formulation, Lauterpacht (1966, 286–287) haughtily intoned that the doctrine of rights abuse comes into play when, "as a result of social changes unaccompanied by corresponding developments in the law, an assertion of a right grounded in existing law becomes mischievous and intolerable."

26. Instead of a generic notion of rights abuse, the common law developed a number of specific causes of action designed to prevent the abuse of *particular* rights. Thus, for the abuse of private property, there is the law of nuisance and of economic waste. For abuse in litigation, there are the rules against malicious prosecution and abuse of process. In tax law, there is the requirement of a "business purpose." Perillo (1995, 40) observes that these causes of action serve much the same function as Continental European law on abuse of rights.

27. Fletcher 2013, 158.

28. Ibid., 151.

29. Ibid., 157.

30. Ibid., 151.

31. Ibid.

32. Ibid., 161–162.

33. Ibid., 161.

34. Ibid., 152.

35. Ibid.

36. Ibid.

37. *Oberlandesgericht Celle,* Opinion of Dec. 5, 1947, in Mattei, Ruskola, and Gidi 2009, 951–953.

38. Fletcher 2013, 151, 159.

39. Larson 1950, 20.

40. See de la Feria and Vogenauer 2011.

41. See, e.g., Eidenmüller 2009.

42. Schammo 2008, 360–365.

43. See, e.g., *Sung Hwan Co. v. Rite Aid Corp.,* 850 N.E.2d 647, 650 (N.Y. 2006) ("The public policy inquiry rarely results in refusal to enforce a judgment unless it is 'inherently vicious, wicked or immoral, and shocking to the prevailing moral sense.'").

44. To similar effect, international trade agreements often expressly authorize parties to prohibit a product's importation when "necessary to protect public morals." WTO Agreement, Article XX(a). Though the Agreement does not define "public morals," a judgment of the Appellate Body has construed it broadly to "denote standards of right and wrong maintained by or on behalf of a community or nation." United States—Measures Affecting the Cross-Border Supply of Gambling and Betting Services, ¶3.278, WT/DS285/AB/R (Apr. 7, 2005).

45. See, e.g., *Leyla Şahin v. Turkey,* App. No. 44774/98, ¶99 (Eur. Ct. H.R. Nov. 10, 2005); *S.A.S. v. France,* App. No. 43835/11, ¶117 (Eur. Ct. H.R. July 1, 2014).

46. *Leyla Şahin v. Turkey,* ibid., ¶109; *S.A.S. v. France,* ibid., ¶129.

47. *S.A.S. v. France*, ibid., ¶131; *Leyla Şahin v. Turkey*, ibid., ¶110.

48. Getzler 2004, 315–316.

49. Herman 1977, 759. Sajó (2006, 29–30) adds that the abuse of rights doctrine "emerged as a reaction against the absolutism of possessive individualism . . . uninhibited individual initiative was increasingly seen in society to be the abusable privilege of the few."

50. Yiannopoulos 1994, 1195.

51. Herman 1977, 749.

52. Lawson 1950, 18.

53. Hazard 1947, 54–55.

54. Elkind 1976, 98.

55. Upon retiring from the bench in September 2017, Posner described himself as "proud to have promoted a pragmatic approach to judging," which he understood to entail "that judges should focus on the right and wrong in every case" (Meisner and O'Connell 2017).

56. Because the legislation rarely defines the key term—"abuse"—the result is to leave hard questions and line-drawing to courts and commentators.

57. Alterini and Cabana 1990, 1102, 1117.

58. Ibid., 1117.

59. Ibid., 1101–1102.

60. Roman law itself harbored a contrary aphorism, *sic utere jure tuo ut alienum non laedas:* one's exercise of individual rights may not inflict undue injury upon another.

61. Waldron 2012, 125–126, 227, 257–259.

62. Whether Waldron is correct in drawing these inferences about the cartoonist's intentions is open to dispute: what Waldron takes to be clearly a deliberate insult to all Danish Muslims, others interpret only as a satire of violent jihadis. Andrew March (2011, 817–818), a scholar of Islamic thought, offers this among other possible readings. Some of these do entail a desire to give offense to those besides terrorists and their sympathizers, yet often in ways from which no diverse society—"liberal" or otherwise, he suggests—should seek to protect its citizens.

March then seriously entertains Saba Mahmood's notion of "moral injury" (2009, 842, 848, 859–861), by which she sympathetically characterizes the visceral reaction to the cartoon among Muslims worldwide, a reaction taking lethal form in some countries. He painstakingly delineates the irremediable vagaries of this beguiling notion. March also observes how easily one might invoke it to defend the antipathy and opposition of most Americans to the prospect of a "Muslim Cultural Center" near the former World Trade Center. One might fairly add that, as best we can discern, strong sentiments amounting to what Mahmood describes as moral injury—discomfiting psychological arousal at others' perceived disrespect for one's spiritual identity—lay at the motivational roots of the 9/11 attacks themselves. These considerations give reason to doubt whether the law should grant any recognition to moral injury where that concept encompasses elements of harm not already enjoying legal protection on other grounds.

63. A stronger case for "abuse of right" in this connection would involve the "misuse [of] the secular license to insult religion as an alibi for creating a hostile environment for fellow citizens of Muslim cultural backgrounds" (March, 2011, 820) in the workplace or neighborhood.

64. But see de Morree (2016, 52–55), indicating that the European Court of Human Rights has sometimes classified "hate speech" as an abuse of the right to free speech.

65. Bulman-Pozen and Pozen 2015, 853. They claim, though without evidence, that the "abuse of right doctrine makes it easier for people in civil law countries to recognize hyperbolic adherence to the law as a potential 'abuse' of the system, rather than an unusually restrained mode of dissent" (i.e., compared to civil disobedience) (853).

66. Eleftheriadis 2009, 9.

67. Ibid., 8.

68. Universal Declaration of Human Rights, Art. 19. See also the International Covenant on Civil and Political Rights, Art. 19(2).

69. This core purpose of the doctrine has not found broader application simply because one easily escapes the accusation of malice by offering some account of how one undertook the questionable conduct in pursuit of material self-interest; and after all, perceived self-interest can credibly account for nearly all of business-related behavior. Often, harmful conduct that at first seems malicious and to offer no immediate gain for the party responsible, may actually serve, on closer scrutiny, to win legitimate bargaining chips in the negotiation of some unrelated dispute. The conduct is then no longer purely malicious. This is perhaps the only place in our law where—curiously, though not perversely—one may need to establish one's crassly materialist motives in order to escape liability for injuring another.

70. See, e.g., *Case of Trabelsi v. Belgium,* ECtHR, App. No. 140/10, 16/02/2015 (barring deportation for prosecution in another jurisdiction, where life imprisonment is permitted); *Case of Hirst v. U.K.,* ECtHR, App. No. 74025/01, 06/10/2005 (barring blanket prohibitions on voting by convicted prisoners); *Cases of Vinter and Others v. U.K.,* ECtHr, Applications Nos. 66069/09, 130/10, and 3896/10, 12/01/2012 (barring sentences of life imprisonment without formally providing for ongoing review, or for release on articulated grounds, known to prisoner upon sentencing).

71. Sandholtz, Bei, and Caldwell (2017) discuss several such major instances of national "backlash," as they describe it, in Trinidad and Tobago, the United Kingdom, Venezuela, Ecuador, the Dominican Republic, and Bolivia. In a case involving Uruguay (Gargarella 2015), the Inter-American Court of Human Rights effectively invalidated the result of a democratic plebiscite. Krisch (2008, 196) further reports several Western European instances of active opposition, from solidly democratic countries, to decisions from the European Court of Human Rights.

72. Stokes, Wike, and Poushter 2016, 27–30; Flogaitis, Swart, and Fraser 2013, 40–44.

73. Stokes 2016; YouGov 2014.

74. Sajó 2006, 42–55.

75. De la Feria and Vogenauer 2011. The quoted words provide the book's subtitle.

76. Sajó 2006, 29. The abuse of rights, he argues, extends to "claiming human (fundamental) rights . . . in ways that violate the fundamental rights of other people." Contributors to the volume "agree that in certain instances fundamental rights are used improperly, with troubling consequences, and that making us aware of such improprieties is necessary for the most efficient and just operation of the constitutional system."

77. Under the heading "Abuse of Rights" (Art. 17), the European Convention on Human Rights provides: "Nothing in this Convention may be interpreted as implying for any State, group or person any right to engage in any activity or perform any act aimed at the destruction of any of the rights and freedoms set forth herein or at their limitation to a greater extent than is provided for in the Convention."

78. In Art. 18, drafters of the European Convention on Human Rights were especially concerned with "the abuse of public power based on the rights of a public authority" (Sajó 2006, 35–36)—that is, the species of rights abuse that democratic states themselves might someday commit if and when their elected leaders take a profoundly illiberal or straightforwardly authoritarian turn.

79. Protocol to the Convention for the Protection of Human Rights and Fundamental Freedoms Right, 1952, Art. 3.

80. De Morree 2016, 23–97.

81. International Covenant on Civil and Political Rights, Art. 17(1); see also European Convention on Human Rights, Art. 8(1).

82. To be clear, I do not contend that such a claim would necessarily entail an abuse of right; that is a more specific assertion than is possible to develop here. For a recent pertinent case, see *YM (Uganda) v. Sec. of State for the Home Dept.*, Royal Courts of London, 2014 EWCA Civ. 1292, in which a Ugandan citizen convicted of terrorist offenses, and thereafter convicted of further crimes, successfully opposed his deportation for four years on grounds that this would violate his "right to family life," protected in the country's Human Rights Act, by allowing his children to be "exposed to AIDS."

83. Brunner 1977, 745.

84. Petrova (2004, 481–482) offers an unusually candid admission to this effect.

85. Waldron (2015) sympathetically entertains this idea in several recent publications, without straightforwardly endorsing it.

86. It should do so—that is, in the absence of compelling considerations to the contrary, presumably consequentialist in character.

87. Waldron (2011, 1130–1131) briefly discusses this practice and the European litigation arising from its prohibition.

88. *U.N. Human Rights Committee, Manuel Wackenheim v. France,* Comm. No. 854/1999, U.N. Doc. CCPR/C/75/D/854/1999 (July 15, 2002).

89. See, e.g., European Convention on Human Rights, Art. 3.

90. Waldron 2015, 122.

91. Waldron (2011, 1135) broaches in passing the possibility that the right to bear children may entail the responsibility not to abort a fetus.

92. Ibid.

93. On the origins of desuetude within Roman law, see Schiller 1994.

94. *Poe v. Ullman* 367 U.S. 497, 502 (1961).

95. A modern case to this effect is *Gilbert v. Barkes,* 987 S.W.2d 772 (1999), from the Kentucky Supreme Court, holding that the cause of action for "breach of promise to marry" no longer exists.

96. Some years after these causes of action fell into disuse, many U.S. states abolished them through statute. Several states continue to permit such lawsuits, however, which sometimes yield substantial damage judgments.

97. Vandervelde 1996, 835.

98. Strange and Cribb 2014, 1.

99. The romantic "dumpee," tempted to litigation, would today do better to commit to memory, if not to entirely heart, the mores of contemporary dating, including the etiquette of breaking up, as formally codified by two Yale law students (Rubin and Heller 1994) in their "Restatement of Love," a delicious mockery of our professional proclivity to juridify everything. They satirically lament how "the lack of codification in this area has left a rent in the otherwise seamless web of the law" (707).

100. Sauer 1978, 82, 84.

101. Hacking 1995, 99–120.

102. Kuran (1995, 4–7, 17–19), still the leading analysis of this, speaks of "preference falsification."

103. Abdalla 1982, 94–95; Lightfoot-Klein 1989, 99.

104. Dugger 2013.

105. Sunstein 1995, 756, 752; see also Waldron 2011, 1114. The incidence of abortion is today significantly lower in the United States than when Sunstein offered the figure of 1.5 abortions per year.

106. Sanger 2017, 22–23, 211–221.

107. Ibid., 211, 215–216.

108. Ibid., 226. There may be considerable value, to be sure, in a blog (or hotlines) pre-committed neither to encouraging nor discouraging abortion but instead to engaging the pregnant woman in a truly open-ended deliberation. To count as genuine, true to the stakes in issue, that conversation would necessarily have to raise certain moral questions inescapably implicated by a prospective decision to end the pregnancy, including questions concerning a possible "abuse of rights." What Sanger proposes—"de-stigmatizing" abortion (in all circumstances)—appears quite different, excluding the very possibility of rights-abuse, indeed of self-scrutiny on ethical grounds of any sort, even if the pregnant woman herself saw fit to raise such issues of her own accord. This suggests that Sanger (and Weitz) seek to entirely bracket out the moral questions as simply immaterial, as arising from a fundamental misunderstanding of what, properly understood, this medical procedure truly entails.

109. Ibid., 216.
110. Ibid., 226.
111. Ibid., 215 (emphasis added).
112. Ibid., 22–23.
113. Ibid., 223 (emphasis added).
114. Ibid., 219.
115. Ibid., 227.
116. Ibid., 225–226.
117. Weitz 2010, 163.
118. Sanger 2017, 226.
119. To so observe is not to deny the moral co-responsibility of male partners to employ contraception, of course. Still, many find it difficult to conceptualize this particular duty as attaching necessarily to any specific legal right deemed correlative to it, and therefore balk at interposing legal obligation. This may simply suggest an inherent limitation, however, in thinking about the general relation between rights and duties in that peculiar fashion (O'Neil 1996, 137–139), so characteristically modern yet historically idiosyncratic.
120. Weber 1958, 147. "The primary task of a useful teacher is to teach his students to recognize inconvenient facts—I mean facts that are inconvenient for their party positions. And for every party position there are facts that are extremely inconvenient." The title of Weber's essay is sometimes alternatively translated "Science as a Vocation."
121. Callahan 2014.
122. This is the same error committed, for instance, by *New Republic* editor Peter Beinart, discussed in the Introduction, during his defense of allowing an Islamic Cultural Center near the former World Trade Center.

## 5. Law and Morality in Ordinary Language and Social Science

1. It is often said that, like the decrepit musculature of the inertly aged, we won't have these rights when we truly need them if we don't use them when they're effortlessly at hand, when we are tempted to take them for granted. The metaphor is now unavailing, as recent studies show it possible for long-sedentary elderly to significantly improve strength and stamina through moderate exercise (Dorgo, Robinson, and Bader 2009, 116).
2. Mansfield 1992, 578.
3. This nonprofit institution, launched in 2002, offers as its mission statement: "We believe that citizens in a free and democratic society must actively shape the relationship between police and their community. That means people must be prepared to intelligently 'flex' their constitutional rights during contacts with police." See https://www.flexyourrights.org/.
4. Sunstein 2005.
5. Pellerano et al. (2017) offer the most recent empirical evidence of such "crowding out." Though many studies have by now confirmed its occurrence, we

lack much evidence of where and why it is stronger in some situations than in others. In many circumstances it may be weak, and therefore easily subject to override if incentives are increased (see, generally, Brennan and Jaworski 2016, 104–110).

6. Kahn 1999, 139.

7. As Lessig (1995, 1016, 1034–1039, 1042) and others observe, censoring disfavored speech is neither the most common nor usually the most effective method by which public authorities establish orthodoxies of viewpoint or of acceptable behavior.

8. Steinhauer 2016; Centers for Disease Control and Prevention 2016; Bogart 2011, 124 (citing statistics indicating that smoking among white teenagers failed to decline for more than a decade, and thereafter began to rise). Today nearly 20 percent of American adults are smokers.

9. Perkins 2003, 22, 86–87, 93–95, 138. Similar processes of interfirm isomorphism appear to affect compliance with environmental regulations (Cialdini 2007).

10. Lessig 1995.

11. On how human affairs become "medicalized"—that is, subject to the legal and cultural authority of the medical profession—see Conrad 2007.

12. Rozin and Singh 1999.

13. Bayer 2008; Callahan 2013, 38–40; but see Wiley 2013.

14. Benson (2008, 357) quotes promotional material from Philip Morris USA announcing, "Our goal is to be the most responsible . . . manufacturer and marketer of consumer products."

15. Kohrman 2005, 922 (describing tobacco advertising in China and elsewhere).

16. In American constitutional law, the regulation of "vice"—aimed at enhancing the population's "health, safety, and morals"—was uncontroversial even in the height of laissez-faire legal thought and doctrine (Hovenkamp 2015, 249–262).

17. Pew Research Center 2010b; Langer 2013; Keleher and Smith 2012, 1323–1324.

18. Ipsos Media 2013; Watercutter 2013.

19. Of efforts in the United States to win gay marital rights through litigation, Klarman (2013, 212) concludes, "Although litigation has clearly furthered the cause of gay marriage in some ways, it has also plainly retarded it in others." He identifies (at 212–215) several such drawbacks to that strategy of social change, notably very powerful "backlash" it regularly elicits among the many people who regard the issue as constitutionally delegated (or simply better consigned, as a normative matter) to the democratic branches of government.

20. Burke 1978, 207.

21. Ito (2010) quotes ACLU legal director Steven Shapiro: "You need a First Amendment to protect speech that people regard as intolerable or outrageous or offensive, because that is when the majority will wield its power to censor or suppress."

22. Public policies designed to gently "nudge" people into health-enhancing life choices thus elicit frequent criticism as unacceptably "paternalistic."

23. See, generally, Schweikard and Schmid (2013), who define collective intentionality as "the power of minds to be jointly directed at objects, matters of fact, states of affairs, goals, or values."

24. Jefferson 1975 [1771], 350.

25. Haidt 2003, 284.

26. Durkheim 1995 [1912], 218–220, 386–387, 398–399.

27. Alexander 1990, 27, 36–62, 47–49, 212–213.

28. Joas 2013, 60.

29. March 2012; compare Waldron 2012, 81.

30. *U.S. v. U.S. Dist. Court for Eastern Dist. of Mich.*, Southern Division, 407 U.S. 297, 314 (1972).

31. *Ward v. Rock Against Racism*, 491 U.S. 781, 797 (1989).

32. This view of freedom as consisting in the anarchic absence of discipline, including self-discipline, finds ample reflection in his early writings and interviews. Later lectures and publications adopt a far more nuanced and sympathetic stance toward self-discipline, however, as essential to reflective self-direction and creative self-fashioning, that is, to the salutary exercise of a genuine and appealing form of personal freedom.

33. Teymoori and Jetten 2016.

34. Austin 1975 [1962].

35. Harkness and Hitlin (2014, 463–465) summarize research in several countries finding differences in modes of expressing the moral emotions. Cross-cultural variation is notably broad concerning understandings of the word "disgust" and its close cognates in other languages (Rozin, Haidt, and McCauley 2000, 642–645).

36. Raised among British industrial workers, Hoggart (2003, 136–143) offered an arresting early sketch of how moralizing language was used in that milieu.

37. On the history of verbal 'dueling' among poor African-American males, often involving mocking accusations of incestuous, adulterous, and other morally suspect behavior, see, generally, Wald 2012, 32–34, 86–87, 103–104, 116–121 (describing "the dozens").

38. Several such works offer compelling accounts, dense in thick description, of how those who live in ethnic urban enclaves experience intensely and eloquently articulate a range of moral sentiments wholly familiar to those of higher socioeconomic status, approximating "mainstream" sentiments in many respects. See, e.g., Goffman 2014, 169, 171–172; Anderson 1999, 33, 36, 39, 44; Anderson 2003, 6, 31, 55–56, 210, 231; Duneier 1992, 26, 45, 65–67, 74, 133–134; Duneier 1999, 79, 341; Labov 1972, 251–253; G. Harkness 2014, 12; Suttles 1968, 172–176; compare Lamont 2000, 119, 128, 143, 146. The consistent subtext to this long tradition of urban sociology, initiated by the early "Chicago School," has been that we invariably find within such enclaves—where worried outsiders see only anomie and anarchy—genuine forms of "moral order" effectively governing whole neighborhoods and the lives of their individual inhabitants; to identify and carefully de-

lineate the exact terms of this moral order proves to be, in fact, the ethnographer's central mission.

Marxist scholars like Wacquant (2002, 1469–1470, 1504), however, find wholly abhorrent this scholarly effort (as he characterizes it) to present ghetto life in a form normatively acceptable, even appealing, to a readership of white upper-middle class college students. Wacquant condemns this scholarship as intolerably "moralistic," by which he means that it accords attention to the notions of personal responsibility evidently at work in the minds of community members as they assess one another's behavior. He would prefer that scholars focus exclusively on the larger economic structures of global inequality to which individual behavior is (in his view) chiefly attributable. In this conception of the social world, there is little place at all for the moral agency of individuals, and any talk of personal responsibility or irresponsibility serves only to conceal this overriding fact. Thus, to portray ghetto dwellers as "paragons of virtue" (ibid., 1469), as today's "moralizing sociology" allegedly does, is to "remain locked within the *prefabricated problematic* of public stereotypes and policy punditry" (emphasis in original). The moral lexicon of ghetto dwellers interests Wacquant scarcely at all, and only insofar as it may reflect their effective indoctrination or resistance to bourgeois ideology—that is, into bourgeois conceptions of morality. That ghetto residents, in their casual conversation, themselves mark out distinctions of moral merit among their peers can, from this standpoint, be only an embarrassment. Wacquant offers no careful argument nor serious evidence to warrant dismissing individual moral agency as entirely an ideological illusion. His repudiation of current urban ethnography on these grounds therefore amounts to no more than a radical militant's demand that we shift the conversation from questions about social and individual mores to ones about world revolution.

One recent ethnography (Chen 2015, 23–28) finds "meritocratic morality"—more often associated with those of higher socioeconomic status—common among laid-off industrial workers: they blame themselves for their plight. The concept of meritocratic morality here refers to the assumption that one's self-worth should rest on one's societal worth as registered by relevant labor markets.

39. Respectability is admittedly a rather "thin" concept, and hence assumes quite disparate forms when thickened (as any serious analysis would require) through attention to empirical specificities of social context.

40. Williams 1981, 27–30.

41. Rawls 1971, 51, 190, 248–249.

42. Scanlon 2008, 4, 187, 194, 201, 206, 213, 219, 235–237.

43. Austin 1956.

44. Dalrymple (pen name of Anthony Daniels), a psychiatrist serving felons in British prisons, offers helpful illustrations. He reports (2015, 18–21, 25–27, 59–63) that his patients consistently invoke self-exculpatory tropes to shift responsibility from their poor choices and harmful acts to their alleged mental conditions, often self-diagnosed. He also observes an increasing use of deterministic psychiatric lexicon, drawn from professional discourse of some years before, infusing the language of those seeking scientific warrant for release from responsibility for

their wrongs. Dalrymple (2017) notes more generally that "it has been known for a long time [citing a nineteenth-century medical treatise] that the delusions of madness take on the coloring of the culture of those who suffer them."

45. But see Shklar (1984) for a rare exception.

46. Wilson (1980, 134) and Stafford (2013, 102), cultural anthropologists studying China, report that statements of critical moral appraisal about other people, behind their backs, find more frequent expression in that country than in the United States.

47. Horton 1996, 38. There is admittedly a small if vigorous countercurrent, lamenting that this very reticence leaves us "with no sense of responsibility in a non-judgmental world" (Sowell 2011, 17).

48. Bennett and Shapiro 2002, 3.

49. Ibid., 4, 8. Thinkers on the Left claim it also leads us "to focus on individual moral failings" rather than on "reforming public spaces" and institutions.

50. This is extravagantly evident in a considerable body of scholarship, including such recent works as Kádár (2017).

51. Osiel 2019.

52. Waldron 2016, 11.

53. Pound 1907, 925.

54. Friedman 1973, ix, 10 (intending "to treat American law . . . not as the province of lawyers alone, but as a mirror of society"); Hall 1989, xi (entitling as "The Magic Mirror" a book with the "purpose . . . to elucidate the interaction of law and society as revealed over time"). Neither author takes this term seriously enough, however, to employ it with much analytic care. Both invoke it simply to suggest that law draws its normative raw materials from the moral and other views prevalent within the social order it is to govern. Scarcely anyone would dispute that proposition, stated in terms so lacking in conceptual crispness or possibility of disconfirmation.

55. Tamanaha (2001, 1–2) cites several influential legal thinkers who endorse the idea, variously understood, that law mirrors society.

56. Greenawalt 1992, 165 (emphasis in original).

57. Goodhart 1953, 151.

58. Winston 2018, 18.

59. Holmes 1881, 36.

60. Sunstein 2007, 159.

61. Ibid., 155.

62. Porter 2007, 100; see also Robinson 2008, 149–150 (on "empirical desert").

63. Political scientists conclude that public opinion is among the weakest influences on U.S. legislation (see, e.g., Grossman 2014, 56–57, 73, 81, 89–90, 98; Gilens 2012, 1, 6, 97, 100–113, 122, 185–186). This influence is also unevenly distributed across the landscape of legal and political issues (Burstein 2014, 161–170).

64. Tamanaha 2001, 3.

65. MacGaffey (1994, 123) observes that though anthropologists are today embarrassed by this nineteenth-century term, they have found no replacement clearly more satisfactory.

66. Political scientists (e.g., Thelen 2010, 45) today examine the sources of such equilibrium states through methods of "comparative statics," drawn from economics.

67. Weisberg 2003, 525. Robinson (2009, 36) suggests that even when lawmakers attend closely to indices of public opinion concerning criminal activity, they misread the evidence. They infer from the prominence of mass media attention to violent crime that the public is more acutely concerned about this problem than survey data suggest.

68. Stearns and Zywicki 2009, 45–60.

69. Farber and Frickey 1991, at 146.

70. These empirical correspondences are, however, consistent with alternative explanations as well.

71. Early ventures in opinion polling found that some three-quarters of Americans opposed Prohibition (Lerner 2007, 2).

72. From 1920 through 1933, the Eighteenth Amendment to the U.S. Constitution banned all sale of alcohol.

73. McGirr 2016, 72–73.

74. Gusfield 1963, 174; but see Beisel 1997, 215–217.

75. Andrews and Seguin 2015, 475. As Gusfield (1963, 7) put it, those favoring Prohibition "sensed the rising power of these strange, alien peoples and used temperance legislation as one means of impressing upon the immigrant the central power and dominance of native American Protestant Morality."

76. Weber (1958, 186–187) employs the term "status groups" in reference to groups whose members are united by a distinctive "style of life," in his words.

77. UN Department of Economic and Social Affairs 2014, 3, 17–27.

78. Grzymala-Busse 2015, 2, 338.

79. World Values Survey 2014; Squires 2010.

80. Pew Research Center 2014.

81. Cooperman et al. 2014, 74; Boorstein and Craighill 2014.

82. Díez 2015, 241–242.

83. Grzymala-Busse 2015, 339.

84. New York Times/CBS News Poll 1998; Hunter 1994, 92–93 (summarizing survey results).

85. Grzymala-Busse 2015, 3 (finding that "stark differences in the extent of religious influence persist across countries that are otherwise similar in patterns of religious belonging, belief, and attendance"). As Engeli, Green-Pedersen, and Larsen (2012, 198) observe, "even though one would expect secularization to produce permissive policies on morality issues, significant conditions of politicization must be met for this to happen."

86. Luker 1984, 7–8, 159–161.

87. Luker was uniformly respectful of her informants, nowhere overtly suggesting that this submerged form of socioeconomic self-awareness amounted to "false consciousness." Her purpose was simply to help explain the emotional intensity of abortion politics, "the inability to have anything resembling a dialogue about [the philosophical issues], . . . to deal with them in reasoned tones" (1984, 3, 1). In more recent years, careful studies of "moral reform" movements (for Britain,

see for instance Roberts 2004, 3–10, 291–295) are keen to distance themselves from strongly class-driven accounts, while nonetheless finding that "the middling ranks" of society did generally provide the bulk of public support.

88. Luker 1984, 7–8.

89. Todd Zywicki, professor of law, George Mason University, personal correspondence, Aug. 28, 2013. Some adherents of public choice seek to save their theory, rescue its capacity to explain even certain moral reform movements, by observing that these movements often involve counterintuitive alliances between 'Baptists' and 'Bootleggers'—that is, moralizers and materialistic rent-seekers (Smith and Yandle 2014, 1–30). This has been true, in particular, of all known efforts to prohibit or otherwise regulate alcohol and marijuana. 'Baptists' find the pertinent conduct morally objectionable, while bootleggers relish the higher prices they can charge when once-lawful commerce goes underground and production, now criminal, becomes a riskier investment. No such counterintuitive alliances suggest themselves, however, for abortion politics.

90. Rent-seeking refers to organized efforts to increase one's share of existing wealth by means other than creating new wealth, as through state regulation serving only to block market entry by potential competitors.

91. Ordinary language throughout the Western world has been quite consistent about which issues count as "moral": those involving marriage, human reproduction, and the end of life (Engeli 2012, 23). As mentioned, this folk categorization is nonetheless ultimately inadequate to social scientific purposes, in that nearly any issue is capable, in the proper circumstances and in the right hands, of arousing indignation at perceived injustice.

92. Pew surveys tracked attitudes toward gay marriage since 1996, and public support was very limited until at least 2008 (Pew Research Center 2010b). As late as 2010, those opposed still outnumbered those endorsing legal change by 48 to 42 percent (see also Keleher and Smith 2012, 1323–1324).

## 6. Divergences of Law and Morals

1. Katz 2011, 197. Katz offers his own account, drawn from social choice theory, for law's lenience toward certain serious violations of prevailing morals. He focuses entirely on criminal law, though, where much depends on whether, in assessing the defendant's blameworthiness, we choose to prioritize his intentions or instead the effects of his acts: good intentions sometimes produce harmful consequences, whereas wicked intentions sometimes do not. When there is great disparity in gravity between intent and effect, our conflicting moral intuitions are often equally strong and so fail to provide consistent guidance. Most pertinent in such situations is simply that whenever common morality is itself deeply conflicted, there is no way to clearly, confidently gauge its measure of correspondence with the law. Yet as Gert (1999, 58) suggests, there are very many situations where the relevant elements of common morality are not so acutely at odds. Professors are simply drawn preternaturally to such peculiar "puzzles," as Katz calls them.

2. Carpenter and Moss (2013) reflect the current state of scholarly thinking concerning the capture of regulatory agencies in particular.

3. Expressions of indignation in such matters prominently entered common parlance in the years following the 2008 financial crisis. "Federal rescue" here refers to the Troubled Asset Relief Program (TARP), created by subdivision (A) of the Emergency Economic Stabilization Act of 2008, Pub. Law No. 110-343, §118, 122 Stat. 3765 (codified as amended in 12 U.S.C. §5228 [2015]).

4. Paletta and Patterson 2010; Graham 2010, 10.

5. According to the California Fair Political Practices Commission (2010, 42), "The California Correction Peace Officers Association spent $1,825,000 to oppose Proposition 5 on the 2008 ballot. That measure sought to limit court authority to incarcerate offenders who commit certain drug crimes."

6. McCarthy 2016b.

7. Gilens (2012, 1, 6) finds that if law and policy better reflected the preferences of all Americans, irrespective of differentials in income and education, we would have "a more progressive tax system, stricter corporate regulation, and a higher minimum wage; foreign policy would reflect a more protectionist trade regime with less foreign aid"—but "policies on 'religious' or 'moral' issues such as abortion and gay rights would be more conservative."

8. Burstein 2014, 161–170.

9. As Wallach (2015) shows, "capture" is more a polemical term and tool of political rhetoric than a genuinely social scientific hypothesis amenable to scholarly research or helpful in thoughtful policymaking. To apply the usual definition of capture requires that one first adopt some determinate view of what policies are truly in "the public interest." Capture then entails industry-influenced departures from these policies. However, what the public interest truly requires in a given policy context is usually a question open to good-faith disagreement, arising from differing premises, all enjoying some basis in reality. One might respond to this objection by confining the definition of capture to situations revealing an actual quid pro quo exchange (i.e., outright bribery). But the concept then covers a far narrower range of circumstances than those to which this theory's advocates lay claim.

10. Gilens 2012, 97, 100–113, 122, 185–186.

11. Achen and Bartels 2016, 41–45.

12. Ibid., 311–325.

13. Rozin, Haidt, and McCauley (2000, 643–644) and Miller (1997, 179–205) suggest how, in certain contexts, disgust is an emotion evincing a distinctively moral resonance.

14. Achen and Bartels 2016, 233–234. Psychologists have demonstrated the transmission of "disgust sensitivity" between parents and children (Rozin, Haidt, and McCauley 2000, 647). There can be little doubt that disgust for one's political opponents, no less than principled adherence to one's own high ideals, can influence electoral behavior.

15. On one influential view (Lukes 1974, 16–20), control over the political agenda involves not only active decision-making by relevant elites but also less

conspicuous sources of systemic bias, "socially structured and culturally patterned, . . . neither consciously chosen nor the intended result of anyone's particular individual choices" (21–22). Yet the operation of these elusive forces remains largely conjectural, as do the determinants of their relative potency on distinct issues, in particular places and periods.

16. Some experimental research (e.g., ESRC 1999, 52) explores the points at which increasing technical complexity leads citizens to disqualify themselves as incompetent to judge a given policy question.

17. Jacob (1988, 12–15) reports his conclusions to this effect from studies of policy formation across several issue-areas, including the reform of laws regulating divorce and child abuse.

18. Two leading legal practitioners in international finance openly acknowledged this fact, taking evident pride in it, during the author's research interviews (for another book) in London and Hong Kong.

19. Pinker 2008. Pinker defines this moralizing "mind-set" as one that "makes us deem actions immoral" ("killing is wrong"), rather than merely disagreeable ("I hate brussels sprouts"), unfashionable ("bell-bottoms are out"), or imprudent ("don't scratch mosquito bites")."

20. See especially the work of Jeffrey Alexander, e.g., Alexander, Giesen, and Mast 2006. Also pertinent here, though very different in methods, is the substantial research in American political science on congressional "agenda-setting" (see, e.g., Grossman 2014, 73–76, 92–93, 99, 101).

21. Alexander 1992, 291–292.

22. Alexander 2011, xi, 3, 66.

23. Hart 2012 [1961], 120–132. Schauer (1991, 31–34) describes this perennial source of under-inclusiveness in legal rules vis-à-vis the policies they are designed to serve.

24. Schauer 1991, 31–34, 47–52.

25. Much work by analytic legal philosophers has employed this single, deceptively simple admonition as convenient fodder for exploring what its alternative understanding might teach about the nature of law and its interpretation. Hart (2012 [1961], 127) initiated the discussion.

26. Kagan 1997, 176–178. The greater trust that Western European citizens historically have placed in their lawmakers helps explain why legal rules on the Continent have regularly diverged decisively from prevailing moral sensibilities over long periods on such issues, in particular, as the defensibility of abortion and capital punishment.

27. The founding statement is the Report of the International Commission on Intervention and State Sovereignty (2001).

28. UN Charter, Art. 2(4); Art. 51.

29. G.A. Res. 60/1, ¶¶138–140 (Oct. 24, 2005).

30. Barack Obama, remarks by the president in Address to the Nation on Libya (2011).

31. Gentry 1991, 353–354.

32. Balko 2013, 62–64, 76–80.

33. Pew Research Center 2015.

34. See Del. Code Ann. Tit. 8, §141(h) (1953). Boards of directors thereby acquire great discretion in determining compensation. The Code provides that corporate bylaws may set limitations as deemed necessary.

35. Walker 2012, 233; MSCI, Inc. 2017.

36. Gilson and Gordon 2013, 876.

37. Das and Glazer (2016) report, "Candidates on both sides are playing to widely held public ire over the banks' role in the financial crisis and their subsequent taxpayer-funded bailouts."

38. On the influence of lobbying by Wall Street interests against proposed reform of financial regulation, see Connaughton 2012, 68, 89–93, 102, 110, 173. Wallison (2015, 4–6, 342–343) offers a contrary view, and blames the 2008 crisis chiefly on Democratic housing policies that promoted home ownership among those lacking basic creditworthiness.

39. Dodd-Frank Wall Street Reform and Consumer Protection Act, Pub. Law No. 111-203, 124 Stat. 1376 (2010). On some major limitations of this legislation, notably including its failure to address the central problem of inter-investor "contagion," see Ricks 2016, 250, 253, 256.

40. This explains the approach to sex work adopted by several Western European countries, such as Belgium and The Netherlands: legalize transactions between sex worker and consumer (though not those of intermediaries), and license all sex workers, requiring their periodic testing for STDs (Bilefsky 2005). Monitoring the sex market for legal compliance also facilitates prosecution of the serious crimes frequently accompanying sex work, notably trafficking in persons.

41. Consistent with prevailing economic theory, Basu (1999, 80, 86) argues that if policies penalizing countries for using child labor "are implemented properly, they are likely to drive children from the carpet industry or garment industry or soccer ball industry to other sectors, some of which are more dismal, such as prostitution."

42. Sunstein 2012, 48.

43. Aquinas 1964 [1274], quest. 95, a.1, and 96, a.2, at pp. 107, 127.

44. The counterargument, beginning with Aristotle, has been that one learns to be moral only by behaving morally, even if initially under some external constraint to do so. One acquires virtue, on this view, only through slow habituation to concrete practices of morally acceptable conduct.

45. Stevick 2014, 175–209.

46. On the political dynamics and increasing frequency of state apologies for mass atrocity, see Celermajer 2009. When compared to mass atrocities themselves, a later refusal to apologize for them may hardly seem a grave wrong. Yet by any other standard, it certainly is. The families of immediate victims certainly regard it as such, as do large portions of the international community. This has certainly been so, for instance, regarding the notable equivocation of Japanese leaders for many years over their country's responsibility for war crimes.

47. See, e.g., *Baena-Ricardo v. Panama,* 2001 Inter-Am. Ct. H.R. (ser. C) No. 72, 88 (Feb. 2, 2001); *Cantoral-Benavides v. Peru,* 2001 Inter-Am. Ct. H.R. (ser. C) No. 88, 81 (Dec. 3, 2001).

48. Drawing on several traditions of thought, Celermajer (2013) constructs a plausible and sophisticated rationale to account for how rituals of official apology for mass atrocities may sometimes have transformative effects on how citizens view their national past and present.

49. On the virtues demanded by liberal citizenship, see Galston 1991, 213–237.

50. Nonetheless, official efforts at inculcating this capacity to recognize and exercise one's moral autonomy may at times be required. Such measures would however exceed those authorized by Rawls's "political liberalism."

51. Robbins and Rumsey 2008, 408–412.

52. Compare Fletcher 1978, 115–118, 141–157.

53. Wardle 1991, 93, 104.

54. Greenhouse (2016) sketches the long history of judicial ambivalence over scrutinizing legislative motive even in these weighty matters, whenever defendants offered plausible pretexts for their conduct. She nonetheless notes that certain Supreme Court Justices have recently devised interpretive methods for discerning unlawful motive where earlier Courts believed that task impossible.

55. See, generally, Verstein (2017), who writes: "The law often avoids consideration of motives, and this impulse is even stronger when motives are mixed. We doubt the power of juries to find mental 'facts,' and we distrust our own motives—paternalism, censorship, thought policing—for demanding that they try" (48).

56. On this proposition legal theorists widely agree, with only modest quibbling at the margins. For one influential formulation, see Fuller 1964, 43–45, 62–64, 105. Justice Scalia (1997, 3, 6–7) offered an especially strong variant of the claim.

57. Kant 2001 [1797], 230–238. On one account, a moral right, understood as "natural" or "human" in character, may be "perfectible"—i.e., amenable to specifying how it binds particular people in particular ways—yet nonetheless resist legal codification. This is true where "human rights should be consolidated with other evaluative concerns that may also deserve ethical attention" (Sen 2012, 94), notably those of public well-being, utilitarian welfare.

58. Evans 2008.

59. Sabel and Simon (2015, 1) offer a compelling illustration. They contend that "new governance" strategies of court-supervised police reform "are better understood in terms of an implicit duty of responsible administration than as an expression of any particular substantive right."

60. Sen (2001, 2004, 2006).

61. He thus insists: "Any system of rights that ignores all claims other than those associated with perfect obligations (in analogy with legal obligations) will miss something of potential significance in the field of social norms. This is a serious loss, and the corresponding conceptual impoverishment has had the effect of taking the notion of human rights to be conceptually muddled and problematic in a way it need not be" (Sen 2001, 9).

62. Scheppele 2011, 18–19.

63. Sen 2004, 346; Sen 2006, 2924.

64. Sen 2001, 17. Sen evidently anticipates that law and social norms or mores will follow different paths. In fact, he says nothing at all about what law's proper

role might be in realizing the moral commitments today often described in terms of human rights.

65. Waldron 1981.

66. Waldron does not explicitly contend the law should protect all such moral rights to do wrong. Yet he clearly believes that the particular rights he discusses in this connection, such as campaign donations to a racist politician, warrant legal recognition and protection.

67. Waldron 2011, 1113.

68. Ingram (1984, 93, 103) describes English *charivaris* "involving some form of political protest . . . design[ed] to draw attention to the malfeasance of . . . governors" and seen by such authorities as "an excuse for disorder on the part of base and troublesome members of the community, ill-qualified to mock the follies of their neighbors." These features of Carnival have sometimes induced dictators, fearful of informal public gatherings, to prohibit its celebration, even in such devoutly Catholic countries as Spain of the 1940s (Richards 1998, 260).

69. Douglass 2008 [1849], 100.

70. Bakhtin (1968, 184–195, 213–223, 387–399) influentially suggested these subversive features of Catholic Carnival. Eagleton (1981, 148–149), a Marxist literary critic, acknowledges that Carnival may have been both transgressive of dominant mores and yet a source of fleeting release or political distraction from enduring oppression.

71. Beyond Carnival itself, scholars (e.g., Coser 1964, 41–48) have ascribed this pacifying effect to a wide variety of leisure and recreational practices. Paquette (1991, 684) argues, regarding petty theft and shirking of hard work on slave plantations, that "properly-managed resistance of the day-to-day variety can further system maintenance and may well be essential to its survival."

72. Thomas 1964, 53.

73. Roach 1993, 60–71.

74. Ibid., 69.

75. In today's Rio de Janeiro, Carnival does not take place at the margins of political authority, still less in resistance to it, for the festival has long been a major source of foreign hard currency. Carnival today involves considerable official planning and legal coordination at the highest levels of regional government. One scholar thus laments that the Brazilian state, in its management of all festivities, "has defanged any hint of popular unrest and channeled all energy into harmless paths of conformity" (Ruiz 2012, 248).

76. Roach (1993) shows how the history of Mardi Gras's legal regulation discloses a "process whereby once transgressive activities become dignified, sanctioned, and even legally protected" (45). Over time, "the law created . . . a space for play, a liminal zone in which dances, masquerades, and processions could act out that which was otherwise unspeakable" (56). This zone made possible both casual, playful interracial interactions and the public assembly of blacks in large numbers, long prohibited. In various forms, "transgression and immunity . . . [were] "eventually written into Louisiana law itself" (66). For one illustration, see *Louisiana Revised Statutes Annotated,* 1950, 9:2796.

77. Gross 2000, 110.

78. This preservative effect could arise only insofar as its miserable victims remain blind to it, or see it as merely a by-product of conduct differently motivated. The aim of "system legitimation"—in sixties-era sociologese—collapses once recognized as such, for what it is.

79. But then, surely they would have been too clever to do so, some may say. They will add that economic elites must have known better than to advertise so incautiously their cunning schemes, for the rest of us to later readily unearth. But this is to ascribe a strong mix of fear and foresight to such elites that appears, for most places and periods, historically anachronistic.

80. See Davis 1975, 119. Ruiz (2012, 249) describes archival sources from late medieval and early modern France and Spain that suggest "a great unwillingness on the part of those who ruled to permit spontaneous outbursts of popular celebration for fear that they might turn into a riot or challenge to established rule."

81. Ingram 1984, 106–110; Ruiz 2012, 250, 260.

82. DaMatta 1991, 116–125.

83. There were several early intimations of this view, as in a passing observation by Giambattista Vico (1948 [1744], 425) that "the monarchs mean to strengthen their own position by debasing their subjects with all the vices of dissoluteness."

84. Kuran (1995, 175) notes one such confusion, in the course of criticizing the influential work of James Scott on "weapons of the weak." Kuran observes, "One can despise an oppressor and still, precisely because of the social conditions created by the oppressor, fail to develop a worldview that is essentially one's own. To show that the oppressed do not accept every element of the oppressor's worldview is not to prove that they remain mentally uninfluenced."

James Scott's work (1985, 29) is nonetheless salutary in urging that we appreciate the subtle, quiet beauty of these unobtrusive demurrals in their own terms. If he also insists upon their "political" character—Kuran's objection—this is not to characterize them as premonitions of anything else, intimations of something grander (i.e., more inspiring to radical intellectuals). Scott's corrective here is also a sober reminder, were any needed, that most expressions of resistance to grinding oppression, unlike the celebration of Carnival among the poor, do not enjoy the law's generous indulgence, still less its benign connivance.

85. Several obvious questions at the heart of the theory go unasked: Just how much immorality is necessary to secure mass quiescence? Even if that question had a discoverable answer, how could ruling elites possibly know it? And could they possibly know how much indulgence of popular immorality threatens to become *too* much, seriously risking more overtly contentious forms of revolt?

86. In passing, one might legitimately wonder how anyone ever first stumbled upon the curious idea to analogize the workings of a social order to those of a steam-cooker, rather than, say—to stick with culinary metaphors—a precariously elevated soufflé (ever on verge of collapse, a more benign trope) or, more menacingly, a meat grinder.

87. Wilson (2007, 144–145) issues the assertions quoted throughout this paragraph, but offers only thin empirical evidence in their support.

88. "An Act for the Punishment and more effectual Prevention of the Crime of Adultery," Parliament of Great Britain, May 26, 1800.

## 7. Convergences of Laws and Morals

1. Mitchell and Tetlock 2006.

2. *New England Coal and Coke Co. v. N. Barge Corp.*, 60 F.2d 737, 740 (2d Cir. 1932) ("[I]n most cases reasonable prudence is in fact common prudence; but . . . a whole calling may have unduly lagged in the adoption of new and available devices. It never may set its own tests, however persuasive be its usages").

3. See, e.g., *Jenkins v. Georgia,* 418 U.S. 153 (1974). *Miller v. California,* 413 U.S. 15, 24 (1973), defines obscenity partly in terms of "contemporary community standards."

4. Atiyah 1979, 260, 408.

5. Leff 1967.

6. For example, *Singer v. Tatum,* 251 Miss. 661 (1965).

7. "Mutual mistake" refers to a misunderstanding by both parties of a material fact on which their contract depends. The mistake renders the contract voidable by either side.

8. "Impossibility" is an excuse for nonperformance of a contract arising when either side finds it effectively impossible to meet its obligations.

9. "Default rules" occupy the unstated background of every contract and serve to complete such agreements when the parties have failed to specify a material condition.

10. So reports Professor Steven Burton, an expert in contract law. Personal communication.

11. Uniform Commercial Code, §1-201(3). Other Code provisions seek to accomplish much the same, but none are employed in litigation as often as drafters contemplated (Bernstein 2015, 63).

12. Whitman 1988, 174.

13. Several works by Lisa Bernstein (e.g., 1999, 777–780) reach this conclusion.

14. Precisely on the basis of this apparent "judicial incompetence," Posner (2000b, 7, 14, 18, 20) argues for a formalist approach to contractual interpretation.

15. See, e.g., *Pabalk Ticaret Limited Sirketi v. Norsolor S.A.,* ICC Award, Oct. 26, 1979, No. 3131, Y.B. Commercial Arb., vol. 9, 109 (1984).

16. Kadens 2012, 1205–1206.

17. Wilkinson-Ryan and Baron (2009, 405) found that human "subjects believe that intentionally breaking a contractual promise is a punishable moral harm in itself."

18. Talley (1999, 118) observes that the heyday of unconscionability in contract law coincided with President Lyndon Johnson's "war on poverty" and "with the

arrival of a number of Left-Democratic-appointed and elected judges, many of whom were favorably disposed to distributionally-minded doctrines"; see, generally, Fleming 2014, 1387.

19. Brown 2000.

20. Collins 2014; Hesselink 2011.

21. This is not to suggest that there exists any near-unanimity of views over what kinds of agreements fall into this category, becoming thereby unenforceable.

22. See, e.g., Robinson 2000, 1839.

23. Ibid. This is puzzling, he observes, because the drafters avowedly viewed the public's retributive moral sentiments as a poor guide to penal policy, which they believed should properly stress deterrence, rehabilitation, and (where unavoidable) incapacitation.

24. Robinson and Darley 1995, 28–33.

25. Green and Kugler 2012a, 58.

26. Green and Kugler 2012b, 484.

27. Hoffman 2014, 243 (discussing Paul H. Robinson's empirical findings).

28. Robinson and Darley 1995, 155.

29. Ibid., 124.

30. Ibid., 42–50.

31. Robinson 2000, 1849–1850; Finkel and Duff 1991, 12, 128. Judge Hoffman (2014, 252) illustrates the rule as follows: "Imagine that John and Judy decide to rob a bank. They both go in, but only John is armed. If John gets killed in a shoot-out with the guards, under the most robust form of . . . the felony-murder rule, Judy can be charged and convicted of first-degree murder. The law blames her as if she had planned and then intentionally caused John's death."

32. Finkel and Parrott 2006, 234.

33. Ibid., 209.

34. Green and Kugler 2012a, 58.

35. Hoffman 2014, 257 (discussing several studies by Paul H. Robinson).

36. Green and Kugler 2010, 533–535.

37. The U.S. Model Penal Code, §6.01 (1962), lists the "degrees of felonies." See also §2.02.

38. Cyber crimes offer a notable example. See, e.g., Economic Espionage Act of 1996, 18 U.S.C. §§1831–1837.

39. See generally, U.S. Department of Education 2011.

40. Unnever, Benson, and Cullen 2008, 163.

41. 18 U.S.C.A. §§2339A, 2339B (2015).

42. *Holder v. Humanitarian Law Project,* 130 S.Ct. 2705, 2716–2717 (2010) (holding that 18 U.S.C., §2339B, does not require that the defendant specifically intend to further terrorist activities; it was enough that he was aware that the group to which he offered material assistance employed terrorist methods).

43. The statute's current iteration version is 18 U.S.C. §2339A (2015), "Providing Material Support for Terrorism."

44. Kugler and Darley 2012, 220; McCarthy 2016b.

45. This term refers to efforts at winning electoral office by promising "tough on crime" policies and, in this fashion, appealing to retributive sentiments regularly strong, by some indicators, among the general public (Roberts et al. 2003, 4–9). Reviewing considerable data, Kugler (2014, 2) observes that though "most of the public believes that judges are insufficiently punitive toward criminal defendants as a general matter . . . this effect is substantially diminished if . . . the public is given the details of specific cases . . . and policy-level information."

46. Model Penal Code, §§223.4, 212.5.

47. Some insight might be gained by comparing the few crimes that, at point of judicial application, authorize such direct recourse to common morality with those—most crimes—that do not, in hopes of explaining why particular offenses fall on this or that side of the line.

48. Svensson and Larsson (2009) conclude from a large empirical survey that there exist "no social norms that hinder illegal file sharing."

49. It is open to much contention whether one may accurately describe any of these three offenses—particularly prostitution, in its most common forms—as truly victimless. Yet it is also true that the harms wrought by large-scale copyright infringement, though "only economic," escape the visibility of most people.

50. Perritt 2012, 96; Keating 2015.

51. Hay 2011 [1975], 17, 37–38.

52. The Statute of Anne (1710) was England's first law of copyright.

53. Thayer 1898, 508–538. It is true that the general population did not receive any public education during the period when common-law rules of evidence were adopted. Even today, with the increasing complexity of scientific and statistical evidence presented at trial, there is good reason to doubt the ability of most people, including many judges, to fully fathom it (Rachlinski 2000, 85, 100–101).

54. Schauer 2006, 165–166, 176–177.

55. And, for negligence and contract, incorporated only partly, at that.

56. U.S. Constitution, Art. 3, §1.

57. Altman 2011, 17, 74.

58. Gilens and Page 2014, 6, 9, 564.

59. Nourse and Schacter (2002, 587–588) describe the central role of lobbyists in drafting much legislation.

60. Kahneman and Tversky 1982, 192–194.

61. Rawls 1971, 126–230. Circumstances of justice are the "conditions under which human cooperation is both possible and necessary." Social cooperation is necessary where individuals lack strong interest in the affairs or welfare of others and have competing interests causing them to make conflicting claims to moderately scarce resources. Cooperation is nonetheless possible because the people coexisting within a single territory are of comparable strength and intelligence, so that no person can dominate all the others; their essential needs and interests are also roughly similar.

62. Engeli 2012, 23.

63. Luker 1984, 7.

64. This is a common-law rule providing that "a nonvested interest in property is not valid unless it must vest, if at all, within twenty-one years after one or more lives in being at the creation of the interest and any relevant period of gestation" (Iowa Code Ann., §558.68).

65. Though social scientists offer a variety of possible explanations (see Weaver 2011 for a meta-analysis), it may be the tedium of much everyday experience for many people that creates the consistent appeal of all "limit experience"—especially the liminal moments between life and death—including that entailing risk of great violence.

66. Rae-Hunter 2012, 38–39.

67. Sherman and Percy (2010, 150) conclude from their data that most people attribute moral agency and responsibility to corporations for misconduct, in ways little different from how people ascribe these traits to ordinary, natural persons.

68. Transfer pricing refers to the methods employed for valuing transactions between business entities under common ownership. Multinational corporations sometimes attempt to reduce their taxes by distorting the prices charged in cross-border deals between enterprises under their control. Taxation authorities then seek to adjust intragroup transfer prices so that these better approximate what would have been charged in an arm's-length purchase (Hines and Summers 2009).

69. Kahneman 2011, 19–30, 415–418. "System 1" refers to our most intuitive reactions. These are spontaneous, effortless, emotional, and opaque to our immediate understanding. System 1 endorses deontological stances on moral questions, though the arguments it prompts consist of post facto rationalizations, psychologists contend (Haidt 2001, 814). Indignation is the essential moral sentiment in System 1 (Kahneman and Sunstein 2007, 1). "System 2" refers to reactions more reflective, controlled, effortful, self-aware, sensitive to trade-offs. Consequentialist reasoning prevails, involving a complex weighing of costs and benefits ensuing from alternative responses to perceived wrongs.

70. Robinson 2009, 35 (reporting empirical results in experimental philosophy).

71. Shklar 1990, 94.

## 8. Questions of Method and Meaning

1. A state may at times not merely indulge or turn its back on rampant illegality but actively encourage it. Totalitarian regimes, caring little for legal niceties, often do not trouble to codify even their deepest normative commitments into positive law (Osiel 1995, 545).

2. For example, Ala. Code §13A-12-1 (2014); Conn. Gen. Stat. §53-302a (2014).

3. The causal mechanisms by which "crowding out" occurs are psychological in nature, and now relatively clear (Brennan and Pettit 2004, 262). When we introduce material incentives or impose punishment to increase desired conduct, we imply that others' conduct requires external control, that they will not do the right thing on their own accord. This belittles them and diminishes their self-esteem. Policies of this sort also reduce their ability, when honoring prevailing mores, to

publicly display their virtuous motives for so doing, which at times matters significantly to them.

4. See, e.g., Glendon 1987, 142. Schwarcz (2002) offers a balanced assessment of the strengths and weaknesses of private ordering, in various forms, for fostering efficiency and other public objectives.

5. See generally, for instance, Kennedy 1982, 1351–1352.

6. Slobogin 1996, 321.

7. Ibid., 324.

8. Slobogin here articulates what he takes to be the widespread stance of his professional colleagues, leaving some doubt about whether these views are his own as well.

9. As Robinson and Darley (2012, 740) put it, "a system perceived as unjust provokes resistance and subversion; inspires vigilantism; and loses the power to stigmatize conduct, to gain compliance in borderline cases, and to shape powerful societal and internalized norms." For these reasons, Green and Kugler (2012a, 58) conclude that "the moral intuitions of the lay public are an increasingly important component of criminal law theory."

10. Compare Roberts 2014, 231–234, 240, 245, with Robinson 2014, 54, 57, 59.

11. A recent work by leaders in this field is Epstein, Landes, and Posner (2013, 101–199).

12. Fear of stigma is not the only reason many hesitate to declare bankruptcy, of course. Also important is often their awareness that they will lose access to all financial credit for a few years.

13. Marx 1972 [1844].

14. Rights to religious freedom and against discrimination on grounds of religious affiliation were, in fact, Marx's point of entry into larger questions about the value and import of legal rights as such. He argued that the more we acquire legal rights and the individual freedoms they embody, the greater the suppression of our *genuine* freedom. That freedom must rest upon our nature as singularly social beings, not as pre-social monads rationally entering into a contract with other such isolated units. Thus, when we assert our claims of legal right against one another, we fundamentally misunderstand ourselves and our essential relation to fellow members of our species.

15. Marx 1972 [1844], 42.

16. Kennedy (1979, 37) once thus proclaimed the need "to try to develop, at the level of conscious communication with other people, the extent to which they are letting their goals be perverted by the hegemonic false consciousness generated by law."

17. A decided minority of Americans, one-third at most, believe their country "is headed in the right direction," according to Rasmussen Reports 2017.

18. Bellah et al. 1985, xiv, xv, xxiii, 8, 20–21, 24, 81–84, 111, 133, 160, 195, 237, 306, 334; see also Wolfe 2001, 79,118–119, 195, 200.

19. Porpora et al. (2013, 4, 197, 205) summarize several empirical studies by Wuthnow, Lamont, and others, employing methods somewhat more reliable than those of Bellah et al. 1985.

20. Wuthnow 1991, 36–38, 98–99.

21. Hochschild 2013, 100 (conducting keyword searches on ProQuest Historical Newspapers). However, a keyword search of books in English employing Ngram Viewer (my analysis) for such terms as "moral duty" and "moral responsibility" discloses no clear temporal trend over the last hundred years.

22. Kesebir and Kesebir 2012. However, these authors also find increasing use of certain communal terms, including "team," "teamwork," and "community." Twenge, Campbell, and Gentile (2012, 4) find increasing use of individualizing vocabulary for the period 1960–2008; to similar effect, see also Nafstad et al. 2009 (employing Norwegian data).

23. Thus, Harvard Law professor Joseph Singer (2000, 16), a founding member of the "Critical Legal Studies Movement," writes that our prevailing way of thinking about property, in particular, as a "bundle of sticks, . . . obscured [that] *owners have obligations as well as rights.* We know this to be true," he immediately adds, "but our language for talking about property denies it. It is a knowledge that we suppress by the way we frame discussions about property" (emphasis in original). See also Moyn (2016): "Human rights wither without a language of duties."

24. Wenar 2015; see also O'Neill 1996, 127–153.

25. To speak of muteness is imprecise here, almost a misnomer, in that today one finds no shortage of recourse to moral vocabulary in politics either American or European. What is lacking is agreed-upon ways of using such language in service of any shared ends. With regard to "moral duty," in particular, it is now surely "a concept [widely employed] outside the framework of thought that made it . . . really intelligible" (Anscombe 1958, 6). That was initially the framework of divine law, though more secular worldviews, including those of liberal moral theory, often find ways to reinterpret and incorporate the expression (or words resembling it) within their own lexicon.

An Ngram Viewer search reveals that the phrase "moral duty" steeply declined in usage (by two-thirds) between 1800 and 1900, and since the latter date has remained stable, being employed only quite infrequently. It is notable that the decline occurred so much earlier than many would suppose. One recognized limitation of Ngram Viewer of some importance here, however, is that the vast increase in scientific publication and associated terminology over the last century inevitably yields a relative decline in *non*scientific wording, notably including terms routinely used to engage in normative analysis and to render moral judgment. Still, scientific publication burgeoned only in the twentieth century, whereas the major drop in references to moral duty took place during the nineteenth.

26. In much of Victorian literary fiction—notably the novels of Henry James, Jane Austen, and the plays of Oscar Wilde—the characters routinely reflect aloud (or through interior monologue) about whether, in their relations with one another, they are adequately honoring self-acknowledged duties. Unlike Austen and James, Wilde—along with Gilbert and Sullivan—are of course parodying this behavior. They satirize the hypocrisy and inflated amour propre often accompanying it, even as they backhandedly register its salience in the self-understanding of a certain,

long-vanished social milieu. In the United States, at least, the discourse of good character and its assumed importance to one's approval by others is today no longer nearly so salient in the lives of even "old money" (Marcus 1992, 179–187). It was not only elite authors of Victorian fiction whose writings veritably dripped with talk of moral duty. During the U.S. Civil War, the private letters of soldiers, written home to loved ones, rang with "concepts of duty, honor, manhood, and community," shows historian James McPherson (1997, 17).

27. Haskell 2005, 246. Others voice similar views. Schneider (1994, 583), for instance, believes that "it is difficult to talk one way and act another. Thus, it is legitimate to wonder how long people may be expected to act well without the spur and sustenance moral language provides." Glendon (1991, 77) offered an early argument that the agitated "rights consciousness" so prevalent in contemporary America, she believes, tends to attenuate an appreciation of one's responsibilities, legal and moral. She thus lamented "the missing language of responsibility" and "the colonizing effect . . . of legal rights dialect . . . on popular discourses." On the basis of considerable interview evidence, Bellah et al. (1985, xiv, xv, xxiii, 8, 20–21, 24, 81–84, 111, 133, 160, 195, 237, 306, 334) argued that many Americans lack even an elementary vocabulary to express their genuine intimations of responsibility to others, beyond a narrow circle of family and immediate friends. Later sociological work (Vaisey 2009, 1675), employing methods more reliable, has found that though American teenagers generally behave in ways consistent with "their choice from a list of moral-cultural scripts," they nonetheless "cannot articulate clear principles of moral judgment." Bellah et al. (1985) found that when defining their notion of a "good life," adults do little better, speaking comfortably only of their desires for greater material comfort and personal self-expression, the latter often couched in ephemeral New Age mantras of the day.

28. Through a careful textual analysis of several human rights treaties, one leading NGO thus found it possible to address "communitarian" critiques by showing how "international human rights standards deal adequately with human responsibilities" (Int'l International Council on Human Rights Policy, 1999, 54). Hence, "there is no need for new global agreements focusing on individual responsibilities." The timing of this report clearly suggests an effort to answer contemporaneous charges that international human rights law reflects only the philosophic individualism of a liberal West and depreciates the more communal values of Asian and African societies.

29. Kohrman 2005, 922.

30. See, e.g., Cal. Penal Code §12071(b)(1)(D)(3)(A) (West 2010) (demanding a ten-day waiting period from time of application to purchase of a firearm).

31. See, e.g., 720 Ill. Comp. Stat. 5/24-1(a)(8) (2010) (prohibiting possession of any firearm, stun gun, Taser, or other deadly weapon in any place licensed to sell intoxicating beverages).

32. The legal requirement to deliberate before acting upon an initial, provisional preference often embodies a policy of gently discouraging without prohibiting the relevant act, "nudging" it to the margins. This has been the logic of recent legislative initiatives over abortion. Such include a 2011 South Dakota enactment

requiring that anyone seeking the procedure first visit a pregnancy help center and undergo a short counseling session, with a view to ensuring that her decision to abort is "voluntary and informed." Legislators believed that the law cannot properly regard such a decision as truly "informed" unless the patient is genuinely aware of alternative responses to her circumstance, notably the possibility of offering her prospective child for adoption. Several states have recently enacted precisely this "informational" requirement. See, e.g., 2011 N.C. Sess. Laws 405, §90-21.82(2)(d), available at http://www.ncga.state.nc.us/Sessions/2011/Bills/House/PDF/H854v6.pdf.

33. Sunstein 2014, 20, 96, 118, 140.

34. Cal. Rev. and Tax Code §30101 (West 1994); Cal. Rev. and Tax Code §30123 (West 1989); Cal. Rev. and Tax Code §30131.2 (West 1999) (gradually increasing the tax rate per pack of cigarettes over time from 37 to 87 cents).

35. Bogart 2011, 23–27, 56, 322–324.

36. The basis of such trust varies by circumstance. The act of placing one's trust may be avowedly irrational or carefully calculated; it may rest on blind faith and supine credulity or, instead, on the prudent estimation of acceptable risk. The latter is what social scientists have had in mind when speaking of "placing trust in trust" (Gambetta 2000, 213–238). In this sense, we employ trust selectively, in greater or lesser measure, as a rational method for managing unavoidable complexity in the face of limited information about those on whom we may rely. So understood, "generalized trust" (Luhmann, 1979, 24–31) is integral to contemporary life, because without it many of modernity's distinctive features would be inconceivable.

37. Durkheim 1960 [1893], 3. He writes that "moral facts are phenomena like any others," and that it is therefore necessary to study "moral life according to the methods of the positive sciences." Ibid.

38. "Long-term consequences do not have explanatory power," Elster (1985, 30) influentially argued, "unless an intentional actor is present who deliberately sacrifices short-term benefits" to that end. Functionalist explanation, he observed, fails to demonstrate any causal connection—through goal-directed action or some unconscious, institutional process of 'natural selection'—between the purported function of an institution and how it came into being.

39. This does not always stop them from trying. In 2009 a British Labor government provisionally proposed an official "reminder" to all UK subjects of the "mutual responsibilities" attendant upon their legal rights. Eleftheriadis (2009, 6) offered a compelling critique of that proposal, which was soon abandoned.

40. An anthropologist thus writes—evocatively, if imprecisely—'the "ordinary" implies an ethics that is relatively tacit, grounded in agreement rather than rule, in practice rather than knowledge or belief, happening without calling undue attention to itself' (Lambek 2010, 1–2). In fact, a premise of today's moral anthropology is that "all human activities are grounded in moral assumptions—often so much taken for granted that they are not perceived as such any more . . ." (Fassin 2012, 5). In its very inarticulateness, however, the moral domain threatens to recede beyond possibility of serious scholarly inquiry, more so than such authors appear to acknowledge.

41. Rawls 1971, 48–51, 120, 432, 434, 579.

42. Leiter 2009, 711.

43. "Philosophers no more created new ethical systems in order to study ethics than grammarians invented new languages in order to study philology," observes Morgan (2007, 298–299). "Socrates . . . begin[s] from current Athenian views of a topic like goodness or justice, proceeding to show its difficulties and potential."

44. Tyson (2017) reports 2014 polling data finding that nearly 60 percent of the U.S. adult population found the use of torture sometimes acceptable in counterterror efforts.

45. Dugan 2015.

46. Newport 2016.

47. Opinion data have long indicated (see, recently, Osberg and Bechert 2016) that Americans are more tolerant of income inequality than are the citizens of other OECD countries, and that most Americans view the notion of "desert" as highly pertinent in establishing a just income distribution (Miller 1992, 564–565). Under the influence of Rawls especially (see Sher 1987, 22–36), moral philosophers largely hold the concept of desert in low regard as a basis of distributive justice, whereas most Americans find that notion highly pertinent to the issue (Gilens 1999, 4–8).

48. Haidt and Graham 2007, 98.

49. Ibid. This finding also suggests that political advocates will more likely succeed in winning initial antagonists to their views on contentious policy issues by recasting these views in terms congruent with opponents' underlying ethical commitments. In other words, progressives should find clever ways to appeal to tradition, authority, sanctity (Feinberg and Willer 2015, 1665).

50. Anderson 1993, 218.

51. Schwitzgebel and Cushman 2014, 359–362.

52. These are the formulations of Rawls, Habermas, and Scanlon, respectively.

53. Williams 1985, 104.

54. Winston 2008, 35. This stance entails, he adds, an effort to "ground public morality in social life, rather than in exercises of a self-reliant intellect. Practical deliberation occurs within an ongoing normative order, implicating existing currents of thought and sensibility, including authoritative precepts and techniques" (ibid., 26).

55. Ibid., 36.

56. These texts range from *The Communist Manifesto* and *Quotations from Chairman Mao* to *Mein Kampf* and—to the pleasant surprise of many—Rawls's *A Theory of Justice*, during the period 1990–2005, at least.

57. Griffiths 1994.

58. These moral practices, conveyed with consistency over long periods—though not truly from "time immemorial"—emerge in such accounts as unpretentiously earthy, appealingly artisanal. And yet even such unadorned efforts to describe them turn implicitly to intellectual sources impeccably sophisticated, to a particular approach to moral theory running from Aristotle through Oakeshott. Still, we must not confuse the empirical expression of common morality in observable human interaction with academic efforts at its descriptive elucidation.

59. This stance should not be confused with the meta-ethical theories variously described as "emotivism," "intuitionism," and "sentimentalism" (Stevenson 1944, 20–36). Such views hold that there exists no rational basis for evaluative statements, that these do no more than express visceral feelings of personal approval and disapproval. This book takes no position on meta-ethics. For present purposes it is enough to observe, as a bare empirical fact, that indignation at perceived wrongdoing often manifests itself in ways observable to others and is to that extent susceptible to social inquiry. Whether or not there exists, behind the expression of that sentiment, anything more ontologically substantial than sentiment itself is not a sociological concern and hence lies beyond this book's compass.

60. It is possible and acceptable to treat resentment as a form of indignation, though the two are sometimes distinguished. Ordinary language often confines the word indignation to the sentiments arising within us when we believe others have been wronged, and speaks of resentment when we consider ourselves to be injustice's victims.

61. Some of these sentiments do regularly enter into the application of legal rules, but without legal warrant. This involves what sociologists call the law "in action" rather than "on the books," which is to say that these situations usually entail sub rosa departures from positive law. Thus, for instance, some will say that, in determining the proper punishment, "mercy" is a sentiment entirely appropriate for judges and jurors to display toward convicted criminal defendants, perhaps even the most remorseless. Yet the Sentencing Guidelines that U.S. federal judges employ grant no authorization (see §5K2.0(a)(2)(A)) to act upon this sentiment, in contrast with remorse on a defendant's part (§3E1.1). Still, one recent empirical study reveals that courts rely upon mercy nonetheless (Bennett, Levinson, and Hioki 2017, 971–972).

62. Thus, for instance, the sentiment of public gratitude clearly found legal expression in creating the official awards by which military personnel receive public recognition for courageous service to their country in war. Yet the moral sentiment inspiring enactment of such a system must be distinguished from the more specific criteria employed for distributing individual commendations under its terms. Thus, in determining whether to grant a Medal of Honor to a particular soldier, the relevant civil servants are not authorized to ask themselves: How much gratitude do we feel here? They ask instead, in the official wording: Has this person performed an act of "personal bravery or self-sacrifice above and beyond the call of duty . . . in actual combat" (Torreon 2015).

63. Admittedly, certain policy issues are more readily amenable to such arousal than others, and only a small number will in fact be widely apprehended in these terms at any given time.

64. Saito 2015.

65. According to the website of the U.S. Environmental Protection Agency, "environmental justice is the fair treatment and meaningful involvement of all people regardless of race, color, national origin, or income, with respect to the development, implementation, and enforcement of environmental laws, regulations, and policies." See generally Schlosberg 2007.

66. Admittedly, to satisfactorily reconstruct the assumptions of social actors from a far-distant time requires both a substantial documentary record and relative candor within it concerning what they believed themselves to be doing. The more controversial a legislative measure is likely to be, the more it will at once bring its presuppositions to consciousness and yet ensure that they are kept close to the chest. Still, a competent historian, enjoying intimate acquaintance with available evidence of the period, can often acquire "a feeling for the climate of a time," allowing her "a knowledge of what one can or cannot expect of people of that period" (Veyne 1984, 151). That is the most one may reasonably expect from a sparse archival record, when pertinent participants are no longer living.

67. This is a fair characterization, for instance, of the hopeful if ingenuous view that "if people are given more responsibility, they will behave more responsibly." That assertion appears in David Cameron's *Conservative Manifesto* (2010), written in connection with his advocacy for repeal of Britain's Human Rights Act, legislation which he hoped to replace with a "Bill of Rights and Responsibilities."

68. Zelizer 1979, 73–79, 97–100; 2011, 21–33, 442; Peck 2003, 149.

69. Clark 1999, 9, 22, 34–35.

70. In contemporary China, the Confucian aversion to candid talk about a loved one's possible death, even about financial ramifications for dependents, rendered long taboo any discussion of life insurance (Chan 2012, 5–8, 37–41, 133–141).

71. See, generally, Quinn 2008.

72. Healy 2004, 308–327.

73. My discussion here draws on Weisberg 1986.

74. This is not to deny the repeated, concerted efforts at legal and political compromise between North and South, with a view to discouraging secession, notably the Missouri Compromise and the Compromise of 1850.

75. Taylor 2006, 216–217. In these three quoted paragraphs, Taylor does not cite pertinent passages from Montesquieu, though I shall take the liberty to do so within his text.

76. Montesquieu 1949 [1748], bk. 21, §§22, 23.

77. Ibid., §24.

78. Ibid.

79. Ibid., §26.

80. Supiot (2007, 77) and especially D'Iribarne (1994, 2009) are rare social thinkers still finding significant inspiration in Montesquieu.

81. Though one could scarcely describe *The Spirit of the Laws* as a modest work, Montesquieu wisely did not, as Hirschl (2009, 205) observes, assay such ambitious macro-social schemas as those of many prominent nineteenth- and twentieth-century theorists (e.g., Maine, Savigny, Hegel, Marx, Durkheim, Parsons); unlike these authors, Montesquieu's argument about the relation between law and mores is neither evolutionary nor functionalist.

82. Montesquieu 1949 [1748], bk. 9, §§5, 6, 14, 25.

83. Ibid., §27, does offer passing thoughts on the impact of law upon prevailing mores, but this analysis is brief, perfunctory, and largely unconvincing—an assessment on which the secondary literature concurs.

84. Spector 2009.

85. Montesquieu 1949 [1748], bk. 19, chap. 23.

86. Ibid., §3.

87. Cultural anthropologists were once highly attentive to this process, describing it initially in terms of the "double institutionalization" of custom (Bohannan 1965).

88. See, e.g., M. Posner 2013.

## 9. Why This Book Is Not What You Had in Mind

1. Hesselink (2011, 621, 632, 642–644, 646–648) observes that the doctrine's "field of application" has become "unlimited," having grown "explosively," well beyond the reach of contract law (at 641, 628, 634–635).

2. Dworkin 1977, 105.

3. Dworkin 1986, 413.

4. Greenawalt 1989, 3.

5. This is the long-standing and ever-evolving debate between legal "positivists" and their diverse opponents, long described as "natural lawyers." The meaning of each term is itself subject to debate and has shifted over time.

6. This is the sense in which Hart (2012 [1961], vi) undertakes "a descriptive sociology," as he calls it.

7. See, generally, L. Alexander 2003.

8. Mill 1989 [1851], xv.

9. A satisfactory definition of paternalism, in the philosophical sense, is "the interference of a state or an individual with another person, against their will, and defended or motivated by a claim that the person interfered with will be better off or protected from harm" (Dworkin 2014).

10. These concerns inspired the U.S. Supreme Court's conclusion in *Lawrence v. Texas* that "moral disapproval, without any other asserted state interest, has never been a rational basis for legislation." 539 U.S. 558, 582 (2003).

11. For an introduction, see Beauchamp 2005.

12. The most influential scholarly writings are anthologized in Posner 2007. One definition of "norm" employed in this literature is "a rule governing an individual's behavior that third parties other than state agents diffusely enforce by means of social sanction" (Ellickson 2001, 3).

13. See, e.g., Lessig 1995, 1044; McAdams 1997, 376–381; Shavell 2002, 241.

14. Scott (2000, 1628) observes the obvious danger of vacuity here.

15. Southwood and Eriksson (2011) endorse this view, evident in how they distinguish "norms" from "conventions." They believe that, in our ordinary usage of these terms, "conventions": (1) exist only insofar as they are followed, (2) arise independently of the desires of those they govern, and (3) are not deeply evaluative (in terms of justice), so their violation often inspires no genuine indignation. By contrast, "norms": (1) can exist irrespective of whether people generally follow them, (2) can arise through our conscious desire to create them, and (3)

are more deeply evaluative, hence often prompt acute emotional arousal at their transgression.

These distinctions have analytic appeal, but it is by no means clear empirically whether ordinary language employs either term consistently and uniquely in these ways. The typology is nonetheless helpful in clarifying that economists who purport to be studying norms are in fact far more interested in conventions. If there is anything specifically of interest about norms (to which I shall here assimilate mores), economics is hence very unlikely to help us identify it. McAdams and Rasmusen (2007, 1576), two leading economists of law, equivocate somewhat in this regard, distinguishing norms distinguished from conventions on the basis of how norms entail "behavioral regularities supported *at least in part* by normative attitudes," by which they mean that people consider that "it is wrong to do otherwise" (emphasis supplied).

16. It is nevertheless crucial to the present approach that what counts as *mala in se* differs considerably by place and period: what is only contingently wrongful over here, will sometimes be deemed inherently so over there.

17. The few exceptions include Mears and Kahan 1996; Sunstein 1996, 905; and Bogart 2013, 21–26, 173–176, 213–214.

18. McAdams 1997, 355.

19. Posner 2000a, 5.

20. These observations are sweeping in scope, and hence seek to present themselves as intellectually bracing. Yet if they are taken in a weak sense, they are banal, for they amount to saying, "If you wish to get on in the world, you must care what others think of you." And if taken in a strong sense, they are preposterous, in suggesting that we are wholly ungoverned by any internal sense of right and wrong, and hence disposed to respect others' rights only when we fear our violations of these will be detected and punished.

If we truly wished to explain relevant features of human behavior through a universal desire for esteem, we would ask a host of questions very different from and more specific than posed by the legal economists of norms: When does our desire for esteem outweigh our myriad other goals (when they conflict), such as personal integrity? And when does esteem within a particular group (say, ethnoreligious) assume priority for us over esteem within another (e.g., our profession)? Such conflicts are the woof and warp of personal, social, and political life.

21. At least one prominent exponent of the economic analysis of law (Scott 2000, 1647) concurs in this view. See also Bogart 2011, 125–127.

22. Etzioni 2000, 165.

23. Feldman (2006) observes the heavy reliance of Japanese tuna traders on a specialized court system, formalized yet expeditious, in resolving disputes over product quality within this discrete vocational community. Due to its small size and insularity, this is the type of milieu predisposed toward more informal procedures of dispute resolution, according to conventional social science.

24. Feldman 2006; Bernstein 1992; West 1997; Ellickson 1991; Greif 2006.

25. See, e.g., Lessig 1995, 1029.

26. Posner 2000a, 3.

27. Ruff (2001, 173) describes the growing moral criticism by eighteenth-century elites of this practice, and its consequent prohibition.

28. Despite periodic attempts to outlaw it through international human rights law, dwarf-tossing continues even in several Western, high-GDP countries, including England, New Zealand, Canada, and France.

29. On recent U.S. efforts to define and discourage "problem gambling," see Bogart 2011, 243–288.

30. Post 2003, 494–495 (quoting Austin Sarat and Thomas Kearns).

31. Ibid., 495n44.

32. Ellickson (1991, 281) and Bogart (2011, 111) are rare in making somewhat stronger claims to this effect.

33. Nelson, Nielsen, and Lancaster (2010) conclude, from a large data set of case filings: "Employment discrimination litigation is not so much an engine for social change . . . as it is a mechanism for channeling and deflecting individual claims of workplace injustice" (196). The authors add that "the mere existence of this [individualized litigation] apparatus may displace other possible strategies of reform" (180).

34. Scholars in socio-legal studies regularly register their ambivalence toward those asserting "atomistic" rights when broader goals of social transformation require more collective forms of mobilization. Thus, Scheingold (2004, 5) influentially describes as "myth" the prevailing American view that "the realization of these rights," of individuals to equal protection and due process, "is tantamount to meaningful change." To view the law in this unduly optimistic way is, in the avowed view of many within the "law and society movement," to treat it as a "fetish."

35. Felstiner, Abel, and Sarat 1980, 644.

36. The terms "rights consciousness" and "legal consciousness" describe the disposition to understand one's relations with others in terms of legal rights and duties (Ewick and Silbey, 1992).

37. Felstiner, Abel, and Sarat 1980, 641. A long-standing line of socio-legal research therefore highlights "the capacity of people to tolerate substantial distress and injustice" without seeking legal recourse (ibid., 633).

38. Ibid., 631.

39. Antidiscrimination claims, in particular, are prominent among those whose discouragement would initially seem indefensible. Socio-legal scholars appear especially exercised over how many such claims are winnowed out at early stages. Nielsen and Nelson (2005, 22–23) thus lament that only 5 percent of people with employment grievances file a lawsuit. This acute scholarly concern appears to assume that a great number of these foregone lawsuits are meritorious. Though data are mixed, credible studies suggest otherwise (e.g., Clermont and Schwab 2009, 128–129). Lex Machina, a data analytics company, recently found (Randazzo 2017) that when Title VII sex discrimination disputes go to trial, defendants prevail over 95 percent of the time. This could simply mean that meritorious cases, which may be many, settle before judgment more often than in other areas of litigation. There is no reason to imagine why that might be so, however, still less any empirical evidence in support of this hypothesis.

40. The assumption that any significant instance of injustice is necessarily, inherently "systemic" discloses itself, upon any close reading, as a ubiquitous undercurrent in socio-legal scholarship. This assumption is frequently defended by reference to the alluring aphorism that our "private troubles" with the world spring inexorably from deeper "public issues," as the radical sociologist C. Wright Mills (1959, 3–8) famously put it. The possibility that one's personal problems—with one's employer or spouse, for instance—may sometimes in fact *not* be significantly attributable to deeper institutional conflicts or social practices is simply, summarily, ruled out by this *ex cathedra* stance. For many scholars, it is in any event less an empirical hypothesis—subject to scientific assessment and potential disconfirmation—than a badge of vocational self-definition, resting on bald assertion as an axiomatic principle of social ontology: this is simply how our world *is*.

41. After reaching this conclusion from an extensive survey of the field, I consulted a couple of its most prominent scholars, who confirmed my view here.

42. Fassin 2008, 334.

43. With this influential turn of phrase, Paul Ricoeur alludes to our pervasive tendency, under the influence of three modern master thinkers, to distrust others' professed motives, ascribing their true intentions instead to material self-interest (Marx), *resentiment* (Nietzsche), or unconscious libidinal desire (Freud).

44. Fassin (2008, 333) observes that among cultural anthropologists "morals are not considered as a legitimate object of study and are looked upon with suspicion." Though he himself has pioneered their recent study, Fassin "insist[s] on the heuristic value of the intellectual discomfort aroused by morals among anthropologists."

45. The result is often, in particular, "to treat moral ideas as 'resources that can be put to strategic use' . . . rather than as things people actually care about" (Hitlin and Vaisey 2013, 63, quoting Ann Swidler).

46. This is a major theme in Garth and Dezalay 1996, vii–viii, 1, 18.

47. Bourdieu (e.g., 1984, 339, 367, 389, 425) consistently seeks to show how moral and even aesthetic disagreements within society amount to dissimulated forms of class conflict, deflected from its proper revolutionary path.

48. Boltanski and Thévenot 2006.

49. Smart 2007, 58–59.

50. Benhabib 1992, 126. "To withdraw from moral judgment is tantamount to ceasing to interact, to talk and act in the human community . . . moral judgment is what we 'always already' exercise in virtue of being immersed in a network of human relations . . . [as] a family member, a parent, a spouse, a sister or brother."

51. Sayer 2011, 143–144.

52. Especially promising in this regard are the recent contributions assembled in Stafford 2013, on the subject of "ordinary ethics in China." Stafford writes, "Our intention in this volume has been to resist putting too much stress on the collective and historical side of things—thereby leaving . . . more space for the individual, reflective, agentive dimensions of ethical practice . . . for explicit ethical deliberation" (23).

53. Sayer 2011, 2.

54. See, e.g., Das et al. 2001; Fassin 2013, 253–259.

55. See, e.g., the short account by Faubion (2011, 168–202) of the life of a friend, a philanthropist from Portugal's hereditary aristocracy.

56. See, e.g., Das 2007, 13–14, 19, 27–28, 34, 47, 53–54, examining the emotional memories, decades later, of poor Indian women raped during the 1947 partition.

57. Raz (2009) offers the leading account of what it means for law to have inherent authority, i.e., irrespective of its particular content.

## 10. The Changing Stance of Lawyers toward Common Morality

1. See, generally, R. Gordon 1984, 51–57; 2010, 453.

2. Model Rules of Professional Resp., Rule 2.1 (2010) provides that, "In rendering advice, a lawyer may refer not only to the law but to other considerations such as moral, economic, social and political factors that may be relevant to the client's situation."

3. Robert W. Gordon resists those who characterize his work as championing a long-lost era of ethically enriched lawyering. His most recent formulation (e.g., 2009, 50) describes the lawyer-statesman ideal, quite modestly, as "a myth with some basis in reality." From the limited historical record, it is difficult to gauge the extent to which contemporary invocations of this era romanticize it, with a polemical view to condemning more contemporary practices.

4. Gordon 1984. Early sociological inquiry into large New York law firms (Smigel 1969, 343) had suggested that, as recently as the mid-1960s, partners there enjoyed greater autonomy from clients than in smaller law firms, representing individuals rather than large companies. More recent findings (Nelson 1988, 271–272; Kirkland 2005, 718; Nelson and Nielsen 2000, 487; Heinz and Laumann 1982, 365–373; Heinz et al. 2005, 114–120, 278–280) reverse these conclusions, discovering that corporate lawyers enjoy very little independence from their clients' expectations and demands.

5. Luban (1988, 719) aptly describes Tocqueville's view that American "lawyers, like aristocrats, have a calling higher than bourgeois commercialism . . . and, like aristocrats, assume responsibility for the common good through public life."

6. Tocqueville 1969 [1840], 263–270.

7. By "cultural authority" I refer to "the probability that particular definitions of reality and judgments of meaning or value will prevail as valid and true" (Starr 1982, 13).

8. When survey researchers asked respondents to rate the ethics of ten occupational groups, lawyers were at the bottom. About one-in-five Americans (18 percent) say lawyers contribute a lot to society, while 43 percent say they make some contribution; fully a third (34 percent) say lawyers contribute not very much or nothing at all (Pew Research Center 2013b).

9. American lawyers today view the ethical standards prevalent among their professional brethren as something well short of aristocratic. One survey found

that two-thirds of California lawyers think fellow attorneys "compromise their professionalism as a result of economic pressure." Another survey discovered that a great majority of Virginia attorneys believe that the increasing lack of professionalism among their number is widespread, not merely a matter of "a few bad apples" (Maryland Judicial Task Force 2003, cited in Ariely 2009, 210).

10. Wendel (2010, 20–43) offers a recent, sophisticated defense of this view.

11. Raz 1999, 40–48.

12. Nelson 1998, 780.

13. Gallagher (2011, 331), in an empirical study of intellectual property lawyers, finds that "patent clients exert a great deal of influence over how discovery is done."

14. Kirkland 2012, 152–175.

15. Suchman 1998, 849.

16. Gordon, personal correspondence, 2016.

17. Langevoort 2011, 4, 26, 27.

18. Radzik 1999, 255.

19. For recent evidence on how much more CEOs of U.S. companies earn than do their Western European counterparts, controlling for relevant variables, see Fernandes et al. 2012.

20. Fischl and Paul (1999, 59–64, 77–87, 137–143, 233–239, 280–282) show how and why this is the objective of most U.S. law professors, especially when writing final examinations. Our goal is to elicit dexterity in discovering and exploring ambiguities in the relevant law and facts, suggesting doubt about the ideal or probable resolution of the questions posed. The winning answer to any of them—however irksome to every real-life client—begins not with "The law provides (requires, prohibits, allows) that . . . ," but instead with "What will actually happen depends on (A, B, C . . . X, Y, Z)."

21. Cohen 1935, 840.

22. Werhane (1999, 71–75) reconstructs the deliberations of Ford's management in deciding to market the Pinto without correcting the relevant defect.

23. *Grimshaw v. Ford Motor Co.* (1981) 119 Cal. App. 3d 757, 174 Cal. Rptr. 348.

24. Unless, of course, they majored in economics as undergraduates.

25. Utilitarianism refers to the view that law should seek chiefly to advance the public's overall well-being, often understood in terms of the happiness of individuals.

26. As to criminal law, at least, Thomsen (2014, 119–145) and Keijser (2014, 101–118) adopt versions of this stance.

27. "I always say, as you know, that if my fellow citizens want to go to Hell, I will help them. It's my job" (Holmes and Laski 1953 [1920], 249).

28. Pozner and Dodd 2004, chap. 1, p. 17; chap. 2, pp. 1–30.

29. Truth—the relevant variety—may emerge nevertheless, to be sure, through the equally vigorous use of this method by both sides to a dispute. And the U.S. Supreme Court is free to speculate in this regard that "cross-examination [is the] greatest legal engine ever invented for the discovery of truth" (*California v. Green,* 399 U.S. 149, 158). There exists no serious evidence, however, for this proposition.

30. Osiel 1990, 2054–2064.

31. Moral pluralists hold that there exist multiple ethical principles (utility and dignity, for instance), equally defensible and fundamental, yet often at odds in their counsel (E. Mason 2011).

32. As Minow and Singer (2010, 908) observe, "Judges and lawyers recognize the presence of conflicting values and then explain why one trumps another . . . Justification using these techniques preserves the conflict of values, rather than suppressing it . . ." (908). Through these methods, we acknowledge that moral "conflict will not go away" (at 919.)

33. Gordon, personal correspondence (2016).

34. Hand 1952, 138.

35. Putnam (2001, 147) offers a similar observation.

36. Bird 2010, 575.

37. Siedel and Haapio 2011a; see also Masson and Shariff 2010; Bagley 2010.

38. Bird 2010, 578–579.

39. Galanter 1998b, 806–807.

40. See, e.g., Mintz Levin, "Preventive Lawyering: Protecting Your Business from the Credit Problems of Others in Your Business Network," Aug. 20, 2009, https://www.mintz.com/news-events/events/view/event/itemid/349.

41. Smaller firms too now market themselves in these terms. See, e.g., Greenberg Glusker, "Preventive Counseling," http://www.greenbergglusker.com/practiceareas/EmploymentLaw/PreventiveCounseling; Grehres Law Group, P.C., "Preventive Legal Advice," https://gehreslaw.com/legal-services/preventive-legal-consultation-with-business-attorney/. For other, non-Western countries, see, e.g., Hassan 2010 (offering conflict-preventive services to Pakistani companies); Sahin Law Firm, http://www.sahin.law/our-working-areas/competition-law (offering this form of counsel to Turkish corporations).

42. Susskind and Susskind 2015, 108. Miller (2017) offers a leading casebook on risk management for corporate lawyers.

43. Adam, Beck, and van Loon 2000. Richter, Berking, and Muller-Schmid (2006, 4) go so far as to claim that this term has "come to be the standard self-description of Western societies," as characterized by current sociological theory.

44. Urging the value of preventive legal planning, one management consultant thus observes, "Rivals will not hesitate to emulate a competitive advantage, thereby nullifying its effectiveness" (Bird 2011, 72). Still, if only for a time, the stronger our defenses become, the more assertive a posture we can afford to take if and when conflict looms. In this more assertive mood and idiom, proponents of preventive lawyering expressly promise clients that such work aims not only at "avoiding legal disputes and liability" but also at "strengthening positive rights" (Brown 1998) and "empowering" clients (Schwerin et al. 2018) in relation to their prospective opponents. Bird and Orozco (2014, 84) offer two compelling illustrations from the practice of patent law.

45. In these terms, Jervis (1978, 169) famously described how "many of the means by which a state tries to increase its security [turn out to] decrease the security of

others," resulting in downward spiral toward increased conflict among states seeking only to avoid it.

46. See especially Siedel and Haapio 2011b, 651–656.

47. Henderson (2017) finds that "compared with the average company, lawyer-run firms experienced 16% to 74% less litigation, depending on the litigation type. Employment civil rights, antitrust, and securities lawsuits were reduced the most."

## 11. Commercial Morality, Bourgeois Virtue, and the Law

1. Christopher Hodges, an Oxford University professor of corporate law, provides a typical statement of this prevailing stance: "The imposition of regulation is not enough. Culture is essential. Enlightened financial regulators across the world have accepted that external regulation cannot be relied on to affect all behavior, and that what is more important is the personal and group values of the human actors and the ethical culture of their organizational groups" (Hodges 2015, n.p.).

2. Friedman 1970, 37 (emphasis added). Alas, Friedman says nothing about which customs, among what group of people, he has in mind, nor about how such customs actually operate to restrain the types of self-dealing he evidently regards as unacceptable.

3. Among the lawful practices Judge Richard Posner (2013) considers morally unacceptable are "packing a corporate board of directors with patsies who do not operate as representatives of the shareholders . . . but are in the pocket of the CEO, the confusing disclosure of credit terms, exploitation of consumers' difficulty in understanding interest rates, and hiring pretty girls to hawk new drugs to physicians." To this list, others would add forms of "creative accounting" falling short of "best practice" standards (McBarnet and Whelan 1999, 67–77) not fully embodied in applicable law.

4. Granovetter (2005, 34), summarizing considerable empirical research to this effect, thus writes that within a social network, "greater density makes ideas about proper behavior more likely to be encountered repeatedly, discussed and fixed; it also renders deviance from resulting norms harder to hide and, thus, more likely to be punished." There is no reason to suppose, however, that the norms so generated will be societally optimal, for they very often involve price-fixing, as Granovetter acknowledges.

5. Wallison 2015, 344–346.

6. The Dodd-Frank Wall Street Reform and Consumer Protection Act mandated that bank holding companies with total consolidated assets of over $50 billion and nonbank financial companies designated by the Financial Stability Oversight Council for supervision by the Federal Reserve submit resolution plans annually, for "stress testing," to the Federal Reserve Bank and the Federal Deposit Insurance Corporation.

7. Ricks 2016, 94.

8. From this standpoint, regulation should also focus on areas where common morality, though resilient, is thoroughly misguided, misconstruing the true stakes for public policy.

9. The suggestion could not fail to be ironic, because prevailing intellectual opinion—not only premodern, but modern as well (including Kant through Matthew Arnold, at least)—has held that "the market is not only a cultural void but an active corrosive agent, obliterating cultivated values wherever it reaches" (Haskell and Teichgraeber 1993, 1). The word "cultivated" here refers to both moral and aesthetic values.

10. Smith 1976 [1759], 364.

11. Franklin 1955 [1790], 101–108.

12. See McCloskey 2006, 2–5; and Hanley 2009, 102–131; both parsing Weber.

13. Novak 1982, 117–118; McCloskey 2006, 22–27, 496–501.

14. Novak 1982, 117–118.

15. Solomon (1992) thus writes, "What we need in business ethics is a theory of practice, an account of business as a fully human activity in which ethics provides not just an abstract set of principles or side-constraints or an occasional Sunday school reminder but the very framework of business activity" (99). Hartman (2013, 262) argues to similar effect.

16. McCloskey 2006, 79–85, 94–95, 349–350, 496–502.

17. The law itself accords this notion some formal recognition, in fact, as when pricing a business enterprise for its sale or valuing the harm inflicted on it by trade libel.

18. Finn 2004, 19.

19. For good reason, Thompson (1988) entitles his social history of this period in Britain *The Rise of Respectable Society.* The acute concern with respectability was by no means confined to moralizing preachers among the middle classes. Similar views were common among Chartists and socialists as well, who viewed excessive consumption of alcohol, in particular, as inimical to their aims of political reform (Roberts 2004, 177, 182–184; Himmelfarb 1995, 43).

20. Moore 1998, 26.

21. Ibid., 25.

22. Thrift 1994, 342; Tickell 1996. Thomas (1992, 8–9) observes that though the social meaning of other gestures has varied greatly over time and space, the equation of moral and physiognomic rectitude has been a veritable constant throughout Western history.

23. Thomas 1992, 10.

24. Moore 1998, 53.

25. Simmel 1955, 61; see also Boltanski and Thévenot 2006 [1991], 27–28.

26. Simmel 1955, 61–63.

27. McCloskey 2006, 4.

28. Coffee 2006, 1–10, 104–106, 326–327.

29. Macey 2013, 90–101.

30. Scholars differ over whether "short-termism" played a major role in bringing about the 2008 financial crisis. For a skeptical view, see Roe 2015.

31. Macey 2013, 88–99.

32. Schwarcz (2008, 204) defines the term, more precisely, as "the risk that a financial firm's failure will impact other financial firms or markets, resulting in a domino-type collapse that ultimately harms the real economy." The "real economy" refers to indices of production and consumption of goods and services, apart from financial services. Other prominent scholars take issue with the concept of systemic risk as "inherently vague," effectively "unmeasurable," and present chiefly "in the eye of the beholder" (Ricks 2016, 250).

33. But see Schwarcz (2016) (advocating "a 'public governance duty'—not to engage in excessive risk-taking that could systematically harm the public," with a view to "align[ing] private and public interests").

34. Morgenson and Rosner 2011, 141.

35. Until well past the mid-twentieth century, bankers at the most venerable City of London firms generally remained at a single employer for their entire professional lives (see, generally, Reader and Kynaston 1998).

36. Brooks 2012.

37. Baltzell 1989, 233, 391.

38. Thrift 1994, 342; Tickell 1996.

39. Granovetter 1985.

40. Durkheim 1960 [1893], 203–204.

41. Sennett 2006, 36, 48–49; Ho 2009, 219, 246, 284.

42. Ho 2009, 283–284; Thrift 2002, 201–203.

43. Gray 2011.

44. MacKenzie 2006, 15–25; Callon 1998, 2.

45. Ho 2009, 294 (emphasis added).

46. Ibid., 251.

47. Ibid., 302.

48. Anderson 2000, 196.

49. Weber 1958, 303, 308.

50. Smith 2003 [1776], bk. 5, chap. 1.

51. Goodhart 1953, 117–118.

52. Hirschman (1986, 105–141) provides a leading modern treatment of this hypothesis.

53. Schama (1987) so titles his study of the period, and begins it with this stern admonition from John Calvin's *Commentary on Genesis:* "Let those who have abundance remember that they are surrounded with thorns, and let them take care not to be pricked by them." See, generally, Schama 1987, 79–85.

54. Abolafia (1996, 127) sanguinely reported, in a chapter entitled "*Homo Economicus* Restrained," that financial "specialists are surprisingly satisfied with their culture of restraint. They seem genuinely proud that the pressures of the rating system have forced on them a higher standard of behavior [higher than the law requires]." Abolafia wrote not long before two major rounds of economic and financial crisis.

55. Bannon (2014) contended that the United States manifests a "crony" and "brutal form of capitalism" whose benefits fall chiefly upon "a very small set of people."

56. Starr (2013) stresses the undoubted obstacles to legislative reform posed by the political influence of the financial industry. One should not minimize, however, the genuine difficulty in drafting reforms that would not do more harm than good. On such difficulties, see, e.g., Romano 2014, 29; Ryznar and Woody 2015, 1691.

57. Smith 2016, xi.

58. Hirschman 1986, 139.

59. Ibid., 135–139.

60. For instance, there is no evidence of any increasing preference among the upper middle class for leisure time over enhanced compensation for long workdays. Moreover, the hypothesis that declines in worktime among upper socioeconomic strata would much weaken capitalism failed, in any event, to consider such powerful countervailing forces as technical innovation, entrepreneurial skill, and corporate savings for research and development.

61. Relying on statistical indicators of relative appetite for risk, Kim (2013, 1–2, 29) plausibly estimates the extent to which different types of financial institutions anticipated a government bailout in the event of their insolvency. Directors of larger institutions anticipated bailout much more often (76 percent probability) than those of smaller banks (52 percent). See also Friedman and Kraus 2011, 45–46.

62. Ho (2009, 291), conducting participant observation for an ethnography of investment bankers, discovered that "many of my informants anticipated not only a crash, but an eventual bailout, on the grounds that Wall Street investment banks were 'too big to fail.'" Scholars and analysts of financial markets now recognize that this anticipation of rescue by a federal "lender of last resort" has become, and continues to present, a pervasive "moral hazard" (Wallison 2015, 21–22).

63. The analysis in this paragraph and the next is much indebted to Rollert (2018, 487–497), from which all quotations are drawn unless otherwise indicated. Rollert teaches business ethics at the University of Chicago, Booth School of Business.

64. Jensen and Meckling (1994, 17) here reject, with considerable derision, the influential sociology of Dimaggio and Powell (1983).

## 12. How We Attach Responsibilities to Rights

1. The most common method of conjoining rights and duties is through contract, whereby counterparties, in anticipation of mutual benefit, each commit to some mix of both. Particular contracts vary so widely in how they effect such conjunctions, however, that it would be perilous to attempt any broad generalizations.

2. These several questions, though tantalizing, must await another day.

3. Waldron 2011. Casting about for terms, uncertain how best to describe the peculiar phenomenon at issue, he alternately calls this "the responsibility-form" of

rights; responsibilities arising "in and around rights"; "rights conceived as responsibilities"; and sometimes simply "a responsibility-right" (ibid., 9), the language I here adopt.

4. Merritt 2016, 6. This does not appear to be Waldron's view, as he accords no primacy to either element of a responsibility-right.

5. Other theorists (e.g., Blustein 1982, 104–114; Archard 2004, 108) persuasively make this argument concerning parenting, in particular.

6. The term refers to "the positive . . . honor, prestige, and power attaching to a position or individual person within a system of social stratification" (Jary and Jary 1991, 494).

7. *Caetano v. Massachusetts,* 136 S. Ct. 1027, 1030 (2016); *D.C. v. Heller,* 554 U.S. 570, 618 (2008).

8. What is distinctive about this view of dignity is its focus on duties, rather than rights; on duties toward oneself in particular, rather than to others; and on the inalienability of rights necessary to honoring these duties, including the right to a basic measure of respectful treatment from others (Hennette-Vauchez 2008).

9. Waldron 2015, 134–136 (emphasis in original).

10. This has centrally involved efforts to obtain rights of monopoly in delivering certain services (Sarfatti-Larson 1977, 31–39, 211–212).

11. On this process, see Starr 1982, 13–19.

12. Slivinski (2015) convincingly shows the empirical weaknesses in arguments for state licensing of many occupational groups, including several that have won such market protection.

13. Calabresi 1970, 21, 39, 73–74; Posner and Rosenfield 1977, 117.

14. See generally *Pruitt v. Allied Chemical Corp.,* 523 F.Supp. 975 (E.D. Virg. 1981).

15. *Evra Corp. v. Swiss Bank Corp.,* 673 F.2d 951, 955 (7th Cir. 1982). For this familiar proposition, Judge Richard Posner here cites the leading case of *Hadley v. Baxendale,* 9 Exch. 341, 156 Eng.Rep. 145, Court of Exchequer, 1854.

16. Certain occupations, such as internal auditor or quality control inspector, offer rare exceptions here, in that reporting on misconduct within the very organization employing such people is integral to their essential role-requirements (Miceli and Near 1991, 147).

17. This is the case, for instance, of the least-cost avoider rationales offered for common-law rules on proximate cause, the negligence standard, and aspects of contributory negligence.

18. Latour 2005, 9–11, 243–245; Martin 2003, 1.

19. Eyal 2013, 869–878. But see Collins and Evans (2007, 2), who defend an avowedly "realist" theory of expertise against efforts by "science studies" to conceive of it wholly in relational terms, a matter of competence-attribution by others within a social network.

20. Williams 1972, 52.

21. *Black's Law Dictionary,* 5th ed. (1979, 1357).

22. Hudson 2009, 498.

23. Visser 2008, 771.

24. Baker 2002, 110.

25. Waldron proposes this understanding of human dignity in several recent pieces, including Waldron 2011, 1120, 1131–1132.

26. This is not to suggest that such a responsibility necessarily entails a further duty to bring such a fetus, once conceived, to parturition; but see Waldron 2011, 1135.

27. American Citizen Participation Study, 1990, http://www.icpsr.umich.edu/icpsrweb/ICPSR/studies/06635); Jacquet 2014, 103.

28. Schudson 1994, 59–62. The history of voting participation within the United States is not pretty. For many early decades, large majorities of eligible citizens vigorously exercised this right, though participation by disfavored minorities was no less vigorously discouraged. In the last half-century, with infrequent exceptions, turnout has been weak, by contemporary international standards, among both majority and minority populations. Curiously, at no point in this history has there existed any consistent official policy of urging people to vote, still less by proclaiming it their moral duty as citizens. To vote was once clearly considered a duty, though enforced only through mores, via informal shaming.

29. Gerber, Green, and Larimer 2010, 411–413, 416. Data also show, however, that most people think that though citizens have a duty to vote, they "have no duty to be informed, to process political information in a rational way, or to vote for just outcomes" (Brennan and Jaworski 2016, 188).

30. Jackman 2001.

31. Parsons 1951, 285–315.

32. Schneider (1994, 525) observes that "when such a society is medicalized, its members are called to heed the leading requirement of the sick role—to devote themselves to healing themselves."

33. The concept has not been central to sociological theorizing for over a half-century now.

34. DiMaggio 1990, 117; Eyal 2013.

35. Abbott 1988, 87–98.

36. Porter 2013, 533. Though Porter endorses the law's movement in this direction, she finds little actual evidence of it (ibid., 545–548).

37. Choose Your Parents Wisely 2014 (citing the Pew Research Center and the U.S. Bureau of Labor Statistics).

38. Myers 2008, 455; Fass 1997, 213–222 (discussing the notorious case of Etan Patz, abducted in 1979, whose murderer was convicted only in 2017).

39. Stearns 2003, 4.

40. Pimentel 2012; Bernstein and Triger 2011. The enforcement of such enhanced standards gains real-life efficacy through the Child Abuse Prevention and Treatment Act of 1974, 42 U.S.C.A.510g, "provid[ing] that in every case involving an abused or neglected child which results in a judicial proceeding, a guardian *ad litem* shall be appointed to represent the child in such proceedings."

41. The pressure upon this area of law has been increasing for over a generation. As Hacking (1995, 238) writes, "The variety of activities covered by the label

'child abuse' has radically expanded during the past three decades . . . New ways to be abusive came into being."

42. Porter 2013, 545 (summarizing case law).

43. Heimer and Staffen 1998, 148, 151–153, 186–187, 243–244. By 2011, American parents were spending on average over four more hours per week on child care than they spent in 1965 (Pew Research Center 2013a).

44. Heimer and Staffen 1998, 153–154, 243–244.

45. Ibid., 7–9.

46. Siebert, Peterson, and Schramm 1956, 105–146.

47. Pickard 2015, 144; Blanchard 1977, 30.

48. Commission on Freedom of the Press 1947.

49. Ibid., 146–151.

50. Ibid., 69, 82, 91. Siebert, Peterson, and Schramm (1956, 73–104) thoughtfully interpret and evaluate the report.

51. Blanchard 1977, 25–27.

52. Commission on Freedom of the Press 1947, 11 ("As new categories of abuse . . . invade valid social interests . . . the extension of legal sanction is justified").

53. Ibid., 69–76.

54. Ibid., 79. The commissioners wrote that "agencies of mass communication . . . are great concentrations of private power. If they are irresponsible, not even the First Amendment will protect their freedom from governmental control. The amendment will be amended . . . everyone concerned with the freedom of the press and with the future of democracy should put forth every effort to make the press accountable, for, if it does not become so of its own motion, the power of government will be used, as a last resort, to force it to be so." The Commissioners added merely in passing that they opposed "censorship" and favored no new statutes inconsistent with the First Amendment, properly interpreted (ibid., 13, 88).

55. Vigorous objections to the perceived abuse of press freedom found similar expression in postwar Europe, spawning official commissions in the UK and new regulation in France (Bell 2001, 50).

56. Luban 1988b, 104–147.

57. Crockett et al. 2010, 855–856; Crockett et al. 2013, 3505–3506; Feng, Krueger, and Luo 2015, 596–599.

58. Is one more likely to assume such costs if one feels bound to do so, under a duty shared by others who will likely appreciate and reward one's efforts, if they ever learn of these? Or rather, is one more likely to enforce social mores, to act virtuously in this regard, if one feels oneself to be acting independently of others' demands, irrespective of what they conventionally expect? The former hypothesis seems more likely, but laboratory experiments have not yet pursued this propitious line of inquiry.

59. The only exception concerned duties under preexisting customary law which new sovereign states automatically assume upon coming into legal existence.

60. UN Charter, Art. 2 (4). The underlying rationale is that by acknowledging the exclusive authority of a sovereign state over what takes place within its terri-

tory, this legal rule serves to diminish potential conflicts between states and enables their political leaders to govern in light their peoples' particular interests and ideals.

61. As before indicated, the UN Security Council has authority under Article 42 to call upon states in a given crisis to employ armed force, i.e., all means "necessary to maintain or restore international peace and security." The Council has, however, exercised this authority on only very few occasions and is unlikely to do so again in the foreseeable future.

62. Hegel 1942 [1821], 208.

63. Lord Peter Julian Millett, *R v. Bow Street Metropolitan Stipendiary Magistrate, Ex parte Pinochet Ugarte* (No. 3) [2000] 1 A.C. 147, 269 (H.L. 1999).

64. See, e.g., Suleiman 1974, 20–24; Caplan 1988, 1–13.

65. Evans (2008), consisting of the 2001 report of the International Commission on Intervention and State Sovereignty.

66. Thoughtful, well-intentioned efforts to this end admittedly abound, but are notably vague. This is conspicuously true, for instance, of the proposed requirement (Zifcak 2012, 34) that more assertive means of intervention may never be employed until every available diplomatic measure in resolution of a humanitarian crisis has been exhausted.

67. The doctrine's most prominent defenders therefore publicly demur from any intention to cultivate new customary international law, even as they privately intimate the contrary.

68. "Soft law" refers to international agreements that lack binding legal force but seek to acquire authoritative recognition and thereby influence institutional conduct (Chinkin 1989). Parties to these understandings are chiefly sovereign states but also such nonstate actors as multinational corporations and intergovernmental organizations. Documents embodying soft law describe themselves as codes of conduct, guidelines, norms of best practice, declarations, recommendations, or statements of principle. These are appealing to states that remain unwilling to make costly commitments to incipient global norms that have attained enough acceptance to preclude explicit disavowal. Drafters often hope, and later strive, to "harden" these provisional documents into new customary international law, or to generate citizen support for incorporating soft law norms into domestic legislation.

69. Theoretically inspired by Dewey's pragmatism, "democratic experimentalism" (Sabel and Simon 2017) urges flexible organizational forms to encourage information-sharing and reciprocal learning by all concerned in a given matter, with a view to periodic improvements in operational procedures and institutional direction.

70. Some empirical evidence suggests that shaming sanctions, such as public reporting of state noncompliance with treaty duties, can at times modestly improve adherence to human rights law (Kelley and Simmons 2014).

71. None of the preceding is to deny, of course, that publicly invoking the language of human rights—in either a moral or a legal sense—will consistently fail to deter those firmly committed to their abuse.

72. *Kaiser Aetna v. United States,* 444 U.S. 164, 179–180 (1979).

73. See Dagan 2006, 1257–1258, 1263–1265, 1269 (discussing German law).

74. Many prominent Anglo-American scholars, at least, deny any such essence. See Waldron 1988, 29 (examining the views of Thomas Grey and Bruce Ackerman).

75. For one recent treatment, surveying the current state of discussion, see Baron 2013.

76. Worthington 2018, 1–2.

77. U.S. Constitution, Fifth Amendment.

78. For instance, Hobhouse 1915 [1913], 3–83.

79. Hardin 1968.

80. Ostrom 1990, 10–13, 17–20, 60–67, 73–77.

81. The clarity of prevailing mores is admittedly only one among several conditions needed to prevent depletion. As historian E. P. Thompson (1976, 337) observed, describing the late medieval and early modern English village, real property held in common "depended not only upon the inherited right, but also upon the inherited grid of customs and controls within which that right was exercised."

82. In a television appearance of the time, William Kristol, editor at large with *The Weekly Standard,* alluded openly to the likelihood that many construction workers would refuse to accept employment on such a building project. He added that arsonists would likely destroy it in any event, before its completion. Kristol then allowed himself a wry smile, unmistakably, and said nothing in explicit criticism of either scenario.

83. Ryan 2015, 72, parsing the long-influential views of Louis Hartz.

84. See Waldron 1988, 157–160.

85. See MacIntyre 1981, 172, for a seminal discussion.

86. MacIntyre (1981, 27) sought to show that "[a] moral philosophy . . . characteristically presupposes a sociology."

87. Strickland 1996, 34–40, 124, 180–181.

88. See Gilbert 1976, 75.

89. U.S. Department of the Air Force 2003. This resistance required expressly objecting to interpretations offered by the Office of Legal Counsel of U.S. law ratifying the Convention Against Torture.

90. In 1908 the American Bar Association (ABA), *Canons of Professional Ethics,* canon 22, established: "An officer of the law [is] charged, as is the lawyer, with the duty of aiding in the administration of justice." The 1983 *ABA Model Rules of Professional Conduct, Preamble and Scope,* ¶1, proclaims: "A lawyer . . . is . . . an officer of the legal system, having a special responsibility for the quality of justice."

91. On the distinctiveness of professional ethics, see Goldman 1980, 1–7, 283–292.

92. In a sociological study of small-town and rural Missouri lawyers, Landon (1982, 459) discovered that they are "very much part of local life, and thus local opinion and values have a salience for practice patterns not typical of larger settings." He further found (Landon 1985, 81) that "in the small town, the lawyer works in a system where expectations of clients, community, and colleagues pos-

sess a high degree of salience for the manner in which he works. The expectations of these separate groups tend to converge on the issue of zealous advocacy and result in the rural attorney's being less likely to exploit the possibilities for adversary combat."

Only 2 percent of American lawyers chiefly serve small towns or rural communities (Pruitt and Showman 2014). Yet nearly 20 percent of the country's population continues to reside there (U.S. Census Bureau 2016, table P2) and to be served by these professionals. We may therefore infer that the attorneys representing at least one-fifth of Americans continue to operate under older understandings of professional duty, more expansive than those of their big-city brethren in the range of social interests accorded some appreciation when contemplating ethical issues.

93. Many American law schools and professors (e.g., Rhode 2015, 143) have concluded that legal ethics is best taught in very practical workplace settings, such as clinics and externships, rather than in classroom discussions infused with sophisticated philosophical ideas claiming more comprehensive relevance.

94. Waldron offers no suggestion of an alternative social ontology, at least, within which such notions as parenting or doctoring would have a more clearly nominalist and constructivist character.

95. Goffman 1985, 132, 139.

96. In Elster (1985), Elster and fellow contributors from Western and non-Western psychology, philosophy, and economics offer one major treatment of this multiplicity.

97. In so doing, they manifest their affection as well, of course, though these feelings are here compatible with those of moral duty.

98. Though I have read some of the relevant literature on shamanism in cultural anthropology, I here rely chiefly on a long conversation with a local shaman in highlands Guatemala, Quetzaltenando, in 2014.

99. For questioning of this sort within the medical profession, see, e.g., Veatch 2001.

100. Kahneman 2011, 13–30, 415–418.

## 13. Common Morality Confronts Modernity

1. Savigny (1814, 11) wrote, for instance, that all law—and certainly the best law—has its origins and foundation in its "organic connection with the essence and character of the people."

2. Only the careless reader will be tempted to assimilate my central argument to that peculiar intellectual tradition. My call for acute legislative attentiveness to the state of social mores in any given area is admittedly congenial with an incrementalist approach to political and legal change. Yet most incrementalists these days—those who seek some theoretical basis for their policy views—espouse "new governance" or "democratic experimentalism," and these scholars often support legal changes unmistakably to the Left (on the American spectrum).

Burke thought it necessary, in highlighting the irreducible place of manners and mores for governing behavior, to simultaneously depreciate the importance of law, as if we necessarily debilitate the former as we increase our reliance on the latter. The stark simplicity of his position is evident in one of his most pithy pronouncements: "Manners are of more importance than laws. Upon them, in a great measure, the laws depend. The law touches us but here and there, and now and then. Manners are what vex or soothe, corrupt or purify, exalt or debase, barbarize or refine us, by constant, steady, uniform, insensible operation" (Burke 1999 [1796], 126). Burke offers no reason, however, to accord a universal primacy to mores, in all places across a society's several spheres of activity. He consequently exaggerates the need for dichotomous choice between these two forms of normativity. Montesquieu's standpoint is subtler and more probing, in posing trenchant questions concerning the myriad interactions between these normative orders—sometimes at odds and in rivalry, sometimes complementary.

Sociologists today remain largely committed to the general idea that the different aspects or spheres of a given social order are, like organs of a living body, finely interconnected, often in nonobvious ways. Yet these connections do not much closely approximate those within an organism, for that metaphor suggests a greater mutual indispensability and receptivity to reciprocal influence than is generally the case within society.

3. Some scholars (e.g., Wilson 2007, x–xiii) question whether the Victorians themselves truly possessed much in the way of common morality. But though Wilson shares some salacious anecdotes, he is obviously too keen—for polemical purposes presumably—to condemn all of "Victorian morality" as little but shallow, upper-class hypocrisy.

4. Habermas 1999, 990.

5. Habermas 1996, 452 (emphasis in original).

6. Veitch 2007, 26. He develops this argument with extended illustrations, notably including the harmful effects of lawful UN economic sanctions on Iraqi civilians during the decade following the 1991 Gulf War.

7. See Singer (2013, 3–9), who observes that for Montesquieu's opponents "juridico-political discourse does not ignore the facts [about social mores] . . . but for this discourse the significance of the facts can only be determined in terms of their accord with the juridico-political norm. As the latter alone constitutes order (and the value and sense conveyed by order), to the extent that the facts do not accord, they appear literally disordered and senseless. It is of secondary importance whether this senseless disorder is attributed to either a shortfall of the law and its enforcement, or to some active, negative principle, which is theological (evil), natural (corruption), or historical (the legacy of a dark and barbarous age)."

8. Manent 1998, 56–64, 75–84; Pangle 1973, 44–45.

9. Austin 1885, 294–295.

10. Mote 1989, 33–43.

11. Bentham 1970 [1782], 246.

12. Perreau-Saussine and Murphy 2007, 1, 2.

13. Uniform Commercial Code, §§1-102(2)(b), 2-202(a), 2-208(1) (1990).

14. In the common law, moral turpitude "involves grave infringement of the moral sentiment of the community" (*Navarro-Lopez v. Gonzalez,* 503 F.3d 1063, 1068, 9th Cir. 2007). The concept finds application in such diverse areas as professional licensing, immigration law, juror disqualification, witness impeachment, and voting rights.

15. This is "autopoiesis," in the idiom of systems theory: any modern legal system insists upon its "impenetrability as a normatively self-sufficient discourse" (Cotterrell 2003, 150, parsing Niklas Luhmann). Nothing may enter law's domain, in other words, without the explicit approval of its official professional gatekeepers, according to criteria they alone establish.

16. Fuller 1940, 111.

17. On humiliation, in particular, and its relation to shame and disgrace, see notably Miller 1995, 9, 118–134, 146, 178–181, 228–236.

18. Jacquet (2015, 177) recounts the recent history and considerable success of such programs.

19. Ibid., 116.

20. Ibid., 178.

21. Stearns 2017b, 53.

22. Stearns 2017a.

23. Foucault 1979 [1975], 9, 10, 13, 61, 107, 112.

24. Nussbaum 2004, 233–234. See also Posner 2000a, 88–98.

25. Whitman 1987, 1059, 1089.

26. "It would be a cruel state," she writes (Nussbaum 2004, 231), "that would string up someone for public viewing." Her coy allusion to lynching (see also 242) is wildly hyperbolic and willfully inflammatory. As Jacquet (2015, 120) observes of the shaming sanctions currently in use, "no one is tied to a pillory, clapped into the stocks, burned at the stake, or publicly hanged."

27. Bibas 2012, 2–11.

28. Ibid., 123–125. Braithwaite (1989) offers an influential formulation of current thinking on "reintegrative shaming," drawing express inspiration from Durkheim's *Moral Education* (1973) [1925].

29. Jacquet 2015, 143–146, 170–176.

30. Based on his considerable policy experience and social scientific inquiry into "restorative justice" programs, Braithwaite (2001, xi) concludes, "If . . . the disapproved actor . . . acknowledges this shame, respects the other's reasons for expressing the disapproval, and the other reciprocates this respect, so that they enter a dialogue about the problem, shame will have been a cause of constructive conflict." In other words, there is an important distinction between an "earned and forfeitable" shame, on one hand, and the type from which individual recovery and societal redemption is impossible, on the other. Shaming can be reintegrative when it is careful not to suggest that "the person being shamed . . . lacks fundamental human rights and worth" (Arneson 2007, 52).

31. See Jacquet (2015, 82–83), on the intentional evocation of disgust as a tactic in official campaigns of public shaming, such as that of Bangladesh against public defecation.

32. On the successes of certain consumer boycotts, see O'Rourke 2005, 126.

33. Jacquet (2015, dust jacket). She surely exaggerates, however, in suggesting that consumer boycotts can have no significant effect "unless nearly everyone participates."

34. To this end, Jacquet declines to suggest any new norm-setting, whether through the law or social mores. She is content to settle—and only at the very end of her book—for a few horrific anecdotes of abusive internet shaming, then abandons the subject.

35. Yet even Kant (2002 [1790], 154) found a special role for "enthusiasm," at least, admitting that "without it, nothing great can be accomplished." Whether enthusiasm can accurately be characterized as an emotion remains open to some question, however (Elster 2016).

36. Morgan (2008, 49) observes several distinct respects in which the emotion of shame is singularly social in nature.

37. Williams 1993, 82.

38. See, generally, Nussbaum 2001, 459–470, 710–713.

39. Deigh 2006, 400, 414.

40. Arneson 2007, 37 (emphasis added).

41. Ibid., 33.

42. Kahan 1999, 65.

43. Deigh 2006, 391.

44. Ibid.

45. Williams 1985, 84, 100; Williams 1993, 8384.

46. Arneson 2007, 48.

47. Deigh's and Arneson's interventions are rejoinders to Nussbaum (2004, esp. 177–188, 223–249). Though Nussbaum emphasizes shame's destructive dimensions, especially in its "primitive" form of "primary narcissism," she acknowledges briefly in passing that it may at times assume a more positive aspect.

48. Williams 1993, 90–91.

49. Ibid., 91–92.

50. Elster 1999, 149–153.

51. Jacquet 2015, 50–59.

52. Ibid., 21–22.

53. Ibid., 22–23.

54. Ibid., 82, 99.

55. Ibid., 41.

56. Ibid., 124. Though many employ social media in hopes of shaming others, the actual effect is often not to strengthen any single, shared morality, but to deepen division among subcommunities with radically different worldviews (Haidt 2017). Serious analysts of shame's place in contemporary society have not yet fully fathomed or grappled with this fact.

57. Jacquet 2015, 8.

58. Ibid., 114.

59. Ibid., 107.

60. Williams (1993, 92) well delineates how the same misconduct can involve both guilt and shame: "When I am a coward or let someone down, what I have done . . . points in one direction towards what has happened to others, and in another direction *to what I am*." (emphasis supplied). With these final words, Williams also shifts the analysis onto the terrain of virtue ethics.

61. Humiliation itself is often assumed as inherently inconsistent with the most minimal human dignity. Yet the term, as employed within ordinary language, actually encompasses a wide spectrum, in the measure of its hurtful intent and effects. These effects range from momentous to very modest, to the pretty "humiliations of day-to-day interaction, the little falls and barely perceptible attacks on our self-esteem and self-respect" (Miller 1995, 133).

62. Link and Phelan 2001, 367.

63. Scholars have found stigma's pernicious influence in "literally scores of circumstances," ranging from urinary incontinence, exotic dancing, and wheelchair use, to leprosy and terminal cancer (ibid., 363–364).

64. The term refers historically to the use of hot irons to permanently brand a person, in punishment for his crimes, and to the bodily perforations suffered by Jesus during his crucifixion.

65. Some may object to my regular reliance on dictionaries as a credible indicator of ordinary usage. Dictionaries and usage manuals offer only one point of entry into real-life linguistic practice, and I draw on many other sources as well. There was once a much greater gap than today between the definitions and rules of usage accepted into such volumes, on the one hand, and actual patterns of everyday speech, on the other. Beginning with the publication of *Webster's Third New International Dictionary* (1961), however, professed "descriptivists" have come to prevail over "prescriptivist" rivals; the gap between popular usage and published definitions has hence greatly narrowed.

66. This term, only very sketchily defined in the relevant sociological literature, refers to circumstances of domination and deprivation so severe as to deprive victims of all recognizable traces of human dignity or respect. Chattel slavery—in its most severe forms at least—presents the archetype.

67. Erving Goffman (1963, 2) wrote that stigma entails the treatment of others as "less than human."

68. Link and Phelan 2001, 377.

69. See O'Rourke 2005; Jacquet 2015; Bartley and Child 2014.

70. Jacquet 2015, 166–169.

71. Corbyn 2015 (quoting Jacquet). In a coauthored study based on laboratory experiments, Jacquet et al. (2011) found that the mild shaming of participants has a notable influence on their responses within game-theoretic scenarios.

72. Bartley and Child 2014, 669, 673.

73. See, for instance, McAdams and Rasumsen 2007, 1575, 1595, 1596, 1609; West 1997, 187–195; Ellickson 1991, 167–183.

74. Ellickson 1991; Bernstein 1992; Feldman 2006; West 1997; Greif 2006.

75. Hunter (2000, 8–13, 26–27, 146–148, 211–213, 217–220) offers the most credible argument to this effect. He shows how U.S. school curricula in what was

once avowedly called "moral education" shifted over the last half-century from efforts to propagate what educators considered enduring principles and virtues, both civic and theologically inspired, to an understanding of morality as simply one aspect of an individual's private quest for personal fulfillment.

76. Beginning only in the 1880s can we have great confidence that, among most people inhabiting its entire territory, there existed in France a subjective sense of shared nationality (Weber 1976, 297–298, 485–496, 546). This was chiefly a result of the unified system of mandatory public education created in these years (ibid., 303–338), a system explicitly committed to creating and preserving a shared national culture.

77. Ellickson 1991, 29–64.

78. Jacquet 2015, 128.

79. These paired ideal-types sought to contrast what was assumed to be the warm communality of village life among extended kin groups in preindustrial society with the alleged impersonality, alienation, anomie, and social antagonism thought to follow from industrialization, urbanization, democratization, and secularization. Early scholars conceived of this simple binary opposition several decades before the advent of genuine ethnography. Careful scholars of more empirical bent, investigating both Western and non-Western societies, long ago exhausted what there was to learn from this crude conceptual contrast, rejecting it in favor of typologies more complexly differentiated and analyses more attentive to historical and geographical particularity.

80. Barros 2003, 189–191.

81. Wozner 2000–2001, 49, 64–66.

82. Ibid., 49.

83. Leviticus 19:17. Cook (2003, 152), parsing this passage, observes that it "is adduced by the rabbis . . . to show that if a man sees something unseemly in his neighbor, it is his duty to rebuke him."

84. Barton 2014, 78 (quoting biblical scholar Walther Eichrodt).

85. Cook 2003, xi.

86. Thomson 1972, 109–142.

87. Rogers, Chuah, and Dockray (2016) describe the current state of regulation in this industry.

88. On this process, see Luhmann 1982, 229–254, 287.

89. Hunter 2000, 8–13, 26–27, 146–148, 211–213, 217–220.

90. Montesquieu 1949 [1748], bk. 8, chap. 11.

91. See, e.g., Putnam 2001, 147.

92. Trivers 1971; Bowles and Gintis 2004, 20–24.

93. Sperber and Baumard 2012, 495.

94. Rasmusen 2007.

95. Bicchieri and Muldoon 2011.

96. Bowles's most recent work on citizenship (Bowles 2016, 150) moves powerfully in this direction, departing from his prior emphasis (Bowles and Gintis 2004) on the centrality of self-interested reciprocity in securing desirable forms of public order.

97. Brinig 2010, 3.

98. See, notably, Bellah et al. 1985, 336; Boltanski and Thévenot 2006 [1991], 25–26.

99. Many sociological and political thinkers "suggest that individualism is necessarily antisocial," as Holmes (1993, 180) observes. Yet properly understood, individualism "can involve a heightened concern *for others* as individuals rather than as members of ascriptive groups" (ibid.).

100. I refer specifically to "act utilitarianism" (introduced by G. E. Moore), the view that one's acts are morally defensible only insofar as they produce greater overall happiness than would alternative courses of action.

101. Skyrms (2004, 1–13) offers one helpful, game-theoretic perspective on the conditions for cooperative interaction.

102. Annas and Densberger 1983–1984, 562–563.

103. Amundsen 1978, 26.

104. For one formulation of this ancient oath, see World Medical Association, *WMA Declaration of Geneva* (Sept. 1948), http://www.wma.net/en/30publications/10policies/g1/.

105. Pappas 1996, 387–389.

106. Best 1980, 211–215.

107. Hull 2014, 64.

108. Crawford 2013, 166–167; Robinson 2016, 257–270.

109. Best 1980, 201–202.

110. Vagts 1959, 361–363.

111. In pursuit of greater social equality, philosophic liberals (with near uniformity) seek to entirely replace honor—of any kind—with respect for human dignity. Yet as Spector (2009, 68–69) observes, "the abstract egalitarianism associated with dignity is not very conducive to emulation and to the development of talents," because basic dignity, unlike honors (whether earned or bestowed by birth), is already inherent in us all.

112. The alternative hypothesis here, not to be casually dismissed, is that elites within these historical vocations were simply once better able to conceal from public scrutiny the many situations—no less numerous than today, perhaps—where these traditional mechanisms of collegial restraint failed of their presumed purpose. It may therefore chiefly be modernity's greater transparency, its reduced asymmetries of information, that have prompted ever more assertive and successfully public efforts to regulate the ethics of armed conflict.

113. Ryan 2015, 62. Some seek to contrast this "political liberalism" with a more "perfectionist liberalism" (associated with Joseph Raz), which seeks to govern not only interactions with the state but human conduct generally. This second form of liberalism prizes the moral autonomy of individuals to choose among equally acceptable conceptions of the good life. And it understands the state's proper tasks to include the active promotion of this self-understanding, as autonomous creatures, among its citizens.

Both these liberalisms differ markedly from the views of many "progressives" today who, like communitarians of some years ago, begin by venturing a broadly solidaristic or fraternal conception of the good society, from which they then deduce certain virtuous qualities for all its members. The state then properly educates and "perfects" its citizens by instilling these virtues, which entail a vision of fused horizons or perception of common fate with all other members, and therefore an expansive regard for and official commitment to ensuring their flourishing.

114. Tomasi 2001, 40 (emphasis added).

115. Ibid., 71.

116. Ibid., 73–77.

117. Rawls 1971, 349.

118. Like the authors of my opening epigraphs, others of diverse theoretical inspiration voice concerns analogous to Montesquieu's, without making these as central a preoccupation. Consider, for instance: Benedict de Spinoza, in his *Tractatus-Politicus* (2007 [1670], 79), in a moralizing register: "He who seeks to determine everything by law will aggravate vices rather than correct them." Much more recently, there is Robert Ellickson (1991, 286), in drier scientific idiom: "Lawmakers who are unappreciative of the social conditions that foster informal cooperation are likely to create a world in which there is both more law and less order." Then we come to Bruno Latour, in a more acerbic tone, from *An Inquiry into Modes of Existence: An Anthropology of the Moderns* (2013, 362): "At various historical moments, the law has been entrusted with the task of bearing morality, religion, science, politics, the State, as if its fine spiderwebs on their own could keep humans from quarrelling, going for the jugular, tearing each other's guts out; as if it were law and law alone that had made us civilized—and even made us human." And finally, Axel Honneth (2013, 67), with Hegelian *hauteur* (and some long-windedness): "Nothing has been more fatal to the formulation of a concept of social justice than the recent tendency to dissolve all social relations into legal relationships, in order to make it easier to regulate these relationships through formal rules. This one-sided approach has caused us to lose sight of the fact that the conditions of justice are not only given in the form of positive rights, but also in the shape of appropriate attitudes, modes of comportment and behavioral routines."

119. Common morality becomes more demanding than tit-for-tat when people are prepared to punish its violation though they receive no personal gain for so doing, even that won by signaling their trustworthiness (Jordan et al. 2016). Though experimental psychology establishes that this willingness does exist, its range of effective operation in modern societies, beyond the laboratory and online research survey, remains quite uncertain.

120. Scanlon 1996, 229–230.

## Conclusion

1. Lazarus et al. 2009, 19.

2. A definitive work on my topic would be impossible, because the questions this book poses are no longer familiar. The hundreds of scholarly works I draw upon also were all written with purposes in mind very different from my own.

3. Above all, the volume seeks to prompt our thought in unaccustomed directions, by viewing the relation between law and morality through the lens, not of Anglo-American analytic philosophy, but of a certain neglected Continental tradition and the fruitful standpoint it still offers. Through an exercise in intellectual disinterment, I resurrect key elements of this tradition from sociology's early French founders, contemporizing their sharpest insights with further conceptual refinement and much recent evidence from across a wide swath of legal life, contemporary and historical, domestic and international.

4. Not since Marx, Weber, and Durkheim. Their ambitious *oeuvre*—its failings notwithstanding—continues, implicitly or explicitly, to provide the theoretical armature for the most valuable (if much humbler) socio-legal scholarship conducted since their day. Most of us are much aware of how far short, by their measure of achievement, we continue to fall.

5. Dickson (2001, 84–102) defends this widely held view of legal philosophy's proper scope.

6. Whether these various methods truly capture differing aspects of the same phenomenon is a problem of some conceptual complexity, requiring more sustained defense than here possible.

7. Foucault 1994, 540 (my translation).

8. Accusations to this effect are ubiquitous. O'Connor (2002), for instance, argues that "attending to the background is necessary because many aspects . . . are anything but harmless and trivial; failing to challenge them means leaving the framework of oppressive systems intact" (5–9). These include "racism, homophobia, violence against women and children" (6). "Not only, then, does the background slip from view, it ceases to be *anything*. There is nothing there to examine, and nothing for which we are responsible" (8, emphasis in original).

9. This study chiefly examines situations where the disparities and resulting tensions between law and mores are salutary and productive, for this goes largely unappreciated, while destructive tensions naturally draw greater attention. Among the circumstances regularly generating unproductive tensions are those involving so-called transplants (Nelken and Feest 2001) of Western law into non-Western societies whose mores remain much at odds with the philosophical understandings of self and society this liberal law often embodies. As Tamanaha (2017, 198) observes, "Transplanted law inevitably functions differently and has different social consequences because it is placed in a wholly different social milieu that it may conflict with, and it is deprived of informal norms and social attitudes that undergirded its functioning at home. With the passage of time, surrounding social arrangements develop in response to and in connection with the transplanted law, sometimes entrenching dysfunctionality, sometimes developing new ways of working."

10. These questions do not occupy the cutting edge of any currently raging debates and are in fact regarded as passé. Yet such timeless questions as Montesquieu's inexorably reassert themselves.

11. Verstein 2017, 48–49.

12. See Epstein (1997, 8, 10, 11), who also writes: "Social norms without legal enforcement do an enormous good. They should not be disparaged simply

because they are not perfect . . . The excesses of big government today often stem from a systematic misevaluation of the relative value of social and legal norms" (15). Less polemically, Pettit (2002, 279) wisely proposes that any adequate "theory of regulation must embody a theory as to when we can expect norms to emerge and stabilize spontaneously in a population." He undoubtedly takes this proposition to encompass norms forming the basis of shared indignation at perceived injustice.

13. It bears reminder (Sheehan and Wahrman 2015) that the endorsement of spontaneous ordering, via endogenous mechanisms of societal self-organization, has historically been no monopoly of the political Right. That versatile notion, variously understood, was shared by many modern and early modern thinkers of differing political stripe, including Thomas Paine (see ibid., 280–283).

14. These summary observations suggest that recent social science was too quick to entirely discard the paired ideal-types of "modern" and "traditional" societies, and that these concepts retain some untapped value.

15. See, e.g., Douthat 2018.

# REFERENCES


Abbott, Andrew. 1988. *The System of Professions: An Essay on the Division of Expert Labor.* Chicago: University of Chicago Press.

Abdalla, Raqiya Haji Dualeh. 1982. *Sisters in Affliction: Circumcision and Infibulation of Women in Africa.* London: Zed Press.

Abercrombie, Nicholas, Stephen Hill, and Bryan S. Turner. 1980. *The Dominant Ideology Thesis.* London: Allen and Unwin.

Abolafia, Mitchel Y. 1996. *Making Markets: Opportunism and Restraint on Wall Street.* Cambridge, MA: Harvard University Press.

Abraham, Kenneth. 1986. *Distributing Risk: Insurance, Legal Theory, and Public Policy.* New Haven: Yale University Press.

Achen, Christopher, and Larry Bartels. 2016. *Democracy for Realists: Why Elections Do Not Produce Responsive Government.* Princeton: Princeton University Press.

Adam, Barbara, Ulrich Beck, and Joost van Loon, eds. 2000. *The Risk Society and Beyond: Critical Issues for Social Theory.* Thousand Oaks, CA: Sage.

Agrama, Hussein Ali. 2010. Secularism, Sovereignty, Indeterminacy: Is Egypt a Secular or a Religious State? *Comparative Studies in Society and History* 52:495–523.

AHC Media. 2003. Mental Retardation and Reproductive Freedom. November 1. https://www.ahcmedia.com/articles/25985-mental-retardation-and-reproductive-freedom.

Ahern, Lawrence. 2005. Homestead and Other Exemptions under the Bankruptcy Abuse Prevention and Consumer Protection Act: Observations on Asset Protection after 2005. *American Bankruptcy Institute Law Review.* 13:585–616.

Ahmari, Sohrab. 2017. How Liberals Killed the Freedom of Movement. *Wall Street Journal,* January 31.

Alesina, Alberto, and Edward L. Glaeser. 2004. *Fighting Poverty in the US and Europe: A World of Difference.* Oxford: Oxford University Press.

Alexander, Jeffrey, ed. 1990. *Durkheimian Sociology: Cultural Studies.* Cambridge: Cambridge University Press.

———. 1992. Citizen and Enemy as Symbolic Classification: On the Polarizing Discourse in Civil Society. In *Cultivating Differences: Symbolic Boundaries and the Making of Inequality,* edited by Michèle Lamont and Marcel Fournier. Chicago: University of Chicago Press.

———. 2011. *Performative Revolution in Egypt: An Essay in Cultural Power.* London: Bloomsbury Academic.

Alexander, Jeffrey, Bernard Giesen, and Jason Mast, eds. 2006. *Social Performance: Symbolic Action, Cultural Pragmatics, and Ritual.* Cambridge: Cambridge University Press.

Alexander, Larry. 2003. The Legal Enforcement of Morality. In *A Companion to Applied Ethics,* edited by R. G. Frey and Christopher Heath Wellman. Malden, MA: Blackwell.

Alford, C. Fred. 2001. *Whistleblowers: Broken Lives and Organizational Power.* Ithaca, NY: Cornell University Press.

Ally, Shireen. 2009. *From Servants to Workers: South African Domestic Workers and the Democratic State.* Ithaca, NY: ILR Press/Cornell University Press.

Alterini, Atilio Anibal, and Robert López Cabana. 1990. El Abuso del Derecho: Estudio de Derecho Comparativo. *Revista Jurídica Argentina La Ley* B:1101–1117.

Altman, David. 2011. *Direct Democracy Worldwide.* Cambridge: Cambridge University Press.

American Community Survey Reports. 2011. *Marital Events of Americans: 2009.* Washington, DC: U.S. Census Bureau.. https://www.census.gov/prod/2011pubs/acs-13.pdf.

American Enterprise Institute. 2012. *Attitudes about Abortion,* compiled by Karlyn Bowman and Andrew Rugg. Washington, DC: AEI Public Opinion Studies.

American Muslims for Palestine. 2014. Seventh Annual Conference for Palestine in the US: Gaza Teaches Life! November 27–29, Chicago. https://web.archive.org/web/20141207040920/http:/www.conference.ampalestine.org/index.php/programs.

Amundsen, Darrel. 1978. The Physician's Obligation to Prolong Life: A Medical Duty without Classical Roots. *Hastings Center Report* 8:23–30.

Anderson, Elijah. 1999. *Code of the Street: Decency, Violence, and the Moral Life of the Inner City.* New York: W. W. Norton.

———. 2003. *A Place on the Corner.* 2nd ed. Chicago: University of Chicago Press.

Anderson, Elizabeth. 1993. *Value in Ethics and Economics.* Cambridge, MA: Harvard University Press.

———. 2000. Beyond *Homo Economicus:* New Developments in Theories of Social Norms. *Philosophy and Public Affairs* 29:170–200.

Anderson, Michelle J. 2003. Marital Immunity, Intimate Relationships, and Improper Inferences: A New Law on Sexual Offenses by Intimates. *Hastings Law Review* 54:1465–1574.

Anderson, Miriam, and Esther Arroyo i Amayuelas. 2011. *The Law of Succession: Testamentary Freedom, European Perspectives*. Groningen: Europa Law.

Anderson, Perry. 2017. *The Antimonies of Antonio Gramsci*. London: Verso.

Andrews, Kenneth, and Charles Seguin. 2015. Group Threat and Policy Change: The Spatial Dynamics of Prohibition Politics, 1890–1919. *American Journal of Sociology* 121:475–510.

Annas, George, and Joan Densberger. 1983–1984. Competence to Refuse Medical Treatment: Autonomy vs. Paternalism. *University of Toledo Law Review* 15:561–596.

Anscombe, G. E. M. 1958. Modern Moral Philosophy. *Philosophy*, 33, no. 124: 1–19.

Anspach, Renee. 1993. *Deciding Who Lives: Fateful Choices in the Intensive-Care Nursery*. Berkeley: University of California Press.

Antenori, Frank, and Hans Halberstadt. 2006. *Roughneck Nine-One: The Extraordinary Story of a Special Forces A-Team at War*. New York: St. Martin's Press.

Appelbaum, Binyamin. 2014. The Vanishing Male Worker: How America Fell Behind. *New York Times*, Dec. 11, http://www.nytimes.com/2014/12/12/upshot/unemployment-the-vanishing-male-worker-how-america-fell-behind.html.

Aquinas, Thomas. 1964 [1274]. *Summa Theologiae*. Edited and translated by Edmund Hill. London: McGraw-Hill.

Archard, David. 2004. *Children: Rights and Childhood*, London: Routledge.

Ariely, Daniel. 2009. *Predictably Irrational: The Hidden Forces That Shape Our Decisions*. New York: Harper Collins.

Armitage, David. 2007. *The Declaration of Independence: A Global History*. Cambridge, MA: Harvard University Press.

Arneson, Richard. 2007. Shame, Stigma, and Disgust in the Decent Society. *Journal of Ethics* 11:31–63.

Associated Press. 2013. Chinese Workers Hold Managers Hostage after Toilet Break Changes. *The Guardian*, Jan 22.

Associated Press/NORC. 2015. Americans Evaluate the Balance between Security and Civil Liberties. http://www.apnorc.org/projects/Pages/americans-evaluate-the-balance-between-security-and-civil-liberties.aspx.

Atiyah, Patrick. 1979. *The Rise and Fall of Freedom of Contract*. Oxford: Oxford University Press.

Austin, John. 1885. *Lectures on Jurisprudence*. London: John Murray.

Austin, John L. 1956. A Plea for Excuses: The Presidential Address. *Proceedings of the Aristotelian Society* 57:1–30.

———. 1975 [1962]. *How to Do Things with Words*. Edited by J. O. Urmson and Marina Sbisà. Cambridge, MA: Harvard University Press.

Autor, David H. 2011. *The Unsustainable Rise of the Disability Rolls in the United States: Causes, Consequences, and Policy Options.* Working Paper No. 17697, National Bureau of Economic Research.

Autor, David H., and Melanie Wasserman. 2013. Wayward Sons: The Emerging Gender Gap in Wages and Education. *Third Way.* http://economics.mit.edu/files/8754.

Bagley, Constance. 2010. What's Law Got to Do with It: Integrating Law and Strategy. *Academy of Management Review* 47:587–639.

Bajos, Nathalie, Agathe Lemarche-Vadel, Fabien Gilbert, Michèle Ferrand, COCON Group, and Caroline Moreau. 2006. Contraception at the Time of Abortion: High-Risk Time or High-Risk Women. *Human Reproduction* 21:2862–2867.

Baker, J. H. 2002. *An Introduction to English Legal History.* 4th ed. London: Buttersworth / LexisNexis.

Baker, Tom. 2008. Liability Insurance at the Tort-Crime Boundary. In *Fault Lines: Tort Law as Cultural Practice,* edited by David Engel and Michael McCann. Stanford: Stanford University Press.

Baker, Tom, and Jonathan Simon, eds. 2002. *Embracing Risk: The Changing Culture of Insurance and Responsibility.* Chicago: University of Chicago Press.

Bakhtin, Mikhail. 1968. *Rabelais and His World.* Translated by Helene Iswolsky. Bloomington: Indiana University Press.

Balko, Radley. 2013. *Rise of the Warrior Cop: The Militarization of America's Police Forces.* Philadelphia: Perseus Books Group.

Baltzell, Digby. 1989. *Philadelphia Gentlemen: The Making of a National Upper Class.* Glencoe, IL: Free Press.

Bankman, Joseph. 2004. The Tax Shelter Problem. *National Tax Journal* 57:925–936.

Bannon, Steven. 2014. Module 3: Should Christians Impose Limits on Wealth Creation? *Dignitatis Humanae Instit.,* July 29. https://www.youtube.com/watch?v=FWXScQaZ2uI.

Barnett, M. L., and R. M. Solomon. 2012. Does It Pay to be Really Good? *Strategic Management Journal* 33:1304–1320.

Baron, Jane B. 2013. Rescuing the Bundle-of-Rights Metaphor in Property Law. *University of Cincinnati Law Review* 82:57–101.

Barros, Robert. 2003. Dictatorship and the Rule of Law: Rules and Military Power in Pinochet's Chile. In *Democracy and the Rule of Law,* edited by José María Maravall and Adam Przeworski. Cambridge: Cambridge University Press.

Bartley, Tim, and Curtis Child. 2014. Shaming the Corporation: Globalization, Reputation, and the Dynamics of Anti-Corporate Movements. *American Sociological Review* 79:653–679.

Barton, John. 2014. *Ethics in Ancient Israel.* Oxford: Oxford University Press.

Barton-Hanson, Renu. 2015. Sterilization of Men with Intellectual Disabilities: Whose Best Interest Is It Anyway? *Medical Law International* 15:49–73.

Bastié, Eugénie. 2017. Nathalie Heinich: La sociologie bourdieusienne est devenue un dogme de la gauche radicale. *Le Figaro* (Paris), April 8.

Basu, Kaushik. 1999. International Labor Standards and Child Labor. *Challenge* 42:80–93.

Bayer, Ronald. 2008. Stigma and the Ethics of Public Health: Not Can We but Should We. *Social Science and Medicine* 67:463–472.

Bayles, Martha. 1994. *Hole in Our Soul: The Loss of Beauty and Meaning in American Popular Music.* New York: Free Press.

Baylor University. 2014. Evangelicals Have Higher-than-Average Divorce Rates, according to a Report Compiled by Baylor for the Council on Contemporary Families. Baylor University, Media Communications, February 5. http://www.baylor.edu/mediacommunications/news.php?action=story&story=137892.

Beach, Mary Catherine, and R. Sean Morrison. 2002. The Effect of Do-Not-Resuscitate Orders on Physician Decision-Making. *Journal of the American Geriatrics Society* 50:2057–2061.

Beauchamp, Thomas L. 2005. The Nature of Applied Ethics. In *A Companion to Applied Ethics,* edited by R. G. Frey and Christopher Heath Wellman. Malden, MA: Blackwell.

Beauchamp, Thomas L., and James F. Childress. 2001. *Principles of Biomedical Ethics.* 5th ed. Oxford: Oxford University Press.

Beckert, Jens. 2008. *Inherited Wealth.* Translated by Thomas Dunlap. Princeton: Princeton University Press.

Beebe, Leslie. 1995. Polite Fictions: Instrumental Rudeness as Pragmatic Competence. In *Georgetown University Round Table on Language Teaching: Ethnolinguistic, Psycholinguistic, and Sociolinguistic Aspects,* edited by J. E. Alatis et al. Washington, DC: Georgetown University Press.

Beeman, William. 1986. *Language, Status, and Power in Iran.* Bloomington: Indiana University Press.

Behr, Eduard. 2011. *Prohibition: Thirteen Years That Changed America.* New York: Arcade.

Beisel, Nicola. 1997. *Imperiled Innocents: Anthony Comstock and Family Reproduction in Victorian America.* Princeton: Princeton University Press.

Belkin, Douglas. 2018. Colleges Bend the Rules for More Students, Give Them Extra Help. *Wall Street Journal*, May 24.

Bell, Daniel. 1996 [1976]. *The Cultural Contradictions of Capitalism.* New York: Basic Books.

Bell, John. 2001. *French Legal Cultures.* London: Butterworth Books.

Bellah, Robert N., Richard Madsen, William M. Sullivan, Ann Swidler, and Steven M. Tipton. 1985. *Habits of the Heart.* Berkeley: University of California Press.

Benhabib, Seyla. 1992. *Situating the Self.* Cambridge, MA: Polity Press.

Bennett, Jane, and Michael J. Shapiro, eds. 2002. *The Politics of Moralizing.* New York: Routledge.

Bennett, Mark W., Justin D. Levinson, and Koichi Hioki. 2017. Judging Federal White-Collar Fraud Sentencing: An Empirical Study Revealing the Need for Further Reform. *Iowa Law Review* 102:939–1000.

Benson, Peter. 2008. Good Clean Tobacco: Philip Morris, Biocapitalism, and the Social Course of Stigma in North Carolina. *American Ethnologist* 35:357–379.

Bentham, Jeremy. 1970 [1780–1782]. *Of Laws in General (The Collected Works of Jeremy Bentham)*. Edited by H. L. A. Hart. London: Athlone Press.

Berberich, Cristine. 2007. *The Image of the English Gentleman in Twentieth Century Literature: Englishness and Nostalgia*. Farnham, UK: Ashgate.

Bernard, Tara Siegel. 2011. Fewer Americans File for Bankruptcy. *New York Times,* July 6. http://www.nytimes.com/2011/07/07/your-money/fewer-americans-filing-for-bankruptcy.html?_r=0.

Bernstein, Gaia, and Tvi Triger. 2011. Over-Parenting. *U.C. Davis Law Review* 44:1221–1279.

Bernstein, Lisa. 1992. Opting Out of the Legal System: Extralegal Contractual Relations in the Diamond Industry. *Journal of Legal Studies* 21:115–157.

———. 1996. Merchant Law in a Merchant Court: Rethinking the Code's Search for Immanent Business Norms. *Pennsylvania Law Review* 144:1765–1821.

———. 1999. The Questionable Empirical Basis of Article 2's Incorporation Strategy: A Preliminary Guide. *University of Chicago Law Review* 66:710–780.

———. 2015. Custom in the Courts. *Northwestern Law Review* 110:63–113.

Best, Geoffrey. 1980. *Humanity in Warfare: The Modern History of the International Law of Armed Conflicts*. London: Weidenfeld and Nicolson.

Bhabha, Homi. 1990. DissemiNation: Time, Narrative, and the Margins of the Modern Nation. In *Narration and Nation,* edited by Homi Bhabha. London: Routledge.

Bibas, Stephanos. 2012. *The Machinery of Criminal Justice*. New York: Oxford University Press.

Biblarz, Timothy J., and Adrian E. Raftery. 1999. Family Structure, Educational Attainment, and Socioeconomic Success: Rethinking the "Pathology of Matriarchy." *American Journal of Sociology* 105:321–365.

Bicchieri, Cristina, and Ryan Muldoon. 2011. Social Norms. *Stanford Encyclopedia of Philosophy*. https://plato.stanford.edu/entries/social-norms/.

Biggs, Andrew. 2015a. Averting the Disability Insurance Meltdown. *Wall Street Journal,* February 23.

———. 2015b. Disabling Entitlement Reform. *Wall Street Journal,* September 7.

Bilefsky, Dan. 2005. Belgian Experiment: Make Prostitution Legal to Fight Its Ills. *Wall Street Journal,* May 26.

Bird, Robert. 2010. The Many Futures of Legal Strategy. *American Business Law Journal* 47:575–586.

———. 2011. Law, Strategy, and Competitive Advantage. *Connecticut Law Review* 44:61–95.

Bird, Robert, and David Orozco. 2014. Finding the Right Corporate Legal Strategy. *MIT Sloan Management Review* 56:81–89.

Black, Donald. 1976. *The Behavior of Law*. Bingley, UK: Emerald Group.

Blanchard, Margaret. 1977. The Hutchins Commission: The Press and the Responsibility Concept. *Journalism Monographs* 49:1–59.

Blassingame, John. 1979. *The Slave Community: Plantation Life in the Antebellum South.* New York: Oxford University Press.

Bloch, Marc, and Scott Moorman. 1993. Working to Rule and Other Alternate Job Actions. *Labor Lawyer* 9:169–188.

Blustein, Jeffrey. 1982. *Parents and Children: The Ethics of the Family.* New York: Oxford University Press.

Bogart, W. A. 2011. *Permit but Discourage: Regulating Excessive Consumption.* Oxford: Oxford University Press.

———. 2013. *Regulating Obesity? Government, Society, and Questions of Health.* New York: Oxford University Press.

Bohannan, Paul. 1965. The Differing Realms of Law. *American Anthropologist* 67:33–42.

Bolgár, Vera. 1975. Abuse of Rights in France, Germany, and Switzerland: A Survey of a Recent Chapter in Legal Doctrine. *Louisiana Law Review* 35:1015–1036.

Bolt, Wilko, and Harold Houba. 2002. *Credible Threats in Negotiation: A Game-Theoretic Approach.* New York: Springer.

Boltanski, Luc, and Eve Chiapello. 2005. *The New Spirit of Capitalism,* Translated by Gregory Elliott. London: Verso.

Boltanski, Luc, and Laurent Thévenot. 2006 [1991]. *On Justification: Economies of Worth.* Translated by Catherine Porter. Princeton: Princeton University Press.

Bongaarts, John. 2013. The Implementation of Preferences for Male Offspring. *Population and Development Review* 39:185–208.

Boorstein, Michelle, and Peyton M. Craighill. 2014. Pope Francis Faces Church Divided over Doctrine, Global Poll of Catholics Finds. *Washington Post,* February 9. https://www.washingtonpost.com/national/pope-francis-faces-church-divided-over-doctrine-global-poll-of-catholics-finds/2014/02/08/e90ecef4-8f89-11e3-b227-12a45d109e03_story.html.

Bosman, Julie. 2016. At Iowa High School, Election Results Kindle Tensions and Protests. *New York Times,* November 19.

Bound, John, Stephan Lindner, and Timothy Waidmann. 2014. Reconciling Findings on the Employment Effect of Disability Insurance. *Journal of Labor Policy* 3:11–23.

Bourdieu, Pierre. 1984. *Distinction: A Social Critique of the Judgment of Taste.* Translated by Richard Nice. London: Routledge.

Bowen, John R. 2001. *Shari'a State, and Social Norms in France and Indonesia.* Leiden: Isim.

Bowles, Samuel. 2016. *The Moral Economy: Why Good Incentives Are No Substitute for Good Citizens.* New Haven: Yale University Press.

Bowles, Samuel, and Herbert Gintis. 2004. The Evolution of Strong Reciprocity: Cooperation in Heterogeneous Populations. *Theoretical Population Biology* 65:17–28.

Bowman, Tim, and Renee Montagne. 2009. Rules of Engagement Are a Dilemma for U.S. Troops. *NPR,* December 11. http://www.npr.org/templates/story/story.php?storyId=121330893.

Braithwaite, John. 1989. *Crime, Shame, and Reintegration.* Cambridge: Cambridge University Press.

———. 2001. Foreword. *Emotions and Violence: Shame and Rage in Destructive Conflicts,* edited by Thomas J. Scheff and Suzanne M. Retzinger. Lexington, MA: Lexington Books.

Bramlett, Matthew, and William Mosher. 2002. Cohabitation, Marriage, Divorce, and Remarriage in the United States, *Vital Health Statistics,* ser. 23, no. 22. http://www.ezjustice.com/Topical_Material/New%20CDC%20Divorce%20Study.pdf.

Brashier, Ralph C. 1996. Protecting the Child from Inheritance: Must Louisiana Stand Alone? *Louisiana Law Review* 57:1–26.

Brennan, Geoffrey, and Philip Pettit. 2004. *The Economy of Esteem: An Essay on Civil and Political Society.* Oxford: Oxford University Press.

Brennan, Jason, and Peter Jaworski. 2016. *Markets without Limits: Moral Virtues and Commercial Interests.* New York: Routledge.

Brinig, Margaret. 2000. *From Contract to Covenant: Beyond the Law and Economics of the Family.* Cambridge, MA: Harvard University Press.

———. 2010. *Family, Law, and the Community: Supporting the Covenant.* Chicago: University of Chicago Press.

Bronsteen, John, Christopher Buccafusco, and Jonathan Masur. 2008. Hedonic Adaptation and the Settlement of Civil Lawsuits. *Columbia Law Review* 108:1516–1549.

Brooks, David. 2012. Why Our Elites Stink. *New York Times,* July 12.

Brown, Evelyn L. 2000. The Uncertainty of U.C.C. Section 2-302: Why Unconscionability Has Become a Relic. *Commercial Law Journal* 105:287–308.

Brown, Louis. 1998. What Is Preventive Law? Whittier Law School. http://cyberinstitute.com/preventivelaw/week1.htm.

Brunner, Chris J. H. 1977. Abuse of Rights in Dutch Law. *Louisiana Law Review* 37:729–746.

Brunner-Huber, Larissa, and Jessica Toth. 2007. Obesity and Oral Contraceptive Use: Findings from the 2002 National Survey of Family Growth. *American Journal of Epidemiology* 166:1306–1311.

Bulman-Pozen, Jessica, and David Pozen. 2015. Uncivil Disobedience. *Columbia Law Review* 115:809–872.

Burke, Edmund. 1999 [1796]. *The Selected Works of Edmund Burke.* Vol. 3, *Letters on a Regicide Peace.* Carmel, IN: Liberty Fund.

Burke, Peter. 1978. *Popular Culture in Early Modern Europe.* New York: NYU Press.

Burkle, Christopher, Paul S. Mueller, Keith M. Swetz, C. Christopher Hook, and Mark T. Keegan. 2012. Physician Perspectives and Compliance with Patient Advance Directives: The Role External Factors Play on Physician Decision

Making. *BioMed Central: Medical Ethics,* April 21. http://bmcmedethics.biomedcentral.com/articles/10.1186/1472-6939-13-31.

Burstein, Paul. 2014. *American Public Opinion, Advocacy, and Policy in Congress: What the Public Wants and What It Gets.* New York: Cambridge University Press.

Butler, Ian. 2003. *Divorcing Children: Children's Experience of Their Parents' Divorce.* London: Jessica Kingsley.

Buzzell, Colby. 2005. *My War: Killing Time in Iraq.* New York: G. P. Putnam and Sons.

Byers, Michael. 2002. Abuse of Rights: An Old Principle, a New Age. *McGill Law Journal* 47:389–431.

Cahn, Naomi. 1997. The Moral Complexities of Family Law. *Stanford Law Review* 50:225–271.

Calabresi, Guido. 1970. *The Costs of Accidents: A Legal and Economic Analysis.* New Haven: Yale University Press.

California Fair Political Practices Commission. 2010. Big Money Talks. http://www.fppc.ca.gov/content/dam/fppc/documents/Education-External-Division/Big_Money_Talks.pdf.

Callahan, Daniel. 2013. Obesity: Chasing an Elusive Epidemic. *Hastings Center Reports* 43:34–40.

Callahan, David. 2014. Who's Who at the Secretive Susan Thompson Buffett Foundation? *Inside Philanthropy,* February 4. https://www.insidephilanthropy.com/home/2014/2/4/whos-who-at-the-secretive-susan-thompson-buffett-foundation.html.

Callimachi, Rukimini. 2015. ISIS Enshrines a Theology of Rape. *New York Times,* August 13.

Callon, Michel. 1998. The Embeddedness of Economic Markets in Economics. *Sociological Review* 46:1–57.

Cameron, David. 2010. *Conservative Manifesto: Invitation to Join the Government of Britain.* London: Conservative Party of Britain.

Campbell, Donovan. 2009. *Joker One: A Marine Platoon's Story of Courage, Sacrifice, and Brotherhood.* New York: Random House.

Caplan, Jane. 1998. *Government without Administration: State and Civil Service in Weimar and Nazi Germany.* Oxford: Oxford University Press.

Capoccia, Giovanni. 2013. Militant Democracy: The Institutional Basis of Democratic Self-Preservation. *Annual Review of Law and Social Science* 9:207–226.

Carlson, Licia. 2005. Docile Bodies, Docile Minds: Foucauldian Reflections on Mental Retardation. In *Foucault and the Government of Disability,* edited by Shelley Tremain. Ann Arbor: University of Michigan Press.

Carpenter, David, and David A. Moss. 2013. *Preventing Regulatory Capture: Special Interest Influence and How to Limit It.* New York: Cambridge University Press.

Carvajal, Doreen. 2013. Museums Confront the Skeletons in Their Closets. *New York Times,* March 24.

Celermajer, Danielle. 2009. *The Sins of the Nation and the Ritual of Apologies.* Cambridge: Cambridge University Press.

———. 2013. Mere Ritual? Displacing the Myth of Sincerity in Transitional Rituals. *International Journal of Transitional Justice* 7:286–305.

Centers for Disease Control and Prevention. 2016. Deaths from Prescription Opioid Overdose. *CDC,* December 16. http://www.cdc.gov/drugoverdose/data/overdose.html.

Chan, Cheris Shun-Ching. 2012. *Marketing Death: Culture and the Making of a Life Insurance Market in China.* Oxford: Oxford University Press.

Chen, Victor Tan. 2015. *Cut Loose: Jobless and Hopeless in an Unfair Economy.* Berkeley: University of California Press.

Chesney, Robert. 2011. Who May be Killed? Anwar Al-Awlaki as a Case Study in the International Legal Regulation of Lethal Force. *Yearbook of International Humanitarian Law* 13:3–60.

Chester, Ronald. 1998. Disinheritance and the American Child: An Alternative from British Columbia. *Utah Law Review* 1998:1–36.

Chidhester, David and Edward Linenthal, eds. 1995. "Introduction." In *American Sacred Space.* Bloomington: Indiana University Press.

Chinkin, Christine. 1989. The Challenge of Soft Law: Development and Change in International Law. *International and Comparative Law Quarterly* 38:850–866.

Chivers, Christopher J. 2010. General Faces Unease among His Own Troops. *New York Times,* June 22.

———. 2012. A Changed Way of War in Afghanistan's Skies. *New York Times,* January 15.

Chokshi, Niraj. 2014. Why Is Use of Disability Benefits So Erratic by County? *Washington Post,* April 4.

Choose Your Parents Wisely. 2014. *The Economist,* July 24. http://www.economist.com/news/united-states/21608779-there-large-class-divide-how-americans-raise-their-children-rich-parents-can.

Cialdini, Robert. 2007. Descriptive Social Norms as Underappreciated Sources of Social Control. *Psychometrika* 72:63–85.

Citizens Against Pro-Obama Media Bias. 2010. Fareed Zakaria, Bret Stephens, Peter Beinart Discuss 9-11 Mosque. http://citizensagainstproobamamediabias.wordpress.com/2010/08/23/fareed-zakaria-bret-stephens-peter-beinart-discuss-9-11-mosque-videotext/.

Citro, Brian, Jeff Gilson, Sital Kalantry, et al. 2014. *Replacing Myths with Facts: Sex-Selective Abortion Laws in the United States.* Cornell Law Faculty Publication No.1399. http://scholarship.law.cornell.edu/facpub/1399.

Clark, Geoffrey. 1999. *Betting on Lives: The Culture of Life Insurance in England, 1695–1775.* Manchester: Manchester University Press.

Clarke, Stewart, and Cornelia Alison-Brentano. 2006. *Divorce: Causes and Consequences.* New Haven: Yale University Press.

Clermont, Kevin, and Stewart Schwab. 2009. Employment Discrimination Plaintiffs in Federal Court: From Bad to Worse? *Harvard Law and Policy Review* 3:103–132.

CNN Politics. 2010. Overwhelming Majority Oppose Mosque Near Ground Zero, Aug. 11. http://politicalticker.blogs.cnn.com/2010/08/11/overwhelming-majority-oppose-mosque-near-ground-zero/.

Coffee, John. 2006. *Gatekeepers: The Professions and Corporate Governance.* New York: Oxford University Press.

Cohen, Eliot A. 1985. Tocqueville on War. *Social Philosophy and Policy* 3:204–222.

Cohen, Felix. 1935. Transcendental Nonsense and the Functional Approach. *Columbia Law Review* 35:809–849.

Cohen, Stanley. 2011 [1972]. *Folk Devils and Moral Panics.* London: Routledge.

Cohen-Cole, Ethan, and Burcu Duygan-Bump. 2008. *Household Bankruptcy Decision: The Role of Social Stigma vs. Information Sharing.* Federal Reserve Bank of Boston Working Paper No. QAU08-6. http://www.bostonfed.org/bankinfo/qau/wp/2008/qau0806.htm.

Collie, Alex, Tyler Lane, Lee Hatherell, and Chris McLeod. 2015. *Compensation Policy and Return to Work Effectiveness (ComPARE) Project: Introductory Report.* Research Report No. 118-1005-R01, October 5. Institute for Safety, Compensation and Recovery Research.

Collins, Harry M., and Robert Evans. 2007. *Rethinking Expertise.* Chicago: University of Chicago Press.

Collins, Hugh. 2014. Implied Terms: The Foundations of Good Faith and Fair Dealing. *Current Legal Problems* 67:297–331.

Collins, Lauren G., Susan Parks, and Laraine Winter. 2006. The State of Advance Care Planning: One Decade after SUPPORT. *American Journal of Hospice and Palliative Care* 23:378–384.

Colton, Matthew. 1997. *Stigma and Social Welfare: An International Comparative Study.* Brookfield, VT: Ashgate.

Commission on Freedom of the Press. 1947. *A Free and Responsible Press.* Chicago: University of Chicago Press.

Connaughton, Jeffrey. 2012. *The Payoff: Why Wall Street Always Wins.* New York: Prospecta Press.

Conrad, Peter. 2007. *The Medicalization of Society: On the Transformation of Human Conditions into Treatable Disorders.* Baltimore: Johns Hopkins University Press.

Cook, Michael. 2003. *Forbidding Wrong in Islam: An Introduction.* Cambridge: Cambridge University Press.

Cooperman, Alan, James Bell, Neha Sahgal, and Katherine Ritchey. 2014. Religion in Latin America: Widespread Change in a Historically Catholic Region. Pew Research Center, November 13. http://www.pewforum.org/files/2014/11/Religion-in-Latin-America-11-12-PM-full-PDF.pdf.

Corbin, Arthur. 1963. Corbin on Contracts. Minneapolis: West Publishing.

Corbyn, Zoë. 2015. Jennifer Jacquet: The Power of Shame Is That It Can Be Used by the Weak against the Strong. *Guardian,* March 6. https://www.theguardian.com/books/2015/mar/06/is-shame-necessary-review.

Coser, Lewis. 1964. *The Functions of Social Conflict.* Glencoe, IL: Free Press.

Costa, Dora, and Matthew E. Kahn. 2003. Civic Engagement and Community Heterogeneity: An Economist's Perspective. *Perspectives on Politics* 1:103–111.

Côté, Stéphane, Paul Piff, and Robb Willer. 2012. For Whom Do the Ends Justify the Means? Social Class and Utilitarian Moral Judgment. *Journal of Personality and Social Psychology* 104:490–503.

Cotterrell, Roger. 2003. Comparative Law and Sociology. In *Comparative Legal Studies: Traditions and Transitions,* edited by Pierre Legrand and Roderick Munday. Cambridge: Cambridge University Press.

Cottrol, Robert J. 1987. Liberalism and Paternalism: Ideology, Economic Interest and the Business Law of Slavery. *American Journal of Legal History* 31:359–373.

Crawford, Neta. 2013. *Accountability for Killing: Moral Responsibility for Collateral Damage during America's Post-9/11 Wars.* Oxford: Oxford University Press.

Crockett, Molly J., Annemieke Apergis-Schoute, Benedikt Herrmann, Matthew D. Lieberman, Ulrich Müller, Trevor W. Robbins, and Luke Clark. 2013. Serotonin Modulates Striatal Responses to Fairness and Retaliation in Humans. *Journal of Neuroscience* 33:3505–3513.

Crockett, Molly J., Luke Clark, Matthew D. Lieberman, G. Tabibnia, and T. W. Robbins. 2010. Impulsive Choice and Altruistic Punishment Are Corrected and Increase in Tandem with Serotonin Depletion. *Emotion: American Psychological Association* 10:855–862.

Crow, Thomas E. 1998. *Modern Art in the Common Culture.* New Haven: Yale University Press.

Cumming-Bruce, Nick, and Steven Erlanger. 2009. Swiss Ban Building of Minarets on Mosques. *New York Times,* November 29.

Curtin, Sally, Stephanie Ventura, and Gladys Martinez. 2014. *Recent Declines in Nonmarital Childbearing in the United States.* NCHS Data Brief No. 162, National Center for Health Statistics, DHHS, Washington, DC.

Dadkhah, Lara. 2010. Empty Skies over Afghanistan. *New York Times,* February 18.

Dagan, Hanoch. 2006. The Social Responsibility of Ownership. *Cornell Law Review* 92:1255–1274.

Dale, Maryclaire. 2011. IRS Awards $4.5M to Whistleblower. *USA Today,* April 8.

Dalrymple, Theodore [Anthony Daniels]. 2015. *Admirable Evasions: How Psychology Undermines Morality.* New York: Encounter Books.

———. 2017. Silence in Paris. *City Journal,* April 3.

DaMatta, Roberto. 1991. *Carnivals, Rogues, and Heroes: An Interpretation of the Brazilian Dilemma.* Notre Dame, IN: Notre Dame University Press.

Das, Anupreeta, and Emily Glazer. 2016. Republicans and Democrats Agree: We Hate Wall Street. *Wall Street Journal,* January 13. http://www.wsj.com/articles/republicans-and-democrats-agree-we-hate-wall-street-1452681567.

Das, Veena. 2007. *Life and Words: Violence and the Descent into the Ordinary.* Berkeley: University of California Press.

Das, Veena, Arthur Kleinman, Margaret M. Lock, Mamphela Ramphele, and Pamela Reynolds, eds. 2001. *Remaking a World: Violence, Social Suffering, and Recovery.* Berkeley: University of California Press.

Davis, David Brion. 2006. *Inhuman Bondage: The Rise and Fall of Slavery in the New World.* New York: Oxford University Press.

Davis, Natalie Zemon. 1975. *Society and Culture in Early Modern France.* Stanford: Stanford University Press.

Dawwas, Amin. 1993. Abuse of Right in the Shari'a and under Modern Arab Civil Codes: A Study in Comparative Jurisprudence. *Islamic and Comparative Law Review* 13:1–18.

Dean, Nick. 2010. ACLJ Asks Commission to Make N.Y. Building a Landmark to Keep 13-Story Mosque from Being Built at Ground Zero. *CNSNews.com*, July 25.

Deenen, Patrick. 2018. *Why Liberalism Failed.* New Haven: Yale University Press.

Deigh, John. 2006. The Politics of Disgust and Shame. *Journal of Ethics* 10: 383–418.

Delacote, Philippe. 2006. *Are Consumer Boycotts Effective?* Economics Department Working Paper, European University Institute, Florence. http://www.webmeets.com/files/papers/ERE/WC3/388/boycott.coordination.pdf.

de la Feria, Rita, and Stefan Vogenauer, eds. 2011. *Prohibition of Abuse of Law: A New General Principle of EU Law?* Portland, OR: Hart.

de Lombard, Jeannine Marie. 2002. Representing the Slave: White Advocacy and Black Testimony in Harriet Beecher Stowe's *Dred. New England Quarterly* 75:80–106.

Democracy Now. 2012. United Nations Probe: U.S. Should Return Stolen Sacred Lands, Including Mt. Rushmore, to Native Americans. May 11. http://www.democracynow.org/2012/5/11/un_probe_us_should_return_stolen.

de Morree, Paulien. 2016. *Rights and Wrongs under the ECHR: The Prohibition of Abuse of Rights in Article 17 of the European Convention on Human Rights.* Cambridge: Intersentia.

de Soto, Hernando. 1989. *The Other Path: The Invisible Revolution in the Third World.* New York: Harper and Row.

Devlin, Patrick. 1959. *The Enforcement of Morals.* Oxford: Oxford University Press.

Dickson, Julie. 2001. *Evaluation and Legal Theory.* Oxford: Hart.

Díez, Jordi. 2015. *The Politics of Gay Marriage in Latin America: Argentina, Chile, and Mexico.* Cambridge: Cambridge University Press.

DiMaggio, Paul. 1990. Cultural Aspects of Economic Action and Organization. In *Beyond the Marketplace: Rethinking Economy and Society,* edited by Roger Friedland and A. F. Robertson. New York: Aldine de Gruyter.

DiMaggio, Paul, and Walter Powell. 1983. The Iron Cage Revisited: Institutional Isomorphism and Collective Rationality in Organizational Fields. *American Sociological Review* 48:147–160.

Dinstein, Yoram. 2010. *The Conduct of Hostilities under the Law of International Armed Conflict.* Cambridge: Cambridge University Press.

D'Iribarne, Philippe. 1994. The Honour Principle in the "Bureaucratic Phenomenon." *Organization Studies* 15:81–97.

———. 2009. National Cultures and Organizations in Search of a Theory: An Interpretive Approach. *International Journal of Cross-Cultural Management* 9:309–321.

Doar, Robert, Karlyn Bowman, and Eleanor O'Neil. 2016. *2016 Poverty Survey,* August 18, American Enterprise Institute and Los Angeles Times. http://www.aei.org/publication/2016-poverty-survey/.

Donadio, Rachel. 2014. Vision of Home: Repatriated Works Back in Their Countries of Origin. *New York Times,* April 17.

D'Onofrio, Brian. 2011. Consequences of Separation/Divorce for Children. *Encyclopedia on Early Childhood Development,* June. http://www.child-encyclopedia.com/documents/DOnofrioANGxp1-Divorce.pdf.

Dorgo, Sandor, Kristynia M. Robinson, and Julia Bader. 2009. The Effectiveness of a Peer-Mentored Older Adult Fitness Program on Perceived Physical, Mental, and Social Function. *Journal of the American Association of Nurse Practitioners* 21:116–122.

Douglas, Mary. 1986. *How Institutions Think.* Syracuse: Syracuse University Press.

Douglass, Frederick. 2008 [1849]. *The Life and Times of Frederick Douglass.* Edited by Henri Bergson. New York: Cosimo Classics.

Douthat, Ross. 2018. Is There Life after Liberalism? *New York Times,* January 18.

Druckman, Yoram. 2012. Comptroller Slams PM in Flotilla Report. *Israel News,* June 13. http://www.ynetnews.com/articles/0,7340,L-4241882,00.html.

Dugan, Andrew. 2015. Solid Majority Continue to Support Death Penalty. Gallup Surveys, October 15. http://www.gallup.com/poll/186218/solid-majority-continue-support-death-penalty.aspx.

Dugger, Celia W. 2013. Report Finds Gradual Fall in Female Genital Cutting in Africa. *New York Times,* July 22.

Duneier, Mitchell. 1992. *Slim's Table: Race, Respectability, and Masculinity.* Chicago: University of Chicago Press.

———. 1999. *Sidewalk.* New York: Farrar, Straus and Giroux.

Dunoff, Jeffrey, Steven Ratner, and David Wippman. 2010. *International Law: Norms, Actors, Process.* New York: Aspen.

Durkheim, Émile. 1938 [1895]. What Is a Social Fact? In *The Rules of Sociological Method,* edited by George Catlin and translated by Sarah Solovay and John Mueller. New York: Free Press.

———. 1960 [1893]. *The Division of Labor in Society.* Translated by W. D. Halls. New York: Free Press.

———. 1973 [1925]. *Moral Education: A Study in the Theory and Application of the Sociology of Education.* Translated and edited by Everett K. Wilson. New York: Free Press.

———. 1995 [1912]. *The Elementary Forms of Religious Life.* Translated by Karen E. Fields. New York: Free Press.

Dworkin, Gerald. 2014. Paternalism. *Stanford Encyclopedia of Philosophy.* https://plato.stanford.edu/archives/spr2017/entries/paternalism/.

Dworkin, Ronald. 1977. *Taking Rights Seriously.* Cambridge, MA: Harvard University Press.

———. 1986. *Law's Empire.* Cambridge, MA: Harvard University Press.

———. 2011. *Justice for Hedgehogs.* Cambridge, MA: Belknap Press of Harvard University Press.

Eagleton, Terry. 1981. *Walter Benjamin, or Towards a Revolutionary Criticism.* London: New Left Books.

Ebenstein, Avraham Y. 2007. *Fertility Choices and Sex Selection in Asia: Analysis and Policy.* Harvard University Department of Economics Working Paper. http://papers.ssrn.com/sol3/papers.cfm?abstract_id=965551.

Eckert, Susan. 2012. Community Collects to Reflect on Hate Speech. *Daily Gazette* (Swarthmore College), April 3.

Editorial Board. 2015. Segregation Destroys Black Wealth. *The New York Times,* September 15.

Efrat, Rafael. 2006. The Evolution of Bankruptcy Stigma. *Theoretical Inquiries in Law* 7:365–394.

Egan, James F. X., Winston A. Campbell, Audrey Chapman, Alireza A. Shamshirsaz, Padmalatha Gurram, and Peter A. Benn. 2011. Distortions of Sex Ratios at Birth in the United States: Evidence for Prenatal Gender Selection. *Prenatal Diagnosis* 31:560–565.

Ehrenhalt, Alan. 1995. *The Lost City: Discovering the Forgotten Virtues of Community in the Chicago of the 1950s.* New York: Basic Books.

Eidenmüller, Horst. 2009. Abuse of Law in the Context of European Insolvency Law. *European Company and Financial Law Review* 6:1–28.

Eleftheriadis, Pavlos. 2009. *On Rights and Responsibilities.* Oxford Legal Studies, Working Paper No. 44/2009. https://papers.ssrn.com/sol3/papers.cfm?abstract_id=1486086.

Eligon, John, and Steven Yaccino. 2012. After Deadly Shooting at Sikh Temple, Neighbors Turn Out to Work for Tolerance. *New York Times,* August 10.

Elkind, Jerome B. 1976. Footnote to the Nuclear Test Cases: Abuse of Right—A Blind Alley for Environmentalists. *Vanderbilt Journal of Transnational Law* 9:57–98.

Ellickson, Robert. 1991. *Order without Law: How Neighbors Settle Disputes.* Cambridge, MA: Harvard University Press.

———. 2001. The Market for Social Norms. *American Law and Economics Review* 3:1–49.

Elster, Jon. 1985. *Making Sense of Marx.* Cambridge: Cambridge University Press.

———, ed. 1985. *The Multiple Self.* Cambridge: Cambridge University Press.

———. 1993. *Political Psychology.* New York: Cambridge University Press.

———. 1999. *Alchemies of the Mind: Rationality and the Emotions.* Cambridge: Cambridge University Press.

———. 2016. Is Enthusiasm an Emotion? Unpublished manuscript. www.hf.uio .no/ . . . /2016/is-enthusiasm-an-emotion. doc.

Emanuel, Ezekiel, and Linda Emanuel. 1992. Proxy Decision Making for Incompetent Patients: An Ethical and Empirical Analysis. *Journal of the American Medical Association* 267:2067–2071.

Emanuel, Linda. 1993. Advance Directives: What Have We Learned So Far? *Journal of Clinical Ethics* 4:8–16.

Engel, David M. 1984. The Oven Bird's Song: Insiders, Outsiders, and Personal Injuries in an American Community. *Law and Society Review* 18:551–582.

———. 2016. *The Myth of the Litigious Society: Why We Don't Sue.* Chicago: University of Chicago Press.

Engel, David and Jaruwan Engel. 2010. *Tort, Custom, and Karma: Globalization and Legal Consciousness in Thailand.* Stanford: Stanford University Press.

Engeli, Isabelle. 2012. "Introduction." In *Morality Politics in Western Europe,* edited by Engeli, Christoffer Green-Pedersen, and Lars Thorup Larsen. London: Palgrave Macmillan.

Engeli, Isabelle, Christoffer Green-Pedersen, and Lars Thorup Larsen 2012. "The Two Worlds of Morality Politics—What Have We Learned?" In *Morality Politics in Western Europe,* edited by Engeli, Green-Pedersen, and Larsen. London: Palgrave Macmillan.

Engstrom, David Freeman. 2017. Bounty Regimes. In *Research Handbook on Corporate Crime and Financial Misdealing,* edited by Jennifer Arlen. Cheltenham, UK: Edward Elgar.

Epstein, Lee, William Landes, and Richard Posner. 2013. *The Behavior of Federal Judges: A Theoretical and Empirical Study of Rational Choice.* Cambridge, MA: Harvard University Press.

Epstein, Richard. 1997. Enforcing Norms: When the Law Gets in the Way. *Responsive Community* 7:4–15.

Ericson, Richard V., and Aaron Doyle. 2004. *Uncertain Business: Risk, Insurance, and the Limits of Knowledge.* Toronto: University of Toronto Press.

Ericson, Richard V., Aaron Doyle, and Dean Barry. 2003. *Insurance as Governance.* Toronto: University of Toronto Press.

ESRC (Economic and Social Research Council). 1999. *The Politics of GM Food: Risk, Science and Public Trust.* Swindon, UK: University of Sussex. https://www.researchgate.net/publication/280154207_The_Politics_of_GM _Food_Risk_Science_and_Public_Trust.

Etzioni, Amitai. 2000. Social Norms: Internalization, Persuasion, and History. *Law and Society Review* 34:157–178.

Eurostat. 2017. Asylum Decisions in the EU: EU Member States Granted Protection to More than 700,000 Asylum Seekers in 2016. *EU News Release,* April 26. http://ec.europa.eu/eurostat/documents/2995521/8001715/3 -26042017-AP-EN.pdf/05e315db-1fe3-49d1-94ff-06f7e995580e.

Evans, Gareth. 2008. *The Responsibility to Protect: Ending Mass Atrocity Crimes Once and for All.* Washington, DC: Brookings Institution.

Ewick, Patricia, and Susan Silbey. 1992. Conformity, Contestation, and Resistance: An Account of Legal Consciousness. *New England Law Review* 26:731–750.

Eyal, Gil. 2013. For a Sociology of Expertise: The Social Origins of the Autism Epidemic. *American Journal of Sociology* 118:863–907.

Farber, Daniel, and Philip Frickey. 1991. *Law and Public Choice: A Critical Introduction.* Chicago: University of Chicago Press.

Farnsworth, Douglass. 2006. Moral Hazard in Health Insurance: Are Consumer Directed Plans the Answer? *Annals of Health Law* 15:251–273.

Fass, Paula. 1997. *Kidnapped: Child Abduction in America.* New York: Oxford University Press.

Fassin, Didier. 2008. Beyond Good and Evil? Questioning the Anthropological Discomfort with Morals. *Anthropological Theory* 8:333–344.

———. 2012. Introduction: Toward a Critical Moral Anthropology. In *A Companion to Moral Anthropology,* edited by Didier Fassin. Hoboken, NJ: Wiley-Blackwell.

———. 2013. On Resentment and *Ressentiment:* The Politics and Ethics of Moral Emotions. *Current Anthropology* 54:249–267.

Faubion, James. 2011. *An Anthropology of Ethics.* Cambridge: Cambridge University Press.

Fay, Scott, Erik Hurst, and Michelle J. White. 2002. The Household Bankruptcy Decision. *American Economic Review* 92:706–718.

Fede, Andrew. 1985. Legitimized Violent Slave Abuse in the American South, 1619–1865: A Case Study of Law and Social Change in Six Southern States. *American Journal of History* 29:93–150.

Feinberg, Matthew, and Robb Willer. 2015. From Gulf to Bridge: When Do Moral Arguments Facilitate Political Influence? *Personality and Social Psychology Bulletin* 41:1665–1681.

Feldman, Eric. 2006. The Tuna Court: Law and Norms in the World's Premier Fish Market. *California Law Review* 93:313–370.

Fella, Stefano, and Carlo Ruzza. 2013. *Anti-Racist Movements in the E.U.: Between Europeanisation and National Trajectories.* London: Palgrave Macmillan.

Felstiner, William L. F., Richard L. Abel, and Austin Sarat. 1980. The Emergence and Transformation of Disputes: Naming, Blaming, Claiming. *Law and Society Review* 15:631–654.

Felter, Joseph, and Jacob Shapiro. 2017. Limiting Civilian Casualties as Part of a Winning Strategy: The Case of Courageous Restraint. *Daedalus* (Winter) 146:44–58.

Feng, Chunliang, Frank Krueger, and Yue-Jia Luo. 2015. Neural Signatures of Fairness-Related Normative Decision Making in the Ultimatum Game: A Coordinate-Based Meta-Analysis. *Human Brain Mapping* 36:591–602.

Fernandes, Nunes, Miguel Ferreira, Pedro Matos, and Kevin J. Murphy. 2012. Are U.S. CEOs Paid More? New International Evidence. *Review of Financial Studies* 26:323–367.

Fick, Nathaniel. 2005. *One Bullet Away: The Making of a Marine Officer.* Boston: Houghton Mifflin.

Finkel, Norman, and Kevin Duff. 1991. Felony-Murder and Community Sentiment: Testing the Supreme Court's Assertions. *Law and Human Behavior* 15:405–429.

Finkel, Norman, and Gerrod Parrott. 2006. *Emotions and Culpability: How the Law Is at Odds with Psychology, Jurors, and Itself.* Washington, DC: American Psychological Association.

Finn, Margot C. 2004. *The Character of Credit: Personal Debt in English Culture, 1740–1940.* Cambridge: Cambridge University Press.

Fiorina, Morris. 2017. *Unstable Majorities: Polarization, Party Sorting, and Political Stalemate.* Stanford, CA: Hoover Institution Press.

Fischl, Richard Michael, and Jeremy Paul. 1999. *Getting to Maybe: How to Excel on Law School Exams.* Durham, NC: Caroline Academic Press.

Fisher, David. 2012. *Morality and War: Can War Be Just in the 21st Century?* Oxford: Oxford University Press.

Fisher, William W., III. 1993. Ideology and Imagery in the Law of Slavery. *Chicago-Kent Law Review* 68:1051–1086.

Fleming, Anne. 2014. The Rise and Fall of Unconscionability as the Law of the Poor. *Georgetown Law Journal* 102:1383–1442.

Fleming, James, and Linda McClain. 2013. *Ordered Liberty: Rights, Responsibilities, and Virtues.* Cambridge, MA: Harvard University Press.

Flessas, Tatiana. 2013. *The Ends of the Museum.* LSE Legal Studies Working Paper No. 14/2013. May 19. https://papers.ssrn.com/sol3/papers.cfm?abstract_id=2271501.

Fletcher, George P. 1978. *Rethinking Criminal Law.* Boston: Little, Brown.

———. 2013. The Right and the Reasonable. In *Fletcher's Essays on Criminal Law,* edited by Russell Christopher. New York: Oxford University Press.

Flogaitis, Spyridon, Tom Swart, and Julie Fraser. 2013. *The European Court of Human Rights and Its Discontents.* Cheltenham, UK: Edward Elgar.

Foa, Roberto Stefan, and Yascha Mounk. 2017. The Signs of Deconsolidation. *Journal of Democracy* 28:5–16.

Foucault, Michel. 1979 [1975]. *Discipline and Punish: The Birth of the Prison.* Translated by Alan Sheridan. New York: Vintage Books.

———. 1994 [1978]. La philosophie analytique de la politique. In *Dits et écrits:1954–1988,* vol. 3: *1976–1979,* edited by D. Defert and F. Ewald. Paris: Gallimard.

Franklin, Benjamin. 1955 [1790]. *The Autobiography of Benjamin Franklin.* New York: Washington Square Press.

Frayne, David. 2015. *The Refusal of Work: The Theory and Practice of Resistance to Work.* London: Zed Books.

French, David. 2015. How Our Overly Restrictive Rules of Engagement Keep Us from Winning Wars. *National Review,* December 21. http://www.nationalreview.com/article/428756/rules-engagement-need-reform.

Friedman, Jeffrey, and Wladimir Kraus. 2011. *Engineering the Financial Crisis: Systemic Risk and the Failure of Regulation.* Philadelphia: University of Pennsylvania Press.

Friedman, Lawrence. 1973. *A History of American Law.* New York: Simon and Schuster.

Friedman, Milton. 1970. The Social Responsibility of Business Is to Increase Profits. *New York Times,* September 13.

Friesen, Jennifer. 2006. *State Constitutional Law: Litigating Individual Rights, Claims, and Defenses.* Vol. 2. New York: LexisNexis.

Fuller, Lon. 1940. *The Law in Quest of Itself.* Chicago: Foundation Press.

———. 1964. *The Morality of Law.* New Haven: Yale University Press.

Fung, Archon, and Jennifer Shkabatur. 2015. Viral Engagement. In *From Voice to Influence: Understanding Citizenship in a Digital Age,* edited by Danielle Allen and Jennifer S. Light. Chicago: University of Chicago Press.

Gabel, Joan, Nancy Mansfield, and Gregory Todd Jones. 2006. The Peculiar Moral Hazard of Employment Practices Liability Insurance: Realignment of the Incentive to Transfer Risk with the Incentive to Prevent Discrimination. *Notre Dame Journal of Law, Ethics and Public Policy* 20:639–654.

Galanter, Marc. 1998a. The Faces of Mistrust: The Image of Lawyers in Public Opinion, Jokes, and Political Discourse. *University of Cincinnati Law Review* 66:805–845.

———. 1998b. Shadow Play: The Fabled Menace of Punitive Damages. *Wisconsin Law Review,* no. 1: 1–14.

Gallagher, William T. 2011. IP Legal Ethics in the Everyday Practice of Law: An Empirical Perspective on Patent Litigators. *John Marshall Review of Intellectual Property Law* 10:309–364.

Gallay, Allan. 1987. The Origins of Slaveholders' Paternalism: George Whitefield, the Bryan Family, and the Great Awakening in the South. *Journal of Southern History* 53:369–394.

Gallup Polling. 2012. Abortion. September 25. http://www.gallup.com/poll/1576/abortion.aspx#1.

Galston, William. 1988. A Liberal-Democratic Case for the Two-Parent Family. In *The Essential Communitarian Reader,* edited by Amitai Etzioni. Lanham, MD: Rowman and Littlefield.

———. 1991. *Liberal Purposes: Goods, Virtues, and Diversity in the Liberal State.* Cambridge: Cambridge University Press.

Gamarekian, Barbara. 1989. Corcoran, to Foil Dispute, Drops Mapplethorpe Show. *New York Times,* 14 June. http://www.nytimes.com/1989/06/14/arts/corcoran-to-foil-dispute-drops-mapplethorpe-show.html.

Gambetta, Diego. 2000. Can We Trust Trust? in *Trust: Making and Breaking of Cooperative Relations,* edited by Diego Gambetta. New York: Blackwell.

Garcés-Conejos Blitvich, Pilar, and Nuria Lorenzo-Dus. 2013. Reality Television: A Discourse-Analytical Perspective. In *Real Talk: Reality Television and Discourse Analysis in Action,* edited by Lorenzo-Dus et al. New York: Palgrave Macmillan.

Garfinkel, Harold. 1956. Conditions of Successful Degradation Ceremonies. *American Journal of Sociology* 61:420–424.

Gargarella, Roberto. 2015. Democracy and Rights in *Gelman v. Uruguay. AJIL Unbound,* November 11. https://asil.org/blogs/symposium.

-constitutionalization-international-law-latin-america-democracy-and-rights -gelman-v.

Garland, David. 1990. *Punishment and Modern Society: A Study in Social Theory.* Chicago: University of Chicago Press.

———. 2008. On the Concept of Moral Panic. *Crime, Media, Culture* 4:9–30.

Garry, Patrick. 1993. *An American Paradox: Censorship in a Nation of Free Speech.* Santa Barbara: Praeger.

Garth, Bryant, and Yves Dezalay. 1996. *Dealing in Virtue: International Commercial Arbitration and the Construction of a Transnational Legal Order.* Forward by Pierre Bourdieu. Chicago: University of Chicago Press.

Geertz, Clifford. 1975. Common Sense as a Cultural System. *Antioch Review* 33:5–26.

Genovese, Eugene. 1965. *The Political Economy of Slavery: Studies in the Economy and Society of the Slave South.* New York: Vintage Books.

———.1974. *Roll, Jordan, Roll: The World the Slaves Made.* New York: Pantheon Books.

Genovese, Eugene, and Elizabeth Fox Genovese. 2011. *Fatal Self-Deception: Slaveholding Paternalism in the Old South.* New York: Cambridge University Press.

Gentry, Curt. 1991. *J. Edgar Hoover: The Man and the Secrets.* New York: W. W. Norton.

Geppert, C. 2010. Saving Life or Respecting Autonomy: The Ethical Dilemma of DNR Orders in Patients Who Attempt Suicide. *Internet Journal of Law, Healthcare and Ethics* 7, no. 1, http://ispub.com/IJLHE/7/1/11437#sthash .l70eMsoF.dpbs.

Gerber, Alan, Donald Green, and Christopher Larimer. 2010. An Experiment Testing the Relative Effectiveness of Encouraging Voter Participation by Inducing Feelings of Pride or Shame. *Political Behavior* 32:409–422.

Gert, Bernard. 1999. Common Morality and Computing. *Ethics and Information Technology* 1:57–64.

———. 2004. *Common Morality: Deciding What to Do.* Oxford: Oxford University Press.

Gert, Bernard, Charles M. Culver, and K. Danner Clouser. 1997. *Bioethics: A Return to Fundamentals.* Oxford: Oxford University Press.

Getzler, Joshua. 2004. *A History of Water Rights at Common Law.* New York: Oxford University Press.

Gilbert, Arthur. 1976. Law and Honour among 18th Century British Army Officers. *History Journal* 19:75–87.

Gilens, Martin. 1999. *Why Americans Hate Welfare: Race, Media, and the Politics of Antipoverty Policy.* Chicago: University of Chicago Press.

———. 2012. *Affluence and Influence: Economic Inequality and Political Power in America.* Princeton: Princeton University Press.

Gilens, Martin, and Benjamin Page. 2014. Testing Theories of American Politics. *Perspectives on Politics* 12:564–581.

Gilligan, Carol. 1982. *In a Different Voice: Psychological Theory and Women's Development.* Cambridge, MA: Harvard University Press.

Gilliom, John. 2001. *Overseers of the Poor: Surveillance, Resistance, and the Limits of Privacy.* Chicago: University of Chicago Press.

Gilson, Ronald, and Jeffrey Gordon. 2013. The Agency Costs of Agency Capitalism: Activist Investors and the Revaluation of Governance Rights. *Columbia Law Review* 113:863–927.

Glantz, Aaron, and Anthony Swofford, eds. 2008. *Winter Soldier: Iraq and Afghanistan, Eyewitness Accounts of the Occupation.* Chicago: Haymarket Books.

Gleick, Elizabeth. 1996. Hell Hath No Fury. *Time,* October 7.

Glendon, Mary Ann. 1987. *Abortion and Divorce in Western Law.* Cambridge, MA: Harvard University Press.

———. 1991. *Rights-Talk: The Impoverishment of Political Discourse.* New York: Free Press.

Glickman, Lawrence. 2009. *Buying Power: A History of Consumer Activism in America.* Chicago: University of Chicago Press.

Goffman, Alice. 2014. *On the Run: Fugitive Life in an American City.* Chicago: University of Chicago Press.

Goffman, Erving. 1963. *Stigma: Notes on the Management of Spoiled Identity.* Englewood Cliffs, NJ: Prentice-Hall.

———. 1985. *Encounters: Two Studies in the Sociology of Interaction.* New York: Macmillan.

Goldberg, Adam. 2006. Reaffirming McClain: The National Stolen Property Act and the Abiding Trade in Looted Cultural Objects. *UCLA Law Review* 53:1031–1071.

Goldberg, Nathan. 2005. Measuring the Impact of Microfinance: Taking Stock of What We Know. Grameen Foundation, December. http://www.givewell.org/files/Cause1-2/Independent%20research%20on%20microfinance/GFUSA-MicrofinanceImpactWhitepaper-1.pdf.

Goldman, Alan H. 1980. *The Moral Foundations of Professional Ethics.* Totowa, NJ: Rowman and Littlefield.

Goodhart, A. L. 1953. *English Law and the Moral Law.* London: Stevens and Sons.

Gordon, Linda. 2003. *The Moral Property of Women: A History of Birth Control Politics in America.* Urbana: University of Illinois Press.

Gordon, Robert W. 1984. The Ideal and the Actual: Fantasies and Practices of New York City Lawyers, 1870–1910. In *The New High Priests: Lawyers in Post-Civil War America,* edited by Gerald Gawalt. Westport, CT: Greenwood Press.

———. 2009. The Lawyer Citizen: A Myth with Some Basis in Reality. *William & Mary Law Review* 50:1169–1206.

———. 2010. The Role of Lawyers in Producing the Rule of Law: Some Critical Reflections. *Theoretical Inquiries in Law* 11:441–468.

Gould, Sheila, and Karen Dodd. 2014. "Normal People Can Have a Child but Disability Can't": The Experiences of Mothers with Mild Learning Disabilities Who Have Had Their Children Removed. *British Journal of Learning Disabilities* 42:25–35.

Graham, Ann. 2010. Bringing to Heel the Elephants in the Economy: The Case for Ending Too Big to Fail. Texas Tech Law School Res. Paper No. 2010-18. https://papers.ssrn.com/sol3/papers.cfm?abstract_id=1565584.

Gramsci, Antonio. 1992. *Prison Notebooks.* Vol. 1. Edited by Joseph A. Buttigieg. New York: Columbia University Press.

Granberg, Donald, and Beth Granberg. 1980. Abortion Attitudes, 1965–1980: Trends and Determinants. *Family Planning Perspectives* 12:250–261.

Granovetter, Mark. 1985. Economic Action and Social Structure: The Problem of Embeddedness. *American Journal of Sociology* 91:481–510.

———. 2005. The Impact of Social Structure on Economic Outcomes. *Journal of Economic Perspectives* 19:33–50.

Graver, Hans Peter. 1997. Consumer Bankruptcy: A Right or a Privilege? The Role of Courts in Establishing Moral Standards of Economic Conduct. *J. of Consumer Policy* 20:161–177.

Gray, John. 2011. A Point of View: The Revolution of Capitalism. BBC, September 11. http://www.bbc.com/news/magazine-14764357.

Green, Stuart, and Matthew Kugler. 2010. Community Perceptions of Theft Seriousness: A Challenge to Model Penal Code and English Theft Act Consolidation. *Journal of Empirical Legal Studies* 7:511–537.

———. 2012a. Public Perceptions of White Collar Crime Culpability: Bribery, Perjury, and Fraud. *Law and Contemporary Problems* 75:33–60.

———. 2012b. When Is It Wrong to Trade Stocks on the Basis of Non-Public Information? Public Views of the Morality of Insider Trading. *Fordham Urban Law Journal* 39:451–484.

Greenawalt, Kent. 1989. *Conflicts of Law and Morality.* Oxford: Oxford University Press.

———. 1992. *Law and Objectivity.* New York: Oxford University Press.

Greenfield, Jeanette. 1995. *The Return of Cultural Treasures.* Cambridge: Cambridge University Press.

Greenhouse, Linda. 2016. The Courts Begin to Call Out Lawmakers. *New York Times,* August 18.

Greif, Avner. 2006. *Institutions and the Path to the Modern Economy: Lessons from Medieval Trade.* Cambridge: Cambridge University Press.

Griffiths, Nicholas. 1994. Inquisition of the Indians? The Inquisitorial Model and the Repression of Andean Religion in Seventeenth Century Peru. *Colonial Latin American Historical Review* 3:19–38.

Gross, Ariela J. 2000. *Double Character: Slavery and Mastery in the Antebellum Southern Courtroom.* Princeton: Princeton University Press.

Grossman, Matthew. 2014. *Artists of the Possible: Governing Networks and American Policy Changes since 1945.* Oxford: Oxford University Press.

Grotius, Hugo. 2001 [1625]. *On the Law of War and Peace.* Translated by A. C. Campbell. Ontario: Batoche Books. http://socserv.mcmaster.ca/econ/ugcm/3ll3/grotius/Law2.pdf.

Grzymala-Busse, Anna. 2015. *Nations under God: How Churches Use Moral Authority to Influence Policy.* Princeton: Princeton University Press.

Gundersen, Astrid, Ellinor Young, and Kaare Torgny Pettersen. 2012. Good Enough Care? A Study of the Difficulties That Norwegian Child Welfare Workers Experience in Working with Mothers Who Have Intellectual Disabilities. *Scandinavian Journal of Disability Research* 15:282–297.

Gusfield, Joseph. 1963. *Symbolic Crusade: Status Politics and the Temperance Movement.* Urbana: University of Illinois Press.

Guttmacher Institute. 2006. State Facts about Abortion: New York. January. https://www.guttmacher.org/fact-sheet/state-facts-about-abortion-new-york.

———. 2011. Trends in Abortion in the United States, 1973–2008. http://www.priestsforlife.org/statistics/trends.pdf.

———. 2016. Facts on Induced Abortion in the United States. September. https://www.guttmacher.org/sites/default/files/factsheet/fb_induced_abortion_3.pdf.

Habermas, Jürgen. 1996. *Between Facts and Norms.* Translated by William Rehg. Cambridge, MA: MIT Press.

———. 1999. Between Facts and Norms: An Author's Reflections. *Denver Law Review* 76:937–942.

Habyarimana, James, Macartan Humphreys, Daniel N. Posner, and Jeremy M. Weinstein. 2009. *Coethnicity: Diversity and the Dilemmas of Collective Action.* New York: Russell Sage Foundation.

Hacker, Jacob S. 2006. *The Great Risk Shift: The New Economic Insecurity and the Decline of the American Dream.* New York: Oxford University Press.

Hacker, Jacob S., and Ann O'Leary, eds. 2012. *Shared Responsibility, Shared Risk: Government, Markets and Social Policy in the 21st Century.* Oxford: Oxford University Press.

Hacking, Ian. 1995. *Rewriting the Soul: Multiple Personality and the Sciences of Memory.* Princeton: Princeton University Press.

Haidt, Jonathan. 2001. The Emotional Dog and Its Rational Tail: A Social Intuitionist Approach to Moral Judgment. *Psychological Review* 108:814–834.

———. 2003. Elevation and the Positive Psychology of Morality. In *Flourishing: Positive Psychology and the Life Well-Lived,* edited by Corey Lee M. Keyes and Jonathan Haidt. Washington, DC: American Psychological Association.

———. 2006. *The Happiness Hypothesis: Finding Modern Truth in Ancient Wisdom.* New York: Basic Books.

———. 2017. The Age of Outrage. *City Journal,* December 17.

Haidt, Jonathan, and Jesse Graham. 2007. When Morality Opposes Justice: Conservatives Have Moral Intuitions That Liberals May Not Recognize. *Social Justice Research* 20:98–116.

Hale, Benjamin. 2009. What's So Moral about the Moral Hazard? *Public Affairs Quarterly* 23:1–25.

Hall, Kermit. 1989. *The Magic Mirror: Law in American History.* Oxford: Oxford University Press.

Hamm, Richard F. 1995. *Shaping the Eighteenth Amendment: Temperance Reform, Legal Culture, and the Policy, 1880–1920.* Chapel Hill: University of North Carolina Press.

Hand, Learned. 1952. *The Spirit of Liberty.* New York: Knopf.
Hanley, Ryan. 2009. *Adam Smith and the Character of Virtue.* Cambridge: Cambridge University Press.
Hardin, Garrett. 1968. The Tragedy of the Commons. *Science* 162:1243–1248.
Hardin, Steven B., and Yasmin A. Yusufaly. 2004. Difficult End-of-Life Treatment Decisions: Do Other Factors Trump Advance Directives? *Archives of Internal Medicine* 164:1531–1533.
Harkness, Geoff. 2014. *Chicago Hustle and Flow: Gangs, Gangsta Rap, and Social Class.* Minneapolis: University of Minnesota Press.
Harkness, Sarah, and Steven Hitlin. 2014. Morality and Emotions. In *Handbook of the Sociology of Emotions,* edited by Jan Stets and Jonathan H. Turner, vol. 2. New York: Springer.
Hart, H. L. A. 1967. Social Solidarity and the Enforcement of Morality. *University of Chicago Law Review* 35:1–13.
———. 2012 [1961]. *The Concept of Law.* 3rd ed. Edited by Penelope Bullock and Joseph Raz. Oxford: Oxford University Press.
Hartman, Edwin. 2013. The Virtue Approach to Business Ethics. In *The Cambridge Companion to Virtue Ethics,* edited by Daniel Russell. Cambridge: Cambridge University Press.
Hasday, Jill. 2000. Contest and Consent: A Legal History of Marital Rape. *California Law Review* 88:1375–1505.
Haskell, Thomas. 2005. Taking Duties Seriously: To What Problems Are Rights and Duties the Solution? In *The Psychology of Rights and Duties,* edited by Norman Finkel and Tathali Moghaddam. Washington, DC: American Psychological Association.
Haskell, Thomas, and Richard Teichgraeber, eds. 1993. *The Culture of the Market: Historical Essays.* Cambridge: Cambridge University Press.
Hassan, Tariq. 2010. Paving the Path for Preventive Lawyering, *The Counsel.* http://counselpakistan.com/vol-1/introduction/introduction.php.
Hassner, Ron. 2009. *War on Sacred Grounds.* Ithaca, NY: Cornell University Press.
Hay, Douglas. 2011 [1975]. Property, Authority and the Criminal Law. In *Albion's Fatal Tree: Crime and Society in Eighteenth-Century England,* 2nd ed., edited by Douglas Hay et al. London: Verso.
Hazard, John. 1947. *Materials on Soviet Law.* New York: Columbia University Papers.
Healy, Kieran. 2004. Sacred Markets and Secular Ritual in the Organ Transplant Industry. In *The Sociology of the Economy,* edited by Frank Dobbin. New York: Russell Sage Foundation.
Hegel, George Wilhelm Friedrich. 1942 [1821]. *Philosophy of Right,* translated by T. M. Knox. Oxford: Oxford University Press.
Heimer, Carol Anne. 1985. *Reactive Risk and Rational Action: Managing Moral Hazard in Insurance Contracts.* Berkeley: University of California Press.
Heimer, Carol Anne, and Lisa Staffen. 1998. *For the Sake of the Children: The Social Organization of Responsibility in the Hospital and the Home.* Chicago: University of Chicago Press.

Heinich, Nathalie. 2017. *Des valeurs: Une approche sociologique.* Paris: Gallimard.

Heinz, John, and Edward Laumann. 1982. *Chicago Lawyers: The Social Structure of the Bar.* Chicago: Russell Sage Foundation.

Heinz, John, Robert Nelson, Rebecca L. Sandefur, and Edward O. Laumann. 2005. *Urban Lawyers: The New Social Structure of the Bar.* Chicago: University of Chicago Press.

Helms, Brigit. 2006. *Access for All: Building Inclusive Financial Systems.* Washington, DC: World Bank.

Henckaerts, Jean-Marie. 2009. Proportionality. In *The Oxford Companion to International Criminal Justice,* edited by Antonio Cassesse. Oxford: Oxford University Press.

Henderson, M. Todd. 2017. Do Lawyers Make Better CEOS than MBAs? *Harvard Business Review* August 24. https://hbr.org/2017/08/do-lawyers-make-better-ceos-than-mbas.

Hennette-Vauchez, Stéphanie. 2008. *A Human Dignitas? The Contemporary Principle of Human Dignity as a Mere Reappraisal of an Ancient Legal Concept.* European University Institute Working Paper, No. 2008/18. http://cadmus.eui.eu/bitstream/handle/1814/9009/LAW_2008_18.pdf.

Henshaw, Stanley. 1998. Unintended Pregnancy in the United States. *Family Planning Perspectives* 30:24–49.

Herman, Shael. 1977. Classical Social Theories and the Doctrine of "Abuse of Rights." *Louisiana Law Review* 37:747–760.

Hernanz, Virginia, Franck Malherbert, and Michele Pellizzari. 2004. Take-up of Welfare Benefits in OCED Countries: A Review of the Evidence. *OCED Library,* 8 March. http://www.oecd-ilibrary.org/social-issues-migration-health/take-up-of-welfare-benefits-in-oecd-countries_525815265414.

Hess, Dan. 2012. The Impact of Religiosity on Personal Financial Decisions. *Journal of Religion and Society* 14:1–13.

Hesselink, M. W. 2011. The Concept of Good Faith. In *Towards a European Civil Code,* edited by Arthur S. Hartkamp, M. W. Hesselink, Ewoud Hondius, et al. Leiden, NE: Kluwer Law International.

Hetherington, Marc, and Thomas Rudolph. 2015. *Why Washington Won't Work: Polarization, Political Trust, and the Governing Crisis.* Chicago: University of Chicago Press.

Hill, Thomas A. 1991. *Autonomy and Self-Respect.* Cambridge: Cambridge University Press.

Himmelfarb, Gertrude. 1995. *The De-Moralization of Society: From Victorian Virtues to Modern Values.* New York: Knopf/Random House.

Hines, James R., Jr., and Lawrence H. Summers. 2009. How Globalization Affects Tax Design. *Tax Policy and the Economy* 23:123–157.

Hirschl, Ran. 2009. Montesquieu and the Renaissance of Comparative Public Law. In *Montesquieu and His Legacy,* edited by Rebecca E. Kingston. Albany: SUNY Press.

Hirschman, Albert O. 1986. *Rival Views of Market Society and Other Recent Essays.* Cambridge, MA: Harvard University Press.

Hitlin, Steven, and Stephen Vaisey. 2013. The New Sociology of Morality. *Annual Review of Sociology* 39:51–68.

Ho, Karen. 2009. *Liquidated: An Ethnography of Wall Street*. Durham, NC: Duke University Press.

Hobhouse, L. T. 1915 [1913]. The Historical Evolution of Property, in Fact and in Idea. In *Property: Its Duties and Rights,* 2nd ed., edited by L. T. Hobhouse and Charles Gore. London: Macmillan.

Hochschild, Arlie Russell. 2013. *So How's the Family? and Other Essays*. Berkeley: University of California Press.

Hodges, Christopher. 2015. *Corporate Behaviour: Enforcement, Support, or Ethical Culture?* Oxford Legal Studies Research Paper No. 19/2015. https://papers.ssrn.com/sol3/papers.cfm?abstract_id=2599961.

Hoffman, Morris. 2014. *The Punisher's Brain: The Evolution of Judge and Jury.* New York: Cambridge University Press.

Hoggart, Richard. 2003. *Everyday Language and Everyday Life.* New Brunswick, NJ: Transaction.

Hohfeld, Wesley Newcomb. 1923. *Fundamental Legal Conceptions.* New Haven: Yale University Press.

Holmes, Oliver W., Jr. 1881. *The Common Law.* Boston: Little, Brown.

Holmes, Oliver W., Jr., and Harold J. Laski. 1953 [1916–1935]. *Holmes–Laski Letters: The Correspondence of Mr. Justice Holmes and Harold J. Laski, 1916–1935,* vol. 1, edited by Mark DeWolfe Howe. Cambridge, MA: Harvard University Press.

Holmes, Stephen. 1993. *The Anatomy of Antiliberalism.* Cambridge, MA: Harvard University Press.

———. 2012. Waldron, Machiavelli, and Hate Speech. In *The Content and Context of Hate Speech: Rethinking Regulation and Responses,* edited by Michael Herz and Peter Molnar. Cambridge: Cambridge University Press.

Honneth, Axel. 1992. Integrity and Disrespect: Principles of a Conception of Morality Based on the Theory of Recognition. *Political Theory* 20:187–201.

———. 2013. *Freedom's Right: The Social Foundations of Democratic Life.* Translated by Joseph Ganahl. Cambridge: Polity.

Hook, Janet. 2017. Political Divisions in U.S. Are Widening, Long-Lasting, Poll Shows. *Wall Street Journal,* September 6.

Hopkins, Daniel. 2010. Politicized Places: Explaining Where and When Immigrants Provoke Local Opposition. *American Political Science Review* 104:40–60.

Hopkins, Daniel, and John Sides, eds. 2015. *Political Polarization in American Politics.* New York: Bloomsbury.

Horn, Ruth. 2014. "I Don't Need My Patients' Opinion to Withdraw Treatment": Patient Preferences at the End-of-Life and Physician Attitudes towards Advance Directives in England and France. *Medicine, Health Care, and Philosophy* 17:425–435.

Horton, John. 1996. Tolerance as a Virtue. In *Toleration: An Elusive Virtue,* edited by David Heyd. Princeton: Princeton University Press.

House of Commons, Home Affairs Committee. 2017. Hate Crime: Abuse, Hate and Extremism Online. Fourteenth Report of Session 2016–17. https://publications.parliament.uk/pa/cm201617/cmselect/cmhaff/609/609.pdf.

Hovenkamp, Herbert. 2015. *The Opening of American Law: Neoclassical Legal Thought, 1870–1970.* New York: Oxford University Press.

Hovenkamp, Herbert, and Christina Bohannan. 2011. *Creation without Restraint: Promoting Liberty and Rivalry in Innovation.* New York: Oxford University Press.

Hudson, Alastair. 2009. *Equity and Trusts.* 6th ed. London: Routledge-Cavendish.

Hull, Isabel. 2014. *A Scrap of Paper: Breaking and Making International Law during the Great War.* Ithaca: Cornell University Press.

Hull, Mary E. 1999. *Censorship in America: A Reference Handbook.* Santa Barbara: ABC-CLIO.

Human Rights Watch. 2011. Sterilization of Women and Girls with Disabilities. November 10. https://www.hrw.org/news/2011/11/10/sterilization-women-and-girls-disabilities.

Hunter, James Davison. 1994. *Before the Shooting Begins: Searching for Democracy in America's Culture War.* New York: Free Press.

———. 2000. *The Death of Character: Moral Education in an Age without Good or Evil.* New York: Basic Books.

Hunter, James Davison, and Joshua J. Yates. 2011. Introduction: The Question of Thrift. In *Thrift and Thriving in America: Capitalism and Moral Order from the Puritans to the Present,* edited by Joshua J. Yates and James Davison Hunter. Oxford: Oxford University Press.

Hunter, Molly. 2016. Local Students Speak Out on Racism. *Daily Iowan,* November 14.

Hursthouse, Rosalind, and Glen Pettigrove. 2016. Virtue Ethics. *Stanford Encyclopedia of Philosophy.* December 8. https://plato.stanford.edu/entries/ethics-virtue/.

Ignatieff, Michael. 2017. *The Ordinary Virtues: Moral Order in a Divided World.* Cambridge, MA: Harvard University Press.

Ingram, Martin. 1984. Ridings, Rough Music, and the "Reform of Popular Culture" in Early Modern England. *Past & Present* 105:79–113.

Institute Montaigne. 2016. *Un Islam français est possible.* http://www.institutmontaigne.org/publications/un-islam-francais-est-possible.

Internal Revenue Service. 2017. *Abusive Tax Shelters and Transactions.* January 23. https://www.irs.gov/businesses/corporations/abusive-tax-shelters-and-transactions.

International Committee of the Red Cross. 2010 [1977]. *Protocol Additional to the Geneva Conventions of 12 Aug. 1949, and Relating to the Protection of Victims of International Armed Conflicts (Protocol I), of 8 June 1977.* Geneva, Switzerland. https://www.icrc.org/eng/assets/files/other/icrc_002_0321.pdf.

International Council on Human Rights Policy. 1999. *Taking Duties Seriously: Individual Duties in International Human Rights Law.* ICHRP: Commentary. http://ichrp.org/files/reports/10/103_report_en.pdf.

Iowa Civil Jury Instructions (2004), Iowa Code §668A.1.

Ipsos Media. 2013. Is TV Helping or Hurting Same-Sex Marriage? *News & Polls*, April 11. https://www.ipsos.com/en-us/tv-helping-or-hurting-same-sex-marriage.

Irving, Shelley. 2011. Comparing Program Participation of TANF and Non-TANF Families before and during a Time of Recession. U.S. Census Bureau. November. http://www.census.gov/prod/2011pubs/p70-127.pdf.

Ito, Susan. 2010. Protecting Outrageous, Offensive Speech. *ACLU Blog*, October 6. https://www.aclu.org/blog/speakeasy/protecting-outrageous-offensive-speech.

Jackall, Robert. 1988. *Moral Mazes: The World of Corporate Managers*. New York: Oxford University Press.

Jackman, Simon. 2001. Compulsory Voting. In *International Encyclopedia of the Social and Behavioral Sciences*, edited by Neil J. Smelser and Paul B. Baltes. Oxford: Elsevier.

Jacob, Herbert. 1988. *Silent Revolution: The Transformation of Divorce Law in the United States*. Chicago: University of Chicago Press.

Jacquet, Jennifer. 2015. *Is Shame Necessary? New Uses for an Old Tool*. New York: Pantheon Books.

Jacquet, Jennifer, Christoph Hauert, Arne Traulsen, and Manfred Milinski. 2011. Shame and Honour Drive Cooperation. *Biology Letters* 7, no. 6. London: Royal Society.

Janser, Lieutenant Colonel Michael J. 2007. *Cognitive Biases in Military Decision Making*. U.S. Army War College, Civilian Research Paper. http://www.dtic.mil/cgi-bin/GetTRDoc?AD=ADA493560.

Jary, David, and Julia Jary. 1991. *The Harper Collins Dictionary of Sociology*. New York: Harper Collins.

Jefferson, Thomas. 1975 [1771]. Letter to Robert Skipwith, August 3, 1771: A Gentleman's Library. In *The Portable Thomas Jefferson*, edited by Merrill D. Peterson. New York: Penguin.

———. 1984. *Thomas Jefferson: Writings*, edited by Merrill D. Peterson. New York: Library of America.

Jenero, Kenneth, and Mark Spognardi. 1996. Defending against the Corporate Campaign: Selected Legal Responses to Common Union Tactics. *Employee Relations Law Journal* 22:119–138.

Jensen, Michael, & William Meckling. 1994. The Nature of Man. https://papers.ssrn.com/sol3/papers.cfm?abstract_id=5471.

Jervis, Robert. 1978. Cooperation under the Security Dilemma. *World Politics* 30:167–214.

Jeynes, William. 2008. Methodological Challenges Facing Researchers in Examining the Effects of Divorce on Children. *Marriage and Family Review* 40:107–130.

Joas, Hans. 2013. *The Sacredness of the Person: A New Genealogy of Human Rights*. Washington, DC: Georgetown University Press.

Jones, Rachel K., Jacqueline E. Darroch, and Stanley K. Henshaw. 2002. Contraceptive Use among U.S. Women Having Abortions in 2000–2001. *Perspectives on Sexual and Reproductive Health* 34:294–303.

Jones, Rachel K., Susheela Singh, Lawrence B. Finer, and Lori F. Frohwirth. 2006. Repeat Abortion in the United States. Occasional Report No. 29, November. http://www.guttmacher.org/pubs/2006/11/21/or29.pdf.

Jordan, Jillian, Moshe Hoffman, Paul Bloom, and David Rand. 2016. Third-Party Punishment as a Costly Signal of Trustworthiness. *Nature* 530:473–476.

Jowers, Kevin F. 2003. Comment, International and National Legal Efforts to Protect Cultural Property: The 1970 UNESCO Convention, the United States, and Mexico. *Texas International Law Journal* 38:145–172.

Kádár, Dániel. 2017. *Politeness, Impoliteness and Ritual: Maintaining Moral Order in Interpersonal Interaction.* Cambridge: Cambridge University Press.

Kadens, Emily. 2012. The Myth of the Customary Law Merchant. *University of Texas Law Review* 90:1153–1206.

Kagan, Robert. 1997. Should Europe Worry about Adversarial Legalism? *Oxford Journal of Legal Studies* 17:165–183.

Kahan, Dan M. 1999. The Progressive Appropriation of Disgust. In *The Passions of Law,* edited by Susan A. Bandes. New York: NYU Press.

Kahl, Colin. 2007. In the Crossfire or the Crosshairs: Norms, Civilian Casualties, and U.S. Conduct in Iraq. *International Security* 32:7–46.

Kahneman, Daniel. 2011. *Thinking, Fast and Slow.* New York: Farrar, Straus and Giroux.

Kahneman, Daniel, and Cass Sunstein. 2007. Indignation: Psychology, Politics, Law. Public Law and Legal Theory Working Paper No. 346. University of Chicago. https://papers.ssrn.com/sol3/papers.cfm?abstract_id=1002707.

Kahneman, Daniel, and Amos Tversky. 1982. *Judgment under Uncertainty: Heuristics and Biases.* New York: Cambridge University Press.

Kaiser Family Foundation / New York Times / CBS News. 2014. Non-Employed Poll. http://www.kff.org/other/poll-finding/kaiser-family-foundationnew-york-timescbs-news-non-employed-poll/.

Katz, Leo. 2011. *Why the Law Is So Perverse.* Chicago: University of Chicago Press.

Kamenev, Marina. 2013. Sterilizing a Child for a Better Life. *Atlantic,* September 19.

Kant, Immanuel. 2001 [1797]. Duties to Oneself. In *Lectures on Ethics,* edited by Peter Heath and J. B. Schneewind, translated by Peter Heath. Cambridge: Cambridge University Press.

———. 2002 [1790]. *Critique of the Power of Judgment.* Edited by Paul Guyer. Translated by Eric Matthews. Cambridge: Cambridge University Press.

Kaufman, Sharon. 2005. *And a Time to Die: How American Hospitals Shape the End of Life.* New York: Scribner.

Keane, Webb. 2016. *Ethical Life: Its Natural and Social Histories.* Princeton: Princeton University Press.

Keating, Lauren. 2015. The Business of Music-Streaming Services: How Deals with Record Labels and Publishers Are Made. *Tech Times,* September 10.

Keijser, Jan W. de. 2014. Penal Theory and Popular Opinion: The Deficiencies of Direct Engagement. In *Popular Punishment: On the Normative Significance of Public Opinion,* edited by Jesper Ryberg and Julian Roberts. Oxford: Oxford University Press.

Keleher, Alison, and Eric Smith. 2012. Growing Support for Gay and Lesbian Equality since 1990. *Journal of Homosexuality* 59:1307–1326.

Kelley, Judith, and Beth Simmons. 2014. Politics by Number: Indicators as Social Pressure in International Relations. *American Journal of Political Science* 59:55–70.

Kennedy, Duncan. 1979. Antonio Gramsci and the Legal System. *ALSA Forum* 6:32–37.

———. 1982 The Stages of the Decline of the Public/Private Distinction. *University of Pennsylvania Law Review* 130:1349–1357.

Kennerly, Maxwell S. 2009. Why False Claims Act Whistleblower Cases Need Awards over $50 Million. *Litigation and Trial Blog,* April 24. http://www.litigationandtrial.com/2009/04/articles/trial/ideas/why-false-claims-act-whistleblower-cases-need-awards-over-50-million.

Kesebir, Pelin, and Selin Kesebir. 2012. The Cultural Salience of Moral Character and Virtue Declined in Twentieth Century America. *Journal of Positive Psychology* 7:471–480.

Khan, Azmat, and Anand Gopal. 2017. The Uncounted. *New York Times,* November 16.

Kahn, Paul. 1999. *The Cultural Study of Law.* Chicago: University of Chicago Press.

Kim, Walter. 1997. The Ties That Bind: Should Breaking Up Be Harder to Do? *Time,* August 18.

Kim, Yunjeen. 2013. *Bank Bailouts and Moral Hazard? Evidence from Banks' Investment and Financing Decisions.* UConn Working Paper. November. http://finance.business.uconn.edu/wp-content/uploads/sites/723/2014/08/Bank-Bailouts-and-Moral-Hazard.pdf.

Kirchin, Simon, ed. 2013. *Thick Concepts.* Oxford: Oxford University Press.

Kirkland, Kimberly. 2005. Ethics in Large Law Firms: The Principle of Pragmatism. *University of Memphis Law Review* 35:631–730.

———. 2012. The Ethics of Constructing Truth: The Corporate Litigator's Approach. In *Lawyers in Practice: Ethical Decision Making in Context,* edited by Leslie Levin and Lynn Mather. Chicago: University of Chicago Press.

Klarman, Michael. 2013. *From the Closet to the Altar: Courts, Backlash, and the Struggle for Same-Sex Marriage.* New York: Oxford University Press.

Klein, Jill Gabrielle, N. Craig Smith, and Andrew John. 2004. Why We Boycott: Consumer Motivations for Boycott Participation. *Journal of Marketing* 68:92–109.

Kleingeld, Pauline, and Eric Brown. 2013. Cosmopolitanism. *Stanford Encyclopedia of Philosophy.* July 1. https://plato.stanford.edu/entries/cosmopolitanism/.

Kleinman, Arthur. 1998. *Experience and Its Moral Modes: Culture, Human Conditions, and Disorder.* The Tanner Lectures on Human Values, Stanford University. http://tannerlectures.utah.edu/_documents/a-to-z/k/Kleinman99.pdf.

Knobe, Joshua, and Shaun Nichols. 2008. An Experimental Philosophy Manifesto. In *Experimental Philosophy,* vol. 1, edited by Joshua Knobe and Shaun Nichols. New York: Oxford University Press.

Kohn, Hans. 1944. *A Study of Nationalism: A Study in Its Origins and Background.* New York: Macmillan.

Kohrman, Matthew. 2005. *Bodies of Difference: Experiences of Disability and Institutional Advocacy in the Making of Modern China.* Berkeley: University of California Press.

Kolben, Kevin. 2011. Transnational Labor Regulation and the Limits of Governance. *Theoretical Inquiries in Law* 12:403–437.

Kolchin, Peter. 1983. Reevaluating the Antebellum Slave Community: A Comparative Perspective. *Journal of American History* 71:579–601.

Koplow, David. 2010. *Death by Moderation: The U.S. Military's Quest for Usable Weapons.* Cambridge: Cambridge University Press.

*Korea Times.* 2016. Korean Air Fires Pilot for Hampering Flight by Joining Work-to-Rule Action, March 7. http://www.koreatimesus.com/korean-air-fires-pilot-for-hampering-flight-by-joining-work-to-rule-action/.

Krause, Sharon R. 2002. *Liberalism with Honor.* Cambridge, MA: Harvard University Press.

Krauthammer, Charles. 2010. Sacrilege at Ground Zero. *Washington Post,* August 13.

KRC/Boston Globe Poll. 1987. Abortion: A New Era. Polling Report, May 22. Boston.

Krisch, Nico. 2008. The Open Architecture of European Human Rights Law. *Modern Law Review* 71:183–216.

Kristof, Nicholas. 2010. Taking Bin Laden's Side. *New York Times,* August 21.

Krueger, Alan. 2017. *Where Have All the Workers Gone?* Brookings Papers on Economic Activity. Federal Reserve Bank of Boston.

Kugler, Matthew. 2014. Book Review of *Popular Punishment: On the Normative Significance of Public Opinion,* edited by Jesper Ryberg and Julian Roberts. http://clcjbooks.rutgers.edu/books/popular-punishment/.

Kugler, Matthew, and John Darley. 2012. Punitiveness toward Users of Illicit Drugs: A Disparity between Actual and Perceived Attitudes. *Federal Sentencing Reporter* 24:217–221.

Kukathas, Chandran. 1998. Liberalism and Multiculturalism. *Political Theory* 26:686–699.

Kuran, Timur. 1995. *Private Truths, Public Lies: The Social Consequences of Preference Falsification.* Cambridge, MA: Harvard University Press.

Labov, William. 1972. *Language in the Inner City: Studies in the Black English Vernacular.* Philadelphia: University of Pennsylvania Press.

Laidlaw, James. 2014. *The Subject of Virtue: An Anthropology of Ethics and Freedom.* New York: Cambridge University Press.

Laksin, Jacob. 2010. The Left's Peretz Problem. *IslamistWatch,* September 30. http://www.islamist-watch.org/5148/the-lefts-peretz-problem.

Lambek, Michael. 2010. Introduction. In *Ordinary Ethics: Anthropology, Language, and Action,* edited by Michael Lambek. Bronx, NY: Fordham University Press.

———. 2015. *The Ethical Condition: Essays on Action, Person, and Value.* Chicago: University of Chicago Press.

Lamont, Michèle. 2000. *The Dignity of Working Men: Morality and the Boundaries of Race, Class, and Immigration.* Cambridge, MA: Harvard University Press.

Landon, Donald D. 1982. Lawyers and Localities: The Interaction of Community Context and Professionalism. *Law and Social Inquiry* 7:459–485.

———. 1985. Clients, Colleagues, and Community: The Shaping of Zealous Advocacy in Country Law Practice. *Law and Social Inquiry* 10:81–111.

Langer, Gary. 2013. Poll Tracks Dramatic Rise in Support for Gay Marriage. *ABC News,* March 18.

Langevoort, Donald. 2011. Getting (Too) Comfortable: In-House Lawyers, Enterprise Risk and the Financial Crisis. *Georgetown Public Law and Legal Theory.* Research Paper No. 11-135. http://papers.ssrn.com/sol3/papers.cfm?abstract_id=1932398.

Las Vegas Bankruptcy Blog. 2012. Why Is There a Social Stigma for Personal Bankruptcy? June 29. http://slf7.wordpress.com/2012/06/29/why-is-there-social-stigma-for-personal-bankruptcy/.

Latour, Bruno. 2005. *Reassembling the Social: An Introduction to Actor-Network-Theory.* Oxford: Oxford University Press.

———. 2013. *An Inquiry into Modes of Existence: An Anthropology of the Moderns.* Cambridge, MA: Harvard University Press.

Lauterpacht, Hersh. 1966. *The Function of Law in the International Community.* Hamden, CT: Archon Books.

Lawless, Robert M., Angela K. Littwin, Katherine M. Porter, John A. E. Pottow, Deborah Thorne, and Elizabeth Warren. 2008. Did Bankruptcy Reform Fail? An Empirical Study of Consumer Debtors. *American Bankruptcy Law Journal* 82:349–406.

Lawson, Frederick. 1950. *Negligence in the Civil Law.* Oxford: Oxford University Press.

Laycock, Douglas. 2010. *Modern American Remedies: Cases and Materials.* 4th ed. Austin, TX: Wolters Kluwer.

Lazarus, Liora, Benjamin Goold, Rajendra Desai, and Qudsi Rasheed. 2009. The Relationship between Rights and Responsibilities. *Ministry of Justice Research Series* 18/09. http://webarchive.nationalarchives.gov.uk/20100512135835/http://www.justice.gov.uk/publications/rights-responsibilities-research.htm.

Lazear, Edward. 2017. The Incredible Shrinking Workforce. *Wall Street Journal,* December 7.

Leff, Arthur Allen. 1967. Unconscionability and the Code—The Emperor's New Clause. *University of Pennsylvania Law Review* 115:485–559.

Leiter, Brian. 2009. Morality Critics. In *The Oxford Handbook of Continental Philosophy,* edited by Brian Leiter and Michael Rosen. Oxford: Oxford University Press.

Lenoir, Rémi. 2003. *Généalogie de la morale familiale.* Paris: Seuil.

Lerman, R. I., and W. B. Wilcox. 2014. *For Richer, for Poorer.* American Enterprise Institute Report. https://www.aei.org/wp-content/uploads/2014/10/IFS-ForRicherForPoorer-Final_Web.pdf.

Lerner, Michael. 2007. *Dry Manhattan: Prohibition in New York City.* Cambridge, MA: Harvard University Press.

Lessig, Lawrence. 1995. The Regulation of Social Meaning. *Chicago Law Review* 62:943–1042.

Levin, Yuval. 2016. *The Fractured Republic: Renewing America's Social Contract in the Age of Individualism.* New York: Basic Books.

Lewicka, Maria. 2011. Place Attachment: How Far Have We Come in the Last 40 Years? *Journal of Environmental Psychology* 31:207–230.

Lewis, Michael J. 2015. How Art Became Irrelevant: A Chronological Survey of the Demise of Art. *Commentary,* July 15. https://www.commentarymagazine.com/articles/how-art-became-irrelevant.

Li, Liangjiang. 2010. Rights Consciousness and Rules Consciousness in China. *China Journal* 64:47–68.

Liddell, Gloria, Pearson Liddell, and Michael Highfield. 2011. Does an Economic Crisis Merit a Prima Facie Finding of Exigent Circumstances or Other Emergency Relief—The Impact of the Credit Counseling Provision of BAPCPA upon Distressed Homeowners in a Severe National Economic Downturn. *John Marshall Law Review* 44:129–178.

Lieberman, Harris, Gaston P. Bathalon, Cristina M. Falco, Charles A. Morgan, Philip J. Niro, and William J. Tharion. 2005. The Fog of War: Decrements in Cognitive Performance and Mood Associated with Combat-Like Stress. *Aviation, Space, and Environmental Medicine* 76: C7–C14.

Lightfoot-Klein, Hanny. 1989. *Prisoners of Ritual: An Odyssey into Female Genital Circumcision.* Binghamton, NY: Haworth Press.

Lindsay, Ronald. 2005. Slaves, Embryos, and Nonhuman Animals: Moral Status and the Limitations of Common Morality Theory. *Kennedy Institute of Ethics Journal* 15:323–346.

———. 2009. Bioethics Policies and the Compass of Common Morality. *Theoretical Ethics and Bioethics,* 30:31–43.

Link, Bruce G., and Jo C. Phelan. 2001. Conceptualizing Stigma. *Annual Review of Sociology* 27:363–385.

Lipman, Frederick. 2012. *Whistleblowers: Incentives, Disincentives, and Protection Programs.* Hoboken, NJ: Wiley.

Livshits, Igor, James MacGee, and Michèle Tertilt. 2010. Accounting for the Rise in Consumer Bankruptcies. *American Economic Journal* 2:165–193.

Llewellyn, Gwyneth, Rannveig Traustadottir, David McConnell, Hanna Bjorg Sigurjonsdott, and Steven Taylor, eds. 2010. *Parents with Intellectual Disabilities: Past, Present, and Futures.* West Sussex, UK: Wiley.

Luban, David. 1988. The *Noblesse Oblige* Tradition in the Practice of Law. *Vanderbilt Law Review* 41:717–740.

Luhmann, Niklas. 1979. *Trust and Power.* Translated by Christian Morgner and Michael King. New York: Wiley.

———. 1982. *The Differentiation of Society.* Translated by Stephen Holmes and Charles Larmore. New York: Columbia University Press.

Luker, Kristin. 1984. *Abortion and the Politics of Motherhood.* Berkeley: University of California Press.

Lukes, Steven. 1974. *Power: A Radical View.* London: Macmillan.
Luttmer, Erzo. 2001. Group Loyalty and the Taste for Redistribution. *Journal of Political Economy* 59:500–528.
Lynch, Holly, Michele Mathes, and Nadia Sawicki. 2008. *Compliance with Advance Directives: Wrongful Living and Tort Law Remedies.* University of Pennsylvania Law School Scholarship Repository. http://papers.ssrn.com/sol3/papers.cfm?abstract_id=1148384.
Macey, Jonathan. 2013. *The Death of Corporate Reputation: How Integrity Has Been Destroyed on Wall Street.* Upper Saddle River, NJ: FT Press.
MacFarguhar, Neil, and Ethan Bronner. 2011. Report Finds Naval Blockade by Israel Legal, but Faults Raid. *New York Times,* September 1.
MacGaffey, Wyatt. 1994. African Objects and the Idea of Fetish. *RES: Anthropology and Aesthetics* 25:123–131.
MacIntyre, Alasdair. 1981. *After Virtue: A Study in Moral Theory.* South Bend, IN: Notre Dame University Press.
MacKenzie, Donald A. 2006. *An Engine, Not a Camera: How Financial Models Shape Markets.* Cambridge, MA: MIT Press.
Mahmood, Saba. 2009. Religious Reason and Secular Affect: An Incommensurable Divide? *Critical Inquiry.* 35: 836–862.
Maitland, Ian. 1997. The Great Non-Debate over International Sweatshops. *British Academy of Management Annual Conference Proceedings* 240–265.
Manent, Pierre. 1998. *The City of Man.* Translated by Marc LePain. Princeton: Princeton University Press.
Mann, Michael. 1973. *Consciousness and Action among the Western Working Class.* London: Macmillan.
Mansfield, Harvey. 1992. Human Rights in Emergencies. *Critical Review* 6:575–585.
March, Andrew. 2011. Speaking about Muhammad, Speaking for Muslims. *Critical Inquiry* 37:806–821.
———. 2012. What's Wrong with Blasphemy? *New York Times,* September 25. http://opinionator.blogs.nytimes.com/2012/09/25/whats-wrong-with-blasphemy/?pagewanted=print.
Marcus, George (with Peter Dobkin). 1992. *Lives in Trust: the Fortunes of Dynastic Families in the Late Twentieth Century.* Boulder: Westview Press.
Marcuse, Herbert. 1965. Repressive Tolerance. In *A Critique of Pure Tolerance,* edited by Robert Paul Wolff, Barrington Moore Jr., and Herbert Marcuse. Boston: Beacon Press.
Martin, John Levi. 2002. Power, Authority, and the Constraint of Belief Systems. *American Journal of Sociology* 197:861–904.
———. 2003. What Is Field Theory? *American Journal of Sociology* 109:1–49.
Martindale-Hubbell Law Digests. 2006a. *Digests of Laws: International Section: Estates and Trusts.* New Providence, NJ: LexisNexis/Reed Elsevier.
———. 2006b. *Digests of Laws of the States: Estates and Trusts.* New Providence, NJ: LexisNexis/Reed Elsevier.

Marx, Karl. 1972 [1844]. On the Jewish Question. In *The Marx-Engels Reader,* edited by Robert C. Tucker. New York: W. W. Norton.

Mason, Elinor. 2011. Value Pluralism. *Stanford Encyclopedia of Philosophy.* July 29. https://plato.stanford.edu/entries/value-pluralism/.

Mason, Lilliana. 2015. Party Polarization Is Making Us More Prejudiced. In *Political Polarization in American Politics,* edited by Daniel Hopkins and John Sides. London: Bloomsbury.

Masood, Salman, and Declan Walsh. 2012. Pakistan Gives U.S. a List of Demands, Including an End to C.I.A. Drone Strikes. *New York Times,* April 12.

Masson, Antoine, and Mary Shariff, eds. 2010. *Legal Strategies: How Corporations Use Law to Improve Performance.* New York: Springer.

Mattei, Ugo, Teemu Ruskola, and Antonio Gidi. 2009. *Schlesinger's Comparative Law.* 7th ed. New York: Foundation Press.

Mazzetti, Mark, Eric Shmitt, and Robert F. Worth. 2011. Two-Year Manhunt Led to Killing of Awlaki in Yemen. *New York Times,* September 30.

McAdams, Richard. 1997. The Origins, Development, and Regulation of Norms. *Michigan Law Review* 96:376–433.

McAdams, Richard, and Eric Rasmusen. 2007. Norms and the Law. In *Handbook of Law and Economics,* vol. 2, edited by Mitchell Polinsky and Steven Shavell. Amsterdam: Elsevier.

McBarnet, Doreen, and Christopher Whelan. 1999. Challenging the Regulators: Strategies for Resisting Control. In *Regulation and Deregulation: Policy and Practice in the Utilities and Financial Services Industries,* edited by Christopher McCrudden. Oxford: Oxford University Press.

McCarthy, Justin. 2016a. Americans Remain Pessimistic about State of Moral Values. *Gallup Polling,* May 25. http://www.gallup.com/poll/191858/americans-remain-pessimistic-state-moral-values.aspx.

———. 2016b. Americans' Views Shift on Toughness of Justice System. October 20. http://www.gallup.com/poll/196568/americans-views-shift-toughness-justice-system.aspx.

McCloskey, Deirdre. 2006. *The Bourgeois Virtues: Ethics for an Age of Commerce.* Chicago: University of Chicago Press.

McGirr, Lisa. 2016. *The War on Alcohol: Prohibition and the Rise of the Administrative State.* New York: W. W. Norton.

McKinsey & Co. 2017. *Women in the Workplace.* Report, October. https://www.mckinsey.com/global-themes/gender-equality/women-in-the-workplace-2017.

McPherson, James M. 1997. *For Cause and Comrades: Why Men Fought in the Civil War.* New York: Oxford University Press.

Mears, Tracey, and Dan Kahan. 1996. Law and Norms Order in Inner City. *University of Chicago Law Review* 63:133–198.

Meisner, Jason, and Patrick O'Connell. 2017. Richard Posner Announces Sudden Retirement from Federal Appeals Court in Chicago. *Chicago Tribune,* September 2.

Merline, John. 2012. The Sharp Rise in Disability Claims: Are Federal Disability Benefits Becoming a General Safety Net? *Region Focus Second/Third*

*Quarter.* https://www.richmondfed.org/~/media/richmondfedorg/publications/research/region_focus/2012/q2-3/pdf/feature3.pdf.

Merritt, Deborah Jones. 2016. *Hippocrates and Socrates: Professional Obligations to Educate the Next Generation.* January 25. Public Law and Legal Theory Working Paper No. 327. Ohio State University, Moritz College of Law. https://papers.ssrn.com/sol3/papers.cfm?abstract_id=2721725.

Merryman, John Henry, ed. 2006. *Imperialism, Art and Restitution.* Cambridge: Cambridge University Press.

Merz, Jon, and Baruch Fischhoff. 1990. Informed Consent Does Not Mean Rational Consent. *Journal of Legal Medicine* 11:321–350.

Mewse, Avril J., Stephen E. G. Lea, and Wendy Wrapson. 2010. First Steps Out of Debt: Attitudes and Social Identity as Predictors of Contact by Debtors with Creditors. *Journal of Economic Psychology* 31:1021–1034.

Miceli, Marcia P., and Janet P. Near. 1991. Whistle-Blowing as an Organizational Process. In *Research in the Sociology of Organizations,* edited by Samuel Bacharach. Greenwich, CT: JAI Press.

Mill, John Stuart. 1989 [1851]. *"On Liberty" and Other Writings.* Edited by Stefan Collini. Cambridge: Cambridge University Press.

Miller, Barbara D. 2001. Female-Selective Abortion in Asia: Patterns, Policies, and Debates. *American Anthropologist* 103:1083–1095.

Miller, Bruce. 1981. Autonomy and the Refusal of Lifesaving Treatment. *Hastings Center Reports*11:22–28.

Miller, David. 1992. Distributive Justice: What the People Think. *Ethics* 102:555–593.

———. 2016. *Strangers in Our Midst: The Political Philosophy of Immigration.* Cambridge, MA: Harvard University Press.

Miller, Geoffrey. 2017. *The Law of Governance, Risk Management, and Compliance.* 2nd ed. New York: Aspen.

Miller, William Ian. 1995. *Humiliation: And Other Essays on Honor, Social Discomfort, and Violence.* Ithaca, NY: Cornell University Press.

———. 1997. *The Anatomy of Disgust.* Cambridge, MA: Harvard University Press.

Millman, Marcia. 1976. *The Unkindest Cut: Life in the Backrooms of Medicine.* New York: William Morrow .

Mills, C. Wright. 1959. *The Sociological Imagination.* New York: Oxford University Press.

Minow, Martha, and Joseph Singer. 2010. In Favor of Foxes: Pluralism as Fact and Aid to the Pursuit of Justice. *Boston University Law Review* 90:903–920.

Mintz, Steven. 2011. American Slavery in Comparative Perspective. Gilder Lehrman Institute of American History, November 20. https://www.gilderlehrman.org/history-by-era/origins-slavery/resources/american-slavery-comparative-perspective.

Mir, Asfandyar, and Dylan Moore. 2018. Drones, Surveillance, and Violence: Theory and Evidence from a US Drone Program. https://dl.dropboxusercontent.com/content_link/Hoh8akiuaC6Ir6RrOQhjRbzwdhk9easRWfVB513WG4XJ3poi8lc4MA9Y8u97hnwT/file.

Mitchell, Gregory, and Philip Tetlock. 2006. An Empirical Inquiry into the Relation of Corrective Justice to Distributive Justice. *Journal of Empirical Legal Studies* 3:421–466.

Modood, Tariq, & Ziva Kastoryano. 2006. Secularism and the Accommodation of Muslims in Europe. In *Multiculturalism, Muslims and Citizenship: a European Approach*, Modood, Tariq, Richard Zapata-Barrero, & Anna Triandafyllidou, eds. London: Routledge.

Moffitt, Robert. 1981. Participation in the AFDC Program and the Stigma of Welfare Receipt: Estimation of a Choice-Theoretic Model. *Southern Economic Journal* 47:753–762.

———. 1983. An Economic Model of Welfare Stigma. *American Economic Review* 73:1023–1035.

Montagu, Alexandre A. 1993. Recent Cases on the Recovery of Stolen Art: The Tug of War between Owners and Good Faith Purchasers Continues. *Columbia Journal of Law and the Arts* 18:75–102.

Montesquieu, Charles-Louis de Secondat. 1949 [1748]. *The Spirit of the Laws.* Translated by Thomas Nugent. New York: Macmillan.

———. 2008 [1721]. *Persian Letters.* Translated by Margaret Mauidon. Oxford: Oxford University Press.

Montopoli, Brian. 2010. Howard Dean on Mosque Comments: "I Am Not Going to Back Off," *CBS News,* August 20. https://www.cbsnews.com/news/howard-dean-on-mosque-comments-i-am-not-going-to-back-off/.

Moore, Barrington. 1998. *Moral Aspects of Economic Growth, and Other Essays.* Ithaca, NY: Cornell University Press.

Morgan, Michael. 2008. *On Shame.* New York: Routledge.

Morgan, Teresa. 2007. *Popular Morality in the Early Roman Empire.* Cambridge: Cambridge University Press.

Morgenson, Gretchen, and Joshua Rosner. 2011. *Reckless Endangerment: How Outsized Ambition, Greed, and Corruption Created the Worst Financial Crisis of Our Time.* New York: New York Times Books.

Morin, Rich, and Renee Stepler. 2016. The Racial Confidence Gap in Police Performance. Pew Research Center, September 19. http://www.pewsocialtrends.org/2016/09/29/the-racial-confidence-gap-in-police-performance/.

Morris, Thomas D. 1996. *Southern Slavery and the Law, 1619–1860.* Chapel Hill: University of North Carolina Press.

Morrow, Glenn Raymond. 1939. *Plato's Law of Slavery and Its Relation to Greek Law.* Buffalo, NY: W. S. Hein.

Mosque-Building and Its Discontents: What the Public Thinks about the Cordoba House Project. 2010. *The Economist,* August 19. https://www.economist.com/blogs/democracyinamerica/2010/08/islamic_cultural_centre_sorta_near_ground_zero.

Mote, Frederick W. 1989. *Intellectual Foundations of China.* 2nd ed. New York: McGraw-Hill.

Moyn, Samuel. 2010. *The Last Utopia: Human Rights in History.* Cambridge, MA: Belknap Press of Harvard University Press.

———. 2016. Rights vs. Duties: Reclaiming Civil Balance. *Boston Review,* May 16. http://bostonreview.net/books-ideas/samuel-moyn-rights-duties.

MSCI, Inc. 2017. Out of Whack: U.S. CEO Pay and Long-Term Investment Returns. https://www.msci.com/ceo-pay.

Mueller, Pam A., Lawrence M. Solan, and John M. Darley. 2012. When Does Knowledge Become Intent? Perceiving the Minds of Wrongdoers. *Journal of Empirical Legal Studies* 9:859–892.

Mullainathan, Sendhil, Eldar Shafir, and Marianne Bertrand. 2006. Behavioral Economics and Marketing in Aid of Decision Making among the Poor. *Journal of Policy Making and Marketing* 25:8–23.

Mullaney, Craig. 2009. *The Unforgiving Minute: A Soldier's Education.* New York: Penguin.

Mutz, Diana C. 2006. *Hearing the Other Side: Deliberative versus Participatory Democracy.* Cambridge: Cambridge University Press.

Myers, John E. B. 2008. A Short History of Child Protection in America. *Family Law Quarterly* 42:449–463.

Nafstad, Hilde Eileen, Rolv Mikkel Blakar, Erik Carlquist, Joshua Marvle Phelps, and Kim Rand-Hendriksen 2009. Globalization, Neo-Liberalism and Community Psychology. *American Journal of Community Psychology* 43:162–175.

Nelken, David, and Johannas Feest. 2001. *Adapting Legal Cultures.* Portland, OR: Hart.

Nelson, Maggie. 2011. *The Art of Cruelty: A Reckoning.* New York: W. W. Norton.

Nelson, Robert. 1998 [1988]. *Partners with Power: Social Transformation of the Large Law Firm.* Berkeley: University of California Press.

———. 1998. The Discovery Process as a Circle of Blame: Institutional, Professional, and Socio-Economic Factors That Contribute to Unreasonable, Inefficient, and Amoral Behavior in Corporate Litigation. *Fordham Law Review* 67:773–808.

Nelson, Robert, and Laura Beth Nielsen. 2000. Cops, Counsel, and Entrepreneurs. *Law and Society Review* 34:457–494.

Nelson, Robert, Laura Beth Nielsen, and Ryon Lancaster. 2010. Individual Justice or Collective Legal Mobilization? Employment Discrimination Litigation in the Post–Civil Rights U.S. *Journal of Empirical Legal Studies* 7:175–201.

Nesser, Petter. 2011. Ideologies of Jihad in Europe. *Journal of Terrorism and Political Violence* 23:173–200.

Neumeister, Larry. 2016. US Terror Attacks' Common Denominator: Anwar Al-Awlaki. *Associated Press,* September 25.

New York Times / CBS News Poll. 1998. *New York Times,* January 18. https://archive.nytimes.com/www.nytimes.com/interactive/2012/01/19/us/politics/19poll-documents.html?ref=politics.

Newport, Frank. 2016. Most in U.S. Oppose Colleges Considering Race in Admissions. *Gallup: Politics,* July 8. http://www.gallup.com/poll/193508/oppose-colleges-considering-race-admissions.aspx.

Nielsen, Laura Beth, and Robert Nelson. 2005. Scaling the Pyramid: A Sociolegal Model of Employment Discrimination Litigation. In *Handbook of Employment Discrimination Research: Right and Realities*, edited by Nielsen and Nelson. New York: Springer.

Nieves, Evelyn. 2005. S.D. Makes Abortion Rare through Laws and Stigma. *Washington Post,* December 27.

Nourse, Victoria, and Jane Schacter. 2002. The Politics of Legislative Drafting: A Congressional Case Study. *New York University Law Review* 77:575–623.

Novak, Michael. 1982. *The Spirit of Democratic Capitalism.* New York: Simon and Schuster.

Nowrasteh, Alex. 2016. Muslim Immigration and Integration in the U.S. and Western Europe. October 31. Cato at Liberty. https://www.cato.org/blog/muslim-immigration-integration-united-states-western-europe.

Nussbaum, Martha C. 2001. *Upheavals of Thought: The Intelligence of Emotions.* Cambridge: Cambridge University Press.

———. 2004. *Hiding from Humanity: Disgust, Shame and the Law.* Princeton: Princeton University Press.

———. 2010. The Capabilities of People with Cognitive Disabilities. In *Cognitive Disability and Its Challenge to Moral Philosophy,* edited by Eva Kittay and Licia Carlson. Indianapolis: Wiley-Blackwell.

———. 2012. *The New Religious Intolerance: Overcoming the Politics of Fear in an Anxious Age.* Cambridge, MA: Harvard University Press.

Nyman, John A. 2007. American Health Policy: Cracks in the Foundation. *Journal of Health Politics, Policy and Law* 32:759–783.

Oakes, James. 1982. *The Ruling Race: A History of American Slaveholders.* New York: Alfred A. Knopf.

Obama, Barack. 2009. Statement by the President, Omnibus Appropriations Act. March 11. https://obamawhitehouse.archives.gov/the-press-office/statement-president-signing-hr-1105.

———. 2011. Remarks by the President in Address to the Nation on Libya, March 28. https://obamawhitehouse.archives.gov/the-press-office/2011/03/28/remarks-president-address-nation-libya.

O'Connor, Peg. 2002. *Oppression and Responsibility: A Wittgensteinian Approach to Social Practices and Moral Theory.* University Park: Pennsylvania State University Press.

Office of the Director of National Intelligence. 2006. Declassified Key Judgments of the National Intelligence Estimate, Trends in Global Terrorism: Implications for the United States. April, Washington, DC. https://www.dni.gov/files/documents/Special%20Report_Global%20Terrorism%20NIE%20Key%20Judgments.pdf.

O'Hanlon, Michael, and Jason Campbell. 2007. Iraq Index: Tracking Variables of Reconstruction and Security in Post-Saddam Iraq. Brookings Institution. https://www.brookings.edu/iraq-index/.

Olsthoorn, Peter. 2017. Situations and Dispositions: How to Rescue the Military Virtues from Social Psychology. *Journal of Military Ethics* 16:78–93.

O'Neill, Onora. 1996. *Toward Justice and Virtue: A Constructive Account of Practical Reasoning*. Cambridge: Cambridge University Press.

Oppenheimer, Mark. 2012. The Loneliness of Doing Right. *New York Times*, February 23.

Orentlicher, David. 2001. *Matters of Life and Death: Making Moral Theory Work in Medical Ethics and the Laws*. Princeton: Princeton University Press.

Orgad, Liav. 2016. *The Cultural Defense of Nations: A Liberal Theory of Majority Rights*. Oxford: Oxford University Press.

O'Rourke, Dara. 2005. Market Movements: Nongovernmental Organization Strategies to Influence Global Production and Consumption. *Journal of Industrial Ecology* 9:115–126.

Orten, James D., and Wade Wilson. 1982. Divorce Applicants: Which Ones Should Go to Marriage Counselors? *Oklahoma Law Review* 35:403–414.

Osberg, Lars, and Elsa Bechert. 2016. Social Values for Equality and Preferences for State Intervention: Is the USA "Exceptional"? Working Paper, Economics Dept., Dalhousie University. https://cdn.dal.ca/content/dam/dalhousie/pdf/faculty/science/economics/RePEc/dal/wparch/Social_Values2.pdf.

Osiel, Mark J. 1990. Lawyers as Monopolists, Aristocrats, and Entrepreneurs. *Harvard Law Review* 103:2009–2066.

———. 1995. Dialogue with Dictators: Judicial Resistance in Argentina and Brazil. *Law and Social Inquiry* 20:481–560.

———. 1999. *Obeying Orders: Atrocity, Military Discipline and the Law of War*. New Brunswick, NJ: Transaction.

———. 2009. *The End of Reciprocity: Terror, Torture, and the Law of War*. Cambridge: Cambridge University Press.

———. 2019. *The Right to Be Rude: The Law and Morals of Incivility* (forthcoming).

Ostrom, Elinor. 1990. *Governing the Commons*. Cambridge: Cambridge University Press.

Owen, Frances, and Dorothy Griffiths. 2009. *Challenges to the Human Rights of People with Intellectual Disabilities*. London: Jessica Kingsley.

Page, Scott E. 2007. *The Difference: How the Power of Diversity Creates Better Groups, Firms, Schools, and Societies*. Princeton: Princeton University Press.

Paletta, Damian, and Scott Patterson. 2010. Banks Falter in Rules Fight. *Wall Street Journal*, April 14.

Pangle, Thomas. 1973. *Montesquieu's Philosophy of Liberalism: A Commentary on The Spirit of the Laws*. Chicago: University of Chicago Press.

Pappas, Demetra. 1996. Recent Historical Perspectives regarding Medical Euthanasia and Physician Assisted Suicide. *British Medical Bulletin* 52:386–393.

Paquette, Robert. 1991. Slave Resistance and Social History. *Journal of Social History* 24:681–685.

Parke, Mary. 2003. *Are Married Parents Really Better for Children?* Center for Law and Social Policy (CLASP), May. http://files.eric.ed.gov/fulltext/ED476114.pdf.

Parsons, Talcott. 1951. *The Social System.* London: Routledge and Kegan Paul.

Patterson, Orlando. 1967. *The Sociology of Slavery: An Analysis of the Origins, Development, and Structure of Negro Slave Society in Jamaica.* Madison, NJ: Fairleigh Dickinson University Press.

———. 1982. *Slavery and Social Death: A Comparative Study.* Cambridge, MA: Harvard University Press.

Pease, Allison. 2000. *Modernism, Mass Culture, and the Aesthetics of Obscenity.* Cambridge: Cambridge University Press.

Peck, Dennis. 2003. Life Insurance as a Social Exchange Mechanism. In *Handbook of Death and Dying,* edited by Clinton Bryant. Thousand Oaks, CA: Sage.

Pellerano, José, Michael Price, Steven Puller, and Gonzalo Sánchez. 2017. Do Extrinsic Incentives Undermine Social Norms? Evidence from a Field Experiment in Energy Conservation. *Environmental and Resource Economics* 67:413–428.

Peretz, Martin. 2010. The New York Times Laments "A Sadly Wary Misunderstanding of Muslim-Americans." But Really Is It "Sadly Wary" or a "Misunderstanding" at All? *New Republic,* September 4.

Perillo, James. 1995. Abuse of Rights: A Pervasive Legal Concept. *Pacific Law Journal* 27:37–97.

Perkins, Wesley. 2003. *The Social Norms Approach to Preventing School and College Substance Abuse.* San Francisco: Jossey-Bass.

Perreau-Saussine, Amanda, and James Bernard Murphy. 2007. The Character of Customary Law: An Introduction. In *The Nature of Customary Law: Legal, Historical and Philosophical Perspectives,* edited by Amanda Perreau-Saussine and James Bernard Murphy. Cambridge: Cambridge University Press.

Perritt, Henry. 2012. New Business Models for Music. *Villanova Sports and Entertainment Law Journal* 18:63–212.

Petrova, Irina. 2004. "Stepping on the Shoulders of a Drowning Man": The Doctrine of Abuse of Rights as a Tool for Reducing Damages for Lost Profits; Troubling Lessons from the Patuha and Himpurna Arbitrations. *Georgetown Journal of International Law* 35:455–482.

Pettit, Philip. 2002. *Rules, Reasons, and Norms: Selected Essays.* New York: Oxford University Press.

Pew Research Center. 2006. Strong Public Support for Right to Die: More Americans Discussing—and Planning—End-of-Life Treatment. *U.S. Politics and Policy,* June 5. http://www.people-press.org/2006/01/05/strong-public-support-for-right-to-die/.

———. 2010a. The Decline of Marriage and the Rise of New Families. November 18. http://www.pewsocialtrends.org/files/2010/11/pew-social-trends-2010-families.pdf.

———.2010b. Support for Same-Sex Marriage Edges Upward: Majority Continues to Favor Gays Serving Openly in Military. *U.S. Politics and Policy,* October 6. http://www.people-press.org/2010/10/06/support-for-same-sex-marriage-edges-upward/.

———. 2012a. Global Opinion of Obama Slips, International Policies Faulted: Drone Strikes Widely Opposed. *Global Attitudes and Trends,* June 13. http://www.pewglobal.org/2012/06/13/global-opinion-of-obama-slips-international-policies-faulted/.

———. 2012b. More Support for Gun Rights, Gay Marriage than in 2008 and 2004. *U.S. Politics and Policy,* April 25. http://www.people-press.org/2012/04/25/more-support-for-gun-rights-gay-marriage-than-in-2008-or-2004/.

———. 2013a. Modern Parenthood: Roles of Moms and Dads Converge as They Balance Work and Family. *Pew Research: Social and Demographic Trends,* March 14, authored by Kim Parker and Wendy Wang. http://www.pewsocialtrends.org/2013/03/14/modern-parenthood-roles-of-moms-and-dads-converge-as-they-balance-work-and-family/.

———. 2013b. Public Esteem for Military Still High. *Religion and Public Life,* July 11. http://www.pewforum.org/2013/07/11/public-esteem-for-military-still-high/#about.

———. 2013c. Views on End-of-Life Medical Treatments: Growing Minority of Americans Say Doctors Should Do Everything Possible to Keep Patients Alive. *Religion and Public Life,* November 21. http://www.pewforum.org/2013/11/21/views-on-end-of-life-medical-treatments/.

———. 2014. Religion in Latin America: Widespread Change in a Historically Catholic Region. *Religion and Public Life,* November 14. http://www.pewforum.org/2014/11/13/religion-in-latin-america.

———. 2015. Beyond Distrust: How Americans View Their Government, November 23. http://www.people-press.org/files/2015/11/11-23-2015-Governance-release.pdf.

Pickard, Victor. 2015. *America's Battle for Media Democracy: The Triumph of Corporate Libertarianism and the Future of Media Reform.* New York: Cambridge University Press.

Pimentel, David. 2012. Criminal Child Neglect and the "Free Range Kid": Is Overprotective Parenting the New Standard of Care? *Utah Law Review* no. 947.

Pinker, Steven. 2008. The Moral Instinct. *New York Times Magazine,* January 13. http://www.nytimes.com/2008/01/13/magazine/13Psychology-t.html.

———. 2011. *The Better Angels of Our Nature: Why Violence Has Declined.* New York: Viking.

Poe, Ted. 2015. Time to Silence Terrorists on Social Media. *CNN,* February 25. http://www.cnn.com/2015/02/25/opinion/poe-terrorism-social-media/index.html.

Porpora, Douglas V., Alexander G. Nikolaev, Julia Hagemann May, and Alexander Jenkins. 2013. *Post-Ethical Society: The Iraq War, Abu Ghraib, and the Moral Failure of the Secular.* Chicago: University of Chicago Press.

Porter, Elizabeth G. 2013. Tort Liability in the Age of the Helicopter Parent. *Alabama Law Review* 64:533–587.

Porter, Jean. 2007. Custom, Ordinance and National Right in Gratian's *Decretum.* In *The Nature of Customary Law,* edited by Amanda Perreau-Saussine and James Bernard Murphy. Cambridge: Cambridge University Press.

Posner, Eric A. 2000a. *Law and Social Norms.* Cambridge, MA: Harvard University Press.

———. 2000b. A Theory of Contract Law under Conditions of Radical Judicial Error. *Northwestern University Law Review* 94:749–774.

———. 2007. *Social Norms, Nonlegal Sanctions, and the Law.* Northampton, MA: Edward Elgar.

Posner, Michael H. 2013. Address the Real Challenges. *New York Times,* May 2.

Posner, Richard. 2012. Physician-Assisted Suicide—Posner. *Becker-Posner Blog,* February 5. http://www.becker-posner-blog.com/2012/02/physician-assisted-suicideposner.html.

———. 2013. Business Ethics—Posner, March. *Becker-Posner Blog,* March 3. http://www.becker-posner-blog.com/2013/03/business-ethicsposner.html.

Posner, Richard, and Andrew M. Rosenfield. 1977. Impossibility and Related Doctrines in Contract Law: An Economic Analysis. *Journal of Legal Studies* 6:83–118.

Post, Robert C. 1986. The Social Foundations of Defamation Law: Reputation and the Constitution. *California Law Review* 74:691–742.

———. 2003. Law and Cultural Conflict. *Chicago-Kent Law Review* 78:485–508.

Pound, Roscoe. 1907. The Need of a Sociological Jurisprudence. *Annual Reports of the American Bar Association* 31:911–926.

Pozner, Larry, and Roger Dodd. 2004. *Cross-Examination: Science and Techniques.* New York: LexisNexis.

Pruitt, Lisa R., and Bradley Showman. 2014. Law Stretched Thin: Access to Justice in Rural America. *South Dakota Law Review* 59:466–528.

Putnam, Robert D. 2000. *Bowling Alone: The Collapse and Revival of American Community.* New York: Simon and Schuster.

———. 2007. E Pluribus Unum: Diversity and Community in the Twenty-First Century—The 2006 Johan Skytte Prize Lecture. *Scandinavian Political Studies* 30:137–174.

———. 2015. *Our Kids: The American Dream in Crisis.* New York: Simon and Schuster.

Putnam, Robert D., and David E. Campbell. 2010. *American Grace: How Religion Divides and Unites Us.* New York: Simon and Schuster.

Pyle, Ralph E. 2006. Trends in Religious Stratification: Have Religious Group Socioeconomic Distinctions Declined in Recent Decades? *Sociology of Religion* 67:61–79.

Quinn, Sarah. 2008. The Transformation of Morals in Markets: Death, Benefits, and the Exchange of Life Insurance Policies. *American Journal of Sociology* 114:738–780.

Rachlinski, Jeffrey. 2000. Heuristics and Biases in the Courts: Ignorance or Adaptation. *Oregon Law Review* 79:61–102.

Radnofsky, Louise. 2016. Millions Eligible for Medicaid Go without It. *Wall Street Journal,* February 1.

Radzik, Linda. 1999. Advocacy and Genuine Autonomy: The Lawyer's Role When the Client Has a Right to Do Wrong. *South Texas Law Review* 40:255–267.

Rae-Hunter, Casey. 2012. Better Mousetraps: Licensing, Access, and Innovation in the New Music Marketplace. *Journal of Business and Technology Law* 7:35–67.

Raine, Tina, Cynthia C. Harper, Corinne H. Rocca, R. Fischer, N. Padian, J. D. Klausner, and P. D. Darney. 2005. Direct Access to Emergency Contraception through Pharmacies and Effect on Unintended Pregnancy and STIs: A Randomized Controlled Trial. *Journal of the American Medical Association* 293:54–62.

Rajan, Raghuram G., and Luigi Zingales. 2003. *Saving Capitalism from the Capitalists: Unleashing the Power of Financial Markets to Create Wealth and Spread Opportunity.* Princeton: Princeton University Press.

Randazzo, Sara. 2017. Harassment Complaints Mount, but Successful Suits Remain Elusive. *Wall Street Journal,* November 23.

Rasch, Vibeke, Hanne Wielandt, and Lisbeth B. Knudsen. 2002. Living Conditions, Contraceptive Use and the Choice of Induced Abortion among Pregnant Women in Denmark. *Scandinavian Journal of Public Health* 30:293–299.

Rasmusen, Eric., ed. 2007. *Game Theory and the Law.* Cheltenham, UK: Edward Elgar.

Rasmussen Reports. 2012. New Low: 47% View Abortion as Morally Wrong Most of the Time. *Politics,* April 20. http://www.rasmussenreports.com/public_content/politics/current_events/abortion/new_low_47_view_abortion_as_morally_wrong_most_of_the_time.

———. 2015. Americans Are Still Supportive of Assisted Suicide. *Politics,* October 15. http://www.rasmussenreports.com/public_content/politics/general_politics/october_2015/americans_are_still_supportive_of_assisted_suicide.

———. 2017. Right Direction or Wrong Track: 39% Say U.S. Heading in Right Direction. *Politics,* May 8. http://www.rasmussenreports.com/public_content/politics/mood_of_america/right_direction_wrong_track_aug21.

Rawls, John. 1971. *A Theory of Justice.* Cambridge, MA: Belknap Press of Harvard University Press.

Raz, Joseph. 1999. *Practical Reasons and Norms.* Oxford: Oxford University Press.

———. 2009. *The Authority of Law: Essays on Law and Morality.* 2nd ed. Oxford: Oxford University Press.

Reader, W. J., and David Kynaston. 1998. *Professionals in the City.* London: Robert Hale.

Reddy, William M. 1997. *The Invisible Code: Honor and Sentiment in Postrevolutionary France, 1814–1848.* Berkeley: University of California Press.

Rees, Joseph. 1994. *Hostages of Each Other: The Transformation of Nuclear Safety since Three Mile Island.* Chicago: University of Chicago Press.

Regan, Milton C., Jr. 2001. Law, Marriage and Intimate Commitment. *Virginal Journal of Social Policy and the Law* 9:116–152.

Rhode, Deborah. 2015. *The Trouble with Lawyers.* New York: Oxford University Press.

Richards, Michael. 1998. *A Time of Silence: Civil War and the Culture of Repression in Franco's Spain.* Cambridge: Cambridge University Press.

Richter, Ingo, Sabine Berking, and Ralf Muller-Schmid, eds. 2006. Introduction. In *Risk Society and the Culture of Precaution.* New York: Palgrave Macmillan.

Ricks, Morgan. 2016. *The Money Problem: Rethinking Financial Regulation.* Chicago: University of Chicago Press.

Ricks, Thomas. 2009. *The Gamble: General David Petraeus and the American Military Adventure in Iraq, 2006–2008.* New York: Penguin Press.

Roach, Joseph. 1993. Carnival and the Law in New Orleans. *Drama Review* 37:42–75.

Roberts, Julian. 2014. Clarifying the Significance of Public Opinion for Sentencing Policy and Practice. In *Popular Punishment: On the Normative Significance of Public Opinion,* edited by Jesper Ryberg and Julian Roberts. Oxford: Oxford University Press.

Roberts, Julian, and Loretta Stalans. 1998. Crime, Criminal Justice, and Public Opinion. In *The Handbook of Crime and Punishment,* edited by Michael Tonry. Oxford: Oxford University Press.

Roberts, Julian V., Loretta J. Stalans, David Indermaur, and Mike Hough. 2003. *Penal Populism and Public Opinion.* Oxford: Oxford University Press.

Roberts, M. J. D. 2004 *Making English Morals: Voluntary Association and Moral Reform in England, 1787–1886.* Cambridge: Cambridge University Press.

Robbins, Joel, and Alan Rumsey. 2008. Introduction: Cultural and Linguistic Anthropology and the Opacity of Other Minds, *Anthropological Quarterly* 81:999–1006.

Robinson, Paul. 2016. The Honor of the Crown: The State and Its Soldiers. In *Honor in the Modern World: Interdisciplinary Perspectives,* edited by Laurie Johnson and Dan Demetriou. Lanham, MD: Lexington Books.

Robinson, Paul H. 2000. Why Does the Criminal Law Care What the Layperson Thinks Is Just? Coercive versus Normative Crime. *Virginia Law Review* 86:1839–1869.

———. 2008. Competing Conceptions of Modern Desert: Vengeful, Deontological, and Empirical. *Cambridge Law Journal,* 67:145–175.

———. 2009. Empirical Desert. In *Criminal Law Conversations,* edited by Paul H. Robinson, Stephen P. Garvey, and Kimberly Kessler Ferzan. Oxford: Oxford University Press.

———. 2014. The Proper Role of Community in Determining Criminal Liability. In *Popular Punishment: On the Normative Significance of Public Opinion,* edited by Jesper Ryberg and Julian Roberts. Oxford: Oxford University Press.

Robinson, Paul H., and John Darley. 1995. *Justice, Liability, and Blame: Community Views and the Criminal Law.* Boulder, CO: Westview Press.

———. 2007. Intuitions of Justice: Implications for Criminal Law and Justice Policy. *Southern California Law Review* 81:1–68.

Robinson, Paul H., and Robert Kurzban. 2007. Concordance and Conflict in Intuitions of Justice. *Minnesota Law Review* 91:1829–1907.

Robinson, Paul H., and Sarah Robinson. 2018. Shadow Vigilantes: *How Distrust in the Justice System Breeds a New Kind of Lawlessness*. New York: Prometheus.

Robitscher, Jonas, ed. 1973. *Eugenic Sterilization.* Springfield, IL: Charles C. Thomas.

Roe, Mark. 2015. The Imaginary Problem of Corporate Short-Termism. *Wall Street Journal,* April 17.

Rogers, Anthony, Jason Chuah, and Martin Dockray. 2016. *Cases and Materials on the Carriage of Goods by Sea.* 4th ed., revised. Abingdon, UK: Routledge.

Rollert, John Paul. 2018. The B-School Experiment and the Rise of Renegade Capitalism. *Critical Inquiry* 44:479–497.

Romano, Roberta. 2014. Regulating in the Dark, and a Postscript Assessment on the Iron Law of Financial Regulation. *Hofstra Law Review* 43:25–94.

Ronen, Yaël. 2009. Avoid or Compensate? Liability for Incidental Injury to Civilians Inflicted during Armed Conflict. *Vanderbilt Journal of Transnational Law* 42:181–226.

Rose, Willie Lee. 1982. *Slavery and Freedom.* Edited by William Freehling. New York: Oxford University Press.

Rosen, Lawrence. 2006. *Law as Culture: An Invitation.* Princeton: Princeton University Press.

Rosenfeld, Jeffrey. 1998. Will Contests: Legacies of Social Change. In *Inheritance and Wealth in America,* edited by Robert K. Miller Jr. and Stephen McNamee. New York: Plenum Press.

Ross, Brian, and Lee Ferran. 2011. How Anwar Al-Awlaki Inspired Terror from across the Globe. *New York Times.* September 30.

Rost, Peter. 2006. *The Whistleblower: Confessions of a Healthcare Hitman.* Brooklyn: Soft Skull Press.

Rozin, Paul, Maureen Markwith, and Caryn Stoess. 1997. Moralization and Becoming a Vegetarian: The Transformation of Preferences into Values and the Recruitment of Disgust. *Psychological Science* 8:67–73.

Rozin, Paul, and Leher Singh. 1999. The Moralization of Cigarette Smoking in the United States. *Journal of Consumer Psychology* 8:3321–3337.

Rozin, Paul, Jonathan Haidt, and Clark McCauley. 2000. Disgust. In *Handbook of Emotions,* 2nd ed., edited by Michael Lewis and Jeannette Haviland-Jones. New York: Guilford Press.

Rubin, Gretchen Craft, and Jamie G. Heller. 1994. Restatement of Love: Tentative Draft. *Yale Law Journal* 104:707–730.

Ruff, Julius R. 2001. *Violence in Early Modern Europe, 1500–1800.* Cambridge: Cambridge University Press.

Ruggie, John. 2007. Business and Human Rights: Mapping International Standards of Responsibility and Accountability for Corporate Acts. UN, Human Rights Council, Report of the Special Representative of the Secretary-General, UN Document A/HRC/4/035, February 19. https://business

-humanrights.org/sites/default/files/media/bhr/files/SRSG-report-Human-Rights-Council-19-Feb-2007.pdf.

Ruiz, Teofilo. 2012. *A King Travels: Festive Traditions in Late Medieval and Early Modern Spain.* Princeton: Princeton University Press.

Ryan, Alan. 2015. Liberalism 1900–1940. In *The Cambridge Companion to Liberalism,* edited by Steven Wall. Cambridge: Cambridge University Press.

Ryberg, Jesper, and Julian Roberts, eds. 2014. *Popular Punishment: On the Normative Significance of Public Opinion.* Oxford: Oxford University Press.

Ryznar, Margaret, and Karen Woody. 2015. A Framework for Mandating versus Incentivizing Corporate Social Responsibility. *Marquette Law Review* 98:1667–1694.

Saad, Lydia. 2001. Doctor-Assisted Suicide Is Moral Issue Dividing Americans Most. *Gallup Politics,* May 31. http://www.gallup.com/poll/147842/Doctor-Assisted-Suicide-Moral-Issue-Dividing-Americans.aspx.

Sabel, Charles F., and William H. Simon. 2015. *The Duty of Responsible Administration and the Problem of Police Accountability.* Columbia Public Law Research Paper No. 14-420, Stanford Public Law Working Paper No. 2507280. http://papers.ssrn.com/sol3/papers.cfm?abstract_id=2507280.

———. 2017. Democratic Experimentalism. In *Searching for Contemporary Legal Thought,* edited by Justin Desautels-Stein and Christopher Tomlins. Cambridge: Cambridge University Press.

Sagan, Scott D., and Benjamin A. Valentino. 2016. Revisiting Hiroshima in Iran: Real American Attitudes about Dropping the Bomb. Paper presented at the Center on International Security and Cooperation, Stanford University, February 27. http://www.mitpressjournals.org/doi/pdf/10.1162/ISEC_a_00284.

Saito, Yuriko. 2015. Aesthetics of the Everyday, *Stanford Encyclopedia of Philosophy.* https://plato.stanford.edu/entries/aesthetics-of-everyday/.

Sajó, András. 2006. Abuse of Fundamental Rights or the Difficulties of Purposiveness. In *Abuse: The Dark Side of Fundamental Rights,* edited by András Sajó. Utrecht: Eleven International.

Sandholtz, Wayne, Yining Bei, and Kayla Caldwell. 2017. Backlash and International Courts. USC School of International Relations, Working Paper. http://www.orfaleacenter.ucsb.edu/sites/secure.lsit.ucsb.edu.gisp.d7_orfalea-2/files/sitefiles/news/conferences/HumanRights2017/Sandholtz_Backlash_HR_Courts_20170118.pdf.

Sandler, James. 2007. The War on Whistleblowers. *Salon,* November 1. http://www.salon.com/2007/11/01/whistleblowers/.

Sanger, Carol. 2017. *About Abortion: Terminating Pregnancy in Twenty-First Century America.* Cambridge, MA: Harvard University Press.

Sarat, Austin. 2004. The Micropolitics of Identity-Difference: Recognition and Accommodation in Everyday Life. In *Engaging Cultural Differences: The Multicultural Challenge to Liberal Democracies,* edited by Richard Schweder, Martha Minow, and Hazel Rose Markus. New York: Russell Sage Foundation.

Sarfatti-Larson, Magali. 1977. *The Rise of Professionalism: A Sociological Analysis.* Berkeley: University of California Press.
Sassaman, Nathan. 2008. *Warrior King: The Triumph and Betrayal of an American Commander in Iraq.* New York: St. Martin's Press.
Satow, Ernest M. 2009. *Satow's Diplomatic Practice.* 6th ed. Edited by Ivor Roberts. Oxford: Oxford University Press.
Sauer, R. 1978. Infanticide and Abortion in Nineteenth Century Britain. *Population Studies* 32:81–93.
Savigny, Friedrich Carl von. 1814. *Vom Beruf unserer Zeit für Gesetzgebung und Rechtswissenschaft.* Heidelberg: Mohr.
Sawyer, R. Keith. 2005. *Social Emergence: Societies as Complex Systems.* Cambridge: Cambridge University Press.
Sayer, Andrew. 2011. *Why Things Matter to People: Social Science, Values and Ethical Life.* Cambridge: Cambridge University Press.
Scalia, Antonin. 1997. Common-Law Courts in a Civil-Law System: The Role of United States Federal Courts in Interpreting the Constitution and Laws. In *A Matter of Interpretation,* edited by Amy Gutmann. Princeton: Princeton University Press.
Scanlon, Thomas. 1996. The Difficulty of Tolerance. In *Toleration: An Elusive Virtue,* edited by David Heyd. Princeton: Princeton University Press.
———. 2008. *Moral Dimensions.* Cambridge, MA: Belknap Press of Harvard University Press.
Schama, Simon. 1987. *The Embarrassment of Riches: An Interpretation of Dutch Culture in the Golden Age.* New York: Knopf.
Schammo, Pierre. 2008. Arbitrage and Abuse of Rights in the E.U. Legal System. *European Law Journal,* 14:351–376.
Schauer, Fred. 1981. Can Rights Be Abused? *Philosophical Quarterly* 31: 225–235.
———. 1991. *Playing by the Rules: A Philosophical Examination of Rule-Based Decision-Making in Law and Life.* Oxford: Oxford University Press.
———. 2006. On the Supposed Jury-Dependence of Evidence Law. *University of Pennsylvania Law Review* 155:165–202.
Schauer, Fred, and Richard Zeckhauser. 1996. On the Degree of Confidence in Adverse Decisions. *Journal of Legal Studies* 25:27–52.
Scheff, Thomas J., and Suzanne M. Retzinger. 2001 [1991]. *Emotions and Violence: Shame and Rage in Destructive Conflicts.* Lanham, MD: Lexington Books/ Authors' Guild.
Scheingold, Stuart. 2004. The *Politics of Rights: Lawyers, Public Policy, and Political Change.* 2nd ed. Ann Arbor: University of Michigan Press.
Scheppele, Kim. 2011. Commentary on the 2011 Grotius Lecture: Amartya Sen's Vision for Human Rights—And Why He Needs the Law. *American Society of International Law Proceedings* 105:12–22.
Schiller, Arthur. 1994. Custom in Classical Roman Law. In *Folk Law: Essays in the Theory and Practice of Lex Non Scripta,* edited by Alison Dundes Renteln and Alan Dundes. New York: Garland.

Schleifer, Ronald. 2011. *Modernism and Popular Music.* Cambridge: Cambridge University Press.

Schlosberg, David. 2007. *Defining Environmental Justice: Theories, Movements, and Nature.* Oxford: Oxford University Press.

Schmidtz, David, and Robert E. Goodin. 1998. *Social Welfare and Individual Responsibility.* Cambridge: Cambridge University Press.

Schmitt, Eric. 2015. U.S. Caution in Strikes Gives ISIS an Edge, Many Iraqis Say. *New York Times,* May 25.

Schneider, Carl E. 1994. Marriage, Morals, and the Law: No-Fault Divorce and Moral Discourse. *Utah Law Review,* no. 2: 503–585.

Schudson, Michael. 1994. Voting Rites: Why We Need a New Concept of Citizenship. *American Prospect,* Fall, 59–62.

Schünmann, Catherine, and Anna Glasier. 2006. Measuring Pregnancy Intention and Its Relationship with Contraceptive Use among Women Undergoing Therapeutic Abortion. *Contraception* 73:520–524.

Schwarcz, Steven L. 2002. Private Ordering. *Northwestern University Law Review* 97:319–349.

———. 2008. Systemic Risk. *Georgetown Law Journal* 97:193–250.

———. 2016. Misalignment: Corporate Risk-Taking and Public Duty. *Notre Dame Law Review* 92:1–50.

Schweikard, David, and Hans Bernhard Schmid. 2013. Collective Intentionality. *Stanford Encyclopedia of Philosophy.* https://plato.stanford.edu/entries/collective-intentionality/.

Schwerin Campbell Barnard Iglitzin & Lavitt, LLP. 2018. Seminars to Empower Union Officers. http://www.workerlaw.com/Seminars/Seminars-to-Empower-Union-Officers.aspx.

Schwitzgebel, Eric, and Fiery Cushman. 2014. Expertise in Moral Reasoning? Order Effects on Moral Judgment in Professional Philosophers and Non-Philosophers. In *Experimental Philosophy,* vol. 2, edited by Joshua Knobe and Shaun Nichols. Oxford: Oxford University Press.

Scott, Elizabeth. 1986. Sterilization of Mentally Retarded Persons: Reproductive Rights and Family Privacy. *Duke Law Journal* 1986:806–865.

———. 2001. Divorce, Children's Welfare, and the Culture Wars. *Virginia Journal of Social Policy and the Law* 9:95–115.

Scott, James. 1985. *Weapons of the Weak: Everyday Forms of Peasant Resistance.* New Haven: Yale University Press.

Scott, Robert E. 2000. The Limits of Behavioral Theories of Law and Social Norms. *Virginia Law Review* 81:1603–1647.

Seagull, Elizabeth, and Susan L. Scheurer. 1986. Neglected and Abused Children of Mentally Retarded Parents. *Child Abuse and Neglect* 10:493–500.

Searle, John. 1983. *Intentionality: An Essay in the Philosophy of Mind.* Cambridge: Cambridge University Press.

Sen, Amartya. 2001. Normative Evaluation and Legal Analogies. Washington University School of Law, Conference on Norms and the Law, 1–21. http://washu.wsoldev.com/centeris/Papers/Norms/sen2.pdf.

———. 2004. Elements of a Theory of Human Rights. *Philosophy and Public Affairs* 32:315–356.

———. 2006. Human Rights and the Limits of Law. *Cardozo Law Review* 27:2913–2927.

———. 2012. The Global Reach of Human Rights. *Journal of Applied Philosophy* 29:91–100.

Sengupta, Rajdeep, and Craig P. Aubuchon. 2008. The Microfinance Revolution: An Overview, *Federal Reserve Bank of St. Louis Review* 90:9–30. http://research.stlouisfed.org/publications/review/08/01/Sengupta.pdf.

Sennett, Richard. 2006. *The Culture of the New Capitalism*. New Haven: Yale University Press.

Seybolt, Tayler, Jan Aronson, and Baruch Fischhoff. 2013. *Counting Civilian Casualties*. New York: Oxford University Press.

Seymour, Jane. 2001. *Critical Moments: Death and Dying in Intensive Care*. Buckingham, UK: Open University Press.

Sgueglia, Kristina. 2011. Polish Paintings, Stolen by Nazis, Repatriated in New York. CNN, September 22. http://www.cnn.com/2011/09/22/us/new-york-stolen-art-returned/.

Shah, Anuj K., Sendhil Mullainathan, and Eldar Shafir. 2012. Some Consequences of Having Too Little. *Science* 338:682–685.

Shane, Scott, and Souad Mekhennet. 2010. Imam's Path from Condemning Terror to Preaching Jihad. *New York Times*, May 8.

Shapiro, Susan P. 2015. Do Advance Directives Direct? *Journal of Health Politics, Policy and Law* 40:487–530.

Sharp, Paul. 2009. *Diplomatic Theory of International Relations*. Cambridge: Cambridge University Press.

Shavell, Steven. 2002. Law versus Morality as Regulators of Conduct. *American Law and Economics Review* 4:227–257.

Sheehan, Jonathan, and Dror Wahrman. 2015. *Invisible Hands: Self-Organization and the Eighteenth Century*. Chicago: University of Chicago Press.

Sheffrin, Steven M. 2013. *Tax Fairness and Folk Justice*. Cambridge: Cambridge University Press.

Shellenberg, Kristen M. 2010. Abortion Stigma in the United States: Quantitative and Qualitative Perspectives from Women Seeking an Abortion. PhD dissertation, Johns Hopkins University. http://search.proquest.com.proxy.lib.uiowa.edu/pqdtft/docview/365705994/138CB36B8D875DDE99F/1?accountid=14663.

Sher, George. 1987. *Desert*. Princeton: Princeton University Press.

Sherman, Nancy. 2010. *The Untold War: Inside the Hearts, Minds and Souls of Our Soldiers*. New York: W. W. Norton.

Sherman, Steven, and Elise Percy. 2010. The Psychology of Collective Responsibility: When and Why Collective Entities Are Likely to Be Held Responsible for the Misdeeds of Individual Members. *Journal of Law and Policy* 19:137–170.

Shklar, Judith. 1964. *Legalism*. Cambridge, MA: Harvard University Press.

———. 1984. *Ordinary Vices*. Cambridge, MA: Harvard University Press.

———. 1990. *The Faces of Injustice*. New Haven: Yale University Press.

Shotwell, Gregg. 2012. *Autoworkers under the Gun: A Shop-Floor View of the End of the American Dream.* Chicago: Haymarket Books.

Siebert, Fred S., Theodore Peterson, and Wilbur Schramm. 1956. *Four Theories of the Press.* Urbana: University of Illinois Press.

Siedel, George, and Helena Haapio. 2011a. *Proactive Law for Managers: A Hidden Source of Competitive Advantage.* Burlington, VT: Gower.

———. 2011b. Using Proactive Law for Competitive Advantage. *American Business Law Journal* 47:641–686.

Simmel, George. 1955. *Conflict and the Web of Group Affiliations.* Translated by Kurt Wolf. Glencoe, IL: Free Press.

Simon, William H. 1996. Should Lawyers Obey the Law? *William and Mary Law Review* 38:217–253.

Singer, Brian, C. J. 2013. *Montesquieu and the Discovery of the Social.* New York: Palgrave Macmillan.

Singer, Joseph. 2000. *Entitlement: The Paradoxes of Property.* New Haven: Yale University Press.

Sinha, Manisha. 2004. Eugene D. Genovese: The Mind of a Marxist Conservative. *Radical History Review* 88:4–29.

Skyrms, Brian. 2004. *The Stag Hunt and the Evolution of Social Structure.* Cambridge: Cambridge University Press.

Slivinski, Stephen. 2015. *Bootstraps Tangled in Red Tape: How State Occupational Licensing Hinders Low-Income Entrepreneurship.* Phoenix, AZ: Goldwater Institute. https://goldwater-media.s3.amazonaws.com/cms_page_media/2015/4/15/OccLicensingKauffman.pdf.

Slobogin, Christopher. 1996. Is Justice Just Us? Using Social Science to Inform Substantive Criminal Law. *Journal of Criminal Law and Criminology* 87:315–333.

Smart, Carol. 2007. *Personal Life: New Directions in Sociological Thinking.* Malden, MA: Polity.

Smigel, Erwin. 1969. *The Wall Street Lawyer.* Bloomington: Indiana University Press.

Smith, Adam. 1976 [1759]. *The Theory of Moral Sentiments.* Indianapolis: Liberty Books.

———. 2003 [1776]. *The Wealth of Nations.* New York: Bantam Classics.

Smith, Adam, and Bruce Yandle. 2014. *Bootleggers and Baptists: How Economic Forces and Moral Persuasion Interact to Shape Regulatory Politics.* Washington, DC: Cato Institute.

Smith, Rogers M. 1997. *Civic Ideals: Conflicting Visions of Citizenship in U.S. History.* New Haven: Yale University Press.

Smith, Steven B. 2016. *Modernity and Its Discontents: Making and Unmaking the Bourgeois from Machiavelli to Bellow.* New Haven: Yale University Press.

Smith, Tom. 2012. Trends in Confidence in Institutions, 1973–2006. In *Social Trends in American Life: Findings of the General Social Survey since 1972,* edited by Peter Marsden. Princeton: Princeton University Press.

Smithson, Ryan. 2009. *Ghosts of War: The True Story of a 19-Year-Old GI*. New York: Collins.

Social Security Advisory Board. 2006. *A Disability System for the 21st Century*. Washington, DC, September. http://ssab.gov/Portals/0/documents/disability-system-21st.pdf.

Solomon, Mildred Z., Lydia O'Donnell, Bruce Jennings, V. Guilfoy, S. M. Wolff, K. Nolan, R. Jackson, D. Koch-Weser, and S. Donnelley. 1992. Decisions near the End of Life: Professional Views on Life-Sustaining Treatment. *American Journal of Public Health* 83:14–23.

Solomon, Robert. 1992. *Ethics and Excellence: Cooperation and Integrity in Business*. Oxford: Oxford University Press.

Sonenscher, Michael. 1989. *Work and Wages: Natural Law, Politics and the Eighteenth-Century French Trades*. Cambridge, UK: Cambridge University Press.

Sousa, Michael. 2014. Bankruptcy Stigma: A Socio-Legal Study. *American Bankruptcy Law Journal* 87:435–482.

Southern Poverty Law Center. 2017a. 917 Hate Groups Currently Operating in the U.S. https://www.splcenter.org/hate-map.

———. 2017b. The Year in Hate and Extremism. https://www.splcenter.org/fighting-hate/intelligence-report/2017/year-hate-and-extremism.

Southwood, Nicholas, and Lina Eriksson. 2011. Norms and Conventions, *Philosophical Explorations* 14:195–217.

Sowa, Nathanial. 2015. Medically Necessary Sterilization of a Minor with Intellectual Disability: A Case Report and Historical Perspective. *North Carolina Medical Journal* 76:59–63.

Sowell, Thomas. 2011. *The Thomas Sowell Reader*. New York: Basic Books.

Spector, Céline. 2009. Honor, Interest, Virtue: The Affective Foundations of the Political in *The Spirit of Laws*. In *Montesquieu and His Legacy*, edited by Rebecca E. Kingston. Albany: SUNY Press.

Sperber, Dan, and Nicolas Baumard. 2012. Moral Reputation: An Evolutionary and Cognitive Perspective. *Mind and Language* 27:495–518.

Spinoza, Benedict de. 2007 [1670]. "The Expediency of Toleration" from *Tractatus Theologico-Politicus*. In *Versions of Censorship*, edited by John McCormick and Mairi MacInnes, translated by A. G. Wernham. Piscataway, NJ: Transaction.

Sprung, C. L., and L. A. Eidelman. 1996. Worldwide Similarities and Differences in the Forgoing of Life-Sustaining Treatments. *Intensive Care Medicine* 22:1003–1006.

Squires, Nick. 2010. Pope Launches Team to "Re-Evangelise" the West. *Telegraph*, June 29. http://www.telegraph.co.uk/news/worldnews/the-pope/7861377/Pope-launches-team-to-re-evangelise-the-West.html.

Stafford, Charles, ed. 2013. *Ordinary Ethics in China Today*. Introduction. London: Bloomsbury.

Stahl, Günter, Martha Maznevski, Andreas Voigt, and Karsten Jonsen. 2010. Unraveling the Effects of Cultural Diversity in Teams: A Meta-Analysis of Research on Multicultural Work Groups. *Journal of International Business Studies* 41:690–709.

Starr, Paul. 1982. *The Transformation of American Medicine.* New York: Basic Books.
———. 2013. A Wasted Crisis? Why Democrats Did So Little to Change Wall Street. *New Republic,* July 15.
Stearns, Maxwell, and Todd Zywicki. 2009. *Public Choice Concepts and Applications in Law.* St. Paul: West.
Stearns, Peter N. 2003. *Anxious Parents: A History of Modern Childrearing in America.* New York: NYU Press.
———. 2017a. Does American Culture Shame Too Much—Or Not Enough? *The Conversation,* November 6. http://theconversation.com/does-american-culture-shame-too-much-or-not-enough-86030.
———. 2017b. *Shame: A Brief History.* Urbana: University of Illinois Press.
Steinhauer, Jennifer. 2016. Senate Passes Broad Bill to Combat Drug Use. *New York Times,* March 10.
Stephens, Bret. 2010. The Mosque at Ground Zero. *Wall Street Journal,* May 25.
Stevenson, Charles L. 1944. *Ethics and Language.* New Haven: Yale University Press.
Stevick, Richard A. 2014. *Growing Up Amish: The Rumspringa Years.* 2nd ed. Baltimore: Johns Hopkins University Press.
Stewart, Amy. 1999. Covenant Marriage: Legislating Family Values. *Indiana Law Review* 32:509–536.
Stockdale, James. 1995. *Thoughts of a Philosophical Fighter Pilot.* Stanford: Hoover Institution Press.
Stokes, Bruce. 2016. Europe's Far-Right Anger Is Moving Mainstream. *Foreign Policy,* December 19. http://foreignpolicy.com/2016/12/19/europes-far-right-anger-is-moving-mainstream/?wp_login_redirect=0.
Stokes, Bruce, Richard Wike, and Jacob Poushter. 2016. Europeans Face the World Divided. Pew Research Center, June 13. http://assets.pewresearch.org/wp-content/uploads/sites/2/2016/06/14095145/Pew-Research-Center-EPW-Report-FINAL-June-13-2016.pdf.
Stolberg, Sheryl Gay. 2010. Obama Says Mosque Remarks Were about Rights. *New York Times,* August 15.
Stolle, Dietlind, Stuart Soroka, and Richard Johnston. 2008. When Does Diversity Erode Trust? Neighborhood Diversity, Interpersonal Trust and the Mediating Effect of Social Interactions. *Political Studies* 56:57–75.
Stone, Deborah A. 1999–2000. Beyond Moral Hazard: Insurance as Moral Opportunity. *Connecticut Insurance Law Journal* 6:11–46.
Strange, Carolyn, and Robert Cribb. 2014. Historical Perspectives on Honour, Violence, and Emotion. In *Honour, Violence, and Emotions in History,* edited by Carolyn Strange, Robert Cribb, and Christopher E. Forth. London: Bloomsbury.
Strickland, Matthew. 1996. *War and Chivalry: The Conduct and Perception of War in England and Normandy, 1066–1217.* Cambridge: Cambridge University Press.
Suchman, Mark. 1998. Working without a Net: The Sociology of Legal Ethics in Corporate Litigation. *Fordham Law Review* 67:837–874.

Suleiman, Ezra. 1974. *Politics, Power, and Bureaucracy in France: The Administrative Elite.* Princeton: Princeton University Press.

Sullivan, Allison R. 2010. Mortality Differentials and Religion in the U.S.: Religious Affiliation and Attendance. *Journal for the Scientific Study of Religion* 49:740–753.

Sullivan, Teresa A., Elizabeth Warren, and Jay Lawrence Westbrook. 1989. *As We Forgive Our Debtors: Bankruptcy and Consumer Credit in America.* New York: Oxford University Press.

———. 2006. Less Stigma or More Financial Distress: An Empirical Analysis of the Extraordinary Increase in Bankruptcy Filings. *Stanford Law Review* 59:213–256.

Sunstein, Cass. 1995. Rights and Their Critics. *Notre Dame Law Review* 70:727–768.

———. 1996. Social Norms and Social Roles. *Columbia Law Review* 96:903–968.

———. 2005. Moral Heuristics. *Behavior and Brain Science* 28:531–542.

———. 2007. If People Would Be Outraged by Their Rulings, Should Judges Care? *Stanford Law Review* 60:155–212.

———. 2012. Show Me the Money: Review of Oren Ben-Gall, *Seduction by Contract Law:* Law, Economics, and Psychology in Consumer Markets. *New Republic,* October 25.

———. 2014. *Why Nudge? The Politics of Liberal Paternalism.* New Haven: Yale University Press.

Supiot, Alain. 2007. *Homo Juridicus: On the Anthropological Function of the Law.* Translated by Saskia Brown. London: Verso.

Susskind, Richard, and Daniel Susskind. 2015. *The Future of the Professions: How Technology Will Transform the Work of Human Experts.* Oxford: Oxford University Press.

Suttles, Gerald. 1968. *The Social Order of the Slum: Ethnicity and Territory in the Inner City.* Preface by Morris Janowitz. Chicago: University of Chicago Press.

Svensson, Mans, and Stefan Larsson. 2009. *Social Norms and Intellectual Property: Online Norms and the European Legal Development.* Lund, Sweden: Lund University.

Sweeney, Michael S. 2010. *Secrets of Victory: The Office of Censorship and the American Press and Radio in World War II.* Chapel Hill: University of North Carolina Press.

Swidler, Ann. 1986. Culture in Action: Symbols and Strategies. *American Sociology Review* 51:273–286.

Swift, Art. 2016. Euthanasia Still Acceptable to Solid Majority in U.S. *Gallup: Social Issues,* June 24. http://www.gallup.com/poll/193082/euthanasia-acceptable-solid-majority.aspx.

Taggart, Lawrence, and Wendy Cousins. 2014. *Health Promotion for People with Intellectual Disabilities.* New York: Open University Press.

Talley, Eric. 1999. Precedential Cascades: An Appraisal. *Southern California Law Review* 73:87–138.

Tamanaha, Brian. 2001. *A General Jurisprudence of Law and Society.* Oxford: Oxford University Press.

———. 2017. *A Realistic Theory of Law.* Cambridge: Cambridge University Press.
Tamir, Yael. 1993. *Liberal Nationalism.* Princeton: Princeton University Press.
Tapp, Christine, Frederick M. Burkle Jr., Kumanan Wilson, Tim Takaro, Gordon H. Guyatt, Hani Amad, and Edward J. Mills. 2008. Iraq War Mortality Estimates: A Systematic Review. *Conflict and Health* 2:1–13.
Taylor, Frank Flagg, IV. 2006. The Politics of Mores and the Tasks of Liberal Statesmanship. PhD dissertation, Fordham University. http://fordham.bepress.com/dissertations/AAI3240065.
Tennyson, Sharon. 2008. Moral, Social, and Economic Dimensions of Insurance Claims Fraud. *Social Research* 75:1181–1204.
Tetlock, Philip, and Aaron Belkin. 1996. *Counterfactual Thought Experiments in World Politics: Logical, Methodological, and Psychological Experiments.* Princeton: Princeton University Press.
Teymoori, Ali, and Jolanda Jetten, et al. Revisiting the Measurement of Anomie. *PLOS One* (July). 11:1–51.
Thayer, James Bradley. 1898. *A Preliminary Treatise on Evidence at the Common Law.* Boston: Little, Brown.
Thelen, Kathleen. 2010. Beyond Comparative Statics: Historical Institutional Approaches to Stability and Change in the Political Economy of Labor. In *The Oxford Handbook of Comparative Institutional Analysis,* edited by Glenn Morgan et al. Oxford: Oxford University Press.
Thomas, Keith. 1964. Work and Leisure in Pre-Industrial Society. *Past and Present,* 29:50–56.
———. 1992. Introduction. In *A Cultural History of Gesture,* edited by Jan Bremmer and Herman Roodenburg. Ithaca, NY: Cornell University Press.
Thompson, E. P. 1976. The Grid of Inheritance: A Comment. In *Family and Inheritance: Rural Society in Western Europe, 1200–1800,* edited by Jack Goody, Joan Thirsk, and E. P. Thompson. Cambridge: Cambridge University Press.
Thompson, F. M. L. 1988. *The Rise of Respectable Society: A Social History of Victorian Britain, 1830–1900.* Cambridge, MA: Harvard University Press.
Thomsen, Frej. 2014. Why Should We Care What the Public Thinks? A Critical Assessment of the Claims of Popular Punishment. In *Popular Punishment: On the Normative Significance of Public Opinion,* edited by Jesper Ryberg and Julian Roberts. Oxford: Oxford University Press.
Thomson, Rudi. 1972. *The Origin of Ostracism.* Copenhagen: Glydendal.
Thrift, Nigel. 1994. On the Social and Cultural Determinants of International Financial Centres: The Case of the City of London. In *Money, Power, and Space,* edited by Stuart Cobridge, Ron Martin, and Nigel Thrift. Hoboken, NJ: Wiley-Blackwell.
———. 2002. Performing Cultures in the New Economy. In *Cultural Economy: Cultural Analysis and Commercial Life,* edited by Paul du Gray and Michael Pryke. Thousand Oaks, CA: Sage.
Thurston, Robert. 1991. The Soviet Family During the Great Terror, 1935–1941. *Soviet Studies.* 43:553–574.

Tibi, Bassam. 2014. *Political Islam, World Politics and Europe: From Jihadist to Institutional Islam.* New York: Routledge.

Tickell, Adam. 1996. Making a Melodrama out of a Crisis: Reinterpreting the Collapse of Barings Bank. *Environment and Planning D: Society and Space* 14:5–33.

Tirman, John. 2011. *The Deaths of Others: The Fate of Civilians in America's Wars.* New York: Oxford University Press.

Tocqueville, Alexis de. 1969 [1840]. *Democracy in America.* Edited by J. P. Mayer. Garden City, NY: Doubleday.

Tomasi, John. 2001. *Liberalism beyond Justice: Citizens, Society, and the Boundaries of Political Theory.* Princeton: Princeton University Press.

Torreon, Barbara Salazar. 2015. Medal of Honor: History and Issues. *Congressional Research Service Report,* August 18. https://fas.org/sgp/crs/misc/95-519.pdf.

Tribe, Laurence. 1981. Jurisdictional Gerrymandering: Zoning Disfavored Rights Out of the Federal Courts. *Harvard Civil Rights-Civil Liberties Law Review* 16:129–156.

Trivers, Robert. 1971. The Evolution of Reciprocal Altruism. *Quarterly Review of Biology* 46:35–57.

Trotsky, Leon. 1942. *Their Morals and Ours.* New York: Pioneer.

Turner, Bryan. 2004. *The New Medical Sociology: Social Forms of Health and Illness.* New York: W. W. Norton.

Tushnet, Rebecca. 1998. Rules of Engagement. *Yale Law Journal* 107:2583–2618.

Twenge, Jean M., W. Keith Campbell, and Brittany Gentile. 2012. Increases in Individualistic Words and Phrases in American Books. *PLOS One* 7 (July 10). http://wkeithcampbell.com/wp-content/uploads/2013/08/Twenge-Campbell-Gentile-2012-PLOSone.pdf.

Tymchuk, Alexander. 2009. Moving toward Integration of Services for Parents with Intellectual Disabilities. *Journal of Intellectual and Developmental Disability* 1:59–74.

Tyson, Alec. 2017. Americans Divided in Views of Use of Torture in U.S. Anti-Terror Efforts. *Pew Research,* January 26. http://www.pewresearch.org/fact-tank/2017/01/26/americans-divided-in-views-of-use-of-torture-in-u-s-anti-terror-efforts/.

UN Department of Economic and Social Affairs. 2014. *Abortion Policies and Reproductive Health around the World.* UN Secretariat: Population Division, New York. http://www.un.org/en/development/desa/population/publications/pdf/policy/AbortionPoliciesReproductiveHealth.pdf.

UN International Criminal Tribunal. 2000. *Final Report to the Prosecutor by the Committee Established to Review the NATO Bombing Campaign against the Federal Republic of Yugoslavia.* PR/P.I.S./510-E, June 13. http://www.icty.org/en/press/final-report-prosecutor-committee-established-review-nato-bombing-campaign-against-federal.

Unnever, James, Michael Benson, and Francis Cullen. 2008. Public Support for Getting Tough on Corporate Crime. *Journal of Research in Crime and Delinquency* 45:163–190.

U.S. Army and Marine Corps. 2007. *The U.S. Army/Marine Corps Counterinsurgency Manual.* Chicago: University of Chicago Press.

U.S. Census Bureau. 2011. *Statistical Abstract of the United States: 2011.* https://www.census.gov/prod/2011pubs/11statab/pop.pdf.

———. 2016. Defining Rural at the U.S. Census Bureau, by Michael Ratcliffe, Charlynn Burd, Kelly Holder, and Alison Fields. Washington, DC: U.S. Department of Commerce.

U.S. Department of Education. 2011. *Analysis of State Bullying Laws and Policies.* Office of Planning, Evaluation and Policy Development. https://www2.ed.gov/rschstat/eval/bullying/state-bullying-laws/state-bullying-laws.pdf.

U.S. Department of the Air Force. 2003. Final Report and Recommendations of the Working Group to Assess the Legal, Policy and Operational Issues Relating to Interrogation of Detainees Held by the U.S. Armed Forces in the War on Terrorism. *USAF: Office of the Judge Advocate General,* February 5. http://balkin.blogspot.com/jag.memos.pdf.

Vagts, Alfred. 1959. *A History of Militarism.* New York: Meridian Books.

Vaisey, Stephen. 2009. Motivation and Justification: A Dual-Process Model of Culture in Action. *American Sociology Review* 114:1675–1715.

Van der Made, Allard, and Pim Heijnan. 2009. A Signaling Theory of Consumer Boycotts. August 12. http://centres.fusl.ac.be/CEREC/document/people/vandermade/boycottsignal10.pdf.

Vandervelde, Lea. 1996. The Legal Ways of Seduction. *Stanford Law Review* 48:831–835.

Van Wolkenten, Megan, Sarah F. Brosnan, and Frans B. M. de Waal. 2007. Inequity Responses of Monkeys Modified by Effort. *Proceedings of the National Academy of Sciences* 104:18854–18859.

Vaughn, Robert G. 2013. *The Successes and Failures of Whistleblower Laws.* Cheltenham, UK: Edward Elgar.

Veatch, Robert. 2001. The Impossibility of a Morality Internal to Medicine. *The Journal of Medicine and Philosophy* 26:621–642.

———. 2003. Is There a Common Morality? *Kennedy Institute for Ethics Journal* 13:189–192.

Veitch, Scott. 2007. *Law and Irresponsibility: On the Legitimation of Human Suffering.* Abington, UK: Routledge-Cavendish.

Verstein, Andrew. 2017. The Jurisprudence of Mixed Motives. *Yale Law Journal* 127:1106–1175.

Veyne, Paul. 1984. *Writing History: Essays on Epistemology.* Translated by Mina Moore-Rinvolucri. Middletown, CT: Wesleyan University Press.

Vico, Giambattista. 1948 [1744]. *Vico's New Science of Life.* 3rd ed. Translated by Thomas Bergin and Max Harold Fisch. Ithaca, NY: Cornell University Press.

Villasenor, John. 2017. Views among College Students regarding the First Amendment: Results from a New Survey. Brookings Institution, September 18. https://www.brookings.edu/blog/fixgov/2017/09/18/views-among-college-students-regarding-the-first-amendment-results-from-a-new-survey/.

Visser, David. 2008. Unjust Enrichment. In *Elgar Encyclopedia of Comparative Law,* edited by January M. Smits. London: Edward Elgar.

Vitchers, Tracey. 2014. Violent Hate Speech Incident at Williams College. *Huffington Post,* January 14.
Vogel, David. 2006. *The Market for Virtue: The Potential and Limits of Corporate Social Responsibility.* Washington, DC: Brookings Institution Press.
Von Wachter, Till, Jae Song, and Joyce Manchester. 2011. Trends in Employments and Earnings of Allowed and Rejected Applicants to the Social Security Disability Insurance Program. *American Economic Review* 101:3308–3329.
Wacquant, Loïc. 2002. Scrutinizing the Streets: Poverty, Morality, and the Pitfalls of Urban Ethnography. *American Journal of Sociology* 107:1468–1532.
Wald, Elijah. 2012. *The Dozens: A History of Rap's Mama.* New York: Oxford University Press.
Waldron, Jeremy. 1981. A Right to Do Wrong. *Ethics* 92:22–39.
———. 1988. *The Right to Private Property.* Oxford: Oxford University Press.
———. 1989. Particular Values and Critical Morality. *California Law Review* 77:561–589.
———. 2011. Dignity, Rights, and Responsibilities. *Arizona State Law Journal* 43:1107–1136.
———. 2012. *The Harm in Hate Speech.* Cambridge, MA: Harvard University Press.
———. 2015. Is Dignity the Foundation of Human Rights? In *Philosophical Foundations of Human Rights,* edited by Rowan Cruft, S. Matthew Liao, and Massimo Renzo. Oxford: Oxford University Press.
———. 2016. *Desanctification of Law and the Problem of Absolutes.* Working Paper, Hebrew University of Jerusalem. https://papers.ssrn.com/sol3/papers.cfm?abstract_id=2848584.
Walker, David. 2012. A Tax Response to the Executive Pay Problem. https://papers.ssrn.com/sol3/papers.cfm?abstract_id=1979791.
Wallach, Philip. 2015. What Is Regulatory Capture? *The New Rambler.* http://newramblerreview.com/book-reviews/political-science/what-is-regulatory-capture.
Wallison, Peter J. 2015. *Hidden in Plain Sight: What Really Caused the World's Worst Financial Crisis and Why it Could Happen Again.* New York: Encounter Books.
Wardle, Lynn. 1991. No-Fault Divorce and the Divorce Conundrum. *Brigham Young University Law Review* 1991:79–142.
Watercutter, Angela. 2013. How Pop Culture Changed the Face of the Same-Sex Marriage Debate. *Wired,* June 27. http://www.wired.com/2013/06/pop-culture-same-sex-marriage/.
Waters, Timothy. 2013. Plucky Little Russia: Misreading the Georgian War through the Distorting Lens of Aggression. *Stanford Journal of International Law* 49:176–238.
Weaver, Andrew. 2011. A Meta-Analytical Review of Selective Exposure to and the Enjoyment of Media Violence. *Journal of Broadcasting and Electronic Media* 55:232–250.

Weber, Eugene. 1976. *Peasants into Frenchmen: The Modernization of Rural France, 1870–1914.* Stanford, CA: Stanford University Press.

Weber, Max. 1949. *The Methodology of the Social Sciences.* Edited and translated by Edward Shils and Henry Finch. Glencoe, IL: Free Press.

———. 1958. *From Max Weber: Essays in Sociology.* Edited and translated by Hans Gerth and C. Wright Mills. New York: Oxford University Press.

———. 1978 [1922]. *Economy and Society: An Outline of Interpretive Sociology.* Translated by Ephraim Fischoff et al. Berkeley: University of California Press.

Weisberg, Robert. 1986. Commercial Morality, the Merchant Character, and the History of the Voidable Preference. *Stanford Law Review* 39:1–138.

———. 2003. Norms and Criminal Law, and the Norms of Criminal Law Scholarship. *Journal of Criminal Law and Criminology* 93:467–592.

Weiss, Lois. 2016. Apartments, Islamic Museum to Be Built on Site of Failed Ground Zero Mosque. *New York Post,* May 19. http://nypost.com/2016/05/19/apartments-islamic-museum-to-be-built-on-site-of-failed-ground-zero-mosque/.

Weitz, Tracy. 2010. Rethinking the Mantra That Abortion Should be "Safe, Legal, and Rare." *Journal of Women's History* 22:161–172.

Wenar, Leif. 2015. Rights. *Stanford Encyclopedia of Philosophy,* September 9. http://plato.stanford.edu/entries/rights.

Wendel, W. Bradley. 2010. *Lawyers and Fidelity to Law.* Princeton: Princeton University Press.

Werhane, Patricia. 1999. *Moral Imagination and Management Decision-Making.* New York: Oxford University Press.

West, Mark D. 1997. Legal Rules and Social Norms in Japan's Secret World of Sumo. *Journal of Legal Studies* 26:165–202.

Whitman, James. 1987. What Is Wrong with Inflicting Shame Sanctions? *Yale Law Journal* 107:1055–1092.

———. 1988. Commercial Law and the American *Volk:* A Note on Llewellyn's German Sources for the Uniform Commercial Code. *Yale Law Journal* 97:156–175.

Wikström, Per-Olof, Dietrich Oberwittler, Kyle Treiber, and Beth Hardie. 2012. *Breaking Rules: The Social and Situation Dynamics of Young People's Urban Crime.* Oxford: Oxford University Press.

Wiley, Lindsay. 2013. Shame, Blame, and the Emerging Law of Obesity Control. *UCD Law Review* 47:121–188.

Wilkinson-Ryan, Tess, and Jonathan Baron. 2009. Moral Judgment and Moral Heuristics in Breach of Contract. *Journal of Empirical Legal Studies* 2:405–423.

Williams, Bernard. 1972. *Morality: An Introduction to Ethics.* New York: Harper and Row.

———. 1981. *Moral Luck.* Cambridge: Cambridge University Press.

———. 1985. *Ethics and the Limits of Philosophy.* Cambridge, MA: Harvard University Press.

———. 1993. *Shame and Necessity.* Berkeley: University of California Press.

———. 2005. *In the Beginning Was the Deed: Realism and Moralism in Political Argument.* Edited by Geoffrey Hawthorn. Princeton: Princeton University Press.

Williston, Samuel, and Richard A. Lord. 2010. *A Treatise on the Law of Contracts.* 4th ed. Vol. 8. Rochester, NY: Lawyers Cooperative.

Wilson, Ben. 2007. *The Making of Victorian Values.* New York: Penguin Press.

Wilson, Richard R. 1980. Conformity and Deviance regarding Moral Rules in Chinese Society. In *Normal and Abnormal Behavior in Chinese Culture,* edited by Arthur Kleinman and Tsung-yi Lin. Hingham, MA: Kluwar Boston.

Winston, Kenneth. 2008. What Makes Ethics Practical. *Harvard Kennedy School Working Paper* No. RWP08-013. https://papers.ssrn.com/sol3/papers.cfm?abstract_id=976556.

———. 2015. *Ethics in Public Life: Good Practitioners in a Rising Asia.* New York: Palgrave Macmillan.

———. 2018. "Good Order and Workable Arrangements": Lon Fuller's Critique of Positivism. In *The Cambridge Companion to Legal Positivism*, edited by Patricia Mindus and Torben Spaak, forthcoming.

Witt, John Fabian. 2008. Form and Substance in the Law of Counterinsurgency Damages. *Loyola Los Angeles Law Review* 41:1455–1482.

Wittgenstein, Ludwig. 1953. *Philosophical Investigations.* Edited by G. E. M. Anscombe and R. Rhees. Translated by G. E. M. Anscombe. Oxford: Blackwell.

Wolfe, Alan. 2001. *Moral Freedom: The Impossible Idea That Defines the Way We Now Live.* New York: W. W. Norton.

Wong, Kristina. 2015. U.S. Aim for "Zero Civilian Casualties" Draws Criticisms. *The Hill,* June 24. http://thehill.com/policy/defense/policy-strategy/245932-us-aims-for-zero-civilian-casualties-in-war-vs-isis.

World Values Survey. 2014. Survey of Church Attendance. http://www.worldvaluessurvey.org/WVSContents.jsp.

Worthington, Sarah. 2018. Revolutions in Personal Property: Redrawing the Common Law's Conceptual Map. Forthcoming in *Revolution and Evolution in Private Law,* edited by Sarah Worthington, Andrew Robertson, and Graham Virgo. Portland, OR: Hart.

Wozner, Shai. 2000–2001. Consistency and Effectiveness in Jewish Law as Reflected by the Lekhat'hila-Bedeabad Distinction. *Diney Israel* 20–21: 42–100 (Hebrew).

Wrage, Stephen. 2003. The Ethics of Precision Air Power. In *Immaculate Warfare: Participants Reflect on the Air Campaigns over Kosovo, Afghanistan, and Iraq,* edited by Stephen Wrage. Westport, CT: Praeger.

Wrong, Dennis. 1994. *The Problem of Order: What Unites and Divides Society.* New York: Free Press.

Wuthnow, Robert. 1991. *Acts of Compassion: Caring for Others and Helping Ourselves.* Princeton: Princeton University Press.

Xue, Xinran. 2010. Gendercide: The Worldwide War on Baby Girls. *The Economist,* March 4.

Yates, Joshua J., and James Davison Hunter, eds. 2011. *Thrift and Thriving in America: Capitalism and Moral Order from the Puritans to the Present.* New York: Oxford University Press.

Yi, Zeng, Tu Ping, Gu Baochang, et al. 1993. Causes and Implications of the Recent Increase in the Reported Sex Ratio at Birth in China. *Population and Development Review* 19:283–302.

Yiannopoulos, A. N. 1994. Civil Liability for Abuse of Right: Something Old, Something New. *Louisiana Law Review* 54:1173–1198.

Yong, Ed. 2009. Envious Capuchin Monkeys React Badly to Raw Deals. In *Phenomena: A Science Salon,* by National Geographic. December 5. http://phenomena.nationalgeographic.com/2009/12/05/envious-capuchin-monkeys-react-badly-to-raw-deals.

YouGov. 2014. *Survey Results.* http://cdn.yougov.com/cumulus_uploads/document/5a36trmrkq/InternalResults_140718_Human_Rights_W.pdf.

Zakaria, Fareed. 2010. Build the Ground Zero Mosque. *Daily Beast,* August 6.

Zelizer, Viviana. 1979. *Morals and Markets: The Development of Life Insurance in the United States.* New York: Columbia University Press.

Zhu, Ning. 2011. Household Consumption and Personal Bankruptcy. *Journal of Legal Studies* 40:1–37.

Zifcak, Spencer. 2012. The Responsibility to Protect after Libya and Syria. *Melbourne Journal of International Law* 13:59–93.

Zigon, Jarret. 2011. *HIV Is God's Blessing: Rehabilitating Morality in Neoliberal Russia.* Berkeley: University of California Press.

Zoghbi-Manrique-de-Lara, Pablo. 2010. Do Unfair Procedures Predict Employees' Ethical Behavior by Deactivating Formal Regulations? *Journal of Business Ethics* 94:411–425.

Zuckerberg, Marc. 2017. Building Global Community. August 16. https://www.facebook.com/notes/mark-zuckerberg/building-global-community/10154544292806634/.

Zussman, Robert. 1992. *Intensive Care: Medical Ethics and the Medical Profession.* Chicago: University of Chicago Press.

Zywicki, Todd. 2005. Institutions, Incentives, and Consumer Bankruptcy Reform. *Washington and Lee Law Review* 62:1071–1138.

# ACKNOWLEDGMENTS

"I think you'll be amused by its presumption." With this gesture of self-abasement (the caption of a famous James Thurber cartoon), I've sometimes inflicted this venturesome project, in search of guidance, on friends and professional acquaintances. Those who left their mark on it, to whom I feel much gratitude, include Joëlle Adda, Hervé Ascenio, Tom Baker, Ziv Bohrer, W. James Booth, Sandy Boyd, Curtis Chan, Jovana Davidovic, Hanoch Dagan, Mihailis Diamantis, Paul Dubinsky, Stella Elias, Linda Emanuel, Zephyr Frank, Antoine Garapon, David Garrow, Robert W. Gordon, Paul Gowder, Kent Greenawalt, Andrew Grewal, Ariela Gross, Stephen Holmes, Abdul Khaliq, Elizabeth Knoll, Michèle Lamont, Thomas LeBien, Clark Lombardi, Larry May, Marcin Matczak, Robert T. Miller, Robert Moffitt, David Orentlicher, Todd Pettys, Jason Rantanen, Brad Roth, Julie Saada, Susan P. Shapiro, Céline Spector, Maya Steinitz, Sean Sullivan, Robert Talisse, Frank Upham, Lea Vandervelde, Teresa Wagner, Jeremy Waldron, Roman Zinigrad, and Todd Zywicki. None bear any responsibility for my missteps.

Thanks as well to my many research assistants over several years, and to the several senior military officers, physicians, and attorneys who have shared with me (under promise of anonymity) sobering stories of the ethical challenges—some here recounted—with which their many years of professional experiences regularly confronted them. Having learned so much from him over several years of close correspondence, I owe my greatest debt in this work to Kenneth Winston, a former colleague at Harvard's Center for Ethics and the Professions. I am grateful also to several anonymous readers for Harvard University Press. In early years, I learned enormously from my many teachers in sociology and in the law, at Berkeley, Harvard, the University of Chicago, and at Foley Hoag, a Boston law firm.

The manuscript profited from presentations to the Columbia Law School Legal Theory Workshop, École Normal Supérieure, University of Iowa Legal Studies Workshop, University of Michigan Legal Theory Workshop, Vanderbilt University Philosophy Department, University of Paris/Sorbonne, political theory workshop of the Paris Institute of Political Studies (Sciences Po), and Hebrew University of Jerusalem, at a conference sponsored by the Minerva Institute of Human Rights. The origin of the argument of this book is "Rights to Do Grave Wrong," which I published in the *Journal of Legal Analysis*, Volume 5, Issue 1, June 1, 2013, pages 107–219, https://doi.org/10.1093/jla/las015. © 2018 Oxford University Press. Several institutions offered hospitable milieus in which to write: Stanford University's WSD Handa Center for Human Rights and International Justice; the Institute des Hautes Études sur la Justice, Paris; the School of Law at Sciences Po; and the Centre d'Études des Normes Juridiques, of the École des Hautes Études en Sciences Sociales. Over many years, the University of Iowa, College of Law, provided helpful support.

# INDEX